D1072696

SOCIAL

PSYCHOLOGY

SHELDON COHEN, University of Oregon, and
SOLOMON FULERO

ALICE H. EAGLY, Purdue University

JOHN HARVEY, Vanderbilt University

SARA B. KIESLER, Carnegie-Mellon University, and
EUGENIA GROHMAN

VLADIMIR J. KONEČNI, University of California at San Diego

MICHAEL KUHLMAN, University of Delaware

BERT MOORE, University of Texas at Dallas

ANNE PEPLAU, University of California at Los Angeles

SOCIAL PSYCHOLOGY

DRURY SHERROD

Pitzer College / Claremont Graduate School

First Edition

987654321

Library of Congress Cataloging in Publication Data
Sherrod, Drury.
Social psychology.

Bibliography: p.
Includes indexes.
1. Social psychology. I. Title.
HM251.S563 302 81-8641
ISBN 0-394-32099-9 AACR2

Cover painting: Oscar Bluemner. *Morning Light* (Dover Hills, October). c. 1916. Oil on canvas, 20 x 30". Hirshhorn Museum, Smithsonian Institution, Washington, D.C. Photo by John Tennant.

Chapter-opener photos: Chapter 4—© Alain Nogues/Sygma; Chapter 12—© Joel Gordon 1981; all others—© Leonard Speier 1979, 1980, 1981

Text design: Clint Anglin

Cover Design: Lorraine Hohman

Photo Editor: R. Lynn Goldberg

Photo Researcher: Flavia Rando

Manufactured in the United States of America

To my parents,
NITA and DRURY SHERROD

PREFACE

This book examines human social behavior in light of the most current findings of experimental social psychology. The book's thesis is that social psychology deals with the same aspects of behavior as do novels, poems, and art—essentially, the nature and context of human social experience. Social psychology's unique contribution to understanding human experience is the empirical method.

In presenting this perspective on human experience, the book has several strengths:

Written by experts and edited for consistency. The book gains value in having each chapter written by an expert in that research area. At the same time, all chapters have been closely edited for stylistic and thematic consistency. The result is a book that presents the most current findings in each major research area from the balanced perspective of a recognized expert. Yet a consistent emphasis, style, tone, and level of analysis have been achieved through careful editing of all chapters.

Themes. Three themes are introduced in the first chapter and are highlighted throughout the book in boxes. These themes are:

1. *The Arts.* As noted above, the book asserts that social psychology deals with the same aspects of behavior as those explored by the arts. To illustrate this point, most chapters include at least one Social Psychology and the Arts box comparing the empirical approach of social psychology with an artistic approach to the same phenomenon. The goal is to demonstrate that social psychology deals with enduring aspects of human experience, yet makes a unique contribution through its empirical method.
2. *Dispositional and Situational Influences on Behavior.* The book maintains that social behavior is usually a joint function of internal, dispositional factors and external, situational factors. This theme is explained in Chapter 1 and is emphasized throughout the book. Most chapters contain at least one Dispositions and Situations box examining a recent instance of relevant research that demonstrates the joint role of situations and dispositions as determinants of behavior. Finally, Chapter 14 considers circumstances that influence the relative importance of situational versus dispositional factors in controlling behavior.
3. *Applications.* The book argues that social psychology developed partly because of its potential use in understanding and resolving social problems. To illustrate the applied value of social psychology, Chapter 2, on research methods, focuses primarily on examples of applied research, and Chapter 13 deals with applying social psychology. In addition, most chapters feature at least one Focus on Applications box that shows how theory and research pertain to current problems and issues in the news.

Chapter organization. Part I contains two chapters that introduce the student to theory and research methods in social psychology. The focus then proceeds from the narrow to the general. Part II deals with individual processes and includes chapters on the Self; Attitudes, Beliefs, and Behavior; and Attitude Change. Part III focuses on interpersonal processes and contains chapters on Attribution and Person Perception; Interpersonal Attraction; Aggression; Altruism; and Social Interdependence. Part IV emphasizes the relationship between the individual and social ecology and includes chapters on Groups; the Physical Environment and Social Behavior; and Applying Social Psychology. Part V presents a short epilogue that reviews the themes and topics of the book and offers some general perspectives and conclusions about social psychology.

Current research issues. Each of the chapters incorporates the most current research traditions and findings. For example:

Chapter 3, The Self, emphasizes information-processing approaches to the self and discusses self-schemata, self-awareness, self-consciousness, and self-monitoring;
Chapter 4, Attitudes, Beliefs, and Behavior, features extensive coverage of the relationship between attitudes and behavior and considers information-processing models of attitude formation;
Chapter 5, Attitude Change, includes a balanced treatment of alternative perspectives, with attention to information-processing models of attitude change and a discussion of individual differences in persuasibility;
Chapter 6, Attribution and Person Perception, presents major theoretical approaches to attribution as well as recent criticisms of attribution theory from the perspective of judgment theory; it also incorporates recent research on social cognition;
Chapter 7, Interpersonal Attraction, examines recent research on the development of close relationships and on loneliness;
Chapter 8, Aggression, considers the role of arousal and emotional labeling in aggressive behavior and discusses applied issues such as television violence, gun control, pornography, and drugs;
Chapter 9, Altruism, analyzes alternative theories of altruism, including sociobiology, and summarizes the latest research on affective mediators of altruism;
Chapter 10, Social Interdependence, presents research on bargaining and social exchange in light of the current relevance of commons dilemmas, and it discusses the ecological validity of laboratory gaming research;
Chapter 11, Groups, considers the relevance of classic group research for applied questions such as family crises, and it introduces cognitive perspectives on group processes;
Chapter 12, The Physical Environment and Social Behavior, emphasizes the role of perceived control in understanding spatial behavior, territoriality, and reactions to environmental stress; it also analyzes attentional explanations of the effects of crowding and noise;
Chapter 13, Applying Social Psychology, considers applied issues of aging, population density, racism and the "contact hypothesis," sex roles and sexism, and the psychology of law.

Learning Aids. Each chapter concludes with a summary of its major points , and the book includes a glossary of key terms. A test-item file that features both informational and conceptual questions is available to instructors.

The message of this book is that we are all social beings; our lives take on meaning through others, and our thoughts, feelings and actions are shaped by others and help shape them in return. It is appropriate then for the authors of this book to dedicate our work to those who have touched and enriched our lives and who have allowed us to touch them back. In particular, this book is dedicated to my parents, Nita and Drury Sherrod, whose memory touches and enriches me daily.

Dru Sherrod
Claremont, California
April 1, 1981

ACKNOWLEDGMENTS

Many people have contributed to the creation of this book. Random House acquiring editor Virginia Hoitsma guided the entire project and contributed valuable suggestions for the book's themes. Random House manuscript editor John Sturman shaped the various chapters into their final form and coordinated the book's production with careful attention to detail and good humor. Other members of the Random House staff—Lynn Goldberg, photo editor; Flavia Rando, photo researcher; Lorraine Hohman, designer; and Suzanne Loeb, production supervisor—also deserve thanks for their hard work and imagination.

A number of professional social psychologists made initial suggestions for the book's content and reviewed various portions of the manuscript for scientific representativeness and accuracy as well as teachability. These include:

— C. Daniel Batson, University of Kansas
— Tyler Blake, California State University, Northridge
— Robert L. Burgess, Pennsylvania State University
— Ellen Cohen, University of New Hampshire
— Ebbe Ebbesen, University of California, San Diego
— Mary B. Harris, University of New Mexico
— Ted L. Huston, Pennsylvania State University
— R. Peter Johnson, University of Illinois
— Hilary Lips, University of Winnipeg
— Charles A. Lowe, University of Connecticut
— David M. Messick, University of California, Santa Barbara
— Norman Miller, University of California, San Diego
— Stephen Misovich, Providence College
— Dan Perlman, University of Manitoba
— Dean G. Pruitt, State University of New York at Buffalo
— Michael F. Scheier, Carnegie-Mellon University
— David R. Shaffer, University of Georgia
— R. Lance Shotland, Pennsylvania State University
— Eric Sundstrom, University of Tennessee
— James T. Tedeschi, State University of New York at Albany
— William Underwood, University of Texas at Austin
— Robin R. Vallacher, Illinois Institute of Technology
— Daniel M. Wegner, Trinity University (Texas)
— David Wilder, Rutgers University
— Timothy D. Wilson, University of Virginia

Helpful suggestions for the Social Psychology and the Arts boxes were contributed by Edward Copeland, Professor of English at Pomona College; Ralph Ross, Professor Emeritus of Humanities at Scripps College; and Albert Wachtel, Professor of English at Pitzer College. Finally, I am grateful to the expert contributors themselves, and to Pitzer College and Hamilton College, which supported the preparation of the manuscript by providing secretarial assistance. Special gratitude is due to Beverly Scales, who most carefully and conscientiously typed various versions of the manuscript. Stella Vlastos and Sue Bennett also ably assisted in typing certain chapters.

This project originally began as a revision of a text called *Social Psychology: Explorations in Understanding,* published by CRM in 1974. As this project developed, however, it no longer became appropriate to call it a revision. More than 90 percent of the book is new material. Nonetheless, we would like to acknowledge portions of some of the original contributors' work that appear in the following chapters of this text: Siegfried Streufert in *Chapter 2, Research Methods in Social Psychology;* James N. Jones in *Chapter 4, Attitudes, Beliefs, and Behavior,* and *Chapter 5, Attitude Change;* Genevieve Clapp in *Chapter 7, Interpersonal Attraction;* Robert M. Liebert, Rita W. Poulos, Dalmas A. Taylor, and Robert S. Siegler in *Chapter 8, Aggression;* Bert Moore and Bill Underwood in *Chapter 9, Altruism;* and Genevieve Clapp, Siegfried Streufert, and Susan C. Streufert in *Chapter 11, Groups.*

CONTENTS

PART ONE

INTRODUCTION

PART TWO

THE INDIVIDUAL

PART THREE

INTERPERSONAL

PROCESSES

PART FOUR

THE INDIVIDUAL AND SOCIAL ECOLOGY

BOXES

SOCIAL

PSYCHOLOGY

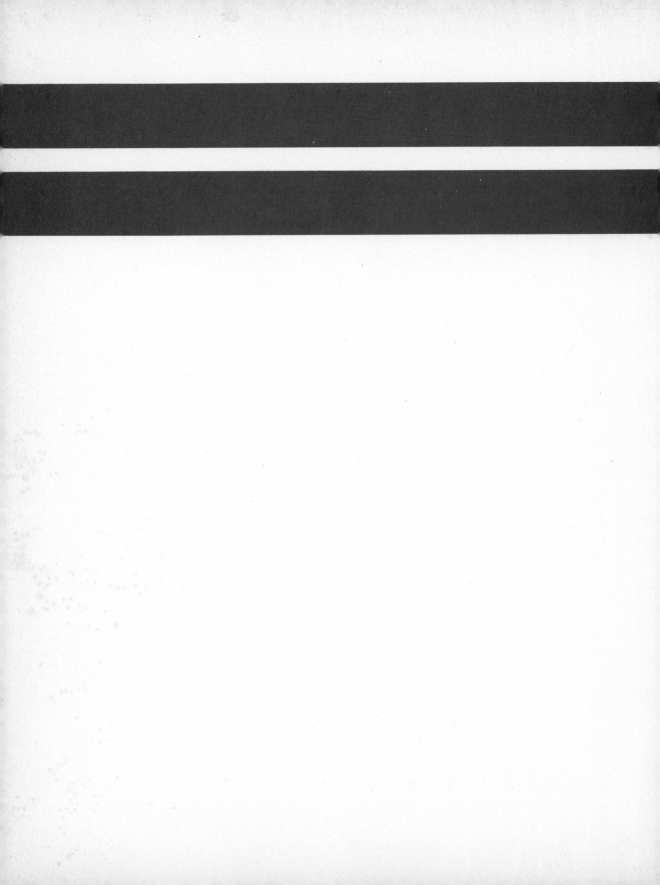

PART ONE

INTRODUCTION

CHAPTER ONE

THE NATURE OF SOCIAL PSYCHOLOGY

Pablo Picasso, one of the twentieth century's most important artists, was once asked, "What is art?" He answered, "What is not?"

Picasso's response seems to suggest that art and human experience are one and the same. Indeed, when we want to learn something about the meaning of human experience, we frequently turn to literature, drama, poetry, and the fine arts. Often we are emotionally moved and intellectually enriched. We gain new insights about self-discovery and self-delusion, about loving and hating, about beliefs, attitudes, and values, about conformity and deviance, about courage and compliance—in short, about human nature and human experience.

But as rich and moving as artistic approaches to human experience may be, art lacks an important dimension. Art represents one person's vision expressed in a highly embellished, involving, and persuasive form. The impact of art derives from an intense focus on unique characters, specific moments, climactic situations. It is not the artist's purpose to offer a representative, objective, unbiased perspective. To the extent that art is one person's subjective view of the world, then, it is unrepresentative of human experience by its very nature. Perhaps it is this subjective quality of art that led to another observation of Picasso's. "Art," he said, "is not the truth. It is a lie about the truth."

If the "truths" of art are unrepresentative, subjective, and potentially biased, where then can we turn for more objective insights about human experience? The authors of this book believe that social psychology offers a unique solution. A glance at the table of contents will demonstrate that social psychology deals with many of the same themes as great art, literature, drama, and poetry. There are chapters on the self, on beliefs and attitudes, interpersonal perception and behavior, love and attraction, aggression and altruism, and on conformity and deviance in groups. In other words, social psychology is the study of human social experience—of the people and social situations in our lives and how they affect us.

Unlike art and literature, however, social psychology approaches these topics *empirically*. That is, social psychologists explore the human condition by gathering data and testing hypotheses, as we will explain in Chapter 2. Whereas art presents feelings and conclusions derived from one individual's personal experience, social psychology presents systematic observations about a number of people's experience under controlled conditions. Thus social psychology parallels art and literature in its focus on human social experience. But as a result of the empirical process, the conclusions of social psychology may be more representative, more objective, and less potentially biased than those of art and literature.

If social psychologists are studying the same "stuff" of the human experience that has occupied writers and artists for centuries, it is legitimate to ask: what can be learned through the empirical approach that is really new? It is only honest to answer that some things will not be new, but they will be presented differently. Other findings will represent observations that you may feel you always knew about human behavior but couldn't put into words. Still other conclusions will be surprising and challenging.

One of the most influential figures in the history of social psychology, Fritz Heider, has asserted that social psychology explains the "naïve psychology of everyday life." Just as we are each a "personal artist," forging and shaping our own experience, so are we each a "personal scientist," observing, questioning, and analyzing our own and others' behavior. Thus we have all spent a lifetime acting as "naïve" social psychologists. We have observed behavior, pondered feelings and thoughts, and asked why.

This lifetime history of functioning as a social psychologist almost guarantees that some of the questions and answers in this book will sound familiar. Yet in the same way that each new work in art or literature provides fresh insights on familiar problems, so social psychology in its empirical approach provides a new and distinctive perspective. Furthermore, in our capacity as "naïve personal scientists," it is likely that we will reach faulty or limited conclusions about human behavior. For example, we all know certain "common-sense" maxims about behavior: "Birds of a feather flock together," but "Opposites attract"; or "Absence makes the

Art and social psychology both focus on human social experience. For example, Pablo Picasso's *Guernica,* painted to commemorate the bombing of a Basque town during the Spanish Civil War in the late 1930s, portrays many of the social forces that we will discuss in this book—among them, aggression, deindividuation, helplessness, propaganda, prejudice, and justice. But Picasso's depiction of pain and persecution was colored by his personal biases; the social psychologist would approach the situation with an objective, empirical outlook. *(On extended loan to The Museum of Modern Art, New York)*

heart grow fonder," yet "Out of sight, out of mind." From our personal experience and common-sense knowledge, we can agree with all of these statements, although each pair is mutually contradictory. Thus common sense fails. What is needed to clarify the contradictions is some analysis of specific circumstances under which the hypotheses are valid. For example, under what specific conditions do opposites attract, and exactly when and what kinds of birds with what types of feathers do in fact flock together?

One goal of social psychology is to reach more valid and representative conclusions about human behavior than are possible on the basis of personal experience alone. Social psychology offers two major advantages that artistic approaches to the human condition lack. First, whether we are great artists or simply common-sense personal scientists, we are probably poor observers. Very likely we make too few and too narrow observations for our conclusions to be representative of many people's experience, perhaps not even our own. And second, our own personal biases always operate to distort our observations and conclusions. The empirical approach of social psychology is an attempt to avoid these problems. Yet the subject matter remains the same, whether one is artist, personal scientist, or social psychologist: the nature and context of human social experience.

SOCIAL PSYCHOLOGY: SCIENCE OR HISTORY?

Despite the empirical approach of social psychology, some practitioners of the discipline have charged that social psychology should more appropriately be viewed as a historical study rather than a scientific study. According to critics such as Kenneth Gergen (1973), social behavior can really be understood only in light of specific cultural and temporal events. The way people behave in one place at one point in time may not at all describe the way other people at a different place and time would behave.

Therefore, scientific laws of general applicability cannot be laid down for social behavior in the same way that laws can be formulated to govern physical objects. Furthermore, these critics argue, even if general laws could be laid down, an individual who was aware of the law could always choose to behave contrary to the law, merely to assert his or her freedom from the law. Thus, if social behavior cannot be lawfully described in social psychology, how can the discipline pretend to be science?

Defenders of the scientific view of social psychology have replied that social behavior is indeed lawful if described in sufficiently abstract terms. For example, one defender, Barry Schlenker (1974), has conceded that it is a culturally and historically limited proposition to assert, "A promise of a lollipop will get children to finish their spinach at suppertime." However, the same statement can be rephrased in universally valid terms—for instance, "Expectations of positive reinforcements will increase the probability of a contingent response."

Although this rephrasing of a specific proposition in universal terms seems valid, the critics of "scientific" social psychology reply that statements of such universal abstracts are hardly useful in predicting or understanding any particular concrete behavior. To make the statement useful requires an interpretation in light of specific historical facts.

One observer of this debate, Clyde Hendrick (1976), has suggested that social psychologists should perhaps lower their sights as scientists. According to this view, social psychologists may continue to formulate propositions regarding human behavior in universal terms. However, the propositions can only be tested within a limited historical context.

This debate may be put in perspective by realizing that social psychology seeks to understand the regularities of human social behavior in a particular time and setting. Just as in the case of literature, some of the findings of social psychology will relate to basic transhistorical, transcultural human experience. A good bet for this type of phenomenon might be a human being's need for perceived competence and control in relating to the surrounding environment. Another might be the tendency to evaluate oneself in comparison with one's peers. In contrast, other findings of social psychology will be valid primarily for a particular historical, cultural period. For example, the factors that influence interpersonal attraction are likely to vary with different cultural norms regarding beauty, social conventions, and desirable behaviors. However, the important scientific contribution of social psychology is its empirical approach to human social behavior. Perhaps the science/history debate can be resolved by asserting that social psychology is both science *and* history. It is the scientific study of human experience in a particular cultural and historical time.

PSYCHOLOGY AND SOCIAL PSYCHOLOGY

Psychology as a discipline deals with individual human functioning, from the biochemistry of the brain to a person's relationship to society. Within this broad spectrum, different specialties in psychology focus on human behavior at different *levels of analysis*. For example, in Figure 1.1 physiological psychology occupies the most basic level because it focuses on the brain and nervous system. On the next level the focus enlarges somewhat, as perception and cognitive psychology examine how we acquire and process information from the outside world. Then the focus increases still further as psychologists interested in learning investigate how organisms interact with their environment to acquire patterns of behavior. At this point the focus enlarges significantly, from a concern with subprocesses of human functioning to an analysis of the individual as a whole. At the next two levels developmental and personality psychologists seek to explain the growth of a human being and the organization of a person's thoughts, feelings, and action into a coherent personality. Closely related to these specialties is clinical psychology, which studies abnormalities or "disorganization" in human development and personality. Then, finally, social psychology enters the picture. Here the focus is broadest of all, since few aspects of human experience are unaffected by social influences or without social im-

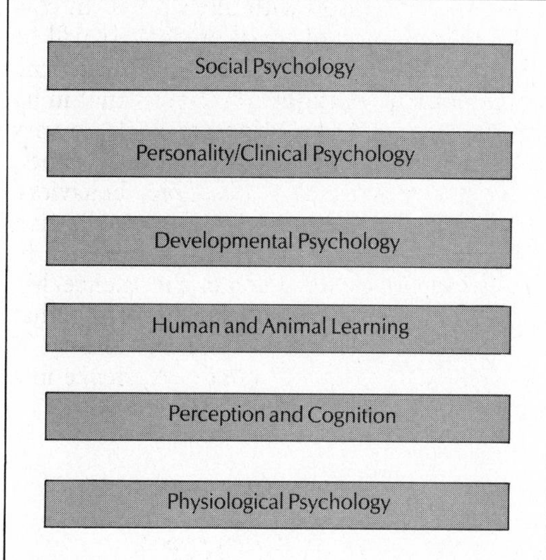

FIGURE 1.1 Levels of analysis in psychology.

plications. Yet social psychology also builds on each preceding level of analysis, since few aspects of human experience are unaffected by factors at the physiological, cognitive, learning, developmental, or personality level.

For example, consider the concrete question that one social psychologist, Judith Rodin (1976), has studied: can crowded housing affect children's ability and motivation to perform in school? To answer the question Rodin set up an experiment. She selected children whose families occupied identical apartments in a large housing complex. These children were alike in every important respect, including parents' income, education, and jobs. The only difference was that some of the children lived in more crowded apartments than others. Rodin brought these children into a social psychology laboratory at Yale University where they were given various tests. She found that children from the most crowded homes made more errors on a puzzle-solving test than children from less crowded homes. Also the children from crowded homes exercised less initiative when given an opportunity to make independent choices.

Now, why should this happen? Why should children from crowded homes make more errors and have less initiative than children from less crowded homes, when these children are similar in most important respects except for the number of people who occupy their apartments? Rodin suggested that the children from crowded homes failed to develop a sense of personal control over their own lives because of the many disruptions and interferences caused by crowding. As a result of these social conditions in their homes, crowded children learn to feel "helpless," and it is this "helplessness" that causes them to give up and perform more poorly than noncrowded children. This explanation sounds plausible, but it is certainly not as simple as it seems at first glance. In fact, the social-psychological concept of "helplessness" may actually involve several different processes at different levels of psychological analysis, as explained below.

A *physiological psychologist* might argue that helplessness is caused by the depletion of a certain neural-transmitter substance, norepinephrine, that is important in the functioning of the central nervous system. For example, J. M. Weiss and his colleagues (1970) have found that helpless animals develop a deficit of this chemical when there is nothing they can do to escape a stressful event like electric shock or submergence in ice water. When there is too little norepinephrine in the nervous system, nerve impulses are not transmitted properly and organisms do not function efficiently. An implication of Weiss's research is that the stress of crowding may cause humans to develop a similar deficit of norepinephrine that can impair ability and motivation.

A *cognitive psychologist* might focus on a different process altogether. These psychologists are concerned with how people attend to information in the environment and how they process that information in their brains. From this perspective, crowded children may simply have to deal with too many inputs for their information-processing system to function effectively. Like a computer, these children may become "overloaded" from excessive inputs due to crowding. In order to focus on the most important stimuli, they learn to "screen out"

Judith Rodin studied children in a large apartment complex to determine whether crowded housing affects their ability and motivation to perform in school. *(Michael Weisbrot)*

much irrelevant background information in the world around them. As a result, they may fail to notice many of the things happening around them, and the strain of so much overload may temporarily deplete their attentional capacity. Consequently, they do not perform as well as if they were less crowded (see Cohen, 1978).

Still other psychologists might be interested in the *personality* of each child and how each child reacts uniquely to his or her living conditions. For example, tests have been developed to measure a personality variable known as "internal control versus external control." People high in internal control believe that they are responsible for their own destinies and the things that happen to them. In contrast, those high in external control see themselves as affected by chance, luck, or fate. Perhaps the constraints of crowding, along with other circumstances, may cause children to develop a personality characterized by a sense of "external control." In other words, these children may develop a generalized expectancy that life is simply beyond their own personal control. Consequently, they may become generally passive.

These examples show that the question of crowding and its effects on children can be approached at several different levels. Each of the explanations may help account for the children's responses on the laboratory tests. The social psychologist interested in understanding and altering the effects of crowding must be aware not only of social factors such as the number of people present in a room, apartment, or neighborhood, but also of the underlying consequences of crowding and how it affects one's social responses. Thus, social psychology depends on findings and concepts in many other areas of psychology in order to understand human social experience.

THE HISTORY OF SOCIAL PSYCHOLOGY

Social psychologists are always pointing out that theirs is a young field within the history of modern psychology. Psychology as a discipline was already dividing into its first competing theoretical camps before social psychology ever appeared on the scene. By the late 1800s American psychologists were locked in a debate about the proper way to study subjective experience. In Germany psychophysical laboratories were already well established in the study of perception and sensation, while in Austria the ideas of Sigmund Freud were outraging the European medical establishment. As these schools of thought waged theoretical battles over the future direction of psychology, social psychology emerged as a purely pragmatic means of answering a concrete question about human behavior.

In 1897 at the University of Indiana, Norman Triplett performed the first social psychology experiment. His research resulted from an interest in bicycle racing combined with the expertise he had gained as a graduate student in psychology. Triplett wondered why bicycle racers almost always had faster times when they competed against another person than when they raced alone against the clock. Triplett thought there must be something in the competitive process that influenced their performance. To test his hunch, he asked schoolchildren to play a game for him. The children "fished" for prizes by cranking a fishing reel that wound up a line attached to a hidden "prize." The goal was to wind up the line as fast as they could. Triplett asked the children to play the game alone some of the time, but at other times to compete against each other in a group. As he had suspected, when the children competed against each other, they hooked their prizes faster than when they fished alone. Triplett tested his finding in a variety of contexts, and he concluded that the presence of another person in a competition serves to make the contestants work harder or, as Triplett put it, "to liberate latent energy not ordinarily available."

While Triplett's finding might seem like an obvious conclusion that you may have realized long ago from your own experience, you will learn in this book that it is not clear why this "obvious" phenomenon occurs. More interesting, the phenomenon also occurs in other species like rats, ants, and cockroaches. It even occurs if cockroaches are merely being observed by other cockroaches. The same holds true for humans, though with humans it is less likely to occur if the observers are blindfolded. And under some circumstances and for some types of behavior, it doesn't happen at all. The phenomenon has come to be called "social facilitation" because the presence of others facilitates certain types of behavior. This phenomenon will be discussed further in Chapter 11.

Social facilitation is a good example of social-psychological research. The research arose out of a concrete question about human interaction. The phenomenon has been tested both in the psychology laboratory and in the real world. There are specific practical implications that may be applied in office, factory, and academic settings. And the research has spawned several alternative theoretical explanations to account for the phenomenon, and the debate is not settled yet.

The example of social facilitation also reflects two trends that have characterized the history of social psychology. Typically, a social psychologist begins, like Triplett, with a *concern about some concrete social problem*, such as the effects of groups on individuals. As theories are advanced and tested, interest often shifts from the specific problem to a *curiosity about the underlying social processes*.

For example, from the 1920s through the 1960s social psychologists were particularly interested in people's attitudes—how they can be measured, formed, and changed. Understanding attitudes seemed crucially important during the 1930s and 1940s as totalitarian governments sought to manipulate public opinion by using mass communication. Because attitudes were thought to be the key to behavior, research on attitudes promised to yield enormously important results for influencing human behavior or, conversely, to help people resist influences on their behavior. Numerous experiments gradually revealed why some communications could wield such persuasive power. However, as research advanced, the practical applications were deemphasized in favor of basic research on the complexities of attitude organization and change. Today, both trends are clearly visible in attitude research: on the practical side social psychologists are exploring how whole communities might be persuaded to adopt more healthy life styles and reduce their rates of

During the 1930s and 1940s totalitarian regimes successfully influenced public opinion through mass communications. In Germany, for example, posters such as this one, which urges women to save their unemployed husbands and doomed children by voting for Adolf Hitler, were instrumental in the Nazis' rise to power. As a result, social psychologists during this period focused much of their attention on how attitudes can be measured, formed, and changed. *(Culver Pictures)*

heart disease (Maccoby and Farquhar, 1975); on the more theoretical side, other psychologists study attitudes to learn how information is stored and organized in the human brain (for example, Wyer, 1974).

The social turmoil in America during the late 1960s and early 1970s left many social psychologists wondering if perhaps their field had strayed too far from its early concerns about concrete social problems and had become too enmeshed in basic research about social processes. Observers talked frequently about the "crisis in social psychology," and some thought the field was floundering as a discipline. Yet in the 1980s the field seems to have reached a new equilibrium between applied research on social problems and basic research on social processes. The concern about social problems is evidenced in research on such topics as crowding and environmental stress, racism and sexism, health and aging, law and social policy. Some of these topics are discussed in Chapters 12 and 13. The curiosity about social processes is seen in research on self-perception and attribution, love and interpersonal attraction, aggression and altruism, to name only a few.

For most social psychologists the attraction of the field is this dual focus on both problems and processes. The discipline not only examines the fabric of human experience, but its findings are also applicable—at least potentially—to changing individual lives and social institutions. Perhaps the typical social psychologist aspires to combine the role of scientist with those of poet-philosopher and social reformer, observing and explaining human experience and researching and designing systems to serve human needs.

THE ROLE OF THEORY IN SOCIAL PSYCHOLOGY

Most observers of the human condition develop theories to explain why people behave the way they do. As we noted earlier, we have all had enough experience observing ourselves and others to derive a number of intuitive theories about everyday behavior. Similarly, novelists, playwrights, and poets usually have their own theories about behavior, expressed either overtly or between the lines.

In the empirical approach of social psychology, theories are more than intuitive feelings lurking between the lines of research. Theory building and theory testing are the most important functions of any science, whether the object of inquiry is subatomic particles or human behavior. Theories allow the social psychologist to formulate "hunches" about behavior in test-

SOCIAL PSYCHOLOGY AND THE ARTS

TESTING THE MUNDANE TRUTHS OF COUNTRY MUSIC

Mickey Gilley is a country-music star and owner of Gilley's nightclub in Pasadena, Texas, the "beer joint" where the movie *Urban Cowboy* was filmed. Not long ago Gilley recorded a song that included the line "Don't the girls all get prettier at closing time."

Wondering about the validity of this sexist but shrewd observation about human behavior, psychologist James Pennebaker and his colleagues at the University of Virginia (Pennebaker, Dyer, Caulkins, Litowitz, Ackreman, Anderson, and McGraw, 1979) decided to set up a tongue-in-cheek empirical test. Gilley himself gave them a hint about how to proceed: "If I could rate them on a scale from one to ten," he sang, "looking for a nine but an eight could fit right in. . . ." To test Gilley's hypothesis, the experimenters selected three bars near the University of Virginia that catered to college men and women. Three male-female teams entered each bar at three different times on a Thursday evening—9:00 P.M., 10:30 P.M., and 12:00 P.M.—so that each couple visited each bar only once. At the bars, each member of the team approached a patron of the same sex and asked the following question: "On a scale from one to ten, where one indicates 'not attractive,' how would you rate the women (men) here tonight?" After the subject answered, the experimenter asked another question: "If you were a (member of the opposite sex) how would you rate the (members of your own sex) here tonight, using the same scale as before?" The subjects were asked to make a global assessment of *all* the opposite- or same-sex individuals in the bar.

Was Gilley's prediction correct? The researchers found that ratings of opposite-sex individuals increased as the night progressed, as the song said, while ratings of same-sex individuals stayed about the same.

© Jeff Jacobson/Magnum

But Gilley's hypothesis was not only confirmed, it was also extended to women as well as men. Apparently, the boys, too, "get prettier at closing time."

Why does this phenomenon occur? The researchers suggested several possible explanations. One comes from social psychology and is called reactance theory (Brehm, 1966). This theory asserts that when an option is threatened—the option in this case being the possibility of making a date for the evening—the attractiveness of the option increases. Another explanation comes from cognitive dissonance theory (Festinger, 1957), which you will read more about later. From this perspective, if a person is committed to going home with someone for the evening, then it might be too dissonant with this person's expectations to go home with an unattractive partner. To resolve this dissonance, the attractiveness of the possible partner is revalued upward. Perhaps Gilley was aware of these subtle psychological processes when he sang, "Ain't it funny, ain't it strange, the way a man's opinions change, when he starts to face that lonely night."

able terms so that the hunches may be supported or rejected. Theories not only serve to explain observed instances of behavior, they also serve to generate predictions about future behavior.

In everyday life, theory building is typically a simple process. For example, we may observe an individual behaving in a group in a quiet manner. On the basis of previous experience, we "theorize" that the person may be shy, and we hypothesize that the individual will avoid attracting attention in social situations. We test our hypothesis by observing the individual in several different contexts, such as at class, at work, and in social settings, and we note whether the individual's behavior supports or refutes our hypothesis. If we come to know the person better, we expand our theory to account for a wider range of behavior, and we try to specify the exact conditions under which the person will behave quietly. When we know someone intimately, we may attempt to theorize broadly enough so that we can explain all past behaviors and predict all future behaviors. However, since it is highly unlikely that we can predict all of a person's future behaviors, no matter how intimately we know him or her, we will probably keep our theories about the person somewhat flexible, so that we can incorporate new observations or new data.

In the same way that we all go through everyday life building theories about our own and other people's behavior, social psychologists build theories about the behavior of people in general. Yet at this stage in its evolution, social psychology cannot offer a few, elegant, all-inclusive, fundamental theories to account for all of human behavior. Instead, social psychology offers a seeming jumble of small, limited, sometimes contradictory "minitheories." There are several reasons for this state of affairs.

First, as we noted when discussing the historical development of social psychology, the field has grown as a series of investigations of specific social problems and processes rather than as a gradual elaboration of basic theory. As a result, the field has developed not systematically, but in fits and starts, depending on the pressing nature of different problems and the interests of different researchers. In contrast, other areas of psychology have developed around major influential theorists. In personality psychology, for example, it is possible to trace the influence of Sigmund Freud and psychoanalysis, B. F. Skinner and behaviorism, and Carl Rogers and the humanistic perspective. There are really no equivalent theoretical "camps" and traditions in social psychology.

Another major factor that accounts for the lack of general theoretical traditions in social psychology is the complexity of human social behavior. Because human behavior is subject to so many influences from within the person as well as from the outside environment, it has not been possible to frame theories at a high level of generality. As a result of these two factors—the problem-centered focus of social psychology and the complexity of human behavior—theories in social psychology have tended to deal with specific responses in specific situations rather than with large-scale questions of "human nature."

While social psychology has not developed a set of general theories to explain behavior, some important theoretical traditions from other branches of psychology have influenced the way that social psychologists *conceptualize* the problems they investigate. In certain instances social psychology is indebted to the general perspectives of *behaviorism* and *gestalt phenomenology*, as discussed below.

BEHAVIORISM

One of the strongest influences on modern psychology is behaviorism. Often identified with the work of B. F. Skinner, behaviorism holds that people engage in behavior in order to gain rewards or to avoid punishments. Essentially, people learn which events in the environment and which of their own behaviors are accompanied by rewards and which events and behaviors are accompanied by punishments, and they respond accordingly. By expanding the notion of "reward" to include everything from nursing a baby, smiling at a child, paying a worker, or even private self-congratulation for a good accomplishment, behaviorists purport to explain virtually every human behavior. While not many social psychologists would consider themselves "strict" behaviorists, behaviorism nevertheless has had a significant impact on social psychology. Certainly, environmental events and the positive or negative consequences of behavior have a pronounced effect on what people do, think, and feel.

Two examples will demonstrate the importance of behavioristic theory in social psychology. First, social psychologists have long been concerned about the origins of aggressive behavior. The study of aggression was one of the first areas in which behaviorism was extensively applied in social psychology. In 1939, John Dollard, Neal Miller, and their colleagues published *Frustration and Aggression*. They argued that aggression does not occur unless an organism's response toward some event in the environment has been blocked or frustrated. For example, they proposed that the lynching of blacks in the South during the 1930s was caused in part by the frustration of cotton planters at declining cotton prices during the Depression.

Dollard and Miller's hypothesis has been criticized and revised over the years, but the study of aggression has remained at the center of social-psychological research. For example, the controversial effects of violent television programs have been interpreted in light of Albert Bandura's social-learning theory (see Bandura, 1977). This theory argues that individuals can learn how to be violent merely by observing other people engage in acts of violence—for instance, on television. Later, when suitable incentives are available, the same individuals who watched and learned violence on television may perform it in real life.

Another area in which learning theory has significantly influenced social psychology is the study of attitude change. Hundreds of experiments have investigated the factors that cause people to change their minds, adopt new opinions, or alter their values. To cite a few examples, research has found that people are amazingly responsive to the promised rewards of increased prestige, wealth, or sex appeal that supposedly follow from buying a certain product such as alcohol or tobacco; that people are more receptive to a sales pitch if they are rewarded with a free dinner or prize, as real-estate developers have discovered; and that people are more likely to accept a product endorsement if it comes from some highly believable source, like the commercials that feature celebrities or real-life consumers.

Aggression and attitude change are but two examples of the many ways in which behaviorism has influenced the study of social-psychological phenomena. Yet social psychologists are not so concerned about events in the outside environment that they ignore the events that occur within a person's head. The impact of behaviorism on social psychology has been tempered by approaches that emphasize individual thought processes and subjective perceptions. These approaches are known as "gestalt" theory and "phenomenology."

GESTALT THEORY AND PHENOMENOLOGY

The term *phenomenology* refers to an individual's subjective experience of the world—the world not as it objectively exists, but as one perceives it. Phenomenology became an important influence in psychology through the work of a group of psychologists in the 1930s who founded the "gestalt" movement. These researchers were initially interested in a perceptual phenomenon in which people tend to organize their sensory impressions of the world into orderly, meaningful patterns, even where such patterns do not necessarily exist. To cite a classic example, why is it that two light bulbs alternately flashing on and off in a dark room do not actually look like two flashing lights but instead take on the form of a single light jumping from place to place? The psychologists who were interested in this phenomenon of perceiving forms and patterns lived in Germany, and since the German word for "good form" or "wholeness" is *gestalt*, their research tradition came to be called the gestalt movement. The original emphasis on sensory perceptions gradually shifted to an exploration of larger questions. For instance, how do people organize their perceptions of the world in general, including themselves, their place in the world, and their attitudes and values? Through this shift of emphasis, gestalt theory opened psychology's door to phenomenology.

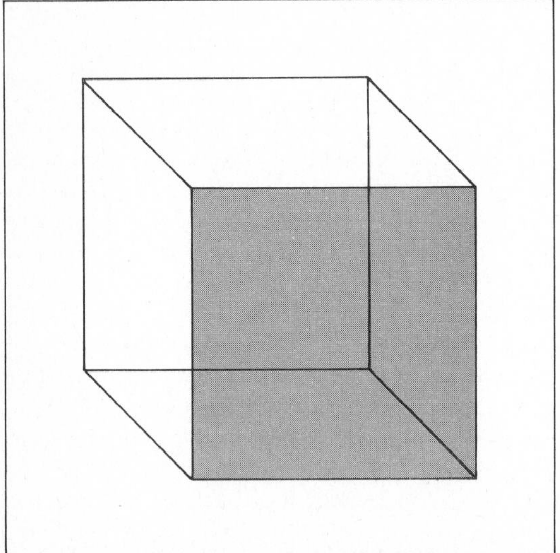

FIGURE 1.2 The Necker cube is a classic case of perceptual ambiguity; the tinted surface appears sometimes as the front of the cube and sometimes as the back. The "gestalt" movement was founded in the 1930s by German psychologists who were interested in perceptual phenomena such as this.

The individual who was most influential in bringing the gestalt perspective to social psychology was Kurt Lewin, a German psychologist who immigrated to the United States in the 1930s. Interested in the study of minorities, prejudice, and interpersonal dynamics, Lewin believed it was not sufficient to view human behavior merely as a response to objective environmental events. Behavior is also influenced by a person's perceptions of the environment or, in Lewin's terms, by a perception of one's "life space." Because the person and the environment were seen as reciprocal parts of a single dynamic "field," Lewin's version of the gestalt perspective became known as "field theory."

The gestalt approach was not Kurt Lewin's only contribution to social psychology. As a researcher, Lewin insisted on rigorous methodology and controlled experimentation. While Lewin himself is not well known today for his own research findings, his perspective has had a major impact on social psychology through the work of many of his students. Throughout the 1950s and early 1960s, the dominant concern of social psychologists was how people sought to organize their perceptions of the world so as to maintain "consistency" and avoid "dissonance" among their different attitudes and behaviors. Lewin's students were among the leading researchers in this area, and their work on attitude formation and change clearly reflected Lewin's emphasis on rigorous research methodology. Yet the narrowness of this research sometimes seemed to diverge from another important value of Lewin's—namely, the social implications and applied value of research.

In addition to Kurt Lewin, a second major theorist also helped extend the gestalt perspective to social psychology. Fritz Heider, another European émigré of the 1930s, shared Lewin's interest in people's needs to organize their perceptions of the world. Heider was particularly interested in an individual's need to maintain harmony or balance among the attitudes and objects that comprise his or her world. Yet Heider's interest extended beyond perceptual organization, and he pioneered another area that led social psychology still further in the phenomenological direction. Heider was curious about the processes through which we come to know and understand another individual, and he presented his ideas in an influential book, *The Psychology of Interpersonal Relations* (1958). He asked how we use information gained from observing the behaviors of others to form theories about their motivations, goals, and personalities. By raising the question of how we attribute causal responsibility for another's actions, Heider laid the groundwork for research in social perception and attribution.

THEORY IN CONTEMPORARY SOCIAL PSYCHOLOGY

Today social psychology combines the behavioristic and gestalt or phenomenological perspectives. Most social psychologists would agree with Lewin that social behavior is mutually dependent on the person and on the environment. Thus social psychology takes account of the individual's perceptual and cognitive processes as well as events and consequences in the environment. However, this orientation is not always made explicit. Some studies seem to deal primarily with processes inside a person's head—how an individual perceives, explains, and organizes the world. Other studies seem to deal mainly with events in the environment—what factors increase or decrease aggression, elicit altruism, influence attraction, or produce conformity. In addition, some research seems to have no specific theoretical basis at all, but is carried out purely for its relevance to real-world issues—for instance, how communication patterns within a group can affect employee satisfaction. In contrast, other research is conducted in order to test one theoretical explanation against another. Probably more than any other branch of psychology, social psychology is characterized by an "openness" regarding what phenomena are appropriate for study and what theoretical perspectives can be applied. It could hardly be otherwise in a discipline that seeks to explain the diversity of human experience.

THE THEORETICAL PERSPECTIVE OF THIS BOOK

The chapters in this book are organized around problems and topics. The focus is narrow in the beginning chapters, dealing with the individual and the ways that social processes influence one's perceptions and shape one's attitudes and values. Then the focus gradually enlarges to a concentration on interpersonal interaction. These middle chapters are concerned with significant social behaviors such as interpersonal attraction and perception, aggression and altruism, and the goals and strategies of interaction among people. Finally, the focus expands still further to an explanation of group processes and the effects on the individual of the surrounding social and physical environments. These final chapters include a discussion of applied social psychology and explore how changes in social systems can produce changes in the individual.

Throughout all of these chapters, across all the phenomena discussed, the book has adopted the perspective on social behavior that Lewin articulated so clearly: behavior is mutually determined by a "Person" and that person's "Environment" or, as Lewin stated it mathematically, $B=f\ (P,E)$. In other words, human actions, thoughts, and feelings are determined by a complex mix of factors, some of them *internal*—in the mind and body of the individual person—and some of them *external*—in the social and physical environments. Under some circumstances, internal factors will be relatively more important than external factors in determining behavior. When this happens, people may seem immune to environmental forces. Under other circumstances, external factors will be relatively more important than internal factors in directing behavior. Under these conditions, people may appear fairly buffeted by environmental forces. Much of the time, though, internal factors and external factors will interact in subtle ways. Because of this subtle interaction, we cannot often understand social behavior unless we look both to the person and to the environment.

In the case of aggression, research has identified a number of external, environmental factors that can influence almost anyone to become more aggressive. For example, when people's desires are frustrated, when they are emotionally aroused, when everyone around them is behaving aggressively, when there are few sanctions against aggression, and when people can't be held personally responsible for their actions, most of these people will become more aggressive than usual. Nevertheless, some people will be more aggressive than others because of factors they carry around within them, regardless of, or in addition to, the situations they encounter.

What about these internal factors? How do they arise in the first place? Are some people more aggressive "by nature," or are these internal aggressive attitudes and predispositions the products of social situations? In the view of social psychology, even a characteristic internal predisposition toward aggression is most likely the product of the social situations in one's past. For example, aggressive individuals probably grew up witnessing violent behaviors routinely performed by parents, siblings, and peers. These people no doubt learned that aggression is an appropriate means to get what they wanted. Because of this social background, these people are probably more attuned to violent events in the environment. For example, they probably select aggressive shows on television, perceive the world in terms of conflict and struggle, and are more aware of their own anger. In this way people become involved in maintaining or "programming" their own aggressiveness. Thus there is almost always a complicated interaction between *internal factors*—a person's attitudes, expectations, and habits, for example—and *external factors*—the social situations in which we live, work, and play. Just as external social situations influence our internal dispositions, so our internal dispositions influence the way we perceive and respond to the social situations we select and encounter. Thus social behavior is a product of a continuous reciprocal interaction between internal personal dispositions and external situational forces.

Yet this process is not an automatic cycle. Once human beings have performed a behavior, such as aggression, they do not simply rest until a host of internal and external factors interact subtly to produce another burst of behavior. Instead, humans often observe their own responses and speculate about the meaning of their behavior. As a result of this analysis of their own behavior, people may arrive at a new view of themselves or a new interpretation of the situation that can influence their future behaviors. For example, if you observe and analyze an aggressive behavior that you have performed, it may become clear that the behavior was largely caused by some situational factor, such as group pressure. If you then wish to reduce the amount of future aggression you might engage in, you could decide to avoid the situations and groups that provoke such behavior. Furthermore, you could decide to remind yourself regularly of your internal values and attitudes that might be inconsistent with engaging in aggression. In this way you could decide to selectively deemphasize certain external situational factors and focus instead on certain internal dispositional factors, in effect shifting the balance from "outside" forces to "inside" forces. In contrast, if you wanted to be less governed by internal doubts or self-limiting constraints, you might act to shift the balance away from "inside" dispositional forces and toward "outside" situational forces. For example, if you thought you were unable to be aggressive even when it was warranted—such as when someone cut in line in front of you—you could seek out social situations that would foster more assertive behavior. You might take part in groups and activities where you could learn how to be more aggressive in asserting your own needs. In this way you would be selectively emphasizing situational factors to alter your own inner dispositions.

The theoretical goal of this book is to explain human social behavior in light of its underlying social-psychological processes. Throughout the coming chapters, we will emphasize how social situations not only influence behavior, but also help shape one's inner dispositions, which in turn affect one's reactions to social situations. We will also examine the circumstances that tend to emphasize one set of factors over another. Finally, we will try to show how all of these processes relate to everyday human experience as well as how they may be applied to understanding and possibly changing human social problems.

SUMMARY

Social psychology involves the empirical study of human social experience. Systematic observations under controlled conditions allow more "truthful" conclusions about human social behavior than nonempirical approaches. Some critics have argued that the findings and theories of social psychology are limited to a particular historical time and culture, and thus social psychology should more properly be viewed as history, not science. While this may be true for some issues, other findings and theories are probably valid across time and cultures if they are stated in sufficiently abstract terms. The important point is that social psychology involves the scientific study of human experience in a particular culture and historical time.

Although social psychology focuses on behavior in response to social situations, it relies on findings in other areas of psychology as well. For example, in order to understand the effects of crowding on social behavior, it may be necessary to consider physiological, cognitive, learning, and personality effects as well.

The history and current state of social psychology reflect two trends: a concern about understanding concrete social problems and a curiosity about explaining social processes. Since the problems and processes of interest have varied over time, social psychology is not characterized by a few major, all-inclusive theories, but by a host of minitheories about particular issues. The general perspective of social psychology is both phenomenological and behavioristic, reflecting Kurt Lewin's emphasis on Persons and Environments as mutual determinants of behavior. For example, many theories in social psychology deal with a person's self-concept, attitudes, expectations, and cognitive processes, while many other theories focus on situational forces that affect such behaviors as attraction, aggression, altruism, and conformity. The goal of this book is to explain how social situations influence behavior and help shape an individual's internal dispositions; an individual's dispositions then subsequently affect a person's response to social situations in a continuous reciprocal interaction.

CHAPTER TWO

RESEARCH METHODS IN SOCIAL PSYCHOLOGY

As the 1970s drew to a close, an event in Cincinnati was heralded by one newspaper as a possible sign of a "new violent era." It was a few weeks before Christmas 1979 and 8,000 young people had been waiting outside Cincinnati's 18,000-seat Riverfront Colosseum. They were waiting for the doors to open to a concert by the British rock group the Who. As the crowd became impatient and restless, someone broke a glass door with a bottle. Others pushed, the crowd surged, and when it was over, eleven people were dead, trampled in the crush.

The explanations by "experts" pointed to many possible causes. The police said that people had been drinking and using drugs and the crowd was rowdy. Others said the crowd was unusually calm for such a concert. A clinical psychologist attributed the crowd's behavior to "latent emotions" and "youthful rebelliousness." A psychiatrist said that the type of person who would attend such a concert "is more likely to be impulsive, show less judgment and be more focused on his experience of the moment." "It is hard to imagine the same thing happening with people waiting outside a Bernstein concert in New York," he said. Another psychiatrist said that the type of music played by the Who, with "screeching, yelling and breaking things up" was "scary and contagious." A psychologist explained the deaths as due to "mob psychology," frustration that a good seat might not be available, and the dehumanization of being part of a huge crowd. Newspaper reporters blamed the Colosseum's first-come, first-served "festival style" seating and questioned whether reserved seats could have prevented the deaths. And, finally, the incident was viewed by another psychiatrist as "part of a growing wave of violence circling the globe, not an episode that will pass over as an unfortunate event."

What really happened in Cincinnati? Were the deaths caused by youthful, impulsive, and rebellious people? Or were these just average youths whose emotions were temporarily aroused by alcohol, drugs, and frustration? Were the people affected by unusual situational factors, like contagious music and a dehumanizing mob? Was it a simple matter of bad seating policies? Or was it a manifestation of a world-wide sociohistorical trend?

From the perspective of social psychology, the cause of the concert deaths is an empirical question. Furthermore, it's a question with implications for both *social processes*—how people behave in anonymous mobs, for example—as well as *social problems*—for instance, how seating policies might affect behavior at rock concerts.

To answer this empirical question we could proceed in several ways. First we could adopt an *observational approach.* At the simplest level we could become *participant observers,* attending different types of concerts and noting how the crowd reacts. We could also employ *unobtrusive measures*—for example, examining the extent of damage to auditorium facilities after a rock concert versus another type of music. If we wanted more detailed information about the people themselves, we might conduct a case study and *interview* the various participants. To be more systematic about it, we might also conduct a *sample survey.* Here we would draw up a questionnaire and administer it to a sample of people carefully selected to be representative of all those who attended the concert. Then on the basis of our observations and people's survey responses, we might conduct *correlational research.* For example, we might correlate ages, educational levels, or musical preferences of concertgoers with the likelihood of these people engaging in violence. We might learn that people who like "screeching" music are more likely to be violent. But, of course, we wouldn't know whether violent people like screeching music or whether the music made them violent.

To answer the question of what really caused the behavior, we need to employ more than observational approaches. We need to adopt an *experimental approach.* Here we could hold all factors constant except the ones we are interested in. For example, if we wanted to know how music affected behavior we could randomly assign all types of people to one of two conditions: they would either hear screeching music or soft music. Then we could give them a chance to behave violently, and we would note if the responses differed in the two different groups. If the people in each group were more or less similar (because they had been randomly assigned), and if the two groups only differed in respect to the type of music they heard (because all other factors were held constant), then any differences in the behavior of the two groups could be explained by the music.

This research could be conducted in a *laboratory experiment*, where we try to create a situation as realistic as possible inside a social psychology lab, or in a *field experiment*, which is simply a controlled experiment conducted in a real-world, or field, setting. For example, instead of playing two types of music in the laboratory, we might conduct some type of measure as people leave two different types of concerts; so long as the people and other circumstances in the two groups were similar, then, again, we could infer that any differences in their behavior could be due to the music. Finally, we might conduct a *simulation* in order to study factors that are too complicated, impractical, or unethical to study in a realistic way in either the lab or field. For example, we might tell people the odds of getting a seat in the first twenty rows at a concert as a function of how large the crowd is and where they are located in the crowd. This information might be presented in the context of a game that is played against other participants or through a computer simulation, and we might observe levels of cooperation and competition as people seek to gain desired goals under different circumstances.

The following sections will present examples of each of these research approaches. We will also examine some of the problems and ethical issues raised by research on human social behavior. We will close with a short discussion of statistics that will help you understand and interpret research findings.

OBSERVATIONAL APPROACHES

Observational approaches to understanding social behavior do not involve a cause-and-effect analysis. They do not involve systematic control of all variables or random assignment of subjects to different conditions. Nevertheless they do allow an examination of what factors, or "variables," tend to occur together. Thus, while observational approaches do not answer conclusively *why* a social phenomenon may occur, they are very useful in answering questions of what, when, where, and how it occurs. In the sections below we will describe various observational research methods, ranging from least to most systematic.

PARTICIPANT OBSERVATION

The most direct way to study social behavior is to participate in the social process and observe what goes on. A classic example of this approach is a study published in 1971 by Laud Humphreys, a sociologist interested in homosexual behavior. Humphreys's specific subject was homosexual contact in public rest rooms, or "tearooms" as they are called among homosexuals. To study this behavior, Humphreys hung out around public rest rooms and offered to serve as "lookout" whenever two men wanted to have sex. In this way he conducted his field observations. The next step involved recording the men's automobile license numbers, tracking them down through the Department of Motor Vehicles, and then disguising himself and conducting an in-person "consumer" survey at the individual's home. Thus he was able to collect additional personal information to round out his participant observations.

While this approach allows a wealth of firsthand data, it is also subject to several possible biases. The individual observer's subjective expectations may color the observations, and the presence of the observer may influence the events that are being observed. In order to avoid these biases, unobtrusive or "nonreactive" measures may be employed.

UNOBTRUSIVE MEASURES

Unobtrusive or nonreactive measures are those that do not intrude on the social process being observed; since individuals are unaware they are being observed, they do not "react" in an unnatural way. One example of an unobtrusive measure dealt with TV viewers' attention to commercials (see Webb, Campbell, Schwartz, and Sechrest, 1966). Rather than asking people whether or not they had seen a particular commercial, the researchers surveyed Water Department records instead. If a sudden drop in water pressure could be detected at exactly the same time a commercial had interrupted a popular TV program, then viewers may have taken advantage of the commercial break to use the bathroom; the drop in water pressure was caused by thousands of simultaneously flushing toilets. Other unobtrusive measures are described in the accompanying Focus on Applications box.

A variant of unobtrusive measures involves concealment. For example, in a social psychology course project at Hamilton College one student rode up and down on top of the elevator in the student union building. His project involved spying through air vents to observe how people reacted to an erotic picture taped to the wall of the elevator when they were either alone or in groups.

Unobtrusive measures can provide valid information, but their practicality is often limited and there may also be ethical problems in observing people's behavior when they are unaware that someone is looking. A more direct observational approach is the interview technique.

INTERVIEWS

Some types of social behavior can best be studied through personal interviews with the people involved. An example of this is how people respond to disasters—such as earthquakes or flash floods—or to personal violence—such as rape. The researcher interested in these problems cannot open up the floodgates of a dam or passively wait for an assault to occur on the street. However, he or she can gather as much information as possible through personal interviews with the victims of such crises.

FOCUS ON APPLICATIONS

UNOBTRUSIVE MEASURES

Here are some nonreactive research techniques mentioned in *Unobtrusive Measures*, by Webb, Campbell, Schwartz, and Sechrest (1966). Because these techniques do not intrude on the behavior being observed, people do not react in an unnatural way.

The floor tiles around the hatching-chick exhibit at Chicago's Museum of Science and Industry must be replaced every six weeks. Tiles in other parts of the museum need not be replaced for years. The selective erosion of tiles, indexed by the replacement rate, is a measure of the relative popularity of exhibits.

The accretion rate is another measure. One investigator wanted to learn the level of whisky consumption in a town which was officially "dry." He did so by counting empty bottles in ashcans.

The degree of fear induced by a ghost-story-telling session can be measured by noting the shrinking diameter of a circle of seated children.

Chinese jade dealers have used the pupil dilation of their customers as a measure of the client's interest in particular stones, and Darwin in 1872 noted this same variable as an index of fear.

Library withdrawals were used to demonstrate the effect of the introduction of television into a community. Fiction titles dropped, nonfiction titles were unaffected.

The role of rate of interaction in managerial recruitment is shown by the overrepresentation of baseball managers who were infielders or catchers (high-interaction positions) during their playing days.

Sir Francis Galton employed surveying hardware to estimate the bodily dimensions of African women whose language he did not speak.

The child's interest in Christmas was demonstrated by distortions in the size of Santa Claus drawings.

Racial attitudes in two colleges were compared by noting the degree of clustering of Negroes and whites in lecture halls. (pp. 2–3)

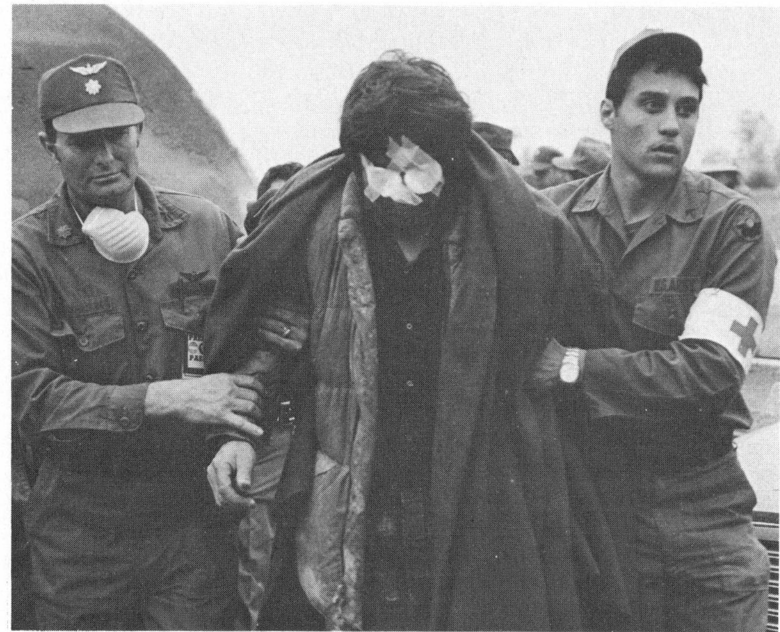

A victim of the eruption of Mount St. Helens, Washington, is taken to a rescue helicopter. The social psychologist interested in how people react in such disasters would probably use personal interviews. *(U.S. Army Photo/UPI)*

An example of research on disasters involves a catastrophic flood that hit Denver in the summer of 1965. Residents of low-lying sections were given a five- to fifteen-minute warning that a twenty-foot wall of water was approaching their homes. When the water arrived some four hours later and crested a few hours after that, bridges were ripped out, houses were destroyed, and the damage amounted to $325 million. Fortunately, no lives were lost because of the advance warning.

Three days after the flood, two researchers began studying people's reactions (Drabeck and Stephenson, 1971). They questioned a random sample of 278 families out of approximately 3,700 families that had been affected by the flood. The average interview lasted about an hour and a half and covered forty-five pages of questions that had been carefully developed to help people reconstruct their actions during the crisis. Answers were recorded verbatim.

The researchers learned that families thought and acted during the flood as groups, not as individuals; that the most effective evacuation warnings did not occur over the mass media but through telephone contacts between friends and relatives; and that people were confused by the initial warning time of fifteen minutes and the actual wait of four hours for the water to appear. Based on these findings, the researchers recommended that the traditional cautions about not tying up telephone lines during an emergency may be counterproductive, since these were the most helpful contacts in mobilizing people. The researchers also recommended that people be given more accurate information so that they can avoid confusion and plan their actions.

Another use of interviews involves reactions to rape (Goodchilds, Johnson, Zellman, and Giarrusso, 1980). Four researchers in Southern California were concerned about rape among acquaintances in young people. Their goal was to understand the processes that lead to forced sex. Since such encounters are typically not reported to the police and may be emotionally difficult to recount, the researchers felt that personal interviews were necessary. To accomplish their goal they selected a sample of young people and drew up a series of questions about experiences and attitudes regarding rape. They also described to each respondent several "vignettes" or social situations, such as the following: a young couple visits a beach; the man puts his arm around the woman's shoulders; they kiss and she touches his leg. Each respondent is then asked whether or not sexual intercourse is likely. The researchers found that males were much more likely to see the young woman's behavior as an invitation for sex than were females. Thus forced sex—or rape—may be partly a reflection of differing expectations between young men and young women. The researchers recommended better sex-role education in the schools as a way of preventing rape among acquaintances.

While interviews can yield helpful information, especially in cases like those above, there are also several types of bias inherent in interviews. The sex and race of the interviewer can affect people's responses as well as the interviewer's phrasing of questions, tone of voice, and inflections. Furthermore, people may not wish to admit certain things in public to another individual—for instance, that they panicked in a crisis or were either the victim or perpetrator of rape. In order to avoid some of these problems, researchers may develop a paper-and-pencil questionnaire and survey a broad cross section of people.

SURVEY RESEARCH

Questions relating to attitudes, opinions, past behaviors, or future behavioral intentions need not require personal interviews. Often such questions deal with ongoing social problems such as energy conservation, racial attitudes, or the use of drugs. To understand these issues may require responses from a great number of people representing a broad cross section of society. In those cases, survey research based on questionnaire responses is usually the most practical and efficient means of obtaining information.

A recent example of such research is a survey of California residents who had installed solar energy in their homes. Environmental researcher Julie Savinar (1980) wondered how those people who had adopted solar energy differed from those people who had not. In particular, California offers its residents an incentive for installing solar equipment by allowing a tax credit on their state income taxes. Savinar wanted to know if the incentive was effective. She obtained a list of people who had installed solar-heating equipment in the past year and mailed them a questionnaire containing questions regarding their background, personality, and motivations for installing such equipment. Surprisingly, she found that the tax credit had little influence on their behavior. Instead, these "solar adopters" were mainly people who saw themselves as innovators. These personality differences became clearer when the same questionnaire was mailed to another group of California residents who were selected for their similarity to the first group except for the fact that they had not installed solar-energy equipment. Their responses revealed that they were not "innovators." Savinar concluded that the tax-incentive plan was not a particularly effective way to encourage solar-energy conversion. Instead, the state might get better results if they directed a publicity campaign specifically to those people who see themselves as innovators.

Another recent example of survey research focuses on a different social problem—teenage contraception. Stuart Oskamp and Burton Mindick (1979) set out to determine why some young women were unable to practice contraception successfully. Previous researchers had attempted to relate failures in contraception to demographic factors such as socioeconomic status and racial and ethnic background. Instead Oskamp and Mindick focused on the individuals' level of sexual knowledge, their attitudes toward contraception, and a personality dimension called "future-time perspective"—that is, whether people are mainly oriented toward the moment or toward the future. The researchers distributed questionnaires to clients at several family-planning centers. They discovered that young women who cannot successfully practice contraception are characterized by inaccurate sexual knowledge, negative attitudes toward contraception, and little future-time perspective.

Survey research can be a useful way of obtaining information about people's attitudes and behaviors toward a broad range of issues.

A researcher who wants to explore the relationship between liberalized pornography laws and an increase in sex crimes would conduct a correlational study. *(© Joel Gordon)*

However, the value of questionnaires depends on the people who are sampled and the questions they are asked. If the respondents are not a representative sample of the population the researcher wishes to study, then their responses are of limited value. Also, if the questions are not clearly worded and the possible answers are not scaled in a way that makes sense to the respondents, then the responses of these respondents will be ambiguous. Furthermore, people may not want to answer questions in a way that would appear unflattering to them. To avoid this "social-desirability bias," questionnaire items must be carefully phrased and anonymity guaranteed. Finally, the questionnaire should be administered in a social setting that will not influence respondents' answers.

CORRELATIONAL RESEARCH

Many observational approaches to social behavior are correlational in nature. They reveal that two factors, or variables, are somehow associated or "co-related." However, as we mentioned earlier, such an approach does not *explain* a relationship; it merely describes it.

Correlations may either be positive or negative. A *positive correlation* between two variables means that an increase in one is associated with an increase in the other; a *negative correlation* between two variables means that an increase in one is associated with a decrease in the other. A correlation of zero means that the two variables have no relationship at all. Correlations are mathematically expressed through a statistic called the *correlation coefficient* (symbolized by r). A correlation coefficient can range from -1.0 to $+1.0$. The more a correlation coefficient departs from zero and approaches either -1.0 or $+1.0$, the higher is the correlation, negative or positive respectively.

Consider the problem facing a social psychologist who is conducting "evaluation research." In evaluation research, the goal is usually to understand how some social policy or program is affecting some segment of society. For example, do liberalized pornography laws cause an increase in sex crimes? Or can counseling juvenile lawbreakers lead to a decrease in juvenile delinquency? The second question was asked by the Police Department of a California community that hired psychologists Mark Lipsey, David Cordray, and Dale Berger (in press) to help them evaluate the impact of their newly instituted counseling program. Rather than sending juvenile offenders to a probation officer, the police began referring these juveniles to counselors. But what was the result, the police wanted to know? Did delinquency *decrease* as a result of this counseling program?

Lipsey and his colleagues determined that juvenile arrests did in fact decrease after the police began referring these young people to counselors. But why? On the surface there appeared to be some association between counseling and arrest rates: as the number of people who were counseled *increased*, the number of people who were arrested *decreased*. In other words, there was a *negative correlation* between counseling and arrest rates. But what caused this correlation? Perhaps the counseling was effective and the counseled juveniles committed fewer repeat crimes. Or perhaps the police felt that juvenile offenses would decrease because of the counseling program, and thus they could afford to be lenient and arrest fewer juveniles. Or perhaps more families moved out of the area at about the same time the police began the counseling referrals, and the lower arrest rates resulted from fewer juveniles in the area. This list of alternative possibilities could go on and on. Fortunately, in this case, the researchers were able to rely on other community information and a sophisticated computer program to demonstrate that counseling was effective in reducing delinquency. But by itself, the correlational approach does not explain cause and effect. In order to understand cause and effect, we must turn to controlled experiments.

EXPERIMENTAL APPROACHES

Experimental research is a means of testing hypotheses about cause-and-effect relationships. It allows an understanding of how one variable affects another variable, all other things being equal. In order to infer such a causal relationship, the experimenter must systematically vary one factor—*the independent variable*—while holding all other factors constant. The experimenter then observes whether these manipulations on the independent variable have some effect on the behavior of an experimental subject. The affected behavior is known as the *dependent variable*, because any changes in this behavior "depend on" the changes in the independent variable. If all other factors in the environment are held constant, and if the participants in the experiment are randomly assigned in order to control for any systematic differences in the people involved in each experimental condition, then any changes observed in the dependent variable can be clearly attributed to the experimenter's manipulations on the independent variable. To understand this more clearly, consider the following example of a laboratory experiment.

LABORATORY EXPERIMENTS

Why do people litter? Robert Krauss, Jonathan Freedman, and Morris Whitcup (1978) set out to answer this question. If the factors that influence littering can be understood, then perhaps social policies can be developed that will discourage littering. Previous research (Robinson, 1976) employing observational methods had suggested that littering is heavily influenced by the amount of litter already present in an environment; in other words, people seem to litter more in environments that are dirty than in environments that are clean. But why? Does litter cause more littering, or do "litterers" frequent littered places? What is the connection between litter and littering?

In order to test this relationship between litter and littering, Krauss, Freedman, and Whitcup conducted a laboratory experiment. Their independent variable was the amount of litter present in a room. The dependent variable was whether subjects littered. Each of these variables had to be translated from an abstract concept to specific procedures. In other words, the variables had to be defined in *operational terms*. The operational definition of the independent variable—litter—was simple: in the "litter" condition, the experimenters strew a room with crushed paper cups, candy bar wrappers, a newspaper, a paper bag, a crushed soft-drink can, some string, and bits of cellophane; in the "nonlittered" condition, the room was swept clean. Neither room had a trash receptacle.

The operational definition of the dependent variable—subjects' propensity to litter the environment—required more creativity. The experimenters needed to supply all subjects with some item to litter. They achieved this by telling subjects that they were participating in an experiment on "the physiological correlates of creative thought." For the purposes of the experiment, it would be necessary to take "palm prints" before and after creative work. In order to take palm prints, the experimenters swabbed each subject's hand with a "greenish oil" and then, after the print was taken, with Vaseline which subjects were told to leave on for sixty seconds. The subject was also given some tissues. The measure of littering was whether subjects left their tissues in the waiting room or took the tissues with them to dispose of properly. The subjects were undergraduate students who were recruited by telephone and paid $2.00 for their participation.

The experimenters found that 30 percent of the subjects in the littered environment simply left their tissues in the room, while only 6.7 percent of the subjects in the nonlittered environment left their tissues behind. These findings supported the hypothesis that litter begets litter.

Like observational methods, laboratory experiments are also subject to potential biases. So much research in social psychology is based on controlled laboratory experiments that we must give careful attention to those biases, for they can limit the validity and generalizability of laboratory research. Some important potential biases are the following.

DISPOSITIONS AND SITUATIONS

ON LITTERING

What factors affect littering, and how can littering be reduced? These questions were studied by William C. Finnie (1973) on the streets of Philadelphia. Two hundred seventy-two people were observed as they purchased a hot dog from vendors on different streets in the downtown business district; some of the streets were more littered than others. In addition, Finnie and his students either placed extra litter cans on the streets or removed all the litter cans from the streets. They were interested in the effects on littering of two situational variables: the general cleanliness of the environment and the presence or absence of litter cans. They also noted subjects' age as a possible dispositional influence on littering. The measure of littering was whether subjects discarded the hot dog wrapper on the street.

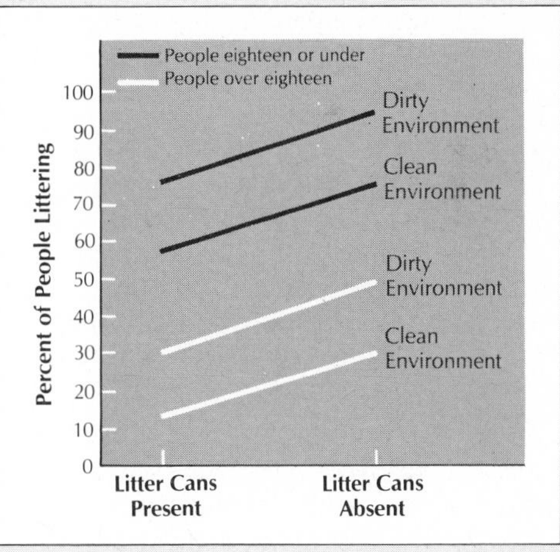

Finnie's results were straightforward. Both situational and dispositional variables affected people's tendency to litter. As shown in the graph below, people littered more in the dirty environment than in the clean environment, and they also littered more when no trash cans were available. Furthermore, people under eighteen were much more likely to litter than those over eighteen.

Representativeness of subjects is important to the validity of a laboratory experiment. *(© Burk Uzzle/Magnum)*

REPRESENTATIVENESS OF SUBJECTS In order to be able to generalize from the findings in a laboratory experiment to a larger population, the subjects in the experiment must be representative of the larger population. In the strictest sense, representativeness can only be obtained if everyone in the larger population has an equal chance of being selected as a subject in the experiment. In a practical sense, of course, this is impossible. Most researchers simply use as subjects whoever is available—typically undergraduate college students, as in the littering experiment above. In some types of research, the use of undergraduate students may pose no problem; for example, if the research involves memory for faces, it is likely that undergraduates remember strangers' faces just about as well as anyone else. However, undergraduates may be more sensitive to certain types of experimental manipulations than the average person in the general population. For example, undergraduates may be more concerned about identity issues than older persons, and thus they may be unusually susceptible to manipulations of self-esteem, self-awareness, and so forth. Undergraduates may even have different littering tendencies than the population at large, for one study has found that people under eighteen litter more than people over eighteen do (Finnie, 1973; see the Dispositions and Situations box on page 29). Thus, in interpreting experimental research, you should keep in mind who the subjects are and how representative their responses might be of the population at large.

EXPERIMENTER EFFECTS In a famous series of experiments reported in 1966, Robert Rosenthal showed that experimenters can influence the outcome of their experiments in subtle ways. As a result, the experimenter may unintentionally produce the findings he or she is setting out to test. Such effects can occur in numerous ways. Rosenthal showed that experimenters may alter their words, voice inflections, and nonverbal behaviors to coincide with their expectations about the subjects. For example, an experimenter may be more animated and appear more encouraging when a subject responds in a way that coincides with the experimenter's hypothesis, or an experimenter may respond differently to one sex of subject than to another.

The best way around these problems is for the experimenter to be "blind" to the subject's experimental condition. In other words, if the experimenter is unaware of what condition the subject is in—for instance, a littered or nonlittered environment—then the experimenter cannot subtly influence the subject's behavior in order to produce a specific result. Better still, the experimenter may be someone who is hired to run the study and who is completely unaware of the experiment's hypothesis. If these safeguards are not feasible, then as much of the instructions as possible should be printed, tape-recorded, or otherwise automated. The goal is to prevent the experimenter from unconsciously influencing the results in any way.

DEMAND CHARACTERISTICS Other biases in laboratory research are contributed by the subjects themselves. For example, when subjects are able to determine the hypothesis of the research, they may respond so as to confirm the hypothesis, thinking they are helping out the experimenter. Or on the other hand, they may respond so as to disconfirm the hypothesis, thinking they will teach the experimenter a lesson for presuming to predict their behavior. Even when subjects incorrectly guess at the hypothesis, their behavior still may confound the results, so long as they are not responding naturally (see the Focus on Applications box on page 32).

One way that experimenters deal with this potential problem is through deception. In other words, they try to lead subjects astray from the real purposes of the study. In the littering experiment discussed above, subjects were told that the experiment dealt with "creative thinking." This "cover story" not only concealed the real purposes of the study, but also provided a rationale for giving subjects a tissue. But imagine how biased the results would be if subjects were told they were taking part in a littering experiment and were then handed an item to litter. In a situation like this, deception may be essential. Of course, deception does create ethical problems, which can sometimes become serious, depending on the type of deception involved. We will have more to say about ethical problems in a later section.

FIELD EXPERIMENTS

Many of the problems of laboratory research can be avoided by conducting experiments in the real world, or in the "field," as it is called. In field experiments the *independent variable* often is not manipulated by the researcher but instead is a naturally occurring phenomenon. A researcher interested in the effects of noise on behavior might locate similar groups of people who live or work in areas of high versus low noise and then measure their behavior as a result of differential noise exposure. Similarly, the *dependent variable* often is not a response to a questionnaire or a response on some finely calibrated measuring instrument, but instead is a naturally occurring behavior that experimenters record and measure. For instance, a researcher interested in littering might count or weigh the amount of actual litter discarded by people on a city street. In addition, field experiments are sometimes a combination of a naturally occurring independent variable and a precisely measured response, or a carefully manipulated independent variable and a naturally occurring response. What defines a field experiment is that it occurs in the field instead of in a social psychology laboratory. Yet, cause-and-effect analyses are still possible because the subjects are assumed to be randomly distributed in the various experimental conditions, and all other factors are either controlled or "matched" so that subjects are similar across all conditions.

Field experiments are becoming more and more popular in social psychology. They have the advantage of "ecological validity" over laboratory research; that is, their findings are immediately valid in the real world, because the "ecology" of the real world is the setting for the research in the first place. In addition field experiments generally avoid many of the prob-

FOCUS ON APPLICATIONS

DEMAND CHARACTERISTICS

How far will people go in a psychology experiment? Martin Orne (1962) argues that because of "demand characteristics" in the psychology experiment, people will do things in the laboratory that they would not do in real life. For example, Orne says that it may be impossible to devise an experiment that subjects will perceive as completely "meaningless." In one case, subjects were given a stack of paper, each page containing rows of random digits. The experimenter instructed subjects to add all the rows of numbers successively, and after accurately completing each page, to tear it into a minimum of thirty-two pieces. Although subjects were given no justification for this task, they continued the apparently meaningless behavior far beyond the tolerance limits of the experimenters. In other studies, people continue in such seemingly purposeless tasks as eating unsalted soda crackers until they can eat no more, trying to balance a marble on a small steel ball, or attempting to ladle spilled mercury into a tiny bottle with a wooden paddle (Frank, 1944) simply because an experimenter asked them to.

But does this cooperation extend to actions that are dangerous and likely to cause injury? Apparently so, according to a study conducted by Orne and his colleague, Frederick Evans (1965). The experimenters set up three dangerous and harmful tasks.

1. A poisonous Australian snake, the fourteen-inch-long red-bellied black snake, was placed in a compartment by an assistant wearing long, thick gloves. The experimenter asked each subject to pick up the snake with his or her bare hands and place it in a bag. Just before the subject reached into the compartment, an invisible glass screen was lowered into place in order to prevent the subject from receiving a mortal wound.
2. Next, the assistant placed a glass beaker in the compartment and slowly poured in fuming concentrated nitric acid. A copper coin was dropped into the acid, and the subject watched the coin dissolve for approximately a minute. The experimenter asked each subject to reach into the beaker as quickly as possible and to pick up the coin with a bare hand and to plunge the hand into a nearby solution of soapy, lukewarm water.
3. Finally, while the subject was distracted, the beaker of acid was replaced with a harmless colored solution. The experimenter then asked the subject to pick up the beaker of "acid" and to throw it into the assistant's face.

How far did subjects go with these requests? When six hypnotized subjects were asked to carry out each of the tasks, only one refused. Then six additional subjects were not hypnotized, but were asked to simulate hypnosis by pretending to be deeply hypnotized; of these, all six complied with each of the requests. Finally, a group of six normal, waking subjects were run through the experiment as a control group; of these, two refused to handle the poisonous snake, but five of the six thrust their hands in the acid and went on to throw it in the assistant's face.

What went on in the minds of these simulation subjects and control-group subjects? Why should normal individuals carry out potentially lethal acts in the context of a psychology lab? When Orne asked the subjects these questions, he found that all of them thought they would be safe, because they were in a psychology experiment. They believed that the snake had been defanged, or that the solution was not really acid (even though they had seen it dissolve a coin), or that the assistant would duck. In other words, just being in a psychology experiment somehow made it all right to do almost anything. This is exactly Orne's point about demand characteristics: experimental subjects can be amazingly cooperative simply because they are in an experiment, and their behavior in the laboratory may not always reflect their behavior in the real world.

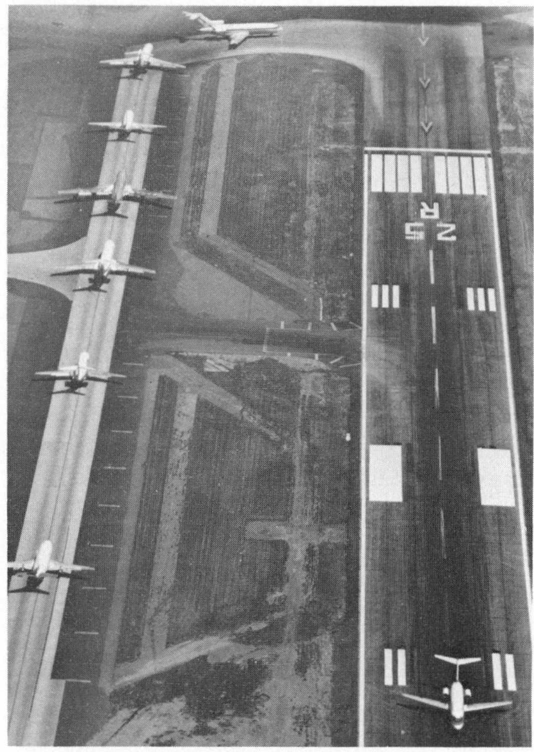

Airplanes awaiting takeoff at Los Angeles International Airport. Cohen, Evans, Krantz, and Stokols conducted a field study using aircraft noise at this airport as the independent variable and the reactions of elementary-school children as the dependent variable. *(© George Hall 1980/Woodfin Camp & Assoc.)*

lems of laboratory experiments discussed above. First, field experiments avoid the problem of nonrepresentative subjects because the participants are "real people" in the daily course of their lives, not college students reacting to a staged event. Second, field experiments can avoid the biases of experimenter effects because the experimenter is less directly involved in manipulating conditions and measuring reactions. Thus the experimenter has less of a chance to influence the outcome. Finally, field experiments can avoid the biases of demand characteristics because the subjects are often unaware they are even taking part in an experiment.

An excellent example of a field study was recently conducted by Sheldon Cohen, Gary Evans, David Krantz, and Daniel Stokols (1980) on the effects of aircraft noise on children's behavior and health. Their independent variable was the noise made by aircraft landing at Los Angeles International Airport. Their dependent variable was how elementary-school children reacted to this noise. To conduct their experiment, the investigators compared children from schools directly under an air corridor with children from quiet schools in a nearby neighborhood. The noisy schools received 300 overflights a day, or about one every two and a half minutes during school hours. These "noisy school" children were "matched" with the "quiet school" children on the basis of grade, ethnic and racial background, and parents' income level, occupational level, and educational level. In other words, children in both schools were similar in terms of age, social class, and race.

The investigators learned that the children from noisy schools had higher blood pressure, were slower to solve and more likely to fail a puzzle-solving task, and gave up sooner on the task than children from quiet schools (see Figure 2.1). In this case, the independent variable was a naturally occurring phenomenon—aircraft noise—while the dependent variable was

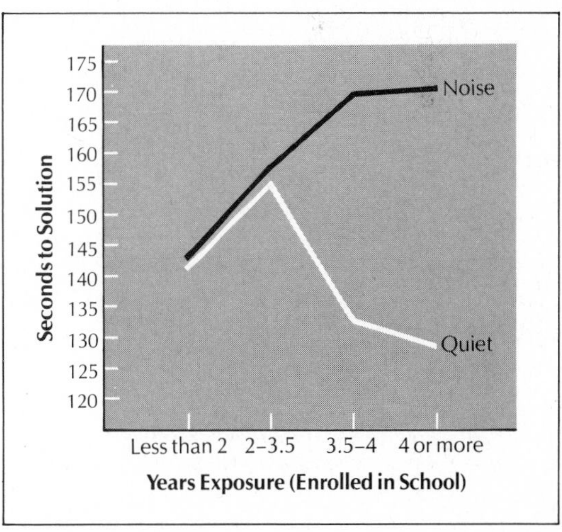

FIGURE 2.1 **In their study of noise and learning, Cohen, Evans, Krantz, and Stokols (1980) found that the longer children had been enrolled in schools subject to aircraft noise, the slower they were to solve the test puzzle.**

precise responses on measures of blood pressure and puzzle-solving ability.

It is also possible for an experimenter to manipulate the independent variable in a field setting. In a study on littering, for example, Robert Cialdini (1977) systematically littered a campus pathway at Arizona State University with one, two, four, eight, or sixteen pieces of paper, or else the pathway was picked clean. As a student approached this pathway, he or she was handed a public-service circular. The measure of the dependent variable—littering—was simply how many people threw away the circular in each of the litter conditions. Cialdini found that the more littered the pathway, the more likely were students to throw down the circular.

Each of these field experiments demonstrates that cause-and-effect relationships can be established in the real world as well as in the laboratory. However, there are certain limitations to field experiments. Generally, it is not possible to randomly assign subjects to experimental conditions. Instead, the experimenter must be satisfied with matching subjects, so that people are as similar as possible in each condition. Also, field research is limited to some extent to phenomena that are easy to locate or manipulate in the field, such as noise and litter, and to responses that are easily observable, such as physiological reactions or gross behaviors. When the researcher is interested in more subtle phenomena, such as self-justification, social perception, or causal attributions for behavior, it becomes harder to conduct the research in the real world. There are often too many contaminations and confounding factors to get a clear reading of such subtle phenomena. Thus, while the field is an excellent place to study social problems, it is often an unsatisfactory place to study intricate social processes. In fact, when the phenomena are particularly intricate or complex, they may best be approached through laboratory simulations.

SIMULATION

A simulation is a way of representing reality in a simplified form while maintaining the essential components of the real event. Simulations are useful in social psychology when the investigator is interested in more complicated variables than are usually feasible in laboratory and field experiments. Because the actual event cannot be staged in the laboratory or observed in the field, it is presented in a simulated form. For example, how do people react to several days of imprisonment? How do they respond when locked in competition with another person over scarce resources? How do people make decisions in a crisis when each of their actions results in new information to consider?

Each of these questions pertains to people's reactions over a period of time to a whole set of surrounding events. Each of these questions has also been studied through a simulation. Philip Zimbardo and his colleagues (Zimbardo, Haney, Banks, and Jaffe, 1973) constructed a simulated prison in the basement of the Stanford University Psychology Department and observed how college students playing the roles of prisoners and guards behaved over a six-day period. Their surprising results will be discussed in Chapter 8. In another type of simulation, Morton Deutsch (1973) had college students play a realistic "trucking game" where two players could each block the other's access to the fastest route between two points on a game board. These results will be discussed in Chapter 10.

Many game-type simulations involve an elaborate preprogrammed series of countermoves for any move made by the subject. For instance, Siegfried Streufert and his colleagues (Streufert, Kliger, Castore, and Driver, 1967) developed a game to study how decision makers behave under limited warfare conditions. Their simulation takes place in a room that resembles a strategic command post, complete with a three-dimensional map of a fictitious country named Shamba, a telephone, video-communication equipment, flags, and many other props. The participants read a manual on the historical background of Shamba and on the current conditions there, and are informed about their resources, capacities, and so on. After a two-hour reading period and a strategy consultation with one another, they are ready to play the game. They believe that they are playing against another team representing an opposing nation. The team members can divide up their work or operate as a unit. The way in which they handle the simulated problem is up to them.

The events in the simulation are carefully preprogrammed so that the illusion of reality is maintained. However, the teams are receiving information (via written messages, telephone calls, or video news broadcasts) that has been predetermined by the experimenters. In this fashion, the experimenters control the conditions at the beginning of the simulation, and they also know exactly what information is being received by the participants at any point in time. In other words, all teams in any experiment can receive information in exactly the same way (the same information in the same or random order).

Involvement is the key characteristic of a good simulation. Participants in simulations often refuse to quit even after hours. They can get carried away with ongoing situations, perhaps confusing reality with simulated events. The advantages of the simulation are that it measures behavior similar to naturally occurring human behavior, that it usually elicits feelings of involvement from subjects that heighten their sense of realism, and that the experimenter has control over events as they proceed. There are some disadvantages as well. The simulation is a compromise between such real-world techniques as the survey and the standard laboratory experiment, which permit more precise control over variables by experimenters. As a compromise, the simulation necessarily has advantages and disadvantages and is probably most effectively used in combination with other approaches, particularly with the standard laboratory experiment, which can usually yield more precise information about relationships among clearly defined conditions.

CONVERGENT VALIDATION

All approaches to studying human behavior can have certain limitations or characteristic biases, as we have pointed out. Therefore, the researcher must carefully consider the strengths and weaknesses of any research approach in light of the particular behavior in which he or she is interested.

One way to reduce the possibility of biases is to adopt more than one research approach to the same problem. For example, a researcher interested in littering may first interview people, then conduct a sample survey, then carry out a controlled laboratory experiment, and finally verify the results in the real world with a field experiment. If each of these different approaches yields the same findings, then the researcher can be confident about the validity of the findings. Such an approach to research is called "convergent validation" (Campbell and Fiske, 1959) because several different research methods converge on the same finding. Thus it is possible to overcome many of the biases inherent in different approaches to human behavior. But another type of problem encountered in studying social behavior involves ethical issues.

ETHICAL ISSUES IN RESEARCH

In the past decade, social psychologists have become increasingly concerned with the ethical implications of their research. The 1970s began with American involvement in an unpopular Asian war, with America's cities being torn by racial conflict, and with American politics and society shaken by a series of political assassinations. What could social psychology offer to help solve these problems?

Many social psychologists felt that too much research was being conducted for selfish or parochial reasons and not enough was being dedicated to significant social problems. In the past ten years, however, more and more research has focused on social problems. Many of these studies have been described in the preceding pages—studies dealing with rape, contraception, energy conservation, littering, and aircraft noise. Yet, ethical issues still trouble social psychologists, and two of these issues in particular deserve special attention.

The first has to do with the creation of false impressions. In numerous studies the experimenter creates a reality for the experimental subjects that has no basis in fact. For example, subjects may be informed that another person likes them, that others' decisions are better than theirs, that they are inflicting intense pain on others, that the building they are in is burning down, and so on. To put it bluntly, these are all lies. Although most researchers probably do not enjoy duplicity for its own sake and are fully willing to admit its ethical shortcomings, many researchers maintain that duplicity is an occupational hazard. The earlier discussion of experimentation provides a rationale. Scientific knowledge depends a great deal on our capacity to test the effects of isolated factors. The natural environment seldom offers an opportunity to observe the effects of a single factor and to hold all others constant. Thus the experimenter often resorts to creating a situation in the laboratory where one factor is manipulated and all others are held constant, as we have described.

The subject cannot be informed of the experimenter's manipulation until after the effects on the subject have been observed, because this information might well bias the subject's reactions. Perhaps it would encourage even more than the usual attention to responses that are socially desirable. Alternatives to this approach are continuously being sought, and most experimenters attempt to minimize the "unreal" aspects of the situation. However, conducting research with enough validity that its results can help solve social problems may require a certain amount of deception on the part of experimenters.

A second important problem stems from the pain that is often inflicted on experimental subjects. Psychologists who are interested in contributing findings that can be used to alleviate conflict, reduce aggression, or understand stress often create situations in which people experience undue emotional stress. The experiment may place subjects in a state of conflict, inflict physical pain, or induce stress. In many instances subjects for research are informed beforehand of the noxious aspects of the research. However, because of problems of biased results, subjects are not always so candidly apprised of the situation. In almost all cases the experimenter introduces as little pain or stress as he can; ethical considerations prevent laboratory study of some issues, such as the psychology of extreme pain. In addition, investigators almost invariably talk with participants after unpleasant experiences to inform them about why the pain was inflicted and to assure them of the value of their contribution to knowledge. In almost all cases in which subjects have been deceived or have experienced discomfort, a debriefing session has followed. The attempt is made to ensure that no one leaves with a false picture of what has happened or with a feeling of having been uselessly abused.

The ethics of social-scientific study is one type of research problem. A different sort of problem is that of making clear conclusions about relationships between independent and dependent variables. Statistics, a branch of mathematics, is useful to social psychologists in "describing" the degree to which a finding is *significant*, or unlikely to have occurred by chance alone.

THE PLACE OF STATISTICS IN RESEARCH

What is statistics? The word is certainly familiar enough. So are the television commercials that attempt to persuade viewers that a particular product is better than brand X by overwhelming these viewers with statistics. The fact is that the manufacturers of any product, or the promoters of any cause or candidate, can "prove" the superiority of even the shoddiest commodity by using statistics selectively. It seems that many people in this age of advertising have a reverence for numbers that is often undeserved. Advertisers, political propagandists, and others frequently capitalize on this reverence. A closer look at what statistics actually can and cannot reveal is in order.

Statistics are often used to compare two classes of persons, objects, or events. These classes will be easy to compare if all members of the first group are similar to one another, if all members of the second group are also similar to one another, and if all members of the first group are different from all members of the second group. For example, if one group contains only children and the other group contains only adults, then it can be stated that the members of the first group are younger than those of the second, and clear-cut comparisons can be made.

Unfortunately, it is not usually that easy to compare two groups. The membership of groups frequently overlaps, characteristics are often similar, and differences may be small. One is justified in saying that two groups are different from each other if one knows (1) the characteristics of all their members and (2) the fact that one member who differs from all the others is present in only one group. Say, for example, that the racial characteristics of two groups are being compared. If one group contains only lower-class whites from the South and the second group contains one middle-class black person from the North among several lower-class southern whites, then the two groups are indeed different. To be aware of such a difference, it is necessary to research the appropriate characteristics of the total *populations* of both groups. A "population" refers to the total membership of a group, class of objects, or class of events. Studying entire populations is often unwieldy if the populations are large. Consequently, social scientists usually must be content with a *sample* of the relevant population—that is, with a representative group of population members. For example, if a researcher wanted to know whether or not the French are better lovers than Americans, it would be impossible to test and interview every French person and every American. On the other hand, if only one French person and one American were studied, the investigator might find that the American is a better lover or that the French person is a better lover or that they are equally good lovers. In the first instance the researcher's prejudice may be unconfirmed. In the second it may be confirmed, and the finding that the two persons did not differ in their love-making abilities would probably confuse the investigator. But what would any of these results imply about the abilities of French people and Americans as lovers? Nothing.

Rather than focus on an individual who may be the exception rather than the rule, the investigator usually selects a sample of persons from the populations being studied, taking care that the sample is as representative of the general population as possible. Only then can results be relatively reliable, so that other researchers following the same research design would probably obtain the same results.

If you were a researcher studying the relative love-making abilities of French and American people and were concerned about basing your data on a sample large enough to permit comfortable generalizations about the populations at large, you might select 500 Americans and 500 French persons and *match* subjects from rural areas with subjects from urban areas, laborers with professionals, males with females, and so on. In other words, the French sample would include the same proportion of, for example, female subjects as would be included in the American sample. You might develop a paper-and-pencil "lover's test" that distinguishes between "good" and "bad" lovers. Undoubtedly, some Americans would score high on the test. So would some French subjects. Other American and French subjects would score low. Still others would score in the middle range. You would have two distributions of scores: one for the French, one for the Americans. You could address two central questions with statistics on the basis of these distributions: (1) Are the French and American distributions different from each other? (2) How sure can one be that the differences obtained (if any) between the sample distributions of the French and American subjects accurately reflect actual differences between the populations of French and American people? The answer to this latter question is typically given as a probability statement. For example, if you had found that the French indeed make better lovers and that the probability of French superiority in this respect was beyond the .05 *level of significance*, or 5-percent *level of confidence*, you could state with reasonable confidence that the probability that your sample differences reflect population differences is better than 95 percent. Or you could express this finding from the opposite direction and say that your conclusion about French love-making abilities has only a 5-percent chance of being wrong. These are both ways of saying that you are confident that the differences you found between your samples reflect differences in the population; in both instances, the odds would be 20 to 1 that your

If you were to study the sunbathing habits of New Yorkers and Parisians, you would need to obtain matching samples from both populations. *(© Jim Anderson 1980/Woodfin Camp & Assoc.; © Patrick Bruchet/VIVA 1980/Woodfin Camp & Assoc.)*

results reflected real population differences. Had the odds been 100 to 1, you could be even more confident in your conclusions, stating that your hypothesis can be accepted at the .01 level of significance, or 1-percent level of confidence. Had your results fallen below the .05 level of significance, then you would not be warranted in concluding that your hypothesis is accurate, because the odds are too great that the results could be due to chance variation. Clearly, then, the term *significance* does not mean that data are "important"; it refers, rather, to the confidence with which one can believe that the results reflect a characteristic of some larger population.

USES AND ABUSES OF STATISTICS

Statistics per se are not of value to the scientist. They may be fun, unpleasant, or whatever, depending on the individual's point of view, but they are not "science." Rather, they are a tool for the scientist, just like the hammer is a tool for the carpenter. The better the hammer and the more appropriate the hammer for the kind of nail being used, the more successful the carpentry job will be. The same is true of statistics. There are many statistical methods. All of them can be used either to confuse or to elucidate issues.

Consider two simple examples. If you are told by an authoritative television personality that nine out of ten lawyers prefer chocolate bars over hard candy, then you have been given insufficient information (the claim has been altered somewhat here in order not to embarrass the manufacturer). The implication is that many lawyers were sampled. In fact, the sample might have consisted of only ten lawyers, nine of whom worked for the chocolate-bar company that produced the advertisement. This is an example of a probability statement that is not accompanied by information about how the probability was obtained. Or you may be told that you should eat fruit sugar because it gets into the bloodstream twice as fast as cane sugar. If fruit sugar takes fifteen minutes to enter the bloodstream and cane sugar takes thirty, that would be quite a difference. But if one takes two milliseconds and the other takes four, then the real difference is not significant enough to warrant a change in your shopping habits; it only sounds impressive. This is a descriptive statement that lacks sufficient information. Both of these examples represent abuses of statistics.

Erroneous or misleading use of statistical methods can occur in social-psychological research. For example, recall the hypothetical study of French and American love making. Among the assumptions on which the study was based was that there would be a paper-and-pencil test measuring the ability to be a good lover. But just as the statistical underpinnings of the TV commercials described above were questionable, the love-making test is also questionable. Is the test *valid*? That is, does it actually measure love-making excellence, or does it measure something else? For example, it may not be surprising that French subjects appeared to excel if the test had been developed by a French researcher, who was particularly sensitive to what the French consider good loving. Americans may have different beliefs, may enjoy different activities, and consequently the test may be valid in France but less valid in the United States. Or the test may tend to elicit socially desirable responses from both French and American subjects, so that differences are more revealing of what are considered socially acceptable sexual activities than they are of differences in what the subjects actually do. In either case, the results obtained in this hypothetical experiment may not mean what they are interpreted to mean.

One should be aware of another characteristic of statistics. Often data are reported that suggest that a significant relationship between two variables has been found. For example, if the reported significance level is .05 or better, the probability that this finding would be obtained erroneously is less than 5 percent. What does this "significance" imply? As discussed earlier, if all the relevant characteristics of two populations are known to an investigator, then only one observation is a sufficient basis for drawing conclusions about that population. By implication, the larger the sample (the more closely it approaches the size of the population), the smaller the difference required to be significant. For example, if data are obtained from six or seven subjects in each of two samples, then there can be practically no overlap between their distributions if a difference is to be statistically significant. If, on the other hand, the samples contain hundreds of subjects, then very small differences will be significant. From a statistical, or mathematical, standpoint, this makes sense. However, from a practical standpoint, the implications of sample size should be understood: when a researcher reports a significant difference between two groups, two subjects, or two conditions, the size (and thus the importance) of this difference should be noted. The difference may well support a theory, it may well be interesting, but it may or may not be a large difference and thus may or may not have practical application.

SUMMARY

Social-psychological research involves both observational approaches and experimental approaches. Observational approaches include participant observation, unobtrusive measures, interviews, and surveys. Participant observation involves taking part in an event and observing what goes on. However, the observer's expectations may bias what is observed, and the observer's presence may affect what goes on. Unobtrusive measures allow observations of naturally occurring events without intruding on the event, although these measures are not always practical and often provide little detail. More information can be gathered through interviews with the people involved in a particular event. However, the nature of the interviewer, the interviewer's phrasing of questions, and the interviewee's reluctance to admit certain types of information to another person can affect the result of interviews. To avoid these problems, a survey based on a series of carefully worded questions may be administered to a selected sample of the population. However, if the sample is not representative of the population of interest, if the questions are not worded and scaled clearly, and if the respondents do not answer truthfully, the responses may be of little value.

Observational approaches to human behavior represent correlational research. They allow a conclusion that certain variables "occur together" or are somehow associated. However, correlational findings do not allow a cause-and-effect analysis. In order to examine causes and effects we must turn to experimental research.

Experimental research measures the effect of a selected independent variable on a particular dependent variable, when all other factors are held constant and subjects are randomly assigned to experimental conditions. Experimental research includes laboratory experiments, field experiments, and simulations. In a laboratory experiment, the experimenter manipulates the independent variable and precisely measures an individual's responses on the dependent variable. However, laboratory experiments may be biased because the subjects may not be representative of a larger population, the experimenter may subtly influence the results, and the subjects themselves may try to guess the hypothesis and alter their behavior accordingly. Some of these problems can be avoided in field experiments, in which the independent variable is either manipulated or occurs naturally in the real world and the dependent variable is measured in the real world as well. While such experiments can have greater "ecological validity," they are not always appropriate for certain types of responses, their findings may be less precise, and subjects must often be "matched" across conditions instead of being randomly assigned. When the variables of interest are too complicated, extended, or unethical to measure in a laboratory or field experiment, simulations may be employed which represent reality in a simplified form while maintaining the essential components of the real event. However simulations sometimes allow less control over variables than other types of experimental research.

Whatever research methods are adopted, it is always a good idea to employ more than one approach, thus allowing for convergent validation. When the same finding can be obtained in the lab and in the field, the experimenter can be confident that the results are not due to artifacts.

Social psychologists are often troubled about two types of ethical problems. The first is the frequent use of deception in research, although to inform subjects of a research hypothesis in advance might bias their responses. The second is the physical or emotional pain caused to subjects by certain types of manipulations, although subjects are generally informed in advance when research may be painful and thoroughly debriefed afterward about the necessity of the manipulation.

Statistics are a means of comparing the significance of differences between two groups. In order to infer that two groups are reliably different, the researcher must show that a pattern of differences would occur by chance only in one in twenty times (.05 level of confidence) or one in one hundred times (.01 level of confidence); thus the differences would be due to genuine differences in the two samples and not to chance occurrences. However, statistics can sometimes be misleading. Unless sufficient information is provided about the nature of the sample, the research measures, the type of statistical analysis performed, and the actual differences measured, the statistics may be irrelevant.

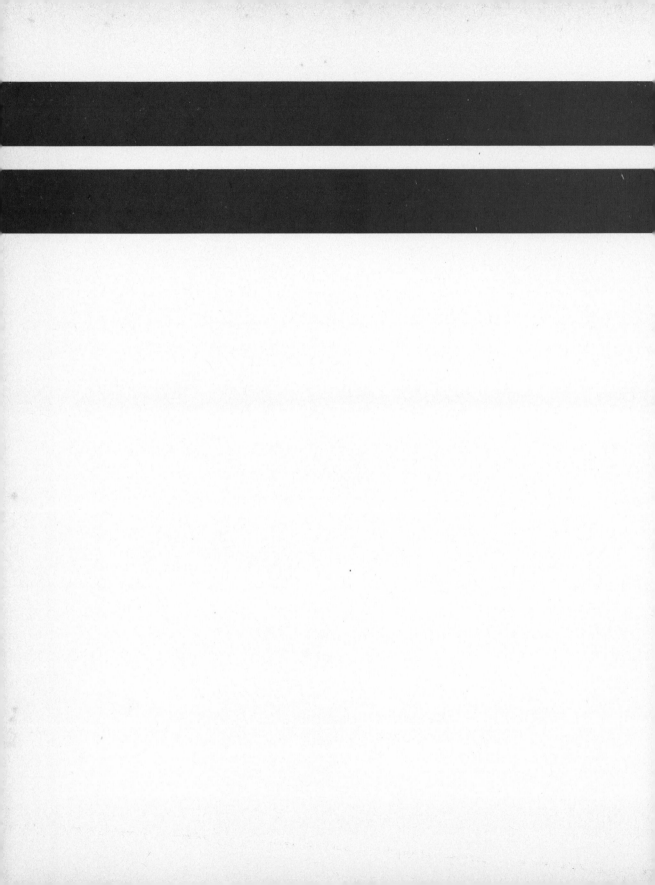

PART TWO

THE INDIVIDUAL

CHAPTER THREE

THE SELF

On an early February evening in 1974, a young woman was finishing dinner with her boyfriend in the small apartment they shared near the University of California campus at Berkeley. Without warning, a band of masked strangers burst in, seized the woman, and dragged her away. Her boyfriend and her family were not to see her again for almost two years, and when they did, she was not the same person who had disappeared into the night.

The woman was Patty Hearst, daughter of newspaper publisher Randolph Hearst and heiress to the Hearst fortune. Her captors were a radical political group calling themselves the Symbionese Liberation Army. Their original goal was to hold Ms. Hearst as a hostage until her father could ransom her with a multimillion-dollar food giveaway to the poor people of Oakland, California. But she was not released when the ransom was paid. Instead, she was bound and held in a dark closet, then detained under guard, and gradually "reeducated" by her captors.

Two months later, on April 3, her captors released a photograph and tape recording of Ms. Hearst. The picture showed her posing in front of the seven-headed cobra symbol of the Symbionese Liberation Army, wearing a beret and brandishing a carbine. On the tape she announced that she had joined the radical group and had taken the name of Tania. She denounced her father as a "corporate liar" and told her boyfriend, "I've changed—grown. I've become conscious."

Tania spent the next twenty months with her captors. She participated in a bank robbery and an assault on a sporting-goods store. When she was finally captured by the FBI on September 18, 1975, she defiantly maintained her new identity. Yet over the next few months as she awaited her trial, visited in jail by her family, old friends, lawyers, and psychiatrists, Tania began to change. She gradually became her "old self" again.

Despite the pleas of her defense lawyer, F. Lee Bailey, that she had been brainwashed, Ms. Hearst was convicted for her part in the bank robbery and imprisoned. A few months later she was pardoned by the court due to the unusual circumstances of her case. Today she is living quietly in suburban San Francisco, married to the man who had been her security guard.

Few of us undergo such a radical self-transformation as Patty Hearst. But most of us question our identity at one time or another. Many of us spend much of our time in a quest for our "real self." We also seek out ways to forget ourselves. Sometimes, when we are immersed in our best work or when we have been touched by another person, we feel truly at one with ourselves. At other times, despite our best efforts to be genuine, we may feel that we are merely playing a role we haven't really chosen. Yet even when our behavior is most inconsistent, we still believe there is something beneath the surface that represents our self. And if we lose touch with this self for a long period of time, we can become profoundly depressed.

Our cultural traditions echo the individual's search for self. In one of the oldest themes of Western thought, Socrates admonished the individual to "know thyself." Shakespeare's *Hamlet* includes the memorable line "to thine own self be true, and it must follow, as the night the day, Thou canst not then be false to any man." A frequent theme of modern literature is self-alienation and self-discovery. For example, in the twentieth-century classic *Steppenwolf*, Hermann Hesse tells the story of a man who decides to commit suicide on his fiftieth birthday if he cannot find his real self. Yet as the story unfolds, the man learns that he is not a single self but a series of selves, like the layers of an onion.

The nature of the self has absorbed psychologists as well as writers and philosophers. In fact, the origin of the self was one of the original concerns of social psychologists, and the self is still the focus of much research. This chapter will present the major classic and contemporary approaches to the self in social psychology.

We will begin by considering how the self has been defined by both laypersons and psychologists. Then we will examine the development of the self, looking first at the effects of various social influences on the self and then at the importance of an individual's own percep-

William Shakespeare wrote, "To thine own self be true." *(Culver Pictures)*

tions and theories about his or her identity. Once we understand the nature and development of the self, then we will see how the self works to help regulate our behavior and organize our perceptions of the world. However, we will also learn that the self is not always an important determinant of our behavior and perceptions, especially when we are not aware or conscious of ourselves. Thus, we will carefully examine various conditions that tend to make us more or less self-aware, as well as the consequences of self-awareness. Similarly, we will look at people who are self-conscious "by nature." We will compare these conditions with the state of "deindividuation," or a complete loss or submergence of self in an overwhelming situation. We will contrast impression management, or self-monitoring, with authentic self-disclosure and look at some determinants and consequences of these two divergent approaches to self-presentation. We will close by looking once again at the nature of the self and we will try to suggest an answer to the question of what one's "real self" is.

THE NATURE OF THE SELF

If you were asked to describe yourself, chances are you would provide several different types of information, according to research by Chad Gordon (1968). You might begin by describing your body, for example, your sex, race, age, height, and weight. Then you might present other objective facts about yourself, such as your occupation, information about your family and home, and perhaps your birthplace and circumstances of growing up. In providing this information, you would be offering some of the details of your *physical self*, but you would probably not stop here. After locating yourself physically in space and time, you would then possibly move on to say something about your personality—about the characteristic ways you think, act, and feel. You might mention that you are bright, outgoing, active, honest, and sensitive. You might also include your expectations about life, your values, and your goals. In providing this information, you would be offering a summary of the types of behaviors you perform and why you think you perform them. In other words, you would be describing your *personality*. Next, if the conversation were somewhat intimate and you were being self-disclosing, you might reveal how you feel about yourself, and how you evaluate your body, personality, and abilities. You might disclose how you compare yourself to others and how you assess your chances for success and happiness. In providing this information, you would be offering your subjective view of yourself, or your *self-concept*. Finally, you might conclude that your real self was still beyond anything you could observe or report. You might maintain that you also have a *spiritual self* that is something like the individual "soul" as described by some Western religions, a "universal essence" as described by some Eastern religions, or an "organismic potentiality" as described in humanistic psychology.

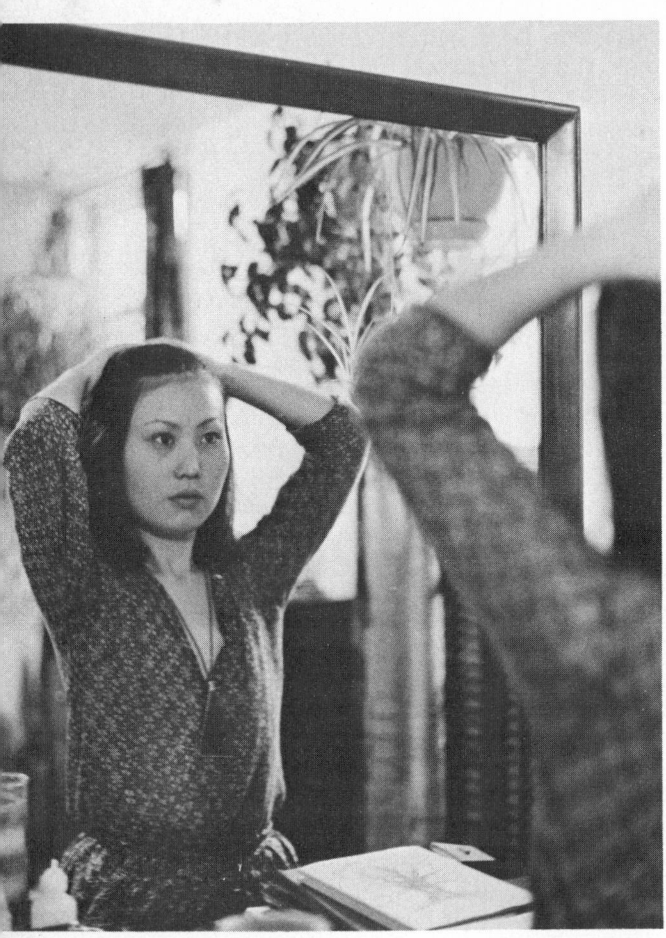

We traditionally view ourselves in four ways: a physical self, a personality, a self-concept, and a spiritual self. *(© Shelly Rusten 1977)*

The preceding paragraph presents four different ways that people have traditionally viewed themselves: a physical self, a personality, a self-concept, and a spiritual self. Each of these has figured into psychologists' approaches to the self.

As early as 1892, one of the founders of American psychology, William James, identified several different components that make up an individual's self. James believed that each person possesses a "material me," composed of a person's body, family, home, and personal possessions; a "social me," made up of a person's view of himself or herself through the eyes of others; and a "spiritual me," described as a person's awareness of his or her own mental processes. James's categories roughly overlap with the four views of self we outlined above, since he seems to combine an individual's personality and "soul" together in the same category of the "spiritual me."

Over the years, as researchers have tried to understand how an individual's sense of self forms, changes, and influences behavior, they have focused particularly on a single aspect of the self: this was James's "social self," or what later researchers came to call one's self-concept (see Wylie, 1974). It is this aspect that represents how one appears to oneself, or, in other words, how a person *views* his or her physical self, personality, and spiritual, potential self. Thus, it is one's self-concept that is most influenced by other people's reactions to oneself and by the hypotheses one forms about oneself. Similarly, it is one's self-concept that is most influential in regulating behavior and organizing perceptions. And it is one's self-concept that is important when one becomes self-aware, self-conscious, or self-disclosing. In this chapter, then, when we refer to the "self," it is primarily a person's self-concept that we will be talking about. It is the self-concept that represents who we are to ourselves.

In the next section we will examine how the self-concept develops and how it changes as the result of social interaction. Specifically, we will consider three types of *social influences* on the self-concept: other people's evaluations of ourselves, social comparison with others, and our responses to other people's behavior.

SOCIAL ORIGINS OF THE SELF-CONCEPT

EFFECTS OF OTHER PEOPLE'S EVALUATIONS

In 1922 a pioneer social psychologist, Charles Horton Cooley, sought to explain the origin of the self in a book called *Human Nature and the Social Order*. In this book Cooley argued that our self-concept arises out of interaction with other people and is composed of three main elements: the imagination of our appearance to others; the imagination of others' judgment of our appearance; and some sort of self-feeling, such as pride or shame. In Cooley's view, then, the self-concept is mainly a reflection of the individual in the eyes of others, a reflection that Cooley came to call "the looking-glass self."

This view of the self as a product of social interaction was developed more explicitly by George Herbert Mead (1934), an early philosopher-sociologist-psychologist. Mead saw the self not as an entity, but as a *process*. He explained the process as including two phases, a subject and an object, or, in Mead's terms, the "I" and the "me." For Mead, the "I" was composed of the impulses that initiated an act and the sensations of carrying out the action. But in the same way that one's actions attract attention and make one a social object to others, one can also become a social object to oneself. Thus because one is capable not only of acting but also of being aware of one's actions, one develops a "me." As the "I" acts and the "me" responds with approval or disapproval, the individual develops a self-concept. What made Mead's argument uniquely social was his view that one cannot become aware of oneself as an object until one is first aware that others view oneself as an object. This awareness of others' reactions begins to dawn when an infant first realizes that his or her behavior meets with approval or disapproval from others, especially the parents. Eventually, the child no longer needs to wait for the reaction of others, but can anticipate their reaction in advance. In so doing, the child learns to take the role of others.

Mead's ideas form the basis of the approach in sociology known as *symbolic interactionism*, so named because it assumes that people imagine symbolically how they will appear to others and then plan their behavior accordingly. The importance of this approach for understanding the origin of the self is that one comes to perceive oneself as one thinks one is seen by others. In other words, the self-concept is a view of oneself that is largely learned from others, particularly the *significant others* in one's life, such as parents, peers, teachers, and lovers.

Although Mead himself conducted no research to support his theorizing, subsequent investigators have confirmed the importance of other people's evaluations in influencing one's view of oneself. One of the clearest demonstrations of Mead's ideas was conducted by Richard Videbeck (1960). Videbeck asked thirty students from a high-school speech class to read several poems aloud to an individual they believed to be a speech expert. Half of the students received a positive evaluation of their speech abilities from the expert, and half received a negative evaluation, regardless of their actual performance. After receiving the expert's evaluation, the students rated themselves on several dimensions and these ratings were then compared with ratings the students made on the same dimensions before the experimental session began. The results showed that the students increased their ratings of the abilities that were praised by the expert and decreased their ratings of the abilities that were criticized by the expert. More interestingly, the students also altered their evaluations of abilities that were not even mentioned by the expert but that were only related to the judged abilities. Thus, the reaction of a significant other influenced the students' views of themselves.

Other research has determined that people's views of themselves are affected more strongly by others' reactions when the others are high in credibility (Bergin, 1962) and sincere (Gergen, 1965), and when their reactions are fairly discrepant from the ways that people initially see themselves (Bergin, 1962). In light of the research, it is easy to see what an impact parents, teachers, and admired peers can have in shaping an individual's self-concept. To the extent that these significant others are expert, credible, sincere, discrepant with one's initial self-perspective, and consistent in their evaluations over time, their reactions will strongly influence the way an individual views himself or herself. Thus, one important influence on the origin of the self-concept is that we learn it directly from others.

EFFECTS OF SOCIAL COMPARISON

People's self-evaluations are not only influenced by direct feedback from others, but they are also affected *indirectly* during social interaction.

In fact, the most common way that others shape our own self-views may be the comparisons we make between ourselves and others as we go through our daily lives. Leon Festinger's *social-comparison theory* (1954) explicitly states that our self-evaluations are influenced by our comparisons with others. According to Festinger, we have a basic learned need to evaluate ourselves. When we lack an objective standard by which to judge our performance, we have no choice but to use the performance of others as our standard for judging ourselves. And even when an objective standard is available—for example, how much weight a weight lifter can lift—our own performance on the standard is only interpretable in light of how well other people perform on the same standard. Thus, in order to evaluate ourselves, we are frequently comparing ourselves with others as we seek to answer questions such as "How attractive am I?" "How successful am I?" "How loving am I?" Of course, as Festinger acknowledges, we do not compare ourselves with just any others, but only with those who are similar to ourselves, in Festinger's terms, "co-oriented others."

An experiment by Stanley Morse and Kenneth Gergen (1970) nicely demonstrates how social comparison affects our feelings about ourselves. These researchers placed a bogus advertisement in the campus newspaper for part-time job help. When students showed up at the university research institute to apply for the job, they unwittingly became part of a social psychology experiment. After being given the application forms, they were ushered into an adjacent room to fill out the forms. When each applicant had completed the first half of the form, which included a self-rating, he or she was joined by another applicant who was actually a confederate of the experimenter. For half the subjects, the second applicant was an extremely impressive person whom the researchers refer to in their report as "Mr. Clean." This individual was sharply dressed and carried an attaché case, from which he removed several sharpened pencils, a philosophy book, and a sta-

According to the social-comparison theory, we often compare ourselves to others as a means of self-evaluation. *(© Ira Berger 1980)*

tistics text, which he stacked on the table. In contrast, the other half of the subjects were exposed to a confederate the experimenters refer to as "Mr. Dirty." This individual was sloppy, unclean, and smelly, and he tossed onto the table a worn copy of a sleazy paperback novel. Shortly after one of these two types of confederates entered the scene, the real subject was given some more forms which included an additional self-rating scale. The results showed that the subjects who were exposed to Mr. Dirty felt more positive about themselves on the second set of self-ratings than on the first, while those exposed to Mr. Clean felt more negative. In addition, subjects who previously had been found to have the least stable self-concepts were more strongly affected by exposure to either confederate than were subjects who had more stable self-concepts. In other words, the subjects' self-concepts were affected by social comparison, and those who were least sure of themselves were affected most strongly.

EFFECTS OF OTHER PEOPLE'S BEHAVIOR

So far we have seen that our self-concept is affected directly by other people's evaluations of our behavior as well as indirectly by the comparisons we make between ourselves and others. There is considerable evidence that we also behave differently in response to different people's behavior, and that our self-concept changes as our behavior changes. In an interesting series of experiments, Kenneth Gergen and his colleagues have demonstrated how flexible an individual's self-concept can be in response to other people's behavior. In one study Gergen (1965) measured college women's self-esteem several weeks before the actual experiment took place. Then later he asked the women to respond to the same self-esteem items, but this time they had to announce their self-ratings verbally to another person. The other person was a female confederate who reinforced the subjects every time they said something positive about themselves. The reinforcements were smiles, nods, and subtle "uhm-hmmms." The results showed that the reinforced subjects described themselves more positively than subjects who received no reinforcements, when compared with their original self-ratings. Moreover, these positive shifts persisted on a subsequent measure of self-esteem conducted when the experiment was over. In a related study, Gergen and Wishnov (1965) again asked college students to fill out self-ratings several weeks prior to an experiment. Then in the experiment the students were asked to describe themselves along the same dimensions, but this time to a confederate who was either very egotistical or very humble. As expected, students interacting with the egotist became more positive in their self-descriptions while those confronted with humility emphasized their shortcomings. And not only did the students' self-descriptions change as a function of the other person's behavior, the majority of the students claimed that they had been completely open and honest during the exchange, no matter which type of confederate they had faced or how they had changed their self-descriptions! Finally, in a closely related study, Gergen and his colleagues (Jones, Gergen, and Davis, 1962) asked students to present themselves to an interviewer as if they were applying for a job. Half of the students were told to be completely honest while the other half were urged to say anything necessary to gain the interviewer's favor. When the interview was over, half of each group heard that the interviewer was either favorably impressed or not. The students were then asked to rate how honest their self-descriptions had actually been during the interview. Surprisingly, those who felt their descriptions were honest were not those who had been instructed to be honest but those who had favorably impressed the interviewer, regardless of whether their initial instructions had emphasized honesty or pragmatism. As Gergen *et al.* conclude, the self-descriptions that were felt to produce the more positive results were seen as the more "real" self.

Each of these experiments demonstrates that one's self-concept is often influenced by the behavior of others. We may present different selves around different people, and our self-concept may change accordingly; however, can each of these selves represent our "real" self?

Kenneth Gergen's research suggests that an individual may be capable of a multiplicity of "real" selves. *(Ken Heyman)*

MULTIPLE SELVES

In light of the apparent flexibility of an individual's self-concept, Gergen has questioned the validity of the notion of a single, "real" self (1968). Traditionally, the self has been viewed as a stable structure, something like an entity within the person. Even Mead, who emphasized the social determinants of the self, saw the self-concept as a fairly consistent, global entity that endured over time once it had developed through social interaction. Similarly, a modern-day symbolic interactionist, Ralph Turner, has suggested that while people may play different roles and take on different "self-images," their basic self-concept remains fairly stable over time (1968). However, Gergen argues that we should perhaps replace our long-cherished notion of a single, "real" self with a view that allows for *multiple selves*. From this perspective the self is not a structure but a process, not a single entity but a multiplicity. An individual might be capable of a number of "real" selves, as suggested by Gergen's research cited above, with each self being authentic in a particular setting. According to Gergen, this view need not necessitate an abandonment of the notion of individual continuity, but a recognition of the adaptiveness and flexibility inherent in human nature. Thus, the phrase "to thine own self be true" might be reinterpreted as being true to one's own capacity for multiplicity.

In this section we have presented evidence that the self-concept develops and changes partly as the result of three types of *social influences*: direct evaluations from others, indirect social comparison with others, and reactions to the behavior of others. A different type of influence on the self-concept does not involve the reactions or behaviors of other people in social interaction. Instead, it involves the conclusions that people arrive at about themselves simply on the basis of observing their own behavior. This type of influence is discussed in the next section.

SOCIAL PSYCHOLOGY AND THE ARTS

ON MULTIPLE SELVES

The twentieth-century classic *Steppenwolf*, by Hermann Hesse, describes a man who feels divided into two selves—one "man" and one "wolf." In the passage below, Harry, the man/wolf, learns that even this dualistic self-theory may be too narrow for the "thousands" of selves of which he is capable.

> The division into wolf and man, flesh and spirit, by means of which Harry tries to make his destiny more comprehensible to himself is a very great simplification. . . . Suppose that Harry tried to ascertain in any single moment of his life, any single act, what part the man had in it and what part the wolf, he would find himself at once in a dilemma, and his whole beautiful wolf-theory would go to pieces. For there is not a single human being, . . . not even the idiot, who is so conveniently simple that his being can be explained as the sum of two or three principal elements; and to explain so complex a man as Harry by the artless division into wolf and man is a hopelessly childish attempt. Harry consists of a hundred or a thousand selves, not of two. His life oscillates, as everyone's does, not merely between two poles, such as the body and the spirit, the saint and the sinner, but between thousands and thousands.
>
> We need not be surprised that even so intelligent and educated a man as Harry should take himself for a Steppenwolf and reduce the rich and complex organism of his life to a formula so simple, so rudimentary and primitive. Man is not capable of thought in any high degree, and even the most spiritual and highly cultivated of men habitually sees the world and himself through the lenses of delusive formulas and artless simplifications—and most of all himself. For it appears to be an inborn and imperative need of all men to regard the self as a unit. However often and however grievously this illusion is shattered, it always mends again.

Source: Hermann Hesse, *Steppenwolf* (New York: Holt, 1963; originally published 1929): 57–58.

THE SELF AS A THEORY

Another way of viewing the formation of an individual's self-concept is to assume that people are active information processors who seek to make sense of their world and themselves. According to this view, people watch themselves as they behave and speculate to themselves about the meaning of their behavior. For example, a young man who notices that he has a hard time making decisions might stop and ask himself, "Why do I do that? Is that really me?" As people seek to answer these sorts of questions, they consider various types of explanations for why they act the way they do. Most important, they make *inferences* about what type of person they must be if they behave the way they do. This inference process results in a gradual build-up of hypotheses about one's own identity. Over time the hypotheses are tested and are either accepted or rejected. If accepted, these hypotheses help shape an individual's self-concept, along with the social influences we discussed in the previous section. In the example above, the young man who sees himself repeatedly being unable to make decisions might conclude that his behavior reflects an underlying uncertainty about values, needs, or directions. This process of observing one's own behavior and forming hypotheses has recently received much attention from social psychologists, and it provides a useful alternative explanation of how the self-concept develops and changes.

One proponent of this view is Seymour Epstein (1973), who has stated his position in terms of a riddle about the nature of the self. What is it, Epstein asks, that consists of organized concepts; that assimilates knowledge yet itself is an object of knowledge; that is changeable, but must maintain a degree of stability;

that is unified and differentiated at the same time; that is necessary for solving problems in the real world; and that is subject to sudden collapse, producing total disorganization when this occurs? His answer is that the self-concept is actually a "*self-theory.*" It is a theory that all individuals unwittingly construct about themselves in order to explain their own experience.

Epstein's views were influenced by personality theorist George Kelly (1955), who viewed the individual human being as a "personal scientist." Just as a scientist conducts experiments, observes the results, and theorizes about their meaning, Kelly argued, so does the individual in everyday life observe his or her personal experience and theorize about the meaning. It is this process of observation and reflection that leads individuals to develop a theory about their own identity, or, in Epstein's words, a self-theory.

If the individual is a good scientist, his or her self-theory should be broad enough to incorporate all the relevant data of his or her life and flexible enough to be revised when experience contradicts the theory. The more complex one's experience, the more differentiated one's self-theory. If the individual is a poor scientist, he or she may lack objectivity, perhaps failing to submit the self-theory to a valid test or refusing to admit when the self-theory is inadequate or disconfirmed by experience. In this way, people may hold on to comfortable but perhaps "outmoded" selves.

Why do we formulate such a theory about ourselves in the first place? According to Epstein, there are three main reasons. First, it is necessary to have a self-theory in order to behave effectively in a complex world. Without a self-theory we would be unpredictable to ourselves and, therefore, unable to maximize pleasure and minimize pain. Second, the self-theory allows us to organize the data of experience in a manner that can be coped with effectively. Without a self-theory to guide our attention and help process information, we might become "overloaded" with random inputs and thus be unable to cope with the buzzing confusion of the world. And third, the self-theory helps maintain self-esteem, since people without an adequate self-theory seem to feel confused about their own identity, uncertain about the future, and often depressed.

SELF-PERCEPTION AND ATTRIBUTION

Epstein's view of the self-concept as a self-theory fits well with an important and very influential theoretical perspective in contemporary social psychology known as *attribution theory.* Many social psychologists are currently involved in studying how people process information about themselves and others. A major focus of this research is the type of explanations or "attributions" people make when they observe human behavior, both in others and themselves, and try to explain what causes it. For example, when you see someone shouting angrily at another person, you may ask yourself, "Why is that person shouting like that?" You may even ask the same question when you observe yourself shouting angrily at another person—"Why am I shouting like this?" The answer you arrive at will influence how you interpret the behavior you observe. For example, you might attribute the person's shouting to a disturbing event in the environment, such as a threatened assault by another individual. Or, failing to locate some apparent cause in the environment, you might attribute the shouting simply to irritability of the shouter. In the same way, you might attribute your own shouting to some outside force such as a threatened attack, or, in the absence of such a force, you might attribute it simply to your own irritability. And if you find yourself shouting over several occasions without sufficient provocation, you may theorize that you are in fact a fairly irritable person. If you arrive at such a conclusion, your theory about your own irritability would be an inference based on observations of your own behavior.

The process of inferring responsibility for one's own behavior has been described by Daryl Bem in his very influential *self-perception theory* (1965, 1972). Although Bem's theory will be presented in more detail in Chapter 4, it is necessary to introduce some of his basic ideas here in order to understand more fully how people generate theories about their own behavior. Bem argues that people observe and seek to explain their own behavior in the same way that they observe and seek to explain other persons' behavior. Of course, when we observe our own behavior, and we know that the behavior reflects some clear, preestablished attitude or personal attribute, then it is easy to explain. For instance, we may be yelling at the person down the hall, but we know that we are yelling because she won't turn her stereo down and the music is bothering us. But what about those instances when we aren't immediately aware of any outside influence on our behavior and we are still shouting? Bem has an explanation for this. He suggests that when we lack a clear explanation for our behavior, we search for an explanation. First, we look for causes in the surrounding situation. If the music isn't loud, for example, and we have nothing against the person down the hall, then we lack any apparent explanation for our shouting. At this point, Bem suggests, we begin to look within ourselves for an answer. If we still can't find a reasonable explanation for our behavior, then we must make an inference. As discussed above, we formulate a hypothesis about why we might be behaving as we are. For example, we might hypothesize that we are easily irritated. Then we proceed to test this hypothesis by observing further instances of our behavior. For instance, we may note whether we shout irritably at several other people as well as the person down the hall and whether we shout fairly often and not just on one unusual occasion. If we accept the hypothesis regarding our irritable nature, then we have elaborated a part of our self-theory.

Bem's self-perception theory has been tested in a number of contexts, as we will see elsewhere in this book. For example, on the basis of observing their own behavior, people have been found to infer attitudes toward all types of issues (see Chapter 4), to infer a wide range of behavioral intentions and even personality traits (see Chapter 6), and to infer emotions as strong as fear and passionate love (see Chapter 7). Perhaps the most surprising finding in these studies is how uncertain people often are regarding the real reasons for their behavior and how easily they can be led to make a false inference about the causes of their behavior. One experiment makes this point rather dramatically. Stuart Valins (1966) led college males to make false inferences about their sexual arousal in response to pictures of attractive nude women in erotic poses. As the men viewed the slides, they believed that they were hearing their own heartbeat amplified through a microphone attached over their heart. Instead, what they actually heard was a tape recording of a heartbeat, and the heartbeat changed its pace from a steady drumming to a more random fluctuation when certain slides flashed on the screen. At the end ot the experiment as a favor for being in the study, the men were allowed to take a few of their favorite slides home with them. The main measure in the experiment was which slides the men chose. The results showed that the men tended to choose the slides that they thought had caused their heartbeat to change pace. Since no other explanation could account for their changing heart rate, these men may have inferred that they must be attracted to the slides that made their heart change pace, even though the amplified heartbeat was not actually their own and all the slides had been previously judged equally attractive by a panel of judges. Whether the men actually inferred that they were attracted or merely wanted to test a tentative hypothesis about their attraction by examining the slides at home, the results are an interesting demonstration of self-perception, or "self-misperception," as the case may be.

Subsequent research has demonstrated that people's self-perceptions and misperceptions are largely influenced by the ways they focus their attention. Recall that Bem's theory of self-perception involves a two-step process. When people are uncertain about the causes of their behavior, first they look to the external environment for an explanation. If they cannot locate a satisfactory external explanation, they make an inference about a possible internal explanation. However, this process can be short-circuited if people's attention is directed away from likely causes for their behavior in the external environment. Then, people may infer personal responsibility for their behavior when it is unjustified. This point has been demonstrated in an

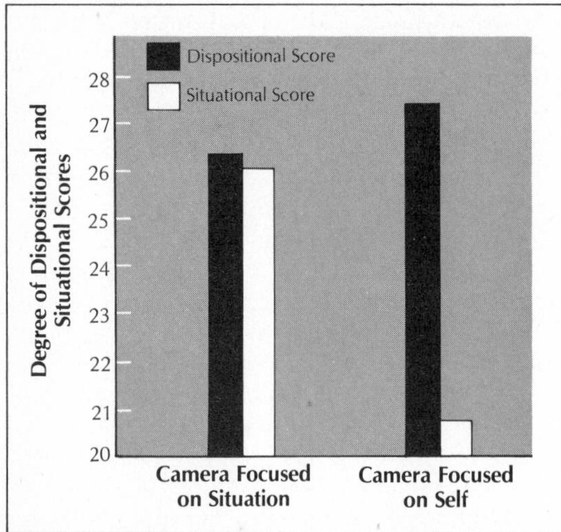

FIGURE 3.1 When people participated in a getting-acquainted conversation and then watched a videotape of the interaction, their causal attributions for their behavior differed, depending on the focus of the camera. With the camera focused on the surrounding situation, they attributed responsibility about equally to dispositional and situational factors; with the camera focused on themselves, they attributed responsibility mainly to their own dispositions. (Based on data from Storms, 1973.)

experiment by Michael Storms (1973). Storms asked pairs of unacquainted students to engage in a getting-acquainted conversation while being videotaped and surrounded by observers and one-way mirrors. Later he asked them to rate themselves in terms of how friendly, nervous, talkative, and assertive they were during the conversation. Storms also asked the students to attribute responsibility for their behavior either to situational factors, such as the cameras, observers, and mirrors, or to personal factors, such as their personality, character, and mood. Before rating themselves, some of the students viewed videotapes taken from their own initial perspective—focused outward on the experimental situation. As shown in Figure 3.1, these students viewed their behavior as about equally influenced by situational factors and by their own personalities. However, other students viewed videotapes focused on themselves as they appeared to others during conversation. These students were also asked to explain their behavior as reflecting either the situation or their own personalities, but their explanations were very different from the former group. These students—with their attention directed away from the situation and focused back on themselves—tended to see their behavior as reflecting their own personalities fairly strongly and not as highly influenced by the surrounding situation. In other words, the students' inferences about themselves were influenced by their focus of attention, whether outward on the situation or inward on themselves. This suggests that people's self-theories may change as their focus of attention changes.

Many factors influence an individual's focus of attention, and these will be discussed later in the chapter. However, one factor that is very close to Storms's videotape experiment has to do with the effects of memory on attention. Recent research by Bert Moore, Dru Sherrod, Tom Liu, and Bill Underwood (1979) suggests that memory may produce shifts in attentional focus, much like those manipulated by Storms, so that recalling one's past behavior may be like watching oneself on videotape. As a person recalls an instance of past behavior, the individual tends to focus on the behavior itself rather than on the surrounding situation. In order to demonstrate this point, the researchers replicated Storms's "getting-acquainted" experiment, but instead of showing the subjects different perspectives on videotapes, they asked the subjects to explain their behavior either immediately or three weeks later. As shown in Figure 3.2, those subjects who provided immediate explanations for their behavior tended to see situational influences as more important than personality factors in accounting for their behavior. However, those subjects who returned three weeks later tended to see their personalities as more important than the surrounding situation. Compare the parallels in Figure 3.1 and Figure 3.2. Apparently the passage of time can affect our focus of attention much like viewing ourselves on videotape. Perhaps this is why we often look back on the past with regret and embarrassment for our mistakes rather than recalling the situa-

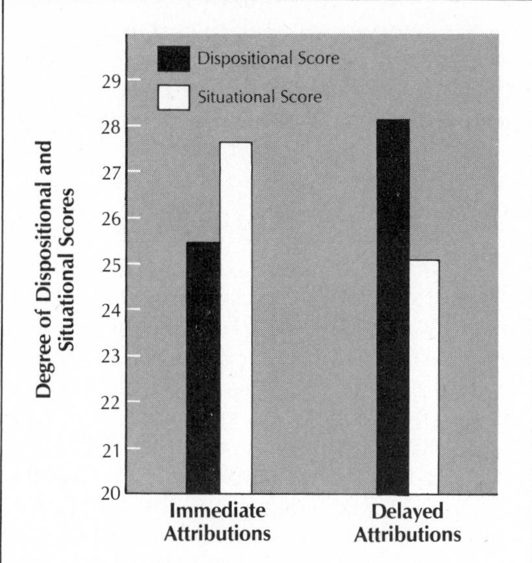

FIGURE 3.2 When people participated in a getting-acquainted conversation and attributed responsibility for their behavior either immediately or three weeks later, their attributions differed, depending on how much time had passed. Immediately after the conversation they attributed more responsibility to situational factors than to dispositional factors; three weeks later they attributed more responsibility to dispositional factors than to situational factors. (Based on data from Moore, Sherrod, Liu, and Underwood, 1979.)

tional factors that may have influenced our regrettable behaviors.

Thus, the research suggests that people do not always function as good scientists when they are theorizing about themselves, despite their best intentions. Many factors can bias and distort people's self-perceptions as they seek to construct their self-theories. Consequently, one's self-theory may be inaccurate, oversimplified, or even a gross distortion of reality. Nevertheless, the self-theory still exerts a profound influence on individual functioning, whether or not it is truly valid.

So far, we have seen how an individual's self-concept may develop as a function of various social influences and how a person's self-theory may take form through the inferences he or she makes about his or her own behavior. In the next section we will examine how one's self-concept or self-theory works to regulate behavior and organize perceptions.

HOW THE SELF FUNCTIONS

Traditionally, psychologists who were interested in the self viewed the relationship between an individual's self-concept and behavior as unidirectional; that is, the self-concept was thought to influence behavior, but behavior was not thought to influence the self-concept. Such theorists also tended to view the self in rather undifferentiated global terms (see Wylie, 1974). For instance, they sought to measure an individual's general self-concept or general level of self-esteem and then to predict behavior as a function of the general self-concept (see Rogers, 1959).

In contrast to this view, radical behaviorists have sought to explain behavior entirely as a function of environmental determinants. From this perspective, the self-concept was unobservable and unnecessary except as a convenient shorthand for prior environmental influences (see Skinner, 1971; Stuart, 1972).

As we argued in Chapter 1, however, there is a third ground between these two positions. According to this third view, behavior is determined neither by the self-concept alone nor by the environment alone, but is a joint function of both persons and environments. While this approach is historically associated with Kurt Lewin, its modern version is most fully expressed in the writings of social-learning theorists such as Albert Bandura (1978) and Walter Mischel (1973, 1979). Bandura, for example, has recently argued that there is always a *reciprocal relationship* between a person, the environment, and the person's behavior. To understand how this reciprocal relationship pertains to the self, consider an individual's self-concept as one of the most important aspects of the total person. The meaning of a reciprocal relationship, then, is that one's self-concept, one's behavior, and the environment all mutually influence each other.

Consider the case of a woman who sees her most important characteristic as "sensitivity." Initially, this individual could have learned how to be sensitive from her environment, perhaps by being exposed to parents who were themselves sensitive and by being reinforced by parents and friends when she behaved in a sensitive manner. As others began to label her as sensitive, she gradually came to apply this label to herself, or, as the symbolic interactionists argue, she came to see herself "through the eyes of others." Then, as she observed her own behavior in a variety of contexts, she was able to test and refine a theory regarding the extent of her own sensitivity. But just as her self-concept was developing as a result of environmental learning, social influences, and self-inferences, so her self-concept was at the same time influencing the very same elements that shaped its development. For example, as the woman came to label herself as sensitive, she probably began to seek out environments that allowed her to exercise her sensitivity. Perhaps she went out of her way to seek out people who may have needed help. Then, whenever she found an opportunity, she probably continued behaving in a sensitive manner so as to maintain her self-concept as a sensitive person. Thus, the three elements—self-concept, environment, and behavior—were constantly influencing each other, so that it is difficult, if not impossible, to say that one is cause and the others are effect.

The situation is still more complicated than the simple relationship we have described. In Bandura's view the self is not made up of a single global self-concept. Instead, it is a *self-system* composed of numerous self-concepts, each pertaining to specific circumstances and behaviors. For example, a young man might see himself as a successful athlete but a poor scholar, at ease with men but nervous in the company of women, assertive with peers but submissive around authority figures. Each of these self-concepts helps determine how the young man views the world and how he behaves in different situations.

Bandura's notion of a self-system composed of numerous self-concepts is similar to Epstein's description of a self-theory composed of numerous hypotheses about the self. Both theorists see the self as a collection of subprocesses that organize information and regulate behavior. In the following sections we will examine recent research that explores how the self operates to organize information and regulate behavior.

THE ROLE OF THE SELF IN INFORMATION PROCESSING

If the self serves to organize information, then a person's self-theory or self-system should influence how he or she perceives the world. For example, if a woman sees herself as "dependent" and "conforming," then she should view the world in a different light than a woman who sees herself as "independent" and "in control." The woman who sees herself as dependent might be especially sensitive to situations in which she appears submissive. She might recall these instances more easily than those occasions when she was genuinely assertive, even though there might be a number of such occasions in her life. But because these instances fail to conform to her "dependent" self-view, she is likely to distort her perceptions and memories of events and to process information about her behavior incorrectly. In so doing, her self-view would be maintained, although it would be a distortion of reality.

Social psychologists have just begun to investigate how the self affects perceptions and memory. One experiment by Hazel Markus (1977) demonstrates the important role of the self in information processing. Markus reasoned that one's self-theory is composed of a number of propositions or "minitheories" about oneself on different dimensions, such as dependence and independence. Together these theories function as *schemata*, or a framework for processing information, much like a filing system in the brain. For each relevant dimension of an individual's behavior, the individual develops a *schema*, which might be visualized as something like a file drawer. For example, as you observe yourself behaving in a particular way over time, you develop a schema about that behavior just as you might set up a file drawer to hold all the information about a particular topic. Just as it would be hard to keep track of all the details about a certain topic if you didn't have a file drawer on that topic, it is difficult to process information about a behavior without a schema for that behavior. In our earlier example, the woman who saw herself behaving submissively on a number of occasions would no doubt have established a schema for her dependent behavior. The existence of the schema would then make it easier for her to process information relevant to her dependency.

Markus's experiment dealt with the issue of dependency. First, she identified individuals who defined themselves strongly in terms of dependence/independence by virtue of their ratings on a self-rating scale. She inferred that those who saw themselves as strongly dependent or independent must have a self-schema for that dimension, while those who did not rate themselves highly on that dimension must not have such a self-schema. Markus reasoned that if the self functions as a schema which facilitates information processing, then the individuals without a firm self-schema on the dimension of dependence/independence should have a harder time processing information relevant to this dimension than those individuals who do have such a schema. This is exactly what she found. She asked her subjects to read a list of adjectives related to dependence/independence—adjectives such as *conforming* or *assertive*—and to decide whether the adjectives described them or not. The individuals who originally rated themselves as highly dependent or independent and who, therefore, were assumed to have a well-developed schema on this dimension were able to make faster judgments than those without a schema. The individuals with a schema were also able to cite more instances of their own actual behavior and to predict their future behavior more confidently relevant to dependence/independence than were those without a schema. Furthermore, when individuals with a schema were given false feedback about themselves that contradicted their self-schema, they were more resistant to accepting this information than were those without a schema. In other words, a self-schema on a particular dimension helps to organize and process information about oneself more efficiently.

A self-schema also has other implications for how we process information. T. B. Rogers and his colleagues suggested that a self-schema should not only help organize *existing* information about an individual, as Markus demonstrated in her experiment, but it should also help the individual to sort, organize, and make sense of *new* experiences or new information. In other words, Rogers proposed that when people react to new experiences or information, they ask themselves, "Is this me?" If the new experiences or information are important to the individual's self-theory, then these experiences and information will be attended to and processed in a different manner than if they are not important.

To test his ideas, Rogers (1977) asked subjects to read a list of 60 sentences similar to those found on a personality test—sentences such as "I would like to travel freely from country to country." Then later he showed them this list of 60 sentences combined with another list of 60 sentences they had not seen before. The test was to pick out of the total list of 120 items the 60 sentences they had seen before. Rogers found that the people who were good at correctly identifying the original items had followed a certain information-processing strategy when they read the sentences the first time around. Essentially they had tried to decide whether the items described themselves or not. People who did not make such a self-referent decision had a harder time identifying the original items. Rogers then performed a second experiment in which he specifically asked subjects to decide whether each of the first 60 items described themselves or not. The group that used this self-referent strategy was much more accurate at identifying the original items the second time around when these items were imbedded in the larger list than the group who did not use such a self-referent strategy. And in a related experiment, Rogers and his colleagues (Rogers, Kuiper, and Kirker, 1977) found that such a self-referent strategy is more effective than several other standard systems for memorizing information. The reason that self-reference is so effective as a memory strategy, they theorized, is because the self already exists as a well-structured schema or system of categories in one's head. Thus, associating information with one's preestablished self-schema allows one to process the information more effectively.

The role of the self-schema in organizing new information was further explored in a third experiment by Rogers, Rogers, and Kuiper (1979). Previous research in personality had found that once we develop a theory about another person's personality—such as labeling an individual an introvert or an extrovert—then we tend to misperceive new information about him or her to make it conform with our theory about his or her personality (Cantor and Mischel, 1977). Rogers and his colleagues showed that the same misperceptions occur when an individual processes information about himself or herself. For example, the more self-descriptive an adjective was, the more the subjects believed that they had been previously exposed to that adjective in a prior word list, even though they had actually not seen the adjective before. Presumably, the existence of a self-schema biased subjects' perceptions of the new adjectives, so that the more similar the adjective was to their schema, the more likely were subjects to infer that they had seen the adjective before. Thus an individual's self-schema serves an important function in organizing new information in memory and in influencing perceptions.

SELF-AWARENESS AND SELF-REGULATION

We have seen that the self functions as a system or schema that helps process information. Yet the self is much more than an information-processing network. It is also composed of ideals, values, and standards that can directly influence our behavior. Unless we are consciously thinking about these values and standards, however, the influence of this "ideal self" is significantly reduced. When we become aware of our values and standards though, this ideal self can play an important role in determining our behavior. Thus, *self-awareness* is a crucial step in the process of self-regulation.

"Self-awareness theory" was first developed by Shelly Duval and Robert Wicklund (1972; Wicklund, 1975), who argued that human attention can be focused in two ways: we can either direct our attention outward toward the environment or inward toward ourselves. According to Duval and Wicklund, when we direct our attention toward ourselves, we become aware not only of our appearance, but also of our thoughts and feelings, our values and standards. For example, all of us have experienced that acute awareness of self that can be triggered by walking into a room and having everyone stare at us, by standing before a large group, by staring at our image in a mirror, or by hearing our voice on a tape recorder. Our immediate reaction is to wonder whether we're "all right." In answering this question, we usually focus on our values and standards and compare them against our behavior. The way we answer this question leads to a number of interesting consequences, which are discussed below.

SELF-AWARENESS AND SELF-CRITICISM When people become aware of their values and standards and compare them to their behavior, there are two possible outcomes: either the behavior matches or exceeds their standards, or the behavior falls short of their standards. When behavior falls short of a person's standards, the individual has several choices: (1) behavior can be changed to align with the person's standards; (2) standards can be changed to align with behavior; (3) the discrepancy can be accepted; or (4) the individual can try to escape the state of self-awareness and thus avoid dealing with the discrepancy. In their original statement of the theory, Duval and Wicklund assumed that most people's standards exceed their typical behaviors. When behaviors cannot be changed to reduce the discrepancy, then self-awareness leads to self-criticism or attempts to escape whatever caused the self-awareness.

Initial research by Duval and Wicklund and their colleagues seemed to suggest that their expectations were correct and that self-awareness indeed appeared to make people more self-critical. For example, when female college students rated their real self versus their ideal self, the students felt a greater discrepancy between their real and ideal selves if they were listening to tape recordings of their own voices than if they listened to a recording of another woman's voice (Ickes, Wicklund, and Ferris, 1973). Similarly, male college students rated their self-es-

Nervous gestures and habits may help people distract themselves from self-criticism. *(Ann Chwatsky)*

teem lower when they had to work in front of a large mirror after receiving negative information about their personalities than if there was no mirror present (Ickes, Wicklund, and Ferris, 1973). In each of these experiments subjects seemed to be more self-critical when the tape recordings and mirrors made them self-aware.

Self-aware subjects not only appeared more self-critical, they also attempted to avoid the circumstances that made them self-aware. In one experiment, college women who had received negative information about their creativity and intelligence sought to avoid a state of self-awareness by leaving the experimental room sooner when there was a large mirror on the wall (Duval, Wicklund, and Fine in Duval and Wicklund, 1972: pp. 16–20). And when college men received a negative evaluation of their physical appearance from a female student, they spent less time listening to their own tape-recorded voices than if they had received a positive evaluation (Gibbons and Wicklund, 1976). In both of these studies, when people were feeling self-critical, they tried to avoid things that focused their attention on themselves.

Finally, when subjects were unable to avoid the things that made them self-aware, they sought to escape self-criticism by distracting themselves from focusing too much on themselves. For example, a British social critic, Lord Chesterfield, noted in 1774 that people engage in nervous habits such as "putting a finger to the nose or twirling a hat" when they feel "ashamed in company." In an experiment that Wicklund interprets as supporting this proposition, smokers who sat for half an hour in front of a large mirror were observed to take more puffs, to spend more time holding their cigarette, and to flick their ashes more often than smokers who did not have to confront their image in a mirror (Liebling, Seiler, and Shaver, 1974). And in related research, Duval and Wicklund found that when college women were made self-aware by hearing their own written work read back to them, they felt more confident about their work and their attitudes if they were allowed to distract themselves by such trivial tasks as squeezing a handgrip or rotating a disc (in Duval and Wicklund, 1972: pp. 193–205). These experiments suggest that when people cannot alter their behaviors, they seek to avoid self-awareness by distracting themselves. And distractions such as smoking or playing idly with some object in one's hand may often be successful in minimizing the self-criticism frequently caused by self-awareness. However, self-awareness is not necessarily a negative state and need not lead to self-criticism or escape and distraction, as the research cited in the next section demonstrates.

SELF-AWARENESS AND SELF-PRAISE Are the consequences of self-awareness really so negative as Duval and Wicklund initially believed? Aren't there times when one's behavior clearly matches or exceeds one's standards—for example, when we are especially pleased with our physical appearance, when we are unusually confident of our abilities, or when we are simply feeling good? Aren't there times when it's pleasant to contemplate one's image by standing before a mirror, appearing in public, or focusing on one's feelings? Indeed, what accounts for narcissism if people generally want to avoid their own images?

In 1975 Robert Wicklund revised the original theory to explicitly acknowledge the consequences of self-awareness following a success experience. Recall that the theory originally stated that self-awareness should normally lead to self-criticism since an individual's aspirations are generally thought to exceed capacities. Thus, focusing on oneself would most likely produce an awareness of a negative discrepancy between ideals and actuality. Although Wicklund still believes this is the most likely result of self-awareness, he conceded in his revision of the theory that people may also experience a *positive* discrepancy when their behavior *exceeds* their aspirations.

Several of the experiments discussed above bear on this point. For example, when male students received *positive* information about their personalities prior to being exposed to a mirror, they subsequently rated their self-esteem higher than those who were not exposed to a mirror (Ickes, Wicklund, and Ferris, 1973). Also when college men received positive evaluations about their physical appearance from a female student, they spent more time listening to their own tape-recorded voices than those men who received negative evaluations (Gibbons and Wicklund, 1976). Thus, people may experience either a positive discrepancy or a negative discrepancy when they become self-aware. The important point in Wicklund's revision of the theory is that self-awareness intensifies either self-criticism or self-praise, whichever one is experiencing.

More recent research has further clarified the consequences of self-awareness. In an important revision of the theory, Charles Carver (1979) has argued that an individual's reactions to self-awareness depend not only on the nature of the discrepancy between standards and behavior, but also on the individual's expectations about whether he or she will be able to alter his or her behavior in the future. In one experiment subjects who believed they would have no opportunity to improve a poor performance were more likely to avoid self-awareness than subjects who expected a chance to improve their performance (Steenberger and Alderman, 1979). In another experiment, when subjects who had first failed at one task were given a chance to work on a second one, self-awareness manipulations caused them to persist longer if they expected to improve than if they expected no improvement (Carver, Blaney, and Scheier, 1979). Thus, people's reactions to self-awareness depend not merely on their immediate successes or failures but also on their expectations about the future.

SELF-AWARENESS AND SELF-ATTRIBUTION Self-awareness also influences the attributions we make about our behavior. As we discussed earlier, when people seek an explanation for their behavior, they may explain it in one of two ways: either their behavior is a reflection of their personality, ability, and effort or their behavior is caused by situational factors beyond their control. However, when one's attention is focused inward on oneself rather than outward on the surrounding environment, one is more likely to feel that one's behavior reflects personal responsibility rather than situational influences. Thus self-awareness can intensify self-blame and self-credit.

In one experiment (Duval and Wicklund, 1973) female undergraduates heard descriptions of hypothetical situations such as the following: "You're driving down the street about five miles over the speed limit when a little kid suddenly runs out chasing a ball and you hit him." When asked how responsible they would feel for the accident if they were the driver, subjects who were sitting before large mirrors felt more responsible than those who were not confronted with the mirror. Similarly, when the women pictured themselves in positive situations (for example, "You received an A on a paper that a friend turned in for you, although she added some clarifying comments in a conversation with the professor"), the subjects assigned more responsibility to themselves for the positive outcome when they were in front of a large mirror than if no mirror was present. Increases in self-blame were obtained in other experiments when subjects were made self-aware by a videotape camera (Arkin and Duval, 1975) or by performing in front of dissimilar observers (Sherrod and Goodman, 1978). It is important to note, however, that when people can distract themselves from focusing on their own performance, as in the experiments where subjects squeezed a handgrip or rotated a disc, they are less self-blaming than if they are unable to distract themselves.

SELF-AWARENESS AND SELF-CONSISTENCY We spoke earlier about the problems of self-consistency when we noted that social behavior is often inconsistent over time and across different situations. For example, a person may appear prejudiced in one situation but not in another, friendly in one setting but not in another, conscientious on some occasions but not on others, and sometimes assertive but at other times meek (Mischel, 1968; Bem and Allen, 1974). One of the major paradoxes of social psychology is how a person might behave so discrepantly over time and situations yet still retain a stable notion of him- or herself as recognizable and continuous. One reason may be that an individual's sense of self or identity may not always be an important influence on his or her behavior. Outside influences are often so vivid and compelling that one doesn't always stop to reflect on personal standards before engaging in some behavior. However, if self-awareness makes people more aware of their personal standards, as Duval and Wicklund argue, then we might expect self-aware individuals to be more attentive to their standards and to behave more in accord with these standards. In other words we would expect self-aware persons to behave more consistently over time than people who are not self-aware. Furthermore, if conditions of self-awareness make people more attentive to themselves and their standards, then people should be more accurate in rating their attitudes and personalities if they fill out the forms in the presence of mirrors.

Robert Wicklund and his colleagues tested the hypothesis that self-awareness increases self-consistency (Pryor, Gibbons, Wicklund, Fazio, and Hood, 1977). In one study, male subjects rated their sociability while sitting in front of a mirror or not. Later they were observed as they interacted with another person, and their actual behaviors were scored for sociability. For those men who rated their sociability before a mirror, the actual behaviors correlated much higher with their self-ratings ($r = .68$) than for those who rated themselves without the mirror ($r = .08$). Thus, self-awareness increased the accuracy of their self-ratings. Similarly, when female subjects were given a series of problems to work out and were later asked to rate how interesting the problems were, there was a higher correlation between their ratings of the problems and their actual behavioral involvement with each problem if the ratings were made before a mirror ($r = .74$) than if no mirror was present during the ratings ($r = .13$).

Frederick Gibbons (1978) followed up on this research by making subjects self-aware while they were performing a behavioral test rather than during their self-ratings, as in the above experiments. He first measured male subjects' attitudes toward erotic stimuli and one month later asked them to study pictures of nude women and rate them for "excitability." If the pictures were evaluated while the subjects were sitting in front of a mirror, their excitability ratings correlated more highly with subjects' general attitudes toward erotic stimuli than if no mirror was present. In the same study, Gibbons also measured other male subjects for their general level of "sex guilt." Later when they were asked to read and rate pornography in terms of how arousing and how enjoyable it was, the sex-guilt ratings and pornography ratings correlated more highly if subjects read the pornography in front of a mirror than if no mirror was present. Other researchers found that mirror-induced self-awareness caused male subjects to behave less aggressively toward an innocent female subject than those men who performed without a mirror (Scheier, Fenigstein, and Buss, 1974). Apparently the mirror served to remind the men of their internal standards not to aggress against a female victim who had done nothing to provoke the aggressor. However, when aggression was made a desirable standard for female subjects in an experiment, then self-awareness served to make them *more* aggressive (Carver, 1975). The point is that self-awareness brings behavior more in line with a person's standards—whatever they may be—because it focuses attention on those standards.

In several ways, then, it has been shown that self-aware people are more attuned to their standards and behave more in accord with their standards than people who are not self-aware. However, if people in front of mirrors are asked to attend to their mood and emotions instead of their standards, then self-awareness can lead people to behave more in accord with their current emotions than with their general standards. For example, in a study of aggression, Michael Scheier (1976) made some subjects angry by having a male confederate badger them with critical, sarcastic comments as they tried to solve a difficult puzzle. When these subjects were later given a chance to administer electric shock to the kibbitzer, the presence of a mirror caused them to administer more shocks than if no mirror was present. Thus, the mirror seemed to make them focus more on their anger. In another study college males were asked to attend to their emotions and bodily reactions as they looked at pictures of nude women. Men who were in front of mirrors rated the pictures as more attractive than did men who were not in front of mirrors (Scheier and Carver, 1977). Similarly, if people are asked to read material designed to affect their mood, mirrors make them more responsive to the material (Scheier and Carver, 1977). Thus, it can be said that mirrors help people to be "truer" to themselves; it just depends on whether the self they are attending to is their general standards or current emotions.

SELF-CONSCIOUSNESS AND SELF-REGULATION

Are people only self-aware in the presence of mirrors, cameras, audiences, and in other unusual situations? Must something in the environment jolt their attention away from the surroundings and back toward themselves as an object in the environment? You probably know from your own experience that this is not true. Many of us spend a good deal of time thinking about ourselves, our feelings, abilities, satisfactions, and dissatisfactions. No doubt some of us spend more time than others. Thus, it is reasonable to approach the issue of self-awareness not merely as a temporary *state*, induced by mirrors, cameras, etc., but also as an enduring *predisposition* to focus on oneself. Perhaps there are those of us who spend so much time focusing attention on ourselves that we behave as if we are in front of a mirror, even when we are not. Indeed, the only mirror may be the one in our minds.

Allan Fenigstein, Michael Scheier, and Arnold Buss (1975) developed a scale to measure one's tendency to focus attention on oneself. They titled their scale the *Self-Consciousness Scale* in order to distinguish the enduring predisposition or trait of self-focused attention from the temporary state of self-awareness. It has become conventional to distinguish the two different research areas by using the term *self-awareness* to refer to an externally induced focus on oneself and the term *self-consciousness* to refer to an enduring predisposition to focus attention on oneself. As we will see, there are many similarities between the state of self-awareness and the trait of self-consciousness.

The Self-Consciousness Scale is a twenty-three-item scale scored from 0 (extremely un-

FIGURE 3.3 The items shown here are taken from the Self-Consciousness Scale (Fenigstein, Scheier, and Buss, 1975). They represent the dimension of "private self-consciousness." The average score for college men on these ten items is 25.9; for college women, 26.6.

Score each statement below from 0 to 5 (0 = extremely uncharacteristic; 5 = extremely characteristic).

1. I'm always trying to figure myself out. . . . . _____
2. Generally, I'm not very aware of myself* . . . . _____
3. I reflect about myself a lot . . . . _____
4. I'm often the subject of my own fantasies . . . . _____
5. I never scrutinize myself* . . . . _____
6. I'm generally attentive to my inner feelings . . . . _____
7. I'm constantly examining my motives . . . . _____
8. I sometimes have the feeling that I'm off somewhere watching myself . . . . _____
9. I'm alert to changes in my mood . . . . _____
10. I'm aware of the way my mind works when I work through a problem . . . . _____

TOTAL _____

*These two statements are worded in a reverse direction. Before calculating your total score, reverse the numbers on these items; that is, if you score 5, count it as 0; if you score 1, count it as 4; and so on.

characteristic) to 4 (extremely characteristic). It is composed of three subscales: private self-consciousness—a private mulling over the self; public self-consciousness—an awareness of the self as a social object; and social anxiety—apprehension about presenting oneself socially. Since private self-consciousness is closest to the state of self-awareness that we discussed above, our focus in this section will mainly be on the dimension of private self-consciousness. The items on the private self-consciousness subscale are shown in Figure 3.3.

SELF-CONSCIOUSNESS AND SELF-ATTRIBUTION

The consequences of self-consciousness are similar in many respects to those of self-awareness. Recall that people in front of mirrors assumed more personal responsibility for hypothetical outcomes than when mirrors weren't present. Similarly, people who are high in self-consciousness also assume more responsibility for hypothetical outcomes than people low in self-consciousness (Buss and Scheier, 1976). For example, one hypothetical situation was the following: "Imagine that you are driving down the expressway when suddenly the woman in front of you slams on her brakes and you run right into the back of her. To what degree did your actions cause this outcome and to what degree did the actions of the woman cause this outcome?" When asked to respond to this situation, people who were highly self-conscious attributed more responsibility to themselves than those who were low in self-consciousness.

SELF-CONSCIOUSNESS AND SELF-CONSISTENCY

When we discussed the effects of mirrors on people, we concluded that mirrors seemed to help people "know themselves" better. In front of mirrors, people behaved more in accord with their internal standards and feelings than when mirrors weren't present. Similar effects have been found for people who score high on the Self-Consciousness Scale. For example, Scheier and his colleagues (Scheier, Buss, and Buss, 1978) found that individuals' aggressive behav-

DISPOSITIONS AND SITUATIONS

SELF-KNOWLEDGE AND SUGGESTIBILITY

In the text we have seen that people in front of mirrors are more attentive to their own inner states and more responsive to emotions such as anger or sexual arousal than those not placed in front of mirrors. In other words, mirrors can help people to "know themselves" better. But can such self-knowledge also make people more resistant to situational influences?

Michael Scheier, Charles Carver, and Frederick Gibbons (1979) set out to test this notion in two interesting experiments. In the first, they showed moderately arousing slides of nude females to fifty-five undergraduate men at the University of Miami. The men were also exposed to strong situational pressures designed to influence their ratings of how aroused they felt by the slides. Half of the men were told by the experimenter, "By the way, you might as well know before you even start that the guys we've run so far with this particular set of slides have been reporting that they really aren't arousing at all—I mean, not at all. I've noticed that they've been circling points way over there on the left side of the page." The other half of the men heard a different message: "Well, it looks like you're one of the lucky ones. The guys we've run so far with this set of slides have been reporting that they're really pretty arousing. I've noticed that they've generally been circling points way over here on the right side of the page."

In each of these experimental conditions, half of the men watched the nude slides on a rear projection screen that went black in between slides; the other half watched on a screen that turned reflective in between slides. Thus, the second half saw their own image after each slide.

The experimenters predicted that the mirrors would make the men more attentive to their own inner states—their actual emotional reactions to the slides—and, therefore, less influenced by the strong situational pressure exerted by the experimenter. This is exactly what the researchers found. As shown in the table below, the men who saw their own reflections were less affected by the experimenter's remark than the men who saw only the slides. In other words, the mirror helped them to know their own inner feelings and thus resist the situational pressure to perceive the slides as more or less arousing than they actually were.

MEAN AROUSAL SCORES IN EACH EXPERIMENTAL CONDITION

	NO MIRROR	MIRROR
High-Arousal Instructions	78.69	70.00
Low-Arousal Instructions	39.85	45.63

Source: M. F. Scheier, C. S. Carver, and F. X. Gibbons, "Self-Directed Attention, Awareness of Bodily States, and Suggestibility," *Journal of Personality and Social Psychology* 37 (1979): 1576–1588.

The experimenters demonstrated the same point in a second experiment, but instead of measuring sexual arousal they measured taste, and instead of inducing self-attention with mirrors they used subjects who were either high or low in dispositional self-consciousness. In this case, high self-consciousness subjects were less influenced by the experimenter's pressure in rating a solution of peppermint extract than were the low self-consciousness subjects. In other words, high self-consciousness allowed them to be more sensitive to the solution's actual taste.

In each experiment the subjects' responses were influenced both by their inner states and by situational forces. But when attention is directed to one's inner state, that disposition becomes a relatively more important determinant of one's response.

Incidentally, you might note that the experimenter's remarks in the above studies amounted to extremely strong demand characteristics, as discussed in Chapter 2. However, self-directed attention was able to reduce the influence of these remarks on the subjects' behavior.

ior correlates higher with their previous ratings of their own aggressiveness for people who are high in self-consciousness ($r = .66$) than for people who are low in self-consciousness ($r = .09$). Similarly, if people are made angry and are then given a chance to aggress against their attacker, highly self-conscious persons are more aggressive than persons low in self-consciousness, thus suggesting that highly self-conscious people are more in tune with their emotions (Scheier, 1976).

Self-consciousness also influences people's expressions of emotions other than anger. For example, Scheier and Carver (1977) showed that highly self-conscious males rate slides of nude women as being more attractive and slides of maimed bodies as being more unpleasant than males low in self-consciousness. Also when highly self-conscious persons were asked to read statements designed to manipulate their moods, they rated themselves as more affected by the mood manipulations than persons low in self-consciousness (Scheier and Carver, 1977). In addition, when highly self-conscious persons and persons low in self-consciousness were shown slides of handicapped or normal persons, self-consciousness had no effect on ratings of the normal person, although highly self-conscious individuals rated the handicapped person more positively than individuals low in self-consciousness (Scheier, Carver, Schultz, Glass, and Katz, 1978). Apparently, self-consciousness leads people to be more attuned to their sympathy for the handicapped. Thus, self-consciousness has been shown to intensify a wide range of human emotions, from aggression, sexual attraction, and repulsion to elation and sympathy. Apparently, the tendency to focus attention frequently on oneself—on one's inner feelings and reactions—leads people to be more aware of their standards and emotions and to behave more in accord with them.

An interesting paradox that is not entirely answered by the research is what happens when one's standards and emotions contradict each other? For example, if you generally oppose violence but feel extremely angry because you were the victim of an unprovoked attack, what would you do if you had an opportunity to aggress against your attacker? Would high self-consciousness lead you to behave more in accord with your standards, and thus turn the other cheek, or with your emotions, and thus respond in kind? The answer seems to be that it depends on whether your standards or your emotions are stronger, and whether you are attending more to your current bodily sensations or your long-term values and beliefs.

LOSS OF SELF-AWARENESS AND DEINDIVIDUATION

As we have just seen, self-awareness is important for self-regulation. When people's attention is focused on themselves they are more aware of their internal standards and feelings and they behave more in accord with these standards and feelings. In other words, they are "truer" to themselves. Yet what happens when attention is focused away from oneself and onto the environment? What happens, for example, when the individual is totally involved in an absorbing movie, an exciting group discussion, or an angry mob? The self certainly does not cease to exist in these situations, but to the extent that one's attention is focused away from oneself, one may be unaware of oneself. Consequently, one's behavior should be less determined by internal standards and feelings and more influenced by external situational forces. In other words, self-regulation decreases, and people may in fact behave as if they did not have a well-developed self-concept or an inner set of values, standards, and ideals.

In most situations an individual's attention fluctuates between the environment and the self. Even when one is absorbed in a movie, one can easily divert attention away from the movie and back to oneself. However, some situations can be so absorbing and so intense that one's attention is entirely focused outward, and it may be difficult to switch attention back toward oneself. Such a state is termed *deindividuation*, and it has been defined as loss of self-awareness due to immersion in a group activity (see Dipboye, 1977; Diener, 1979). Some people may begin to experience this feeling at parties, for example, as individuals are packed onto a crowded dance floor with music blasting, lights flashing, and dancers merging into a writhing mass. Soci-

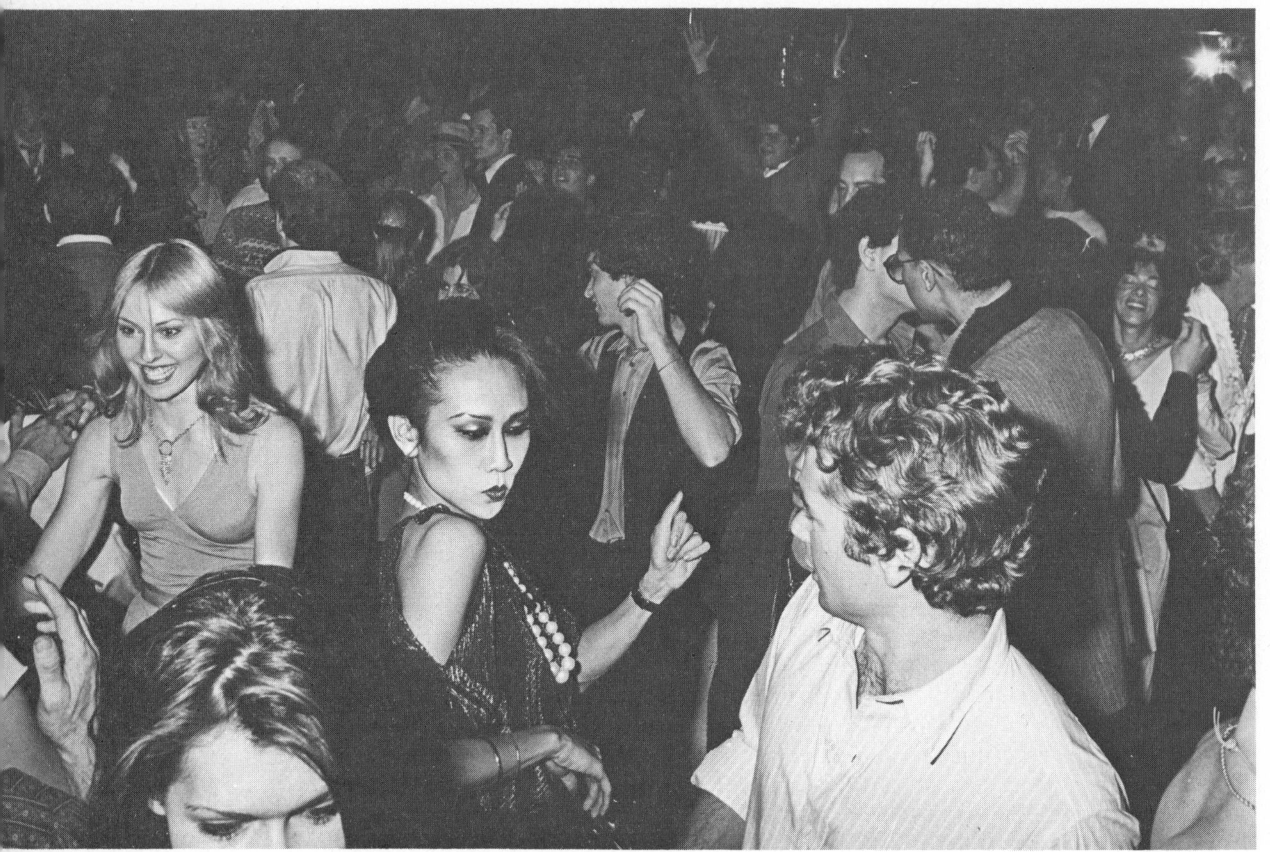

Deindividuation may occur in settings such as a crowded dance floor, where the intensity of a group activity can diminish self-awareness. *(Mike Norcia / Sygma)*

ologist-philosopher Le Bon (1879) referred to this phenomenon as a "group mind" and believed that it could cause individuals to behave in ways that were uncharacteristic of them and contradictory to their own standards. A vivid and horrifying example of deindividuation is the My Lai massacre that took place during the Vietnam War. As described by Seymour Hersh in his book, *My Lai Four* (1972), a group of American soldiers entered a Vietnam village that contained only old men, women, and children and systematically murdered all of the inhabitants and burned their huts. The soldiers were not murderers "by nature." They were simply average people caught up in the madness and fear of war, and their brutal behavior can be seen partly as the result of deindividuation.

RESEARCH ON DEINDIVIDUATION

Social psychologists have adopted several approaches to the study of deindividuation. The term was first used in 1952 by Leon Festinger, Albert Pepitone, and Theodore Newcomb, who observed a group of college students involved in a highly absorbing conversation featuring outspoken criticism of their parents. The researchers found that the more involved the students were in the conversation, the less likely they were to remember who in the group had made what specific points. The researchers concluded that in a highly involved group interaction, individuals are "not seen or paid attention as individuals" (p. 382).

A more systematic theory of deindividuation was offered in 1969 by Philip Zimbardo, who described certain "input variables" that could produce deindividuation and result in certain antisocial "output behaviors." Among the factors that could produce deindividuation, Zimbardo listed anonymity, group size and activity, sensory overload, and physical involvement in the group activity. These conditions were predicted to create a loss of self-observation, self-evaluation, and concern about others' evaluations. The result would be uninhibited behavior, freedom from normal self-controls, impulsiveness, emotionalism, and actions colored by the surrounding situation. In support of his theory, Zimbardo performed an experiment in which he deindividuated college women by shrouding them in hoods, placing them in groups of four in a dark room, and giving them an opportunity to shock a female victim. In contrast, other women were "individuated" by wearing large prominent name tags and taking part in the experiment in a bright room. Zimbardo found that the deindividuated women delivered longer shocks and failed to discriminate between deserving and undeserving victims. In contrast, the individuated women administered shorter shocks and were more lenient toward the undeserving victim than the deserving victim.

More recently, Edward Diener (1979) explicitly linked the phenomenon of deindividuation with theory and research on self-awareness. Noting that earlier approaches emphasized a lack of self-consciousness during deindividuation, Diener defined deindividuation as a lack of self-awareness and self-regulation caused by certain situational factors that may be present in some groups. Diener's definition has two important components: first, the *external situational factors* inherent in a group, such as group uniformity, an external focus of attention, and physical activity; and, second, the *internal state of deindividuation*, composed of lack of attention to one's own behavior and lack of awareness of oneself as a distinct entity.

Diener and his colleagues have performed several clever and interesting experiments to test their ideas. In one study, trick-or-treaters were the subjects, and the experiment took place as these children came to the door on Halloween night in masks and costumes. The children were ushered into the living room where they were shown a large bowl of individually wrapped candy bars and another bowl of nickels and dimes. The experimenter told them that they could take one candy bar, and then he left the room. A hidden observer noted whether the children took extra candy or any of the money. When the children came alone and their anonymity was removed by asking them their names, only 7.5 percent of them stole extra candy and money. But when the children came in groups and they remained anonymous, 57.2 percent of them took extra candy and money (Diener, Fraser, Beaman, and Kelem, 1976). In an interesting variation on this study, the next Halloween the researchers performed the same study but this time set up a large mirror just behind the candy bowl. The results showed that the mirror reduced stealing, but only if the children's anonymity had been removed by first asking them their name. The mirror did not have any effect on the anonymous group of costumed children (Beaman, Klentz, Diener, and Svanum, 1979).

While these two studies provide suggestive evidence that certain situations cause lowered self-awareness and antinormative behavior, Diener has performed two studies that establish these links more explicitly. In the first experiment (Diener, 1979) college students took part in group interactions that were designed to create feelings of deindividuation or not. For example, in the deindividuation groups, two real subjects took part with six confederates who led the group through a series of activities designed to produce high group unity and group involvement. These included group singing, "elevating" a prone individual high into the air, forming interlocking arms to prevent an assistant from breaking into the circle, and performing African dancing to loud Burundi drum music with the lights dimmed. In contrast, subjects in a self-aware condition wore large name tags, wrote essays about themselves, and read personal information to each other. Subjects from both the deindividuation and self-awareness groups were then given an opportunity to choose several different tasks to work on in the second half of the experiment. The tasks were of two types: "disinhibition" tasks requiring bizarre behaviors such as eating unusual foods and smearing paint, and "inhibition" tasks composed of standard paper-and-pencil exercises. Subjects also rated themselves on self-consciousness and the degree to which they felt a loss of individual identity. The results showed that the deindividuation subjects chose more of the disinhibition tasks and rated themselves as less self-conscious and as having less of a sense of individual identity than the self-aware subjects. The study clearly demonstrated that external situational factors in groups can produce lowered self-awareness and release uninhibited behavior.

In a second experiment, Diener wanted to see if he could produce a similar sense of deindividuation through purely verbal interaction rather than the intense physical activity of the previous experiment. This time subjects were provided with an absorbing external focus of attention by having the groups discuss the topic of sexuality. In a condition designed to decrease subjects' self-awareness, confederates in the group discussed topics such as homosexuality, premarital sex, bestiality, pornography, and incest in a highly interesting and animated way. In a contrasting condition designed to heighten subjects' self-awareness, the confederates discussed the same topics but in a halting, boring repetitive way. Also in each type of conversation, half of the groups heard confederates who behaved in a highly uninhibited style, telling about explicit incidents, cursing, and using sexual slang, while half of the groups heard confederates who behaved in a very inhibited way, avoiding the topics of sex, and telling boring stories. The sessions were tape-recorded and the real subjects' behavior was subsequently analyzed for evidence of deindividuation. For example, how much cursing and how much self-revelation about sexual behavior were expressed by the subjects, and how explicit were descriptions of sexual incidents? In addition, at four points during the conversation, subjects were asked to rate their level of self-consciousness during the preceding minute. The results indicate that subjects in the low-self-awareness groups behaved in a more deindividuated way than subjects in the high-self-awareness groups. Furthermore, the confederates' uninhibited behavior influenced mainly those subjects in the low-self-awareness conditions. In other words, subjects were responsive to the uninhibited confederates, but mainly when the subjects themselves were not self-aware. It is also interesting to note that correlations were performed between subjects' initial attitudes toward sexual liberalness and their degree of uninhibited sex talk in the group. These correlations were high only for subjects who were in the high-self-aware groups, while the correlations were very low for those subjects in the low-self-aware groups. Thus, as we saw earlier, attitudes and behavior correlate highly when people's attention is focused on themselves and their own standards. However, when one's attention is focused outward, in a highly absorbing group conversation, for example, there is little correlation between attitudes and behavior.

In these two experiments, then, Diener has shown that when an individual's attention is focused outward toward highly involving group interaction—whether physical activity or absorbing conversation—the individual will have lower self-awareness, will express a greater liking for the group, and will behave in an uninhibited, counternormative way than when his or her attention is focused inward. Thus, deindividuation can be seen as the extreme opposite of self-awareness.

DEINDIVIDUATION: VALUABLE OR HARMFUL?

We have presented the topic of deindividuation as if it were a negative, irrational, antisocial state. It involves turning attention away from one's own internal standards, following the group, and behaving in ways that probably contradict one's own values. Essentially, deindividuation violates the cultural maxims "know thyself" and "to thine own self be true." But is this necessarily wrong or harmful?

Perhaps an individual's sense of self may be narrow and restricting, essentially preventing growth. No doubt all of us have felt the debilitating straitjacket that acute self-consciousness can impose on us. Many of the rituals of modern social life are engaged in purely because they help release us from self-consciousness and help foster deindividuation and remove inhibitions. Certainly, this is a principal motive in the use of alcohol and drugs, in attending crowded parties and dances, or in vacationing in locales where one is entirely unknown.

Some theorists and researchers have seen a definite positive advantage in deindividuation experiences. Many psychologists and therapists associated with the human-potential movement see deindividuation experiences as essential to leaving behind the "social self," composed of rigid standards and expectations, and getting in touch with an "inner self," defined as capacities and potentialities for experience yet untried. For example, Abraham Maslow (1968), frequently identified as the "father of humanistic psychology," believed that "self-actualization" requires a willingness to blend the rational and the irrational, to accept one's inner impulses even when they contradict one's standards, and to be able to act "pleasantly zany." Research has shown that deindividuated people are more open and disclosing with others, apparently because deindividuated people have less fear of being identified and criticized for expressing inappropriate feelings (Maslach, 1974). Deindividuated people also enjoy group experiences and feel closer to one another because of the intense mutual involvement of deindividuation (Festinger, Pepitone, and Newcomb, 1952; Cannavale, Scarr, and Pepitone, 1970; Diener, 1978, 1979b).

Deindividuation may work for either good or ill. When an individual's personal standards are narrow and restricting, it may feel quite "liberating" to be submerged in a group and to have the opportunity to try out new "selves." On the other hand, submergence in a group may also lead to behaviors that are undesirable or demeaning. In the final analysis, the value of deindividuation depends on the particular individual's own standards and the nature and direction of group activities.

IMPRESSION MANAGEMENT

We have seen that people who focus attention on themselves behave differently than people who focus attention on their environment. In particular, when people are self-conscious or self-aware, their behavior is more in tune with their internal standards and is, therefore, more consistent over time than the behavior of those who are not self-conscious or self-aware. But there is still another kind of self-awareness. For example, some people such as actors or politicians are especially skilled at presenting themselves differently in different settings. These people are able to "calculate" and manage their behavior in order to make a desired impression and to appear in tune with a wide variety of situations. Their behavior is often inconsistent, yet these people do not lack self-awareness. Instead, they are highly aware of their own behavior and of the social appropriateness and social consequences of their behavior. What is this type of self-awareness, and what leads some people to be better at it than others?

Mark Snyder (1974, 1979) proposed a *self-monitoring theory* that is different from the type of self-awareness we have considered. What Snyder's theory pertains to is not an individual's awareness of inner values and standards, but *an awareness of one's behavior as it appears to others.* Snyder asserts that some people are more sensitively attuned to their behavior than others are. In Snyder's terms some people are better at "monitoring" the social appropriateness of their behavior. These "self-monitors" tend to look outside themselves for cues about how they should be responding in different situations. They are skilled in managing and expressing a wide range of emotions. Because self-monitors are concerned about the situational appropriateness of their behavior, they are relatively *situationally controlled* individuals.

In contrast, individuals who are low self-monitors are less concerned about the impressions they make and less responsive to the surrounding social environment. These people are less attuned to the situational appropriateness of their behavior and are more attuned to their internal feelings and standards. As a result, low self-monitors are more likely to appear stable and consistent over time, regardless of the situation or what kind of people they are with. Low self-monitors, then, can be seen as relatively *dispositionally controlled* individuals. (To avoid confusion, keep in mind that self-monitoring refers to an awareness of external *behavior* rather than inner ideals and feelings. Thus, an individual who is high in self-monitoring is not necessarily high in self-awareness.)

In order to identify high and low self-monitors, Snyder constructed a scale he called the Self-Monitoring Scale (1974), which measures sensitivity to the social appropriateness of one's behavior, as shown in Figure 3.4. To validate the scale, Snyder observed high and low self-monitors on several dimensions. For example, professional stage actors were found to score higher on the scale than typical undergraduate students; high scorers were able to convey a variety of emotions more accurately on videotape than low scorers when their expressive behaviors were judged; and in an ambiguous situation, high scorers were more attentive to cues about appropriate behavior than low scorers.

The most important point about the Self-Monitoring Scale is that it allows some prediction about the degree of consistency one should expect in an individual's behavior over time. People who score high on the scale—that is, high self-monitors—are more varied in their behavior over time because they are attuned to subtle shifts in the situation and they modify their behavior accordingly. In contrast, low self-monitors are less varied and more consistent in their behavior over time, because they are less attuned to the surrounding situation and less aware of the social appropriateness of their own behavior.

This difference between high and low self-monitors has been demonstrated in a variety of ways. One of the more unusual predictions involves whether or not people salt their food before tasting or after tasting. McGee and Snyder (1975) reasoned that situationally controlled persons would probably taste their food first to see if it needed salt. In contrast, they predicted that dispositionally controlled persons would probably salt their food before tasting it. To test their predictions, they watched a number of people in restaurants to see whether these people salted before or after tasting. These diners were then approached and asked to fill out a questionnaire. The questionnaire contained a list of twenty adjective pairs (for example, realistic-idealistic, cautious-bold). Subjects were asked to check which of the two adjectives in each pair described them better, or they could choose a third option by checking "it depends on the situation." The results showed that those people who salted their food *before* tasting checked more than twice as many adjectives to describe themselves as did those who salted *after* tasting; the latter group tended to say their behavior "depends on the situation." In other words, people who salt *before* tasting see themselves as having more personality traits than people who salt after tasting. Accordingly, the behavior of those who salt before tasting should be more controlled by internal dispositions, while those who salt after tasting should be more influenced by situations. Although the Self-Monitoring Scale was not employed in this particular study, the authors suggest that those individuals who taste before they salt and who ascribe fewer personality traits to themselves and rely more on situational cues are also the same people who are high self-monitors.

The relationship between self-monitoring and behavioral consistency was made more explicit in a second study. Snyder and Monson (1975) presented subjects with descriptions of three behaviors having to do with generosity (offering a seat to a middle-aged lady on a bus), honesty (returning extra change to a cashier), and hostility (expressing anger to a classmate who pulled a chair out from under you). Subjects were asked to rate how they might respond if they performed each of the three behaviors under different situational conditions—for example, if they were in a bad mood, if a friend were present, or if they had just failed at something important. As expected, people who scored high on the Self-Monitoring Scale rated their probable behavior as more variable, or more dependent on the situation, than low self-monitors. Furthermore, when subjects were asked to rate a friend's behavior in each of the same situations, high self-monitors rated their friends as *less* variable than themselves, while low self-monitors rated their friends as *more* variable than themselves.

Snyder and his colleagues have also shown that despite an individual's dispositional tendency toward high or low self-monitoring, certain kinds of situations can increase an individual's awareness of situational pressures on behavior or, conversely, can increase an individ-

Answer "true" or "false" for each question. The scoring key is listed below.*

1. I find it hard to imitate the behavior of other people. . . . . ______
2. My behavior is usually an expression of my true inner feelings, attitudes, and beliefs . . . ______
3. At parties and social gatherings, I do not attempt to do or say things that others will like . ______
4. I can only argue for ideas which I already believe . . . . ______
5. I can make impromptu speeches even on topics about which I have almost no information . . . . ______
6. I guess I put on a show to impress or entertain people . . . . ______
7. When I am uncertain how to act in a social situation, I look to the behavior of others for cues. . . . . ______
8. I would probably make a good actor . . . . ______
9. I rarely need the advice of my friends to choose movies, books, or music . . . . ______
10. I sometimes appear to others to be experiencing deeper emotions than I actually am. . . ______
11. I laugh more when I watch a comedy with others than when alone . . . . ______
12. In a group of people I am rarely the center of attention . . . . ______
13. In different situations and with different people, I often act like very different persons . . ______
14. I am not particularly good at making other people like me . . . . ______
15. Even if I am not enjoying myself, I often pretend to be having a good time . . . . ______
16. I'm not always the person I appear to be . . . . ______
17. I would not change my opinions (or the way I do things) in order to please someone else or win their favor . . . . ______
18. I have considered being an entertainer . . . . ______
19. In order to get along and be liked, I tend to be what people expect me to be rather than anything else . . . . ______
20. I have never been good at games like charades or improvisational acting . . . . ______
21. I have trouble changing my behavior to suit different people and different situations . . . ______
22. At a party I let others keep the jokes and stories going . . . . ______
23. I feel a bit awkward in company and do not show up quite so well as I should . . . . ______
24. I can look anyone in the eye and tell a lie with a straight face (if for a right end) . . . . ______
25. I may deceive people by being friendly when I really dislike them . . . . ______

*"Correct" responses: (1) F, (2) F, (3) F, (4) F, (5) T, (6) T, (7) T, (8) T, (9) F, (10) T, (11) T, (12) F, (13) T, (14) F, (15) T, (16) T, (17) F, (18) T, (19) T, (20) F, (21) F, (22) F, (23) F, (24) T, (25) T.

FIGURE 3.4 The Self-Monitoring Scale. Questions are scored in the direction of high self-monitoring. Give yourself one point for each "correct" response. Individuals who score more than 15 points are considered high self-monitors; individuals who score less than 9 points are considered low self-monitors. (From Snyder, 1974.)

ual's awareness of internal values and attitudes. Snyder and Swann (1976) found that when people were asked specifically to reflect on their attitudes prior to engaging in a behavior, then their behavior was more consistent with their attitudes than if their attitudes had not been made particularly salient. On the other hand, when a strong situational force was introduced into the picture, there was very little relationship between attitudes and behavior.

In summary, the research on self-monitoring closely parallels the research on self-awareness and self-consciousness. Because high self-monitors are highly attuned to their social images and the surrounding situation, their behavior tends to vary with the situations in which they find themselves. On the other hand, because low-self monitors are less attuned to their social images and the surrounding situation, their behavior is less varied.

SELF-DISCLOSURE AND AUTHENTICITY

Throughout this chapter we have been primarily concerned with an individual's self-concept or self-theory: how it develops, whether it is single or multiple, how it affects information processing and regulates behavior, and what circumstances lead an individual to be more or less aware of the self-theory and to behave in accord with it. But we have left out one final and important question: Is one's self-concept or self-theory the same thing as one's "real" self? Furthermore, is it even possible to have a "real" self, or should we speak in terms of "real" selves? Can the self that seems most real be contradictory at different times and places? This question of the self's authenticity cannot be easily answered by referring to social-psychological research. However, some theories help point to an answer.

Many humanistic psychologists place a high value on authenticity and genuineness. Representative of this approach is the work of clinical psychologist Sidney Jourard. Jourard's book *The Transparent Self* (1971) argues that "transparency" or "self-disclosure" is necessary for positive mental health. In fact, Jourard argues that one cannot really know oneself until one has first disclosed oneself to others. In Jourard's words, "Every maladjusted person is a person who has not made himself known to another human being" (p. 32). According to Jourard, an individual with a healthy personality "will display the ability to make himself fully known to at least one other significant human being" (p. 32).

In order to evaluate his claims, Jourard developed a Self-Disclosure Scale that measures how disclosing individuals have been to other people in their lives, as shown in Figure 3.5. In practice, however, it has been difficult to evaluate Jourard's claim that mental health requires authentic self-disclosure. Although some studies have found a relationship between psychiatric disorders and low self-disclosure, other studies have obtained no relationship at all (see Cozby, 1973; Chaikin and Derlega, 1974).

Despite the difficulties in relating self-disclosure and mental health, self-disclosure may be important to an individual's functioning for another reason. Recall the importance of social comparison in the development of an individual's self-theory. As we noted earlier, the research indicates that people evaluate themselves in light of how they compare with other people. In order to evaluate your feelings about yourself and to determine whether your self-view is harsh, lenient, or realistic, it is important to know how other people feel about themselves. One of the most significant and frequently demonstrated consequences of self-disclosure is a phenomenon called the *dyadic effect*; that is, when you self-disclose to someone else, that person will probably self-disclose back to you (see, for example, Worthy, Gary, and Kahn, 1969). Furthermore, the more intimate and the more extensive your self-disclosure, the more intimate and the more extensive the reciprocal disclosure of the person to whom you have revealed yourself (Derlega, Harris, and Chaikin, 1973; Rubin, 1975). Thus, if social comparison is an important influence on an individual's self-theory, and if self-disclosure facilitates social comparison by causing individuals to reveal their feelings about themselves, then self-disclosure may be an important step in de-

For each question below, rate the degree to which you have disclosed information about that topic to any other person at any point in your life, according to the following scale: 0 = never; 1 = almost nothing; 2 = in general, but not specifically; 3 = some specific details; 4 = most of the important details; 5 = complete disclosure.

1. What are your views on the way a husband and wife should live their marriage? .... _____
2. What are your usual ways of dealing with depression, anxiety and anger? .... _____
3. What are the actions you have most regretted doing in your life and why? .... _____
4. What are your personal religious views and the nature of your religious participation if any? .... _____
5. What are the ways in which you feel you are most maladjusted or inmature? .... _____
6. What are your guiltiest secrets? .... _____
7. What are your personal views on politics, the presidency, foreign and domestic policy? .... _____
8. What are the habits and reactions of yours which bother you at present? .... _____
9. What are the sources of strain and dissatisfaction in your marriage (or your relationship with the opposite sex)? .... _____
10. What are your favorite forms of erotic play and sexual love making? .... _____
11. What are your hobbies, how do you best like to spend your spare time? .... _____
12. What were the occasions in your life on which you were the happiest? .... _____
13. What are the aspects of your daily work that satisfy and bother you? .... _____
14. What characteristics of yourself give you cause for pride and satisfaction? .... _____
15. Who are the persons in your life whom you most resent? Why? .... _____
16. Who are the people with whom you have been sexually intimate? What were the circumstances of your relationship with each? .... _____
17. What are the unhappiest moments in your life? Why? .... _____
18. What are your preferences and dislikes in music? .... _____
19. What are your personal goals for the next ten years or so? .... _____
20. What are the circumstances under which you become depressed and when your feelings are hurt? .... _____
21. What are your most common sexual fantasies and reveries? .... _____

TOTAL _____

FIGURE 3.5 The Self-Disclosure Scale. The average score for high and low self-disclosers varies, depending on age, sex, region of the country, socioeconomic background, and so on. You may wish to compare your score with friends or with the class average. (From Jourard, 1971.)

veloping a realistic self-concept. For example, if a young man had anxieties about sexual performance, and he believed that the anxieties were unique to him, then the anxieties might lead him to develop an overly critical self-evaluation. As a result he might avoid sexual intimacy altogether. However, if mutual self-disclosure with close friends revealed that most

Self-disclosure encourages reciprocal disclosure from one's confidants and therefore helps to avoid unrealistic self-evaluations. *(Elizabeth Hamlin / Stock, Boston)*

people felt anxieties about sexual performance from time to time, then the young man would not make the false inference that he was uniquely incapacitated. As a result, he could arrive at a more realistic self-theory and regulate his behavior accordingly.

Research has also revealed other aspects of the dyadic effect. A number of studies have found that men are generally less self-disclosing than women, especially to other men, though this effect varies with different populations (see Cozby, 1973). Also most people are more disclosing to strangers than to friends, apparently because they fear no rejection from strangers (Derlega, Wilson, and Chaikin, 1976). Finally, the dyadic effect does not appear to occur because mutual intimacy produces mutual liking, but because of a norm of reciprocity (Lynn, 1977). Apparently, reciprocity in self-disclosure occurs because inequity creates tension and most people would prefer to avoid tension.

WHAT IS THE "SELF" IN SELF-DISCLOSURE?

The question with which we began this section concerns the authenticity of the "self" that is disclosed in self-disclosure. As we have seen in this chapter, the self means many things. It may mean one's body, one's characteristic ways of thinking and behaving, one's feelings about oneself, or even one's "spiritual essence." However, we have seen that one's feelings about oneself change under different social conditions. And one's behavior can vary widely over time and place, depending partly on whether an individual is focusing attention on the self-theory or on the environment. Indeed, under conditions of extreme deindividuation, individuals respond primarily as a member of a group, as if they have no self at all.

Thus, it is appropriate to ask: What is the "authentic self" that is disclosed in self-disclosure? Is the self merely a summary of past behaviors, thoughts, and feelings? If so, what happens when some aspects of our experience are inconsistent with other aspects of our experience? Which is more "authentic"? Furthermore, what about the extremes of behavior that we may have performed under self-awareness versus deindividuation?

An answer to this paradox is suggested by George Herbert Mead. Recall that Mead viewed the self as a dualism, the "I" and the "me." Essentially, the "I" is an individual's *organismic capacity* for acting, thinking, and feeling; the "me" is the individual's *awareness* of acting, thinking, or feeling. In any individual, there can be as many "me's" as there are variations in experience; yet there is only one "I." Thus, to be fully self-disclosing, one must disclose the full variety of one's experience—in other words, the multiplicity of one's "me's." In so doing, one begins to suggest the nature and capacity of the "I."

A different, but related, view is expressed by Alan Watts (1966), a Zen philosopher who approaches the self from the viewpoint of Eastern religions. Just as Mead distinguished between the "I" and the "me," Watts distinguished between the "I" and the "ego." For Watts, the "ego"—one's awareness of oneself—is always false because it is limited by one's experience. The only real authentic self is the "I"—defined purely as one's capacity for experience. Paradoxically, then, we can never "know" our real self, for whenever we put boundaries around our experiences and seek to objectify ourself, we only arrive at the false ego. For Watts, as for many mystics, we cannot come to know ourselves until we cease trying to "know" ourselves. For many mystics the riddle of the self is that it cannot be "known"; it can only be "experienced." In other words, if the "real" self is the "I," defined as our capacity for experience, we can only come to know this "I" as we begin to surrender our limited self-theory and accept self as pure experience.

SUMMARY

The notion of the self has several meanings. It may refer to the physical body, to an individual's personality, to one's self-concept, or to a spiritual self. Most research on the self deals with the self-concept. Mead and others have suggested that the self-concept is determined by social interaction. Research has shown that the self-concept is influenced by other people's reactions, by social comparison, and by the effects of other people's behavior. Because an individual's self-concept varies in social interaction, Gergen has suggested that the self-concept should actually be viewed as a system of multiple selves.

Another way of explaining the self-concept is to view the self as a theory—essentially a hypothesis that individuals develop in order to explain the data of their lives. This view is consistent with Bem's self-perception theory, which argues that we infer internal responsibility for our behavior when we lack a sufficient external explanation. Our self-theories and self-inferences may be erroneous, however, if we fail to account for all the relevant data in arriving at our hypotheses.

Once the self-concept or self-theory develops, it serves to organize perceptions and regulate behavior. Recent research suggests that the self functions as a system of schemata in memory. These self-relevant schemata, or information-processing categories, influence what we attend to in the world and how efficiently we encode and retrieve information about the world.

The self also comprises values and standards that regulate behavior. To the extent that individuals are more attentive to these internal values and standards than to the external environment, their behavior reflects these values and standards. Circumstances that induce self-awareness, such as mirrors and cameras, help focus attention on the self rather than on the environment. Similarly, some people are more dispositionally self-conscious than others. Self-awareness and self-consciousness both result in a matching of behavior to inner standards, increase self-attributions of responsibility for behavior, and increase consistency between internal standards and behavior. However, unusual conditions of extreme group involvement, sensory overload, and anonymity can produce a state of deindividuation that is characterized by little self-awareness or self-regulation.

Some humanistic psychologists assert that the "real" self can be discovered through self-disclosure. Other psychologists question whether "authentic" self-disclosure is possible in light of the wide variation among a person's behaviors, thoughts, and feelings—or among a person's several selves. Perhaps the most real or most authentic self is an individual's organic capacity for experience rather than any specific assortment of past experiences.

CHAPTER FOUR

ATTITUDES, BELIEFS, AND BEHAVIOR

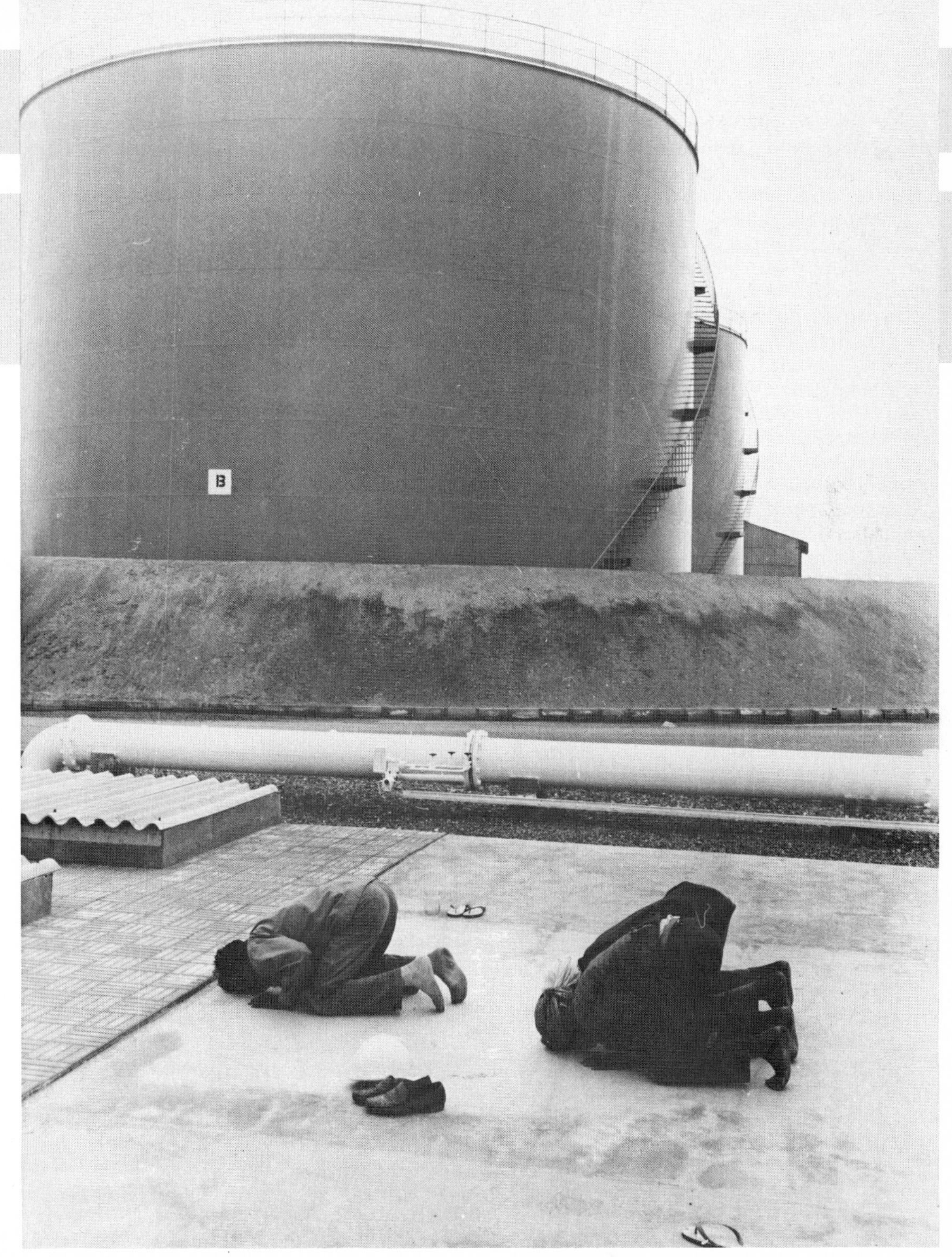
B

In the early morning hours of March 28, 1979, a nuclear power plant on Three Mile Island, Pennsylvania, suffered a major breakdown. Because of a cooling-pump malfunction, the reactor core overheated and was in danger of a catastrophic meltdown. At the same time a hydrogen gas bubble formed in the plant's reactor vessel and threatened to explode. For seventy-two hours engineers had no control over events, and the nation awaited a possible nuclear diasaster. Pregnant women and children within a five-mile radius of the plant were evacuated by order of the governor of Pennsylvania because radioactive steam had escaped into the atmosphere. Thousands more prepared to flee. Across the country millions of others had recently viewed the popular movie *The China Syndrome*, which frighteningly portrayed a similar accident in a fictional nuclear power plant. Although the real-life hydrogen leak at Three Mile Island was eventually brought under control with apparently little harm to human life, public attitudes toward nuclear energy were profoundly shaken. What had appeared to be a safe and inexhaustible energy supply became an ominous uncertainty. If changing public attitudes favor dwindling oil supplies and environmentally polluting coal over development of nuclear energy, the impact may be felt in daily lives—all because people's *attitudes* change from positive to negative.

What are attitudes? How do they influence behavior? How do various conflicting attitudes fit together in a person's head, and how do they form in the first place? Are attitudes simply conditioned by our environment, or are they products of a sophisticated information search? And how can they be measured in order to predict behaviors? These are the questions this chapter addresses.

An *attitude* is defined as a relatively enduring disposition to evaluate persons, events, or objects in a favorable or unfavorable way. The study of attitudes is not concerned with temporary mood states or brief flights of fancy, but with the thoughts and feelings that people have on a relatively frequent, consistent, and long-term basis.

Attitudes are generally studied in relation to two other aspects of human behavior: the *beliefs* people hold about attitude objects and the *actions* they take toward attitude objects. Because attitudes are evaluations, exploring an individual's attitude toward nuclear energy would mean studying his or her general feelings toward the issue: To what extent does the individual regard nuclear energy as good or bad? Yet attitudes must also be related to beliefs, because one's general evaluations are tied to one's beliefs or cognitions about attitude objects. For example, one person's most salient belief about nuclear energy might be that it provides needed electric power for homes and industry. Another person might view nuclear energy as an extremely dangerous threat to human health and life. No doubt the attitudes of these two individuals would differ, along with their beliefs. Finally, attitudes must be related to actions, because people often encounter situations that require actions or behaviors in relation to attitude objects. For example, persons holding attitudes about nuclear energy might be invited to join an antinuclear demonstration, be expected to vote in an election containing a referendum on nuclear energy, be asked for their opinions on nuclear energy, and so on.

Attitude theory and research vary in their relative emphasis on the evaluative, cognitive, and behavioral components of attitudes. As we will see, a great deal of attitude theory focuses on the cognitive issue of relating evaluations to beliefs and on the behavioral issue of relating evaluations to actions. These issues have been important to social psychology for several decades. Indeed, attitudes have long been a central area of study in social psychology, as illustrated by Gordon Allport's comment in 1935 that "the concept of attitude is probably the most distinctive and indispensable concept in contemporary American social psychology." The study of attitudes remains important to social psychology today, and many of the central issues of attitude theory—such as the relation between attitudes and behaviors—have been enduring questions for social psychologists. In the following sections, we will discuss the relationship between attitudes and beliefs and between attitudes and behavior.

ATTITUDES AND BELIEFS

To understand the relationship between attitudes and beliefs think for a moment about the city of Paris. No doubt quite a few thoughts come to mind—for example, you may think of Paris as a romantic city with sidewalk cafes, an attractive city with graceful monuments and buildings, a cultural city of museums and art galleries, a historical city, a European city, and so on. Social psychologists refer to the thoughts or cognitions that you have concerning Paris as your *beliefs* about the city. Each belief consists of an association that you have made in your mind between Paris and some characteristic—in other words, you may associate Paris with romance, culture, history, and other attributes.

Do the beliefs that you hold about the city of Paris relate in a systematic way to your evaluations? If there is a relation between evaluations and beliefs, a person who thinks Paris is a terrific city would have different beliefs than a person who evaluates Paris unfavorably. Not surprisingly, there is a general correspondence between evaluations and beliefs: individuals with positive evaluations of Paris have predominantly favorable thoughts (for example, that Paris is beautiful, lively, sophisticated), and individuals with negative evaluations have predominantly unfavorable thoughts (for example, that Paris is large, unfriendly, and expensive).

Knowing that there is a general correspondence between evaluations and beliefs does not provide a precise understanding of how evaluations and beliefs relate. Various attitude theorists have attempted to provide an explanation that is more exact—in fact, precise enough to be expressed by a mathematical equation. In order to understand such an approach, it is necessary to think of each individual belief as expressing some degree of evaluation. A positive thought such as the idea that Paris is a *very lively city* expresses favorable evaluation, while a negative thought such as the idea that Paris is *overly large* expresses unfavorable evaluation. The degree of favorable or unfavorable evaluation expressed by each belief could be represented on a scale running from, say, +3 for very positive evaluation through 0 for neutrality to −3 for very negative evaluation.

An attitude object—such as the city of Paris—may elicit a wide range of beliefs. Some people have positive evaluations of it—for example, that Paris is beautiful, historic, and elegant; others have negative evaluations—for example, that Paris is too large and slum-ridden. *(© Britton-Logan 1973 / Photo Researchers; © C. Raimond-Dityvon / VIVA 1980 / Woodfin Camp & Assoc.)*

Although the idea of a mathematical theory of attitudes may seem imposing to many people, these theories are essentially simple. In fact, the most popular mathematical approach assumes that persons' overall evaluations of an attitude object are averages of the positive or negative evaluations expressed by their beliefs about the attitude object. The beliefs that a person holds about Paris determine his or her attitude about Paris. For example, a person who has three favorable beliefs about Paris and one unfavorable belief would average together the three positives and the one negative belief, with the result that his or her overall evaluation would be positive.

According to the averaging approach, an individual's evaluation of an attitude object is not revealed by the *number* of beliefs the person holds. Some attitude objects, such as the city of Paris, tend to elicit many beliefs. Because most people have encountered a lot of information about such attitude objects, these objects are associated with a large number of attributes. In other cases, people may have few beliefs about an attitude object. For example, most Americans may have relatively few ideas concerning the attributes of the city of Portland, Oregon (although the citizens of that city and persons who have visited it would have a rich array of beliefs about Portland). Despite the fact that most Americans have many more beliefs about Paris than about Portland, their attitudes toward (that is, evaluations of) the two cities may be similar—perhaps moderately favorable toward both cities. To illustrate this principle, imagine that five beliefs come to mind when you think about Paris: it is *expensive* (assume you slightly devalue this attribute, −1), has a *beautiful, romantic atmosphere* (assume +3), has *several major museums* (+2), and is *historically interesting* (+1) and *very large* (0). Imagine that thinking about Portland brings to mind only two thoughts: it is in the *Pacific Northwest* (+1) and is a *small city* (+1). If you perceive these attributes and place these values on them, your thoughts about Paris

$$\frac{(-1)+(+3)+(+2)+(+1)=(0)}{5} = \frac{+5}{5} = +1$$

and about Portland

$$\frac{(+1)=(+1)}{2} = \frac{+2}{2} = +1$$

would both average to +1. With respect to how positive or negative your overall evaluation is, then, it doesn't matter that your evaluation of Paris is based on a larger number of thoughts than your evaluation of Portland.

The averaging approach to relating attitudes and beliefs, which is called *information integration theory*, has been investigated extensively by Norman Anderson and his associates (Anderson, 1980). Research has shown that averaging the amounts of positive or negative evaluation expressed by a person's beliefs about an attitude object generally yields a good estimate of his or her overall attitude toward that object. Despite such relatively accurate predictions on the basis of averaging, several other simple mathematical equations (such as one that *adds* evaluations rather than averages them) have also been proposed and have some advantages under certain circumstances. Together, these approaches have provided good evidence that attitudes can be viewed as summaries of the positive or negative aspects of people's beliefs about attitude objects.

ATTITUDES AND BEHAVIOR

DO ACTIONS CORRESPOND TO ATTITUDES?

For many years social scientists considered the study of attitudes a shortcut to predicting behavior. In fact, the main reason attitudes became a major focus of research was that attitudes were seen as *causes* of behavior. Persons with favorable attitudes toward an attitude object were assumed to engage in positive behaviors that support or enhance the attitude object; those with unfavorable attitudes toward an attitude object were assumed to engage in negative behaviors that oppose or weaken the attitude object. If attitudes cause behaviors, then one would expect persons with positive attitudes toward nuclear energy, for example, to praise nuclear power in conversations with friends, write to their legislative representatives to support pronuclear legislation, and engage in other pronuclear actions. Persons with negative attitudes toward nuclear energy would be expected to affix "No More Nukes" bumper stickers to their cars, write opposing letters to their legislators, participate in antinuclear demonstrations, and so on.

Even though the assumption that behaviors correspond to attitudes seems reasonable, a number of social scientists have questioned whether an individual's behavior can be accurately predicted from knowledge of that individual's attitudes. An early study that raised this question examined the correspondence between prejudiced attitudes toward Chinese and discriminatory behaviors toward a particular Chinese couple. This study was conducted by social scientist LaPiere (1934), who traveled twice across the United States and up and down the Pacific coast—a total of ten thousand miles—with two Chinese friends. LaPiere and the Chinese couple were received in 66 hotels, auto camps, and tourist homes and were served in 184 restaurants. They were refused service only once. Six months after these visits, LaPiere sent copies of a questionnaire to the same establishments the trio had visited. The questionnaire asked: "Will you accept members of the Chinese race as guests in your establishment?" Of the 81 restaurants and 47 hotels that replied, 92 percent replied that they would *not* accept Chinese customers, and the remainder checked "Uncertain, depends upon circumstances." It is clear that these written replies did not correspond to the actual behavior of the respondents.

Even though the LaPiere study does not provide a very good general test of the relationship between attitudes and behaviors, it is often cited in textbooks, in part because it was one of the first attitude-behavior studies. Among the many possible criticisms of the study is that the proprietors of the restaurants and other establishments may not have recognized the couple as Chinese, and even if they did, their behavior may have been directed primarily toward LaPiere, who was white, rather than toward his Chinese friends. Further, the "members of the Chinese race" that the owners had in mind when they responded to the questionnaire may not have been as Westernized or as well dressed and prosperous-appearing as the man and woman who accompanied LaPiere. Also, the responses to LaPiere's letters were probably written by the owners of the establishments, although the Chinese couple was dealt with by desk clerks and waitresses. It is thus possible that "management policy" pertaining to such interracial contact was unknown by clerks, waitresses, and others in the lower echelons.

After LaPiere's provocative study, however, dozens of researchers used more sophisticated methods to study the attitude-behavior relation. Many of these studies also obtained relatively low correspondence between questionnaire measures of attitudes and measures of behavior. A number of these studies were reviewed by Allan Wicker in a paper published in 1969. Wicker claimed that the correlation between attitudes and behaviors is seldom as high as .30 (that is, seldom more than 9 percent of the variability in a behavior is accounted for by an attitude). In fact, Wicker found that the average correlation between attitudes and behaviors in the studies he reviewed was only a low .15. Since Wicker's review, the idea that attitudes and overt behavior are not closely related has been expressed with increasing frequency. In fact some social psychologists have despaired that the attitude concept is of any use in studying behavior (Abelson, 1972).

In the mid- and late 1970s the tide seemed to have turned again in discussions of the attitude-behavior relation. After several years of increasing pessimism concerning attitude-behavior predictions, researchers found that certain social behaviors may be fairly accurately predicted from verbally expressed attitudes. For example, Martin Fishbein and Fred Coombs (1974) found that voters' attitudes toward 1964 presidential candidates Barry Goldwater and Lyndon Johnson correlated highly with voters' reported voting behavior in this election. Other research successfully predicted intentions to have children and engage in birth control (Davidson and Jaccard, 1975). Still other studies ex-

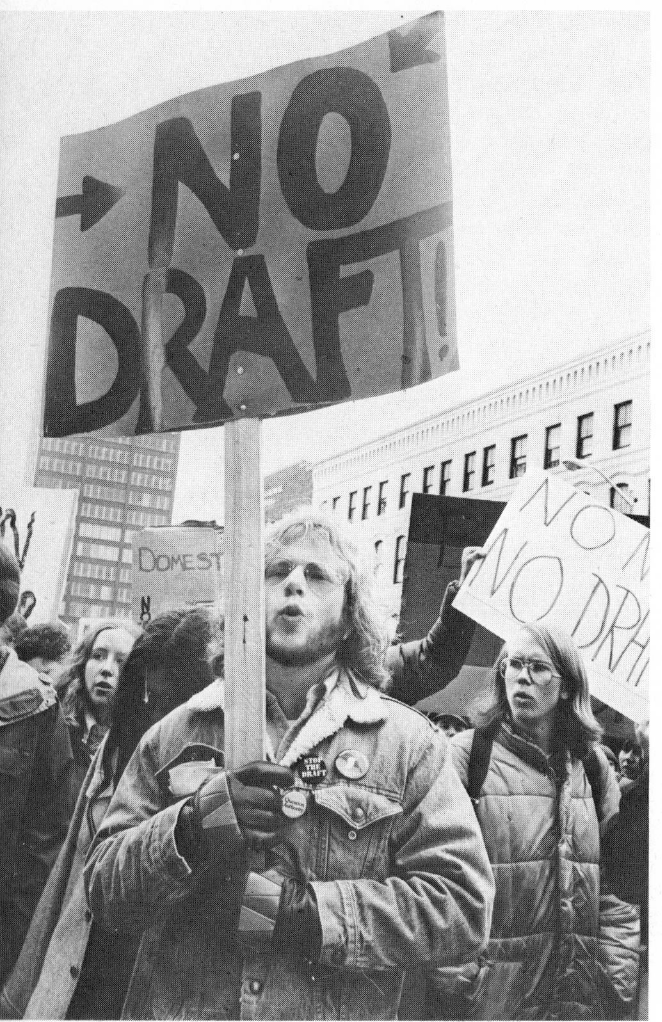

Certain social behaviors can be predicted from expressed attitudes. For example, we would expect a person who participates in an antidraft rally to hold antidraft attitudes. *(© Joan Liftin 1980 / Woodfin Camp & Assoc.)*

amined church-attendance intentions and behavior (King, 1975) as well as blood-donation intentions and behavior (Pomazal and Jaccard, 1976). All of these studies obtained satisfactory predictions of behavior from verbally expressed attitudes.

Why do these studies find that attitudes predict behavior, while other studies, such as LaPiere's, find little or no relationship? To answer this, it is necessary to probe the circumstances under which attitudes relate to behaviors. Through the work of Martin Fishbein and Icek Ajzen (1975) as well as other attitude researchers, understanding of these circumstances has grown in the past few years.

One important principle is that attitudes and behaviors are found to relate most strongly when researchers define them *similarly, in terms of specificity or generality.* Think once again about attitudes as evaluations—as dispositions to hold favorable or unfavorable beliefs about things, persons, or events. Then it is clear that the object of the evaluation can be defined very generally (for example, psychology) or more specifically (for example, an introductory psychology course at a particular university). Also, behaviors can be defined in terms of a general class of behaviors (for example, all behaviors relating to psychology) or a specific behavior (for example, studying for a particular psychology exam).

Thus, attitudes predict behaviors if the attitudes and behaviors in question are defined at an equivalent level of specificity. In other words, specific attitudes can predict appropriate specific behaviors with considerable success, and general attitudes can predict correspondingly general classes of behaviors with considerable success. An example of a specific attitude predicting a specific behavior is the following: attitudes toward a particular psychology exam should predict the extent to which students study for the exam. In contrast, an example of a general attitude predicting a general class of behaviors is the following: attitudes toward psychology as a whole should predict fairly well the *average tendency* to engage in various behaviors generally relevant to learning more about psychology (for example, reading magazine articles about psychology, talking about psychology to friends, taking psychology courses). Fishbein and Ajzen (1975) have suggested the term *multiple-act criterion* to refer to a general behavioral index based on an average or combination of different specific behaviors.

USING GENERAL ATTITUDES TO PREDICT GENERAL BEHAVIORAL TENDENCIES

Russell Weigel and Lee Newman (1976) demonstrated that general attitudes correspond quite well to broad behavioral measures encompassing several relevant behaviors. Weigel and Newman surveyed residents of a New England town to determine their environmental attitudes, indicative of their concern about conservation and pollution issues. Three months later the same residents were contacted several times and given opportunities to participate in various organized ecology projects, such as signing a petition opposing nuclear-power-plant construction and participating in a paper and bottle recycling program. When Weigel and Newman compared residents' environmental attitudes to each of the ecology-related behaviors separately, the correlations were quite low. However, when residents' environmental attitudes were compared with a combined index of several different behaviors—that is, a multiple-act criterion—the correlation between environmental attitudes and the combined behavior index was much higher. This fairly strong attitude-behavior relation using the multiple-act criterion is especially impressive in view of the fact that the participants were unaware of any connection between the attitude survey and the later opportunities to engage in ecology-relevant behaviors. Therefore, the findings are not due to town residents merely trying to appear consistent.

The reason that general attitudes usually predict multiple-act criteria much better than they predict single acts is that single acts are usually affected by many factors. For example, the specific behavior of participating in a recycling program on a given day no doubt is a product of how much time a person has available that day and how much material he or she happens to have that is appropriate for recycling. While environmental attitudes are no doubt one determinant of this behavior, they are certainly not the only determinant and perhaps not even the major determinant. Prediction of specific behaviors from a general attitude is weak, then, because a general attitude cannot encompass all of these other determinants of behavior. However, if a researcher sums over several behaviors that are all at least partially determined by a particular attitude, the multiple-act criterion that results tends to be more strongly related to the general attitude. In other words, several fairly weak behavioral indicators of an attitude can be summed together to create a stronger composite index.

USING SPECIFIC ATTITUDES TO PREDICT SPECIFIC BEHAVIORS

What happens when a researcher wants to predict a single specific behavior and not a multiple-act criterion? One way to achieve this goal is to choose a similarly specific attitude as the predictor. Thus, recycling behavior is likely to be predicted more exactly from attitudes toward recycling than attitudes toward the environment. An attitude as specific as an individual's attitude toward recycling takes into account not only general attitudes about ecology and the environment but also a variety of other factors—for example, that he or she may be unenthusiastic about recycling because of lack of time. Substituting specific attitudes for general attitudes is not always a satisfactory alternative, however, because a researcher ends up with a multitude of attitudinal predictors, each effective only for predicting a particular behavior. Still, specific attitudes will do the job of predicting specific behaviors with some accuracy. Weigel, Vernon, and Tognacci (1974) demonstrated this fact in a study of the extent to which residents of a medium-sized western city would commit their time and energy to the activities of the Sierra Club. The residents with least behavioral commitment refused even to allow their names to be given to the local Sierra Club chapter, while the most committed residents volunteered to donate their time to work on a Sierra Club subcommittee. Other residents were in between these extremes. Weigel, Vernon, and Tognacci attempted to predict residents' behavioral commitment from various attitude measures. Very general attitude measures, such as attitude toward a pure environment, yielded poor prediction. Moderately specific attitude measures,

DISPOSITIONS AND SITUATIONS

PREDICTING A VOTE ON NUCLEAR ENERGY

In the 1976 general election voters in Oregon had an opportunity to vote on a nuclear-energy referendum—the Oregon Nuclear Safeguards Initiative. The goal of the referendum was to place restrictions on nuclear-power-plant construction. Would it be possible to predict voters' decisions in the voting booth, social psychologists asked? If so, on what basis could the prediction be made?

Social psychologists Carole Bowman and Martin Fishbein (1978) saw the Oregon referendum as an opportunity to test the relationship between a voter's attitude toward nuclear energy and a voter's behavior in the voting booth. They applied a theory developed by Fishbein and Ajzen (1975). This model asserts that behaviors are best predicted not by an individual's general attitude toward some issue such as nuclear energy, but on the basis of an individual's "behavioral intention." Behavioral intention, in turn, depends on two components: (1) an individual's attitude toward a specific action—such as voting for the antinuclear referendum; (2) normative or situational influences, specifically, what people who are important to the individual think he or she should do—such as voting for the referendum. How important would be the influence of dispositional factors (the voter's attitudes and beliefs about nuclear energy) and situational factors (social norms)?

The psychologists mailed a questionnaire to a sample of 500 voters in Portland, Oregon. Eighteen percent of the sample answered the questionnaire. Among the questions were ones concerning voters' behavioral intentions ("I intend to vote 'Yes' on the Oregon Nuclear Safeguards Initiative"), voters' attitude toward this action (for example, "good-bad," "wise-foolish," "harmful-beneficial"), and voters' perceptions of normative influences ("Most people who are important to me think I should vote 'Yes' on the Oregon Nuclear Safeguards Initiative"). Other questions assessed voters' beliefs about the consequences of this action.

After the election, the people who returned the questionnaire were telephoned and asked how they had voted. Almost everyone revealed his or her vote. As expected, actual voting behavior was very strongly predicted by voting intention (the correlation between intention and behavior was .89). In turn, voting intention was predicted by voters' attitude toward the action (correlation = .91) and by voters' perceptions of normative influences (correlation = .72). Furthermore, attitudes toward the act of voting for the initiative were influenced by a number of beliefs about the safety of nuclear energy and nuclear-waste disposal.

Incidentally, the ballot initiative failed by a margin of 45 percent to 55 percent. Results of the present study showed that both "Yes" and "No" voters tended to agree on the possible risks and dangers of nuclear energy. They differed mainly in their evaluations of these risks: those who opposed the initiative were concerned mainly about the costs of restricting nuclear energy; those who favored the initiative felt that the benefits would outweigh the costs.

such as attitudes toward conservation and toward pollution control, predicted somewhat better. A more highly specific measure, attitude toward the Sierra Club, provided the best prediction.

Research by Icek Ajzen and Martin Fishbein (1973) has demonstrated that actual behaviors can usually be predicted successfully from attitudes toward behaviors, which is one type of very specific attitude. Their approach assumes that attitude toward a behavior (for example, attitude toward signing an antinuclear-power petition) determines one's intention to engage in the behavior (intention to sign the antinuclear-power petition) and that the intention to engage in the behavior is the direct determinant of carrying out the behavioral act (actually signing the petition). So one good way of finding out what people will actually do is to determine how they evaluate the behaviors that are available in a situation.

Despite the increased accuracy of predictions based on specific attitudes, most researchers are not interested in attitudes toward specific behaviors, but in more general attitudes—for example, attitudes toward the environment, toward religion, toward women, toward racial groups, and so on. General attitudes are more interesting because they seem to relate to a variety of behaviors across different settings and situations. Yet such general predictions across behaviors and situations are not easily achieved unless the research investigates multiple-act criteria rather than single behaviors.

STREET ETIQUETTE.
The refined couple, and the couple who make themselves ridiculous.

Social norms—the ways in which people believe one should behave in given situations—have a great effect on how we act. *(Culver Pictures)*

THE "OTHER VARIABLES" APPROACH TO IMPROVING ATTITUDE-BEHAVIOR CORRESPONDENCE

Despite the difficulties of predicting single acts from general attitudes, many researchers remain interested in the task. These researchers typically supplement general-attitude measures with measures of "other variables" that also serve as predictors of behavior. This approach can be a good one because the major barrier to obtaining high correspondence between general attitudes and particular behaviors is most often the fact that variables other than attitudes also influence behaviors. In particular, situational variables and personality variables are often more important than are attitudes themselves.

SITUATIONAL INFLUENCES ON BEHAVIOR

The type of situational characteristic most widely studied by attitude researchers is *social norms*—the expectations that people have concerning how other people should behave in a given situation. If, for example, college students expect their fellow students to dress in jeans and casual clothes rather than suits and dresses, these expectations would constitute a norm concerning proper student attire. Norms have a major impact on behavior. Most people are very much influenced by the social approval they receive for behaving in accord with others' expectations, and by the disapproval for going against others' expectations. Social norms, then, are some of the "other variables" that influence behavior along with people's general attitudes. Using both general attitudes and norms to predict specific behaviors is usually more successful than relying on general attitudes alone.

Whether social norms or general attitudes are the more important determinant of particular behaviors is a critical issue. Certainly, there are circumstances in which norms and other characteristics of situations are more important than one's attitudes. If you stop for a red traffic light when driving, this behavior is probably not strongly related to your attitude toward traffic laws, toward stop signs, toward stopping at stop signs, or to any other attitude. You stop because you are aware that there are penalties for disobeying traffic rules, and you may also expect that your companions would disapprove of running a red light. In contrast, other settings impose few normative constraints on behavior. At a large party, for example, there may be little guidance from the situation concerning which persons you ought to talk to or avoid, and you are likely to behave mainly in accord with your likes and dislikes toward the people at the party and the topics they appear willing to discuss with you. In general, then, there are circumstances in which general attitudes toward people and things are the most important determinants of single behaviors; there are other circumstances in which features of the situation are more important; and there are still other circumstances in which both general attitudes and situational factors are fairly important.

PERSONALITY INFLUENCES ON BEHAVIOR Another class of "other variables" that influences the relationship between general attitudes and specific behaviors is an individual's personality dispositions or traits. These dispositions are frequently helpful in specifying the conditions under which attitudes relate to behaviors. For example, Ross Norman (1975) investigated a personality disposition known as "affective-cognitive consistency"—the extent of agreement between an affective index of an individual's attitudes (based on the individual's rating of his or her positive or negative feelings toward an attitude object) and a cognitive index (based on a summation of the individual's beliefs about the attitude object). Norman found that subjects high in affective-cognitive consistency were more likely to act in accord with their attitudes than subjects low in affective-cognitive consistency. Specifically, people who had a favorable attitude toward volunteering to be a subject in psychological research were more likely to actually volunteer when they were high in affective-cognitive consistency than when they were low in this trait.

Another variable that affects whether general attitudes correspond to specific behaviors has recently been investigated by Mark Zanna, Russell Fazio, and their colleagues (Zanna and Fazio, 1977). This variable is the extent to which an individual's attitudes are based on direct behavioral experience with the attitude object. Attitudes based on direct experience tend to be more predictive of later behavior than attitudes formed through indirect experience not involving direct contact with the attitude object. Among the studies demonstrating this point is one that related students' attitudes toward participation in psychological research to a specific behavior—the number of experiments in which students were willing to participate (Fazio and Zanna, 1978). An interesting finding emerged. Students who had direct experience with previous psychology experiments held attitudes that related strongly to their behavior, willingness to take part in future experiments. However, the behavioral intentions of students lacking this direct prior experience could not be predicted from their attitudes. Further research by these investigators has suggested that attitudes based on direct experience are more predictive of behavior because they are relatively clear and well defined and seem to be held more confidently than attitudes based on indirect experience.

ATTITUDES VERSUS PERSONALITY TRAITS AS PREDICTORS OF BEHAVIOR

The debate among social psychologists concerning whether attitudes predict behaviors is similar to a debate among personality psychologists regarding whether personality traits predict behavior. Like general attitudes, personality traits are usually not efficient predictors of single behaviors. Walter Mischel (1968) made this point quite persuasively by reviewing numerous studies of personality and behavior and showing that correlations between personality traits and seemingly relevant behaviors are almost always low. Mischel's pessimism about the value of personality traits as predictors of behavior set off a wide-ranging debate concerning the predictability of behaviors from traits. The solutions offered by personality psychologists have mirrored the suggestions of attitude researchers on the problem of predicting behavior from attitudes. For example, Seymour Epstein (1979) has shown that general behavioral indices, which sum behaviors over several occasions or situations, can be readily predicted from personality traits, even though prediction of single behaviors is difficult. Many other personality psychologists have adopted an "interactionist" position, advocating the use of situational characteristics along with personality traits as predictors of behavior (for example, Endler and

Magnusson, 1976). Still other psychologists have suggested that additional characteristics of individuals determine the conditions under which traits predict behaviors. For example, Daryl Bem and Andrea Allen (1974) showed that individuals who identify themselves as consistent on a particular trait dimension, such as conscientiousness, are more likely to engage in behaviors consistent with that trait across a variety of situations than are persons who identify themselves as variable on that trait dimension.

In the next section we turn from considering how attitudes relate to beliefs and behaviors to the question of how different attitudes relate among themselves.

ATTITUDE STRUCTURE

If you were to sit for a while and attempt to count your attitudes (rather than your blessings), you would easily come up with a long list. This counting exercise would quickly illustrate the fact that people have many attitudes. Because of this multiplicity of attitudes, it becomes important to ask whether individuals' attitudes bear any relation to one another. Is each attitude independent from others, or are the attitudes linked in some manner so that they form larger structures? Such questions about how attitudes relate to each other are part of a broader set of concerns that social psychologists refer to as issues of attitudinal and cognitive structure.

There are many ways of thinking about structure, and several theories of attitudes have implications for understanding structural relationships. One of the most widely known viewpoints concerning attitude structure stems from a perspective generally referred to as *cognitive consistency theory*. Cognitive consistency theory is not a single theory, but a set of related theories that first became popular in the late 1950s and the 1960s. These theories not only seek to explain attitude structure, but also deal with the effects of inconsistencies that arise among attitudes or beliefs that are structurally linked. Cognitive consistency theories differ in the terminology that they use to define consistency and inconsistency in cognitive structures. However, they all share the important idea that structures containing attitudes and beliefs that are inconsistent or in disagreement with one another are unpleasant, and the psychological tension created by this unpleasant state leads to changes in the structures. One type of structural change that often resolves the inconsistency is a change in the attitudes and beliefs that make up the structure.

BALANCE: KEEPING OUR COGNITIONS IN ORDER

The cognitive consistency theory with the clearest implications for attitude structure is *balance theory*, which derives primarily from the work of Fritz Heider. In 1958 Fritz Heider published *The Psychology of Interpersonal Relations* in which he discussed an organizational principle he called balance. Although he had presented the balance principle in his earlier work, with the publication of this book it became the focus of considerable research.

To understand balance theory, it may be helpful to think about an everyday situation in which you disagree with someone you like. Say, for example, that you and your mother disagree on the issue of abortion. Your mother thinks that liberal abortion laws would be a great mistake. You, though very fond of your mother, are a strong advocate of abortion.

If you were to represent this situation of disagreement using the language Heider provided in balance theory, you would focus first on yourself as the person or perceiver, represented by the letter *P*, whose attitudes and beliefs are described. The two other elements in this system usually are the other person, represented by the letter O, and an attitude object, represented by the letter X. In the abortion example, the other person O is your mother and the attitude object X is liberal abortion laws, an object of concern to both you and your mother. As shown in Figure 4.1, you, your mother, and liberal abortion laws can be regarded as linked together into a *P*-O-X triangle structure.

Because you favor liberal laws, the link between you and liberal laws has a positive value. This link is entered as a positive sign in Figure 4.1. Because you and your mother get along, the

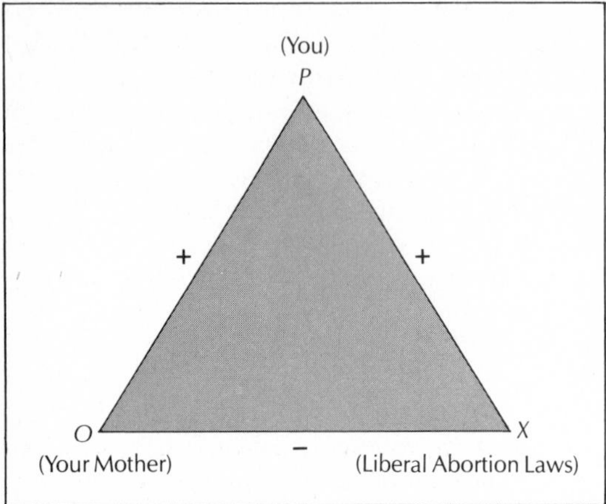

FIGURE 4.1 Multiplying the signs that represent the attitudes shown here produces a minus, revealing imbalance. According to Heider (1958), a person would strive to relieve this imbalance.

link between you and your mother is positive. And finally, the link between your mother and liberal abortion laws is negative, because you know that your mother thinks liberal laws would be a mistake. These links between *P*, *O*, and X are attitudinal in nature: they specify your evaluation of a person (your mother), an issue (liberalized abortion laws), and your perception of someone else's evaluation of an issue (your mother's attitude toward liberal laws).

Although this abortion triangle depicts only attitudinal relations, it is important to know that Heider thought the elements in a cognitive structure could be linked by two different types of relationships—namely, attitudinal relations, which Heider termed "liking" or "sentiment" relations, and unit relations. The liking or sentiment relation refers to the positive or negative evaluation that may be the defining aspect of a relation between any two elements of a structure. Unit relationships exist to the extent that two or more things are perceived as being associated—or dissociated in the case of a negative unit relation—on some basis other than liking. For example, when people are related as husband and wife or as father and daughter, the two persons constitute a unit. The unit relation would be negative if the husband and wife got divorced or the father disowned the daughter. Two things may also be perceived as belonging together in a unit because they are part of each other or one belongs to the other.

How do these *P-O-X* structures involving sentiment and unit relations become consistent or inconsistent? Return to the example of your mother and liberalized abortion laws. This situation is bound to be uncomfortable because you disagree with someone you like. Balance theory labels this uncomfortable quality *imbalance* or *inconsistency*. Balance theorists determine whether a structure is inconsistent by the formal device of multiplying the signs of the relations in the triangle structure. For example, in Figure 4.1, when the two positive relations (between you and your mother and between you and liberal abortion laws) are multiplied by the negative relation (between your mother and liberal abortion laws), the overall product is negative: $(+) \times (+) \times (-) = (-)$. This resulting negative sign is the mathematical representation of imbalance. In general, balance theory regards a cognitive structure as imbalanced if the product of the signs of the relations is negative and as balanced if the product of the signs is positive.

An experiment by Elliot Aronson and Vernon Cope (1968) illustrates how the balance principle influences human behavior. The experimenter in this study either made himself an enemy of the subjects by telling them some unflattering information about themselves in a stark and brutal manner or became their friend by delivering the information in a gentle manner that allowed them to save face. Subjects subsequently overheard the liked or disliked experimenter receive from his supervisor either a very favorable or a very unfavorable evaluation of a report he had written. The subjects were then given an opportunity to help the supervisor by making a number of phone calls to recruit volunteers to participate in a research project. Subjects' decisions whether or not to help the supervisor can be predicted on the basis of the supervisor's attitude toward the experimenter and their own attitude toward the experimenter. Subjects were quite willing to help the supervisor if he had dealt harshly with the enemy experimenter or praised the friend ex-

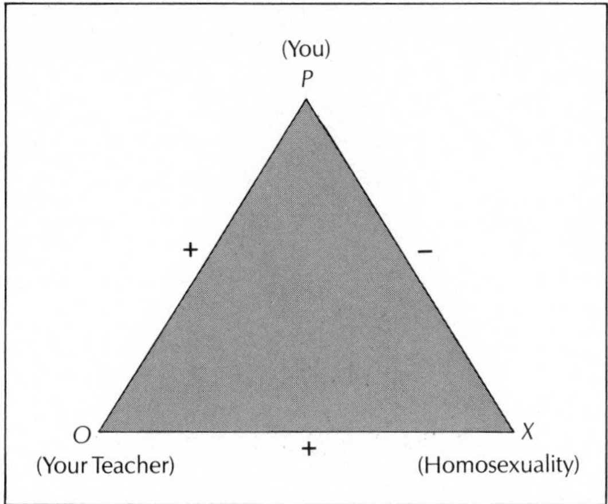

FIGURE 4.2 Balance theory represents both attitudinal (or sentiment) and unit relations. In this figure, your teacher and homosexuality are linked by a positive unit relation. You and the teacher and you and homosexuality are linked by attitudinal relations. Because the product of the signs on the relations is negative, the structure is imbalanced.

perimenter, but they were relatively unwilling to help if he had praised the enemy or dealt harshly with the friend. These findings suggest that subjects completed their cognitive structures so that the overall structure involving the subject (*P*), the supervisor (O), and the experimenter (X) was balanced.

When imbalance occurs, according to Heider, psychological pressures are brought to bear to set the organizational apparatus right—in other words, to restore balance to the structure. Consider the example given in Figure 4.2, which depicts a situation in which you discover that a favorite teacher (positive sentiment relation) is homosexual (positive unit relation). If you disapprove of homosexuality (negative sentiment relation), your cognitive structure is imbalanced and would therefore be unstable. Mathematically, the product of your two positive attitudes and the one negative attitude, $(+) \times (-) \times (+) = (-)$, indicates imbalance.

The imbalance could be reduced in at least three ways. You could decide that you dislike the teacher—a decision that would change the plus sign between you and your teacher to a minus. After this sign change, multiplying the plus sign representing the unit relationship between your teacher and homosexuality times the two minus signs representing your attitudes toward the teacher and toward homosexuality would yield a positive product: $(+) \times (-) \times (-) = (+)$.

Another possible resolution might be that you decide homosexuality is a good thing after all—perhaps because it is a genuine expression of your teacher's truest feelings. This viewpoint would change the sign of the relationship between you and homosexuality to a plus. Then multiplication of the plus sign for the unit relationship between your teacher and homosexuality and the plus signs representing your attitudes toward the teacher and toward homosexuality would produce a plus: $(+) \times (+) \times (+) = (+)$.

Alternatively, you could dissociate your teacher and homosexuality by deciding that the teacher is actually not a homosexual. Then the teacher and homosexuality would not form a unit, and the sign on the relation would become a minus. In this last case, multiplication of the minus sign representing the unit relationship, the minus sign representing your attitude toward homosexuality, and the plus sign representing your attitude toward the teacher would yield a positive product: $(-) \times (-) \times (+) = (+)$.

Note that in all three resolutions of the structure relating you, the teacher, and homosexuality, the product of the signs of the relationships is positive. This indicates that the structure has become balanced. Which of the three resolutions would be most likely to occur? Balance theory has some difficulty predicting which of these (or other) changes would occur in an unbalanced structure. There have been various efforts to solve this prediction problem. One such effort (Osgood and Tannenbaum, 1955) suggests that the resolution depends on how polarized or extreme the perceiver's attitudes are toward the elements of the triad: the more extreme an attitude is, the less likely it is to change.

Even though balance theory has some difficulty in predicting which change will take place

FOCUS ON APPLICATIONS

BALANCE THEORY IN ADVERTISING

The accompanying advertisement appeared in major American newspapers on Sunday, February 3, 1980. Placed by a group calling itself America's Electric Energy Companies, the ad attempts to unbalance the reader's attitude structure regarding nuclear energy.

The advertisement gets your attention by appearing objective. The two silhouettes present a number of beliefs on each side of the issue. The first line of the copy asserts, "There are two sides to the issue of nuclear power." It goes on to say that "Americans are bombarded with conflicting views and statements." Few of these conflicting views are actually presented, however, and little is done to untangle the confusion. Instead, the ad tries to link the critics of nuclear energy with persons and issues that readers are likely to oppose. For example, "those leading the attack on nuclear power" are described as "actors and actresses, rock stars, aspiring politicians and others who think America has grown enough."

Next, in strict adherence to the principles of balance theory, the ad goes on to link these actors, rock stars, and politicians with assaults on a variety of other seemingly constructive energy sources: geothermal energy, hydroelectric plants, a new oil refinery, new natural-gas pipelines, more coal-fired power plants, and synthetic fuels. And if the reader hasn't gotten the point, the ad makes the connection clear: "One wonders what they are *for*, and how they propose meeting America's energy needs?"

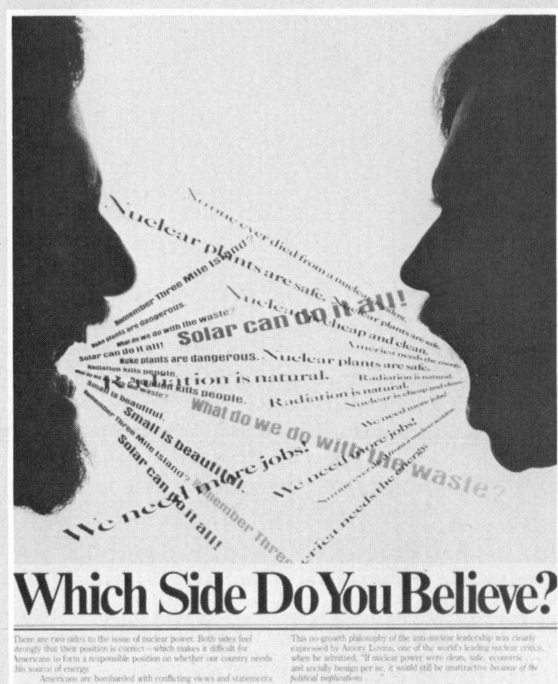

Courtesy, America's Electric Energy Companies

in an unbalanced cognitive structure, it has been successful in predicting people's preferences for balanced structures over unbalanced structures and in specifying whether change will take place—that is, whether a given structure is stable or unstable. According to the theory, balanced structures are pleasant and stable, and imbalanced structures are unpleasant and unstable. Numerous empirical tests of balance theory have presented subjects with structures that are balanced or imbalanced by the multiplicative rule, and have asked them to rate the stability or pleasantness of the structures or to provide other responses that indicate their stability and pleasantness. For example, in a study by Theodore Newcomb and his colleagues (Price, Har-

You can easily see the issues in terms of Heider's balance triangle:

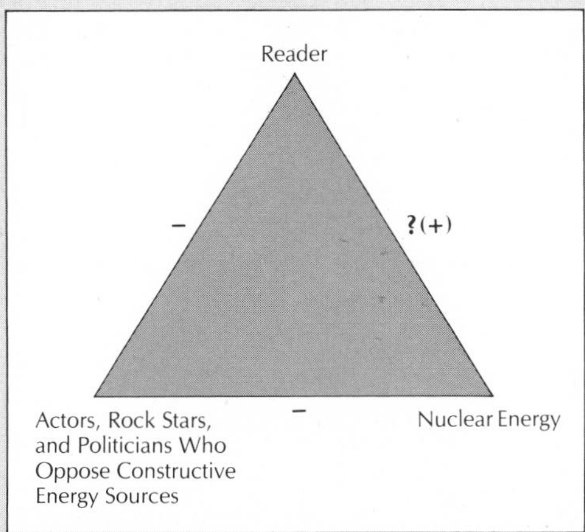

Then, to complete its case, the ad seeks to establish positive links between nuclear energy and many organizations that readers are likely to respect. For example, it asserts that nuclear energy has been endorsed by "the AFL-CIO . . . the NAACP . . . the National Governor's Conference . . . Consumer Alert . . . and many more." Furthermore, the reader learns that the health and safety record of nuclear power has been endorsed by several prestigious scientific organizations. Again, the issues can be drawn in light of Heider's triangle:

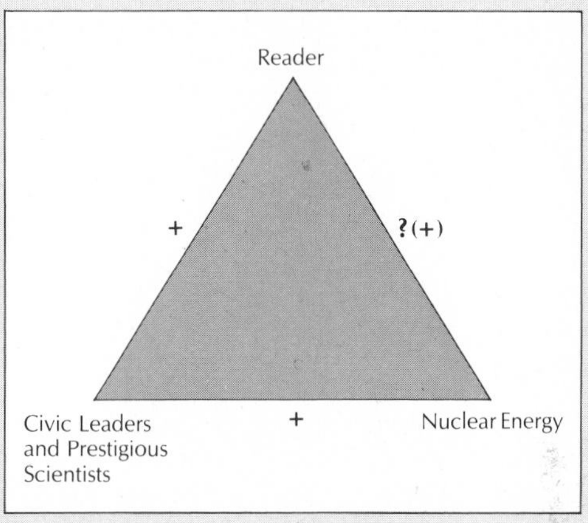

In order to maintain psychological balance and a consistent attitude structure, the resolution is clear: readers must replace their attitude of uncertain confusion regarding nuclear energy with an attitude in favor of nuclear energy. Most interestingly, however, the entire advertisement provides very few facts about nuclear power, except to concede that it is not risk-free. Yet neither is any other source of energy, the reader learns, and besides, according to America's Electric Energy Companies, "America needs energy." If it is true that Americans also need consistency in their attitude structure regarding nuclear power, then perhaps the advertisement was successful.

burg, and Newcomb, 1966) subjects provided the names of their best friends as well as persons whom they disliked. Then the investigators asked the subjects to imagine that one of these persons liked or disliked another. For example, if Susan were your best friend but you disliked Jeffrey, you might have been asked to imagine that Susan strongly likes Jeffrey. This structure would be imbalanced because a positive relation (you like Susan), a negative relation (you dislike Jeffrey), and a positive relation (you think Susan likes Jeffrey) have a negative product. Subjects rated these and other structures according to how pleasant or uneasy the situations made them feel. On the whole, this experiment and other similar studies have shown that imbalanced structures are more unstable and more unpleasant than balanced structures.

There are also a number of additional factors that influence how stable and pleasant a structure is—for example, agreement between *P* and *O*. Everything else being equal, people prefer to agree with each other. Consequently, in addition to a preference for balanced over imbalanced structures, most individuals prefer structures in which *P* and *O* agree rather than disagree in their evaluations of the third element in the structure (Zajonc, 1968).

PSYCHOLOGICAL IMPLICATIONS: SEARCH AND RESISTANCE

Heider's balance theory has provided the basis for other, more complex models of attitudinal consistency (Cartwright and Harary, 1956; Rosenberg and Abelson, 1960). Each of these models points out interesting features of psychological balance. One of these models evolved because Robert Abelson (1968) was intrigued with the way in which balance needs either motivate a search for new information or close us off from additional facts. Abelson termed a basic unit of cognitive organization the *implicational molecule*, which is a self-contained set of statements that, taken together, is psychologically consistent. It is important to the perceiver that all the elements within these molecules fit together. If a molecule is incomplete, or if there is a nonfitting element, the molecule will require cognitive reorganization.

The three most striking characteristics of implicational molecules are that (1) they tend toward completion, (2) completed molecules are resistant to change, and (3) molecules with nonfitting elements produce pressure to relieve the inconsistency.

The following sentences represent an incomplete molecule:

1. Jim sent Amy flowers.
2. Amy was surprised.

The above sentences suggest the following action to complete the molecule:

3. Amy thanked Jim.

Whether or not sentence 3 is added, the temptation is to complete the molecule begun with sentences 1 and 2 by searching for a resolution something like that of sentence 3. Suppose you are faced with the following incomplete molecule:

1. Jim loathed Amy.
2. Amy loved flowers.

To make these two elements consistent, a sentence like the following might be expected to provide the missing link:

3. Jim did not send Amy flowers.

However, suppose that you knew the following sentence was true:

3. Jim sent Amy flowers.

This third sentence is a nonfitting element that makes the three elements difficult to organize in terms of a single implicational principle. But a fourth sentence like the following can complete the molecule:

4. Amy had hay fever.

This sentence completes a four-sentence implicational molecule that is organized around a principle that might be defined as duplicity. If you felt a "need to explain" the situation when you encountered the surprising third sentence, you were experiencing the pressure to search out elements that would reduce the inconsistency in the implicational molecule.

People do not always seek to resolve inconsistency, however. According to Abelson, people sometimes organize their attitudes and beliefs into such self-contained molecules that their implications are isolated from one another and quite resistant to change. One empirical demonstration of this phenomenon is an experiment by Gordon Bear and Alexandra Hodun (1975), in which subjects were taught an implicational principle and then were given information either confirming the principle or contradicting it. Information confirming an implicational principle was more likely to be recalled accurately than contradictory information. Further, subjects often inaccurately recalled contradictory information as confirmatory and fabricated missing information as confirmatory. This study illustrates the strong pressures that exist to keep attitudes and beliefs neatly packaged in terms of implicational molecules and to avoid acknowledging their inconsistency.

Research on balance theory and related issues such as the implicational-molecule concept has been extensive, and most of the research has supported at least some form of the theory. At the same time, other theorists interested in cognitive consistency developed a theory of a different sort known as cognitive dissonance theory. In fact, cognitive dissonance theory, developed by Leon Festinger (1957), is now more widely known than balance theory. According to Festinger, when a person simultaneously holds two cognitions or thoughts that imply the opposite of each other, he or she is thrust into a state of *dissonance*. Because dissonance is an unpleasant state, the tendency is to attempt to rid oneself of it. The methods that people use to reduce dissonance are fascinating and frequently include attitude change. Because Festinger's theory is particularly useful for the study of attitude change, it will be considered in detail in the next chapter.

Rather than seeking consistency and familiarity at all times, we often look for novelty, surprise, and excitement. *(© Charles Harbutt / Magnum)*

CONSISTENCY THEORY AND THE SEARCH FOR NOVELTY AND VARIETY

Whether people's striving for balance and consistency among their attitudes is as all-encompassing as cognitive consistency theory suggests is a matter of some debate. For example, Daryl Bem (1970) had this to say about the hypothesis that the need to eliminate inconsistencies is the central motive in attitude organization:

> I don't believe it. At least not very much. In my view, a vision of inconsistency as a temporary turbulence in an otherwise fastidious pool of cognitive clarity is all too misleading. My own suspicion is that inconsistency is probably our most enduring cognitive commonplace.

A theory that has people trying to eliminate all the inconsistencies in their lives overlooks the fascination people often have for mysteries, puzzles, surprise endings, scientific problems, and incongruous juxtapositions. Rather than seeking the simplest, most congruent, and most familiar state of affairs, we often seek the excitement of novelty, surprise, and mystery.

Any theorist who insists that either consistency or variety is the basic motive of human behavior is sure to be deluged with solid examples of the opposing tendency. To see consistency as the sole motive is to ignore the toleration for inconsistency that characterizes the creative contributions of many artists, writers, scientists, philosophers, and explorers. And to see nothing but the search for variety is to commit a comparable oversight. Perhaps an answer to this paradox can be found in the work of Daniel Berlyne (1960), J. M. Hunt (1963), and other psychologists who suggest that there is an optimal level of consistency or congruity between cognitions that is neither so high that it creates panic and confusion nor so low that it creates boredom. Individuals may reach their own personal compromises between their needs for consistency and for variety. For example, people often find ways to exercise needs for novelty without disturbing the consistencies they cherish most. They can brighten otherwise monotonous lives by becoming absorbed in crossword puzzles or mystery stories. If they cannot solve all of the puzzles or mysteries, their lives are not significantly disturbed. When they are successful, they feel competent at resolving inconsistencies.

OTHER APPROACHES TO ATTITUDE ORGANIZATION

Although cognitive consistency provides the best-known and most widely researched approach to attitude organization, other psychologists have suggested different theories. Milton Rokeach (1960) proposed that attitudes are organized along a hierarchy, with some beliefs more central than others in an individual's cognitive structure. The most central beliefs are *primitive beliefs,* which function as the axioms or basic postulates of our belief system. These are basic beliefs about the nature of physical reality (for example, that the sky is blue) as well as basic beliefs about oneself (for example, that I am a woman). Primitive beliefs are seldom challenged, but, if they are, the person holding the beliefs becomes extremely upset. Other beliefs, somewhat less central to cognitive structure, concern the nature of authority. Examples are one's basic beliefs about God or about democracy as a political system. Beliefs more peripheral than these are derived from one's beliefs about authority. For example, one's beliefs about the Social Security system may be derived from more central beliefs about the nature of a democratic society. Still other psychologists have discussed cognitive structure in terms of general principles such as how abstract or how concrete structures are (Harvey, Hunt, and Schroder, 1961) or how simple or how complex they are (Bieri, 1966).

In the next section we turn from considering how attitudes are organized to the question of how they develop in the first place.

ATTITUDE FORMATION

You form new attitudes continuously throughout your life as you gain information about attitude objects with which you were previously unacquainted. In addition, your existing attitudes are changed and transformed in response to new events. The process of attitude formation can be described in many ways. Some psychologists carry out longitudinal studies investigating how attitudes of a certain type, such as religious or political attitudes, develop throughout childhood and adolescence. Yet, social psychologists generally have confined their work to understanding the basic psychological processes that underlie the formation of attitudes of *all* types. This approach focuses on general psychological theory rather than on particular attitudes or even on particular types of attitudes. The research relevant to those general theories most often utilizes laboratory experiments rather than survey research or public-opinion findings.

Psychologists have adopted two major perspectives on the basic processes by which attitudes are formed—a *learning* perspective and an *information-processing* or *cognitive* perspective. From a learning perspective, attitudes are formed through learning processes similar to the classical and operant conditioning studied by animal learning researchers. Other social psychologists prefer to think about attitude formation as a cognitive process that occurs through the receipt of information about attitude objects. The learning approach links social psychology with learning research and leads to the design of experiments that directly parallel basic conditioning experiments carried out with animals. The information-processing approach links attitude theory with cognitive psychology and suggests laboratory research in which various patterns of attitudinally relevant information are presented to subjects.

LEARNING-THEORY APPROACHES TO THE STUDY OF ATTITUDE FORMATION

CLASSICAL CONDITIONING Familiar to most introductory psychology students is a process first demonstrated by Russian physiologist Ivan Pavlov called classical conditioning. By means of classical conditioning, animals learn to make specific responses to particular cues that are associated with (but not the same as) the objects that originally produced the responses. Some psychologists have since suggested that a conditioning process may be responsible for much attitude formation.

According to this viewpoint, human beings learn attitudes in the same way that Pavlov's dogs learned to salivate when presented with a sound or a light. A typical conditioning procedure with human subjects is to pair a neutral stimulus, perhaps a nonsense syllable (such as *zak*), with an unconditioned stimulus, often electric shock, so that the unconditioned response of anxiety and arousal generalizes from the shock to the nonsense syllable (Razran, 1961). In this way, the nonsense syllables, which subjects evaluated as neutral at the outset of the experiment, take on negative connotations because they were consistently paired with electric shock. This classical-conditioning process can easily be reinterpreted as a process of attitude formation. From an attitudinal perspective, the aversive arousal, originally associated with the shock and then transferred to the nonsense syllable, can be viewed as negative evaluation or a negative attitude.

Many laboratory experiments have demonstrated that social attitudes can be acquired through classical conditioning (Staats and Staats, 1958). Generally, words or nonsense syllables are repeatedly paired with stimuli that already have positive or negative value. Then subjects' evaluation of the words or nonsense syllables is tested to see if the feelings elicited by the positive or negative stimuli have transferred to the words or nonsense syllables. In an especially interesting demonstration of how attitudes can be conditioned, Mark Zanna, Charles Kiesler, and Paul Pilkonis (1970) recruited fifty female subjects, ostensibly for the purpose of "developing a more sensitive and instantaneous physiological measure than the old standard ones, like heart rate." The women were forewarned that they would be shocked a random number of times at predetermined intervals in the experiment and that they would be signaled when the shocks were beginning and ending. (Interestingly, these researchers used female subjects because the pretesting of the women had indicated that females were made more anxious by the shock than males.) For one group of women the onset of the shocks was signaled by the word *light* and the termination was signaled by the word *dark*. These signal words were reversed for a second group of subjects, while a control group heard only the signals *begin* and *end*.

To discover the true effects of these procedures on subjects' evaluations of the words *light* and *dark*, the researchers took great pains to assure that subjects' responses were not affected by "demand characteristics." One criticism of earlier research on attitudinal conditioning was that subjects may have become aware of the experimenter's hypothesis and then responded so as to confirm the hypothesis that attitudinal conditioning had taken place. Such a subject might think, "Ah, ha! It must be that I am supposed to give unfavorable ratings to the syllables that signaled when the shocks were starting, and I am supposed to give favorable ratings to the syllables that signaled when the shocks were ending." This process would not be attitudinal conditioning, but a complex cognitive process of figuring out the experiment and then delivering the responses that subjects believed the experimenter desired. This criticism is a powerful one in view of Monte Page's (1969, 1974) repeated demonstrations that, in "higher order" conditioning experiments involving pairings of nonsense syllables with favorable or unfavorable words, apparent attitudinal conditioning can be explained simply in terms of subjects going along with the perceived demands of the experimental situation.

Zanna, Kiesler, and Pilkonis wanted to provide a clear laboratory demonstration that attitudinal conditioning does occur, and to do so they had to rule out the possibility that subjects were merely providing the responses they thought the experimenter desired. Therefore, subjects' attitudes toward the words *light* and *dark* were measured in an entirely different situation than the original shock-conditioning set-

SOCIAL PSYCHOLOGY AND THE ARTS

CLASSICAL CONDITIONING OF ATTITUDES

Futuristic novels—Aldous Huxley's *Brave New World* (1932) and Anthony Burgess's *A Clockwork Orange* (1962), for example—frequently contain chilling examples of attitudinal conditioning. In the following excerpt from *Brave New World,* the Director of Hatcheries and Conditioning (D.H.C.) is demonstrating attitudinal conditioning as practiced in the infant nurseries.

The nurses stiffened to attention as the D.H.C. came in.

"Set out the books," he said curtly.

In silence the nurses obeyed his command. Between the rose bowls the books were duly set out—a row of nursery quartos opened invitingly each at some gaily coloured image of beast or fish or bird.

"Now bring in the children."

They hurried out of the room and returned in a minute or two, each pushing a kind of tall dumb-waiter laden, on all its four wire-netted shelves, with eight-month-old babies, all exactly alike (a Bokanovsky Group, it was evident) and all (since their caste was Delta) dressed in khaki.

"Put them down on the floor."

The infants were unloaded.

"Now turn them so that they can see the flowers and books."

Turned, the babies at once fell silent, then began to crawl towards those clusters of sleek colours, those shapes so gay and brilliant on the white pages. As they approached, the sun came out of a momentary eclipse behind a cloud. The roses flamed up as though with a sudden passion from within; a new and profound significance seemed to suffuse the shining pages of the books. From the ranks of the crawling babies came little squeals of excitement, gurgles and twitterings of pleasure.

The Director rubbed his hands. "Excellent!" he said. "It might almost have been done on purpose."

The swiftest crawlers were already at their goal. Small hands reached out uncertainly, touched, grasped, unpetaling the transfigured roses, crumpling the illuminated pages of the books. The Director waited until all were happily busy. Then, "Watch carefully," he said. And, lifting his hand, he gave the signal.

The Head Nurse, who was standing by a switchboard at the other end of the room, pressed down a little lever.

There was a violent explosion. Shriller and ever shriller, a siren shrieked. Alarm bells maddeningly sounded.

The children started, screamed; their faces were distorted with terror.

"And now," the Director shouted (for the noise was deafening), "now we proceed to rub in the lesson with a mild electric shock."

He waved his hand again, and the Head Nurse pressed a second lever. The screaming of the babies suddenly changed its tone. There was something desperate, almost insane, about the sharp spasmodic yelps to which they now gave utterance. Their little bodies twitched and stiffened; their limbs moved jerkily as if to the tug of unseen wires.

"We can electrify that whole strip of floor," bawled the Director in explanation. "But that's enough," he signalled to the nurse.

The explosions ceased, the bells stopped ringing, the shriek of the siren died down from tone to tone into silence. The stiffly twitching bodies relaxed, and what had become the sob and yelp of infant maniacs broadened out once more into a normal howl of ordinary terror.

"Offer them the flowers and the books again."

The nurses obeyed; but at the approach of the roses, at the mere sight of those gaily-coloured images of pussy and cock-a-doodle-doo and baa-baa black sheep, the infants shrank away in horror; the volume of their howling suddenly increased.

It is unlikely that such techniques of attitudinal conditioning would be as effective in the real world as they are portrayed here. Attitudes are formed through more processes than classical conditioning, and attitudes develop and change throughout life. But classical conditioning is one process that contributes to attitude formation and change.

Source: Aldous Huxley, *Brave New World* (New York: Bantam, 1958; originally published 1932): 13–14.

ting. When the conditioning trials were completed, subjects were told that the experiment was over and they were asked to report to another part of the building to participate in what was described as a different experiment. In this second setting another experimenter measured subjects' positive and negative feelings toward each item on a long list of words that happened to include the words *light* and *dark*. The experimental words were embedded in the much longer list so that subjects would not become suspicious that there was a connection between the two experiments.

One result of this test was that all groups of subjects evaluated the word *light* more positively than the word *dark*. This preference for *light* suggests that the subjects had differing prior attitudes toward the words *light* and *dark*. However, the contrast between the evaluations of *light* and *dark* was most exaggerated when *dark* had signaled shocks and *light* had signaled relief. The difference between the evaluations of the two words was smallest when *light* signaled shock and *dark* indicated relief. Thus, both words were evaluated more positively than usual when they had been paired with relief and more negatively when they had been paired with pain. These conditioned responses also generalized to the semantically related words *white* and *black*. Although *white* was uniformly evaluated more positively than *black*, the difference was smallest when *light* had indicated the onset of shock.

The experiment by Zanna and his colleagues provides evidence that attitudes can be formed when people come to associate neutral persons or objects with rewarding or punishing events and that these effects are not always explained by the demands of the experimental situation. This experiment helps explain how attitude conditioning takes place in everyday life. For example, we might take on our parents' political or social attitudes simply because these attitudes have been associated with various rewarding events such as parental affection, attention, assistance, the relief of pain, and even pleasant meals. Further, the conditioning perspective suggests that we might not like people with whom our major contact is in hot, crowded subways or that we might be particularly drawn to those ideas we encounter in courses taught by attractive, entertaining teachers. The conditioning viewpoint is intriguing because it suggests that randomness and arbitrariness characterize the formation of attitudes. Perhaps people base their attitudes on pairings of attitude objects with positive and negative events rather than on the intrinsic properties of attitude objects.

The applicability of conditioning tech-

The classical conditioning perspective suggests that we may dislike people we most often encounter in an unpleasant environment such as this subway car. *(© Danny Lyon / Magnum)*

Research has shown that music can enhance persuasion. Here, John Hall, Graham Nash, James Taylor, Jackson Browne, Bonnie Raitt, and Carly Simon perform at a "no-nukes" rally at New York's Madison Square Garden. *(Photo © Lynn Goldsmith 1980 / The Museum of Modern Art / Film Stills Archive)*

niques in increasing the effectiveness of almost any message presents alarming possibilities. It might permit people to manipulate situations so that others will form attitudes, not because of the characteristics of the attitude objects themselves, but because of the contexts in which the attitude objects are presented. Irving Janis, Donald Kaye, and Paul Kirschner (1965) demonstrated the power of context by giving some subjects soft drinks to enjoy while these subjects read a persuasive communication. Those given soft drinks were more persuaded by what they read than those who were not given soft drinks. Similarly, Mark Galizio and Clyde Hendrick (1972) had some subjects listen to pleasant guitar music as an accompaniment to persuasive messages presented in the form of folk songs. The songs proved more persuasive when accompanied by guitar music than when heard without the music. One interpretation of these experiments is that the positive feelings associated with the soft drinks and guitar music became associated with the persuasive messages via a classical-conditioning process.

INSTRUMENTAL CONDITIONING Learning processes other than classical conditioning have also been studied by attitude researchers. In particular, some psychologists have suggested that attitude learning is usefully viewed as *instrumental* or *operant conditioning*. Just as a rat in a Skinner box learns to engage in those responses that are followed by rewarding events and to avoid responses that are followed by punishing events, humans learn to hold attitudes that enhance rewarding consequences and minimize punishing consequences.

One major effort to view attitudes in terms of rewarding and punishing consequences is the classic work of Carl Hovland, Irving Janis, and Harold Kelley, who published in 1953 a book entitled *Communication and Persuasion*. Sponsored by the Yale Communication Research Program, this book was the first in a series of volumes about attitude change. The theoretical orientation that guided Hovland, Janis, and Kelley was learning theory, particularly the learning theory associated with Clark Hull and others, which viewed learning as an instrumental process by which responses become habitual to the extent they are followed by positive reinforcement. The authors considered attitudes to be internal, implicit evaluative responses that motivate individuals to approach or avoid given objects, persons, groups, or symbols. Hovland, Janis, and Kelley argued that an attitude is formed (or becomes "habitual") when its overt expression or internal rehearsal is followed by the actual experience of or the anticipation of positive reinforcement. This perspective suggests that attitudes are formed or changed by presenting individuals with the positive or negative consequences of holding certain attitudinal positions. These consequences can be conveyed to people either directly by having them experience positive or negative consequences or indirectly by describing these consequences. As an example of experiencing rewarding consequences directly, consider an individual who finds that holding a certain attitude results in a lowering of anxiety in relation to a particular problem. This attitude would become habitual. Such an individual might form a negative attitude toward potentially carcinogenic food additives (and therefore intend to avoid such additives) and find that this orientation reduces anxiety about developing cancer. In this example, the rewarding consequence of anxiety reduction is directly experienced by the individual. This example can be contrasted to instances in which the rewarding consequences of holding a particular attitude are merely described, and therefore people experience them indirectly or vicariously. A description of the rewarding consequences of holding a particular attitude could be accomplished, for example, by suggesting that successful and attractive persons hold the attitude. Advertisers, as we all know, are fond of this technique.

In general Hovland, Janis, and Kelley thought that basic learning processes underlie much of the seemingly complex learning that is carried out in relation to attitude objects. These basic learning processes may be difficult for an observer to discern because they are embedded in complex events of everyday life—reading newspapers, listening to others' views on issues, etc. These learning processes can be understood more clearly when situations are simplified and attitude change is brought into the laboratory to be observed under controlled conditions. Hovland, Janis, and Kelley's research program on attitude change and attitude formation attempted to reveal basic learning processes, while studying attitude learning in a context that was admittedly simplified but yet not radically dissimilar from everyday life. So rather than pair words and rewarding or punishing events in a structured and artificial manner (to parallel learning experiments carried out with animals), the authors presented their research participants with information in the form of written and filmed communications. Some of these studies are reviewed in the next chapter, where more detailed consideration is given to attitude change.

SOCIAL LEARNING Still other psychologists have viewed attitude formation as a *social learning* process. Albert Bandura (1972) and other social psychologists have studied social learning and concentrated on a process called *modeling*, whereby one person copies, or models, his or her behavior after the behavior of another person. From this perspective, individuals learn new responses not only by directly experiencing the positive or negative outcomes of their responses, but also by observing the outcomes of others' responses. That we learn from observing others' reactions to events is widely accepted, and certainly attitudes are learned in this way. For example, if you were to observe a friend taste a particular soup when you were at lunch in a restaurant one day, and the friend made an unpleasant face and explained that the soup was "just awful," you would no doubt acquire a negative attitude toward the soup even in the absence of direct experience with it.

A precise understanding of how attitudes are learned by a social learning process is a matter of continuing interest to social psychologists. Bandura, in claiming that the process is largely *cognitive* in nature, means that people learn by coming to understand what events are associated with or followed by other events. From this perspective, a child does not learn to say "please" by some automatic conditioning process, but instead comes to understand that "please" is often followed by positive and helpful responses from parents and other nurturing adults. Yet, other psychologists have suggested that social learning is at least sometimes a more direct and automatic process not necessarily mediated by conscious awareness of what follows from what. Indeed, the controversy concerning whether or not attitude learning is merely a cognitive process by which people figure out what goes with what and infer what is demanded in a situation has plagued all research on attitude learning. Because it is difficult to prove that human attitude learning processes are not occurring at a complex, cognitive level, the amount of attitude research carried out in terms of a strictly conditioning perspective that does not take account of cognitive processes has decreased markedly in the last decade. The majority of researchers have turned to viewpoints that regard attitude formation and change as some type of complex cognitive processing often referred to as *information processing*.

INFORMATIONAL APPROACHES TO THE STUDY OF ATTITUDE FORMATION

Most of our attitudes are formed in response to information that we receive about attitude objects. How we receive and combine items of information are important processes in the scientific study of attitude formation. Although the information-processing viewpoint is not necessarily inconsistent with learning approaches, especially those learning approaches that view learning as a cognitive process, the emphasis in informational theories is on understanding how people function as sophisticated problem-solvers and as evaluators of new information. The individual is assumed to receive and evaluate incoming information and to form a new attitude based on this information or to integrate the new information with information already stored in memory. Like learning processes, informational approaches are many-sided, and different theorists have tackled different aspects of the general process.

Because the complexity of the information-processing tasks we perform on a daily basis is astounding, the work that information-processing attitude theorists have cut out for them is unlikely to be completed soon. Consider the attitudes that most Americans have formed toward China. Some Americans receive information from at least occasional contact with Chinese or Chinese-Americans, and a few American travelers have visited China. However, attitudes toward China are mainly a distillation of photographs, written descriptions, television presentation, films, and information acquired through formal education in social-studies, history, and political-science courses.

When we are mainly dependent on indirect information about an attitude object, such as the case of China, our attitudes are determined by others, including scholars, media managers, politicians, and political activists. The perceiver must, of course, take into account the reliability of the source as well as the information's content. Business executives, labor leaders, and politicians sometimes convey certain images primarily to support their desired goals. Some information, such as advertising, is clearly intended to persuade people, while, at the other extreme, information deemed "educational" is portrayed as presenting "facts" about reality. Of course, the line between persuasion and education is not always clear. Formal education dispenses legends as well as truths and does not always make clear which is which.

How are these informational processes

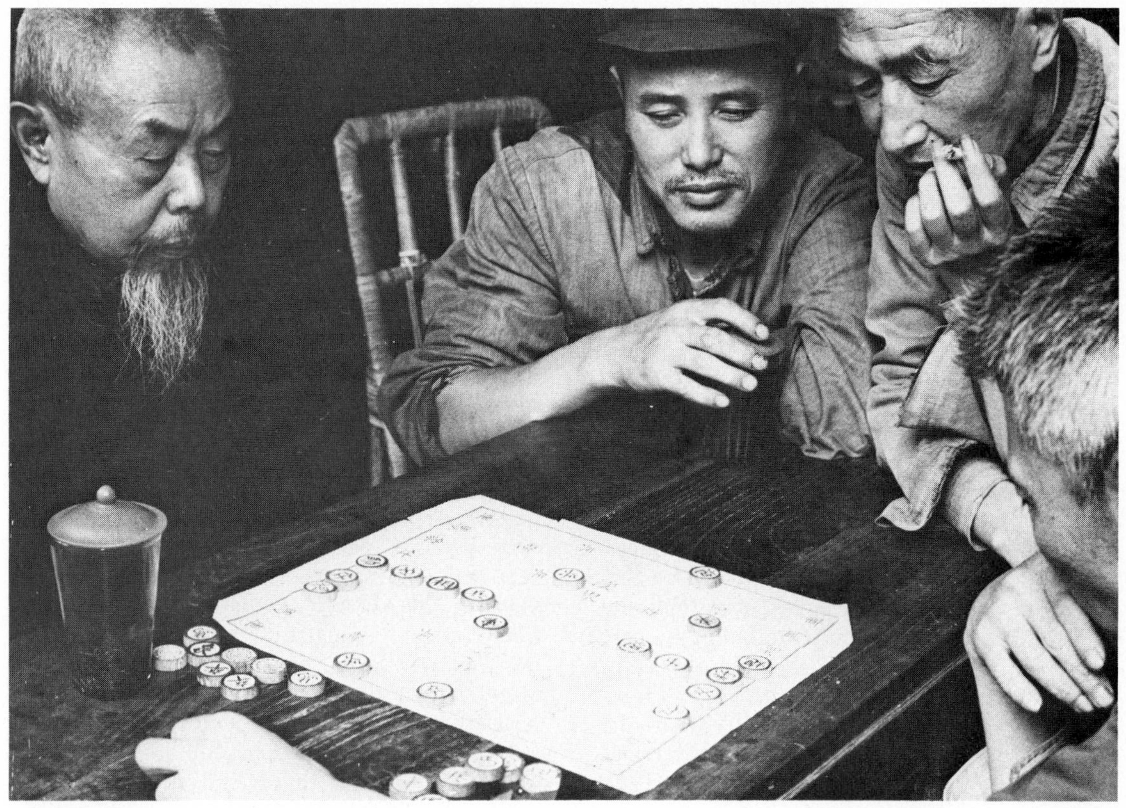

The attitudes of most Americans toward China have been determined by a combination of media presentations and formal education, rather than by firsthand experience. *(© Paolo Koch / Rapho / Photo Researchers)*

taken into account by information-processing theories of attitude formation? Some informational theories, such as Norman Anderson's (1971, 1980) information integration theory (noted earlier in this chapter), assume that an individual forms an attitude by bringing together into an overall impression a number of discrete items of information. These items of information are averaged, and this averaging process can often be described by a simple mathematical "averaging" equation. For example, if you learn that your new neighbor is *shy*, *energetic*, and *compassionate*, your overall attitude toward the neighbor would be an average of the evaluative meaning attached to these traits. Anderson's approach also allows each item of information to be weighted on the basis of the credibility of the source of the information and other factors that contribute to the importance of each item

Other information-processing theories (Rosenberg, 1956; Fishbein and Ajzen, 1975) also emphasize that the perceived attributes of the attitude object are combined to yield an attitude. These theories also take into account the perceived probability of an attribute being associated with an attitude object. For example, an individual might think that increased Social Security benefits for elderly people are *humanitarian* (perceived as a very good quality, +3), *expensive for employed people* (perceived as −2), and *inflationary* (perceived as −3). Further, this individual might be quite certain that an increase in benefits would be humanitarian and expensive, but less certain of the inflationary implications. Therefore, the *humanitarian* and *expensive* attributes might have "subjective probabilities" of .9 assigned to them by this individual, and *inflationary* might have a subjective probability of only .5. It should be noted that these likelihoods or subjective probabilities allow individuals to take into account the reliability or credibility of the source of an item of information. For example, if a perceiver is not sure that a speaker is being completely honest, the probability of the attribute conveyed by the speaker would be considerably less than 1.0. Suppose you suspect that a high-level government economist merely echoes the president's viewpoint on Social Security and thereby distorts the truth in order to support official government policy. This economist's statement that increasing Social Security payments is inflationary would introduce the attribute *inflationary* into your beliefs with considerable uncertainty attached to it.

When the various attributes of an attitude object are taken into account, attitudes are generally predicted by summing (over the attributes) the evaluation of each attribute multiplied by the subjective probability that the attitude object actually includes that attribute. For the Social Security example, the *humanitarian* trait (+3) would be multiplied by a subjective probability of .9, the *expensive* trait (−2) by a probability of .9, and the *inflationary* trait (−3) by a probability of .5. The sum of these products, which is −.6, indicates a slightly negative overall attitude toward increasing Social Security benefits for the elderly.

The emphasis on subjective probabilities is sometimes called an *expectancy-value* theory of attitudes because it takes into account persons' expectancies about whether or not attitude objects have various characteristics and how people evaluate those characteristics. The method is useful because often we are not sure about an attitude object's characteristics. This uncertainty is especially true when we lack direct experience with an attitude object or must infer internal traits such as honesty from external cues. The subjective probability (or expectancy) term in expectancy-value theories takes account of the fact that we often make guesses about characteristics of attitude objects. Using expectancies has the effect of weighting characteristics that are just guesses less heavily than characteristics of which we are certain. Various empirical studies have shown that prediction of attitudes from beliefs is often improved by the inclusion of this expectancy term (Fishbein and Ajzen, 1975).

Still other information-processing models focus on the adequacy of perceivers' reception of new information (McGuire, 1972) or on the processes involved in deciding whether to believe the information. In describing how perceivers decide whether information is valid, Robert Wyer (1974) has suggested that they evaluate the belief statements and conclusions given in persuasive messages. Such an evaluation, which is assumed to proceed according to rules of inference employed by the perceiver, is described in more detail in the next chapter.

SELF-PERCEPTION OF OWN BEHAVIOR AS A SOURCE OF ATTITUDES When you are asked how you feel about something, have you ever done a quick review of your recent behaviors in relation to it and decided how you feel on the basis of how you have behaved toward that object? As discussed in Chapter 3, Daryl Bem (1970) has argued that we commonly decide what our attitudes are by first observing our behavior in relation to the attitude object and then deciding how we must feel about that object. If Bem is correct, you would obtain your answer to the question "Do you like psychology?" by reasoning such as the following: "I must like psychology since I'm always taking psychology courses and reading books about psychology." Bem's idea is that we come to know our attitudes (and emotions and other internal states as well) at least partially by inferring them from observations of our own overt behavior and the circumstances in which this behavior occurs.

Along with the other theories described in this section, Bem's viewpoint, which is known as *self-perception theory*, portrays individuals as information processors and problem solvers, but it emphasizes a particular type of information—namely, one's own behavior—as the key to understanding how people may infer their own attitudes. Bem's point is that we do not always behave *because* of our attitudes, but that we sometimes behave *before* we develop clear attitudes or even in contradiction to our attitudes. In such situations we may then use our behaviors as a basis for inferring our attitudes.

Probing Bem's point more deeply, a skeptic might protest that individuals possess in their memories a large amount of *stored information* about most common attitude objects and therefore should look to the evaluative implications of this stored information, as well as to their own current behavior, in arriving at their attitudes. Need you, then, decide whether you like psychology merely by noting that you are currently taking a psychology course and right now reading a psychology book? Wouldn't you also review some of the knowledge that you have about psychology as a discipline and decide whether you like psychology from this broader perspective, which encompasses stored information and past behavior as well as current behavior? Bem has argued that very often internal cues (or stored information) concerning our attitudes and other states are minimal, ambiguous, and not very salient to us. For example, maybe you knew very little about psychology and were uncertain how you felt about it before taking this course. In the absence of clear-cut alternative information, then, we may look to our own current behavior and the circumstances in which it occurs to find out what our attitudes really are. For instance, you might conclude, "Well, I almost never miss a psychology class, I read the psychology assignments before my other work, and I'm always talking to my friends about it. I guess I must really like psychology."

There have been many demonstrations of the fact that one's own behavior can be a potent source of information concerning one's own attitudes. One of the most striking demonstrations is an experiment that Bem (1965) conducted, making use of "truth" and "lie" signals that functioned as external cues telling subjects whether their own behavior was a good guide to their attitudes. In the first phase of this experiment, subjects each underwent a training procedure in which they answered simple questions about themselves. Subjects had been instructed to answer these questions truthfully in the presence of an amber light and to give false answers in the presence of a green light. This procedure was intended to establish one light as a cue that the subject was telling the truth and the other as a cue for lying.

During the next phase of Bem's experiment, the subject was required to look at cartoons and then to read a statement about the humorousness of the cartoon, such as "This cartoon is very funny" or "This cartoon is very unfunny." Also one of the lights was turned on just before the subject answered (either the truth light or the lie light went on, in a random sequence). After the subject gave the required opinion about the humorousness of each cartoon, the light turned off and the subject indicated how he or she genuinely felt about the cartoon. These ratings showed that subjects' attitudes corresponded more closely with their behaviors when the statements had been made in the presence of the "truth" light than when they had been made in the presence of the "lie" light. This finding illustrates that subjects used their own behavior—their opinion statements about the cartoons—to infer their own attitudes, but moderated this inference by taking into account the circumstances under which the behavior occurred—namely, whether external cues suggested that they were lying or telling the truth. Surprisingly, subjects relied on the lights, rather than their own perhaps vague opinions to infer whether they were actually lying or telling the truth. In general, then, behavior is a guide to one's own attitudes as long as there are no external circumstances that seem to have coerced one into engaging in behaviors inconsistent with one's attitudes and beliefs.

Bem's theory is not as formal as some of the other information-processing viewpoints reviewed in this section. He has not provided a mathematical model, for example, of how information from one's own behavior, from external cues, and from other sources combines to determine one's overall attitude. His insight concerning behavior as a major informational base of attitudes is important, however, and has stimulated considerable research. Further, Bem's viewpoint has far-reaching implications for designing techniques to change people's attitudes. It suggests that it may not be necessary to use argumentation and other methods of changing underlying beliefs in order to accomplish attitude change. Sometimes it may suffice to change *behavior* in desired directions, and appropriate changes in attitudes will follow. Changing attitudes by changing behavior is a topic explored in more detail in Chapter 5.

HOW, THEN, ARE ATTITUDES FORMED?

The question with which this long discussion began—how are attitudes formed?—has led to a consideration of both conditioning and information-processing theories. Like so many other seemingly simple questions about psychological processes, the question concerning attitude formation does not lend itself to a simple answer. To know what answer to the question is most correct at this point in the history of attitude research is to know something about how theory testing has proceeded—that is, one must know which approach has accounted for a greater range of empirical findings and has led to more effective and cumulative research. In terms of criteria such as these, information-processing theory is currently more successful than learning theory. Yet the information-processing perspective is not fully satisfactory as a theory because it currently exists as a set of often-competing models elaborating different aspects of attitude formation. Perhaps these approaches will coalesce in the next decade into a more comprehensive theory of attitude formation and change. In the meantime, information-processing approaches to understanding attitudes constitute one of the most dynamic areas of theory development in social psychology. In the final section of this chapter, we will discuss techniques for measuring attitudes.

ATTITUDE MEASUREMENT

Because the study of attitudes has been an active part of social psychology for a long time, a well-developed technology exists for measuring attitudes. Most methods of measuring attitudes employ questionnaires. Such questionnaires generally assess evaluations of attitude objects by presenting respondents with sentences that state beliefs about the attitude object. Recall that a belief consists of an association between the attitude object and some characteristic or quality—for example, "Nuclear power plants are extremely hazardous for people living near them." In an attitude questionnaire respondents are usually asked to indicate whether they agree or disagree with each of a series of such belief statements concerning an attitude object. In view of the importance of the study of attitudes within social psychology, it is necessary to understand something about how investigators choose these belief statements and interpret respondents' agreement and disagreement with them.

Before explaining how belief statements are selected for inclusion in questionnaires, it should be mentioned that researchers occasionally measure attitudes, not by presenting a series of belief statements, but by asking respondents a single question. An example of this single-question method is a question such as the following one designed to measure attitudes on the nuclear power issue: "How favorably or unfavorably do you evaluate nuclear power plants?" Responses such as "very favorably, somewhat favorably, undecided, somewhat unfavorably, very unfavorably" would be provided just beneath the sentence. Although such a question directly assesses evaluation of an attitude object, the use of a single question to measure an attitude is typically not favored by psychologists. The reason for employing a larger set of items is that responses to any one question are only partially a function of evaluation of the attitude object. Responses are also affected by various other factors (such as the wording of the question). These irrelevant factors create error in the measurement of the attitude, and, for this reason, response to any one question, taken alone, tends often to be a quite imperfect index of an attitude. If responses are instead averaged or summed across a set of questions, a more valid measure is obtained, even though answers to any one question provide an imperfect index of the attitude. The measure has more adequate validity because the error inevitably associated with the individual items tends to cancel across the various items when responses to the items are summed or averaged.

If a researcher desires to obtain a set of questions or items all assessing evaluation of an attitude object, it is wise to have the items differ considerably in content so that they will not all be limited by the same kinds of error. This goal is met if each item expresses a different belief about the attitude object—a belief that links the attitude object (for example, nuclear power plants) with some attribute or characteristic that is relevant to the attitude object (for example, thermal pollution). Each item states a particular belief, and respondents are asked to indicate agreement or disagreement with each item. The favorability of the attitude is inferred from a count or summary of the extent to which respondents agree with favorable belief statements (for example, "Nuclear power plants provide the best solution to the energy crisis") and disagree with unfavorable statements (for example, "Nuclear power plants cause thermal pollution").

The belief statements selected for an attitude measure are carefully chosen to meet certain criteria. These criteria insure that the statements do in fact assess favorable or unfavorable sentiments held by the respondents in relation to the attitude object. There are several systems for choosing appropriate statements. Each of these systems is known as an *attitude scaling method.* Several well-known scaling methods will be described in order to illustrate how belief statements are chosen for attitude scales.

THE THURSTONE METHOD

In 1928 Louis Thurstone asserted unequivocally in the *American Journal of Sociology* that "attitudes can be measured." It was Thurstone's view that attitude measurement could be accomplished by eliciting the beliefs that individuals hold about attitude objects.

Like other attitude theorists, Thurstone viewed attitudes as varying along an evaluative continuum ranging from favorable to unfavorable. Thus, to say someone has an attitude toward abortion is to assert that the person can be placed on a continuum of viewpoints on this issue, ranging from complete endorsement of abortion to complete opposition.

Thurstone suggested that a researcher construct an attitude scale by first choosing an attitude object and then collecting a wide range of belief statements expressing favorable or unfavorable sentiments about the attitude object. In the case of abortion, this preliminary set of statements might include the following:

— Abortion is morally wrong under all circumstances.
— Abortion is a form of murder.
— Abortion is every woman's right.
— Abortion provides an excellent method of population control.

The researcher then determines the location of the statements on the evaluative continuum. Numerical values (called "scale values") representing these locations on a scale running from 1 to 11 are derived by having judges sort the statements into eleven piles according to the degree of favorable or unfavorable evaluation each one expresses. For example, the statement that abortion is a form of murder might be given a rating of 1 (very antiabortion) by a judge, and the statement that it provides an excellent method of population control might be rated 11 (very proabortion). Each statement is given a numerical value that is an average of the ratings assigned by the judges. Then the researcher narrows down the list of statements to a group of twenty-five or fewer statements that judges tend to agree have particular locations on the evaluative continuum. The final statements are selected to meet certain other criteria as well. For example, statements should be chosen to represent an evenly graduated scale from negative to positive attitudes.

Figure 4.3 presents a Thurstone scale pertaining to the issue of birth control. The procedure for measuring an attitude with such a scale is very simple. The final statements are presented to respondents, who are asked to indicate the statements with which they agree. Each respondent's attitude score is the average scale value of the statements that he or she endorses.

Item	Scale Value
The practice of birth control should be punishable by law	1.3
Birth control is morally wrong in spite of its possible benefits	3.6
Birth control has both advantages and disadvantages	5.4
Birth control is a legitimate health measure	7.6
Birth control is the only solution to many of our social problems	9.6
We should not only allow but enforce limitation in the size of families	10.3

FIGURE 4.3 On a Thurstone scale, items are spaced along an eleven-point scale, and respondents endorse the statement or statements that come closest to expressing their own attitudes. These items are a few of those appearing on a scale of attitude toward birth control. High scale values are associated with positive attitudes toward birth control. A respondent's attitude is represented by the average scale value of the statements he or she endorses. (From Thurstone, 1931.)

THE LIKERT METHOD

Although Thurstone's method was the first comprehensive effort at attitude-scale construction, a procedure developed in 1932 by Rensis Likert has exceeded it in current popularity. To construct a Likert scale, a researcher presents a group of respondents with a large preliminary pool of items expressing favorable or unfavorable beliefs about the attitude object. The subjects respond in one of five ways: strongly agree, agree, undecided, disagree, strongly disagree. For items expressing favorable beliefs, an arbitrary score of 5 is given to the strong-agreement response, a score of 4 to the agreement answer, and so forth, with a score of 1 reserved for extreme disagreement. In order that high numbers always signify a favorable evaluation, scoring is reversed for items expressing unfavorable beliefs so that 5 represents strong disagreement, 4 disagreement, and so on.

If an item is to be included on a Likert scale, respondents' responses to the item must relate strongly to responses to the other items in the scale. For this reason, in constructing an attitude-toward-abortion scale, a researcher must compare responses to the various abortion items, and those items relating most strongly to the set of items in the preliminary pool of items are selected for the scale. The scale that results from successful application of this "item analysis" procedure is said to be internally consistent—that is, responses to all the items are highly correlated.

The items selected are then used to assess attitudes of new groups of respondents. Responses are given on the same five-point scale with answers ranging from "strongly agree" to "strongly disagree," and the total attitude score is the sum of these agreement responses. Figure 4.4 shows items from a Likert scale of attitude toward farming.

The scale represents each individual's evaluation of farming as the sum of his or her agree or disagree responses to these and other similar items.

THE GUTTMAN METHOD

Another early attempt to measure attitudes was carried out by Emory S. Bogardus in 1928. Bogardus sought to measure how much social distance people wish to maintain between themselves and various ethnic groups. For example, do people want full integration with members of various groups? Or do they want members of certain groups to remain as far away as possible, so that the members of these ethnic groups would perhaps not even be permitted to visit the country in which the respondents resided?

What are your opinions of the following statements? Your answer is correct if it expresses your true opinion. This is not a test and you are not to be graded. DO NOT OMIT ANY ITEM. In each case encircle the letter or letters which represent your own ideas about each statement.

SA—strongly agree; A—agree; U—undecided; D—disagree; SD—strongly disagree

1. Farming is a pleasant vocation	SA	A	U	D	SD
2. Farm work is drudgery	SA	A	U	D	SD
3. As a life's work, farming would be terrible	SA	A	U	D	SD
4. The farm is a wonderful place to live	SA	A	U	D	SD
5. The independence of farm life appeals to me	SA	A	U	D	SD
6. Living on a farm is just too much hard work	SA	A	U	D	SD

FIGURE 4.4 On a Likert scale, subjects indicate the degree to which they agree or disagree with each item. The Likert items shown here assess attitude toward farming. Items 1, 4, and 5 are worded so that "agree" responses indicate a positive attitude toward farming, and items 2, 3, and 6 are worded so that "disagree" responses indicate a positive attitude. Responses are summed across these and the other items appearing in the scale. (From Myster, 1944.)

In modern terms, Bogardus's social-distance measure is a measure of attitude toward ethnic groups.

Bogardus's technique was to name a particular group and to ask respondents to check which one of seven relationships they would be willing to engage in with members of this group. For example, if a respondent is willing to accept a person into the most intimate relationship (kinship by marriage), a score of 1 would be assigned; a 2 would be given if a person is willing to admit members of the racial or ethnic group into his or her social club, and so on. A score of 7 is given to respondents who inject the most distance between themselves and others—these are respondents who would entirely exclude members of the group from the country. Results of a study conducted in the 1920s using the Bogardus scale are shown in Table 4.1.

Bogardus's instrument was generalized by Louis Guttman (1944, 1950) so that it became a method for scaling any attitude. Guttman's insight was to recognize that the Bogardus items are hierarchical in their meaning. Accordingly, if an individual would accept members of a group into close kinship through marriage, it is reasonable to assume that all of the items describing behaviors that are less intimate would also be endorsed. Similarly, if a person wants to exclude members of a certain group from the entire country, then none of the closer relationships should be acceptable to that individual. In other words, items appropriate for such a scale have the hierarchical property that persons agreeing with any item also agree with those of lower rank on the scale. If a hierarchical set of items is obtained, an individual's attitude score is the rank of the most extreme item he or she endorses since items of lower rank on the scale would ordinarily be accepted also.

THE SEMANTIC-DIFFERENTIAL METHOD

The semantic differential is a popular attitude-measurement technique that asks respondents to rate an attitude object on a number of adjectival scales. This technique was developed by Charles Osgood, George Suci, and Percy Tannenbaum (1957) as a part of their general efforts to measure the meaning of interpersonal

TABLE 4.1 RESPONSES TO BOGARDUS'S SCALE FOR MEASURING ACCEPTABLE RELATIONSHIPS (SOCIAL DISTANCE)*

ETHNIC GROUPS	1 CLOSE KINSHIP BY MARRIAGE	2 PERSONAL CHUMS IN SAME CLUB	3 NEIGHBORS ON SAME STREET	4 EMPLOYMENT IN SAME OCCUPATION	5 CITIZENSHIP IN SAME COUNTRY	6 VISITORS ONLY TO SAME COUNTRY	7 EXCLUDED FROM SAME COUNTRY
English	93.7%	96.7%	97.3%	95.4%	95.9%	1.7%	0.0%
Americans (Native White)	90.1	92.4	92.6	92.4	90.5	1.2	0.0
Norwegians	41.0	56.0	65.1	72.0	80.3	8.0	0.3
Indians	8.1	27.7	33.4	54.3	83.0	7.7	1.6
Jews (German)	7.8	2.1	25.5	39.8	53.5	25.3	13.8
Negroes	1.4	9.1	11.8	38.7	57.3	17.6	12.7
Hindus	1.1	6.8	13.0	21.4	23.7	47.1	19.1

*Based on sample of 1,725 white Americans.

Source: Adapted from E. Bogardus, *Immigration and Race Attitudes* (Boston: D. C. Heath, 1928): 25.

experience. A semantic-differential instrument consists of an attitude object followed by rating scales anchored by pairs of bipolar adjectives, such as good and bad, hot and cold, easy and hard, and so on. Respondents' ratings on these scales express their beliefs about the attitude object. Figure 4.5 shows a set of scales arrayed to obtain ratings of the attitude object "nuclear power plants."

Researchers can easily obtain ratings of attitude objects on a variety of adjective dimensions. Nine dimensions are used in Figure 4.5, but why not ninety? The reason is that extensive research has shown that most adjective dimensions can be usefully grouped in three distinct categories. The largest number of adjectives, such as *good-bad* and *happy-sad*, reflect evaluation. This aspect of meaning is, of course, the same as that studied by attitude researchers. A second group of interrelated dimensions, including *strong-weak* and *easy-hard*, reflect perceived strength—or *potency*, as the semantic-differential investigators have termed it. The third basic component of meaning is termed *activity* and includes dimensions such as *fast-slow* and *young-old*. The potency and activity components of meaning do not link closely to attitude research, which concentrates on evaluation and the specific beliefs that express evaluative meaning. So most attitude researchers are concerned merely with the evaluative dimension of the semantic differential.

Semantic-differential attitude scales are easily constructed because past research has established that certain adjectives express evaluative meaning. If respondents rate an attitude object on a set of such adjective dimensions, and each person's ratings are summed across the various dimensions, a simple measure of attitudes can be easily obtained.

HOW TO CHOOSE A SCALING METHOD

All of the scaling methods reviewed in this chapter produce adequate measures of attitudes, if the methods are correctly implemented. In fact, the result of using different scaling methods to construct scales for the same attitude typically is that the scales correlate very highly. Researchers make decisions about which scale to use primarily on the basis of ease of constructing the scale and ease of administering it to respondents. In terms of these two considerations, no scaling method is preferable over all of the others. Constructing a Likert scale, for example, involves some time and effort since an item analysis must be performed on responses that a preliminary group of subjects gives to a

Nuclear power plants are:

harmful	1	2	3	4	5	6	7	beneficial
active	1	2	3	4	5	6	7	passive
hard	1	2	3	4	5	6	7	soft
wise	1	2	3	4	5	6	7	foolish
good	1	2	3	4	5	6	7	bad
weak	1	2	3	4	5	6	7	strong
calm	1	2	3	4	5	6	7	excitable
beautiful	1	2	3	4	5	6	7	ugly
slow	1	2	3	4	5	6	7	fast

FIGURE 4.5 On a semantic-differential scale, respondents rate the attitude object (nuclear power plants) on a number of adjective scales. Respondents are instructed that ratings closer to the end of the scale indicate a more extreme level of the attribute appearing at that end. The evaluative scales ("harmful–beneficial," "wise–foolish," "good–bad," "beautiful–ugly") assess attitudes toward nuclear power plants.

large set of items, although with modern computers the statistical analyses involved can be quickly calculated. Once constructed, however, a Likert scale is usually easily incorporated into an experiment or a survey because responding to the sorts of opinion statements generally included in Likert scales is an easily understood task having something in common with everyday life experiences. Contrast these advantages and disadvantages of the Likert method with those of the semantic differential. A semantic-differential scale is much more easily constructed. Standard adjectives are paired with the attitude object, and the experimenter is ready to go. However, the task the respondent must perform when completing a semantic-differential scale is unusual. Many people lack prior experience rating attitude objects on scales such as *hard-soft* and *wise-foolish* and may find the task rather bizarre. Therefore, in making a decision about how to measure an attitude, investigators must balance these and other considerations and use the method that best suits their purposes and the prior experiences of the research participants.

SUMMARY

The study of attitudes occupies a central role in social psychology. Attitudes are relatively enduring dispositions to evaluate persons, events, or objects in a favorable or unfavorable way. One major focus in the study of attitudes is the relationship of attitudes to beliefs. Beliefs are the associations that people make between attitude objects and the objects' characteristics or attributes. Each belief expresses some degree of evaluation. An individual's attitude can be predicted from a summary or average of the amount of positive or negative evaluation expressed by those beliefs about the attitude object that are salient to him or her.

Whether attitudes relate strongly to relevant behaviors has remained a controversial issue among social psychologists. Recent research has shown that attitudes relate strongly to relevant actions only if attitudes and actions are defined and assessed in certain ways. Particularly important in this regard is the principle that attitudes and behaviors need to be defined at a corresponding level of generality in order to be highly correlated. It follows that general attitudes are relatively good predictors of correspondingly general behavioral composites, and specific attitudes, such as attitudes toward particular behaviors, are relatively good predictors of specific behaviors. General attitudes usually are weak and inefficient predictors of single behaviors, but predictions of this type can often be improved by taking additional variables into account along with attitudes. Features of social situations such as social norms as well as personal characteristics (other than attitudes themselves) have been shown to enhance the predictability of behaviors when used in conjunction with general attitudes.

The structural relations among attitudes can be described from the perspective of cognitive balance theory, which maps attitudinal and unit relations among the perceiver, another person, and an impersonal entity. The resultant triangle describes the relations between two persons who either agree or disagree about an issue. The theory specifies which structures are balanced and which are imbalanced and predicts that imbalanced structures are unstable and will change over time to one of the balanced structures. There are also several other ways of understanding how attitudes and beliefs relate to one another, such as implicational principles and the idea that attitudes and beliefs vary in their centrality in a cognitive structure.

The formation of attitudes has been studied from various perspectives, including learning theories. Although learning-theory approaches such as classical conditioning and instrumental learning have provided a useful way of thinking about attitude formation, the empirical studies stemming from learning theory have encountered difficulty in demonstrating that attitude formation is anything other than a complex cognitive process mediated by awareness of contingencies between events or by an understanding of what is demanded by the arrangements that subjects encounter in psychological experiments. The chapter reviewed in detail one of the very few studies that provides a demonstration of attitude conditioning that cannot easily be accounted for by assuming that subjects are learning an idea about how the experimenter wishes them to behave.

Information-processing approaches to the study of attitude formation have increased in popularity in recent years. The different varieties of information-processing theory emphasize issues such as how information is evaluated and integrated. Expectancy-value theories assume that the perceived characteristics of the attitude object are weighted according to the perceiver's assessment of how likely it is that the attitude object has each characteristic. The self-perception perspective emphasizes that people form their attitudes to a great extent on the basis of information provided by their own behavior.

The measurement of attitudes generally

takes place through the use of attitude scales, which present a series of belief statements to respondents. Each item of an attitude scale presents respondents with a sentence stating a belief about the attitude object, and respondents indicate how much they agree or disagree with each sentence. Examples of such attitude scaling techniques include the Thurstone, Likert, Guttman, and semantic-differential methods.

CHAPTER FIVE

ATTITUDE CHANGE

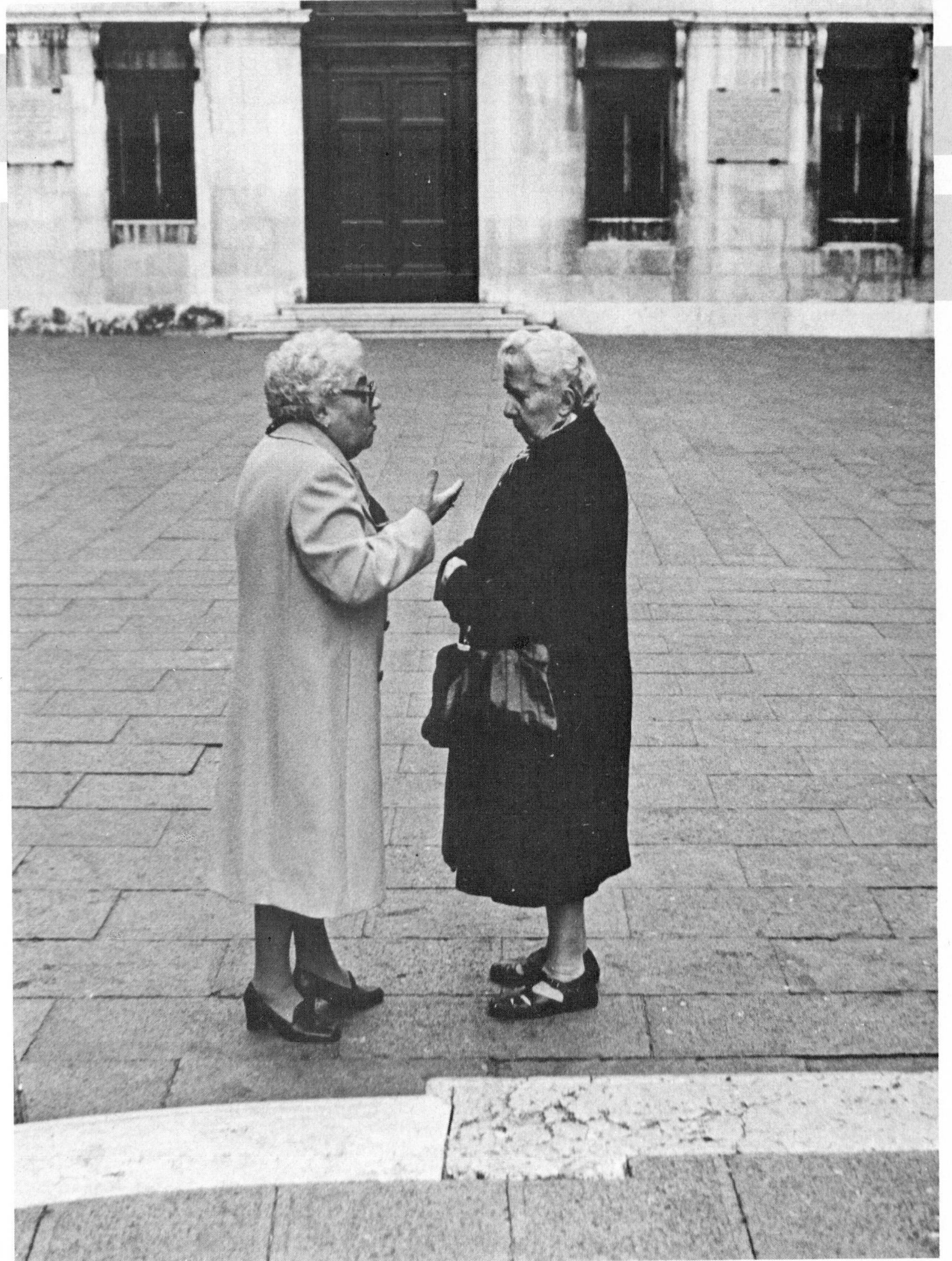

Around 9:30 on an autumn evening in 1973, Peter Reilly, a popular eighteen-year-old high-school senior in Canaan, Connecticut, left the local teen center with a friend in his white 1968 Corvette. About twenty minutes later, after dropping his friend off, Peter came home to a horrible sight. His mother's bloody body was sprawled on the floor, her throat repeatedly slashed by a razor, her legs broken by stomping, and her clothes pulled over her head. Peter called an ambulance and the state police and then ran to a neighbor's house. The police took Peter to the station for questioning, where he spent the night and the next day being interrogated and tested on a polygraph. Convinced of his innocence, Peter waived the right to consult a lawyer. Yet after twenty-five almost sleepless hours of constant questioning, Peter had surprisingly confessed to the murder of his mother. Despite the fact that Peter later retracted his confession, a jury convicted him of manslaughter and he was sentenced to six to sixteen years in prison.

At that point a writer named Joan Barthel became interested in the case and reported the circumstances of Peter's interrogation and confession in a magazine article and a book (1976). The apparent irregularities attracted the attention of the American Civil Liberties Union as well as a number of celebrities, who helped raise money to petition for a new trial. Because of the irregularities and the fact that the state prosecutor on the case withheld evidence that might have cleared Peter, a superior court judge threw out the conviction. In light of the new evidence the state of Connecticut decided not to retry the case, and today Peter Reilly is a free man.

But what pressures during the interrogation could have changed Peter's attitude from a firm belief in his own innocence to a confession of guilt in the razor-blade, stomping murder of his mother? Tape-recorded transcripts of the interrogation reveal subtle and fascinating techniques by which the police persuaded Peter of his own guilt. These techniques will be explained in our discussion of attitude change and persuasion.

DO CHANGED ATTITUDES CHANGE BEHAVIORS?

Most people undergo substantial shifts in attitudes during their lives. These shifts are not often as sudden and dramatic as Peter Reilly's. In fact, they are usually so gradual that they are not even experienced as important changes. Yet because attitudes can influence behavior, social psychologists have long been interested in the processes that lead people to "change their minds." Linked with mass communications, the psychology of persuasion raises the possibility of manipulating attitudes and behavior on a broad scale—for example, in Hitler's racist propaganda or recent campaigns to reduce smoking or encourage the use of seat belts. At the same time, critics have pointed out that attitude-change experiments seldom find corresponding changes in actual behaviors following attitude change (Festinger, 1964).

As explained in Chapter 4, attitudes predict with considerable success the *overall favorability* of an individual's behavior toward a class of attitude objects. If an individual's attitude toward feminism, for example, changes from opposition to support, we would expect a shift in the entire spectrum of that individual's behavior on women's issues. In order to change the general character of people's behavior in a given area, then, their attitudes must change. In contrast, to induce change in a single behavior, it is sufficient simply to expose individuals to appropriate situational pressures. The point is well known to parents. They can induce their child to do homework on a particular evening by manipulating situational contingencies ("You study, or else I will ground you for the weekend"). However, to convince a reluctant son or daughter to study on a regular basis, even in the absence of threats or inducements, general changes in attitudes toward studying are required. Attitude change, then, has the effect of altering the kinds of behaviors that people carry out in relation to an attitude object *across a variety of settings.*

THEORETICAL PERSPECTIVES ON ATTITUDE CHANGE

How do changes in attitudes come about? In everyday life, when people explain why their attitudes have changed, they offer varied reasons. They may cite new information that they received from newspapers, television programs, or friends. Or they may have felt uncomfortable with an attitude because it conflicted with other beliefs and values. This multiplicity of explanations in everyday life is mirrored by social psychologists' lack of a single voice in their scientific explanations of attitude change. As discussed in Chapter 4, both learning and information-processing theory have been used to explain how attitudes are formed. These same perspectives are also important to the study of attitude change. In fact, many of the theoretical issues raised in relation to attitude formation are essentially the same issues that must be addressed in relation to attitude change.

THE LEARNING PERSPECTIVE

The first major research program on attitude change was carried out by Carl Hovland and his associates at Yale University in the 1950s. These researchers adopted a *learning perspective*, which, as Chapter 4 noted, explained attitude formation and change in terms of incentives and reinforcements for holding and changing attitudes (Hovland, Janis, and Kelley, 1953). For example, in the Peter Reilly case, Peter's interrogators tried to convince Peter how good it would feel to confess, even though Peter was sure he hadn't committed a crime. The learning perspective proved useful to attitude-change research for many years, but has gradually given way to information-processing theories, which allow researchers to be more systematic in analyzing the complex cognitive processes involved in changing attitudes.

THE CONSISTENCY PERSPECTIVE

Another useful approach to attitude change is the cognitive consistency perspective introduced in Chapter 4's discussion of attitude structure. The consistency principle asserts that people change their attitudes and beliefs in order to achieve consistency among a set of related attitudes. This approach does not regard the individual primarily as a problem solver and processor of information. Instead, it suggests that attitude change is rooted in motivational processes. The unpleasantness and tension believed to accompany inconsistency motivate the perceiver to change his or her attitudes in order to reach a more pleasant and tension-free state. Among consistency theories, dissonance theory is most effective for predicting attitude change. For example, Peter Reilly's interrogators tried to make Peter feel guilty about small things he had done to his mother, such as throwing a flashlight at her once. If Peter could feel guilty about a small act, it would be dissonant to maintain his innocence in the large act. Some of the research inspired by dissonance theory will be elaborated on in the second half of the chapter.

THE SELF-PERCEPTION PERSPECTIVE

A third approach to attitude change is the self-perception perspective, introduced in Chapter 4 as an explanation of attitude formation. Bem's self-perception theory suggests that when attitudes are weak, ambiguous, or unformed, people may infer their own attitudes by observing their behavior and the circumstances in which it occurs. This approach views the individual primarily as a rational problem solver, seeking answers to such questions as "Why did I do that?" When no satisfactory explanations can be found, the individual may infer an attitude to account for behavior. In the Peter Reilly case, the lie detector indicated that Peter was nervous when asked about his mother's murder. The police also suggested that Peter may have "blacked out" and thus couldn't remember committing the murder. Needing an explanation for his arousal on the polygraph and doubting his own innocence during a "black out," Peter inferred that he must be guilty.

THE INFORMATION-PROCESSING PERSPECTIVE

To the extent that it is possible to discuss recent attitude-change research in terms of a single broad framework, that framework is provided by the family of theories introduced in Chapter 4 as information-processing theories. The relevance of this perspective to attitude change is clear. From an information-processing perspective, attitude change is the product of new information. An attitude, as explained in Chapter 4, is an average or summary of the salient beliefs that an individual has about an attitude object. When a new belief is averaged in with existing beliefs, the resultant evaluation often shifts.

For instance, Peter Reilly didn't see himself as a murderer, but he was presented with new information he found hard to deny—namely, the polygraph results. Yet if information is all that is needed to change attitudes and beliefs, why doesn't all new information result in attitude change? As various information-processing theories have suggested, there are a number of reasons why people may not change their attitudes even though they are presented with new information that challenges their existing evaluation of an attitude object. One barrier to attitude change is that there may be defects in individuals' understanding of new information. This idea was developed in detail by William McGuire (1972), who argued that attitude change is a product of three sequential processes. According to McGuire, in order for attitude change to take place, individuals must first *pay attention* to the information. Then they must *comprehend* the information to which they have attended. Next, they must personally accept or *yield* to the information that they have comprehended. From McGuire's perspective, failures or defects at any of these stages lessen or even prevent attitude change. Unfortunately for Peter Reilly, there were no defects in these stages. The polygraph was described as "reading his brain and heart," and Peter was forced to pay attention, comprehend, and yield to its conclusions. Most of the research in this chapter pertains to why people yield to information, but some findings are best understood in terms of the information-reception processes of attention and comprehension.

Obviously, a lot of the information that we receive in everyday life is quickly rejected as invalid. Should you run into someone who claims that the world will come to an end within three weeks—or that you just murdered your mother—chances are you would reject this person as crazy or some kind of fanatic. In other words, you would not yield to such a viewpoint. A current major theme of social psychology is understanding how people judge the validity of

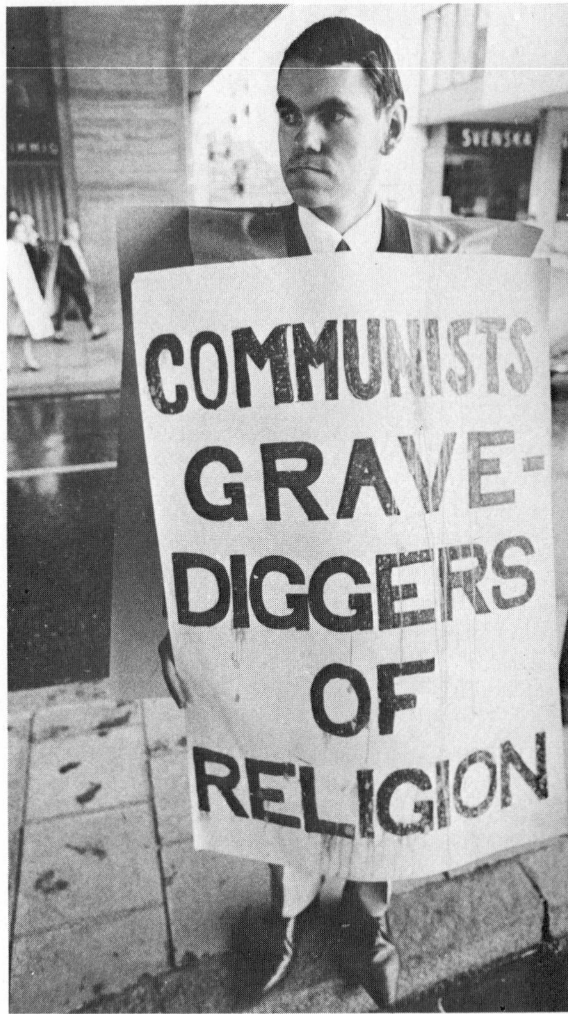

We quickly reject the validity of messages presented by people whom we perceive as fanatics. *(© Leif Skoogfors 1980/Woodfin Camp & Assoc.)*

information. As we will see in this chapter, people have a number of ways of screening incoming information to determine whether it accurately represents reality.

In the next section we will concentrate on attitude change via persuasion by others. In persuasion settings, members of an audience are exposed to a message consisting of a communicator's position on an issue and one or more arguments supporting that position. Several components of persuasion settings can affect attitude change, and it is important to take into account at least these four components of such situations: (1) the communicator; (2) the message itself; (3) the medium or channel through which the message is presented; and (4) the audience.

The final section of the chapter considers self-persuasion, the changes in attitudes that occur as a product of one's own behavior. The behavior that has been studied most often is counterattitudinal advocacy—advocating a position on an issue opposed to one's initial attitude, such as arguing in favor of abortion when in fact you oppose it. Through counterattitudinal advocacy and other behavior, people often change their own attitudes. Both cognitive dissonance theory and Bem's self-perception theory will be explored as possible explanations for self-persuasion effects.

ATTITUDE CHANGE THROUGH PERSUASION BY OTHERS

THE COMMUNICATOR: WHOM SHOULD YOU BELIEVE?

To what extent does your belief in what you hear or read depend on characteristics of the communicator? Are you more likely to buy a deodorant if it is endorsed by a celebrity than by an unknown actor? The question of *communicator credibility* was explored systematically by Carl Hovland and his research group in the 1950s with their learning-theory perspective on attitude change. Later theorists suggested that characteristics other than credibility, such as *attractiveness* and *power*, also enhance a communicator's persuasiveness. Recently, various information-processing perspectives have examined how a communicator's characteristics influence the processing of a communicator's message.

COMMUNICATOR CREDIBILITY The Hovland research group investigated two aspects of communicator credibility: (1) *expertise*, or how well informed and intelligent the audience believes the source is; and (2) *trustworthiness*, or how valid and accurate the audience believes the source's presentation is. In general, the expectation was that the more credible a communica-

FIGURE 5.1 There are four principal components of persuasion settings: (1) the communicator or influencing agent; (2) the message, including its content, style, and organization; (3) the medium or channel through which the message is presented; and (4) the audience or recipients of the communication.

tor appeared to be, in terms of either expertise or trustworthiness, the more persuasive he or she would be. This expectation was consistent with Hovland's learning-theory approach. Effective communicators, he argued, are able to convince the audience that positive consequences will follow from accepting the communicator's viewpoint. For example, a communicator with high prestige, such as a sports superstar, would represent to the audience the kinds of opinions that are respected and approved. Audience members would anticipate receiving social approval to the extent that they adopted the viewpoint of such a communicator. In general, then, high communicator credibility should lead the audience to expect positive consequences if it adopted the communicator's views; in contrast, the audience should expect negative consequences to follow from adopting the views of a low-credibility communicator.

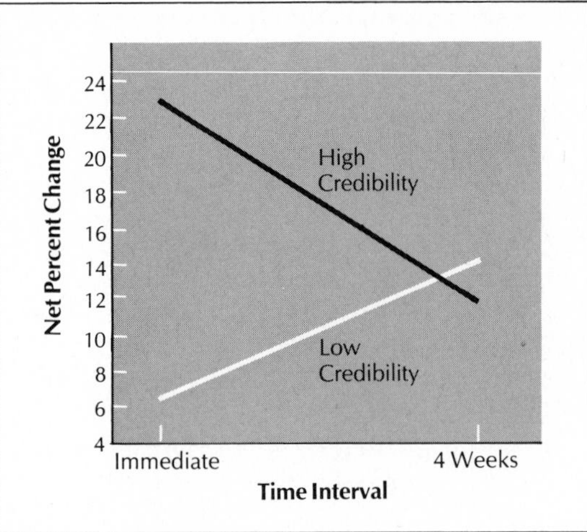

FIGURE 5.2 Hovland and Weiss (1951) found that the short-term effects of communicator credibility on attitude change disappear with time.

A Classic Experiment The prototype for studies of communicator credibility is an experiment conducted by Carl Hovland and Walter Weiss (1951). In this experiment, Hovland and Weiss presented four persuasive messages, such as that atomic-powered submarines could feasibly be built at that time or that television would force movie theaters out of business by 1955. Each message was presented as coming from one of two sources—a high-credibility source or a low-credibility source. For example, the atomic-submarine message was attributed either to J. Robert Oppenheimer, a respected American physicist (high credibility), or to the Russian newspaper *Pravda* (low credibility). The actual content of the communication was always the same, regardless of the source.

Subjects' opinions on the four issues were assessed by questionnaires before and after the subjects read the persuasive communications. As expected, greater opinion change occurred for the high- than the low-credibility sources. Also, presentations from high-credibility sources were judged to be fairer and their conclusions more justifiable than presentations from low-credibility sources.

The most surprising finding occurred four weeks later. Even though the high-credibility sources had produced greater attitude change than low-credibility sources immediately after the communication, this difference was no longer apparent after four weeks. Messages from the high-credibility sources had become less believable over time while messages from the low-credibility sources had become *more* believable over time. Hovland and Weiss called this phenomenon the *sleeper effect.* Why should a message from a low-credibility source become more believable over time? Hovland and his colleagues concluded that people initially link together the content of a message with its source, but that over time content and source become dissociated. Content is remembered while the source is more quickly forgotten. For example, it may be a familiar experience to remember a rumor but not to remember where you heard it.

Recent research has demonstrated that the sleeper effect is not as common as Hovland believed, but under a limited set of circumstances the opinion change produced by a low-credibility source does increase over time (Gruder, Cook, Hennigan, Flay, Alessis, and Halamaj, 1978). However, as Gillig and Greenwald (1974) have shown, the more reliable effect of communicator credibility is that opinion change produced by a high-credibility source decreases

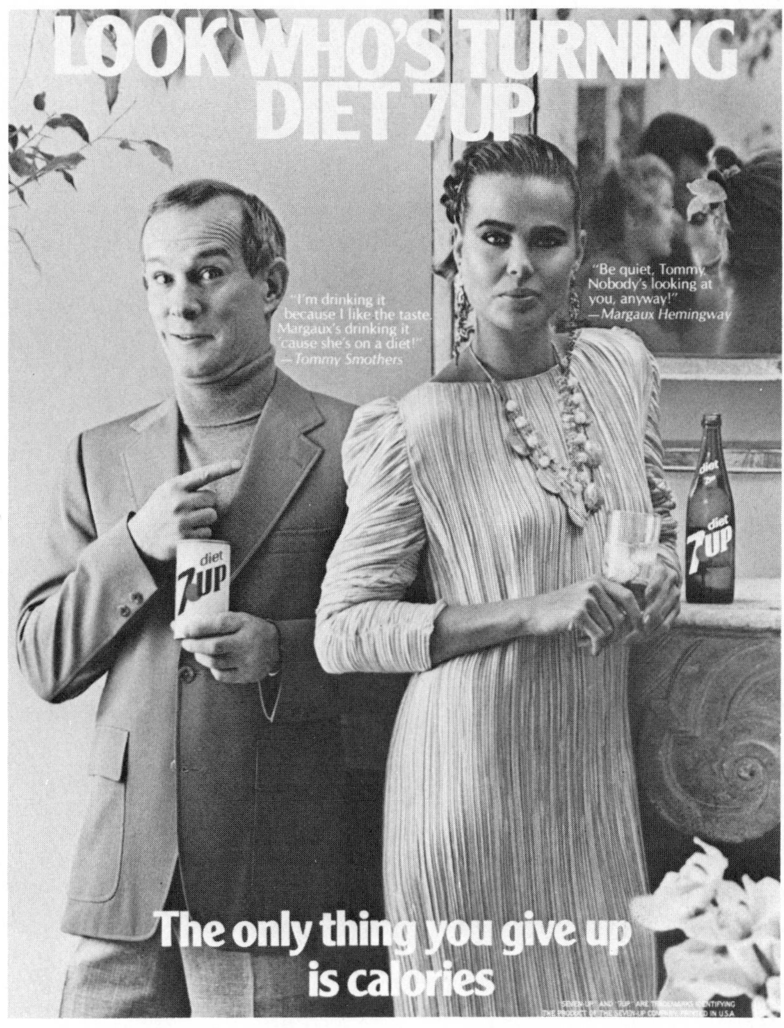

Celebrity and physical attractiveness increase the credibility and persuasiveness of a communicator. As a result, advertisers frequently use well-known personalities to sell products. *(Courtesy, The Seven-Up Company)*

over time. All things considered, persistence of opinion change over time depends on several features of the communication situation, including the credibility of the communicator (Cook and Flay, 1978).

OTHER COMMUNICATOR ATTRIBUTES Other researchers have investigated a wealth of communicator characteristics that affect the persuasiveness of messages. For example, in quite a few studies communicators' physical appearance has been varied. At least under some conditions, communicators are more persuasive if they are *physically attractive* (Horai, Naccari, and Fatoullah, 1974). Communicator attributes such as race, sex, grooming, and style of dress also affect the persuasiveness of messages, as do body position and other nonverbal behaviors. Even the speed of a communicator's speech has been shown to affect opinion change, with communicators who speak fast being more persuasive than those who speak slowly (Miller, Maruyama, Beaber, and Valone, 1976).

Why do communicator attributes such as these affect persuasion? There is no simple answer to this question. Some researchers have tried to identify a small number of dimensions or general attributes that may determine a communicator's persuasiveness. Such efforts have usually agreed on the importance of a *credibility* dimension, which includes both expertise and trustworthiness, but have argued over the value of an *attractiveness* or likability dimension and sometimes a *power* or means-control dimension as well.

Credibility and expertise affect persuasion because the expert can provide a better, more accurate account of the world and, therefore, is likely to be believed more readily than someone who lacks expertise. Attractiveness influences opinion change because recipients want to please or emulate an admired communicator who conveys personal warmth or who is a member of a similar ethnic or religious group. Power affects persuasion because a communicator with high social status, job status, or wealth may control rewards and punishments that in turn influence recipients' behavior. Power of this type is effective so long as recipients are directly under a communicator's surveillance.

Specific attributes of communicators (such as physical appearance, gender, speed of speech, and so on) affect persuasion primarily through their impact on these general dimensions by which communicators are judged. Theories of attitude change, then, should be able to explain how persuasion differs when one rather than another of these general dimensions is salient to the recipient of a message. Herbert Kelman (1961) developed a theory along these lines, and this discussion reflects his thinking.

Persuasion seems to proceed differently when communicators' persuasiveness is based primarily on credibility rather than on attractiveness. In a demonstration of this effect Ross Norman (1976) presented subjects with a message arguing that people should sleep less than the usual eight hours. Half of the subjects received this communication from an attractive, but not expert, source (a physically attractive male undergraduate portrayed as active in athletics, music, and student government) and half from an expert, but not attractive, source (a physically unattractive, middle-aged man portrayed as a professor of physiological psychology and author of a book on sleep). Norman also varied whether the communicator merely gave a simple statement of his opinion or gave a more elaborate presentation based on six supporting arguments. Norman found that the expert was an effective persuader only if he provided justifying arguments. The attractive source was effective whether or not he provided supporting arguments. These findings suggest that the complex information processing required for evaluating detailed arguments may be limited to settings in which credibility is a major consideration. If attractiveness is more salient than credibility, a simpler process may operate whereby the audience decides whether to believe a message simply on the basis of who the communicator is. Perhaps it is noteworthy that most TV commercials emphasize attractiveness over expertise, though advertisers do occasionally take the opposite tack, as when expert crimebuster Clarence Kelley, former head of the FBI, plugs a gem-identification service. And sometimes both attributes are combined, as when an attractive model who changes her make-up several times a day extols a particular skin cream.

INFORMATION PROCESSING AND COMMUNICATOR CREDIBILITY How do recipients of persuasive messages function as information processors? Recent attempts to answer this question have applied the major information-processing theories of attitudes discussed in Chapter 4. For example, Norman Anderson's (1980) *information integration theory* regards persuasive messages as items of information that recipients integrate with their existing attitudes. The effect of source credibility is treated as a "weight" that amplifies the value of the information in the message. This model has been tested in a number of experiments, including one by Birnbaum, Wong, and Wong (1976) in which two communicators each described an individual in terms of a single trait adjective, such as "friendly." Subjects then judged this individual's likability. Communicator credibility was varied by mentioning that the communicator had known the described individual for three years, for three months, or had met him only once. Subjects' judgments of the individual's likability were more strongly affected by communicators who had known him longer. More important, exact predictions of subjects' judgments were made by assuming that information from sources with longer acquaintanceship would be weighted more heavily by subjects and that this weighting could be represented mathematically by a "multiplying model." In other words, the information in a communicator's message is multiplied by a "weight" that corresponds to how credible the communicator is.

Another information-processing approach to communicator credibility emphasizes causal attributions for a communicator's behavior. For instance, communicators are seen as more credible when their persuasiveness appeals cannot be attributed to external situational forces or to their own interests. An experiment illustrating this was performed by Alice Eagly, Wendy Wood, and Shelly Chaiken (1978). Subjects read the transcript of a campaign speech given by a candidate for mayor in a town plagued by industrial pollution. The candidate took a pro-environment position and argued that the offending plant should be shut down. Subjects were told that the candidate was either a long-time supporter of environmentalist causes or a long-time supporter of business and labor interests. In addition they were told that the speech had been delivered either to a proenvironment

FOCUS ON APPLICATIONS

PSYCHOLOGICAL TACTICS IN POLICE INTERROGATION

The following article from *The New York Times* indicates how successful police officers may be when they incorporate psychological tactics into their interrogation procedures. These tactics derive directly from attitude-change research and can be seen in the Peter Reilly case as well.

HAUPPAUGE, L.I.—. . . 43 homicides were recorded last year in Suffolk County, compared with 1,518 in New York City. Members of the 27-man homicide squad say the ratio of cases to investigators has allowed them the time not only to investigate stubborn cases repeatedly, but also to conduct lengthy, psychologically orchestrated interrogations of suspects that have frequently led to confessions that did not involve the use of physical force.

"The number of confessions we get are the result of good, thorough investigations, and three- to four-hour interrogations," said Detective Dennis Rafferty, 38, a 10-year veteran of the squad. "We use psychology—we try to relax them, offer them coffee, a cigarette, and we minimize their crime by telling them we can understand how someone like them could do such a thing. Some of these people have never been talked to like a gentleman."

The detective continued: "We're not talking about cold-blooded hit men. Most people who murder are upset when they're caught, and they want to get the guilt off their chest. We have to use psychology—it's the only thing we've got left. Brutality went out with the 1930's James Cagney movies."

Sidney R. Siben, an attorney whose firm, Siben & Siben, handles one of the largest criminal practices in Suffolk County, asserted in an interview that "the majority of the force are decent, but there are several bad boys who hit first and ask questions later."

Mr. Siben agreed that, as a rule, the homicide squad was careful not to use physical force, although he said there were occasional incidents. But more often, he said, the psychological techniques are less passive than those described by Detective Rafferty.

According to Mr. Siben, a client of his, a youth, had been seized recently by the homicide squad and questioned in connection with the murder of a 13-year-old boy, John Pius of Smithtown.

Mr. Siben's client was held in custody for 48 hours, and the police refused to tell his parents where he was.

"They scared the hell out of him and got a confession, but he had no connection with the murder at all," Mr. Siben said. The boy's family may sue the county, he added.

Source: Frances Cerra, "Police in Suffolk Attribute Record to 'Psychology,'" *The New York Times*, June 25, 1979.

group or to a probusiness group. The environmentalist was not especially persuasive since his knowledge of pollution was seen as biased by his environmentalist commitments. In contrast, when the industrial supporter took the same proenvironment position, he was regarded as less biased and therefore was more persuasive.

When either candidate was presented as talking to a proenvironment audience, the candidate was not especially persuasive. He was regarded as taking the proenvironment position simply because of pressures from the audience. In contrast, when the candidate gave the identical talk to a probusiness audience, his environmentalist position was clearly unexplainable in terms of audience pressures. He was seen as less biased and therefore was more persuasive.

PETER REILLY'S COMMUNICATOR Before leaving the topic of the communicator, let us return to the case of Peter Reilly. How did the communicator's characteristics affect Peter's confession? It appears that they were important in several ways, based on the tape transcripts. Peter's interrogator, Sergeant Kelly, repeatedly emphasized his own expertise and trustworthiness. According to Kelly, he had operated the polygraph for twelve years. He helped some people prove their innocence, and others to confess when they "knew they were guilty but didn't know how to tell somebody." Kelly even claims that he once sent a girl to a mental hospital; she still sends him Christmas cards and underneath she writes the word "Thanks." In a bid to make himself more attractive to Peter, Kelly emphasizes the things they have in common, like the fact that Kelly's brother-in-law also owns a Corvette just like Peter's. Furthermore, Kelly admits that he, too, argues with his mother and that he's done "crazy things" in his own life. Kelly confides, "I'm not going to sit here and tell you I'm an angel." Kelly also doesn't let Peter forget his (Kelly's) power to control Peter's fate. After hours of questioning, Kelly holds out the promise of cigarettes and Coke if Peter will talk. When Peter complains of being hungry and tired, Kelly replies, "Once we get this out, you're going to eat like you've never eaten before. Once you get this out, you'll sleep for a week. Because your conscience will be free."

THE CONTENT OF PERSUASIVE MESSAGES

When you're constantly exposed to all sorts of persuasive messages, how do you decide what to believe? Probably it depends most on the content of the communication. Do the ideas make sense? Do the recommendations and conclusions seem to follow logically from the arguments that are given? Of course, as this chapter makes clear, it is also important to know *who* is talking. Yet to some extent individuals are able to forget about the communicator's identity and to concentrate mainly on what is being said. The content of messages has been described by psychologists in contrasting ways. For example, messages can be examined in terms of their logical structure: Does the premise lead logically to the conclusion? Or they can be analyzed with respect to how one-sided they are: Does the communicator include opposition arguments or only present arguments favoring his or her own position? Also the motivational basis of a message can be examined, and one particular type of appeal, the fear appeal, has been extensively studied. These aspects of message content—logical structure, inclusion of opposition arguments, and fear appeals—will be examined in the following sections. Although these three subjects are arbitrary, they were chosen because they illustrate particularly well how information-processing models approach the study of persuasion.

LOGICAL ANALYSIS OF ARGUMENTS AND CONCLUSIONS How do people take account of what is said in persuasive messages? First they screen the information in terms of what they already know about a topic, and then they analyze the fit between the various parts of the message. Most messages can be regarded as a set of premises or arguments followed by a conclusion. In a presidential campaign speech, for example, a candidate's arguments are likely to be claims about the good consequences that would follow from his or her policies (lower taxes, less inflation, international peace, better medical care, and so on). The conclusion drawn by the candidate would be that the listener should vote for him or her in the coming election. Assuming you had not already firmly decided to vote for the candidate, would you allow such a speech to persuade you to do so? You probably would give the candidate your vote if you believed that all of those good things would follow his or her election.

Despite the communicator's efforts to get you to accept his or her arguments, no doubt you would not be easily convinced of all of them. Some would probably be incompatible with what you already know about the issues. Thus, you would judge each argument in light of your other beliefs and the new information given in the message. Then you could attach a "subjective probability" to each argument. This subjective probability would constitute your own personal estimate of how successful the candidate's policies would be—for example, in lowering taxes.

You would also take into account the relevance of each argument to the conclusion that you should vote for the candidate. For some people, the argument that an administration would change farm policy would have little relevance to their voting decisions because these people aren't concerned about agriculture and know nothing about agriculture policies. These people might believe the message's arguments about farm policy but their belief would have no bearing on their voting decisions. On the other hand, if individuals were very concerned with, say, urban problems, then arguments about urban issues would be highly relevant to their vote. According to this approach, a listener's acceptance of a persuasive message takes into account two things: the subjective probability attached to each argument in the message; and the subjective relevance of each argument to the recommended conclusion. In other words, arguments are most effective when they are believable (that is, have high subjective probability) and pertain to the conclusion (have high subjective relevance).

An extensive research program on logical analysis of persuasive arguments has been conducted by Robert Wyer (1974), and the ideas in this section reflect his work. For example, in a study by Wyer and Goldberg (1970), subjects received persuasive communications designed to increase (or decrease) their belief in premises such as the following: "Drug companies charge excessive prices for the pills they produce." The researchers then examined the impact of these communications on subjects' belief in related conclusions, such as "The size of drug companies' profits should be placed under the control of the federal government." In order to predict how much a subject's belief in a conclusion would change, Wyer and Goldberg determined the subjective relevance of premise to conclusion for each subject. For example, should the size of drug companies' profits have anything to do with federal regulation of the drug industry? By using subjective probability measures and assuming that subjects' reasoning corresponded to mathematical laws of probability, Wyer and Goldberg successfully predicted how much the persuasive communications would change subjects' beliefs in conclusions.

ONE-SIDED VERSUS TWO-SIDED ARGUMENTS AND RELATED ISSUES Is a message more persuasive if it presents only one side of an issue or if it also presents and refutes the opposing side? On the one hand, the apparent bias of a one-sided presentation may diminish the communicator's credibility and make even a persuaded audience vulnerable to opposition arguments later on. On the other hand, introduction of opposing arguments risks providing the audience with a rebuttal to the position advocated in the message.

A Classic Experiment To examine the effects of one-sided versus two-sided arguments, Carl Hovland, Arthur Lumsdaine, and Fred Sheffield (1949) exposed World War II soldiers to communications arguing that Germany's surrender would not result in a quick end to the war. One group of soldiers only heard arguments supporting the message—that is, that Germany's surrender would be followed by a long, protracted war with Japan. A second group heard the same supporting arguments but also was given opposition arguments predicting that when Germany surrendered, Japan's weaknesses would result in an early end to the war. The soldiers' beliefs about the length of the war following Germany's surrender were measured both before and after the communication. Hovland and his colleagues found that the relative effectiveness of the two types of communication depended on the soldiers' *initial opinions* concerning the length of the war. Soldiers who initially opposed the communicator's conclusion were more persuaded by the two-sided message than by the one-sided message—perhaps because the opposing arguments in the two-sided message were especially salient to the soldiers who themselves were initially on the opposition side. However, soldiers who *initially* were on the same side of the issue as the communicator were more persuaded by one-sided messages than by the two-sided ones. Perhaps when audience members are already convinced, the communicator loses effectiveness by bringing to the members' attention opposing material that they were not previously aware of.

A major advantage of presenting (and refuting) opposition arguments is that people who have heard the opposition arguments and their refutations are then more likely to withstand opposition attacks later on. The practical implications of this finding are enormous, since ordinarily when we bother to convince people of a point of view, we hope that they will stay convinced. The importance of refuting opposition is considered in the next section.

Immunization The long-term advantages of exposure to opposition arguments led to an extensive research program by William McGuire (1964) on how people resist persuasion. McGuire argued that giving people a weak form of opposition arguments "immunizes" them against later opposition attack because it stimulates their attitudinal defenses. Thus, individuals are able to resist subsequent attempts at persuasion because they have already encountered and refuted the arguments of the opposition. McGuire tested his theory by attacking "cultural truisms," or beliefs that are so widely shared they are seldom attacked. The belief that it is good to brush one's teeth regularly is a cultural truism. People have seldom heard toothbrushing criticized, and they have no experience in dealing with such criticism. Do you realize, however, that toothbrushing may damage your gums and wear down the enamel of your teeth? Receiving a brief statement of arguments against the toothbrushing truism is thought by McGuire to "immunize" or protect the toothbrushing belief against attack, provided that the recipient is able to ward off the initial weak attack. These weak attacks on truisms are called *refutational defense treatments* by McGuire, and they are often accompanied by some specific information countering the weak attack. In a refutational defense condition of a McGuire experiment, a subject would receive a weak attack on a truism—such as toothbrushing damages gums and enamel—and then would receive information countering this weak attack. Later, the subject would be exposed to a major, full-scale attack on his or her belief. In the full-scale attack a more elaborate rationale would be given—for example, explaining how and why toothbrushing harms gums and enamel. Do people withstand such attacks on truisms? Refutational defense treatments impart a great deal of resistance to attack. Since people have already encountered a weakened form of the attack and are prepared to refute it, they are motivated and experienced in arguing against, or "counterarguing," a message attacking their own beliefs. However, when counterarguing can be disrupted, as discussed in the next section, persuasive messages may be especially effective.

Counterarguing and Distraction Hovland's research on the value of opposition arguments in a two-sided message as well as McGuire's work on refutational defenses suggested that a covert *counterarguing* process often occurs when individuals receive a persuasive message. In other words, while listening to or reading persuasive messages, people often silently think up arguments attacking the communicator's points. The role of counterarguing in resisting persuasion has been studied in detail by Timothy Brock and his associates. After earlier research by Festinger and Maccoby (1964) demonstrated that distractions can enhance the persuasiveness of messages, Robert Osterhouse and Timothy Brock (1970) showed that distraction increases persuasion because it disrupts the process of counterarguing. If an individual tries to listen to a message and is distracted from it at the same time (for example, by flashing lights, or by a film going on in the same room), he or she has little cognitive capacity remaining to think up counterarguments. And with less counterarguing, messages are more persuasive.

The distractions that Osterhouse and Brock

SOCIAL PSYCHOLOGY AND THE ARTS

"LEND ME YOUR EARS"

One of the most noted persuasive appeals in the English language is Marc Antony's speech at Caesar's funeral in Shakespeare's tragedy *Julius Caesar.* Many effective techniques of attitude change are skillfully employed in this oration. First, Marc Antony asks his audience to "lend me your ears"—in effect, to hear him out and suspend counterargument. He goes on to weaken the citizens' resistance by disclaiming any attempt at persuasion: "I come to bury Caesar, not to praise him." Then Marc Antony employs a two-sided argument, a technique that is more effective when the audience initially opposes a speaker's message, as the Romans initially oppose Marc Antony. He says: "The evil that men do lives after them; The good is oft interred with their bones; So let it be with Caesar." The clever orator then plants several supportive arguments well within his audience's latitude of acceptance: "He hath brought many captives home to Rome, Whose ransoms did the general coffers fill"; "When that the poor have cried, Caesar hath wept"; and "I thrice presented him a kingly crown which he did thrice refuse." "Was this ambition?" Marc Antony asks his audience, shrewdly allowing them to draw their own conclusions. Gradually he challenges the credibility and trustworthiness of Brutus, who had taken part in Caesar's assassination and had sought to justify the act at Caesar's funeral: "And Brutus was an honourable man," Marc Antony repeats, more and more skeptically each time. Finally, Marc Antony raises the specter of cognitive dissonance: "You all did love him once,—not without cause: What cause withholds you, then, to mourn for him?" How can the citizens rejoice at Caesar's death as they simultaneously recall their love for him and mourn his loss? When Marc Antony completes his speech, his persuasive powers have worked their way. The next line in the play comes from a citizen in the audience who confides to a compatriot, "Methinks there is much reason in his sayings."

Friends, Romans, countrymen, lend me your ears;
I come to bury Caesar, not to praise him.
The evil that men do lives after them;
The good is oft interred with their bones;
So let it be with Caesar. The noble Brutus
Hath told you Caesar was ambitious:
If it were so, it was a grievous fault;
And grievously hath Caesar answer'd it.
Here, under leave of Brutus and the rest,—
For Brutus is an honourable man;
So are they all, all honourable men,—
Come I to speak in Caesar's funeral.
He was my friend, faithful and just to me:
But Brutus says he was ambitious;
And Brutus is an honourable man.
He hath brought many captives home to Rome,
Whose ransoms did the general coffers fill:
Did this in Caesar seem ambitious?
When that the poor have cried, Caesar hath wept:
Ambition should be made of sterner stuff:
Yet Brutus says he was ambitious;
And Brutus is an honourable man.
You all did see that on the Lupercal
I thrice presented him a kingly crown,
Which he did thrice refuse: was this ambition?
Yet Brutus says he was ambitious;
And, sure, he is an honourable man.
I speak not to disprove what Brutus spoke,
But here I am to speak what I do know.
You all did love him once,—not without cause:
What cause withholds you, then, to mourn for him?
O judgement, thou art fled to brutish beasts,
And men have lost their reason!—Bear with me;
My heart is in the coffin there with Caesar,
And I must pause till it come back to me.

Source: William Shakespeare, *Julius Caesar,* in *The Complete Works of William Shakespeare* (New York: Oxford University Press, n.d.): 598.

and other researchers have used to disrupt counterarguing are relatively mild. They do not affect comprehension of a message, but only the process of counterarguing. If distractions are extreme, as in an experiment by Haaland and Venkatesan (1968), people no longer even understand the arguments in a message and are then *less* persuaded because of this failure of reception.

Recent research has shown that mild distractions increase persuasion only when counterarguing is the dominant covert response to a message (Petty, Wells, and Brock, 1976)—that is, if people would ordinarily argue against the message while they listen to it. Counterarguing is most likely to be dominant when messages are strongly opposed to subjects' initial opinions, supported by weak arguments, delivered by a low-credibility communicator, or characterized by other negative features. In contrast, when thoughts favorable to a message are dominant, distraction lessens recipients' ability to produce these favorable thoughts and thereby has the effect of *reducing* opinion change.

PERSUASION THROUGH FEAR Persuasive communications are often built around negative appeals—the communicator threatens negative consequences if his or her viewpoint is not accepted. Such appeals are, of course, common in everyday life. The image of the perpetual fires of Hell is a compelling one that conjures thoughts of hot, burning flames forever sapping the body and consuming the mind. Dante recorded his visions of such an Inferno, and these images have since fueled the sermons of many a clergyman. Other agents of socialization, including parents, have also been known to rely on scare techniques. If you suck your thumb, warts will grow on your nose. If you don't brush your teeth, they'll rot. Even as an adult, you have been admonished that speed kills, that smoking causes cancer, and if you do not have a college degree, you will not find a good job. Do such threats further the communicator's purpose or hamper it?

From the learning-theory standpoint of Carl Hovland's research group, the effects of fear were of particular interest. Fear, they believed, can motivate attitude change. Their approach, commonly known as the *fear-as-a-drive* model, pertains to situations in which a communicator arouses fear by describing threatening events and then follows the fearful message with reassuring recommendations. Mental rehearsal of these reassuring recommendations was assumed to reduce the fear and thereby reinforce the rewarding event that induced acceptance of the recommendations.

A Classic Experiment In a study on fear arousal Irving Janis and Seymour Feshbach (1953) had subjects watch a fifteen-minute illustrated lecture on dental hygiene. High-school freshman subjects saw one of three different versions of the lecture, designed to elicit either high fear, moderate fear, or low fear. The high-fear message suggested that tooth decay could spread to other parts of the body and lead to ailments such as arthritis, kidney damage, and partial blindness. In addition, the high-fear message addressed the viewer directly as "you" and featured a disturbing slide show of diseased gums and decayed teeth in vivid color. The moderate-fear message did not emphasize the sometimes dangerous side effects of tooth decay and was characterized by impersonal language and black-and-white photographs. The low-fear message used X-ray pictures and photographs of completely healthy teeth.

As expected, the strong appeal produced the greatest concern about decayed teeth and diseased gums. However, the most frightening appeal was not the most persuasive. In fact, Janis and Feshbach found that the *minimal* appeal produced the most resistance to subsequent "counterpropaganda"—a message that argues against the original recommendations. Furthermore, subjects given the low-fear message actually followed the recommendations made in the communication more closely than did those subjects given the more fear-provoking messages.

Why did Janis and Feshbach's findings fail to support their hypothesis that more fear should produce more attitude change? Apparently, a high level of fear caused their subjects to avoid thinking about the recommendations in order to minimize reminders of the fearful communication. This avoidance reaction is

Dante's *Inferno,* which urges its readers to lead virtuous lives, is a classic example of persuasion through fear. Here, Dante and Vergil, his guide, visit the Ninth Circle of Hell, where traitors and people who have committed violence against family members are doomed to spend eternity frozen up to their faces in ice. *(Culver Pictures)*

likely to occur if the recommendations in a message seem inadequate to deal with the dangers described. Perhaps Janis and Feshbach's subjects realized that toothbrushing is a weak measure for dealing with tooth decay, which is often caused by poor diet, genetic factors, and inadequate childhood exposure to fluoride.

Fear Arousal and the Parallel Response Model
Subsequent research has shown that the generality of Janis and Feshbach's finding that minimal fear is more persuasive than higher levels of fear is somewhat limited. As Howard Leventhal's review of this research literature (1970) suggested, it is more common for studies to find that the *more* fear-inducing a communication, the *more* attitude change it produces.

In an effort to improve on the learning-theory approach, Leventhal (1970) proposed what he termed a *parallel response* model. This approach suggests that fear communications produce two parallel and relatively independent reactions: *fear control* and *danger control.* Thus, message recipients are motivated to contain and reduce their fear (fear control) as well as to cope with the danger described in the message (danger control).

Fear control should be understood as an

emotional process. In contrast, with danger control people function as problem solvers—they think about the dangers described in the message and assess the resources they have available for avoiding these dangers. The information in the message is processed as part of this rational, problem-solving process of danger control. Accepting the message's recommendations is an aspect of danger control, provided that the message describes an appropriate way of dealing with the dangers.

The parallel response theory does not claim that the emotional reaction of fear is the cause of attitude change, as the fear-as-a-drive approach did. Rather, fear control and danger control are regarded as parallel and contemporaneous. Under some circumstances, however, there may be some relation between fear control and danger control. Especially with serious threats that elicit strong emotional responses and strong coping reactions, one type of reaction may delay or interfere with the other. A very strong, immediate emotional reaction to a message may delay or interfere with coping behavior. Such people may be "frozen" or "paralyzed" by fear and therefore temporarily unable to cope with the danger that was described. In the classic Janis and Feshbach study, the strong emotional reactions elicited by the strong fear appeal may have interfered with subjects' coping with the dangers that were described. In contrast, strong coping behavior may delay or interfere with emotional responses. Such people may be so busy coping with danger, as in a potential automobile accident, that they experience a flood of fear only after the danger is averted. As Leventhal (1970) has shown, the parallel response model is consistent with many findings in the fear-appeal research literature. Also, the approach's emphasis on persuasion as part of a danger-control process illustrates yet another effort to understand persuasion in terms of information processing.

MESSAGE CONTENT IN THE PETER REILLY CASE

It is fair to say that Peter Reilly was subjected to considerable fear arousal as the police tried to persuade him of his guilt. At the same time, Peter was told exactly what he could do to relieve the fear—confess. Also the subjective probability and relevance of confession to fear reduction were directly manipulated by the police.

Peter protests that he is sure he didn't kill his mother, and Sergeant Kelly replies, "I think you're so ashamed of last night, you're just trying to block it out of your mind." Kelly then threatens with a variety of fears unless Peter confesses: "As long as you don't get this straightened out, you'll never have a day of peace. . . . Your so goddamed ashamed of it, you're afraid to come out with it. . . . So how are we going to resolve this? Do you want me to start yelling at you? . . . Peter, you're ashamed, and you're afraid you'd go into a mental hospital. . . . You're afraid we're going to lock you up and throw away the key."

Kelly then implies that if Peter confesses, after just three months of psychiatric treatment Peter may be free: "Three months out of your life . . . that's not a very long time. It is not the end of the world." Finally Peter breaks, "I want to tell you how I did it now. But I'm still not sure I did do it."

THE MEDIUM OF COMMUNICATION

Persuasive communications are delivered by means of a medium or channel of transmission. The communications may be written, oral, or nonverbal (if conveyed through gestures and facial expressions), and may be transmitted through such mass media as television, radio, newspapers, and magazines. As early as the 1930s researchers have examined the effects of communication media on the persuasiveness of messages. For example, Hadley Cantril and Gordon Allport wrote a book in 1935 entitled *The Psychology of Radio*. Findings have not proven especially consistent, but overall live or videotaped messages have tended to induce greater opinion change than oral or audiotape messages, which, in turn, are more persuasive than written messages. Despite these findings, researchers have not examined in much detail why communication media differ in persuasive power. The reason for this lack of attention seems to be that most of the attitude-change theories that have been popular since the 1950s have not been very useful for understanding media effects.

An exception is William McGuire's (1972) sequential processing theory, which, as noted early in the chapter, emphasizes reception and yielding to information. McGuire's emphasis on reception is interesting in light of research on the best media for presenting difficult or complicated messages. Whereas oral presentations are generally more persuasive than written messages, this is not the case when the material is difficult to understand. If reception is a mediator of persuasion, and if difficult material is easier to receive in writing than orally, then written messages should be more persuasive for difficult material. However, when material is easy to understand, the more usual superiority of oral messages should be found.

In a recent study confirming the importance of reception processes, Shelly Chaiken and Alice Eagly (1976) exposed subjects to either an easy-to-understand message or a difficult-to-understand message. These messages were written, audiotaped, or videotaped. With difficult material, reception appeared to play an important role. Comprehension of difficult material was better for the written message than for the videotaped or audiotaped messages, and consequently the written message was more persuasive. With easy material, comprehension was equivalent for the three communication media, and persuasion was greatest when the message was videotaped, moderate when audiotaped, and least when written.

Why should live or videotaped messages be generally more persuasive than written messages? Perhaps the communicator's identity is more salient when physical appearance and nonverbal behaviors are visible. Assuming that most studies have used communicators with likable and positive images, videotaped or live messages would gain persuasiveness because of the greater salience of the communicator. Supporting this idea is recent research by Virginia Andreoli and Stephen Worchel (1978). Their study varied communicators' trustworthiness. They found that trustworthy communicators were much more effective than untrustworthy communicators with a "television" presentation, whereas the differences between media were much smaller with a "radio" and a written presentation.

The persuasiveness of communication media is also a product of the history of use of the various mass media in a society. Are television news reports generally seen as more objective in America, where they are produced by independent networks, or in Europe, where they are under state control but free of private interests? Are newspapers considered more or less trustworthy than television and radio? In natural settings, then, different media have acquired different reputations concerning reliability and trustworthiness in relation to content of varying types. Acquired reputation no doubt has a major impact on the persuasiveness of communication media in everyday life.

THE MEDIUM AND PETER REILLY Though Peter Reilly's interrogation was conducted face to face, the most persuasive information was pre-

Since the end of World War II, television has become perhaps the most persuasive medium of communication in the United States. *(© Joan Liftin / Woodfin Camp & Assoc.)*

sented electronically—through the polygraph or lie detector. Sergeant Kelly tells Peter that the polygraph machine costs $2,000 and is the best one made. When Peter asks how it works, he is told "It works on your heart. That's your conscience, right? All we're trying to do is arrive at the truth. And the truth will be on that tape." After a few test questions, when Peter is asked to lie deliberately, he is told that he's a "textbook reactor." Kelly declares that Peter's "heartbeat changes" when he's asked if he hurt his mother. "The polygraph can never be wrong," Kelly asserts, "because it's reacting to *you*." When Peter swears that he doesn't remember hurting his mother, Kelly contends, "The charts don't say that . . . that shows me from your heart that you hurt your mother last night." Gradually Peter concedes. "I know consciously I didn't do it. Subconsciously, I don't know."

CHARACTERISTICS OF THE AUDIENCE

In most persuasion settings, members of the audience differ in their reactions to communications. It is not surprising that reactions to communications are usually highly variable since people differ in their past experiences in relation to topics, communications, and the contexts in which influence is exerted. These differing experiences lay the groundwork for the differing reactions.

The term *persuasibility* is often used to refer to individual differences in reactions to persuasive messages. One of the interesting questions about persuasibility is whether some individuals are generally more persuadable or less persuadable than others, regardless of content, communicator, medium, or any other aspect of persuasion settings. In one early study conducted by Hovland and his colleagues (Hovland and Janis, 1959), subjects received several different types of persuasive communications. The researchers found a small but consistent tendency for persuasibility to be positively correlated across the various communications. They concluded that to a moderate extent persuasibility is a personality trait manifested across a wide variety of settings. For the next few years, researchers tried to identify personality traits associated with persuasibility, but with limited success, as discussed in the next section.

EFFECT OF PERSONALITY TRAITS ON PERSUASIBILITY Research on personality and persuasibility initially focused on personality traits such as self-esteem and anxiety as influencing an individual's response to persuasive messages. However, as noted in reviews of this area (Eagly, 1980; McGuire, 1968), findings have tended to be inconsistent. Consider the case of self-esteem. Persons with high self-esteem have proven to be less influenced than persons with low self-esteem in many persuasion studies, yet in other studies they have turned out to be more persuaded than those with low self-esteem. Still other studies find persons with medium self-esteem to be most affected, though at least one study found the opposite—that medium-self-esteem persons are the least affected by persuasive messages.

What is going on here? Because of the diversity of findings relating self-esteem and other personality traits to persuasibility, recent research has tried to specify the conditions that mediate the effects of personality traits on persuasibility. For example, William McGuire argued that both message reception (attention and comprehension) and yielding are important in understanding how personality traits affect attitude change. Often, persons high in self-esteem may be better able to *receive* messages (because they tend to be more competent and verbally skilled), but persons low in self-esteem are more likely to *yield* to the message (because they lack confidence). Therefore, knowing how a personality trait such as self-esteem will affect opinion change requires knowing whether reception processes or yielding processes or both will determine persuasibility in a given situation.

Research on audience characteristics has suffered from many of the same problems encountered in early research on how attitudes affect behaviors. As noted in Chapter 4, attitude researchers once expected general attitudes to show strong relationships to specific behaviors. Persuasibility researchers evidently hoped that general personality traits such as self-esteem would have a strong impact on how people

DISPOSITIONS AND SITUATIONS

ARE WOMEN MORE PERSUASIBLE THAN MEN?

For years social psychology textbooks informed their readers that women were more easily influenced than men. The reason was that women were thought to be socialized into a sex role that emphasized "passivity and yielding" while men were taught to be "independent thinkers." Is this true?

Alice Eagly (1978) set out to verify this widely accepted "finding." First, she noted that most writers who make this claim about women's greater persuasibility refer to the same few experiments as evidence. Yet when Eagly surveyed research articles in all social psychology journals over the past three decades that reported sex differences in influenceability, she found little support for the claim. For example, out of 62 published articles on persuasibility, 82 percent reported no differences between men and women; and out of 61 articles on group pressure and conformity, 62 percent reported no difference.

What about the minority of these studies that do report women to be more influenceable than men? Eagly has two important observations: first, most of these were published prior to 1970 and the rise of the women's movement; second, most of these also employed topics on which males were generally more knowledgeable than women, such as political and economic matters. Interestingly, in one experiment that varied the nature of the persuasive material (Sistrunk and McDavid, 1971), women were found to be more conforming than men in their responses on a "masculine" task. Yet on a "feminine" task (such as nutrition or food preparation), men were found to be more conforming than women. Thus, Eagly concludes that the minority of studies which did find women to be more persuasible than men were influenced by the historical context of the research as well as the content of the persuasive messages.

One other point is worth considering. Although the majority of studies on group pressure and conformity found women to be no more conforming than men, a sizable minority of 38 percent did find women to be more influenceable than males. Yet these group-pressure situations may be a special case. For example, considerable research (see Deaux, 1976) suggests that women in groups are more oriented toward interpersonal goals than males. As a result, women are often more accommodating in groups in order to maintain positive social relationships with their partners. Thus, in the minority of group-pressure studies where women were more conforming than males, they may not have actually been persuaded by the group but were merely responding in a cooperative way in order to facilitate the group process.

Overall, then, there is little evidence for the often-reported "finding" that women are more persuasible than men. What accounts for the prevalence of this stereotype? Eagly suggests that the stereotype may reflect a reality that existed prior to 1970; and to the extent that it is still accepted, it may represent a "cultural lag." Furthermore, the stereotype may be based on observations made in day-to-day family and work settings, where women have traditionally been placed in subordinate roles and where they may have behaved in an accommodating way for the sake of group harmony. Finally, the appearance of this stereotype in psychology textbooks may reflect a tendency on the part of textbook writers (often male) to select citations from the available research that support their own biases.

react to particular persuasive messages. Such specific behaviors are not usually much affected by very general personality traits, however, just as specific behaviors are not usually affected very strongly by general attitudes. Thus, one good approach to improving prediction in persuasibility research would be to use *multiple-act criteria* in assessing persuasibility. This approach was noted in Chapter 4's discussion of the attitude-behavior problem. General personality traits, such as self-esteem, should predict a general class of behaviors more effectively than single specific behaviors. Unfortunately, most studies of personality and persuasibility have measured attitude change by means of a single behavior or a very small set of questionnaire responses.

Another useful direction in persuasibility research would be to consider situational variables along with personality. This approach is similar to the "other variables" approach that provides a method of improving attitude-behavior predictions. From this perspective, a personality variable should be employed as a predictor along with aspects of the communicator, the message, or the medium of communication. For example, the effects of self-esteem on persuasibility would depend on situational variables such as the favorability of the information that is presented. High-self-esteem persons are especially persuaded by information with favorable implications for themselves, and low-self-esteem persons by information with unfavorable implications for themselves (Leventhal and Perloe, 1962). One promising approach, then, to understanding the effects of audience characteristics is to consider how these dispositional variables interact with features of the situational context to affect the audience's past history or "frame of reference," as discussed in the next section.

FRAMES OF REFERENCE AS AUDIENCE CHARACTERISTICS Consider a situation in which two people judge the temperature of a pail of water. The actual temperature is, say, 65 degrees. The measure of beliefs about the water temperature is simple. Each person is instructed to put his or her hand in the water and report whether the water is either very cold, cold, moderately cold, moderately warm, warm, or very warm. One individual reports that the water is moderately warm, and the other says it is moderately cold. Prior to putting their hands in the water, the person who thought the water rather warm had stuck her hand in 30-degree water, and the person who thought the water rather cold had stuck his hand into 120-degree water. The two individuals had thereby acquired different frames of reference, and consequently their judgments were affected. Unless researchers know the frames of reference people use, the researchers are not aware of the judgmental predispositions that affect individuals' reactions.

In the final book produced by the Yale attitude-change program—a volume entitled *Social Judgment* (1961)—Muzafer Sherif and Carl Hovland showed that the same message from a communicator will not be perceived the same way by all who are exposed to it. Just as prior experience with hot or cold water affects judgments of water temperature, people judge incoming messages on the basis of their prior experience with related topics.

As explained in Chapter 4, an individual's prior experience with an attitude object can be summarized in terms of his or her attitude toward that object. The attitude is a summary of the evaluative aspects of an individual's beliefs about the attitude object and of the evaluative implications of the individual's own behaviors in relation to the attitude object. When an attitude is firmly held, it may provide the individual with a reference point or interval anchor for judging related content. Thus, if worship of (a positive attitude toward) a wrathful God who punishes sinners is central to a person's thinking, that person may disapprove of things as diverse as coffee, card playing, and the writings of Shakespeare.

Sherif and Hovland suggested that an individual's attitudes in a particular domain can be represented as a psychological reference scale. Figure 5.3 shows a reference scale of attitudes toward prohibition. Note that this scale is a series of belief statements located at differing points along the attitude continuum and is therefore similar to the Thurstone scale described in Chapter 4. Each individual's preferred attitudinal position can be located at some point on the reference scale and constitutes an anchor in relation to which other attitudinal positions are judged. Although people generally find one position on the scale that is most acceptable, they can usually agree with other positions as well. The statements on the reference scale that are acceptable to an indi-

FIGURE 5.3 Sherif and Hovland (1961) used this reference scale for assessing subjects' frames of reference on the issue of alcoholic-beverage prohibition.

(A) Since alcohol is the curse of mankind, the sale and use of alcohol, including light beer, should be completely abolished.

(B) Since alcohol is the main cause of corruption in public life, lawlessness, and immoral acts, its sale and use should be prohibited.

(C) Since it is hard to stop at a reasonable moderation point in the use of alcohol, it is safer to discourage its use.

(D) Alcohol should not be sold or used except as a remedy for snake bites, cramps, colds, fainting, and other aches and pains.

(E) The arguments in favor of and against the sale and use of alcohol are nearly equal.

(F) The sale of alcohol should be so regulated that it is available in limited quantities for special occasions.

(G) The sale and use of alcohol should be permitted with proper state controls, so that the revenue from taxation may be used for the betterment of schools, highways, and other state institutions.

(H) Since prohibition is a major cause of corruption in public life, lawlessness, immoral acts, and juvenile delinquency, the sale and use of alcohol should be legalized.

(I) It has become evident that man cannot get along without alcohol; therefore there should be no restriction whatsoever on its sale and use.

vidual fall within a range that Sherif and Hovland termed the *latitude of acceptance*, and the statements that are not acceptable fall within a *latitude of rejection*. Statements that are neither acceptable nor unacceptable fall within a *latitude of noncommitment*. Sherif and Hovland, with their colleagues, have studied the ways in which such personal reference scales reflect what is and is not acceptable to people. Consider the following study.

Alcohol was still prohibited in public places in Oklahoma in 1959. A referendum was held then to enable Oklahoma to remain dry or to join the rest of the nation in legalizing liquor. During the campaign preceding the referendum, Carl Hovland, O. J. Harvey, Muzafer Sherif (1957) selected from newspapers both favorable and unfavorable arguments regarding prohibition. From this lengthy set of statements, judges chose the nine statements listed in Figure 5.3 as being representative of the controversy. These statements ranged from very much opposed to the sale of liquor—the "dry" position—to very much in favor of the sale of liquor—the "wet" position.

The researchers instructed subjects to read the nine items and to indicate which were acceptable and which were not acceptable. Researchers found that the latitude of rejection for people with the most extreme view—either for or against prohibition—was greater than for those who held more moderate views. Furthermore, when a person was subsequently presented with an additional statement that was relatively moderate but nevertheless opposed to his or her position, that person tended to judge the statement as being more extreme than did other persons. For example, when subjects heard a moderately wet speech, those who adhered to the driest position judged the speech as being much wetter than did subjects who agreed with the speaker's stand. Therefore, whether the stimulus is a pail of water or a speech, judgments are highly dependent on the frame of reference that is provided by one's own position on an issue.

The persuasiveness of a message depends on where it falls along an individual's own latitude of acceptance and rejection. According to Hovland and Sherif, when communications fall within an individual's latitude of acceptance, they cause opinion to change toward the message. Within this latitude of acceptance, the greater the *discrepancy* or distance between the recipient's initial position and the position advocated by the message, the greater will be the attitude change. However, when communications fall within an individual's latitude of rejection, Hovland and Sherif expected very little attitude change. As communications become increasingly discrepant within the latitude of rejection, they would be easily dismissed as too extreme to be given serious consideration, and attitude change would decrease.

Several studies have examined the persuasiveness of a message as a function of its discrepancy from recipients' initial opinions. For example, Bochner and Insko (1966) exposed subjects to a message advocating that for "maximum health and well-being" people should get eight, seven, six, five, four, three, two, one, zero hours of sleep per night. The communication was attributed either to Sir John Eccles, Nobel prizewinning physiologist, or to Mr. Harry J. Olsen, director of the Fort Worth YMCA. Subjects' opinions about sleep are shown in Figure 5.4 as a function of the communicator's identity and the discrepancy between subjects' initial opinions (that eight hours of sleep are desirable) and the communicator's opinion. As the figure indicates, communications that are distant from subjects' opinions were less persuasive than those that were closer, especially when the source of the communication was the YMCA director, who had only moderate credibility. Thus, communications that fall within a person's latitude of acceptance are more persuasive than communications that fall within the latitude of rejection. Furthermore, as demonstrated by Bochner and Insko, the width of an individual's latitude of acceptance or rejection is affected by communicator credibility and other aspects of the situation.

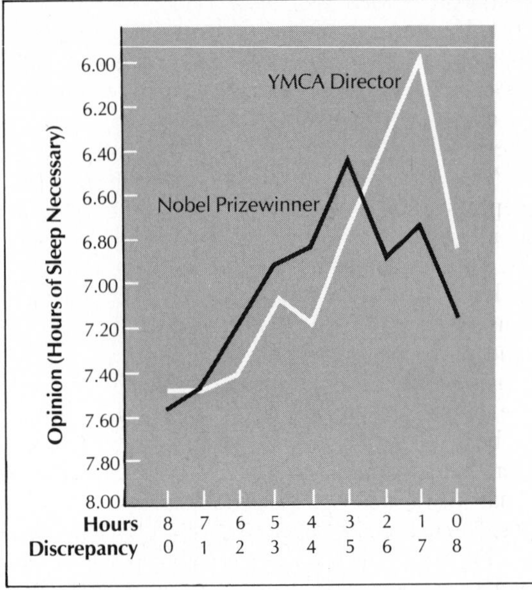

FIGURE 5.4 Bochner and Insko (1966) examined the relation between opinion change and how discrepant messages about sleep were from subjects' existing opinions. When the communicator was a Nobel prizewinner, more opinion change was obtained at the larger discrepancies than it was when the communicator was a YMCA director.

AUDIENCE CHARACTERISTICS IN THE PETER REILLY CASE We have discussed two audience characteristics that affect persuasibility: personality traits and frames of reference (latitudes of acceptance or rejection). Each of these might have had some influence on Peter's yielding to the police. Though we don't know much about Peter's personality, friends described him as easygoing, friendly, and funny. A neighbor who heard of Peter's arrest said that "he didn't have a mean bone in his body." Even his interrogator, Sergeant Kelly, described Peter as "very cooperative." A chilling example of Peter's cooperativeness is seen in the following response to Kelly's questioning: "If I did it, I don't remember it. What I told you is exactly how I remember it. Is there any way they can kind of pound it out of me? To find out if I did it? I mean dig deeper into me?" Perhaps it was Peter's trusting, cooperative personality that made him so susceptible to the police tactics of persuasion.

Peter's frame of reference and latitude of acceptance may have also been altered through the interrogation. Although Peter started out with a firm belief in his own innocence, the police led Peter to doubt his own innocence. In terms of the research discussed above, Peter's frame of reference toward himself was changed from innocence to potential guilt and his latitude of acceptance thus expanded to include the belief that he himself might be the murderer. For example, when Peter is first asked if he has any doubts about his innocence, he replies, "If I had any doubts, I'd try to help myself. I'd see a doctor." Later when Kelly tells Peter the polygraph is never wrong, Peter says, "This test is giving me doubt right now. Disregarding the test, I still don't think I hurt my mother." Still later Peter says, "I want to tell you I did it now. But I'm still not sure I did do it." Finally, Peter is convinced. "I don't remember doing the things that happened. I believe I did it now."

Peter Reilly's case vividly demonstrates how persuasive communications can change beliefs and attitudes—even a belief as important as one's own innocence or guilt. Subtle factors associated with the source, medium, content, and audience of the communication were all influential. In the next section we turn to the issue of self-persuasion, and we will see how Peter may have been led to convince himself of his own guilt.

ATTITUDE CHANGE THROUGH SELF-PERSUASION

When we want to change someone's mind about something, it is natural to think first of persuasive arguments as the most likely method. If we can only talk to the people whose minds we wish to change, we may be able to convince them through reason and understanding. However, you know from past experience that persuasion is often not easily accomplished; voters are unaware of their long-term interests, parents intransigent, lovers unsympathetic. All our attempts at persuasion are of no avail. As this chapter has noted, people are often able to resist changing because they have counterarguments available. Moreover, as persuasability research has suggested, some people may even be chronically resistant to persuasion of all types. Barring an easy victory through persuasion, then, it is frequently worthwhile to utilize self-persuasion techniques. If the individual whose mind you desire to change can be induced to advocate the desired point of view, he or she may become quite accepting of the viewpoint, surprising even himself or herself.

Counterattitudinal advocacy—advocating a position opposed to one's initial attitude—has generated an enormous amount of research over the past twenty-five years. Why should arguing against your own position produce such an unexpected reversal of opinion? What conditions are necessary to create this effect? There will be much to say about these issues later. But first let us consider some of the earliest research to demonstrate the dramatic effectiveness of self-persuasion techniques. This research focused on role playing and its consequences.

ROLE PLAYING AND ATTITUDE CHANGE

People are more likely to believe what they hear when they hear their own voices saying it. Egocentric as such findings may seem, people are very often more persuaded by themselves than by other people. Irving Janis and Bert King (1954) demonstrated this tendency by comparing subjects' response to messages that subjects themselves had delivered versus messages delivered by other people. Subjects were run in groups of three, and each subject gave the other two subjects an informal talk based on a prepared outline. Subjects were instructed to give their talks as a sincere advocate of the point of view represented in the outline. Subjects changed more toward the advocated position when they actively participated in the communication than when they passively listened to it.

ACTIVE PARTICIPATION AND ROLE PLAYING There are many possible interpretations of why Janis and King's role-playing subjects manifested greater attitude change than the passive listeners. Perhaps in order to comply with the experimenter's request to play an active role, the subjects found it necessary to improvise arguments and thereby may have tailored their arguments to be especially effective for themselves. On the other hand, subjects' feelings of satisfaction from having performed competently as a communicator may have reinforced the ideas they communicated. Thus the content of the message may have been more associated with rewards in the active condition than in the passive condition.

To clarify these issues, Bert King and Irving Janis (1956) carried out a second experiment in which they varied (1) the degree to which subjects improvised arguments, and (2) the degree to which subjects felt satisfied with their performance. All subjects first read a completely prepared script silently to themselves. Then subjects either read aloud from the script, a task that required no improvisation, or talked extemporaneously without being allowed to refer to the script, a task that demanded considerable improvisation in presenting the arguments. The experimenters also varied the satisfaction of the subjects who were required to improvise by giving the subjects either favorable or unfavorable ratings of their speeches.

Improvisation had a major impact on attitude change. Among the subjects who improvised, 87.5 percent showed overall opinion change in the direction advocated in the talk, whereas among the subjects who read from the script, only 54.4 percent changed toward the advocated position. Although subjects' attitudes were not affected by the experimenter's evaluation of their performance, other research has shown that opinion change can be affected by such feedback. The experiment did demonstrate, though, that role playing is a more effective attitude-change technique when people have to improvise their own arguments.

Anthony Greenwald (1969, 1970) argued that a major reason why role players change more toward the positions they advocate is that they are open-minded to information opposing their initial views but supporting their anticipated roles. Especially if a person has to make up his or her own arguments, role-supporting information is quite useful. Even *expecting* to play a role causes subjects to yield to role-supporting information, provided that they had not already considered and rejected this information.

The findings of these and other studies suggest that communicators can increase the effectiveness of messages by enlisting the active participation of the audience, especially if this participation requires audience members to improvise relevant arguments on their own. Commercial jingles that viewers repeat to themselves long after the commercials are over capitalize on the power of active participation. Yet the most effective version of this technique evidently requires not rote repetition, but adding something of one's own. It is interesting that religions often involve ceremonies requiring improvisation—for example, silent prayer after unison repetition of standard prayers, and, especially in evangelical Christian groups, testimonies to the congregation about one's own personal religious experiences. Groups committed to behavior change, such as Weight Watchers and Alcoholics Anonymous, also make extensive use of personal testimony in their programs, as do certain group-therapy programs such as Est.

EMOTIONAL ROLE PLAYING Research on role playing has demonstrated many times that people tend to believe their own performances. One study is especially noteworthy, though, because it dealt with people's attitudes and behaviors toward a real-world dilemma, cigarette smoking. Quitting smoking is almost always difficult, yet Irving Janis and Leon Mann (1965) achieved dramatic results by forcing smokers who could not stop on their own to confront their smoking problem in a personal way. The smokers had to role-play the traumatic experience of being told by their doctor they had lung cancer. Janis and Mann referred to this particularly vivid role-playing procedure as *emotional role playing*.

All twenty-six women that Janis and Mann selected as subjects were between the ages of

The active involvement of an audience can increase the persuasiveness of a message. Personal testimony in groups such as this evangelical Christian congregation is an especially effective form of audience participation. *(© Charles Harbutt / Magnum)*

eighteen and twenty-six and were moderate to heavy smokers, consuming at least fifteen cigarettes daily. After the experimenters assessed their subjects' attitudes toward smoking, they assigned some women to role-play a cancer victim and asked others to passively listen to a tape recording of a role-playing subject. Each woman was asked to imagine that the experimenter was a doctor to whom she had gone for treatment of a bad cough. The scenes to be enacted occurred during the woman's third visit to the doctor, when she received the results of the X-ray and other medical tests. The experimenters gave each woman in the role-playing group the following five scenes and asked each to act out the scenes as realistically as she could.

SCENE 1: *Soliloquy in waiting room.*
A woman is worried about her diagnosis and experiences conflict about whether or not to smoke another cigarette.

SCENE 2: *Conversation with physician as he gives diagnosis.*
The experimenter tells the woman that he will be frank and honest and unfortunately has bad news. She has a small malignant mass just under the right lung (shows actual X-ray) and an operation is needed as soon as possible. There is a moderate possibility of successful surgery.

SCENE 3: *Soliloquy while physician phones for hospital bed.*
The woman expresses her feelings about the bad news.

SCENE 4: *Conversation with physician about arrangements for hospitalization.*
The physician asks the woman for information about medical coverage and family background and tells her that she will be in the hospital about six weeks.

SCENE 5: *Conversation about causes of lung cancer.*

> Physician talks about the patient's smoking history and asks if she is aware of the link between smoking and lung cancer. He discusses the urgent need to stop smoking.

The experiment was powerful. The role-playing experience not only changed attitudes, but also influenced subjects to decrease their cigarette smoking. Specifically, role-playing subjects changed more than passive subjects toward (1) believing that smoking causes lung cancer, (2) fearing personal harm from smoking, and (3) intending to quit smoking. Also, when asked two weeks later about their smoking habits, subjects who had played the role reported smoking an average of 10.5 fewer cigarettes per day than they had been two weeks earlier (down from 24.1 to 13.6 cigarettes, on the average). In contrast, the drop in cigarette consumption among subjects who had not played the role was only 4.8 cigarettes, or less than half the drop reported by the role players. Apparently, the vivid personal experience of role playing goaded Janis and Mann's subjects into greater vigilance in curbing their smoking.

And the results lasted. Janis and Mann conducted their original sessions in July 1963. Two follow-up surveys of the same women were made in March 1964 and in January 1965 (Mann and Janis, 1968). In addition to the group that had played the role and the group that had not, a third group of women from the same school, a control group, had received no treatment—neither role playing nor tape recordings. Follow-up interviews of the women in all three groups were conducted by telephone, so that these women were divorced from the original experimental setting. The smoking patterns of the three groups during the eighteen months that followed the role playing are shown in Figure 5.5. In all three groups, cigarette consumption dropped approximately five cigarettes daily per subject after the Surgeon General's Report linking smoking to lung cancer was published in February 1964. Yet the effects of role playing persisted for at least eighteen months. At the end of that time, role-playing subjects were smoking as many cigarettes per day as they had been just after the role-playing experience. The Surgeon General's Report apparently reinforced the effects of the role playing and kept cigarette consumption at relatively low levels. The effects of the government warning were most enduring for subjects who had played the role; these effects dissipated somewhat for subjects who had listened to the recording of a role-playing subject; and the effects dissipated completely for the control subjects, who had received no treatment. These findings provide dramatic evidence that role playing can have powerful effects on behaviors as difficult to modify as smoking behavior.

ROLE PLAYING AND PETER REILLY Similar dramatic effects of role playing are seen in the Peter Reilly case. After the police convince Peter that he has doubts about his innocence and that it will feel good to confess, they begin feeding him details of the crime and asking him to improvise how he might have done it. For example, consider the following dialogue, from the actual tape transcripts of Peter's interrogation:

> KELLY: Last night the animal instinct took over. And you fought back to protect yourself.
> PETER: Maybe I'm imagining it, but it seems to be coming out.
> KELLY: How does the straight razor come in?
> PETER: I don't know. I may be imagining it, slashing at her throat with a straight razor.
> KELLY: Did you step on her legs or something? While she was on the floor. And jump up and down?
> PETER: I could have. . . . You just say it, then I imagine I'm doing it.
> KELLY: Let's run through the whole thing again.

An important implication of the role-playing technique is that attitude change may *follow* behavior change. This contrasts with the conventional wisdom that attitudes must change *before* behavior can be expected to change. For example, the conventional wisdom was often invoked in the 1950s and early 1960s by white segregationists when they advocated delaying integration. It was claimed that integration should not proceed too quickly—before whites' attitudes toward blacks had become more favorable. In contrast to this perspective, role-playing research suggests that social change

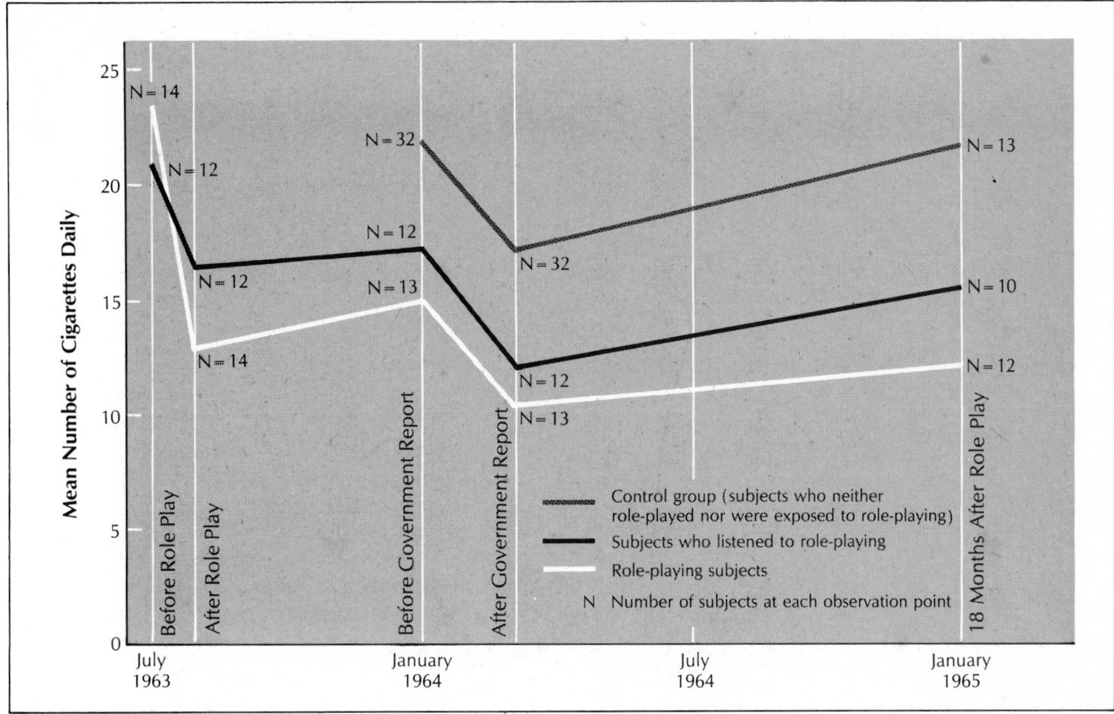

FIGURE 5.5 Mann and Janis (1968) showed that playing the role of a cancer victim can reduce cigarette consumption. While the 1964 Surgeon General's report on the harmful effects of smoking caused short-term reduction of smoking among all three groups studied, long-term results were most pronounced in the role-playing group.

may be hastened by inducing people to adopt socially desired behaviors, regardless of unchanged attitudes. In fact, legislating desegregation may have had a more powerful impact on prejudiced racial attitudes than would have been achieved by even the most extensive information campaign aimed at persuading people. Inducing desired behaviors can be a powerful attitude-change technique, but, as discussed in the next section, it is not always effective. Some of the conditions when it is most effective are described below in the discussion of dissonance theory and counterattitudinal advocacy.

COGNITIVE DISSONANCE AND COUNTERATTITUDINAL ADVOCACY

One interpretation of the success of counterattitudinal role playing in changing attitudes is that role playing arouses *cognitive dissonance*, which is then reduced through attitude change.

But in order to understand how dissonance theory pertains to role playing, it is helpful to know a little more about the theory itself. In 1957 Leon Festinger published *A Theory of Cognitive Dissonance*, in which he laid out the rudimentary aspects of the theory. Attitudes and/or beliefs (Festinger called them *cognitive elements*) are in a state of dissonance with one another if one implies the opposite of the other. Such is the case, for example, when a student goes to the movies even though he or she feels obligated to study for an exam being given the next morning. These cognitions are considered dissonant because going to the movies implies having no obligation to study—the opposite of having to study.

The basic premise of dissonance theory is

that discrepant cognitions produce an uncomfortable psychological state called dissonance that people are motivated to reduce or eliminate. In his original statement, Festinger proposed that individuals have at their command three ways of reducing dissonance.

1. These persons may change their cognitions regarding their own behavior—that is, reinterpret their actions so that the actions become consistent with their attitudes and previous actions. In the movie example, the student might come to perceive the movies as a short "break" in a long evening of study.
2. They may change their cognitions regarding the environment—in other words, change attitudes and beliefs about aspects of the environment. In the movie example, the student might decide that the exam will be so easy that no studying is needed.
3. They may add new, consonant cognitive elements. This procedure cannot eliminate dissonance entirely, but it can swamp the dissonant elements with consonant cognitions and thereby diminish the effects of the dissonant elements. In the movie example, the student might come to believe that going to the movie was necessary, despite the upcoming exam, because the movie was truly exceptional, was being shown for the last time that night, would be especially entertaining and educational, and a good friend who was going really hated to go alone, and so on.

Which resolution is chosen in a given situation? Not surprisingly, the resolution depends on the circumstances. Dissonance theorists have been particularly interested in exploring circumstances, such as counterattitudinal role playing, in which individuals are required to behave in a way that is inconsistent or dissonant with their previous behaviors and attitudes. In such circumstances, people are unlikely to change their cognitions regarding their own behavior. It is simply too difficult to change or deny the facts of what one has done, particularly if the behavior is recent and is unambiguous in meaning. Also, because adding consonant elements does not completely eliminate the dissonance, people tend to use this form of resolution only

Aesop's fable of the fox and the grapes illustrates an important principle of dissonance theory: when people experience dissonance, they tend to change their attitude toward the object that is responsible for the dissonance. The fox wants to sample the luscious grapes hanging on the vine. He cannot reach them, however, so he decides that they are unappetizing.

when they cannot reduce dissonance through one of the other methods. Therefore, the form of dissonance reduction that occurs most often in such circumstances is changing one's cognitions regarding the environment. In other words, when people experience dissonance, they typically change their attitude toward whatever object in the environment that is causing the dissonance. It is in this sense, then, that dissonance theory evolved into an effective theory of attitude change. For example, Festinger (1957) gave a dissonance-theory interpretation to Janis and King's findings on the effects of role playing on attitude change. Role-playing subjects, Festinger argued, would have found it dissonant to publicly say things they did not believe. Therefore they came to believe the communications they delivered.

Research on cognitive dissonance has tried to identify the circumstances under which counterattitudinal advocacy results in attitude change toward the advocated position. In particular, dissonance research has demonstrated that when people perceive themselves as *forced* to behave publicly in ways that contradict their private beliefs, little dissonance is created and their attitudes do not change. In contrast, when people are led to engage in the same behavior, but allowed to feel that the choice was their own, dissonance is aroused. To reduce the dissonance, attitudes fall into line with actions, as shown by the following experiment.

THE $1 AND $20 EXPERIMENT One of the best-known studies in social psychology is a dissonance study conducted by Festinger and J. Merrill Carlsmith (1959). This experiment compared the amount of attitude change when subjects feel little dissonance—that is when they are *forced* to engage in a counterattitudinal behavior—versus a great deal of dissonance—that is, when they feel the behavior is freely chosen. Festinger and Carlsmith had college-student subjects spend an hour performing two very boring tasks: putting spools onto a tray and turning pegs on a board. Then each subject was requested by the experimenter to tell the next subject that the experiment had been fun and exciting. The experimenter claimed that his assistant, who was supposed to introduce the experiment to the next subject, had failed to show up. He offered the subjects money for performing this service and for being on call in the future if help was needed again. He also told them that the decision to "help out" in the experiment was up to them, though in fact it was difficult for subjects to refuse. In this and other dissonance experiments, the experimenter must apply just enough pressure so that people will comply but still feel that they have a choice. The experimenter offered half of the subjects $1 and the other half $20 for telling the next subject that the experiment was interesting (the counterattitudinal behavior).

After making this statement to the person they believed would be the next subject, the subjects were referred to an interviewer, who was supposedly associated with their introductory psychology course and not with the experiment. The subjects were asked to evaluate, among other things, the degree to which they had enjoyed the experimental tasks—that is, the tasks involving the spools and pegs. Subjects who had been paid $1 for praising the tasks reported enjoying the task *more* than did subjects who had received $20. In fact, on a scale of +5 to −5, the task was rated −.05 among subjects paid $20 and +1.35 among subjects paid only $1 (control subjects who had not told a lie at all rated the task −.45). In other words, subjects who were paid only $1 to advocate a counterattitudinal position changed more toward that position than subjects who were paid $20.

According to dissonance theory, saying something you do not believe is dissonant unless you have a good reason for doing it. Subjects paid $1 did not have a very good reason for lying about the experiment. They could not reduce dissonance by denying that they made the statement since the memory of this quite unambiguous behavior was fresh in their minds. They could not easily add consonant cognitions in terms of additional justifications because the situation did not suggest any justifications. Thus, in order to reduce dissonance, subjects paid only $1 decided that the task had not been so boring after all, and they changed their attitudes concerning the boring tasks. In contrast, subjects paid $20 were not making their counterattitudinal statements without a good reason—on the contrary, they had a very good justification (a substantial amount of money) for saying something they did not believe. Their behavior was consonant with the reward they received, and consequently there was relatively little dissonance to reduce. Festinger argued, in general, *the less the justification* (in terms of money, for example) for engaging in a counterattitudinal behavior, *the more attitude change* occurs in the direction of the behavior.

FURTHER RESEARCH ON THE EFFECTS OF MONETARY REWARD ON COUNTERATTITUDINAL ADVOCACY Notice that Festinger and Carlsmith's finding is just the opposite of what many learning theories might predict concerning attitude change. Irving Janis and his associates (for example, Elms and Janis, 1965) drew attention to the reinforcing potential of the reward in the Festinger and Carlsmith experiment and suggested that, according to learning theory, a larger monetary reward ought to bring about greater attitude change than a smaller reward. Janis's own research on this problem had a somewhat ambiguous outcome, but did show that under some circumstances monetary reward increases the attitude change that follows from counterattitudinal advocacy.

Later research has helped clarify the conditions under which findings similar to the original Festinger and Carlsmith study are obtained. In fact, later dissonance research discovered numerous limiting conditions for what is now known as the "dissonance effect"—that is, more attitude change under low- than under high-justification conditions. The theory has attempted to adjust for these limiting conditions, and continual reworking of the theory has taken place. The evolution of dissonance theory is the subject of a book by Robert Wicklund and Jack Brehm titled *Perspectives on Cognitive Dissonance* (1976).

One such limiting condition, noted earlier, is that people must feel their counterattitudinal acts are freely chosen in order to experience much dissonance (Linder, Cooper, and Jones, 1967). Evidently, people must think that they are taking personal responsibility for a dissonant action in order for attitude change to follow the action, and freedom of choice enhances the perception of personal responsibility.

In other dissonance research, the dissonance effect of more attitude change with less reward has occurred only when the counterattitudinal behavior—such as lying to the next subject—leads to adverse or unwanted consequences (for example, Cooper and Worchel, 1970). If the next subject does not seem to be convinced that the experiment will be interesting and enjoyable, people think they have done no harm. Then they experience little dissonance and little attitude change. Furthermore, the dissonance effect occurs if subjects convince a person whom they like but not if they convince a person whom they dislike (Cooper, Zanna, and Goethals, 1974). The list of these limiting conditions grows continually, but converging evidence points to the overriding importance of two limiting conditions: people must assume *personal responsibility* for the consequences of their behavior; and the consequences must be *undesired* and *unwanted.*

ALTERNATIVE DISSONANCE PARADIGMS The findings of the $1 and $20 experiment were genuine and have been confirmed repeatedly, not only by numerous close replications, but also by experiments involving quite different types of counterattitudinal behavior. The justification for engaging in counterattitudinal behavior has taken diverse forms in these experiments.

The Forbidden-Toy Experiments In one type of study, the *forbidden-toy experiments* (Aronson and Carlsmith, 1963), children are told that they should not play with a certain toy. The justification for staying away from the toy is varied. In the high-justification condition the threat is severe, and in the low-justification condition the threat is mild. In the original forbidden-toy experiment, conducted by Aronson and Carlsmith (1963), a child was first allowed to play with several toys and was then asked to rank the toys in order of preference. Next, one of the toys the child liked most was placed on a table, and the experimenter said that the child could not play with it. In the severe-threat condition, the child was told that playing with the toy would result in the experimenter being very angry and taking all of the toys away. In the mild-threat condition, the experimenter merely promised to be "annoyed" if the child disobeyed.

The experimenter then left the room, and none of the children in either the high- or low-threat condition played with the forbidden toy during this temptation period. Upon returning, the experimenter once again asked the child to rank each toy and thereby was able to find out whether the child's attitude had changed toward the forbidden toy. What does dissonance theory predict about attitude change in this case? The theory predicts that little change should occur in the severe-threat condition. The behavior of not playing with the toy is dissonant with the attitude of liking the toy. However, the severe threat provided a great deal of justification for staying away from the toy. In contrast, the mild-threat condition provided very little justification for staying away from the toy, and therefore the behavior of not playing with the toy was very dissonant with liking the toy. This dissonance could be reduced by devaluing the toy as not really very attractive or amusing. Indeed, Aronson and Carlsmith found that the children valued the prohibited toy less highly in the mild-threat condition than in the severe-threat condition (and less highly than a no-threat control group as well).

The effects of mild and severe threats in the forbidden-toy experiment have been enduring. One experiment by Jonathan Freedman (1965) varied the level of threat used to prevent children from playing with a very attractive robot toy. Even when children were brought back into the room with the robot *forty days* after receiving the threat, only 33 percent of the children in the mild-threat condition played with the robot whereas 78 percent of the children in the severe-threat condition played with the robot.

These dissonance experiments using threats as justifications embody important lessons concerning the role of force in controlling behavior. Agents of social control such as police often face a choice between using a great deal of force to obtain compliance with a rule or "keeping a low profile" by using the minimum force. The dissonance experiments suggest that long-term control of behavior is best facilitated by using the minimum amount of force that still induces compliance. Under such conditions, people are likely to change their attitudes to make them consistent with their law-abiding or rule-following behavior. Such internalized changes in attitudes increase the likelihood that future behavior will be consistent with the prevailing laws and rules even though this behavior is not under the direct surveillance of police and other agents of social control. The point is one that parents and future parents should take note of. The use of a high level of threat to induce children to obey can no doubt cause temporary compliance, but it is unlikely to encourage the internalization of parental attitudes.

Decision-Making Experiments Among the numerous additional applications of dissonance theory is a body of research pertaining to the attitudinal consequences of decision making. The question in these experiments is: What happens to our attitudes when we have to choose between two equally desirable alternatives? Festinger claimed that a decision between attractive alternatives inevitably creates dissonance. Dissonance results from losing the attractive features of the forgone alternative and having to accept the unattractive features of the chosen alternative.

In an early study of the attitudinal implications of decision making, Jack Brehm (1956) recruited female college students as subjects, ostensibly for a market-research study on product preferences. Each subject was told that she would be recompensed for her time with a gift from one of the manufacturers. Eight products, each worth between $15 and $30 (for example, a fluorescent desk lamp), were placed in front of the subjects. Each woman inspected the items and rated each item's desirability. The experimenter explained that, to insure that everyone would receive a gift she liked, each student would choose between two products. Which two a subject chose from was determined by the experimenter in such a way that either both of the products were very attractive to her (high dissonance), based on the ratings she had already completed, or one product was very attractive and the other had considerably less appeal (low dissonance). After the women had chosen their gifts, they were asked again to rate the desirability of each product. Table 5.1 shows that, as predicted, subjects who chose be-

TABLE 5.1 REEVALUATION OF PRODUCTS (BREHM)

CHOICE	CHANGES IN EVALUATION*		TOTAL DISSONANCE REDUCTION†
	CHOSEN PRODUCT	REJECTED PRODUCT	
One Attractive Product	+.11	0	.11
Two Attractive Products	+.38	−.41	.79

*The figures in the table represent the difference between a first and second rating on a scale from 1.0 (not at all desirable) to 8.0 (extremely desirable).

†Because reduction in dissonance may be accomplished both by raising the desirability of the chosen object and by lowering the desirability of the unchosen one, the totals here represent the algebraic difference in change of ratings (plus and minus signs are disregarded).

Source: Adapted from J. W. Brehm, "Postdecision Changes in the Desirability of Alternatives," *Journal of Abnormal and Social Psychology* 52 (1956): 386.

tween two attractive items experienced the greatest attitude change. They evaluated the chosen product more favorably and the nonchosen product less favorably than they had before. The subjects who chose between an attractive and an unattractive alternative showed little reevaluation of the two alternatives because they experienced little dissonance from such an easy choice. Many studies since Brehm's have confirmed the conclusion that people tend to glorify the options they choose and derogate those that they forgo. A number of these experiments are published in Festinger's *Conflict, Decision, and Dissonance* (1964). Certainly, there are many fascinating practical implications of the dissonance approach to postdecisional attitude change. Could the dissonance principle help to explain why so many colleges have loyal alumni who are convinced that their own college is the best they could have possibly attended?

PETER REILLY'S DISSONANCE On top of the other persuasion tactics employed by the police, it seems that Peter Reilly must have experienced quite a lot of cognitive dissonance. A common strategy of interrogators is to make their suspects feel guilty. Cognitions of both guilt and innocence are clearly dissonance-arousing.

In Peter's case Sergeant Kelly started with little things: "You've never done anything that you're really ashamed of in your life, have you?" Peter explains that he was once approached by a homosexual. Kelly probes further: "Besides that, anything else that you're really ashamed of?" Later Kelly moves in closer with a key question. "Have you ever hit your mother in the past?" Peter says that he threw a flashlight at her three months ago, then apologized. Kelly plants the greatest seeds of guilt when he convinces Peter that the polygraph reads his heart. At this point Peter has one cognition about his own behavior: the polygraph says he's guilty. This contrasts sharply with a second cognition about his behavior: Peter believes he didn't kill his mother. Kelly subtly redefines the accusation of murder so it's easier for Peter to accept: "You're not a criminal. You did a crazy thing. . . . I'm not saying you're nuts. You're

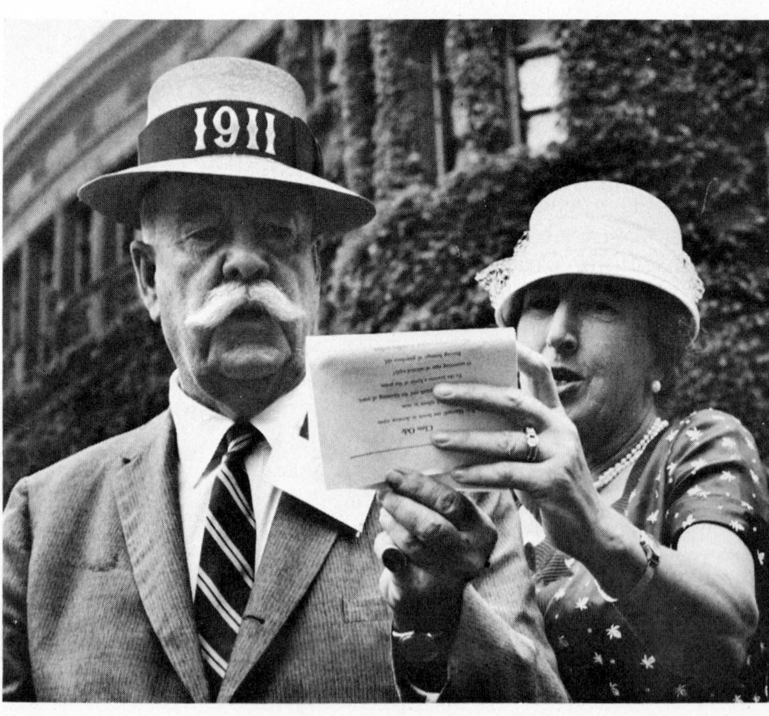

Research confirms that people tend to glorify alternatives that they have chosen and belittle those that they have rejected. Many college alumni, for example, are certain that their alma mater is the best one they could have possibly attended. *(© Inger McCabe/Rapho/Photo Researchers)*

confused. . . . Do we have a cold-blooded killer sitting here or do we have a guy with a problem that needs to be straightened out?"

How can Peter resolve the dissonance? He can't deny the polygraph evidence; as Kelly says, it's right there "in the charts." He can't add consonant elements to his belief in his own innocence because Kelly keeps refuting all Peter's protests: "There's no doubt in my mind from these charts that you did it." Finally, Peter resolves the dissonance in the only way left; he changes his attitude: "I believe I did it now."

SELF-PERCEPTION THEORY AND COUNTERATTITUDINAL ADVOCACY

An alternative to the cognitive dissonance explanation of counterattitudinal advocacy was contributed by Daryl Bem (1965), whose ideas about inferring attitudes from behaviors were introduced in Chapter 4. Bem agreed with the findings produced by dissonance theorists but challenged their theory. In particular, Bem denied the central assumption of dissonance theory—that dissonance is a state of psychological tension, which motivates attitude change. Instead, Bem reasoned from an information-processing perspective. He argued that subjects in dissonance experiments are acting as observers of their own behavior and that they simply infer their attitudes from their actions. Outside observers look at the behavior of others and judge it in relation to the circumstances in which it occurs. If observers see a cause for another person's behavior in some external circumstance, then they are not sure whether the behavior follows from the individual's attitudes and beliefs or is merely a response to the external events. However, if external causes seem to be lacking, observers are likely to interpret the behavior as a product of the individual's inner dispositions—in other words, of his or her attitudes and beliefs.

Consider the Festinger and Carlsmith experiment from the viewpoint of an observer who sees someone endure a boring task, hears that person exalt the experience to someone else, and knows that the person was paid $1 to do so. In guessing the real attitude of the subject toward the seemingly dull task, the observer can disregard the possibility of financial motivation; compensation was a mere $1. The lack of financial motivation suggests that the subject's real attitudes are responsible. In this situation, the observer will probably assume that the other person's attitudes and behavior are consistent. In contrast, if the subject has been compensated $20, the observer is likely to conclude that the financial incentive is sufficient to explain the behavior; thus, the observer would not account for the behavior on the basis of the subject's private views.

Bem suggested that people regard their own behavior much as an observer would. In the Festinger and Carlsmith $1 condition, subjects would surmise that the environment provides no sufficient incentive for their actions; their actions must reflect the subjects' true attitude toward the task, which the subjects consequently recall as more interesting than it had seemed at an earlier point. In this way, according to Bem, subjects changed their attitudes, not to reduce an unpleasant motivational state, but as an integral part of inferring their attitudes from their behaviors and the circumstances in which these behaviors occurred.

To support this line of reasoning, Bem (1967) replicated the Festinger and Carlsmith study with subjects serving as observers rather than as counterattitudinal advocators. The observer subjects heard a tape recording of a college sophomore, Bob Downing, stating that he had participated in an experiment involving two motor tasks, which he described, just like those in the Festinger and Carlsmith experiment. Control subjects then rated Bob's attitude toward the task. The experimental subjects were told that Bob had accepted an offer of either $1 or $20 to tell the next subject that the tasks had been fun. The observer subjects then heard Bob telling a young woman in the waiting room that the tasks had been fun and enjoyable. When Bem had his observer subjects estimate Bob's attitude toward the tasks, their estimates were nearly identical to the evaluations of the tasks that Festinger and Carlsmith's role-playing subjects had given. Thus, if outside observers could estimate the real subjects' attitudes based only on their knowledge of the behavior and the surrounding circumstances, then it is plausible that the real subjects might have arrived at their own attitudes in the same way.

Considerable controversy has surrounded this and other of Bem's replications involving observer subjects. Bem's theory states that individuals rely on their behavior as a guide to their attitudes primarily when their original attitudes are weak, ambiguous, or uninterpretable. Then the individual is functionally in the same position as an outside observer and must use his or her own behavior as a guide to knowing what his or her attitudes are. Critics claimed that subjects in Festinger and Carlsmith's study did not have weak, ambiguous, or uninterpretable attitudes: they knew the experiment was boring. Thus Bem should have given his observers one salient piece of information that Festinger and Carlsmith's subjects would have had—namely, their own attitudes prior to the experiment. Providing this information did make it impossible for observer subjects to replicate the findings of dissonance experiments. However, Bem and McConnell (1970) countered by demonstrating that role-playing subjects who perform dissonant actions cannot correctly recall their own initial attitudes at the time of the final attitude assessment. In other words, people's original attitudes may actually become ambiguous and uninterpretable after they engage in counterattitudinal behavior. This finding suggests that Bem was correct in not giving his observer subjects information about initial attitudes.

THE SEARCH FOR A RESOLUTION OF THE CONTROVERSY The controversy between dissonance and self-perception interpretations of counterattitudinal advocacy has continued for more than a decade. The controversy has important implications for social psychology and relates to the general issue of whether observers and actors differ in their attributions (see Chapter 6). A number of researchers have carried out experiments purporting to test differences between dissonance and self-perception predictions. For example, dissonance researchers argue that increasing the *salience* of individuals' initial, predissonance attitudes should *increase* attitude change because the counterattitudinal behavior becomes more dissonant. In contrast, self-perception theory predicts that salience should *decrease* attitude change because it increases the clarity of one's initial attitudes and thereby decreases reliance on external cues. Yet, other researchers questioned the logic of these predictions. They argued that dissonance theory could also predict less change when initial attitudes are salient because salience may increase commitment to one's attitude and therefore increase resistance to change. There is even a complicated rationale whereby self-perception theory might predict greater change with more salient initial attitudes. In view of the tangled nature of such debates, many psychologists have concluded that it is questionable whether either theory can make predictions about the effects of counterattitudinal behavior that cannot be accounted for by the other theory.

OVERSUFFICIENT-JUSTIFICATION EXPERIMENTS One area in which dissonance theory and self-perception theory make differentiated predictions is known as *oversufficient justification* (Nisbett and Valins, 1971). Experiments on oversufficient justification give people a reward for doing what they would otherwise do spontaneously. An example of oversufficient justification is giving a child a reward for playing with an attractive new toy. A reward is thoroughly unnecessary to induce a child to play with a new toy. The action of playing with the toy is *proattitudinal,* not counterattitudinal. Therefore, it is difficult to argue that such actions are dissonant.

Consider situations of oversufficient justification from the viewpoint of self-perception theory. If individuals receive large external rewards for engaging in attitude-consistent actions, they would tend to view the actions as caused by the rewards, not by their own positive attitudes. In the toy situation, the child would reason, "I must be playing with this toy because they'll give me a reward for doing it." If the behavior can be explained by the external reward, the child would not think that his or her liking for the toy accounted for playing with it. It follows, then, from self-perception theory that external rewards should undermine intrinsic interest or "turn play into work." This prediction has been confirmed in a number of studies (Lepper and Greene, 1975; Lepper, Greene, and Nisbett, 1973) and has important general implications for the uses of external rewards and punishments to change attitudes and control behavior.

An Illustrative Study To better illustrate the operation of the oversufficient-justification principle, let us briefly examine a study by Mark Lepper, David Greene, and Richard Nisbett (1973). They observed three- to five-year-old children in a nursery school and noted that one of the children's favorite activities was drawing with Magic Markers. A week later the experimenters returned to the nursery school and told one-third of the children that they would receive a special award that day for drawing with the Magic Markers (the reward was a certificate with a gold seal and ribbon); another third received the same award for drawing with the markers, but had not expected the reward; the final third received no reward. Then one to two weeks later the experimenters returned and observed the children as they played. As predicted, the children who had received no award and those who had received an unexpected award showed more spontaneous interest in the activity than those children who had received an expected award. The no-award and unexpected-award groups did not differ in spontaneous interest. Thus, Lepper and associates

FOCUS ON APPLICATIONS

OVERSUFFICIENT JUSTIFICATION IN JEWISH FOLKLORE

The effect of oversufficient justification, as explained in the accompanying section, has great intuitive appeal. To demonstrate this, Edward Deci cites the following Jewish fable in his book *Intrinsic Motivation* (1975). Deci concedes: "There are some people who assert that we never really discover anything new, but rather that we just rediscover things." The tailor below demonstrates what research has confirmed—that external rewards can undermine intrinsic interest in a task.

In a little Southern town where the Klan was riding again, a Jewish tailor had the temerity to open his little shop on the main street. To drive him out of the town the Kleagle of the Klan set a gang of little ragamuffins to annoy him. Day after day they stood at the entrance of his shop. "Jew! Jew!", they hooted at him. The situation looked serious for the tailor. He took the matter so much to heart that he began to brood and spent sleepless nights over it. Finally out of desperation he evolved a plan.

The following day, when the little hoodlums came to jeer at him, he came to the door and said to them, "From today on any boy who calls me 'Jew' will get a dime from me." Then he put his hand in his pocket and gave each boy a dime.

Delighted with their booty, the boys came back the following day and began to shrill, "Jew! Jew!" The tailor came out smiling. He put his hand in his pocket and gave each of the boys a nickel, saying, "A dime is too much—I can only afford a nickel today." The boys went away satisfied because, after all, a nickel was money, too.

However, when they returned the next day to hoot at him, the tailor gave them only a penny each.

"Why do we get only a penny today?" they yelled.

"That's all I can afford."

"But two days ago you gave us a dime, and yesterday we got a nickel. It's not fair, mister."

"Take it or leave it. That's all you're going to get!"

"Do you think we're going to call you 'Jew' for one lousy penny?"

"So don't!"

And they didn't.

Source: N. Ausubel, ed., "Applied Psychology," in *A Treasury of Jewish Folklore* (New York: Crown, 1948): 440–441.

concluded that the expected award had undermined the children's intrinsic motivation for drawing.

The implications of research on oversufficient justification are clear. Parents and teachers in particular should be cautious in rewarding children for activities that they find inherently enjoyable. If, for example, a child likes schoolwork, a monetary reward for high grades may diminish some of the intrinsic interest in the work. But, as noted by Lepper and associates, additional research is necessary to specify more clearly the conditions under which the oversufficient-justification effect occurs if clear-cut practical recommendations are to be set forth. There is little doubt that external reward may sometimes be very effective in eliciting and maintaining behavior, such as the token economies that have been successfully employed in classroom settings (O'Leary and Drabman, 1971). However, such techniques may have a countereffect on those individuals whose behavior is already maintained by their own inherent interest in an activity.

A POSSIBLE RESOLUTION OF THE DISSONANCE VERSUS SELF-PERCEPTION CONTROVERSY In view of the success of self-perception theory in the case of oversufficient justification, it appears that self-perception theory may be more appropriate than dissonance theory in accounting for the effects of *proattitudinal* behavior; on the other hand, dissonance theory may be more appropriate than self-perception theory for accounting for the effects of *counterattitudinal* behavior, especially when original attitudes are strong and unambiguous. This resolution has been proposed by Russell Fazio, Mark Zanna, and Joel Cooper (1977).

How satisfactory this resolution will prove to be can only be determined by research. Certainly, the self-perception processes postulated by Bem are important, although their implications may not be as general as he claimed. Bem's theory tended to lead some researchers too narrowly to the conclusions that (1) motivational processes such as dissonance reduction have no bearing on attitude change, and (2) internal attitudes and beliefs are an unimportant source of information for inferring one's own attitudes and beliefs. A variety of research evidence has suggested that motivational processes probably do play a role in the attitude change that follows counterattitudinal behavior and that people are aware of their internal states and attitudes at least some of the time. In general, then, a more balanced view of the roles of self-perception and dissonance processes is emerging in the recent research literature.

SELF-PERCEPTION THEORY AND THE CASE OF PETER REILLY Self-perception theory is especially applicable in the case of Peter Reilly. Recall that the police convinced Peter he had a lapse of memory. Once Peter distrusted his own memory he became a perfect candidate for attitude change through self-perception. As required by Bem's theory, Peter's internal cues were weak, ambiguous, and uninterpretable. He essentially became an observer of himself, trying to infer what might account for the polygraph reading.

When Peter denies his involvement in the murder, Kelly refers to the polygraph test and asks, "Then why the reaction?"

Peter plaintively seeks an explanation: "I don't know. Maybe it's just nervousness. I mean, my mom did die."

But Kelly rejects Peter's explanation: "The polygraph can never be wrong."

Gradually, Peter begins to doubt his own inner feelings: "I've been drilled and drilled and drilled. I'm getting tired. They told me that . . . I could have forgotten . . . that really shook me."

Peter desperately needs an explanation of the polygraph results, and, just as Bem's theory predicts, Peter finally infers his own guilt in order to explain the test. "I don't remember doing the things that happened. I believe I did it now."

When the interrogation is over and Peter has confessed, he feels the impact of what he has done. "I don't want to get tossed in a cell."

Kelly replies, "I just work here."

THEORETICAL ADVANCES RELATED TO DISSONANCE THEORY Despite the challenge from self-perception theory, dissonance researchers have continued to publish studies at an impres-

Peter Reilly talks to reporters after he learns he has been granted a new trial for the slaying of his mother. His case shows that attitudes can be changed through both persuasion by others and self-persuasion. *(UPI)*

sive, though somewhat diminishing, pace to the present day. Indeed, the long-term validity of dissonance theory is astonishing, especially in view of the vigor of the attack from self-perception theory and other standpoints. Nevertheless, the decades of experimentation have brought to dissonance researchers an embarrassment of "limiting conditions" for the dissonance effects that were proclaimed in the early period. Many observers think the theory has become unwieldy as it has attempted to encompass these numerous limiting conditions, such as those noted earlier in relation to the counter-attitudinal-advocacy paradigm.

How best to modify dissonance theory in order to account for the many limiting conditions is not entirely clear. Elliot Aronson (1969) proposed that subjects in dissonance experiments are trying to preserve a positive self-concept. According to Aronson, what creates dissonance in the Festinger and Carlsmith experiment is the discrepancy between cognitions: "I am a decent, truthful human being" and "I misled a person by conning him into believing something that is just not true, and I will have no chance to set him straight because I probably will never see him again." Aronson's self-concept interpretation, with its emphasis on morality, is similar to the view that people must take personal responsibility for unwanted consequences of their behavior in order to experience dissonance. Behavior leading to unwanted consequences would surely cause moral misgivings or a twinge of guilt. Yet quite a few other dissonance situations seem to have no implications of immorality. For example, in experiments by Wilhelmy

(1974) and Wilhelmy and Duncan (1974), subjects who merely agreed to taste bitter liquids experienced attitude change. Agreeing to taste bitter liquids is dissonant with one's negative attitude toward them, but this dissonance is merely hedonically unpleasant and certainly does not arouse concerns about morality. Kelman and Baron (1974) distinguished between *moral dissonance* and *hedonic dissonance* and suggested that these two kinds of dissonance may have different dynamics.

Another interpretation of dissonance research, called impression management theory, was suggested by James Tedeschi, Barry Schlenker, and Thomas Bonoma (1971). This viewpoint suggests that people desire to present themselves favorably to others as well as to preserve a positive self-identity. Counterattitudinal advocacy threatens that individuals will appear socially unattractive and immoral to other people as well as to themselves. This self-presentational dilemma is, of course, resolved by changing one's attitude.

The evolution of dissonance theory continues. The original theory is burdened by the growth of complicated limiting conditions that are difficult to encompass within Festinger's original logic. Many social psychologists appear to have lost interest in the dissonance approach because the simple elegance of its original explanations could not be maintained. Those attracted to simple explanations continue to seek an overall motivational principle that will explain existing findings—if not reducing dissonance, preserving a positive self-image or presenting a favorable impression to other people. Yet other social psychologists have stuck by the very patched-up structure that now constitutes dissonance theory, and they continue to conceptualize their research in terms of cognitive dissonance.

The most notable conclusion of this chapter is that many processes influence attitude change. Attitudes can be changed through persuasion based on learning theory and information-processing principles. Attitudes can also be changed through self-persuasion based on cognitive dissonance or self-perception theory. Which particular strategy proves most effective in a given situation depends on countless complex factors, as the chapter has made clear. Human beings are not simple creatures, and how they form and change their attitudes toward themselves and their world is complicated. When all the attitude-change strategies are focused on a single belief, however, as in the case of Peter Reilly, human beings appear singularly vulnerable.

SUMMARY

This chapter has considered research on persuasion and on self-persuasion. In persuasion situations a communicator gives his or her position on an issue and one or more arguments supporting the position. Persuasion is regarded as the degree to which members of an audience agree with the communicator's position after hearing his or her presentation. Several components of persuasion settings affect the persuasiveness of messages: the communicator, the message itself, the medium through which the message is presented, and the audience.

Much of the research on persuasion has concentrated on how people process the information in persuasive communications and on how various components of persuasion settings affect the processing. In particular, theory has focused on the role of information-reception processes and on the determinants of perceiving information as valid and yielding to it.

Another method of changing attitudes is to induce individuals to advocate viewpoints that differ from their own. Early research showed that playing a role discrepant from one's attitudes and beliefs was very effective in inducing attitude change. Later research has attempted to discern the conditions that enhance or lessen attitude change under these circumstances. Primary among these efforts is the work of Leon Festinger and others on cognitive dissonance theory. These researchers claimed that counterattitudinal advocacy creates dissonance, which is then reduced (at least under certain circumstances) by attitude change toward the position that was advocated.

The dissonance interpretation of counterattitudinal advocacy was challenged by Daryl Bem's self-perception theory. Self-perception provides a plausible accounting for many dissonance findings, and it has been difficult to choose between the two theories on the basis of empirical evidence. However, recent research has suggested that self-perception theory may be best suited to account for self-persuasion effects that are a product of proattitudinal behaviors, while dissonance theory may be more appropriate for explaining the effects of counterattitudinal behavior. Yet, despite the challenge from self-perception theory, dissonance theory has continued to evolve in response to new findings that limit the circumstances under which dissonance effects occur.

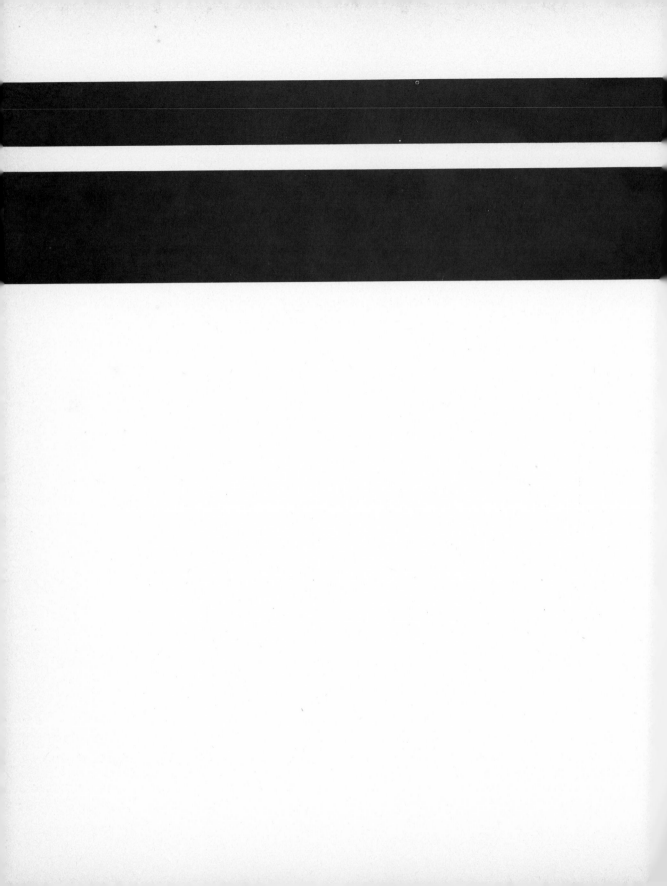

PART THREE

INTERPERSONAL PROCESSES

CHAPTER SIX

ATTRIBUTION AND PERSON PERCEPTION

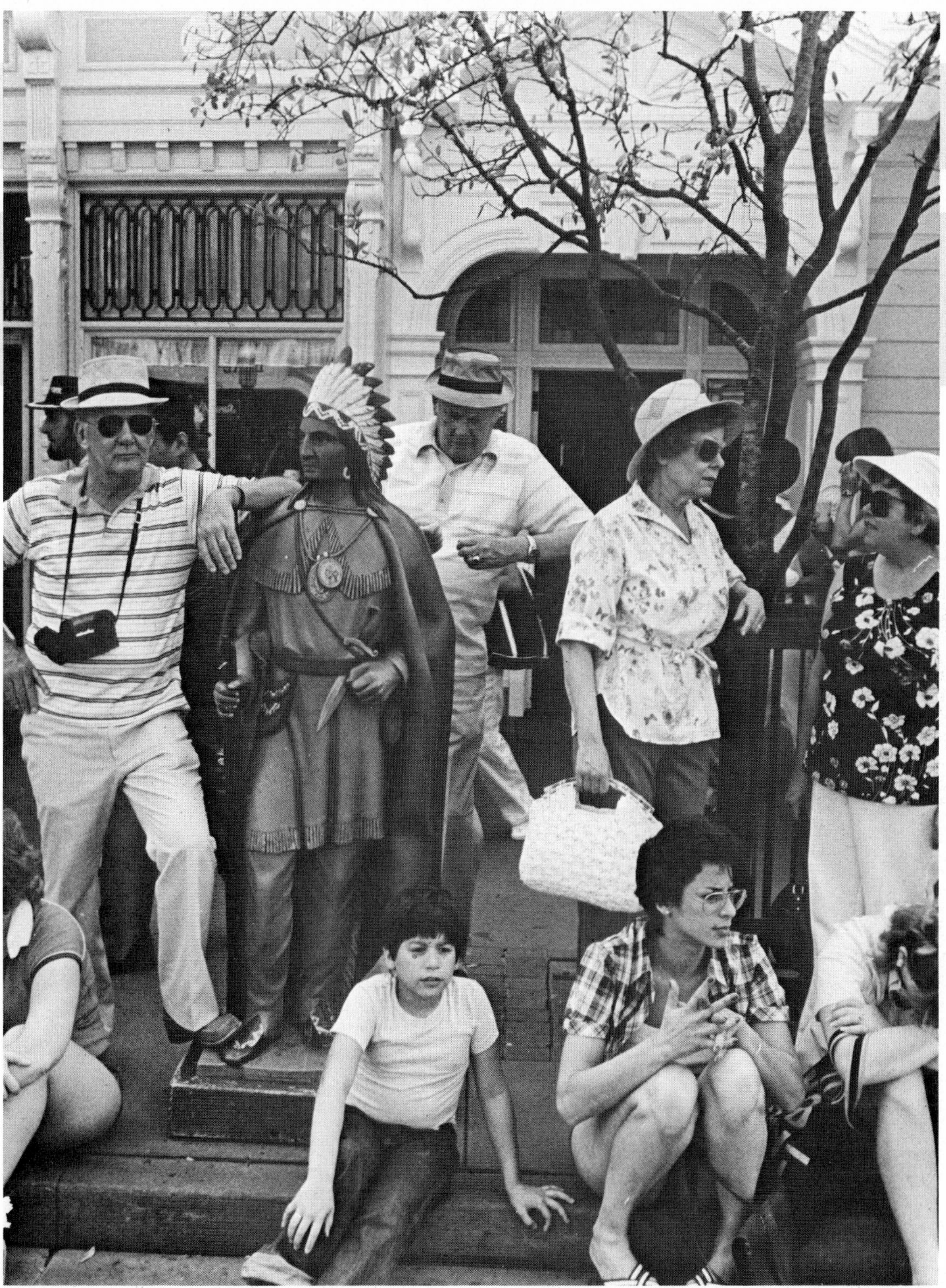

Rennie and Joe Morgan live in a small Maryland college town near Chesapeake Bay. Joe is a philosophy professor and Rennie trains horses. Their marriage, like most close relationships, rests on their ability to know and understand each other—to be accountable in their actions toward each other. When Rennie has sex with Joe's best friend, Jacob Horner, Rennie and Joe's relationship is threatened. It is important that they understand why it happened so they can decide what to do.

This is the central dilemma in the novel *The End of the Road*, by John Barth. Did Jacob have a premeditated plan to take his best friend's wife to bed? Was Joe testing Rennie by deliberately encouraging her closeness with Jacob? Was Rennie falling in love with her husband's friend? Or was it all just an accident—a chance touching of shoulders in a darkened hallway when Joe was away from home?

Such questions may sound melodramatic, but in literature, as in psychology, explaining behavior and attributing responsibility for actions are often no simple matters. To take another example, consider what happens when you quarrel with a person you love. The argument may be due to (1) hostile feelings you may be developing toward your lover; (2) your lover's developing hostility toward you; (3) external circumstances surrounding the argument; (4) any combination of your feelings, the other's feelings, or the circumstances; or (5) some other complicating factor such as a rival lover for either or both of you. How we interpret such situations determines how we cope with the important dilemmas and decisions of our lives.

The area of psychology that is concerned with the intricacies of how we explain behavior is called attribution theory and person perception. These two areas of research are typically defined in an overlapping fashion.

In its most basic form, *attribution theory* is concerned with how people *explain* (*assign causes for*) personal and interpersonal events. It may focus on how an individual tries to understand a personal feeling ("Why do I get the chills whenever I come into this classroom?"). Or, as in the quarrel between the lovers, it may focus on how a person explains an interpersonal encounter or situation. In a broader sense, attribution theory also is concerned with how people assign *responsibility* to the self and others. Attributions of causality and responsibility may or may not be highly related. For example, a child may cause a valuable lamp to tip over and crash, but the babysitter may be deemed responsible because he or she neglected to supervise the child closely.

Person perception simply involves the act of encountering and forming an impression of another person, whether through face-to-face interaction, on film, through hearing or reading, or simply by seeing someone at a distance. Thus, in person perception there is no necessary attributional process of explaining causality or imputing responsibility—though, indeed, it may happen, depending on the nature of the encounter. Both person perception and attribution may be carried out in a very rapid—even unconscious—fashion. However, this rapid process is more likely to characterize person perception than attribution, which often involves elaborate, long-term deliberation about how events and experiences go together.

Why do people make attributions and form impressions of others? The answer most often advanced is that we need to *predict* and *control* the events that occur in our everyday lives (Heider, 1958; Kelley, 1967). People cannot easily live with chaos. The ability to predict and control events allows us to organize our lives and develop expectations about what we will face in the future. Relevant to our earlier example of the argument with a lover, Robert Weiss (1975) has found that people deal with separation from close relationships much more easily if they can explain who is responsible for what and can account for the cause-and-effect sequence involved in the crumbling of the relationship. Presumably, people who cannot construct these accounts will lack a feeling of control over future relationships and are likely to remain insecure and distressed long after a breakup. In addition to a need for prediction and control of events, people may make attributions and form impressions quite simply because they are intrinsically curious about their world.

Person perception involves encountering and forming impressions of another person, and two individuals may perceive a third person in quite different ways. For example, people have debated for centuries whether or not the enigmatic subject of Leonardo da Vinci's *Mona Lisa* is smiling. *(Alinari-Scala / EPA, Inc.)*

In this chapter we will first examine the nature of person perception. "How do we form impressions of others?" and "How much do first impressions count?" are some of the questions we will explore. Next we will consider how person perception relates to stereotyping and what factors lead to false impressions of entire groups of people. Then we will look at foundation works on attribution and compare several classic theories about how people seek to explain others' behavior. We will also examine more recent extensions of attribution research to areas such as actor/observer differences in attributions, attributions for success and failure, sex differences and attribution, and attribution therapy. Finally, we will consider some criticisms of the attribution approach from theorists who believe that human beings are not always as rational as attribution researchers presume.

PERSON PERCEPTION AND IMPRESSION FORMATION

Impression formation is concerned with the initial impressions we form about others. Such impressions are the first step in a process that may result in a more elaborate perception or attribution about others. "What is he like—can you tell from his voice?" "I wasn't impressed in my meeting with her; she seemed aloof." We often hear such statements after someone has just met another person for the first time, whether in person or indirectly. We generally form these impressions quickly, based upon a few discrete pieces of information about the other person.

Suppose you hear a friend describing a man in your neighborhood as a rather hard-working, ambitious, and responsible individual. But you also learn that the man is somewhat impersonal in his dealings with others. What kind of general or global impression do you form of this man based upon these discrete traits? What if the man were imputed to have all of the above traits except that instead of being impersonal, he is very open and friendly in his relations with others? Would your overall impression be quite different than one based on the knowledge that he is somewhat impersonal? The pioneering work of Solomon Asch (1946) examines how people take a set of discrete traits ascribed to another person and then form a global impression of that person.

Asch's theoretical perspective was derived from gestalt psychology with its emphasis upon the principles of perception. One of these principles is that the whole is greater than the sum of its parts; that is, any group of characteristics generates an impression different from the impressions formed when each characteristic is presented separately. This line of reasoning is well illustrated in Asch's classic "warm-cold" study, which is related directly to the above example.

THE "WARM-COLD" STUDY AND CENTRAL TRAITS

In this study, Asch presented subjects with a list of traits that all referred to the same person: "intelligent," "skillful," "industrious," "warm," "determined," "practical," and "cautious." Another group of subjects read the same list, with the substitution of "cold" for "warm." Subjects were then asked to write a brief sketch of the person and to indicate which trait out of several pairs of traits (for example, "happy-unhappy") the individual would probably possess. Asch found that exchanging the word "cold" for "warm" profoundly affected subjects' impression of the stimulus person. If the list included "warm," subjects tended to infer that the person was also generous, happy, good-natured, humorous, and sociable. If the list included "cold," subjects tended to infer that the person was also ungenerous, unhappy, irritable, humorless, and ruthless. Thus, subjects appear to have been able to form general impressions of the stimulus person based on a few discrete pieces of information about that person; and, most important, they formed very different general impressions based on the "warm-cold" variation. Asch concluded that in these particular lists of traits warm and cold were *central traits* because of their great importance in influencing the ultimate impression.

In subsequent work, Asch found that substituting "polite" for "blunt" in a list identical to the one described above made considerably less difference in the overall picture formed by the subjects. He also found that if "warm" is inserted into a list containing the words "obedient," "weak," "shallow," "unambitious," and "vain," it loses its potency in producing a relatively favorable impression of the stimulus person. Asch interpreted these findings as indicating that a trait (such as warm or cold) may be central in one set of accompanying traits but quite peripheral in another. Further, he suggested that some traits (such as polite and blunt) may not be central in any list of traits.

SUBSEQUENT WORK ON CENTRAL TRAITS

An interesting replication of Asch's original results was reported by Harold Kelley (1950). He distributed written descriptions of a guest speaker in a psychology course before the lecturer spoke. The descriptions included seven adjectives similar to those used by Asch. Half of the students received a description containing the trait warm; the other half received a description containing the trait cold. Later, the lecturer came to the class and led a discussion for a few minutes, after which the students were asked to give their impressions of the lecturer. Consistent with Asch's results, the "warm-cold" variation produced big differences in the impression formed by the students. Students who had expected the lecturer to be warm generally tended to rate him more positively than did those who had expected him to be cold. Also, students who had expected the lecturer to be warm interacted with him more freely and initiated more discussions with him than did those who had expected him to be cold. Kelley's results suggest that central traits attributed to another person may play an important role in influencing not only impressions, but actual behaviors toward the person. These results greatly extend the generality of the findings reported by Asch.

IMPLICIT PERSONALITY THEORY AND CENTRAL TRAITS

Why are people able to form integrated impressions of another person based on such limited information? Bruner and Tagiuri (1954) have suggested that each of us as perceivers carries in our head an *implicit theory of personality*. This theory, in effect, is an understanding of which traits are usually associated with or implied by other traits. As an illustration of how these theories work, consider the case where we hear that a certain individual is warm. Based on our knowledge of human characteristics that usually go along with being warm, we may readily infer that the person is easy to be with, sociable, and someone with whom to share meaningful experiences. Implicit theories of personality help us

Each of us possesses an implicit theory of personality that enables us to make quick evaluations of other people. *(Michael Weisbrot)*

make rapid overall assessments of other people based on limited knowledge of these people. However, the theories may sometimes lead the perceiver to adopt erroneous and stereotypic views of other persons.

What determines if a trait is central or not? An integrative analysis by Wishner (1960) represents the most conclusive current view of how to predict which traits will be central in impression formation. In formulating his analysis, Wishner made use of the leads provided by Bruner and Tagiuri's implicit personality theory and subsequent research. He suggested that any trait will be central to the extent that it is perceived as closely related to other traits on which an individual is rated. In other words, the greater the number of characteristics to which a trait is viewed as being related and the stronger the perceived relationships, the greater will be its impact on subjects' impressions of a stimulus person.

In line with this reasoning, Wishner found that the traits of warm and cold were perceived as being closely linked to the other traits used by Asch, such as generosity or happiness; that is, statistically speaking, there were high intercorrelations between these two traits and the other traits in Asch's list. In contrast, the traits of polite and blunt were not intercorrelated very highly with the other traits. Thus, in Asch's study the reason these traits were peripheral rather than central was apparently due to the low perceived relationship between them and the other traits on the list. However, Wishner showed that polite and blunt could be made into central traits if they were inserted into a list containing traits with which they were highly correlated. Therefore, we should be able to predict what traits will be central in a list if we know how each trait correlates with every other trait: central traits simply have the highest intercorrelations with all the other traits.

ORDER OF INCONSISTENT INFORMATION

Do people base their early impressions of others on initial information or on later disconfirming information? For example, who is liked more—a person who is seen as first wise and then deceptive, or one who is seen as first deceptive and then wise? If the perceiver's impression is based on initial information, a *primacy effect* is said to occur. But if the impression is based on later information, a *recency* effect is said to occur.

Again, Asch (1946) paved the way for this line of work with his early investigations of impression formation. In one study, Asch showed subjects a list of six adjectives that supposedly described an individual, and then he asked the subjects to form an impression of the person. Half of the subjects were presented with the following list: "intelligent," "industrious," "impulsive," "critical," "stubborn," and "envious." The other half received this same list but in reverse order. Asch found that the first group formed more favorable impressions of the stimulus person than did the second group. For example, the first group saw the person as happier and more sociable than did the second group. Asch suggested that the meaning of the latter traits was assimilated toward the meaning established by the former traits. That is, the latter traits were perceived so as to be consistent with the former traits.

More recent work on order effects, especially research by Norman Anderson and his colleagues, has revealed that the primacy effect may be a potent and reliable phenomenon. Anderson's research (1968) suggests that perceivers may assign less weight to information that is presented later in a series. In other words, people may tend to *discount* information that disconfirms earlier information.

But the research on order effects is complicated, and under certain conditions a recency effect can occur. For example, if subjects read a paragraph describing a man as introverted, then perform an irrelevant task, and then read a second paragraph describing the same man as outgoing, subjects are likely to remember the second paragraph better than the first (Luchins, 1948). Under still other conditions, neither a primacy nor a recency effect may be found—for example, if subjects are induced to attend equally to all pieces of information in an entire set (Hendrick and Costantini, 1970).

COGNITIVE SETS AND INCONSISTENT INFORMATION

People also tend to perceive and recall information differently depending on their cognitive set. For example, imagine that you are a young reporter and are given the task of writing a succinct profile of a politician running for office. You concentrate closely on the politician, hoping to develop a description of the individual that the average reader will find clear and easy to remember. Given this set to transmit information about the candidate, do you emphasize the consistent parts of the candidate's personality (for example, that she has a nice family and is active in civic affairs) and exclude the inconsistent parts that might confuse the reader (for example, that she is a nice person with whom to work, but has a serious drinking problem)? Or, if you heard the information but did not have to transmit it clearly to someone else, would you organize the information differently and emphasize different aspects?

Research addressing these questions was carried out by Arthur Cohen (1961), based on Zajonc's (1960) theory of "cognitive tuning." According to this theory, a person who has a set to *transmit* information to others (as the reporter did) will tend to look for consistent pieces of information and ignore the inconsistent information that would complicate the transmission. In contrast, a person who has a set to receive information can be more flexible and critical in evaluating the information. To demonstrate how cognitive tuning applies to person perception, Cohen (1961) asked subjects to form an overall impression of a person described with low, moderate, or highly contradictory pieces of information. Some subjects were given a set to transmit their impressions to others. Other subjects believed that they would receive a message about the person being observed.

Cohen found that subjects who were tuned (or oriented) to transmit information were inclined to discount contradictory elements in their impressions and to polarize their assessments of the stimulus person as compared to the subjects who were tuned to receive information. Thus, regardless of how contradictory the information about the stimulus person was, transmitters apparently felt that they had to block out irreconcilable facts in order to transmit a clearer picture.

COMBINING IMPRESSIONS

What happens when a person hears a series of positive statements made about someone else? Does the person's impression grow more positive with each new positive characteristic? Or are the characteristics averaged together to form an overall impression? Investigators have differed about whether *summation* or *averaging* better reflects the processes by which people combine impressions of others.

Norman Anderson (1968) compiled a list of 555 adjectives and asked college students to rate how much they would like a person who had each of these traits. Some traits were found to be highly positive, others moderately positive, and others highly negative. For example, "sincere" was perceived as the most likable trait, and "liar" the most detestable. Using adjectives such as these, Anderson (1965) asked subjects to rate an individual's likability when the individual was described as having a series of traits of different values. For instance, an individual was described as "sincere" (a value of +3) and then "cautious" (a value of +1). Did subjects add these trait values to give the individual an overall likability rating of +4, or were the traits averaged for a likability rating of only +2? As illustrated in Figure 6.1, subjects were more likely to average the traits rather than add them in combining impressions.

Yet other researchers have reported evidence supporting a summation model. Fishbein and Hunter (1964) found that if subjects are given five strongly positive traits about another individual, greater liking is produced than if subjects are given only two strongly positive traits. An averaging model would have predicted no difference between conditions in this study. (If each trait had a +4 value, the average in each condition would be +4, whether it was based on five traits or two.)

FIGURE 6.1 Note the differences that are possible in overall impressions when evaluations of traits are combined according to the additive approach versus the averaging approach.

Positive traits	*Value*	*Negative traits*	*Value*
Condition 1		Condition 1	
Trait #1	+4	Trait #1	−4
Trait #2	+4	Trait #2	−4
	Add = +8		Add = −8
	Average = +4		Average = −4
Condition 2		Condition 2	
Trait #1	+4	Trait #1	−4
Trait #2	+4	Trait #2	−4
Trait #3	+2	Trait #3	−2
Trait #4	+2	Trait #4	−2
	Add = +12		Add = −12
	Average = +3		Average = −3
Finding: Condition 1 greater liking than Condition 2.		Finding: Condition 1 less liking than Condition 2.	

To account for results such as these, Anderson (1968) refined his averaging approach to a weighted averaging model. According to this revised theory, people form an overall impression by averaging all traits but giving more weight to polarized (highly positive or highly negative) traits. In most research testing rival models, the weighted averaging model has been shown to be a relatively powerful predictor of global impressions of others.

The important implication of this and other research on impression formation is the very complexity of the processes involved. When the possible biases caused by central traits and the order of information are processed through our own cognitive sets and implicit personality theories, our combined impressions of others in the world are probably more complex than even the weighted averaging model would suggest. And we have examined just a few of the processes that influence our impressions of others. In light of this research, people should be justifiably cautious in forming their first—and maybe even their second and third—impressions of others.

PERSON PERCEPTION AND STEREOTYPING

Stereotyping, or perceiving an individual as possessing certain traits and behaviors that are considered undesirable, may be conceived as a special subcategory of person perception. Walter Lippmann (1922) first introduced the concept of stereotype to refer to people's erroneous, overgeneralized, negative attitudes and perceptions about other persons or groups of persons. A stereotypical attitude or perception is an integral part of the more general phenomenon of prejudice. An individual's prejudice toward others may contain several component stereotypes such as "They are dirty"; "They are clannish"; "They are domineering." Gordon Allport (1954) suggests that people employ stereotypes in order to justify their prejudices and associated behavior (for example, "We exclude them from our organization because they would try to take control of everything if we let them in").

THE PRINCETON STUDIES OF ETHNIC STEREOTYPING

A series of studies done at Princeton University between 1933 and 1967 reveals the stereotypes held by white male Princeton students toward different racial groups and how these stereotypes changed over the years. Katz and Braly conducted the first survey in 1933 using a very simple procedure in which students simply read a list of eighty-four diverse character traits (for example, "intelligent," "superstitious," "happy-go-lucky," "lazy," "artistic," and "industrious"). Subjects were asked to select those traits they believed most characteristic of each of ten different ethnic groups: "Americans," Chinese, English, Germans, Irish, Italians, Japanese, Jews, Negroes, and Turks.

These Princeton men perceived Jews as shrewd, mercenary, industrious, grasping, and intelligent. "Americans" were seen as industrious, intelligent, materialistic, ambitious, and progressive. Negroes emerged as superstitious, lazy, happy-go-lucky, ignorant, and musical. The authors concluded that the high degree of agreement in stereotyping indicated cultural forces which led to a "public attitude." They argued that prejudiced attitudes consist of both public and private attitudes. Private attitudes were conceived to be based upon individual feeling and experience, while public attitudes involved acceptance of cultural labels. Katz and Braly viewed stereotypes as deplorable because "to the realist there are no racial or national groups which exist as entities and which determine the characteristics of the group members" (p. 289).

Katz and Braly's work was replicated in the early 1950s (Gilbert, 1951) and again in the late 1960s (Karlins, Coffman, and Walters, 1969). Over the years these investigations found a considerable reduction in negative stereotyping for all groups that were rated. Jews and blacks, in particular, were rated increasingly more favorably over the three measurement periods. However, negative traits such as superstitious, lazy, and ignorant still were attributed to blacks to a significant degree.

These Princeton studies reveal that social stereotypes are changing in terms of trait content. But the tendency to stereotype still is

Negative stereotypes of ethnic and other groups are an integral component of prejudice. Throughout much of New World history, for example, the Native Americans were stereotyped as vicious savages. *(Culver Pictures)*

present and this tendency is especially true in the ratings of blacks. There are many questions that remain unresolved in this area of work. One central question concerns the perceived social desirability of particular stereotypes in different groups and at different historical times. For example, would a university student who held deep-seated prejudices be willing to acknowledge in a campus questionnaire that he or she viewed a whole group of people as lazy and ignorant? Thus, stereotypes reveal prejudice, historical changes in our perceptions and impressions of others, and our sensitivity to what others may think about us if we admitted the full extent of our prejudice.

More recent research on stereotyping has turned from documenting the existence of stereotyping to an analysis of stereotyped thinking. Why do people overgeneralize from their observations about a single individual or a small number of persons to form conclusions about an entire group? What role do mass media play in this process by presenting extreme instances rather than representative cases? These questions will be considered later in the chapter after looking at research on attribution and judgment.

FOUNDATION WORKS ON ATTRIBUTION

HEIDER'S NAÏVE ANALYSIS OF ACTION

The development of attribution theory can be traced to a book published in 1958 by Fritz Heider entitled *The Psychology of Interpersonal Relations*. This book not only laid the foundation for work on attribution theory, it also represents a monumental contribution to understanding person perception and other social-psychological processes and suggests how these formerly independent areas of work might be integrated. Before the publication of Heider's book, the attribution field did not exist. His analysis greatly enhanced the then emerging research on how people perceive others, and it pinpointed attribution as a central activity in our knowledge of others and of ourselves. Heider analyzed in detail how people go about answering questions such as: "What did he mean by that action?" "What is she really like when you get to know her?" "If Joe likes Ed and dislikes Tom, what will happen if Ed likes Tom?"

Heider referred to his analysis as the "naïve analysis of action" because he was concerned about the everyday events in most people's lives and how people try to understand and explain these events in "common sense" terms. However, in no sense did Heider's analysis represent a naïve conception. Its sophistication is such that researchers and scholars have yet to probe adequately many of the eminently researchable ideas contained in his book.

At the very heart of Heider's analysis is the view that perception, whether of the social or nonsocial world, involves a search for structure. People are seen as trying to put together organized, meaningful explanations about the myriad of events that they observe in the world around them. This perspective is essential if people are to limit the occurrence of unpredictable and uncontrollable situations.

Many principles that underlie person perception have parallels in the field of nonsocial, or object, perception. For example, in an early experiment Heider and Simmel (1944) showed subjects a short film depicting three geometric figures—a circle and two triangles—as they moved into and around a large rectangle. Subjects described the action in anthropomorphic terms, attributing motives and causes to the geometric figures, which were seen as "fighting" and "chasing each other" around the "house." In the same way, people also attribute dispositions to persons as a means of explaining actions. One reason this occurs, Heider believes, is that "behavior engulfs the field." In other words, a stimulus person's behavior is so overwhelming that it often engulfs the perceiver's view of the social context in which the behavior occurs, just as an inanimate figure in an abstract drawing may obscure perception of the field surrounding the action. As we shall see later, this idea represents a core element in explaining why an observer's causal attributions for behavior may differ from the attributions made by an actor himself or herself.

Heider admits that there are also some differences in the principles underlying social and nonsocial perception. For example, constancy and invariance (always seeing the person as displaying the same traits) are not perfect in social perception as they are in nonsocial situations. Heider suggests that people operate very much like quasi-scientists in their attributional analyses. In the same way that scientists seek to establish cause-and-effect explanations, people observe an event and then, often in a logical, analytical way, attempt to disentangle and rearrange connections among the various effects and possible causes. Heider does not contend that people are always objective and rational in their attributional behavior. He points out, for example, that sometimes people make attributions that are not based on enough information or on an adequate analysis of the information, or people reflect their own psychological needs and motivations as opposed to an objective assessment of available information. Heider (personal communication, 1977) also suggests that attributions may be made very quickly and that in a typical day people may make hundreds of attributions about both mundane questions ("What caused that big noise?") and questions of grave import ("Why did she leave me after so long and at this critical time in my life?").

Heider thought that people make two major types of attributions, as reflected in the following examples:

— "He committed the robbery because his wife needed to have an operation."
— "He committed the robbery because he is a hardened, habitual criminal."

The first statement represents an *external attribution*; it attempts to explain the robbery as caused by something in the environment. The second statement represents an *internal attribution*; it seeks to explain the robbery as caused by something in the person who committed the act. External attributions refer to the physical and social circumstances surrounding the action, while internal attributions refer to the actor's dispositional state, such as his or her ability, motivation, attitude, or emotions. In view of Heider's principle that behavior engulfs the field, he believed that people tend to explain events in dispositional terms (internal attributions) rather than situational terms (external attributions). However, the degree of dispositional responsibility that people might attribute for an action depends on the perceived influence of two types of forces—environmental and personal—as explained below.

CONDITIONS OF ACTION Heider proposed that an action outcome usually depends on a combination of environmental force and personal force. He used the term *environmental force* to refer to important external factors such as the difficulty of a task. The term *personal force* he conceived to involve principally the internal factors of ability ("can" in Heider's words) and motivation ("trying"). Heider felt that people are very sensitive to the extent to which "can" and "trying" are involved in a person's behavior. For example, we may predict great success for people who do not have very high ability but who try very hard to succeed at difficult tasks. In our common-sense understanding of events, Heider suggests that we somehow form a calculus of "can," "trying," and environmental force elements, thereby estimating the amount of dispositional responsibility involved in an event. For example, only if an actor's *ability* exceeds the *task difficulty* does the actor attain the dispositional state of "can." Similarly, only if an actor *intends* a behavior and *exerts effort* toward that end does the actor attain the dispositional state of "trying." Only when these criteria apply can the actor be held dispositionally responsible for an action. A more detailed theory of these processes was worked out by Jones and Davis, as described below.

JONES AND DAVIS'S THEORY OF "CORRESPONDENT INFERENCES"

Edward Jones and Keith Davis (1965) adopted Heider's principles of attribution to develop a theory of "correspondent inferences." This theory basically seeks to explain how an observer comes to attribute intent and internal responsibility to another person. Jones and Davis's formulation was the first to state attributional processes in testable terms, and it set the stage for an upsurge in research on attribution.

ATTRIBUTION OF INTENT AND DISPOSITION In Jones and Davis's theory, a correspondent inference is an inference about an individual's intent and disposition that corresponds with or follows directly from his or her behavior. How is such an inference made? According to Jones and Davis it depends on the effects of an individual's behavior.

Consider the example depicted in Figure 6.2: Bill makes a hostile remark to Don that results in much emotional distress on the part of Don. We might infer that Bill *intends* to abuse Don verbally, and furthermore we might infer that Bill has a malicious *disposition*. On the other hand, we might infer that Bill bears Don no ill will, in which case the effects are not intended and we do not think that Bill has a malicious disposition. But how do we decide whether Bill intended to harm Don and whether Bill is malicious?

According to Jones and Davis, we first try to ascertain the actor's *knowledge* and *ability* regarding the effects of the actor's behavior. In the example above, did Bill know that his remarks would have such a harmful effect on Don? Is Bill capable of making remarks that would cause distress in Don? If we know that Bill fully understood the impact of his remarks and that Bill was capable of such remarks (perhaps he knew something about Don that could hurt him), then we can reasonably infer intent.

"NONCOMMON" AND EXTREME EFFECTS: THE CENTRAL DETERMINANTS OF CORRESPONDENT INFERENCE To proceed further and confidently infer a disposition that corresponds with an actor's behavior, we need two additional

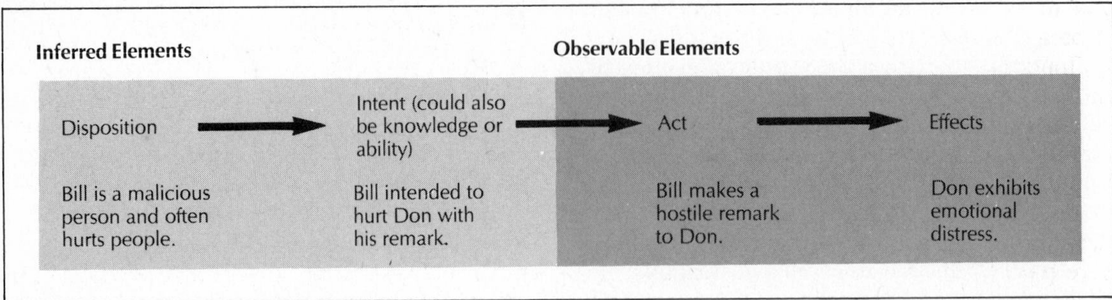

FIGURE 6.2 Jones and Davis's correspondent-inference paradigm. Note that the inference about Bill's intent and disposition is made backward—from the effects of the act to inferred characteristics of Bill. (Adapted from Jones and Davis, 1965.)

types of information about the effects of the behavior. The first type has to do with the unique effects—or in Jones and Davis's terms, the "noncommon" effects—caused by a particular behavior. For example, assume that Bill could make either a hostile remark to Don or a firm but polite request. Both responses might express Bill's displeasure with Don and suggest that Don alter his behavior, but only the hostile remark would also hurt Don's feelings. In other words, the effect of hurting Don's feelings is unique to the hostile remark. If we knew that Bill could have chosen either course of action, but that in fact he chose the hostile remark, then we could infer that he chose it because of its unique effects; that is, Bill intended not only to express displeasure and to ask Don to alter his behavior, but also to hurt his feelings. Thus we may more confidently infer that Bill has a malicious disposition.

The second type of information we use to infer a disposition with confidence has to do with the extremity of the behavior and the social desirability of its effects. For example, if a behavior is appropriate for a particular situation and its effects are desirable, then anyone would do it; we cannot confidently infer much that is unique about the person or much about the person's underlying dispositions. In contrast, if the behavior is inappropriate for a particular setting and its effects are undesirable, then something unique about the person must have caused him or her to behave that way. In this case, we can more confidently infer dispositional responsibility, or in Jones and Davis's terms, we can make an inference about an underlying disposition that corresponds with the actor's behavior. In our own example, if Bill made his hostile remark at a party in Don's honor with Don's close friends present, then we could be more confident in our inference that Bill is a malicious person.

A classic study by Jones, Davis, and Gergen (1961) shows how people perceive an individual whose behavior is extreme, or out of role, for a particular situation versus an individual whose behavior is appropriate and in role. According to the theory, extreme or out-of-role behavior should be more informative than in-role behavior about the intent and disposition of the person involved.

In this experiment, subjects listened to tape recordings in which a stimulus person was interviewing for a job either as an astronaut or a submariner. Before listening to the taped interview, subjects were instructed that the ideal astronaut should be a person who is essentially inner-directed (autonomous, can get along well without others); the ideal submariner was described as a person who is essentially other-directed (gregarious, likes frequent contact with others). In the actual interview, the stimulus person, who also understood the requirements for the job, described himself either as a person who was fit for the job (in-role condition) or as a person who was not fit for the job (out-of-role condition). Subjects were then asked to give their impressions of the person on several traits and to rate how confident they were in their impressions.

Jones and his associates found that subjects had stronger impressions and were more confident about these impressions in the out-of-role condition than in the in-role condition. For example, astronaut candidates who described themselves as gregarious and dependent on others—despite the solitary nature of the job—were perceived as more revealing of their true selves than those candidates who described themselves as exactly suited for the job. In other words, out-of-role behavior was seen as more informative about the person's inner nature than in-role behavior.

And the same point has been made in several other studies. In one case, a stimulus person who took an extreme position on an issue was seen as more sincere than a stimulus person who took a moderate position (Eisenger and Mills, 1968). Presumably, extreme behavior is a powerful indicator that a stimulus person is acting in line with his or her beliefs and not simply responding to the constraints of the specific situation.

As noted by Kelley Shaver (1975), however, we have to exercise care in assessing when a behavior will be perceived as extreme or low in social desirability. Behavior that is viewed as extreme and inappropriate by one group may be considered to be normal and appropriate by another group. For example, "streaking," the mid-1970s fad of taking off one's clothes and running naked through the streets, may be high in social desirability if one identifies with a collegiate peer group. However, the same behavior probably will be viewed as quite low in social desirability if one identifies with an antiobscenity organization.

In conclusion, Jones and Davis's theory of correspondent inference and related research (including a refinement of the theory by Jones and McGillis, 1976) epitomizes the contemporary approach to person perception. Clearly, the emphasis is on *situational* factors that influence the *process* of perceiving others. While Jones and Davis's approach represented an extension of Heider's original ideas, it remained for Harold Kelley to provide a systematic framework for attribution theory.

The appropriateness of a behavior varies from group to group and situation to situation. *(© David Hurn 1967 / Magnum)*

KELLEY'S MODEL OF ATTRIBUTION AND "COVARIATION"

Harold Kelley (1967) developed a comprehensive theory of attribution processes that explains not only our perceptions of other people's behavior, but also our perceptions of our own behavior. Kelley's analysis integrated previous approaches and provided needed impetus and cohesion to research on attribution. Kelley believed that people often make causal attributions in the same way a scientist would go about analyzing data. To decide if a behavior should be attributed to something within the person (internal factors) or to something in the environment (external factors), people employ the principle of *covariation*. That is, people observe

DISPOSITIONS AND SITUATIONS

"WHY DID IT HAPPEN TO ME?"

You are a young adult in the prime of your life. Suddenly you have an accident that leaves you paralyzed. It may have happened in an automobile, on the ski slope, or on a flight of stairs, but it will change your life. You cannot help but ask, "Why did it happen to me?"

How you answer this question is more than an attempt to make sense out of random tragedy. It can also influence how you cope with the tragedy. And basically it's an issue of causal attribution.

In Chicago, Ronnie Janoff-Bulman and Camille Wortman (1977) interviewed twenty-nine victims of spinal-cord injuries, people between the ages of sixteen and thirty-five who had been left either paraplegic (paralyzed in the lower half of the body) or quadriplegic (paralyzed from the neck down). Each person was asked if he or she had ever asked himself or herself the question "Why me?" They were also asked to what extent they blamed the accident on each of the following factors: self, other people, environment, or chance. Nurses and social workers were then asked to rate how well the victims were coping.

The most popular response to the open-ended question "why me?" was that God had a reason for victimizing the person. As one said: "There must be a reason for it. Could it be that He had a reason for it? Maybe someone else needs my legs more than I do." Other people blamed chance ("Just a freak accident; it could have happened to anybody"); predetermination ("Fate took its turn"); probability ("It was bound to happen"); deservedness ("If you do wrong, you reap what you sow"); and reinterpreting the accident as a valuable lesson ("This was the best way to slow me down").

The most interesting results of the study were the correlations between the victims' coping ability and whether they blamed themselves or other factors. The more victims blamed themselves for their misfortune, the better they coped with it. Apparently, blaming oneself is a way of perceiving meaning and order in the world—of making things seem more personally controllable. If one's life is subject to chance or forces beyond one's own control, then it becomes more difficult to cope, because tragedy would be unpredictable.

In a study of rape victims, Ronnie Janoff-Bulman (1979) found a similar pattern of results. Rape victims frequently blame themselves for being raped, despite the fact that the National Commission on the Causes and Prevention of Violence (1969) concluded that only 4.4 percent of all rapes were precipitated by the victim. Why, then, do so many women blame themselves? Some writers have suggested that women are socialized to view themselves as a victim. But the high incidence of self-blame may also represent an attempt to assert personal control over one's own life.

Janoff-Bulman obtained results in her study of rape victims that suggested that self-blame may in fact be an attempt to reassert control. She found two types of self-blame among rape victims: behavioral, in which the rape was attributed to modifiable behaviors ("I should not have walked alone in that neighborhood"); and characterological, in which the rape is attributed to unchangeable factors within the person ("I'm immature and can't take care of myself"). More women employed behavioral self-blame than characterological self-blame. This tendency is consistent with the suggestion that blaming one's own behaviors allows a perception of personal control over one's life. Even though one's past behaviors may have resulted in tragedy, there is the hope that things may be different in the future. Without a sense of personal control, there is little hope.

a behavior under a number of conditions and try to decide what factors occur together or "co-vary" with the behavior. In this way, people try to verify whether they have correctly linked cause and effect.

For example, imagine you are observing a friend who is enjoying a new food for the first time. Is the food really that good or is your friend simply a "food freak"—someone who would enjoy almost any new food? In other words, should your friend's liking for the food be attributed to an external factor (the new food itself) or to an internal factor (your friend's personality, tastes, etc.)? To answer a question such as this, Kelley says we must consider three basic factors:

1. *Distinctiveness.* Is the observed behavior distinctive to a particular entity or does the person respond this way to all entities? For example, is your friend's enthusiasm distinctive to the new food in particular, or does your friend respond this way to all foods in general? If your friend's response is distinctive to this particular food, then it suggests that the food may be unusually good; if your friend responds this way to all foods in general, then the behavior reveals more about the friend than the food. Thus, when a behavior is high in distinctiveness, it leads to an external attribution (the behavior was caused by a particular entity or event); when a behavior is low in distinctiveness, it leads to an internal attribution (something about the person must have caused the behavior).
2. *Consensus.* Do other people respond the same way to the entity or is the behavior unique to the individual observed? For example, do others agree that the new food is especially good or that your friend's enthusiasm is unique? If other people respond the same way, then it suggests that the food is in fact delicious; if others do not share your friend's enthusiasm, then it reveals something unique about your friend's taste. Thus, when a behavior is high in consensus, it leads to an external attribution (something in the environment caused everyone to respond the same way); when a behavior is low in consensus, it leads to an internal attribution (something within the individual led to a unique response).
3. *Consistency.* Does the person behave the same way over time and across modalities? For example, does your friend respond just as enthusiastically to the new food each time it is eaten, regardless of the circumstances, and does your friend also like the food's aroma and texture as well as its taste? If your friend responds the same way across time and modality, then it suggests that the food is truly pleasurable; however, such a response also reveals something about your friend, because it suggests that your friend has a genuine liking for the food, regardless of when, where, or how it is encountered. In contrast, if your friend's response to the food varies across time and modalities, then it reveals little about either the food or your friend; instead, it suggests that some factor of chance or circumstance may have caused the original response, such as being on vacation or eating the food at a special restaurant. Thus, when a behavior is high in consistency, it leads to both external attributions (a particular entity or event causes a certain response, regardless of time and modality) and internal attributions (something within the person leads to the same response across time and modalities). But when a behavior is low in consistency, it is difficult to make any stable attribution to either an external factor or an internal factor.

Several investigators have reported evidence supporting Kelley's (1967) ideas. In one such study, Leslie McArthur (1972) examined the causal attributions people made for another person's behavior. McArthur presented subjects with statements describing a person's response to a certain stimulus (for example, "Tom is enthralled by the painting") and three accompanying statements providing information about high or low consensus (high: "Almost everyone who sees the painting is enthralled by it"), high or low distinctiveness (high: "Tom is not enthralled by almost every other painting"), and

External Attributions	Internal Attributions
1. **High Distinctiveness** A person's behavior is distinctive toward a particular entity.	1. **Low Distinctiveness** The same behavior is shown toward other entities as well.
2. **High Consensus** Other people behave the same way toward a particular entity.	2. **Low Consensus** The individual's behavior is unique and is not shared by other people.
3. **High Consistency** The individual responds in the same way toward a particular entity regardless of time, circumstances, or modalities.	3. **High Consistency** The individual responds in the same way toward a particular entity regardless of time, circumstances, or modalities.

FIGURE 6.3 Conditions allowing external attributions and internal attributions in Kelley's theory.

high or low consistency (high: "In the past, Tom has almost always been enthralled by the same painting"). For each set of information, the subjects were asked to decide what probably caused the event to occur. They could attribute it to something about the person, something about the stimulus, something about the particular circumstances, or some combination of two or more of the three factors. McArthur found that people tended to attribute the response to the stimulus (that is, something about the painting) when the response was described as being high in distinctiveness, high in consensus, and high in consistency. In contrast, she found that people were likely to attribute the response to the person (that is, something about Tom) when it was characterized by low consensus, low distinctiveness, and high consistency. Overall, McArthur's results support Kelley's theory and suggest that people may be quite sophisticated in their analysis of information as they make causal inferences about behavior.

CAUSAL SCHEMATA Kelley does not claim that his model is appropriate for all the causal attributions we make in daily life. In fact, Kelley (1971a) believes that it is not actually descriptive of most day-to-day attributions (recall the type of "raw perception" attributional analysis Heider proposed). According to Kelley, the inferential problem is only occasionally so imposing that it necessitates a full-blown attributional analysis. Furthermore, we often do not have the time to engage in a complete analysis, even if it were necessary. The pace and complexity of modern life frequently require hasty deliberations in which decisions are made mainly on the basis of present feelings, thoughts and perceptions, our own past experiences, or the advice of others. Kelley contends that past experience can provide individuals with a store of knowledge and that individuals can call on this store of knowledge when an inference has to be made quickly. This backlog, or store of knowledge, of causal relations represents what Kelley refers to as "causal schemata." In Kelley's view, a *causal schema* may be thought of as a script that tells an actor how to make sense out of events, what to expect, and how to react to certain situations. Although Heider does not explicitly acknowledge such a backlog of past experience, he, too, seems to be advancing a notion similar to causal schemata in his assertion that people make hundreds of attributions every day.

According to Kelley's conception, causal schemata are learned, stored in the person's memory, and then activated by environmental cues. They presumably generalize across a broad range of objects and situations and may be activated by numerous types of cues. For example, a person who observes two people embracing affectionately and happily at an airport terminal might readily infer that the people have a warm friendship and that they have just been reunited. On the other hand, the sight of tears might suggest that they are about to be separated from one another. These situations are so familiar in one's past experience that a full attributional analysis is unnecessary. An observer simply relies on a well-learned schema to explain the behavior.

SOME EVIDENCE ABOUT THE CAUSAL-SCHEMATA MODEL Kelley's causal-schemata model has not yet received sufficient empirical attention. One causal-schema prediction that has been tested, however, is the notion that the more extreme a behavior, the more likely it is that an observer would attribute responsibility for that behavior to multiple causes. This prediction was tested in a study by Cunningham and Kelley (1975). These investigators asked subjects to make attributions about hypothetical social events that varied in their extremity of effect. An example of an extreme effect in this study was "Norm always avoids Al," whereas an example of a moderate effect was "Norm sometimes avoids Al." The more extreme the effect, the more likely were observers to attribute responsibility for that effect to multiple causes—for example, Norm does not like people very much, and Al is not a very pleasant person to be around. Cunningham and Kelley found relatively strong support for the hypothesis across a wide array of hypothetical social situations.

Important questions about causal schemata remain to be studied. For example, how do causal schemata develop? Do people have different types of causal schemata at different stages of development? How advanced do schemata become in the cognitive development of most people?

DISCOUNTING Another instance when a full-scale attributional analysis is unnecessary involves discounting. Consider the case where an average student consistently flatters an instructor about the quality of the instructor's lectures. Suppose no other student in the class flatters the instructor, who also typically does not receive high ratings as a teacher. While the student who does the praising may claim that the lauding of the teacher was well deserved, an attributor might readily *discount* this claim and instead infer that the student was merely trying to ingratiate himself or herself with the instructor to achieve a high grade in the course. When are certain possible causes discounted? According to Kelley (1971b): "The role of a given cause in producing a given effect is discounted if other plausible causes are also present" (p. 8). In the example above, the attributor might discount the student's praise for the teacher because another plausible cause for the student's behavior—ingratiation—is also present.

A well-known pair of studies by Thibaut and Riecken (1955) illustrates how the discounting principle works. In one of these studies, an undergraduate student worked on a task with two other subjects, both of whom were actually the experimenter's accomplices. One of the confederates was a high-status person (he had just finished his Ph.D. requirements), while the other was a low-status person (he had just finished his freshman year of college). Part of the experiment required the real subject to request help from the confederates. Later the subject was asked why each of the other persons had complied with the request for help: Was it because the other wanted to help (an internal cause) or because the other had been pressured to help (an external cause)? The results showed that subjects attributed the high-status person's compliance to the internal cause and the low-status person's compliance to the external cause.

To understand how this study relates to the discounting principle, consider the possible causes for the compliance. Both the high- and low-status helpers could have complied for either internal causes (the helper's own preference) or external causes (the subject's persuasive power). In the case of the high-status helper, the subject's power is not a plausible cause for compliance; since there is no other cause that could lead to a discounting of the helper's motives, compliance is attributed internally. In the case of the low-status helper, however, the subject's power is a plausible cause for compliance, and, given the two plausible causes (the subject's power or the helper's own preference), the role of the internal cause is discounted; thus, the low-status person's behavior is attributed to external pressure.

Although Kelley (1971b) has reviewed a large body of evidence relating to the discounting principle, a number of major questions remain to be investigated. For example, what decisional rules do people use in deciding which of several seemingly equivalent causes to discount?

THREE APPROACHES TO ATTRIBUTION: A BRIEF COMPARISON

Heider's naïve analysis of action (Heider and Simmel, 1944; Heider, 1958) was the seminal work for later theory and research in attribution. Heider emphasized an individual's common-sense search for meaning in events. He treated attributions like "raw" perceptions, suggesting that people could quickly formulate numerous cause-and-effect linkages. Heider distinguished between internal and external causes of behavior, and he proposed circumstances that allow the inference of dispositional responsibility.

Jones and Davis (1965) presented the first empirically grounded statement about attribution processes. These theorists were concerned primarily with person perception, not self-perception. They were particularly interested in how perceivers make attributions about the intents and dispositions of other people. Correspondent inferences about dispositional causes are possible, Jones and Davis suggested, when a behavior's effects are unique (noncommon with other behaviors) and extreme (not predictable within a situation).

Kelley's work has had three aims: (1) synthesizing earlier treatments of person perception and self-perception; (2) developing a formal model of how people deliberately analyze information about a behavior's distinctiveness, consensus, and consistency in making causal attributions; and (3) analyzing how people sometimes use accumulated knowledge from their past experience in observing behavior to make attributions very quickly.

EXTENSIONS OF ORIGINAL ATTRIBUTION THEORY

BEM'S CONTRIBUTION TO ATTRIBUTION THEORY

Daryl Bem's (1967, 1972) theory of self-perception was discussed in Chapter 3. We will now describe only those aspects of his work that relate to attribution. As Kelley recognized in his integrative analysis (1967), Bem's work on self-perception was a necessary complement to Jones and Davis's work on person perception. Interestingly, although Bem's ideas were originally proposed as an alternative explanation for cognitive dissonance phenomena and attitude change (see Chapters 4 and 5), his work has now become an important part of the attribution literature.

Bem (1972) claims that people come to know their own attitudes, emotions, and other internal states partially by inferring them from observations of their own overt behavior and the context in which this behavior occurs. The strikingly unorthodox implication of Bem's analysis is that people sometimes do not know what they think, feel, or believe until they see themselves act. From this perspective, human beings are viewed strictly as information processors who make inferences about their own internal dispositions in the same way they would if they were trying to explain the behavior of another individual they had observed.

Bem argues that when an individual's own internal cues are weak, ambiguous, or uninterpretable, that individual is functionally in the same position as an outside observer. To understand our own behavior under such circumstances, we would first have to look to the context in which it occurs. If we cannot attribute our behavior to some external force, then we must make an inference about our own internal dispositions. For example, consider the case in which Sue seeks to understand her friend Ann's political ideology. Sue observes that Ann voted

Conservative in the last election and that no one coerced her to do so. Sue infers that Ann must be a Conservative. Now consider the case from Ann's own perspective. If Ann had never voted before, and she had no strong political philosophy prior to the election, her own internal attitude might be ambiguous, weak, and uninterpretable. To explain her own behavior, she might say to herself, "Well, I voted for the Conservative candidate and nobody forced me to; I guess I must be a Conservative." On the other hand, assume that Ann knows she has voted for the Liberal candidate in the past and that she has endorsed the views of the Liberal party for many years. In this case, Ann's own inner state is *not* ambiguous, weak, or uninterpretable. She knows clearly that her political philosophy is Liberal and that her recent Conservative vote should be attributed to the particular candidate running on the Conservative ticket rather than to an internal disposition. Under circumstances such as these, Bem concedes that the individual is *not* functionally in the same position as an outside observer, because the individual knows more about her own inner states than would an outside observer. In fact, under these circumstances, Sue, the observer, may err if she relies solely on Ann's behavior in the seemingly noncoercive context of the voting booth to infer that Ann is a Conservative. Because observers often utilize different information than actors in arriving at causal attributions, their explanations of behavior frequently differ, as the next section explains.

According to the divergent perspectives hypothesis, variations in attributions may result from actor-observer differences. Thus, the fans at a football game may blame the quarterback's incompetence for an incomplete pass, while the quarterback himself would be likely to attribute the incomplete pass to the actions of other players on the field. *(© George Whiteley 1973 / Photo Researchers)*

JONES AND NISBETT'S DIVERGENT PERSPECTIVES HYPOTHESIS

One of the richest extensions of attribution research has focused on the differing perspectives of actors (those who perform a behavior) versus observers, and how these differing perspectives influence the causal attributions of each. Edward Jones and Richard Nisbett (1971) have formulated a highly provocative statement about actor-observer differences in attribution—the *divergent perspectives hypothesis*—and their work has influenced much research.

As a way of illustrating divergent perspectives in attribution, let's consider the situation confronting a quarterback who fails to complete several passes on third down and long yardage in an important game. Fans may view the quarterback's incomplete passes as an indication of the quarterback's incompetence. On the other hand, the quarterback himself may attribute the incomplete passes to the rushing linemen of the opposing team and to his own linemen's inability to hold back the opponent. These divergent attributions of fans versus the quarterback may be at least partially due to their different perspectives. The fans focus on the quarterback as the most important stimulus on the field and tend to ignore the surrounding events; the quarterback, in contrast, focuses entirely on the surrounding events. Partly as a result of such divergent perspectives, the fans make an internal attribution for the failed passes (to the quarterback's own incompetence) while the quarterback himself makes an external attribution for the failed passes (to the play of the offensive and defensive linemen).

Pursuing some of Heider's (1958) insights, Jones and Nisbett proposed that actors and observers alike are subject to a pervasive bias in their causal attributions: *actors are likely to attribute responsibility for their behavior to situational influences, whereas observers are likely to attribute responsibility for the same behavior to stable dispositions within the actors.*

Jones and Nisbett think there are two principal reasons for actors' and observers' divergent attributions. First, actors and observers possess *different information.* Actors know more about their own past experiences and inner feelings than do observers. Thus actors are aware that their behavior may have differed in the past, whereas observers must rely on the actors' current behavior to infer inner dispositions. To use Kelley's terms, observers probably lack information about the distinctiveness and consistency of the actors' behavior.

The second reason for actors' and observers' divergent attributions is that *different aspects of the available information are salient for actors and observers.* Because actors' sensory receptors are poorly located for observing themselves in action, they tend to direct their attention to the situational cues surrounding them. For the observers, however, the actor is the most salient cue, and surrounding factors are merely background for the actor's behavior. Consequently, actors tend to explain their behavior as a response to the salient situational factors that surround them, while observers tend to assign major responsibility to the actors themselves.

SOME EVIDENCE ABOUT THE DIVERGENT PERSPECTIVES HYPOTHESIS Two experiments have provided the most direct and compelling evidence in support of Jones and Nisbett's divergent perspectives hypothesis. Richard Nisbett and his associates (Nisbett, Caputo, Legant, and Maracek, 1973) created a situation in which observer-subjects watched actor-subjects either comply or not comply with an experimenter's request that the actors volunteer their time to help out with a service project for their university. Later, when asked to predict whether the actors would also volunteer for similar projects in the future, the observers assumed that actors would help out in the future as well; actors thought it would depend on the circumstances. In other words, observers explained the actors' behavior as reflecting stable internal dispositions; actors saw the same behavior as a response to external circumstances. In further support of the divergent perspectives hypothesis, Nisbett and associates found that male college students explained their best friends' choice of girlfriends and college majors as a reflection of their friends' dispositional qualities, but they explained their own similar choices in terms of attractive characteristics of the girlfriends and majors.

Michael Storms's (1973) study, discussed in Chapter 3, also provides clear evidence that actors and observers explain the actor's behavior differently. Even more interesting, Storms showed that actors' and observers' attributions could be reversed if their perspectives on the actor's behavior were reversed. By videotaping half of the actors from an observer's perspective and then playing it back to those actors, actors were allowed to see themselves as observers do. Similarly by playing a videotape for half of the observers that was made from the actors' perspective, observers were allowed to see the world through the actors' eyes. The other half of the subjects saw their original perspectives on videotape. For those subjects whose perspectives were not reversed, actors made the predicted situational attributions for their behavior while observers saw the same behavior as reflecting internal dispositions of the actors. However, when perspectives were reversed, actors' attributions became more dispositional and observers' attributions more situational, as shown in Figure 6.4. Thus Storms's study demonstrates that focus of attention is an important determinant of causal attributions, as Jones and Nisbett hypothesized.

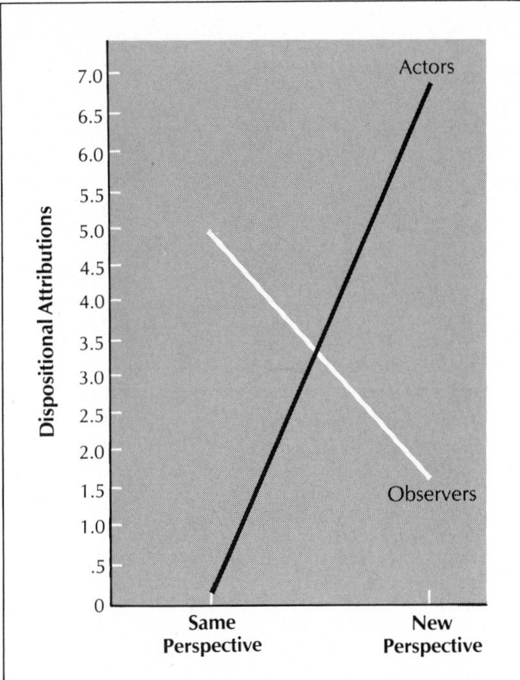

FIGURE 6.4 Actors' and observers' attributions as a function of perspective. Actors who saw their original perspectives on videotape made situational attributions for their behavior (in the graph shown here, a low dispositional score is a high situational score), while observers who saw their original perspectives made dispositional attributions for the actor's behavior. When the perspectives were reversed, however, the attributions reversed, too; actors made dispositional attributions, and observers made situational attributions. (Adapted from Storms, 1973.)

SOME QUALIFICATIONS OF THE DIVERGENT PERSPECTIVES HYPOTHESIS While observers frequently underemphasize the importance of situational influences on an actor's behavior, as the above research demonstrates, they are not always blind to those factors. Jones and Nisbett make no predictions about circumstances under which observers may be more or less attuned to situational factors, but several experiments have investigated these circumstances. In one of these studies, John Harvey and his associates (Harvey, Arkin, Gleason, and Johnston, 1974) exposed observers to an actor whose behavior led either to an expected or unexpected effect. When the effect was *discrepant* with observers' expectation (for example, when a positive effect had been expected, but a negative effect occurred), observers attributed much more responsibility to the actor than when the effect was not discrepant. Harvey and associates argued that a discrepancy between expected and actual events makes the actor's behavior highly salient and hence draws observers' attributions to the actor. (Note the similarity between this explanation and the previously mentioned hypothesis by Jones and Davis [1965] that socially inappropriate, out-of-role behavior results in greater dispositional attributions.)

In a second study, Harvey and his associates (Harvey, Harris, and Barnes, 1975) exposed observers to an actor whose behavior had either a moderately negative or a strongly negative effect on another person. The results showed that the more negative the effect, the more responsibility the observers attributed to the actor. Perhaps the observers felt a greater need to predict or control the actor's behavior the more negative it was, and thus they made more dispositional attributions.

An important reformulation of the divergent perspectives hypothesis was recently proposed by Thomas Monson and Mark Snyder (1977), who suggested a number of qualifying propositions. These qualifications include the following conditions:

1. When a behavior has been performed in a situation *chosen* by the actor, actors are likely to make more dispositional attributions than observers. In situations not chosen by the actor, actors are likely to make more situational attributions than observers.
2. Individuals may differ in a *general way* in their inclinations to make situational or dispositional inferences, regardless of their role as actors or observers.
3. When an act leads to an outcome that is *not intended,* actors are likely to make more situational attributions than observers.
4. When observers are led to empathize with actors, observers' attributions should be similar to actors' attributions (Regan and Totten, 1975).

SOCIAL PSYCHOLOGY AND THE ARTS

THE OBSERVER'S PERSPECTIVE: ASSIGNING ROLES

This chapter began with an incident from John Barth's novel, *The End of the Road.* This same novel also contains an incident that demonstrates Jones and Nisbett's proposition about actors and observers. As explained in the accompanying section, observers are likely to view an actor's behavior as reflecting stable dispositions within the actor, while actors themselves are likely to be aware of situational influences on their behavior.

In the passage below, Barth suggests that social interaction may require this simplification on the observer's part, even though it is "an arbitrary distortion of the actors' personalities." In the same way that dispositional attributions for another's behavior may be necessary in order for the observer to gain a sense of prediction and control over social events—according to attribution theorists—Barth argues that "such role assigning . . . is apparently necessary if one would reach the ends he desires."

The following passage describes Jacob Horner's attempt to pick up Peggy Rankin, a woman he met at the beach. From her perspective as an actor, Peggy Rankin points out many situational factors that have influenced her feelings, ranging from events during the past two weeks to Jacob's behavior. From his perspective as an observer, however, Jacob sees Miss Rankin in dispositional terms—as a "Forty-Year-Old Pickup."

> "Don't you understand how you make me feel? Today is my last day at Ocean City. For two whole weeks not a soul had spoken to me or even looked at me, except some horrible old men. Not a *soul!* Most women look awful at my age, but I don't look awful: I just don't look like a child. There's a lot *more* to me, damn it! And then on the last day you come along and pick me up, bored as you can be with the whole thing, and treat me like a whore!"
>
> Well, she was correct.
>
> "I'm a cad," I agreed readily, and rose to leave. There was a little more to this matter than Miss Rankin was willing to see, but in the main she had a pretty clear view of things. Her mistake, in the long run, was articulating her protest. The game was spoiled now, of course: I had assigned to Miss Rankin the role of Forty-Year-Old Pickup, a delicate enough character for her to bring off successfully in my current mood; I had no interest whatever in the quite complex (and no doubt interesting, from another point of view) human being she might be apart from that role. What she should have done, it seems to me, assuming she was after the same thing I was after, was assign me a role gratifying to her own vanity—say, The Fresh But Unintelligent Young Man Whose Body One Uses For One's Pleasure Without Otherwise Taking Him Seriously—and then we could have pursued our business with no wounds inflicted on either side. As it was, my present feeling, though a good deal stronger, was essentially the same feeling one has when a filling-station attendant or a cabdriver launches into his life-story: as a rule, and especially when one is in a hurry or is grouchy, one wishes the man to be nothing more difficult than The Obliging Filling-Station Attendant or The Adroit Cabdriver. These are the essences you have assigned them, at least temporarily, for your own purposes, as a taleteller makes a man The Handsome Young Poet or The Jealous Old Husband; and while you know very well that no historical human being was ever *just* an Obliging Filling-Station Attendant or a Handsome Young Poet, you are nevertheless prepared to ignore your man's charming complexities—*must* ignore them, in fact, if you are to get on with the plot, or get things done according to schedule.
>
> . . . We are all casting directors a great deal of the time, if not always, and he is wise who realizes that his role-assigning is at best an arbitrary distortion of the actors' personalities; but he is even wiser who sees in addition that his arbitrariness is probably inevitable, and at any rate is apparently necessary if one would reach the ends he desires.

Source: John Barth, *The End of the Road* (New York: Bantam, 1967; originally published 1958): 27–28.

Despite these proposed qualifications, Jones and Nisbett's proposition about divergent perspectives has many practical implications. Anyone who needs to understand and be understood by another person—such as teachers and students, managers and workers, husbands and wives, and parents and children—should keep in mind that actors and observers frequently see the same behavior differently. To understand the other's behavior, perhaps one should adopt the other's perspective.

TABLE 6.1 WEINER AND ASSOCIATES' CLASSIFICATION SCHEME FOR THE PERCEIVED DETERMINANTS OF ACHIEVEMENT BEHAVIOR

STABILITY DIMENSION	LOCUS OF CONTROL DIMENSION	
	INTERNAL	EXTERNAL
Stable	Ability	Task Difficulty
Unstable	Effort	Luck

Source: B. Weiner et al., *Perceiving the Causes of Success and Failure* (Morristown, N.J.: General Learning Corp., 1971).

ATTRIBUTION ABOUT CAUSES OF SUCCESS AND FAILURE

Another extension of attribution theory concerns people's attributions about the causes of success and failure. According to Bernard Weiner and his colleagues (1971), people infer causal responsibility for another person's success and failure at a task mainly on the basis of four factors: a perception of the other person's *ability*; how much *effort* the person seemed to exert on the task; how *difficult* the task was; and how much *luck* influenced the outcome. In this scheme, ability and effort are properties internal to the person, whereas task difficulty and luck are external factors. In addition, ability and task difficulty are relatively stable or invariant, whereas luck and effort tend to be more variable. This scheme is summarized in Table 6.1.

A study by Irene Frieze and Bernard Weiner (1971) illustrates how these factors influence causal attributions. These investigators employed Kelley's principles of attribution to understand perceptions of success and failure. Their subjects were given information about a person's prior success or failure at similar tasks (the consistency of the behavior), and the performance of others at the task (social consensus). The subjects were then asked to attribute responsibility for the person's immediate success or failure to the four factors outlined above: ability, effort, task difficulty, and luck. The data revealed these patterns: (1) outcomes with high consensus were ascribed to characteristics of the task—for example, that it was unusually easy or hard; (2) success was generally ascribed to internal factors, while failure was attributed to external factors; (3) behavior inconsistent with past performance was attributed to the unstable factors of luck and effort; and (4) the greater the degree of prior success or failure, the greater the tendency for immediate success or failure to be attributed to high or low ability.

Weiner and his colleagues believe that our perceptions of "effort," or "trying," are important determinants of how much we reward people for their task performance. In fact, effort appears to be an even more important determinant of rewards and punishments than ability. According to Weiner and his associates, this is a reasonable basis for evaluating others' performance. It is likely that teachers, for example, can set up environmental conditions to stimulate the effort that other people, such as students, expend; however, ability is presumably unaffected by environmental conditions and, therefore, less emphasized in evaluating achievement.

An interesting question is how children learn the importance of these factors as they begin to evaluate other people's performance. According to one study (Weiner and Peter, 1973), as children of both sexes develop, they first focus on intent (effort) as they evaluate someone's performance; then around age twelve they begin to place greatest weight on outcome (how well a person did), and this trend continues into adult life. This developmental drift toward the outcome dimension, as opposed to the intent dimension, in evaluative judgment is reinforced by society—even though emphasis on outcome would seem to be a more primitive stage of development.

Weiner and his associates have investigated many questions relating to attributions for success and failure (see Weiner, 1974, for a comprehensive review of work in this area). This work may have important implications for education and for understanding how people develop cognitive sets for evaluating the performance of others.

SEX DIFFERENCES AND ATTRIBUTION

In recent years, many researchers have begun to study sex differences in behavior. Some of their work has focused on attribution processes. Attribution enters into sex stereotyping because we frequently make different inferences about the reasons for a person's behavior on the basis of a person's sex. If a woman graduates at the head of a medical-school class, for example, people may explain her success quite differently than if a man takes top honors in the class. Because this behavior may seem unusual for a woman, people may think that the woman put most of her energy into studying and that she is probably inadequate in social relations. The successful male, however, may be seen as following an expected course, one that does not reflect inability in social relations. One probably can think of many other situations where a woman's behavior—even though it is identical to that of a man in the same situation—often produces a negative and stereotypic attribution. Common examples include women walking the streets at night, sitting alone in a park, or having a drink alone at a bar.

Kay Deaux (1976) has provided an interesting summary of research on sex differences and attribution, and her work demonstrates how people's attributions often reflect sex biases. In one study (Deaux and Emswiller, 1974) both men and women tended to perceive successful performance by a man on a "masculine" task (a mechanical problem) as due to ability, while successful performance by a woman on the same task was attributed to luck. Deaux argues that this attributional stereotype is mediated by expectancy (that is, how well a particular sex should do on a particular task) and that expectancies must change before stereotypes, and perhaps discriminatory behavior, will change.

Research shows that our attributions often reflect sex biases. For example, we are likely to attribute a man's becoming an astronaut to his ability, but we might regard the same achievement in a woman as the result of luck or single-mindedness. *(René Burri / Magnum)*

ATTRIBUTION IN CLOSE RELATIONS

A recent research concern for social psychologists is the area of close, long-term, affective relationships. Attribution no doubt plays a major role in our behavior in close relationships. We make inferences about whether or not others will be receptive to us, whether or not they really love us, whether or not they secretly want out of a relationship, and so on. Even in long-term relationships, people are constantly evaluating the intents and meanings of each other's actions. It seems especially important that we think we understand others whom we love, have loved, or want to love. Thus, we spend much time analyzing our lovers and love situations, sometimes in an unconscious fashion. Perhaps the most poignant attributions we make in close relationships are our attempts to explain why relationships have come to an end.

A study by Harvey, Wells, and Alvarez (1978) reveals some of the breadth and intensity of attributions people make when separating from a marriage of over two years duration. When asked why they felt the separation had occurred, some of these people's major attributions included romantic involvement outside of marriage; insensitivity and lack of affection and sexual intimacy; quest for freedom from the constraints of marriage and desire for a new life style; different values and habits; and commitment to end the relationship (involving an escalation of verbal or sometimes physical abuse, threats to end it, and actual trial separation). Further, Harvey and his associates found that people who are separated often spend much time questioning why their relationships ended, involving sleepless nights of private rumination and many lengthy discussions with friends. These periods of quandary are accompanied by emotional, self-deprecating, obsessive thoughts such as the following:

> "I need somebody now. I'm falling apart inside. My insecurity is showing. I feel as though I have very little to hang on to."

> "I'm terribly confused. I need help! Somebody please tell me what I'm doing."

> "I'm feeling that there is no hope for my ever finding anyone with whom to spend what is left of my sometimes miserable life."

One investigation in this area has found pronounced differences in how males and females explain conflict in close relationships (Orvis, Kelley, and Butler, 1976). Male and female college students, most of whom had been living together for some time, were asked to give their individual explanations for conflicts that had arisen in their relationships. The findings of this study relate well to Deaux's work on sex differences in attribution and to Jones and Nisbett's proposition about actor-observer differences.

In terms of sex differences, these investigators found that the female's behavior in a close relationship is more often attributed to the environment, to other people, to inability, and to insecurity about the relationship than is the behavior of the male. These attributions appear to be consistent with common stereotypes of women as more dependent and weaker than men.

Relevant to the divergent perspectives hypothesis, actors were found to explain their behavior as caused by environmental circumstances, such as other people or objects, as well as to the actor's emotional state and the actor's preferences or beliefs. In contrast, the partner often explained the actor's behavior in terms of the actor's characteristics and the actor's negative attitude toward the partner. While these attributional patterns partially support Jones and Nisbett's hypothesis, they also show how attributions in close relations may be made by both actors and partners to communicate to one another feelings of justification and exoneration or blame and accusation.

ATTRIBUTION OF EMOTION

Consider a man who frequently has unexplainable feelings, for example, headaches and stomach sickness, when he wakes up in the morning. This man's emotional state and related behavior will no doubt be greatly different depending on whether he interprets his physical state as evidence of serious illness (such as brain tumor) or as evidence of a temporary reaction to severe urban pollution. He probably will search for clues (for example, by examining how he feels in other ways and at other times and by inquiring about how others feel early in the morning) as to why he feels the way he does. If he infers that pollution is not causing his physical state, he will most likely be very anxious and seek immediate medical help; but if he infers that it is pollution, he will probably just go about his life without too much anxiety, though perhaps with even greater disdain for his plight of having to live in a polluted city. This man's attribution of the basis for his state may greatly influence how he subsequently feels and behaves. We may analyze the man's situation and find that two main clusters of factors go into his attributional analysis: his experience of physiological reactions (headaches) and his perception of environmental circumstances in which he finds himself (the extent to which the air is polluted and whether other persons mention similar physical symptoms). These are the two clusters of factors that are most important in the attributional approach to emotional states, which began with the work of Stanley Schachter and Jerome Singer (1962).

SCHACHTER AND SINGER'S APPROACH Schachter and Singer proposed that individuals in a state of physiological arousal for which they have no immediate explanation will feel a need to evaluate their state. In order to evaluate their unknown state, individuals presumably will focus on their social context and label their state in terms of emotion-related cues present in this context. Schachter and Singer also proposed that if aroused individuals have an explanation for their physiological state, they will not have this evaluative need and consequently will not search their social context for an understanding of their state. In sum, the basic postulate of this approach to emotion may be stated succinctly as: *physiological arousal + situational cues relevant to the arousal = emotional state.*

In their test of these ideas, Schachter and Singer (1962) designed a realistic experimental setting to manipulate subjects' arousal and explanations for their arousal. To enhance credibility, they conducted the study at a medical research center. College students were recruited for a study that purportedy concerned how a certain vitamin compound, Suproxin, affects vision. If they agreed to continue their participation in the study, subjects were told they would be given a small injection of the vitamin compound. There were three conditions in which subjects actually were injected with epinephrine, which causes autonomic arousal (such as heart pounding or flushed, warm face), and one condition in which subjects were actually injected with a saline solution that does not cause arousal or have other noticeable effects. In those who received epinephrine, arousal symptoms began to occur in about 5 minutes.

Explanations for the arousal were varied by giving subjects information about the presumed side effects of the vitamin. There were three information conditions:

1. Epinephrine informed, in which the real effects of epinephrine were described as the side effects. These subjects were expected to understand how they would feel and, accordingly, attribute their aroused state to the drug.
2. Epinephrine ignorant, in which Suproxin was said to have no side effects. These subjects were not expected to have an appropriate explanation for their aroused state and thus were expected to search their social context for an explanation.
3. Epinephrine misinformed, in which a variety of irrelevant effects, such as itching sensation and numbness in feet, were reported to accompany injection of the vitamin. These subjects were not expected to attribute their arousal to the drug, because its effects did not correspond with those they expected; hence, they were expected to search their social context for an explanation.

Subjects given the placebo (those to whom a saline solution had been administered) were give the same instructions as subjects in the epinephrine-ignorant condition.

After the injections had been administered, the experimenter brought in another subject (actually an accomplice) who was supposedly undergoing the same treatment. The experimenter told both subjects that the part of the study concerning effects on vision would begin in about 20 minutes, after the Suproxin had started to take effect. The subjects waited together during this time interval. The accomplice's job was to act out one of two emotional charades intended to supply the subjects with contextual cognitions. In one condition, the accomplice displayed a series of euphoric actions (wadded up paper and practiced jump shots into the wastebasket). In the other condition, the accomplice showed an increasing amount of anger about the personal nature of the questions (questions concerning the extramarital sexual behavior of his mother); he ultimately ripped up the questionnaire and stomped out of the room.

During this interaction, the subjects' behavior was observed from behind a one-way mirror, and the extent to which they imitated the accomplice was recorded. After the interaction period the experimenter asked subjects a series of questions about their mood at that time.

The results of the Schachter and Singer experiment provided considerable support for their predictions. The groups injected with epinephrine did report more arousal symptoms than did the group that received saline injections. Thus, as expected, physiological arousal was created by epinephrine injection. How well were the predictions for cognitive labeling supported by the data?

Table 6.2 presents the findings for subjects' actual behavior in the interaction situation. When the accomplice acted euphoric, the subjects in the ignorant and misinformed conditions imitated him more than did subjects in the informed condition. These results are clearly in line with Schachter and Singer's predictions. However, Table 6.2 also shows that there was a relatively great amount of imitation of the euphoric accomplice by the subjects who had been injected with saline: according to Schachter and Singer's theory, these subjects, who presumably were not physiologically aroused, should not have exhibited any more euphoria or anger than did the informed subjects—but they did. The data for the subjects who received saline are rather important, and Schachter and Singer's interpretation of these data will be examined after we have presented the results for the conditions involving the angry accomplice.

Table 6.2 shows that when the accomplice acted angry, the subjects showed the expected pattern of imitating the accomplice more when they were ignorant than when they were informed about their physiological state; no epinephrine-misinformed condition was run with the angry accomplice. Also, subjects injected with saline showed more anger than expected, in comparison to the informed subjects.

Without presenting the specific data, we should note that the mood responses, reported on the postexperimental questionnaire, for subjects in conditions with both the euphoric and angry accomplice paralleled the data for actual behavior; that is, their feelings of anger or euphoria corresponded to their display of these emotions.

Overall, Schachter and Singer's results indicate that persons who were aroused and did not have adequate explanations for their arousal labeled their emotional states in terms of emotion-related cues present in their social contexts.

TABLE 6.2 EFFECTS OF PHYSIOLOGICAL AROUSAL AND INFORMATION ABOUT AROUSED STATE ON EMOTIONAL BEHAVIOR*

	ACCOMPLICE	
STATE OF AROUSAL	EUPHORIC	ANGRY
Nonaroused (saline-injected)		
Ignorant	16.00	.79
Physiologically aroused (epinephrine-injected)		
Informed	12.70	−.18
Ignorant	18.30	2.28
Misinformed	22.60	—

*The higher the score, the more euphoria or anger the subjects displayed. An epinephrine-injected, misinformed condition was not run with the angry accomplice.

Source: Adapted from S. Schachter and J. E. Singer, "Cognitive, Social and Physiological Determinants of Emotional State," *Psychological Review* 69 (1962): 379–399.

This labeling process occurred for subjects in conditions with both the euphoric and angry accomplice. The most problematic aspect of these results pertains to the finding that subjects who received saline injections also showed a slight tendency to label their emotional states in terms of available situational cues. This latter finding is puzzling for the Schachter and Singer conception, because the saline-injected subjects did not report arousal (nor were they expected to). Schachter and Singer interpreted these subjects' behavior as possibly indicating that they may have informed themselves that they were aroused, actually may have become somewhat aroused, and then may have labeled their state in light of the accomplice's behavior.

Schachter and Singer's research suggests that attribution processes may be important in understanding some emotional disorders and in treating some emotional problems. For instance, people may falsely attribute responsibility for some emotional disorders to themselves and suffer unnecessary self-blame as a result; on the other hand, people may simply *think* they are aroused, without actually being aroused, and interpret their perceived arousal in light of the surrounding social situation.

IMPLICATIONS FOR PSYCHOTHERAPY During periods of intense depression, students may seek assistance from a therapist or counselor. In discussing the student's problems, the therapist may discover that the depression is related directly to a sense of failure in school and in interpersonal relations. Often such failures are attributed by depressed persons to their own incompetence and inadequacy. For example, students may feel that because they are not making good grades and are not attracting interesting people for relationships, they must be incompetent misfits. An attributional approach to such problems might involve a causal analysis that emphasizes how outcomes were influenced by environmental factors. The therapist may attempt to shift a depressed person's attributions for failures from internal blame to a more external focus. For example, students might be shown how academically competitive their school is, and they might be given tips on how to become socially attractive. Presumably, such a shift in attributions would facilitate a positive self-image and help relieve depression.

RESEARCH ON ATTRIBUTION THERAPY Research has shown how attribution therapy might be effective in changing people's maladaptive behaviors. In an early demonstration of the potential usefulness of this approach Lee Ross, Judith Rodin, and Philip Zimbardo (1969) encouraged laboratory subjects to reattribute their fear of electric shock to a different event. As a result, these subjects felt less fearful of the shock. Based on this finding, Ross and associates suggested that phobic patients may be helped by therapeutic procedures that lead them to reattribute their fearful arousal to some external stimulus.

Such a procedure was actually employed in an attribution therapy program for insomniacs, conducted by Michael Storms and Richard Nisbett (1970). Some subjects in the program were given a placebo (an inactive "drug" such as a sugar pill) described as capable of producing arousal symptoms. Other subjects were given a placebo described as capable of producing relaxation symptoms. Both groups were told to take the "drug" just prior to bedtime. As predicted, those who expected the drug to produce arousal symptoms reported later that they had gotten to sleep significantly faster than did the subjects who expected the drug to produce relaxation symptoms. Presumably, subjects in the aroused condition must have attributed their usual arousal at bedtime to the drug, not to their own anxieties, and thus they were able to fall asleep faster than normal. On the other hand, subjects who expected to be relaxed must have attributed their usual bedtime arousal to even greater-than-usual anxieties, since the pill was having no effect; thus it took them even longer to fall asleep than normal.

The effect found by Storms and Nisbett (1970) has been referred to as the *attribution boomerang effect.* In other words, when arousal caused by phobias and anxieties can be reattributed to an inert placebo substance, then people may feel less concerned about the real causes of their anxieties and thus experience less arousal. This is the opposite of the traditional placebo effect, in which subjects become more aroused after being told a pill will arouse them. Future research is needed to determine when a placebo effect will occur versus when an attribution boomerang effect will occur. Storms and Nisbett's study indicates that people's physiological state (whether or nor they are experiencing a natural state of arousal such as insomnia) may interact with their attributions to influence their emotions and behavior.

LABELING AND ATTRIBUTION

Psychiatric diagnoses involve attributions about the causes of behavioral disorders. When these attributions are biased or incorrect, they may lead to frightening possibilities, as demonstrated by Stanford psychologist David Rosenhan (1973).

Rosenhan and several of his graduate students, who would probably be considered normal, each made appointments for intake interviews at a psychiatric hospital. During these interviews, they feigned certain mental-illness symptoms such as "hearing voices." Practically all of these pseudopatients were admitted to the hospital and labeled by attending psychiatrists as schizophrenic—the most common form of serious mental illness or psychosis. Most of them spent a few weeks in the hospital, acting perfectly normal all the time. They observed how the psychiatrists' diagnostic labels, or attributions about their reported behavior, became perpetuated in the perceptions and behavior of the hospital staff. For example, the pseudopatients spent a lot of time taking notes about what was going on. Although their fellow patients generally perceived them to be normal and merely conducting research or checking up on the hospital, the staff (including the doctors) saw the note taking and observational behavior as symptomatic of their disturbed condition—perhaps reflecting compulsive schizophrenic behavior. The attribution had "taken," and almost anything the pseudopatients did was interpreted as somehow indicative of their supposed schizophrenia.

Rosenhan's data suggest that once people are perceived in a certain way by others, they may have a difficult time escaping or refuting the attribution, regardless of how erroneous it may be. Although persons may know quite well that they are not schizophrenic at the start of their hospital stay, they may find it hard to resist attributing the state of schizophrenia to themselves after a few months of interaction with others who consistently make this attribution to them.

CRITIQUES AND REVISIONS OF ATTRIBUTION THEORY

Do people really operate in such a logical, calculating way as attribution theorists maintain? Do they carefully weigh information before making a social judgment, much like an impartial scientist or even a computer? According to recent research in decision-making theory (Slovic, Fischhoff, and Lichtenstein, 1977), the answer is "definitely not." In fact, people are often illogical and fallible in their causal inferences. Furthermore, such errors of judgment can have serious real-world consequences—for example, in the development of stereotypes.

LIMITATIONS IN PEOPLE'S COGNITIVE-ATTRIBUTIONAL ABILITIES

In an important integrative statement, Baruch Fischhoff (1976) criticizes attribution theorists' view of the individual as an "intuitive scientist" who organizes and processes information in a systematic way. In contrast, Fischhoff states that the work of judgment researchers reveals people to be inept at all but the simplest inferential tasks—and sometimes even at these. In Fischhoff's view, people are seen as "muddling through a world that seems to let them get through life by gratuitously allowing for a lot of error" (p. 421). Thus, while contemporary attribution researchers make explicit assumptions about people's causal inference sophistication (see Jones and McGillis, 1976), judgment researchers have often gone in the opposite direction, looking for even more biases in people's judgments and for ways in which fallible people can be wholly or partially removed from their own decision-making processes.

In an influential demonstration of fallibility

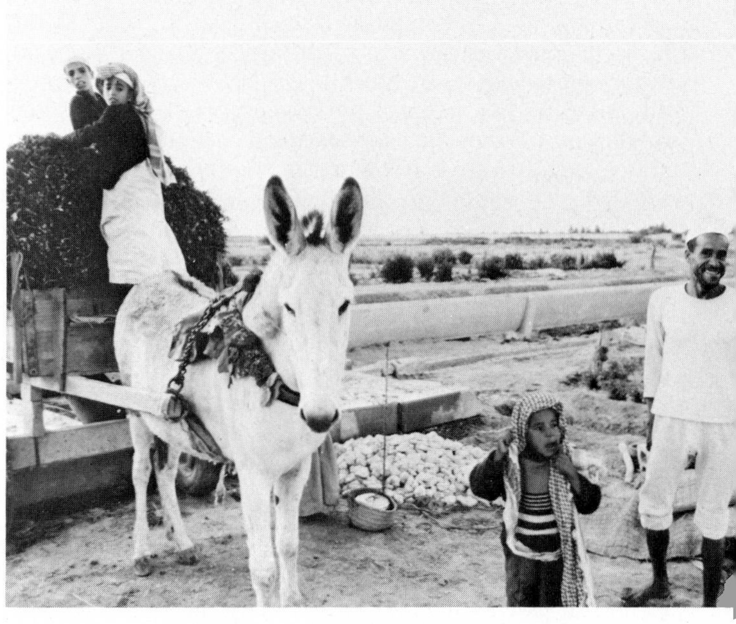

We tend to recall frequently occurring events more easily than those that do not happen often, and this phenomenon can bias our judgment. For example, since we hear regularly about rich Arab oil sheiks, we may forget the fact that most Arabs are poor. *(© Robert Azzi 1979 / Woodfin Camp & Assoc.; © Tony Howarth / Woodfin Camp & Assoc.)*

in judgment, Daniel Kahneman and Amos Tversky (1973) showed that people are often wrong in their recollection and prediction of events. People are frequently confronted with more information than they are able to process. To cope with this overload, they develop "heuristics," or a simple way to organize and codify information. According to Kahneman and Tversky, one important heuristic deals with *availability*. An event is judged likely or frequent if it is easy to recall or to imagine relevant instances. In real life, events that occur frequently are typically easier to recall than events that happen less often; similarly, likely events are easier to imagine than unlikely ones. Thus, the more available something is in memory, the higher is the probability that it is a frequent or likely event. But this common-sense process is also subject to major biases. For example, something may be easily available in our memory because of its prominence and not because of its actual frequency; because of a few prominent oil sheiks, for example, we expect all Arabs to be rich. On the other hand, we may assume that something is unlikely simply because it is not easily available in our memory, despite its actual frequency.

To demonstrate their point, Kahneman and Tversky performed an experiment in which they presented subjects with information about "category base rates" in a population—that is, how many members of a certain category are represented in an overall population, such as the number of women in medical school. Subjects also read a description of a particular member of the population and were asked to judge the probability that the individual belonged to a given category. For example, subjects heard that a population consisted either of 70 engineers and 30 lawyers or 30 engineers and

70 lawyers. Then they read a personality description of a man and were asked to judge the probability that the man was in fact an engineer. Logically, they should have guessed a higher probability when they were told he was part of a population made up of 70 percent engineers than one with only 30 percent engineers. However, subjects' estimates differed very little, regardless of the make-up of the population. The subjects failed to consider base-rate information (that is, the fact that there were many more engineers than lawyers in the population) even though they admitted that the predictive value of the personality information was very low.

Recent research on stereotyping (Rothbart, Fulero, Jensen, Howard, and Birrell, 1978) shows how the concept of availability may be relevant to the formation of *stereotypes*. Rothbart and his associates found that individuals with extreme characteristics (such as persons who have been involved in serious crimes) can be more readily remembered than the same number of individuals with mild characteristics (such as individuals who have been involved in minor crimes). Because of their greater availability in memory, the extreme individuals are estimated as more frequent in a general population than the less extreme individuals. This research suggests how stereotypes may be influenced by mass media. Since much of our information about minority groups is filtered through the news media, and since the information usually defined as newsworthy represents extreme forms of behavior, news reports of extreme individuals can lead to an overrepresentation of extreme behaviors in our images of these groups. For example, seeing blacks on television news frequently associated with murder may lead to an overgeneralized conception of blacks as a group committing murder.

A similar point has been made by David Hamilton and Robert Gifford (1976), who argue that the key determinant of stereotyping is not prejudice, but *distinctiveness*. Essentially, when a member of a distinctive group performs an extreme behavior, then an "illusory correlation" can be established between that group and the extreme behavior. For instance, being a black is distinctive and committing a murder is distinctive; thus, an illusory correlation may be established so that blacks as a group are highly associated with murder in people's thinking.

In light of this research, Fischhoff (1976) claims that attribution theorists show great respect for people's intuitive capacities at the price of being able to do relatively little to help them. In contrast, he suggests that judgment theorists, who view people as much less able processors of information, have developed useful ideas for helping people manage their decisions and learn from experience.

CONSENSUS AND THE LAW OF SMALL NUMBERS

We have seen that people tend to ignore base-rate information and that they overgeneralize from a few distinctive cases. But what happens when both types of information are available? Which is more important in influencing people's decisions?

Consider the following example. While alcohol is a factor in a majority of traffic accidents in America, this statistic is less likely to influence a motorist's decision to drink and drive than is a single encounter with a grisly alcohol-related highway fatality. Richard Nisbett and his colleagues have demonstrated that people are relatively insensitive to consensus information, but that they weigh heavily a few, small, possibly nonrepresentative cases in making inferences and predictions (Nisbett, Borgida, Crandall, and Reed, 1976). These researchers asked subjects to estimate whether a particular member of a population would behave in an extreme way (for example, give another person high levels of electric shock) when they knew that extreme behavior was common for the population or when they knew that extreme behavior was atypical. It turned out that people made about the same estimates regardless of what they knew about the population. However, subjects were willing to infer that extreme behavior was common in a population when they knew of as few as two cases, described in vivid, concrete terms. Finally, subjects attributed equal responsibility for extreme behavior to a person's inner dispositions, regardless of whether extreme behavior was common in the situation.

This work by Nisbett and his colleagues

FOCUS ON APPLICATIONS

RISKY ASSUMPTIONS

What are the chances of accidental death in America? How likely are you to die from homicide, cancer, botulism, or tornadoes? What about diseases such as diabetes, stroke, tuberculosis, or asthma? If you're like most people, you probably overestimated the risk of death from dramatic, sensational causes such as homicide or tornadoes and underestimated the risk from unspectacular diseases that claim one victim at a time.

Why do people make such errors of judgment? According to the research of Kahneman and Tversky, discussed in the accompanying section, people judge an event as likely if it is easy to imagine or recall. This is called the "availability heuristic." However, the ease of imagining or recalling an event doesn't always represent its frequency in reality. For example, Paul Slovic, Baruch Fischhoff, and Sarah Lichtenstein (1980) found that newspapers carry three times as many articles about homicides as they do about diseases; yet diseases kill one hundred times more people than homicides do. Thus, people overestimate the risk of death by homicide and underestimate the risk of death from disease.

To study the nature of people's errors in judgment, the researchers asked forty members of the League of Women Voters in Eugene, Oregon, to estimate the likelihood of death from thirty different causes, ranging from nuclear fallout to accidents involving home appliances. Their estimations were then compared with those of fifteen experts across the country whose professions involved risk assessment. As shown in the accompanying table, the lay people agreed with the experts that some hazards, like power mowers, were low in risk, and others, like handguns, were high. But they thought nuclear energy to be much more dangerous than did the experts and they underestimated the dangers of x-rays and contraceptives.

Could it be that the experts themselves were wrong? Many policy blunders based on expert advice would suggest that experts may make the same errors of judgment that nonexperts are subject to. Slovic, Fischhoff, and Lichtenstein cite several instances of experts' errors. For example, scientists failed to recognize the harmful effects of x-rays until their use was widespread; designers of the DC-10 failed to realize that decompression in the cargo compartment could affect the plane's control system; and technicians at the Three Mile Island nuclear power plant turned a minor incident into a major accident by misdiagnosing a reactor problem. Apparently, experts can become overconfident when a hazard is rare, or they may fail to check carefully for a problem they cannot imagine happening.

A similar situation in our own lives may be a failure to use automobile seat belts. Most of us are seldom, if ever, involved in auto accidents. Thus the risk of an accident

demonstrates surprisingly that people may make attributions and predictions based on logically weak—though very concrete—information but that these same people may be insensitive to logically compelling information.

QUALIFICATIONS TO THE COGNITIVE-LIMITATIONS POSITION

Research on the fallibility of human judgment represents a valid critique of the assumptions made by attribution theorists. However, some qualifications are necessary. Fischhoff's conclusions that attribution concepts offer little help in solving real-life problems can be challenged by the research on attribution therapy and the role of attribution in labeling processes. Furthermore, the conclusion by Nisbett and his colleagues that consensus is a weak determinant of attributions as well as predictions has been challenged by several investigators (for example, Wells and Harvey, 1977). These researchers

and the need for a seat belt seem unlikely. The researchers suggest that we should all be sensitive to circumstances that may distort our judgments.

RANKING RISKS: VOTERS AND EXPERTS

Asked to rank the risk of dying in the U.S. from 30 activities and technologies, League of Women Voters members agreed with experts on items like power mowers and handguns, but disagreed about radiation technologies like nuclear power and x-rays, and about contraceptives and non-nuclear electric power. League members, one of several groups the authors studied, represented the opinions of educated, informed citizens. The ranking 1 represents a judgment of the most risk; 30, of the least.

VOTERS		EXPERTS
1	Nuclear power	20
2	Motor vehicles	1
3	Handguns	4
4	Smoking	2
5	Motorcycles	6
6	Alcoholic beverages	3
7	General (private) aviation	12
8	Police work	17
9	Pesticides	8
10	Surgery	5
11	Fire fighting	18
12	Large construction	13
13	Hunting	23
14	Spray cans	26
15	Mountain climbing	29
16	Bicycles	15
17	Commercial aviation	16
18	Electric power (non-nuclear)	9
19	Swimming	10
20	Contraceptives	11
21	Skiing	30
22	X-rays	7
23	High school and college football	27
24	Railroads	19
25	Food preservatives	14
26	Food coloring	21
27	Power mowers	28
28	Prescription antibiotics	24
29	Home appliances	22
30	Vaccinations	25

Source: **P. Slovic, B. Fischhoff, and S. Lichtenstein, "Risky Assumptions,"** ***Psychology Today*** **14 (June 1980): 44–48.**

have shown that when consensus is meaningful and salient, it is a powerful determinant of attributions, as would be expected from Kelley's (1967) model.

SCRIPTS AS AN ALTERNATIVE TO DELIBERATIVE ATTRIBUTIONAL ANALYSIS

A different criticism of attribution theory argues that people can be relatively "mindless" in performing complex actions. According to this view, people not only err in their judgments, as the above research demonstrates, but they frequently make no judgments at all. Robert Abelson (1976) and Ellen Langer (1978) argue that large units of varied behavior can be chunked together to form fewer coherent cognitive units that require little attention and can be *overlearned* (for example, the flushing of a toilet). These units are called scripts, which Abelson (1976) defines as "a coherent sequence of events expected by the individual, involving him either as a participant or as an observer" (p. 33). The basic ingredients of scripts are features abstracted from many single vignettes (for example, the images of an event that has recently occurred). These common features help group similar experiences together and also help differentiate contrasting ones. With experience, these scripts, or common features, come to be processed instead of the original vignettes, thus leading to relatively "mindless" behavior.

In order to demonstrate scripted behavior, Langer, Blank, and Chanowitz (1978) conducted a study in a university library, using as subjects persons who were about to use a copy machine. Subjects were presented with a request that was either easy to comply with or difficult, and the requester either provided justifying information or did not, as seen in the examples below.

1. Request only—"Excuse me, I have five (or twenty) pages. May I use the Xerox machine?"
2. Real information—"Excuse me, I have five (or twenty) pages. May I use the Xerox machine because I'm in a rush?"

The researchers predicted and found that so long as the requested compliance was not effortful (only five pages), then the subjects would simply follow a script to be compliant. That is, they would simply do what was requested without thinking—performing a "do as you're told" script, as it were. However, when twenty pages had to be copied, subjects were found to abandon scripts and "thoughtfully" process the information, resulting in relatively little compliance when no justifying information was provided. Langer and associates conclude that many of the mundane interactions of everyday life probably rely on scripts rather than on the active processing of incoming information as required in making attributions.

While the script argument of Abelson and Langer seems to provided an important alternative to traditional attributional analysis, we all can think of many events when we seem to be overly *reflective* and to engage in an inordinate amount of attributional analysis. Such a case may be the loss of a lover, as we discussed in the research on close relationships.

In summary, we seem to be amazingly adaptive in the way we process information: we appear equally capable of complex causal attributions, illogical errors of judgment, and "mindless" scripted behavior. Our actual behavior seems to depend on several factors, including prior knowledge about the object of analysis, the salience of situational information, and our motivations for accurate prediction.

SOME THOUGHTS ON THE FUTURE OF ATTRIBUTION RESEARCH

We have discussed the major perspectives and concepts in contemporary attribution theory. As should be clear from our discussion, attribution theory is a general, multifaceted explanation of how people process social information and draw conclusions about their own and others' behavior. In the last several years, attribution theory has had an immense impact on social psychology. It seems likely that this intense interest in attribution theory will continue for at least another decade. There are still many unanswered questions with respect to the theory and many substantive areas to which attribution theory could be fruitfully applied. Perhaps the most essential future theoretical development will be a more precise integration of various components of the attribution process, such as the information-processing component and the motivational component.

The following quotes from Harold Kelley, Edward Jones, and Fritz Heider indicate the optimism and direction these preeminent attribution theorists feel for the future of attribution work.

> KELLEY: I think the very way it [the attribution approach] developed—it wasn't some bright idea that somebody had, that somebody forced on somebody's data or tried to extend by brute force. It came out of a lot of phenomena that social psychologists have looked at and tried to interpret. I just can't imagine that the phenomena that are hooked into that kind of cognition will change or be modified. They'll never go away. We'll always have

to have that kind of explanation (Jones and Kelley, 1978: p. 384).

JONES: I think there is a potential collision in sight with the psychotherapist, the dynamic psychologist [and the attribution theorist]. Maybe the collision has already occurred. It seems to be that the boundary of attributional notions is going to get established somewhere and that there is going to be a wave of returning to try to understand the irrational and the emotional, the phenomena that I don't think attribution theory is well designed to handle. In general social psychology doesn't have much to say about the intense affects, the strong emotions (Jones and Kelley, 1978: p. 384).

HEIDER: It is all-pervasive and important. I think it can go anywhere. Attribution is part of our cognition of the environment. . . . Whenever you cognize your environment you will find attribution occurring (Heider, 1976: p. 18).

SUMMARY

Attribution and person perception deal with how we come to know and understand behavior. Person perception involves the act of forming an impression of another person. Attribution theory is concerned with how people explain or assign causes for their own or others' behavior. Why do we form impressions or make attributions in the first place? Presumably because we need to predict and control the events in our everyday lives and develop expectations about the future.

Solomon Asch was a pioneering researcher in person perception. His work on central traits showed that exchanging the word "warm" for "cold" in a list of adjectives greatly affected subjects' impressions of a stimulus person. Later research determined that central traits are those adjectives that correlate most highly with every other adjective in the list. Our understanding of which traits usually occur together amounts to an implicit personality theory. Asch also showed that the meaning of subsequent traits in a list could be affected by the traits that precede it—a primacy effect; when later traits in a list are more influential, it is a recency effect. Generally, the primacy effect leads people to discount later information. People's perception of others is also determined by their cognitive set—for example, being set to transmit information to another person. And when a series of traits are combined to form an overall impression, people may adopt an averaging approach, an additive approach, or a weighted averaging approach, depending on how polarized the adjectives are. Finally, stereotyping can be viewed as a subcategory of person perception—essentially a biased perception of other persons because of our expectations about negative traits and behavior that supposedly occur in minority groups.

The foundations of attribution theory can be traced to three influential approaches: those of Heider, Jones and Davis, and Kelley. Heider referred to his approach as "the naïve psychology of everyday action." In their search for causal explanations for behavior, Heider thought people made two types of major attributions: an external attribution to something about the environment and an internal attribution to something about the person. Furthermore, he thought personal forces involved mainly ability ("can") and motivation ("try"). Jones and Davis adopted Heider's principles in formulating their systematic theory of correspondent inferences—basically an attempt to specify when behavior "corresponds with" internal intents and dispositions as opposed to external environmental forces. For example, when the effects of a behavior are unique or extreme, the behavior is more likely to be seen as "correspondent" with internal dispositions. Kelley then developed a more integrated model of attribution that applied equally well to another person's behavior or to one's own. Kelley's model emphasized three factors: a behavior's distinctiveness to a particular cause; its consensus with other persons' responses to the same cause; and its consistency over time, situations, and modalities. However, people's attributions do not always involve such a complex analysis. Often people explain behavior in light of causal schemata, or a general "rule of thumb" about why people act the way they do in common situations. People's expectations also lead them to discount certain types of information.

Attribution theory has been extended by other investigators to many social phenomena.

Daryl Bem's self-perception theory asserts that when internal attitudes are weak or uninterpretable, people explain their own behavior in the same way an outside observer would, by looking for an external cause and then inferring an internal explanation if external causes appear unlikely. In a related approach, Jones and Nisbett developed a theory of actor/observer differences, which explains that actors often arrive at different attributions than observers do because actors typically possess more information than observers and also actors have a different perspective on the mutually available information. Although numerous experiments confirmed this hypothesis, later research outlined certain qualifications on the general proposition. Other investigators extended attribution theory to accounting for success and failure in achievement behaviors, to sex differences in explaining men's and women's behavior, to an understanding of close relationships, to attributing internal emotions, and to psychotherapy.

Recently, the assumptions of attribution theorists have been criticized on several grounds. Judgment theorists have shown that people are often fallible and illogical in their judgments and predictions because they overgeneralize from information that is easily available in memory and neglect such information as category base rates. For example, the distinctiveness of extreme behavior when it is performed by a minority-group member can lead to an illusory correlation, which may be the basis of stereotyping. Similarly, a few vivid instances of behavior can influence predictions about future events more than consensus information about that behavior's incidence in the population as a whole. Finally, other critics have argued that people often behave "mindlessly," responding to someone on the basis of scripts, or common features abstracted from many single vignettes, and thus make no attributions at all.

Key figures in attribution theory expect attribution to continue to be a major concern of social psychologists because it is a pervasive phenomenon. At the same time, many feel that models of human information processing will have to allow as much room for impulsive, biased, "mindless" perceptions and behaviors as for the complex causal inference analyses that underlie attribution assumptions.

CHAPTER SEVEN

INTERPERSONAL ATTRACTION

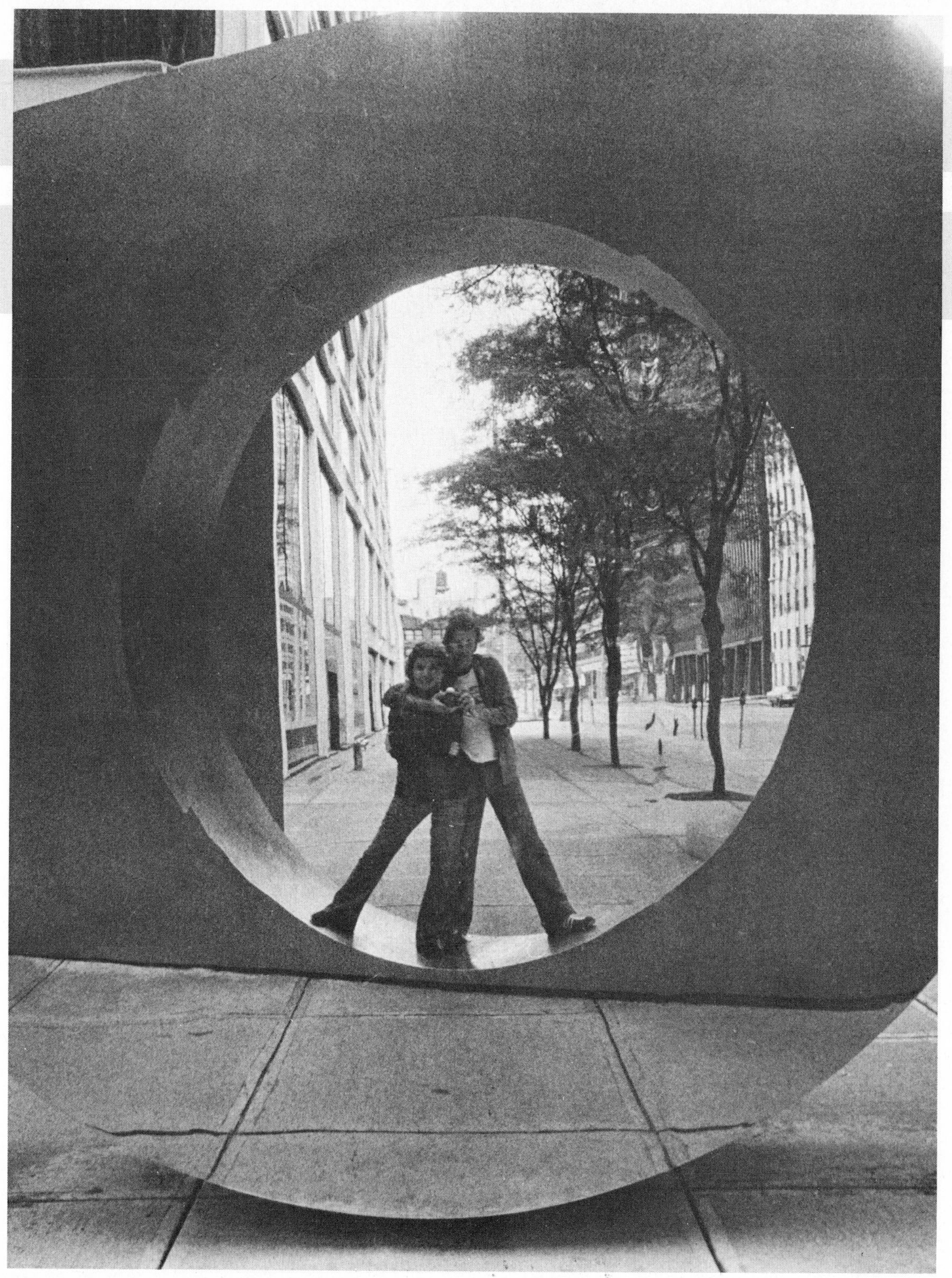

The most profound human experiences are connected with love—with seeking, finding, and losing love. To feel unloved can be devastating, as the following profile of a Southern California college student makes painfully clear.

> A young woman sits on the edge of her narrow bed inside a small dorm room staring at a bright poster her roommate has taped to the wall. It's some rock star, she knows, but she can't remember which one. Not that it matters. Nothing much matters any more.
>
> Not the fact that now in her second semester at the University of Southern California she feels like a caged animal each time she enters this small cubicle.
>
> Not the fact that she hates her roommate, who is so busy with sororities and dates that she's never around anyway—except in the mornings. But then mornings can be the worst times.
>
> Nor does it matter anymore to her that she's about to flunk out of school, disgracing her father, who has long since given up hope that she, like himself, would one day become a successful surgeon. Or that she has gradually turned into a 5′2″, 155-pound blob, humiliating her svelte mother, who still can't believe Eleanor, 21, is a product of her very own, perfect body.
>
> It does not even matter anymore that Paul, her high-school sweetheart and the only person whom she ever felt genuinely loved and accepted her, has explained with painful delicacy that they should simply become "friends."
>
> When the phone rings, suddenly shattering the silence of Saturday night in the dorms, Eleanor stares at it, counting its insistent rings. Ten times. It is not for her, she knows, because nobody ever calls her. She has no friends.*

We ponder the joys and sorrows of intimate relationships, and our poetry, literature, and popular music mirror the human longing for love. Some people turn to newspaper columns and paperback books for helpful information on how to find and attract others, as well as how to manage and understand their intimate relationships. Other people, like Eleanor, struggle with the problem of loneliness.

*Bella Stumbo, "The Lonely Young," *Los Angeles Times*, April 28, 1975.

All of these issues have concerned social psychologists, and much research has focused on interpersonal attraction and, more recently, love and loneliness. In approaching these topics, social psychologists have considered three broad questions: First, why is the need to affiliate such a basic element in human life? What factors cause people to seek human company? Second, why are people more attracted to some individuals than to others? What factors influence our selection of friends and lovers? Third, how do relationships develop from a casual acquaintanceship into an enduring friendship or marriage? In this chapter, each of these three topics—affiliation, interpersonal attraction, and the development of close relationships—will be examined. The chapter concludes with a discussion of loneliness—the painful experience of emotional and social isolation.

AFFILIATION

The experiences of men and women who have been deprived of human contact for long periods of time attest to the strength of our need to affiliate. Shipwrecked sailors and prisoners in solitary confinement, for example, have reported feelings of overwhelming psychological distress. The extreme and often unexpected reactions that people can have to social isolation are illustrated in the autobiography of Admiral Richard Byrd. In 1933, Byrd volunteered to spend six months alone in a small weather station in the Antarctic. Byrd was initially eager to "taste peace and quiet and solitude long enough to find out how good they really are." Byrd was well supplied with food, books, and even a radio to contact the outside world. At first he enjoyed his isolation, but within a few weeks his enthusiasm turned to loneliness and depression. Ultimately, he became apathetic and withdrawn; he ruminated obsessively about religious questions and experienced hallucinations.

Personal accounts such as this suggest that the pain of social isolation initially increases over time to severe levels, but is often followed by a state of apathy. It is common for isolated individuals to think and fantasize about familiar people, and even to hallucinate that others are present. Isolated individuals who keep busy with survival activities and physical or mental exercise may suffer less. In general, however, the psychological consequences of long-term isolation are extreme.

The severity of reactions to prolonged social isolation might lead us to speculate that there is an innate basis for the affiliative tendency. One proponent of this view is John Bowlby (1969), who has studied the attachment behavior of young children toward their mother. Bowlby observed that young children engage in behaviors that maintain physical proximity with their mother or that restore proximity if it is disrupted. These include behaviors like crying and smiling that signal the mother to attend to the child, and also behaviors such as clinging or following in which the child approaches the mother. Bowlby believes that in the evolutionary history of the human species, such attachment behaviors have had strong survival value. Children who maintained close contact with caretakers may have been less vulnerable to predators and other environmental dangers, and so had a better chance of living to adulthood. While the pattern of behaviors described by Bowlby can be readily observed, not all psychologists agree with his view that attachment behaviors are inherited.

According to learning theorists, affiliation is a learned, secondary drive rather than an innate, primary drive. In this view, infants learn to associate human caretakers with the satisfaction of basic needs for food, warmth, and protection. Each time the parent feeds or cuddles the child, human contact is associated with pleasurable experiences. Through repeated pairings of a human caretaker with the reduction of hunger, thirst, and discomfort, the child learns to value and seek out people.

A third explanation for the tendency to affiliate emphasizes the fact that people are the source of a wide range of important resources. For example, the stranded survivors of a plane crash may exchange crucial information about gathering food, protecting themselves from the weather, or finding the route to safety. They may also offer each other sympathy and companionship during a time of stress. Robert Weiss (1974) has identified six of the most important resources provided by social relationships.

1. *Attachment* is the sense of security and comfort that is provided by our closest relationships. Children may be strongly attached to their parents; adults experience this sense of intimacy with dating partners, spouses, or other loved ones.
2. *Social integration* is the sense of having shared interests and perceptions of the world that is often provided by relationships with friends. Such relationships offer companionship and give mutual assistance.
3. *Reassurance of worth* is provided when other people attest to the individual's competence. The knowledge that others value our skills and appreciate our personal qualities is an important contributor to our self-esteem.
4. *A sense of reliable alliance* is most often provided by relationships with family and relatives. In times of crisis, people often turn to their relatives for financial aid or other forms of assistance.
5. *The obtaining of guidance* is provided by others who help us to clarify our own beliefs and formulate plans of action. People may turn to friends for guidance, but also to teachers, counselors, ministers, or doctors.
6. *The opportunity for nurturance* occurs when we know that another person depends on us for his or her well-being. Taking care of another person may provide the individual with a sense of being needed and important.

Weiss's list is useful because it emphasizes the diversity of rewards and resources provided by social relations. The desire to have someone support our opinions, give helpful advice, or merely laugh at our jokes contributes to the general tendency to affiliate.

We have briefly considered three general explanations for the widespread tendency to affiliate—innate characteristics, learning, and social resources. But the desire to affiliate is not equally strong in all situations. Social psychologists have been particularly concerned with

Social relationships provide us with several important resources including social integration, reassurance of worth, a sense of alliance, and the availability of guidance. *(© Jill Freedman / Magnum)*

identifying situations that influence the strength of affiliative tendencies. Both fear and uncertainty are important factors.

AFFILIATION AND THE REDUCTION OF FEAR

Personal accounts of reactions to social isolation suggest a link between isolation and psychological stress. This observation led psychologist Stanley Schachter (1959) to hypothesize that frightening situations may increase the desire to affiliate with others. The results of Schachter's simple but classic experiment supported this hypothesis.

The women undergraduates who took part in Schachter's experiment were recruited for a study on the effects of electric shock. Upon arriving for the experiment, students were met by a serious-looking man in a white lab coat who introduced himself as Dr. Gregor Zilstein of the Medical School's Department of Neurology and Psychiatry. For half the participants, Dr. Zilstein's description of the study was deliberately designed to arouse a high degree of fear:

> I feel I must be completely honest with you and tell you exactly what you are in for. These shocks will hurt, they will be painful. . . . What we will do is put an electrode on your hand, hook you into apparatus such as this [points at the equipment behind him], give you a series of electric shocks, and take various measures such as your pulse rate, blood pressure, and so on. (p. 13)

In the low-fear condition, the electrical equipment was removed from the room, and participants were reassured that the study was harmless:

> Do not let the word "shock" trouble you; I am sure that you will enjoy the experiment. . . . What we will ask each of you to do is very simple. We would like to give each of you a series of very mild electric shocks. I assure you that what you feel will not in any way be painful. (p. 13)

After these instructions, students were asked to wait for a few minutes while the equipment was set up. They were given the choice of waiting alone in a pleasant room supplied with reading material or in an empty classroom together with other participants in the same study. Each woman indicated in writing whether she preferred to wait alone, with others, or had no preference. At this point the study ended, and no shocks were ever actually administered.

Results strongly supported Schachter's predictions as shown in Table 7.1. In the high-fear condition, two-thirds of the women preferred to wait with others. In the low-fear condition, only one-third of the women preferred to wait with others. This and other research support the general principle that frightening situations increase the desire to affiliate.

TABLE 7.1 SCHACHTER'S STUDY OF THE EFFECTS OF FEAR ON AFFILIATION

	WOMEN PREFERRING TO WAIT		
CONDITION	TOGETHER	DON'T CARE	ALONE
High Fear	63%	28%	9%
Low Fear	33%	60%	7%

Source: S. Schachter, *The Psychology of Affiliation* (Stanford, Calif.: Stanford University Press, 1959): 18.

Two qualifications to this basic pattern should be noted, however. First, while fear typically increases affiliative tendencies, other types of stresss may actually lead people to prefer being alone. In particular, if people believe that their psychological distress is embarrassing or inappropriate, they may avoid being with others. This is illustrated in a study by Sarnoff and Zimbardo (1961). Some of the college men who participated in this study were exposed to fear conditions similar to those used by Schachter. Others were assigned to conditions designed to arouse "oral anxiety." In the high-anxiety condition, men were told that they would have to suck on baby bottles, rubber nipples, and breast shields—a task that many college men might find embarrassing. As predicted, men who anticipated painful electric shocks were eager to affiliate with others, but men who anticipated having to suck on anxiety-arousing objects preferred to be alone. In stressful situations where other people may increase the individual's discomfort, affiliation is avoided.

Second, even when people are frightened, they are selective in their choice of companions. In a later study, Schachter again led women to believe that they would receive electric shocks. As before, some of the women had the option of waiting alone or with other participants in the same study, and, as before, most women in the high-fear condition preferred to wait together. However, some participants were offered a different choice. They could either wait alone or wait with other women who were not taking part in the study but were waiting to see their advisors. Given this choice, none of the women in the high-fear condition wanted to wait with the dissimilar others. In times of stress, people prefer to affiliate with others who are in the same predicament. In Schachter's words, "Misery doesn't love just any company, it loves only miserable company."

We have seen that when people are frightened, they typically want to be with others. But does social contact actually reduce their fear? Research evidence is mixed (Epley, 1975). Wrightsman (1960), for example, found that students who were frightened showed a greater reduction in fear after waiting in groups than after waiting alone. It appears, however, that the behavior of one's companions may be a crucial factor. If a frightened individual is exposed to people who are calm in the face of danger, his or her fear may be reduced. But if one's companions are more intensely distressed or hysterical, they may actually increase the person's fears.

AFFILIATION AND THE REDUCTION OF UNCERTAINTY

Another factor contributing to increased affiliation during times of stress may be the person's desire to compare his or her own reactions to those of others. As explained in Chapter 3, Leon Festinger's social-comparison theory (1954) asserts that when people are uncertain about the reality of a situation, they may turn to others to provide cues about what is happening. In one of Schachter's studies, he asked participants why they had chosen to wait alone or with others. One woman in the high-fear condition explained, "I wanted to wait with other people to see how they would react." Another wrote, "I thought that the others probably had the same feelings toward the experiment that I had, and this thought made me want to be with someone" (Schachter, 1959: p. 41). Schachter believed that the need for self-evaluation heightened the desire for affiliation in this high-fear condition:

> In a novel, emotion-producing situation, unless the situation is completely clear-cut the feelings one experiences or "should" experience may not be easily interpretable, and it may require some degree of social . . . comparison to appropriately label and identify a feeling. (p. 26)

Thus, uncertainty about how to react to a frightening situation may lead to affiliation.

It should be noted, however, that the desire for self-evaluation occurs not only when an individual is frightened, but in a wide variety of other situations as well. Many of the important questions that people want to know about themselves—How attractive am I? How good a sense of humor do I have? How lovable am I?—can only be answered on the basis of social comparisons. Thus, we might compare our appearance to that of our friends, observe whether other people laugh at our jokes, and note whether people seek our company. From this perspective, a major reason for affiliation is the desire to evaluate ourselves in reference to others.

Festinger's theory of social comparison predicts that the greater the uncertainty a person experiences, the greater his or her desire to affiliate will be. This pattern was demonstrated empirically in an ingenious study by Gerard and Rabbie (1961). They employed a procedure similar to Schachter's for creating fear. But before participants decided whether to wait alone or with others, some were given fictitious information about their own emotional reactions, some received information about their own reactions as well as those of other participants, and some received no information at all. The researchers reasoned that students who already knew how other participants were reacting would feel very little uncertainty, and so would have little desire to affiliate. In contrast, students who received information concerning only their own reaction, or who were given no information would be uncertain and so would prefer to wait with other people. Strong evidence was found to support these predictions.

Festinger's theory also predicts that people prefer to compare themselves to others who are similar in ability, attitudes, or personalities. The amateur tennis player wants to know how his or her performance stands up against other amateurs, not against trained professionals. Similarly, the frightened women in Schachter's experiments were eager to affiliate with other women participating in the study, but they did not want to spend time with nonparticipants. Furthermore, people who are frightened would rather affiliate with someone like themselves than with someone who is much less frightened and who therefore would help to calm their fears. John Darley and Elliot Aronson (1966) used the Schachter procedure to frighten college women. The women were then given a choice of waiting with a woman who was slightly more frightened than they were themselves or who was much less fearful. The frightened subjects chose the woman who was slightly more frightened. This finding suggests that the subjects' desire to affiliate was probably motivated by a desire for social comparison. While the less fearful woman might have helped to calm the subjects' fears, she would have been less similar to the subjects, and thus less relevant for social comparison.

INDIVIDUAL DIFFERENCES IN AFFILIATION

Psychologists have found that the need to affiliate is increased in situations of fear or uncertainty. Despite such situational influences, however, there are also obvious differences among individuals in affiliation. In everyday life, we observe some people who prefer to suffer alone, while others seek company. Some people prefer to spend their leisure in solitary hobbies, while others prefer to relax with friends. One of the most interesting individual differences in affiliation noted by Schachter concerns birth order. In frightening situations, first-borns and only children are more eager to affiliate than later-borns. Evidence also suggests that first-borns and only children may actually benefit more from being with others in times of stress than later-borns. This has been found both in laboratory studies such as Schachter's and in real-life situations. Shortly after a major earthquake in Los Angeles, two enterprising social psychologists (Hoyt and Raven, 1973) investigated reactions to the emergency. When asked how many people they had talked to during the first fifteen minutes after the earthquake, first-borns reported talking to significantly more people than did later-borns.

One explanation for this effect of birth order concerns the childrearing practices of new parents. With their first child, parents may be more cautious and protective, responding to the least problem or sign of discomfort immediately. As a consequence, first-borns learn that other people are a ready source of comfort and reassurance. But, with experience, parents discover that children are not as fragile as they imagined, and so parental behavior becomes more blasé and less vigilant. As a result, later-born children may learn to be more self-reliant.

In this section we have seen that the need to affiliate is an important facet of human life. But beyond a general need to affiliate with others, especially when we are frightened or uncertain, what attracts us to *specific* others? In the next section we will examine the question of interpersonal attraction and explore what factors draw one person to another.

ATTRACTION

Why are we more attracted to some people than to others? Why do we hit it off well with one classmate, but take an immediate dislike to another? What factors affect our choice of friends or lovers? According to Ellen Berscheid and Elaine Walster (1978), "the psychological principle which threads throughout all theories of interpersonal attraction is the principle of reinforcement: we like those who reward us and we dislike those who punish us" (p. 26). In this section, we review psychological research that has specified more precisely the important types of rewards that affect interpersonal attraction.

PROXIMITY: GEOGRAPHY AS FATE

It's not surprising that people often marry the girl or boy "next door." Physical proximity is a strong determinant of whom we know and like. A classic study by Leon Festinger, Stanley Schachter, and Kurt Back (1950) demonstrated the effects of proximity on friendship development. These researchers studied patterns of friendship among couples who were living in married-student housing at the Massachusetts Institute of Technology. For the most part, the students did not know one another before moving into the apartment complex. Furthermore, the residents had no choice regarding the units to which they were assigned. The housing complex consisted of seventeen separate two-story units, and each contained ten apartments as illustrated in Figure 7.1. The researchers measured both the *physical distance* (feet and inches) between doorways to apartments and the *functional distance* (an index calculated by counting each apartment door as one unit and by adding an extra unit when residents had to go up or down stairs to visit). They also asked each resident to name his or her three closest friends in the housing project. As indicated in Figure 7.1, the closer any two residents lived to one another, the more likely they were to be friends. For example, next-door neighbors were more likely to be friends than were neighbors two doors away. Both physical and functional distance affected friendship. For example, students were more likely to be friends with someone who lived on their own floor than with someone who lived exactly the same number of feet away but on another floor. In short, the apartment to which an individual happened to be assigned and the architectural design of the building were influential determinants of friendships.

FIGURE 7.1 Festinger, Schachter, and Back (1950) studied the friendship patterns that developed in seventeen married-student housing units, like the one diagrammed here, at the Massachusetts Institute of Technology. The fewer the number of doors between apartments, the more likely it was that students were close friends.

Choice of Close Friends and Physical Distance

Number of Doors Separating Apartments	Percentage Choosing
1	41.2
2	22.5
3	16.2
4	10.3

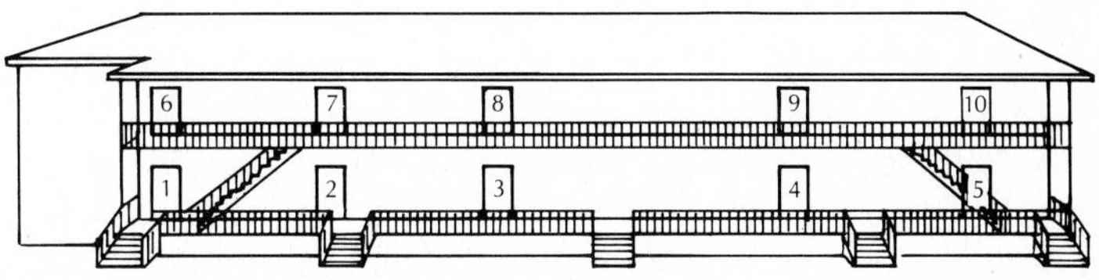

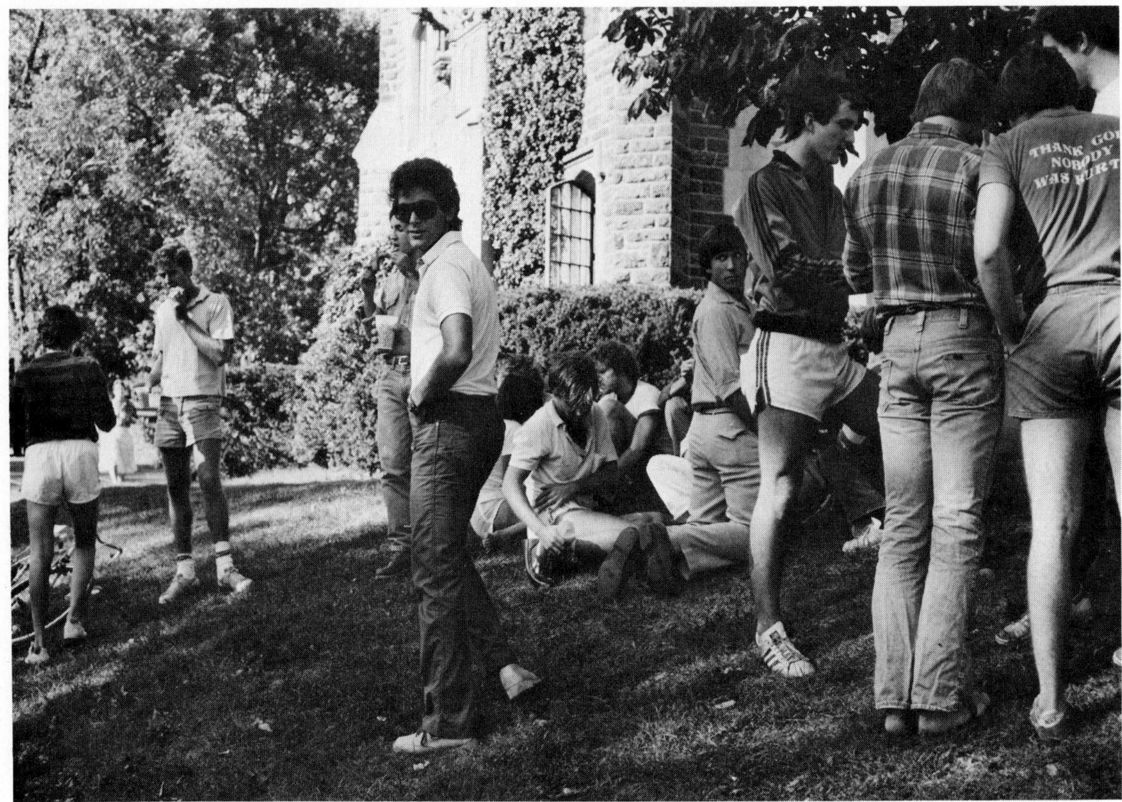

Proximity increases the opportunities for relatively effortless interaction between individuals—such as these dormitory residents—and thus facilitates liking. *(© R. Lynn Goldberg 1980)*

The link between proximity and friendship has been demonstrated in such diverse settings as a police academy (Segal, 1974), a jet bomber (Kipnis, 1957), and a suburban community (Whyte, 1956). Studies have even shown that the selection of a marriage partner is related to physical proximity (Katz and Hill, 1958).

There are several reasons why proximity leads to liking. Intuitively, it makes sense that one must get to know others before liking them, and the closer they are, the more available they are for interaction. An important factor is the relative ease with which people can interact with those in close proximity. No special arrangements are needed to chat with a neighbor over the backyard fence or in a shared elevator. Although the rewards we obtain from a neighbor may be only mildly pleasant—a friendly smile or "hello"—they are obtained with a minimum of effort and personal cost. In contrast, relationships with people who live or work at a distance are maintained only through some degree of effort. Even a good friendship may wither if the friends move apart and discover that the costs of maintaining their relationship have become substantial; the greater the effort required, the greater the fear of awkward encounters. Proximity greatly reduces the costs of interaction.

FAMILIARITY One consequence of proximity is that another person's behavior may become increasingly familiar and predictable. There is considerable evidence that merely being exposed to a person can increase our liking for him or her. This is also true of being exposed to an object. Extensive research by Robert Zajonc (1968) and his colleagues has shown that repeated exposure to impersonal objects such as Chinese characters as well as to people can produce increasingly positive attitudes. In one study, Zajonc (1968) showed subjects photographs from a college yearbook. Some photos were shown only once, others twice, five times, ten times, or twenty-five times. Next Zajonc asked the subjects how much they thought they would like the people in the photographs. Subjects' evaluations bore a direct relationship to the frequency of exposure: the more times they had seen a face, the more they expected to like its owner. The same effect has been demonstrated for repeated exposure to actual people. For example, Saegert, Swap, and Zajonc (1973) set up an experiment in which undergraduate women had to sit in pairs in a small booth for a judgment task. Some of the partners met only once; others were paired two, five, or ten times. The results showed that the more times a pair had been in the booth together, the more they liked each other.

Research suggests several important conditions that must be met for repeated exposure to increase liking (Stang, 1974). First, the person or stimulus must be relatively unfamiliar to begin with. Repeated exposure to a person whom you already know and dislike will not enhance liking (see, for example, Perlman and Oskamp, 1971; Brockner and Swap, 1976). Second, exposure should occur at moderate rather than at very high levels. Overexposure to a person or stimulus can lead to satiation or even boredom (Miller, 1976; Zajonc, 1968). Finally, for optimal effectiveness the person should be exposed to several different people or stimuli at different frequencies. Knowledge of these conditions led a team of researchers (Grush, McKeough, and Ahlering, 1978) to make predictions about the effectiveness of media advertising on political campaigns. In their analysis, repeated exposure to candidates through TV or radio ads should have little effect on presidential elections since candidates are already well known and citizens have preexisting attitudes about the candidates. In contrast, primary elections for congressional seats should be more easily influenced by a "media blitz." In primary elections candidates are often relatively unknown, and several different candidates typically vie for a single seat. Under such circumstances, repeated media exposure should enhance the candidate's appeal to voters. A careful analysis of the 1972 congressional elections demonstrated the importance of repeated exposure. As predicted, liking (measured by actual voting) was related to frequency of media advertising, but only when candidates were initially unknown to voters. These and other studies indicate that the effects of increased familiarity depend not only on the frequency of exposure, but also on our initial reactions to the stimulus or person.

BALANCE THEORY Another explanation for the impact of proximity on liking is provided by Fritz Heider's balance theory, as explained in Chapter 4. Heider (1958) distinguished between two types of relationships. A *unit relationship* exists when two persons or objects are perceived as belonging together. Unit relationships can be based on many factors. A person can be in a unit relationship with a neighbor (based on proximity), with a relative (based on kinship), with a fellow participant in a psychology experiment (based on common fate), and even with an object (based on ownership). In some sense, the pair in a unit relationship is seen as belonging to a larger unit. A *sentiment relationship* refers to the positive or negative feelings a person has toward an individual or object.

A basic principle in Heider's theory is that people strive to maintain balance or harmony among unit and sentiment relationships. It is psychologically satisfying to know that one's relatives are pleasant and successful people or to have a likable next-door neighbor. In these cases, our unit relationships and sentiment relationships are in balance. In contrast, it is psychologically uncomfortable for an imbalance to exist between unit and sentiment relationships. For example, imagine being assigned to a college roommate whom you personally find to be unfriendly and disagreeable. It is distressing to dislike a person with whom one must share living quarters. In such cases, people are motivated to restore balance. Sometimes this can be done by ending the unit relationship with a disliked person—for instance, by requesting a new roommate. But sometimes the unit relationship is inevitable. Most of us have at times been "stuck" with an undesirable roommate, lab partner, traveling companion, or neighbor. When this happens, we often learn to like the other person. We use psychological means to make the best of a relationship that we are forced to maintain. Thus we may try to understand why our disagreeable associate is so unfriendly, to discover his or her hidden good qualities, or to develop mutual interests.

Sometimes even the anticipation of future interaction can lead us to evaluate another person positively. John Darley and Ellen Berscheid (1967) gave students information concerning two strangers and told them that they would meet one of the strangers. When subjects were asked to give their personal evaluations of the two strangers, they reacted much more favorably to the stranger they thought they would meet than to the stranger whom they did not expect to meet.

In this section we have seen that proximity can increase our chances of liking another person. While this general principle often applies, it is not a foolproof basis for friendship. There are important exceptions to the proximity-leads-to-liking rule. For example, when two people have conflicting interests, continued interaction may aggravate their conflict. This possibility was demonstrated in research conducted by Ebbe Ebbeson, Glen Kjos, and Vladimir Konecni (1976) at a Southern California apartment complex. These investigators found that proximity not only increased liking, but under some conditions it also increased disliking. In other words, when neighbors did not get along, they were likely to feel more antagonistic toward close neighbors than toward distant neighbors. Thus an analysis of interpersonal attraction must consider not only the effects of proximity, but also the characteristics of the people involved and the nature of the social contact of these people.

PERSONAL CHARACTERISTICS: HOW TO BE SOCIALLY DESIRABLE

Although proximity facilitates interaction between two people, many other factors influence their chances of becoming good friends. The personal characteristics of both individuals are important. Recent research has drawn attention to the role of physical attractiveness in social relations. However, other factors such as personal warmth and competence may be even more important determinants of liking.

PHYSICAL ATTRACTIVENESS Although many people downplay the impact of physical attractiveness on friendship because it seems such a superficial criterion, empirical evidence indicates that beauty can affect liking (Berscheid and Walster, 1974). In a study by Karen Dion (1972), for example, women read descriptions of children who had ostensibly behaved badly. Sometimes the description of a particular child was accompanied by a photograph of a very attractive youngster, and sometimes the same description was accompanied by a photograph of an unattractive youngster. (Ratings of the physical attractiveness of the children in the photographs had been made earlier by independent judges.) The women were then asked to attribute responsibility for the child's behavior. The results showed that women were much more likely to attribute blame to a child who had been judged unattractive and to conclude that the disruptive behavior was typical for that child. In contrast, women typically produced excuses for a physically attractive child.

The tendency to assume that "what is beautiful is good" is pervasive. In one study, college students rated attractive people as being happier and more successful, having a better personality, and being more likely to get married than less attractive people (Dion, Berscheid, and Walster, 1972). It is not clear to what extent this popular stereotype contains a "kernel of truth." In a recent study (Goldman and Lewis, 1977), students engaged in three telephone conversations and rated their telephone partners for social skill, liking, and desirability for future interaction. Independent observers rated the physical attractiveness of each student participant. Results indicated that physically attractive students were rated by their telephone partners as being more socially skillful and more likable than were their less attractive counterparts. Since students were not able to see their telephone partner, it appears that physically at-

Physical attractiveness tends to increase likability and can be an asset in many situations. *(© Silverstein 1980 / Sygma)*

tractive students may actually have learned to be more socially adept than less attractive students.

There is evidence that in a variety of situations physical attractiveness may be an asset. Harold Sigall and David Landy (1973) found that men who were accompanied by an attractive woman made a better impression on observers than did men in the company of an unattractive woman. Similar findings have recently been obtained concerning observers' reactions to women who are accompanied by an attractive versus unattractive male companion (Sheposh, Deming, and Young, 1977). Even in instances where observers are supposed to be impartial, such as courtrooms, physical attractiveness is sometimes an asset. Using a simulated jury procedure, Harold Sigall and Nancy Ostrove (1975) gave mock jurors information about a crime, along with a photograph of the defendant. When the woman defendant was accused of a burglary, beauty was an advantage. Jurors gave the pretty burglar a lighter sentence than the unattractive burglar. In contrast, however, when the crime involved a situation in which the woman might have used her good looks—swindling—the attractive defendant was treated more harshly than the less attractive one.

Most studies of the effects of physical appearance on attraction emphasize heterosexual relationships. Considerable attention has been given to the *matching hypothesis,* which postulates that people choose dating and marriage partners whom they perceive as being of approximately the same physical attractiveness as themselves, rather than partners whom they perceive to be much more or much less attractive. Some evidence in support of this hypothesis has been found. For example, in one study researchers arranged a computer-dating situation (Berscheid, Dion, Walster, and Walster, 1971). Participants were asked to describe the kind of date with whom they wanted to be matched. The experimenters then led the participants to believe that the participants would actually be paired with a person who matched their description. The physical attractiveness of each participant was secretly rated by a panel of judges. The researchers found that the more attractive the individual, as rated by judges, the more attractive a date he or she requested. Individuals judged less attractive by the panel's standards requested less attractive dates.

Other studies have not confirmed the matching hypothesis, however. In one study, college students were randomly matched by computer for a dance (Walster, Aronson, Abrahams, and Rottman, 1966). A postdance questionnaire indicated that the intelligence and personality of the date did not seem to influence whether or not the date was liked. In fact, the only variable that seemed to affect liking for the date was his or her physical attractiveness. But, counter to the matching hypothesis, *everyone* liked the most attractive dates best, regardless of their own physical appearance.

These contradictory findings concerning the matching hypothesis can be resolved by considering an additional factor—fear of rejection. In the computer-dating study described first, participants were assured that they would actually meet the person they chose. To minimize their chances of being rejected by their prospective date, they may have selected someone whose looks were similar to their own. In contrast, in the computer-dance study, fear of rejection was not a factor. Liking for the date was assessed after the fact. Because there was no possibility of being rejected, participants may have decided to aim high regardless of their own deficits. Thus the matching hypothesis may be most likely to hold when people are making actual choices that entail the possibility of being turned down by a prospective partner.

Although the benefits of physical attractiveness are evident, they should not be overestimated. Especially as people move from first impressions to forming more lasting relationships, other personality characteristics become important.

PERSONAL WARMTH AND COMPETENCE Zick Rubin (1973) has suggested that the two fundamental dimensions of liking are affection and respect. In Rubin's analysis, *affection* stems from the way another individual treats you personally, and it is experienced as emotional warmth and closeness. A good deal of psychological research (summarized in Chapter 6) indicates that people who are perceived as warm and friendly tend to be liked.

Rubin's second dimension, *respect*, is based on admiration for another person's desirable characteristics or behaviors. We like people we admire and who are competent in terms of social skills, intellectual ability, athletic prowess, or other areas. Not surprisingly, Rubin found that college students evaluated their dating partners and their close same-sex friends as being highly intelligent, having good judgment, and being someone they would recommend for a responsible job. Although as a general rule competence and high ability contribute to liking, there are limits to this principle.

Sometimes a person can be too "perfect" for comfort—too intelligent, too successful, or too charming. In such cases, we may actually like a highly competent person better if we discover that he or she has minor human weaknesses. This effect has been demonstrated in several studies. In one experiment (Aronson, Willerman, and Floyd, 1966), participants listened to a tape recording of a student who was trying out for the "College Bowl" quiz team. Half the participants heard an outstanding performance by the applicant who answered nearly every question correctly; half the participants heard a rather mediocre performance by the applicant. In addition, after the supposed tryout was finished, some of the participants heard each of the applicants make a minor blunder by spilling coffee on his suit. Results clearly indicated that the highly competent applicant was liked a great deal better if he blundered than if he did not. For the mediocre applicant, the reverse was true. He was liked quite well if he did not spill coffee; in the condition where he blundered, his ratings plummeted.

Another exception to the general tendency to like highly competent people is related to gender. Traditional sex roles have dictated that in a dating relationship or marriage, the man should be the more intelligent and professionally successful partner. According to this "norm of male superiority," women should not be more competent than their male partners. The college men interviewed by Mirra Komarovsky (1976) illustrated this traditional pattern. One young man said, "I enjoy talking to more intelligent girls, but I have no desire for a deep relationship with them." Another man commented, "A brilliant girl would give me an inferiority complex; the girls I date are less smart than I" (p. 49).

Empirical support for the persistence of a norm of male intellectual superiority comes from a study of college dating couples (Peplau, 1976; Pleck, 1976). It was predicted that students with traditional sex-role attitudes would be especially sensitive to intellectual competition with their dating partner. In this study, college students first worked individually on a verbal anagram task. A month later they were randomly assigned to work on a similar task either in competition against their dating partner or in cooperation with the partner. In the competitive condition they were told that their individual scores would be directly compared to see "who did better"; in the cooperative condition they were told that they would receive only a single score for their joint performance. As expected, college women with traditionalist attitudes performed more poorly on a verbal task when competing against their boyfriend than when cooperating or working alone (Peplau, 1976). In complementary fashion, college men whose responses to a projective test indicated that they were threatened by women's competence performed at their best when competing against their girlfriend, and did less well in the other conditions (Pleck, 1976). Thus both traditional men and women behaved in a way that preserved the man's relative superiority. In striking contrast, students who had nontraditional attitudes about sex roles did not appear concerned with insuring that the man outperformed the woman. Women with egalitarian attitudes performed at their best in the competitive condition; men who were not threatened by women's ability performed at their best in the cooperative condition. These results suggest that as sex-role attitudes become more egalitarian and the norm of male intellectual superiority begins to fade, women may be liked and respected for their competence as much as men are.

SIMILARITY: BIRDS OF A FEATHER

One of the most frequent questions concerning interpersonal attraction is whether "birds of a feather flock together" or "opposites attract." In order to answer this question, it is helpful to distinguish among similarity based on background characteristics, attitudes, and personality. There is strong evidence that similarity in background and attitudes facilitates liking; but the evidence concerning personality matching is not clear (Berscheid and Walster, 1978).

Research has repeatedly found that friends are more similar in social and economic backgrounds than would be expected by chance. For example, one study (Hill, Rubin, and Peplau, 1976) found that college dating partners were significantly matched on religion, physical attractiveness, Scholastic Aptitude Test scores, plans for graduate education, age, and even height. Furthermore, the researchers retested the same students two years later to see which couples had stayed together. They found that those couples who had initially been closely matched on background variables were more likely to have continued their relationship than were couples with dissimilar backgrounds.

There is also abundant evidence (Bell, 1979) that most husbands and wives are of the same race, social class, economic status, educational level, and religion. For example, fewer than 1 percent of American marriages are interracial (Heer, 1974). Even though Americans are presumably free to marry the partner of their choice, the principle of endogamy—marriage within one's group—is still a potent factor in mate selection. As Goode (1959) has noted, parents often take an active role in ensuring that their children marry appropriately:

> . . . parents threaten, cajole, wheedle, bribe, and persuade their children to "go with the right people," during both the early love play and later courtship phases. Primarily, they seek to control love relationships by influencing the informal social contacts of their children; moving to appropriate neighborhoods and schools, giving parties

Most Americans marry someone of their own race, religion, socioeconomic class, and educational level. *(© Chester Higgins, Jr., 1976 / Photo Researchers)*

> and helping to make out invitation lists, by making their children aware that certain individuals have ineligibility traits (race, religion, manners, tastes, clothing, and so on). (p. 45)

Thus the individual's "free choice" of a marriage partner is often influenced directly by learning to consider some partners more eligible than others.

Another consistent finding concerning attraction is that people with similar attitudes tend to like one another (Berscheid and Walster, 1978). For example, among college couples, dating partners tend to be significantly matched in their attitudes about sexual standards, religion, proper sex roles for men and women, and conceptions of the nature of love (Hill, Rubin, and Peplau, 1976). Early research on the link between attitude similarity and attraction was troubled by the chicken-and-the egg problem of causality. Correlational studies demonstrated that friends and spouses often had similar attitudes, but it was not clear whether attitude similarity was actually the cause of friendship or whether friends influenced each others' attitudes in the direction of greater similarity.

The first clear demonstration that shared attitudes facilitate attraction came from the work of Theodore Newcomb (1956, 1961). For an entire semester, Newcomb provided rent-free cooperative housing for two separate samples of students at the University of Michigan. In return for the free housing, each student participated in several hours of research per week. All the participants were sophomore and junior men, and none of them had been previously acquainted. Before the students arrived in Michigan, they responded by mail to questionnaires measuring their attitudes and values. Attraction among house residents and changes in attitudes were measured throughout the semester. If similarity is a cause of attraction, one would expect that those house residents who were similar prior to meeting each other would become friends, and this is what occurred. In the first weeks of the semester, the only variable related to attraction was proximity; roommates and individuals living on the same floor were more attracted to each other than they were to other residents. As the semester continued, however, similarity of preacquaintance attitudes became the best predictor of attraction. Thus Newcomb's research demonstrated that some degree of attitudinal and value similarity is an important determinant of the attraction process.

Newcomb's field study has been followed by a large number of laboratory experiments concerning the similarity-attraction link. Donn Byrne (1971) and his colleagues have undertaken a systematic program of research on this issue, using the control gained in laboratory research to eliminate the effects of other factors that might influence the relationship of attitudinal similarity and liking. Byrne first studied the influence of shared attitudes on liking between same-sex individuals. To hold constant other factors such as physical appearance, personality, background, or mannerisms that might affect liking, Byrne developed the "phantom other" technique. In his experiments, participants read responses to attitude questionnaires that were ostensibly completed by another person of the same sex (a stranger). In actuality, however, there was no such person, and the questionnaires had been completed by the investigators, who tailored the responses to be either very similar, moderately similar, or dissimilar to the participant's own responses, which had been obtained at an earlier time. After reading the responses of this presumably real (but actually fictitious) stranger, participants estimated how much they thought they would like the other person. In study after study, Byrne (1971) has found that the more similar the stranger's responses are to those of the participant, the more the participant expects to like the stranger.

Byrne's results have been so consistent that he has proposed that a general "law of attraction" has been uncovered. The law states that attraction toward a person bears a linear relationship to the proportion of positive attitudes (or, more generally, rewards) associated with the person (Clore and Byrne, 1974). Figure 7.2 illustrates this linear relationship between shared attitudes and liking. This model assumes that it is reinforcing to have someone agree with you; accordingly, the more a person agrees with you, the more reinforcing is that person, and the greater your attraction to him or her. This pattern has been found among fourth-grade children, college students, Job Corp trainees, surgical patients, and even alcoholics, and in countries as diverse as India, Mexico, and Japan. This relationship appears to hold regardless of the significance or triviality of the attitudes and regardless of the physical attractiveness, race, and gender of the stranger (Byrne, 1971).

Although there is little doubt that similarity does facilitate liking, several qualifications should be noted. First, most evidence that attitude similarity fosters attraction comes from research conducted in fairly contrived laboratory settings. In real life, other factors may override the effects of similarity, especially early in a relationship. In one study, for example, researchers (Curran and Lippold, 1975) set up a dating service and arranged dates for college students. Couples rated each other after the first date, and at this point physical attractiveness was a stronger determinant of liking than was attitude similarity. In order for shared attitudes to have an effect, two people must communicate about their attitudes. It is possible that on blind dates or other first meetings, important similarities are never revealed. Instead, couples

FIGURE 7.2 Byrne (1971) has consistently found a linear relationship between the proportion of attitudes that subjects believed they shared with a stranger and their attraction toward that stranger. Although this relationship has been found among a wide variety of subject groups, Byrne's research has been largely restricted to controlled laboratory settings. Factors outside the laboratory, however, can lessen this tendency.

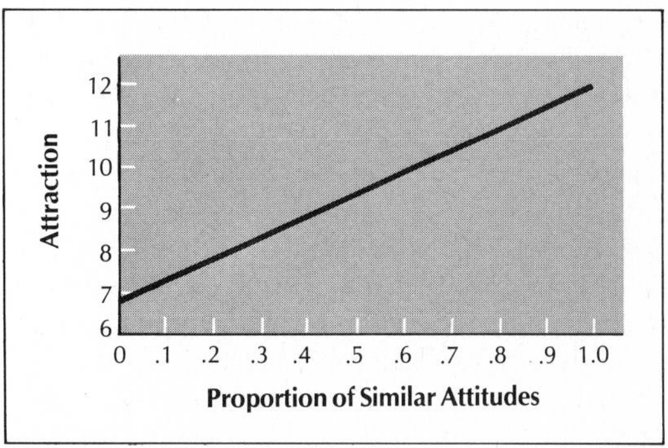

DISPOSITIONS AND SITUATIONS

MEN'S REACTIONS TO MALE HOMOSEXUALS

How would you react to a homosexual student? What would you do if you knew the person was similar to you in most important respects? Would you disregard the individual's sexual orientation and respond instead to the things you have in common? Or would similarity not matter in this case? Or would it depend on how liberal your sex-role attitudes were?

Judith Krulewitz and Janet Nash (1980) performed an experiment to answer these questions. Their subjects were 120 male undergraduates at Iowa State University. These men had filled out an Attitude Toward Feminism Scale, designed to measure their sex-role attitudes. On the basis of their responses to this scale they were classified as traditional, moderate, or liberal in their sex-role attitudes. Equal numbers of men in each of these categories were later asked to participate in a psychology experiment that involved interacting with a partner. Pairs of subjects reported to a laboratory and were seated in separate rooms. Each person was asked to fill out an attitude questionnaire and answer some personal questions.

Subjects believed that the forms would be exchanged with their partners, but actually the forms were intercepted by the experimenter, using a technique developed by Donn Byrne in his similarity/attraction research. The experimenter then filled out a "dummy" form in order to manipulate partners' similarity or dissimilarity. In the "similar" conditions, 50 percent of the items were filled out identically with the partner's form and 50 percent of the items were filled out only one or two points away on the scale; in the dissimilar conditions, 50 percent of the items were answered in extremely opposite directions from the partner and 50 percent were answered one or two points to the opposite side of the neutral response.

The partner's sexual orientation was manipulated so that half of the partners in each similarity condition were perceived as homosexual. This was achieved by writing the following information on the personal data sheet:

> **I don't know if this is relevant or not but I am homosexual. I noticed this questionnaire asked**

may spend much of their time listening to music, dancing, or going to a movie. As a consequence, more readily observable characteristics about the person, such as physical appearance and mannerisms, may play a large role.

Second, there is evidence that in some situations, similarity may actually decrease liking. It is certainly rewarding to be similar to a person who is competent and well adjusted. But would people also find it rewarding to be similar to a person who was emotionally disturbed? Social psychologists David Novak and Melvin Lerner (1968) predicted that in the latter case, similarity might be threatening and so reduce liking. To demonstrate this point, they used a "phantom other" technique similar to Byrne's. Students who participated in the experiment read a questionnaire allegedly completed by another person whose attitudes were either similar or dissimilar to their own. In addition, half the participants learned that their partner had recently been hospitalized for a nervous breakdown and had been seeing a psychiatrist; half the participants received no information about their partner's mental health. As Novak and Lerner predicted, when the partner was "normal," similarity increased liking. But when the partner was "emotionally disturbed," similarity led to avoidance rather than liking.

Third, there is evidence that fear of rejection may influence preferences for similar versus dissimilar others. Walster and Walster (1963) hypothesized that people would be more willing to associate with dissimilar strangers if they

about sexual attitudes, and I thought this might help you somehow.

In the heterosexual condition, the phrase "I am getting married next month" was written in place of "I am homosexual."

Finally, each subject was asked to rate how much he liked his partner and how much he would like to meet him for a short conversation.

How did these men react? It turned out that similar partners were liked more than dissimilar partners. But more important, heterosexual partners were liked more than homosexual partners, regardless of the partner's similarity. Yet these reactions also depended on the men's sex-role attitudes. As shown in the graph below, men with more liberal attitudes were more accepting of the homosexual partner, though even these students liked the heterosexual partner more.

Overall, the results confirm Byrne's similarity/attraction theory, but they suggest that the degree of attraction can also depend on a person's general attitudes, such as an acceptance of nontraditional sex-role behaviors. But like other research using Byrne's laboratory technique, it is unclear how important attitudinal similarity versus sexual orientation may be in interpersonal attraction in a face-to-face encounter in the real world.

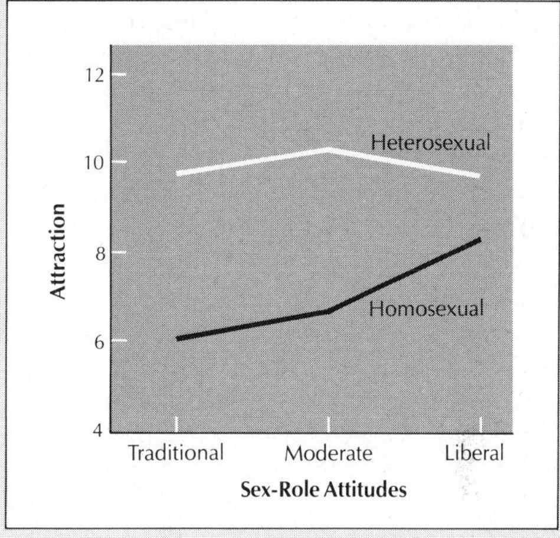

knew in advance that the strangers would like them. To test this prediction, college students were offered the choice of participating in a discussion group with people who were either very similar to themselves (that is, introductory psychology students) or with people who were very dissimilar (that is, psychologists, factory workers). Before selecting a group, some students were assured that people in all groups would be predisposed to like them, and other students were told that group members would be predisposed to dislike them. Results indicated that when students were confident of being liked, they greatly preferred to associate with dissimilar people. In contrast, when students believed that they might be disliked, they were eager to talk to similar others.

A fourth limitation on the link between similarity and attraction in the real world may be an individual's need to be unique (Fromkin, 1972). When a person finds that he or she is just like someone else, then the similarity can detract from the person's sense of uniqueness. Consequently, it may not be particularly rewarding to be around someone who is so similar to oneself.

To summarize, we have seen that both similarity in background characteristics and similarity of attitudes and values can facilitate liking. But there are limitations to this pattern. Sometimes similarity can be threatening, but more often it simply becomes boring. When people agree about basic values and share important attitudes, they may find that differences in background, interests, and opinions add "spice" to their relationships.

NEED COMPLEMENTARITY So far our discussion has not considered the personalities of prospective friends and lovers. Do people tend to like others with similar personalities, or is this a case where people prefer others whose personalities are complementary? Examples of relationships that seem to be based on complementarity rather than similarity are easy to find: the domineering husband and the submissive wife, the highly nurturant person who likes highly dependent friends, the incessant talker who is attracted to good listeners. Illustrations such as these led Robert Winch (1958) and others to formulate a theory of complementary needs. Winch hypothesized that we seek others who can best satisfy our needs. Winch did not deny that partners in a satisfying relationship may be similar in some ways. He maintained, however, that the relationships with the greatest promise of satisfying the participants' needs are those mutually rewarding relationships based on complementarity. In such relationships, each partner, by acting out his or her own needs, simultaneously and effortlessly satisfies the needs of the other.

Winch tested his theory with a sample of twenty-five married couples, and found general support for the theory. But later studies (Banta and Hetherington, 1963; Levinger, Senn, and Jorgensen, 1970) have not supported the theory of complementary needs. Studies have consistently found that in personality characteristics as in attitudes, similarity is the more important basis of attraction. Since the concept of personality complementarity seems so intuitively sensible, it is useful to consider possible reasons why research on complementarity has been so unsuccessful.

First, it may be that need complementarity is more important at a particular stage in the development of a relationship. Alan Kerckhoff and Keith Davis (1962) found evidence that in the early stages of dating, social-status factors such as religion and class were most important. Later these were preempted in importance by similarity of values. Only in a still later stage of the relationship did need complementarity make a difference. Unfortunately, subsequent studies have not been able to replicate this pattern (for example, Levinger, Senn, and Jorgensen, 1970).

Second, it has been suggested that researchers often define personality complementarity too globally. Levinger (1964) observed that a person with a strong need to be dominant might prefer to express this need at work by dominating his or her subordinates, rather than by expressing this need at home. Global measures of dominance and other personality characteristics may be less useful in predicting attraction than more specific measures of needs relevant to close relationships. At least one study (Lipetz, Cohen, Dworin, and Rogers, 1970) found that marital satisfaction was correlated with complementarity of needs specifically pertaining to marriage, although there was no relationship between satisfaction and complementarity of general psychological needs.

Research to date is inconclusive about the importance of personality complementarity to interpersonal attraction. Perhaps future research emphasizing specific personality needs relevant to close relationships may demonstrate the principle of need complementarity. But at present, this principle must be considered unproven.

COMPLEMENTARITY OF SKILLS AND RESOURCES Although the importance of need complementarity in relationships is uncertain, it is clear that other forms of complementarity occur frequently. For example, in the traditional marriage, the wife was typically skilled at domestic tasks and child care while the husband was competent in some occupation and knowledgeable about cars and household repairs. In growing up, boys and girls acquire different skills and interests; as adults, these differences often contribute to patterns of behavioral complementarity in close relationships. It is important to note that traditional sex roles specified not only that men and women should perform different tasks, but also which behaviors constituted "women's work" and "men's work." Even in more egalitarian relationships where task division is not rigidly based on gender, partners may find it a relief that one person prefers doing the laundry while the other enjoys cleaning. Role differentiation is often a sensible, efficient, and enjoyable way of performing necessary tasks. Such divisions of interest, skill, and task performance may be more central to interpersonal attraction than are differences in personality needs.

RECIPROCITY OF LIKING

In his best seller *How to Win Friends and Influence People* (1937), Dale Carnegie offered this advice about how to be liked: "Become genuinely interested in other people; smile; be a good listener; talk in terms of the other man's interests; and make the other person feel important." Psychological experiments have confirmed the soundness of Carnegie's commonsense prescriptions. Evidence suggests that we like people who we think like us, and we dislike others who we perceive as disliking us. This reciprocity-of-liking principle is an important factor in interpersonal attraction.

An early demonstration of this effect was provided by a study conducted by James Dittes and Harold Kelley (1956). These psychologists led student participants in small discussion groups to believe that their fellow group members either liked or disliked them. (The subjects read anonymous evaluations of themselves, ostensibly written by other group members but actually completed by the experimenters.) Dittes and Kelley found that participants who were led to believe that they were liked were more attracted to the group than were participants who believed that they were disliked.

Apparently, people are especially receptive to others' acceptance when feeling insecure. James Dittes (1959) conducted another experiment in which subjects whom he encouraged to feel accepted were again more attracted to the group than were subjects who felt rejected. But this time he probed further. Prior to the experiment, he had subjects respond to a self-esteem scale. Individuals who scored low on this scale were assumed to feel more negative about themselves than were those with higher scores. Dittes compared the reactions to being accepted or rejected of subjects who differed in self-esteem. He found that people with low self-esteem reacted quite differently in the two conditions: when they were accepted, they liked the group a great deal; and when they were rejected, they disliked the group a lot. In contrast, for high-self-esteem subjects, liking for the

A person who can take pride in his or her life and work—artist Georgia O'Keeffe, for example—tends to have high self-esteem. Such a person is less likely to be affected by group acceptance or rejection than is someone with low self-esteem. *(© Dan Budnik 1980 / Woodfin Camp & Assoc.)*

group was not significantly affected by acceptance or rejection. It seems that positive evaluation from others is especially valuable when a person feels insecure about himself or herself (Jones, 1973).

In the Dittes experiment, it was clear to subjects whether they had been accepted or rejected. In real life, however, the messages a person receives from others are often ambiguous. Research suggests that low-self-esteem individuals react negatively to ambiguous evaluations, and tend to dislike the person giving the evaluation. In contrast, high-self-esteem individuals react almost as positively to a person giving an ambiguous message as to one giving a clearly accepting message (Jacobs, Berscheid, and Walster, 1971). Thus, although a person with low self-esteem is more receptive to acceptance from another, the message of acceptance must be clear and unambiguous.

INGRATIATION As we have seen elsewhere in this chapter, general principles always have exceptions. Edward Jones (1964) has studied an exception to the rule that people like those who have unambiguously expressed attraction to them. That exception is *ingratiation*—behavior designed to impress people in order to gain personal advantage. There are various techniques of ingratiation—or "apple polishing," as it is sometimes called. People may deliberately present themselves in a favorable light, shower the target person with compliments, agree with the other person's opinions, or do favors for the other person. Many individuals behave in these ways quite sincerely. These behaviors are only forms of ingratiation when they reflect manipulative intentions.

There are hazards to ingratiation, however, as Jones and others have documented. For example, Hilda Dickoff (1963) found that people were less attracted to an individual who evaluated them favorably if they suspected ulterior motives than if they had no reason to suspect ulterior motives. However, Dickoff also found that people who received unrealistically positive evaluations, even when they suspected flattery, were more attracted to the evaluator than when the evaluator was honest in her evaluations. Apparently flattery *will* get you somewhere, but not as far as when your admiration seems genuine.

THE GAIN-LOSS HYPOTHESIS

There is an impressive array of evidence that reward is important in attraction. However, difficulties arise when the notion of reward is invoked to predict how attraction develops amidst the complexities of real life. For example, the value of any reward can differ from person to person. As indicated previously, another's liking and acceptance are more valuable to a person with low self-esteem than to someone who thinks highly of himself or herself. Also the value of any reward can vary from situation to situation. As we saw earlier, praise is usually a reward, but it loses much of its value when it comes from a flatterer with ulterior motives. Furthermore, the value of a reward can vary with the degree to which it is expected: the more it is anticipated, the less value the recipient is likely to attach to it. One study (Harvey, 1962) found that people respond more positively when they are praised by a stranger than by a friend. Apparently compliments from friends are expected, and, therefore, do not carry as much weight as when they come from unexpected sources. Still another factor that influences the value of a reward is the pattern in which rewards are received. Who would you like more, for example—a person who consistently compliments you or one who initially criticizes you but then becomes complimentary?

Three hundred years ago the Dutch philosopher Benedict de Spinoza observed that "hatred which is completely vanquished by love passes into love and love is thereupon greater than if hatred had not preceded it." This suggests that we would like a person better if he or she were initially cool toward us but later became more enthusiastic in his or her liking for us. Similarly, we may dislike a person more if he or she liked us at first but then became increasingly hostile. Psychologists term this theory the *gain-loss hypothesis*: we like most those people who initially dislike us but warm up to us, and we dislike most those people who initially like us but turn cold. There is some empirical evi-

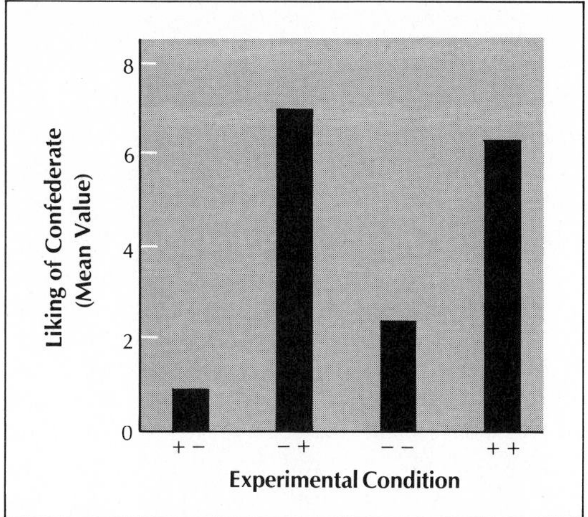

FIGURE 7.3 Aronson and Linder (1965) found that subjects liked a confederate when she consistently approved of them (+ +) and disliked the confederate when her comments about them were uniformly negative (− −). However, subjects liked the confederate *most* when her evaluations progressed from negative to positive (− +) and *least* when her opinions deteriorated from positive to negative (+ −). These results support the gain-loss hypothesis—that people weigh the direction of another person's evaluations more heavily than the absolute number of compliments they receive from that person.

dence that this effect can occur. Elliot Aronson and Darwyn Linder (1965) conducted a laboratory test of this hypothesis. In their experiment, participants accidentally "overheard" themselves being evaluated by another person (secretly a confederate of the researchers). The sequence of evaluations that the subject heard followed one of four patterns: consistently positive; consistently negative; first positive and later negative; or first negative and later positive. The results were striking. As shown in Figure 7.3, the confederate was liked significantly more when the evaluations progressed from negative to positive than when they were consistently favorable. Further, when the confederate's initial compliments turned into negative evaluations, the confederate was liked even less than when the evaluations were consistently negative.

This phenomenon seems to run counter to a simple reinforcement model, since the person who is consistently praised receives more rewards overall than the person who is first evaluated negatively and only later receives positive rewards. Aronson has suggested two possible explanations for this puzzling result. The first is anxiety reduction. If we find that others dislike us, we may experience anxiety, hurt, or self-doubt. But if these others subsequently come to like us, then we not only experience the reward of being liked, but also the pleasure of having our anxiety reduced. Thus, the compliments that come late in the sequence are more rewarding than they would be if they were not preceded by criticisms.

A second possibility is that we assume that people who change their opinions in response to new information are discriminating and discerning. If they are consistently positive or negative, we can minimize the importance of their evaluations by concluding that they are undiscriminating, and may like or dislike just about anyone. When, however, others seem more judicious in their opinions, a gradual increase in positive evaluations is particularly appreciated, and an evaluation that becomes increasingly negative is particularly stinging (Mettee, 1971).

The gain-loss principle has been generalized to real-world relationships, where it is sometimes referred to as "Aronson's law of marital infidelity." Consider the following example:

> Mr. and Mrs. Doting, who have been married for 10 years, are preparing to leave their house for a cocktail party. He compliments her—"Gee, honey, you look great!" She yawns. She already knows that her husband thinks she is attractive.
>
> Mr. and Mrs. Doting arrive at the cocktail party. A male stranger begins to talk to Mrs. Doting, and after a while he says, with great sincerity, that he finds her very attractive. She does not yawn. The compliment increases her liking of the stranger. (Aronson, 1970, p. 48)

Although the preceding scenario has received support in at least one experiment (Clore, Wiggins, and Itkin, 1975), it may not apply so well in the real world. As Ellen Berscheid, Thomas Brothen, and William Graziano (1976) argue, in the real world we do not usually receive evaluations of ourselves in *sequence*, as in the Aronson and Linder experiment; instead, they believe, we are more likely to receive evaluations *simultaneously*—say, from a doting mate and an admiring stranger. When these investigators performed an experiment similar to Aronson and Linder's, the gain effect was replicated if evaluations were received in sequence. But when evaluations were received simultaneously from one evaluator whose statements went from negative to positive and from another whose statements were consistently positive, the latter was liked far more than the former. When evaluations are received simultaneously, the researchers suggest, the contrast between the compliments of the consistently positive evaluator and the initial criticism of the negative-to-positive evaluator leaves the consistent praiser more appreciated overall. Thus, when evaluations are received in sequence, the gain-loss principle may well apply; but when positive evaluations are contrasted simultaneously with negative evaluations—as is often the case in real-world social triangles—Aronson's law of marital infidelity may be found wanting. The important point is that each principle may apply under different conditions, depending on the social context.

In this section we have examined several factors that influence our attraction to other people. First, physical proximity is necessary in order to become familiar with others. Then, personal characteristics such as physical attractiveness, warmth, and competence draw our attention. Basic similarities in attitudes and values hold our interest, though complementarity of personalities may also add spice. Finally, tangible rewards become important in the form of reciprocal liking, praise, and pleasure. However, these rewards may be more meaningful when they come from unexpected sources rather than from those we have already learned to rely on. All of these factors are thought to influence the first stage of attraction. In the next section we examine the interpersonal processes that are important as attraction builds to love.

CLOSE RELATIONSHIPS

Anyone who has experienced the joys and pains of a very close relationship probably suspects that there is more to love and attraction than has been discussed so far in this chapter. In the past, most psychological research on interpersonal attraction has focused on the early stages of the acquaintance process, and has typically studied the development of liking between strangers in a laboratory context. Much less research has examined the nature and development of close relationships outside the laboratory (Huston and Levinger, 1978). In the real world, for example, liking and attraction comprise only one determinant of whether a relationship develops between two people. The case of unrequited love, where one person is strongly attracted but the other is not, illustrates this point. In addition, the level of attraction we feel toward another person is not the sole determinant of our commitment to a relationship with that person. Sometimes people remain in relatively unsatisfying relationships because they perceive their alternatives to be even worse (Thibaut and Kelley, 1959).

In recent years, social psychologists have shown greater interest in studying intimate relationships. In this section, several aspects of close relationships are considered. First, what are the essential elements of a close relationship? Second, what are some important ways in which close relationships differ from one another? Third, how can we conceptualize the stages that occur in the development of a close relationship? And finally, what is love and how does it differ from mere liking?

WHAT IS A CLOSE RELATIONSHIP?

It is easy to identify close relationships. Our relationships with good friends and loved ones are reasonable candidates for being "close." It is not so simple, however, to provide a precise statement on the nature of close relationships. Recently Harold Kelley (1979) has proposed that there are three essential elements to all close personal relationships. Consider the case of Rick and Lisa, a college couple contemplating marriage.

Rick is considering whether to ask Lisa to marry him. This means making a commitment to her, breaking off with old girl friends, and giving up some of his current freedoms. He thinks over the things Lisa has done for him and remembers how wonderful she can make things for him. As he recalls these occasions, he realizes that they have often enjoyed the same things. At the same time he recognizes that some of the things she has done for him were probably not things she would have preferred to do herself.

He thinks of what a good person she is and how much she seems to love him. He also remembers similar occasions when he made sacrifices for her. The first characteristic of Rick and Lisa's relationship to note is their *interdependence.* Rick depends on Lisa and is affected by her moods and her actions. Lisa depends on Rick and cares about the things he has done for her and with her. The experiences of Rick and Lisa, their joys and disappointments, are in some measure intertwined. Rick and Lisa share many common interests and find joint activities rewarding. Sometimes, however, they also experience conflicts of interest. Rick may want Lisa to go with him to a movie, while she may prefer to go to a dance. The mutual dependence of close couples is often reflected in the kinds of problems or conflicts that they report. For example, in one study of college couples (Kelley, Cunningham, and Stambul, 1980), students complained that their partner had different preferences about how to spend leisure time, that the couple had conflicts about the division of tasks, or that one partner interfered with the other's work or studying.

A second feature of close relationships is that partners are *responsive* to each other's outcomes. Partners show sensitivity to each other's needs and preferences by behaving in ways that take the partner into consideration. Rick recognizes that Lisa has "gone out of her way for him" or has "put up with a lot from him." Partners in close relationships sometimes put aside their own immediate wants and preferences in order to please the other.

Finally, partners in close relationships are concerned with understanding each other's *enduring dispositions.* People want to find out what their partner is "really like" and whether their love is real. People take specific interaction events as evidence of the partner's character and feelings. Thus, when Lisa gets angry at Rick for arriving late for a date, she is probably less concerned with his actual tardiness and more concerned about whether this means he is "losing interest in her" or that he is an inconsiderate person. Situations in which one partner goes out of his or her way to please the other may provide especially important information. So if Lisa goes with Rick to the movie despite her own preference to go dancing, Rick may view this as a sign of the depth of her love for him.

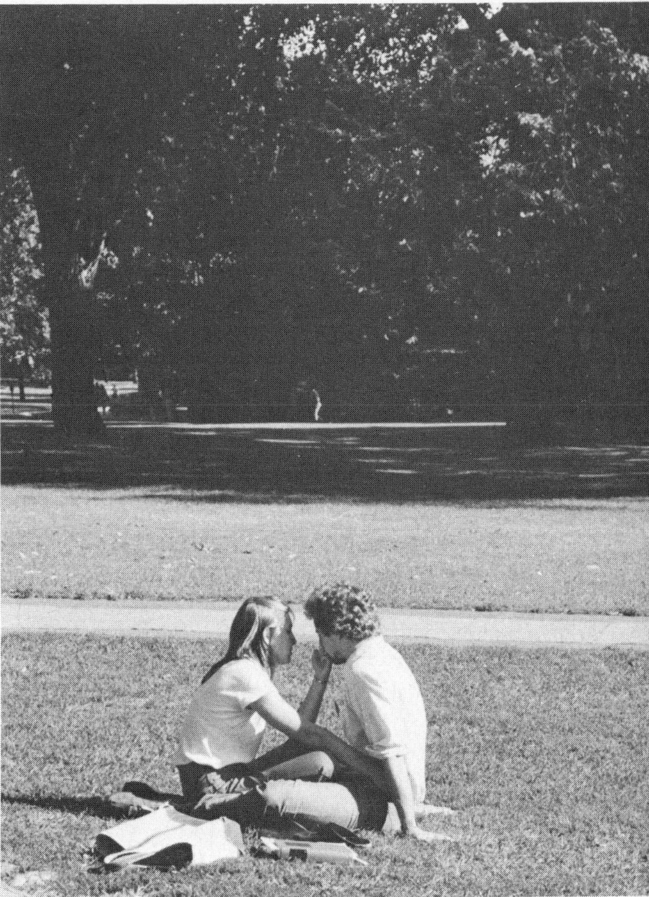

A close relationship is characterized by interdependence, responsiveness to each other's needs and preferences, and concern for understanding each other's enduring dispositions. *(© R. Lynn Goldberg 1980)*

To this rather general description of characteristics of personal relationships can be added more specific features that are common to most close relationships. George Levinger (1977) suggests that close relationships typically involve frequent interaction; it is an indication of closeness that people spend time together. The partners in close relationships are usually in fairly close proximity to one another; physical closeness often accompanies psychological feelings of closeness. Partners in close relationships often share important common goals; they work together on joint projects and make plans for future events together. The mutual exchange of personal information is characteristic of close relationships. Finally, members of close relationships usually care deeply about each other. Indeed, it may be this subjective experience of love and caring that is most salient in everyday conceptions of close relationships.

DIMENSIONS OF CLOSE RELATIONSHIPS

Having considered several elements common to all close relationships, it is also useful to examine important differences among relationships. What are some of the dimensions that distinguish close friendships, parent-child relationships, husband-wife relationships, or the relationship of a psychotherapist and client? Several dimensions have been proposed by theorists (Hinde, 1978; Levinger, 1977; Marwell and Hage, 1970; Wish, Deutsch, and Kaplan, 1976).

INTIMACY Some relationships are relatively superficial while others are very intense. Even among those relationships that a person considers to be "close," there may be noticeable differences in subjective feelings of love and closeness. In a study by Wish, Deutsch, and Kaplan (1976), students perceived as most intense the relationships between husband and wife, parent and child, and close friends. Relationships between a psychotherapist and patient and between a teacher and pupil were seen as somewhat less intense. Most superficial were relationships between casual acquaintances or distant relatives.

STATUS A second important difference among close relationships concerns asymmetry in status, power, or dominance. While some relationships are egalitarian, others are lopsided in terms of power. In the study by Wish and colleagues students perceived the greatest equality among relationships of close friends, spouses, teammates, and business partners. Students perceived considerable inequality in the relationships of parent and child, teacher and pupil, master and servant, supervisor and employee. Relationships in which there is a difference of status or power are often marked by other asymmetries. For example, parents and their young children clearly have different rights and obligations in their relationship. Although psychotherapists usually receive a great deal of personal information from their clients, they typically give very little information in return.

There is currently much controversy about equality of power and status in love relationships between men and women. Young people today expect such relationships to reflect equal power. For example, the students in the Wish, Deutsch, and Kaplan study perceived husband-wife relations as quite egalitarian. And in another study of college students (Peplau, 1979), the great majority said that dating relationships should be equal in power. It is not clear, however, whether most heterosexual couples actually achieve these egalitarian ideals. Peplau found that only half of the college couples she studied believed that their current relationship was actually equal in power; when power was unequal, it was much more likely for the man to have the greater influence. Nancy Henley (1977) suggests that the behavior of men and women in close relationships often mirrors patterns of dominance and submission in society. Men are more likely to touch women and to interrupt women while the women are speaking than vice versa. Similarly, high-status individuals, such as executives, are more likely to touch and to interrupt low-status individuals, such as secretaries, than vice versa. Evidence such as this has led feminist psychologists to argue that imbalances of status and power characterize many male-female relationships.

The dimensions of intimacy and status are only two ways in which close relationships may differ. Other important distinctions concern the extent to which relationships are competitive versus cooperative and the degree of commitment to the relationship in each party. Despite these differences, all relationships seem to develop through similar stages. In the next section we will examine the development of close relationships.

THE DEVELOPMENT OF CLOSE RELATIONSHIPS

George Levinger and J. Diedrick Snoek (1972) have suggested that most of the determinants of attraction typically studied by social psychologists, such as physical attractiveness and proximity, can predict only initial attraction to a new person. Levinger and Snoek attempted to provide a framework for understanding the development of relationships beyond the first phase of initial attraction. They considered the degree of "interpersonal relatedness" in a broad spectrum of relationships—between acquaintances, teammates, close friends, spouses, and parents and children. They postulated three basic levels of relatedness, each one implying a greater complexity of interpersonal feelings and a deeper degree of involvement than the preceding one. Their analysis can be seen as charting the progressive increase in interdependence that occurs as relationships become more intimate.

Table 7.2 shows the characteristics of relationships at each of the three levels. All rela-

TABLE 7.2 A BREAKDOWN OF LEVINGER AND SNOEK'S (1972) THREE LEVELS OF RELATEDNESS

INTERPERSONAL PROCESSES	LEVELS OF RELATEDNESS 1 (AWARENESS)	2 (SURFACE CONTACT)	3 (MUTUALITY)
Communication	Unilateral	Confined to role-required instrumental concerns; no self-disclosure.	Self-disclosure concerning personal feelings and the evaluation of outcomes in the relationship.
Common Knowledge	None	Confined to other's public self-presentation.	Much mutually shared information, including knowledge of each other's personal feelings and biographies.
Process of Interaction	None	Stereotypic role-taking; trial-and-error responses to novel situations.	Spontaneous and free-flowing; person understands how other is affected by the interaction and has concern for his well-being.
Regulation of Interaction	None	By cultural norms; untested implicit assumption that other shares same norms.	By joint construction of some unique pair norms, tested and found appropriate by both persons.
Maintenance of Relationship	None	Of little concern; responsibility for maintenance is perceived to be vested in externally derived roles or organizational requirements. Cost of terminating relationship is low.	Person and other both assume responsibility for protecting and enhancing the relationship. Cost of terminating relationship becomes increasingly high.
Evaluation of Relationship	None	Satisfaction on the basis of self-centered criteria; person compares his outcomes with prior experience and with alternate relationships.	Based on mutual outcomes evaluated against joint criteria, reflecting mutual equity.
Attraction to Other	Based on other's reward potential or "image"	Based on person's satisfaction with experienced outcomes, as well as on other's reward potential. Determined considerably by adequacy of other's role enactment.	Based on affection for other as a unique person and on person's emotional investment, as well as on criteria for surface contact.

Source: Adapted from G. Levinger and J. D. Snoek, *Attraction in Relationships: A New Look at Interpersonal Attraction* (Morristown, N.J.: General Learning Press, 1972).

tionships progress through the levels in sequence, but not all relationships achieve Level 3 or mutuality.

UNILATERAL AWARENESS At Level 1, the beginning of any relationship, the participants—whether individuals, couples, or groups—possess only a unilateral awareness of each other. The student who observes an attractive new classmate from a distance is operating at Level 1. The probability that Susan, for example, will approach her classmate, Jim, rests on many factors, such as physical proximity, Jim's appearance and manners in the classroom, and Susan's own affiliative needs. The decision to initiate interaction will also be influenced by Susan's perception of Jim's accessibility, and perhaps by her current satisfaction with other relationships and her willingness to take the initiative in a social setting. At Level 1, the observer's attraction is based on an image formed from minimal information.

SURFACE CONTACT If Susan and Jim make the transition to Level 2 of relatedness, that of surface contact, they will begin to interact in a restricted and fairly noninterdependent manner. Their interactions will tend to be constrained by their social roles. As students, they may chat with each other about the class or about an upcoming test. They might decide to work together on a course project or have coffee after class. The more they interact, the more likely it is that they will reveal personal things about themselves, although they may not reveal how they feel about themselves or about the relationship. Level 2 allows continual feedback during each interaction and, therefore, facilitates more realistic appraisals of one another and of the association. Most relationships are superficial and are likely to remain at Level 2, if they continue at all. Casual relationships with neighbors, college faculty, or one's dentist illustrate this point. The transition to a deeper relationship will depend on such factors as opportunities for continued interaction, availability of free time, the attractiveness of the rewards received from the other person, and each person's perception of the probability that his or her liking would be reciprocated.

MUTUALITY The transition from Level 2 to Level 3 is one from affiliation to attachment. Level 3 is characterized by interpersonal closeness and interdependence. Each partner's behavior and attitudes are influenced by the other's, resulting in shared behavior and attitudes. A feeling of "we" rather than "I" develops. Mutuality is best conceived as a continuum along which a wide range of behavior is possible. The move toward greater intimacy is generally accomplished by an escalation of self-disclosure and a growing sense of the uniqueness of the other person. Frank communication stimulates attachment between partners and makes information available to each partner concerning the effects that his or her own behavior has on the other. Mutual agreement and accommodation begin to develop, so that mutually satisfying behavior is maintained and behavior that is superfluous or unsatisfying is discarded. Levinger and Snoek maintain that similarity of values and interests, especially in areas relevant to the relationship, increases the probability that individuals will be able to reach this state of accommodation. Similarity may also foster empathy with one another's experiences, which would provide a basis for some of the affection that characterizes close relationships.

In summary, Levinger and Snoek hypothesize that in close relationships new factors enter into the attraction process, such as self-disclosure, open communication, trust, mutual accommodation, and empathy. Unfortunately, social psychological research has only begun to explore the important interpersonal processes that foster increasing mutuality and commitment in relationships. In the next section we discuss a recent attempt to measure intimacy in relationships by developing a "love scale."

LIKING AND LOVING: WHAT'S THE DIFFERENCE?

Early social psychologists paid little attention to love. When they did discuss love, they often defined it as merely an intense form of liking. Some years ago, however, Zick Rubin (1970, 1973) took a different position, suggesting that there are qualitative differences between liking and loving. Not content simply to speculate, he

empirically the distinc-
oving.
and it is unreasonable
ence of love is neces-
ips between parents
t friends, between
in dating and mar-
urposes of his re-
omantic love be-
ex partners. He
ng a large num-
popular concep-
included state-
one, sharing of
e desire to af-
one, and feel-
other. Rubin
udents indi-
c statements
w oyfriend or
gir nd" of the
opp iking and
love hould be
char oward a romantic
partn of feelings toward a friend.
Clear upport was found for this prediction.

On the basis of these results, Rubin constructed two separate self-report scales, one to assess liking and one to assess love, as shown in the Social Psychology and the Arts box (see pp. 222–223). The Love Scale reflected three central concerns: *attachment*, indicated by affiliative and dependency needs; *caring*, the desire to help the other person; and *intimacy*, feelings of trust and absorption with the other. The statements on the Like Scale emphasized perceived similarity, admiration, and respect. Further evidence that liking and love are distinct was obtained in a subsequent study of 182 dating couples from the University of Michigan.

In Rubin's study of dating couples, students who scored high on the Love Scale were more likely than low scorers to say that they and their partner were "in love." High scorers also gave higher estimates of the probability of marrying their dating partner than low scorers. In a laboratory experiment, Rubin demonstrated that students who scored high on his Love Scale spent more time making eye contact with their partner than did low scorers, corroborating the notion that lovers often gaze into each other's eyes. In a follow-up conducted six months later, Rubin investigated whether students with high love scores were more likely to continue dating their partner than students with low love scores. He found that strong lovers were more likely to stay together, but only if they were also high in "romanticism"—the belief that love conquers all. Finally, additional support for the distinctiveness between loving and liking was indicated by the fact that although students liked their dating partners about as much as they did a close friend of their own sex, they showed much greater love for their boyfriend or girlfriend than for their friend. These data provide strong support for Rubin's belief that love is not merely an intense form of liking, but is rather a qualitatively distinct sentiment. They also suggest that romantic love, as measured by Rubin's scale, is one of the characteristics that distinguishes close dating relationships from close platonic friendships. But as we shall see in the next section, there may be different forms of romantic love.

COMPANIONATE AND PASSIONATE LOVE

According to Ellen Berscheid and Elaine Walster (1978), two distinct forms of love can characterize romantic relationships. The researchers define *companionate love* as "the affection we feel for those with whom our lives are deeply intertwined" (p. 177). It is the comfortable feeling of warmth and caring that can exist between individuals who have shared experiences over some length of time. Berscheid and Walster speculate that the major difference between liking and companionate love is the intensity of feelings and the extent of interdependence of the partners.

Passionate love is quite a different emotion. According to Berscheid and Walster, "Passionate love is a wildly emotional state: tender and sexual feelings, elation and pain, anxiety and relief, altruism and jealousy coexist in a confusion of feelings" (p. 177). Perhaps not surprisingly, these psychologists believe that passionate love is often short-lived (see also Walster and Walster, 1978; Cimbalo, Faling, and Mousaw, 1976). But although the wildly romantic

SOCIAL PSYCHOLOGY AND THE ARTS

CAN LOVE BE MEASURED?

In one of the best-known romantic poems in the English language, Elizabeth Barrett Browning tries to measure her love for her husband, Robert:

How do I love thee? Let me count the ways.
I love thee to the depth and breadth and height
My soul can reach, when feeling out of sight
For the ends of Being and ideal Grace.
I love thee to the level of every day's
Most quiet need, by sun and candlelight.
I love thee freely, as men strive for Right;
I love thee purely, as they turn from Praise.
I love thee with the passion put to use
In my old griefs, and with my childhood's faith.
I love thee with a love I seemed to lose
With my lost saints—I love thee with the breath,
Smiles, tears, of all my life!—and, if God choose,
I shall but love thee better after death.

A different attempt to measure love was carried out by social psychologist Zick Rubin (1970). As discussed in the text, Rubin developed a Love Scale and a Like Scale in order to study the nature of love relationships and friendship relationships among students at the University of Michigan.

Heterosexual dating couples were asked to fill out each of the thirteen-item scales with their lover in mind and then with their best same-sex friend in mind. This allowed a comparison between men's ratings of how much they liked and loved their girlfriend versus their best male friend with women's ratings of their love and liking for boyfriends versus best female friends. The students circled the number that best described their feelings about each statement on the scales, excerpted below. The number "1" represents "not at all true; disagree completely." The number "9" represents "definitely true; agree completely."

LOVE SCALE

I would do almost anything for _______.
1 2 3 4 5 6 7 8 9

I would greatly enjoy being confided in by _______.
1 2 3 4 5 6 7 8 9

It would be hard for me to get along without _______.
1 2 3 4 5 6 7 8 9

side of love may be fragile, companionate love is described as a more enduring basis for a long-term relationship.

Berscheid and Walster have proposed a social-psychological theory of passionate love, based on Schachter's more general theory of emotion (see Chapter 6). In their view (1971, 1974), there are two key prerequisites for the experience of passionate love. First, the individual must experience *physiological arousal.* The physical symptoms that people associate with love—heart pounding, stomach aflutter—are crucial. But, according to Berscheid and Walster, these symptoms need not be aroused by the loved person, they can occur for any number of reasons, ranging from sexual arousal to fear or even frustration. Second, the individual must *label these internal cues as "love."* This labeling is often based on situational cues that indicate which emotions are appropriate. If our pounding pulse and fast breathing occur in the presence of a charging wild bear, we are likely to conclude that we are feeling afraid. But if those same symptoms occur in the presence of someone we find attractive, we are more likely to suspect that we are in love. In this two-component theory of passionate love, both internal arousal and external cues play an important part. According to the theory, people may sometimes mislabel their arousal—for instance

LIKE SCALE

Most people would react very favorably to _______ after a brief acquaintance.

1 2 3 4 5 6 7 8 9

I would vote for _______ in a class or group election.

1 2 3 4 5 6 7 8 9

_______ is the sort of person whom I myself would like to be.

1 2 3 4 5 6 7 8 9

How does the average college student score on these scales? With his University of Michigan sample in 1970, Rubin obtained the following results:

	WOMEN	MEN
Love for Opposite-Sex Partner	90.57	90.44
Liking for Opposite-Sex Partner	89.10	85.30
Love for Same-Sex Friend	64.79	54.47
Liking for Same-Sex Friend	80.21	78.38

Note the major differences among men's and women's scores. While opposite-sex partners loved each other to the same degree, women liked their boyfriends significantly more than men liked their girlfriends; and while men and women both liked their same-sex friends about equally, women loved their same-sex friends significantly more than men loved their same-sex friends. Perhaps the differential liking for boyfriends versus girlfriends may be due to sexism; that is, certain items in the Like Scale—such as being elected to a class office or recommended for a responsible job—may have been more descriptive of males than females in 1970. The males would appear more "likable" because they were more likely to receive higher scores on the Like Scale. And similarly, perhaps women love their same-sex friends more than men because it is more appropriate for women to "love" someone of the same sex than for men to feel this way.

So, can love be measured? Let us "count the ways. . . ."

Source: Zick Rubin, "Measurement of Romantic Love," *Journal of Personality and Social Psychology* 16 (1970): 265–273.

by misinterpreting fear as love. This may explain why Ovid, the Roman poet of love, suggested that men might more easily arouse passion in a woman by taking her to watch violent gladiatorial combat (Rubin, 1973: p. 5).

An interesting test of the notion that fear may be misinterpreted as love was conducted by Donald Dutton and Arthur Aron (1974). These investigators had a female confederate approach a male subject as he was crossing a narrow 450-foot-long wooden suspension bridge that sways 230 feet above a rocky gorge in British Columbia, Canada. In a control condition, a male subject was approached by the same female confederate on a wide, sturdy bridge just a few feet above a small rivulet. In both conditions, the confederate asked each subject to make up a story based on an ambiguous picture of a young woman who was covering her face with one hand and reaching out with the other. The confederate then asked subjects to fill out a questionnaire, tore off a corner of it, wrote down her name and phone number, and told the subjects to call her if they were interested in more information about the questionnaire. The results showed that the men on the suspension bridge made up stories with significantly more sexual imagery than the men on the low bridge. The suspension-bridge subjects were also much more likely to call up the confederate than the

Passionate love—a condition marked by physiological arousal and intense, often confused, emotions—recurs as a romantic ideal in literature and films—such as *Susan Lenox: Her Fall and Rise* (1931), starring Greta Garbo and Clark Gable. Companionate love, however, forms a stronger basis for an enduring relationship. *(The Museum of Modern Art / Film Stills Archive)*

men on the low bridge, suggesting that the men on the suspension bridge were more frightened and thus more attracted to the confederate. Interestingly, there were no differences in the responses from the two groups of subjects when the confederate was a male. Similar results were also obtained in the laboratory when anxiety was manipulated by Schachter's technique in the fear and affiliation studies discussed earlier. Dutton and Aron found that men who expected to receive a strong shock were more attracted to a female confederate than men who expected a mild shock, again suggesting that fear may be misinterpreted as love.

JEALOUSY We have observed that the essence of a close relationship is interdependence. A major difference between passionate and compassionate love is the degree of interdependence of the partners. "One might expect . . . that the growth of a relationship from casual acquaintance of two separate and independent individuals into the increased pleasure-giving and mutual need-satisfaction associated with love should be an unalloyed delight" (Berscheid and Fei, 1977: p. 103). But this is not always the case. Increasing interdependence can lead not only to stronger feelings of love, but also to increased vulnerability and to jealousy.

Berscheid and Fei (1977) have attempted to analyze the psychology of jealousy. They propose that high dependency is a prerequisite for jealousy. Unless we truly care about another person and value the rewards he or she provides for us, our fear of losing him or her to a rival should not be very great. But high dependency is not the only condition for romantic jealousy. The second necessary ingredient is insecurity. A person's insecurity about a relationship might be reflected in worrying about losing the partner's affection or wondering just how much the partner really cares for him or her. Thus the prime candidates for jealousy are individuals who are highly dependent and also highly insecure. Who are these people likely to be? One study conducted by Berscheid and Fei suggests that they are often people in the early stages of a romantic relationship where love is growing, or people who aren't sure whether or not they and their partner are really "in love."

Recent contributions to the understanding of close relationships by social psychologists have helped to correct the imbalance in interpersonal-attraction research that has too often ignored the deepest and thus most important relationships. Having briefly surveyed some of the diverse joys and benefits to be gained from close relationships, it is easy to understand why the absence of intimate relationships produces painful feelings of loneliness. The last section of this chapter takes a look at the nature and causes of loneliness.

LONELINESS

From time to time, most people suffer from loneliness. It is common to feel lonely after moving to a new town or following the ending of a love relationship. Although loneliness can occur at any age, there is evidence that young adults may be the loneliest age group. In a large study of 25,000 Americans of all ages, Rubenstein and Shaver (1979) found the highest levels of loneliness among people between the ages of eighteen to twenty-five. Loneliness decreased with age, and was actually lowest among senior citizens. For many people, early adulthood is a time of transition from living with one's parents to living independently and establishing new social relationships outside the family. During this period many people contemplate and actually begin marriage. Thus, this may be a time when the search for intimacy and, for some, the failure to establish intimate relations are especially important.

In the case of Eleanor, the young woman who was described at the beginning of this chapter, many of these factors came together to produce her extreme loneliness. She had re-

Loneliness is a common problem that can occur at any age. Research suggests, however, that it is most prevalent among young adults. *(Rick Smolan)*

Feelings When Lonely:

"Desperation"	"Impatient Boredom"	"Self-Deprecation"	"Depression"
Desperate Panic Helpless Afraid Without hope Abandoned Vulnerable	Impatient Bored Desire to be elsewhere Uneasy Angry Unable to concentrate	Feeling unattractive Down on self Stupid Ashamed Insecure	Sad Depressed Empty Isolated Sorry for self Melancholy Alienated Longing to be with one special person

What People Do When They Feel Lonely:

"Sad Passivity"	"Active Solitude"	"Spending Money"	"Social Contact"
Cry Sleep Sit and think Do nothing Overeat Take tranquilizers Watch TV	Study or work Write Listen to music Exercise, walk Work on a hobby Go to a movie Read Play music	Spend money Go shopping	Call a friend Visit someone

FIGURE 7.4 Rubenstein, Shaver, and Peplau (1979) found four large clusters of both feelings of loneliness and responses to loneliness among a large sample of Americans.

cently moved to a large university; her boyfriend had just broken up with her; she had little in common with her roommate or the other people around her; and she was a disappointment to her parents. Not surprisingly, she felt that nothing mattered anymore. Only recently have social psychologists begun to study people such as Eleanor.

WHAT IS LONELINESS?

Loneliness is a painful psychological experience that occurs when a person's social relations are inadequate. Loneliness has been described as "a gnawing chronic distress without redeeming features" (Weiss, 1973). Although the experience of loneliness can range from fleeting to long-lasting, it is always unpleasant.

The experience of loneliness differs from person to person. Rubenstein and Shaver (1979; see also Rubenstein, Shaver, and Peplau, 1979) found four clusters of feelings and thoughts that often accompanied loneliness among their large sample of Americans, as shown in Figure 7.4. The most common feeling was *desperation.* People described themselves as being helpless, abandoned, hopeless, and afraid. This set of feelings may be characteristic of prolonged loneliness. A second cluster of feelings reflected *impatient boredom* that might accompany milder forms of loneliness. The feelings in this cluster included wanting to be somewhere else, being unable to concentrate, and feeling uneasy. A third cluster of feelings concerned *self-deprecation*: people described themselves negatively as being unattractive, stupid, insecure, or ashamed. Finally, a more resigned and passive state of *depression* was another manifestation of loneliness, with people feeling sad, empty, isolated, alienated, and longing to be with one special person. A theme running through these diverse patterns of thoughts and feelings is that loneliness is an intensely unpleasant experience.

Early in this chapter we indicated that humans show a widespread tendency to affiliate with other people. Loneliness is a sign that a person's social relationships are unsatisfactory in some way. Consistent with the view that affiliation is a basic human need, Harry Stack Sullivan (1953) proposed that loneliness occurs when the need for intimacy is not met. More recently, Robert S. Weiss (1974) has emphasized the fact that relationships provide a diverse range of social resources, including a sense of attachment, social integration, reassurance of worth, and so forth. A consideration of the broad range of possible rewards provided by relationships led Weiss (1973) to postulate that there are two different types of lonelinesss. *Emotional loneliness* occurs when the individual lacks a personal, intimate relationship. Children separated from their parents and individuals who have lost a spouse through death or divorce illustrate emotional loneliness. In contrast, *social loneliness* results when the person feels that he or she is not part of a group, does not have friends who share common interests, is not socially integrated into the community. This might be illustrated by the student who moves away to college and must establish a new circle of friends and associates. In Weiss's view, no single relationship is a safeguard against loneliness. An "adequate life organization" requires a broad set of social relationships.

THE CAUSES OF LONELINESS

It is important to recognize that loneliness is not the same as solitude or aloneness. For many people, time spent alone while hiking, reading, or working on a creative activity can be extremely pleasant. When people deliberately seek solitude, it can be a rewarding experience. Loneliness occurs only when people are distressed or unhappy about the absence of social contact or lack of close relationships. It is possible for people to be alone without being lonely, and also to be lonely in the midst of other people.

Anne Peplau and Daniel Perlman (1979) tried to specify more precisely just when loneliness does occur. In their view, loneliness results when there is a gap between an individual's *actual social relations* and the person's *desired social relations*, as illustrated in Figure 7.5. When a person has fewer or less satisfying relationships than he or she wants, loneliness results. The experience of loneliness is usually precipitated by a change in the person's social life. In some instances, it is the person's actual relationships that change. Thus, the breakup of a dating relationship (Hill, Rubin, and Peplau, 1976), divorce (Weiss, 1976), and widowhood (Lopata, 1969) frequently cause loneliness to occur. In

FIGURE 7.5 The causes of loneliness. According to Peplau and Perlman (1979), loneliness results from a discrepancy between a person's actual and desired social relationships.

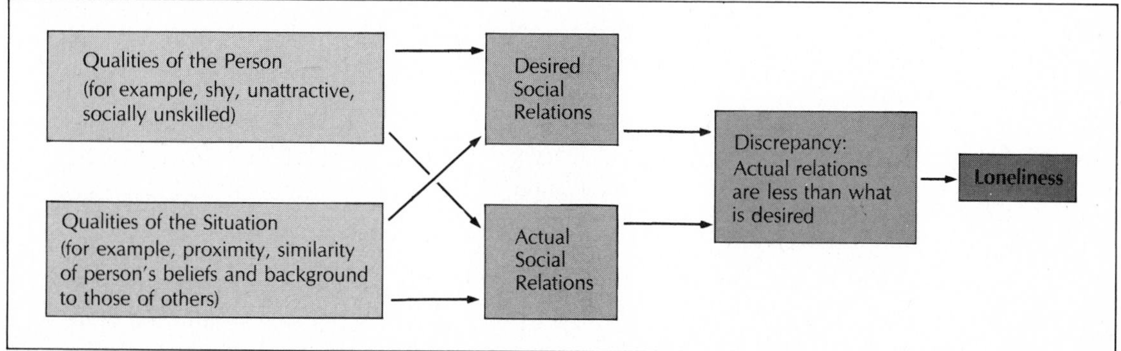

other instances, it is the person's desires for social relations that change and lead to loneliness. For example, during adolescence most teenagers decide that it is time for them to begin dating. If this new desire for a romantic relationship is not accompanied by an actual dating relationship, loneliness may occur.

In addition to specific events that cause the onset of loneliness, it is also useful to identify factors that make some people more vulnerable than others to loneliness. The earlier discussion of interpersonal attraction outlined various characteristics of people and of situations that facilitate liking. Attraction research thus suggests factors that may hinder the formation of relationships and so increase the likelihood of loneliness. Physical proximity may play a part. People whose work or place of residence keeps them socially isolated may have fewer opportunities to begin and maintain social relationships. Personal qualities may also affect people's ability to establish enduring relationships. People who are physically unattractive or who appear to be cool and aloof may find it difficult to make friends. Research indicates that shyness and poor social skills are linked to loneliness (Peplau and Perlman, 1979). Another factor related to loneliness is similarity—the match between the individual and his or her peers. The person who is "different" because of his or her background, ethnicity, attitudes, or values may have a difficult time creating a satisfactory social life.

In a sense, research on interpersonal attraction and research on loneliness are examining opposite sides of the same coin. Both further our understanding of the social-psychological processes involved in beginning and maintaining close relationships. Both emphasize the vital importance of personal relationships for psychological well-being.

SUMMARY

The need for human contact is a powerful force in human social life. When people are deprived of contact with others for long periods, they often become painfully anxious. This need for affiliation is partly based on early learning experiences that occur because of the extreme dependency of the human infant. Some psychologists believe that affiliative tendencies also reflect inherited behaviors that promote attachment to a parental caretaker. As adults, we continue to turn to others for a variety of important social rewards, including love, social approval, and confirmation of our opinions and self-worth.

Certain situations, such as fear and uncertainty, are likely to increase the desire to affiliate. In such situations, we usually prefer to be with others who are in a similar predicament. There are also individual differences in affiliation, as first-borns and only children show greater affiliative tendencies than later-borns, who are more self-reliant and independent even in situations of stress.

Many factors influence our choice of acquaintances and friends. Physical proximity increases the probability of our meeting a person, and makes interaction simpler and less costly. Casual contact based on proximity may lead another person to become familiar. In general, research indicates that familiarity fosters compatibility and liking. Sometimes, however, overexposure leads to satiation and boredom. If initial attitudes toward another person are extremely negative, repeated exposure may serve to increase hostility. A theoretical explanation for the effects of proximity is provided by Heider's balance theory, which states that people strive to maintain consistency between their unit relationships and their sentiment relationships. As a result, there is a tendency either to end relationships with people we dislike or to come to like these other people.

Personal characteristics of another person also influence our attraction to him or her. Especially in first encounters, we are attracted to those whom we consider beautiful. It appears, however, that in actually choosing partners, we follow the matching hypothesis by choosing others who are similar to ourselves in physical attractiveness, thereby avoiding the threat of rejection.

Zick Rubin suggested that two fundamental dimensions of liking are affection and respect. We tend to like people whom we perceive as interpersonally warm and competent. While warmth is equally valuable for men and women, high levels of competence in women can violate sex-role norms. An extremely competent person may also be liked better if he or she exhibits minor human weaknesses.

In addition to proximity and personal qualities, a third important determinant of attraction is similarity. There is strong evidence that similarity in background and in attitudes facilitates liking. Byrne's "law of attraction" states that our liking for another person is directly related to the proportion of attitudes we share. However, there are exceptions to the similarity-leads-to-liking principle. Other factors, such as physical appearance, can override the importance of attitude similarity, and when another person has undesirable traits, such as a mental disturbance, similarity may actually decrease liking.

Personality variables also play a part in attraction. Although it is commonly believed that complementarity of personalities fosters attraction (for example, a dominant person likes a submissive person), the evidence for complementarity of personality needs is weak at best.

Reciprocity—developing a liking for those who are attracted to us—often increases the original attraction. An exception is ingratiation, or insincere expression of liking and admiration. If someone seems to have ulterior motives for behaving in a rewarding fashion, his or her "attraction" will not be reciprocated.

A key theme running throughout psychological discussions of attraction is the importance of social rewards. In general, we are attracted to individuals who reward us in some way, though the nature of the rewards can vary from person to person and can be changed by the context of the relationship. In some instances, we are more attracted to a person who is initially cool toward us, but who then becomes a more enthusiastic admirer.

Most research on attraction has focused on brief, superficial interactions between strangers meeting for the first time in a controlled laboratory setting Much less is known about long-term close relationships.

Kelley has proposed that the essential elements in all close relationships are interdependence, responsiveness, and the tendency to interpret the partner's acts as indications of his or her enduring dispositions. Two dimensions along which close relationships differ are the degree of intimacy and the equality of status of the partners. Levinger and Snoek have conceptualized three levels of increasing closeness and interdependence in relationships: unilateral awareness, surface contact, and mutuality. Research indicates that love and liking are qualitatively distinct emotions. It has been suggested that love occurs in two forms, one passionate and the other companionate. Passionate love is a function of both physiological arousal and social labeling.

Social psychologists have recently begun to study loneliness, the common and distressing experience that occurs when a person's social relationships are inadequate. Weiss has distinguished emotional loneliness from social loneliness. Rubenstein and Shaver identified four clusters of feelings and thoughts associated with loneliness: desperation, impatient boredom, self-deprecation, and depression. The causes of loneliness are diverse. Specific events that precipitate the onset of loneliness include the termination of close relationships and moving to a new community. Our vulnerability to loneliness can be increased both by our personal characteristics (physical appearance, competence) and situational characteristics (physical proximity, similarity of backgrounds and attitudes). Research on close relationships and on loneliness are promising new directions for social psychology.

CHAPTER EIGHT

AGGRESSION

WHAT IS AGGRESSION?

VIEWS ON AGGRESSION

INTERNAL DETERMINANTS OF AGGRESSION
- Biological Mediators: Stocking the Arsenal
- Ethology: Preprogrammed Violence
- Psychodynamics of Aggression: Freud's Views
- Frustration and Aggression

EXTERNAL DETERMINANTS OF AGGRESSION
- Imitation of Aggression
- Reward and Punishment

INTERPERSONAL DETERMINANTS AND CONSEQUENCES OF AGGRESSION
- Verbal Attack, Physiological Arousal, and Anger
- Consequences of Direct and "Sublimated" Aggression for Further Aggression

INSTITUTIONAL AGGRESSION
- Passing on the Misery
- Reactions to Authority: "Just Doing My Job"
- Deindividuation: The Faceless Villain

AGGRESSION AND PUBLIC POLICY
- Televised Violence and Aggression
- Pornography and Aggression
- Guns and Aggression
- Alcohol and Aggression

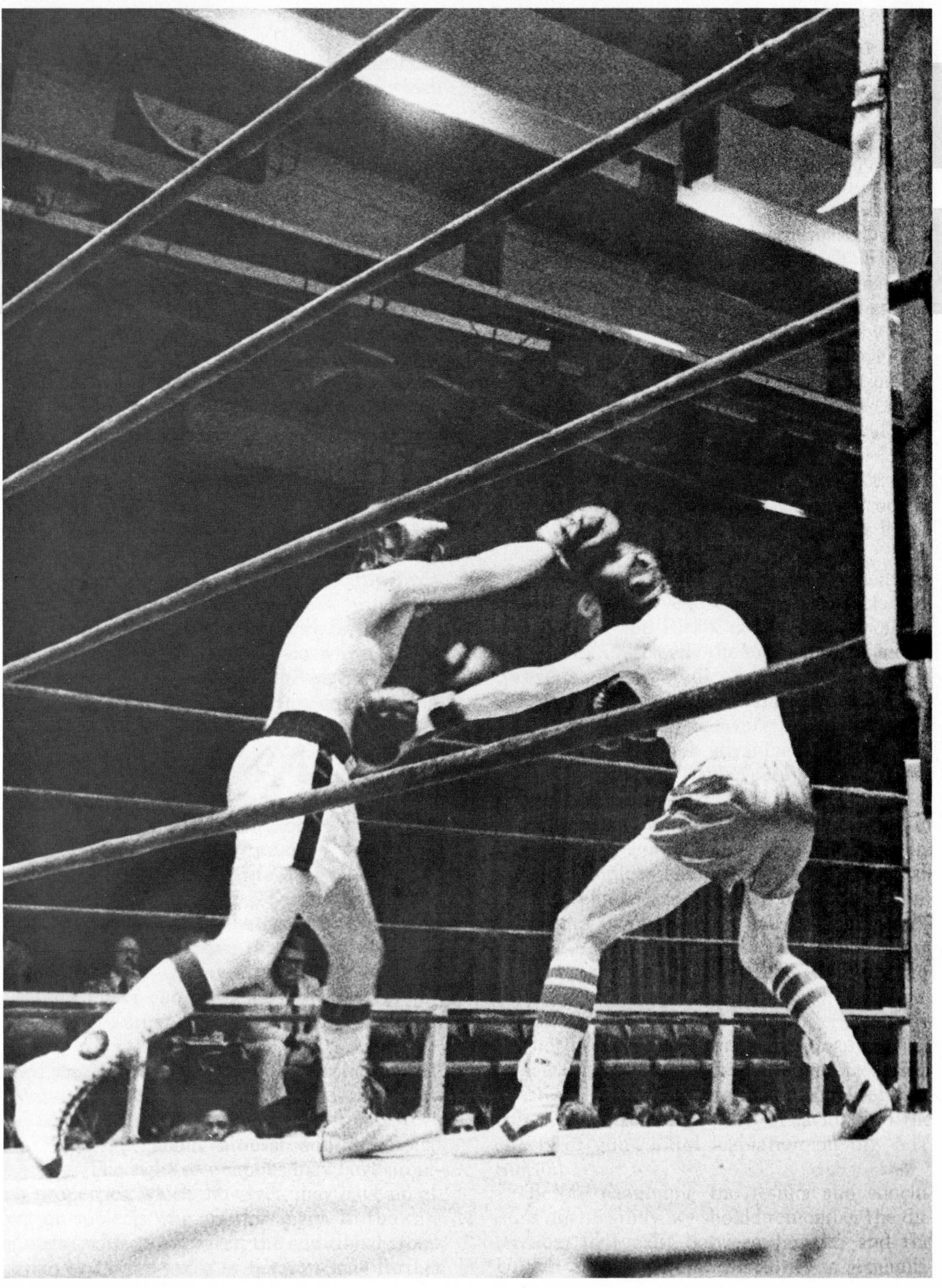

In the still, early morning hours of February 2, 1980, two guards at the New Mexico State Prison in Sante Fe were making their rounds. Most of the 1,200 inmates had finally settled down for the night, except for Dormitory E-2. Here, the guards discovered two inmates drinking a home-brew made from fermented fruit. The drunken prisoners overpowered the surprised guards and raced down to the control center in the middle of the prison. Smashing the 1½-inch thick windows with clubs, they stormed the control room and flicked switches releasing locks in the prison's ten dormitories and cell blocks.

Hundreds of convicts spilled into the hallways, seizing fifteen of the eighteen guards on duty. Other prisoners broke into the pharmacy for drugs, while still others smashed their way into the prison's work rooms for tools that could serve as weapons.

It was thirty-six hours before officials could regain control, and by that time, much of the prison was a burned-out ruin. Thirty-eight prisoners had died—all of them killed by fellow prisoners. Some of the deaths were so brutal that a prison employee said, "These men turned on their own kind the way rats and sharks do." One man was beheaded; others were cremated with blowtorches; some inmates had their arms and legs cut off; and other prisoners were hanged and blinded. When prison officials surveyed the carnage, one observed, "I know I'm never going to believe any of the things they say about human behavior can ever stretch far enough to cover what was done to some of those men."

The New Mexico State Prison riot is shocking because of its savagery, but violence in America is not unusual. In the 1960s the course of national politics was greatly altered by the assassinations of John Kennedy, Robert Kennedy, and Martin Luther King, Jr. In 1978 the mayor of San Francisco, George Moscone, and a city supervisor, Harvey Milk, were fatally shot by a former supervisor who disagreed with them politically. During the gasoline crisis of 1979, murders were committed in three states—Massachusetts, Texas, and California—simply because motorists cut in front of one another in long lines of cars waiting at the pumps. In December 1980 John Lennon was gunned down outside his New York apartment house by a disturbed fan. Newspapers carry daily accounts of robberies, assaults, and rapes, and the events we learn about are but a small fraction of the total number of violent incidents. Less dramatic crimes are often neglected by the media altogether. Still other acts of violence are not even reported to the police.

Violence is by no means unique to the United States. In the past few years, Protestants and Catholics have slaughtered each other in Ireland, black Ugandans have massacred Indian Ugandans, Israelis and Arabs have attacked each other's civilian populations, and Lebanese Christians have confronted Lebanese Muslims. Nor is violence unique to the present. In the Middle Ages, "chivalrous" knights routinely looted and pillaged defenseless villages, killing and raping the inhabitants at will. Renaissance Florentines and Elizabethan Londoners complained of terror in the streets and longed for personal safety. Human history has largely been one of battles and bloodshed. It is small solace to the victims of violence, but aggression is a pervasive problem even in the most diverse societies.

Social scientists, long interested in the problem, have recently increased their efforts to understand the processes underlying violence and aggression and the means by which people can control and reduce such behavior. In this chapter some of the resulting work is examined.

WHAT IS AGGRESSION?

The task of defining aggression is not an easy one. Consider the following actions and try to evaluate them according to whether or not they are aggressive. Then try to formulate your own definition.

1. A driver screams at an old man who is slowly crossing the street against a red light.
2. A baseball player hits a home run.
3. A boxer knocks out his opponent in the eighth round.

4. A farmer slaughters a chicken and prepares it for dinner.
5. A husband and wife argue over who is to take out the garbage.
6. A policeman clubs a robber on the head as the robber is escaping from the scene of a crime.
7. A woman dislikes Jews and avoids them.
8. A disappointed lover slashes his wrists.
9. A chemist accidentally blows up her laboratory; her assistant is killed in the explosion.
10. An assassin takes a shot at the president and misses.
11. A teenager attacks a stranger, kills him, and flees.

These examples introduce a number of issues. One concerns the *target* of the aggressive act. The baseball player who slugs a ball out of the park would not be viewed as an aggressor by many people, yet his swat may closely resemble the strokes of the policeman who uses his club on a thief. A second issue is *legitimacy*. People are more likely to label the policeman as aggressive if they believe his assault is unjustified rather than a necessary duty. Closely related is the important question of *intent*. If the chemist did not plan to demolish the laboratory, then she is not thought of—legally or generally—as an aggressor. Finally, whether *damage* actually occurs or is only attempted must be considered. Is an assassin aggressive if he hits his target but not aggressive if he misses?

As you might expect, there are several definitions of aggression. But the one that most people agree on amounts to this: aggression includes acts of *physical* or *verbal* abuse intentionally directed by one human being at another. Aggression may, therefore, be closely related to violence, which often involves great force, especially physical force, used against others.

No actual harm need occur for an act to be aggressive. The assassin who misses his target as well as the college student who thinks he is delivering electric shocks to another student in an experiment in which the shock box is not connected have acted aggressively. In both cases the individual *intended* to inflict injury, harm, or pain.

The idea of abuse is also important in defining aggression, because it distinguishes between aggressive and assertive behavior. There are times when it is essential to take a stand and be assertive. Thus, if a motorist finds herself trapped in an alley between two large trucks whose drivers have decided to renew an old friendship, she might reasonably suggest that they move their vehicles. Although her behavior could result in an aggressive episode if the truckers take offense, the motorist's initial request would be classified as assertive rather than aggressive.

Finally, it is important to realize that whether or not a behavior will be labeled aggressive depends not only on the various circumstances under which it occurs, discussed above, but also on the culture in which it occurs. Thus, several investigators, notably Albert Bandura (1973), have stressed that the labeling of aggression is a social and cultural process. For example, in many cultures the initiation rites for adolescent boys and girls are extremely painful, often brutal, and yet the tribal people designated to perform the rites are not considered aggressive by anyone concerned. In still other cultures, old men beyond a certain age are killed, sometimes by their sons, with the full approval of both the victims and other people in the society. Recent controversies in this country concerning euthanasia (merciful killing of the terminally ill and suffering patients) and the proabortion/antiabortion debate illustrate this point well. In other words, like other forms of social behavior, aggression is both multiply determined and complexly evaluated in light of a variety of social and cultural norms, which, in turn, determine the consequences of aggression for both the aggressor and the target.

We now turn to some views on the possible causes of aggressive behavior.

VIEWS ON AGGRESSION

Psychologists have devoted considerable attention to mechanisms that may explain aggressive behavior. Some researchers have concentrated on factors within the individual that may lead to aggression. These *internal factors* include biochemical influences, innate tendencies, psychodynamic instincts, and reactions to frustration. Other researchers argue that aggression is not inherent in "human nature" but is a learned response that is shaped and influenced by *factors in the environment.* In the section below we will consider the internal factors that have been hypothesized to explain aggression. First, we will examine the evidence for biochemical influences and then turn to theories that define innate tendencies in nonphysiological terms. Finally, Freud's views and the frustration-aggression hypothesis will be discussed.

INTERNAL DETERMINANTS OF AGGRESSION

BIOLOGICAL MEDIATORS: STOCKING THE ARSENAL

One striking example of biochemistry's role in aggressive behavior was found in a study of laboratory rats by Douglas Smith, Melvyn King, and Bartley Hoebel (1970). Some of the rats used in the experiment were initially killers that killed almost immediately any mice placed in the rats' cages. Others were pacifists: given the opportunity to kill, they consistently refrained from attacking. The investigators believed that a biochemical agent that mediates killing was present in the brain of both groups but was activated in one and not in the other. The researchers therefore anesthetized all the animals and implanted miniature tubes in their brain. As expected, the investigators found that when they injected certain activating drugs (such as carbachol and neostigmine) through the tubes into a certain part of the brain—the lateral hypothalamus—previously peaceful rats became killers. On the other hand, rats that ordinarily killed mice on sight were inhibited from killing when injected with a different drug (methyl atropine).

These researchers also found that the activating or inhibitory effects did not occur if the tube was inserted even one millimeter away from the hypothalamus; that only certain chemicals would produce the effects; and that the stimulating or inhibiting effects on aggressive behavior lasted only for the few hours in which the drug was pharmacologically active. At present, researchers do not know if these drugs would have the same effects on human beings as they do on rats. It is possible, though, that there are at least some parallels.

Brain malfunctions may be responsible for at least some aggressive acts committed by humans. Perhaps best known is the case of Charles Whitman, the sniper who barricaded himself in a tower at the University of Texas and for ninety minutes shot with a high-powered rifle at everything that moved. He wounded twenty-four people, killed fourteen, and even hit an airplane. Whitman's autopsy revealed a tumor the size of a walnut, located in a portion of the brain known as the amygdala. Moreover, Whitman left behind personal notes that reveal that he suffered painful headaches and at times experienced uncontrollable urges to be violent. To some extent, then, human beings' capacities for aggression may be influenced by biological malfunctioning, and this conclusion has led some investigators, particularly ethologists, to conclude that human aggression is instinctual.

ETHOLOGY: PREPROGRAMMED VIOLENCE

In explaining human violence, ethologists—scientists who study animal behavior—have drawn analogies between the aggressive patterns of human beings and other animals. Seen from this perspective, we are unique among animals in both the frequency with which we kill members of our own species and the relative absence of immediate instrumental goals, such as acquisition of food, sex, or territory.

One leading ethologist, Konrad Lorenz (1966), explains the human penchant for aggressive behavior in evolutionary terms. He reasons that animals that are equipped with deadly weapons—poisonous fangs, sharp talons, powerful teeth and jaws—either develop inhibitions against killing members of the same species or become extinct by annihilating one another. Lorenz has observed, for example, that many of nature's potential killers have developed ritualized acts of surrender, so that a battle almost never ends in the death of the weaker participant. He writes:

Konrad Lorenz believes that animals that are naturally equipped with deadly weapons—a dog's powerful teeth and jaws, for example—tend not to kill members of their own species. However, human beings are less suited by nature to aggress; therefore our inhibitions against killing one another are less instinctive and reliable. *(© Bob Adelman / Magnum)*

The wolf turns his head away from his opponent, offering him the vulnerable, arched side of his neck; the jackdaw holds under the beak of the aggressor the unprotected base of the skull, the very place which these birds attack when they intend to kill. . . .

When the loser of a fight suddenly adopted the submissive attitude, and presented his unprotected neck, the winner performed the movement of shaking to death, in the air, close to the neck of the morally vanquished dog, but with closed mouth, that is, without biting. (132–133)

Lorenz believes that human beings, by contrast, are less well equipped by nature for aggression and thus never developed inhibitions against aggression that occur as automatically and dependably as do the wolf's or jackdaw's. In recent centuries, however, we have rapidly developed deadly weapons—but we still lack inhibitory mechanisms that are strong enough to match our destructive potential. According to Lorenz's analysis, we are almost certainly doomed to join other unsuccessful species who failed to survive because of aggression among members of the same species.

Fortunately, there is also some reason for hope, even according to Lorenz's arguments. If people are ingenious enough to develop weapons of mass destruction, there seems no inherent reason why they cannot learn to inhibit their aggressive impulses as well. Although humanity may not have time enough to rely on slow-working evolutionary processes for salvation from its own destructive potential, the possibility exists that people can use language and other forms of communication to shape human evolution.

Animals as diverse as fish, worms, gazelles, and lizards stake out particular areas and put up fierce resistance when intruders encroach on their territory. Many species distribute odorous secretions over their individual turfs so that other animals will be aware of their territorial prerogatives. For example, a wolf or wild dog marks its domain by urinating around the perimeter. Ethologists refer to these actions as manifestations of *territoriality*.

Noting that humans also can be extremely aggressive when defending their homes and personal property, Robert Ardrey (1966) has postulated that people may be territorial animals whose aggressive actions arise from the same instinctual base that motivates their nonhuman counterparts.

We act as we do for reasons of our evolutionary past, not our cultural present, and our behavior is as much a mark of our species as is the shape of a human thigh bone or the configuration of nerves in a corner of the human brain. If we defend the title to our land or the sovereignty of our country, we do it for reasons no different, no less innate, no less ineradicable, than do lower animals. The dog barking at you from behind its master's fence is motivated for reasons that are indistinguishable from those of its master when the fence was built.

Ardrey invokes numerous examples: juvenile gangs fighting to protect their turf, neighbors of similar ethnic backgrounds "joining forces" to keep out those of a different skin color or religion, and nations warring over contested territory. But not all human beings exhibit similar inclinations toward aggression or have similar attitudes toward property. There are tribes of human beings that do not fight over property or material goods; other people simply do not practice any form of aggression (Montagu, 1968). Clearly, then, Ardrey overstates his case. Environmental and social sources of aggression loom as more important than instinct, as is pointed out many times throughout this chapter.

PSYCHODYNAMICS OF AGGRESSION: FREUD'S VIEWS

In his early writing (prior to 1905), Freud proposed the existence of two groups of instincts, sexual and "ego." In this scheme, aggression was not considered a primary instinct, but only a "primordial reaction" elicited when pleasure-seeking and pain-avoiding behaviors were frustrated. Around 1920, in order to provide what he thought was a more satisfactory explanation for some neurotic behaviors, Freud revised his motivational system and proposed a new dichotomy. This consisted of the "life instinct," or Eros (Greek god of love), which included the sexual and self-preservation tendencies of the organism, and the "death instinct," or Thanatos, which encompassed instinctual strivings for self-destruction. Aggression directed at others, according to Freud, resulted from the "death instinct" being blocked by the "life instinct," so that self-destructive tendencies were redirected outward toward the world. In this view, aggression was not considered a response to some external frustration but rather was seen as the expression of an innate aggressive drive. Therefore, aggression could not be alleviated through the peaceable removal of frustration, but was thought to build up continuously over time until the aggressive energy sought release.

Freud's views on the relative importance of the life and death instincts changed as he grew older and witnessed more wars, with the aggressive instinct looming ever larger. He remained constant, though, in his beliefs about the main motivational principle of all instincts: all motives, whether sexual or aggressive, were directed toward ceasing stimulation and reducing tension. The nervous system was considered to be an apparatus that would, if possible, main-

According to Robert Ardrey, a juvenile gang that fights to protect its turf is one example of territorial behavior among human beings. *(© Jean-Pierre Laffont / Sygma)*

tain itself in an altogether unstimulated condition.

The process of *catharsis* represented for Freud an important link in this chain of events. This term can be traced to the writings of Aristotle, who believed that one of the beneficial effects of observing classical Greek tragedies was the "purgation" of the spectators' violent emotions and passions. Freud first introduced the notion of catharsis in the treatment of certain neurotic disorders, where he used the term to refer both to the process and the tension-reducing consequence of emotional expression. In later writings of Freud and his followers, the hydraulic, or "boiling pot," model of aggression became fully developed, with catharsis as the energy-discharging and tension-reducing part of the system. The model is simple. Internal tension, which is both unpleasant and detrimental, is constantly created through the unavoidable accumulation of aggressive energy. When the tension becomes too great, this energy is released by aggressive activity. The consequences of such a release are tension reduction and a temporary decrease in the level and likelihood of subsequent aggression.

Although this model is espoused by all major psychoanalytic schools, including those that reject the "death principle," few other scientists nowadays suscribe to it. In fact, as we will see later in the chapter, most of Freud's (as well as Lorenz's) views on aggression have been shown, by experimental studies, to be untenable.

FRUSTRATION AND AGGRESSION

One of the best-known explanations of human aggression was proposed forty years ago by a group of psychologists at Yale University. The *frustration-aggression* model has influenced thinking and research in several disciplines. Even before the model was formally outlined, many of the ideas that subsequently became a part of it were already familiar from literary works, dictionary definitions, and lay psychological thinking. It almost seems that the frustration-aggression model formalized a truism.

The model pertains to any situation in which an external or internal stimulus activates the organism to set about obtaining a specific goal. The concept of frustration is defined independently of aggression (1) as an external interference with a goal-directed response, but also (2) as the internal condition that exists when a goal-directed response is subjected to interference. Aggression, on the other hand, is defined as an act whose objective is to injure another organism, and aggression is considered to be an organism's primary reaction to frustration. All of these statements were anticipated on the very first page of a book entitled *Frustration and Aggression* (Dollard, Doob, Miller, Mowrer, and Sears, 1939), in the much-quoted, controversial proposition that expresses the frustration-aggression hypothesis: "the occurrence of aggressive behavior always presupposes the existence of frustration and, contrariwise, the existence of frustration always leads to some form of aggression."

Suppose, for example, that James hears an ice-cream truck coming down the street. He wants ice cream and may first try to get the necessary money from his mother. If she refuses, he will be deprived of the ice cream and thus will be frustrated. The goal is consumption of the ice cream; the boy's mother, by making it impossible for him to obtain the goal, is the frustrater. According to the strongest and the most literal version of the hypothesis, James would aggress against his mother. Also, according to the hypothesis, if an observer who was not aware of the preceding events was to see James aggressing against his mother, the observer would be safe in concluding that James had previously been frustrated.

Actually, in subsequent works (Miller, 1941, 1951, 1959), the Yale group softened the original position. The group recognized that a frustrated person may anticipate the consequences of the aggression and thus realize that aggression against certain targets and in certain situations is not desirable, because of punishment and other reasons. Therefore, the Yale group hypothesized that "displacement" may occur, either in the form of attacks on substitute targets (for example, less threatening ones) or in the form of behaviors other than overt physical or verbal aggression (such as muttering under one's breath, imagining sequences of revenge, engaging in hostile humor, and so on).

Despite these revisions, the popularity of the frustration-aggression hypothesis has been declining over the years, for both theoretical and experimental reasons. It became clear that various types of frustration are vastly different in terms of their ability to lead to aggressive behavior. For example, frustrations caused by the arbitrary or capricious behavior of others may quickly lead to aggression, while unintentional impersonal frustrations may be quietly accepted. Furthermore, because of large individual differences, things that are frustrating for some people are not frustrating for others. Also, when frustration is defined as an internal condition rather than a directly observable external interference, a different problem arises, having to do with the difficulties of measuring such an internal condition. Moreover, even when the original first part of the hypothesis is watered down by saying that aggression is only one of many responses to frustration, this is not very helpful unless it is specified under what conditions aggression will or will not occur. As we will see later, other stimuli—such as verbal insults—that would not necessarily be classified as frustrations in the original formulation of the hypothesis have been experimentally shown to be far more powerful elicitors of aggression than are frustrations.

Finally, the second part of the hypothesis has fared especially poorly. It is simply not a fact that aggression is always preceded by frustration. It is farfetched to assume that pilots dropping bombs over inhabited areas are doing this out of frustration. The same is true for many acts of aggression that are performed in order to gain money, to seek subculture approval, or in response to social pressures or norms.

With regard to the research studies, several early studies that have been repeatedly interpreted as strongly supporting the frustration-aggression hypothesis are actually open to other interpretations. One of these studies, by Carl Hovland and Robert Sears (1940), correlated indices of economic prosperity with the number of southern blacks who were lynched between 1880 and 1930. When the price of cotton was high and the white farmers were prosperous, few lynchings tended to occur. In contrast, recessions and depressions seemed to be associated with higher frequencies of lynchings. Hovland, Sears, and many others interpreted this correlation to mean that when times were bad, people were frustrated and vented their frustration through aggression against a powerless, highly visible social group—a behavior tolerated by the authorities. Attractive as this explanation may appear, it is also possible that in the years when the price of cotton was low, there was less employment, more spare time, an increase in alcohol consumption, and so on, among both blacks and whites. Such factors may have led to an increasing number of interracial contacts under adverse circumstances, and to the various alleged "transgressions" on the part of blacks as defined and perceived by whites. Many of the lynchings might have been caused by these incidents that were correlated with the low price of cotton, rather than due to the frustrations induced by the low price of cotton.

Several arguments against the frustration-aggression hypothesis are also applicable against other "internal" theoretical explanations of aggression as well. Sweeping views about the nature and antecedents of aggression—be they of the psychoanalytic, ethological, or frustration-aggression variety—are not nearly as popular today as they used to be. Increasingly sophisticated research has shown that a wide variety of factors plays a part in almost every instance of aggressive behavior. Therefore, researchers have tended to compartmentalize the field of aggression, and to develop small-scale theoretical models to account for specific findings. Although this narrower approach may not at first appear as appealing as having a grand theory that explains everything, it is, upon reflection and upon examination of the experimental findings, more realistic and reasonable. Biochemical, constitutional, sex-related, social, and cultural factors all contribute to some degree to an act of aggression and in all cases are governed to a large extent by the specific details of the situation in which aggression occurs. Such multiple causation of aggressive behavior is made more explicit in the small-scale models of aggression discussed in the next section.

EXTERNAL DETERMINANTS OF AGGRESSION

Even researchers who stress the innate aspects of aggressive behavior would agree that human aggression takes highly complex and subtle forms. Most of the details concerning when aggression is appropriate, what type of aggression to perform, and what consequences to expect from aggression are learned—generally from other people and from one's own past experience. Therefore, in this section, we will consider some of the factors in the external environment that are important in the learning of aggression. First, we will examine learning by imitation and then the effects of specific rewards and punishments.

IMITATION OF AGGRESSION

Other people, starting with one's parents, provide valuable and important learning experi-

We learn a great deal about aggressive behavior—for example, how to perform aggressive actions, when they are appropriate, and how they are rewarded or punished—merely by observation. *(Eugene Richards / Magnum)*

ences. In addition to rewarding and punishing our behavior, they provide examples of the behaviors to be learned and thus spare us the necessity of engaging in the behavior ourselves while we are still totally unskilled in it. In other words, they spare us the painful experiences of learning by trial and error. These "models"—the people we imitate—provide at least four different types of information that are important in determining how aggressive behavior is acquired and maintained. First, models teach us details of aggressive actions: how to strike, how to hurt and insult verbally, how to cause others misery by scheming and taunting. Second, they cue already learned behavior by making various behavioral alternatives more salient, explicitly or implicitly informing us about the courses of action open in a given situation. Third, they provide us with information about when aggression is appropriate, thus passing on the accumulated wisdom (or lack of it) and social norms of the culture in which we live. And fourth, they demonstrate the consequences of aggression, as we observe whether their behavior is rewarded or punished (by the victim or others) and under what circumstances. Even a brief reflection of these issues will reveal the extent to which "modeling" is important in the learning of aggression. Albert Bandura has been responsible for much of the theoretical and experimental work on the role of modeling in the acquisition and maintenance of aggressive behavior. Bandura has written a book on aggression from the viewpoint of his social-learning theory, which has modeling at its core (Bandura, 1973).

Bandura's approach is demonstrated in his now classic experiment on the modeling of aggressive behavior (Bandura, 1965). In this study children watched an adult perform unusual types of aggression against a large inflated doll called a "Bobo doll." One group saw the aggressive model rewarded for clubbing the doll, kicking it around the room, punching it, and shouting such cries as "Sock him in the nose";

another group saw the model punished for the same behavior; and a third group saw the model receive neither reward nor punishment for this behavior. The children who saw the model punished subsequently exhibited less aggression than did those in the other conditions, although when encouraged to recall the model's actions, they were able to reconstruct the model's techniques accurately. Bandura warned that even when aggressive models are punished, they may still be instrumental in teaching observers new ways to aggress as well as pushing the prevailing standards of behavior in the direction of overt aggression. Thus, even if observers do not approve of the model's behavior, the aggressive actions may be reenacted later on by those same observers when the situation suits them.

The discerning reader may have noted that in a strict sense of the definition this last study is not directly concerned with aggression because the target is an inanimate doll. However, a study conducted by Bandura, Dorothea Ross, and Sheila Ross (1963b) revealed that children will also imitate aggressive acts performed against human targets. These investigators showed nursery-school children a television program in which a boy named Johnny is playing with some toys and refuses to let another boy, Rocky, play with him. Rocky proceeds to hit Johnny with a baton, lasso him with a hula hoop, shoot darts at his cars, and defeat him in such a manner that the aggressor winds up with all the toys. At the end of the sequence Rocky departs with Johnny's hobby-horse under his arm and a sack of Johnny's toys over his shoulder.

When the children who saw this scene were asked to evaluate Rocky's conduct, most of them indicated disapproval. But when the experimenters placed them in a somewhat analogous situation, those who had seen Rocky's victory behaved in a dramatically more aggressive manner than did those who had either seen the same sequence with a different ending (in which Johnny successfully counterattacked) or who had not seen a movie at all. The effect was personified by the actions of a four-year-old girl who had expressed severe disapproval of Rocky's behavior during the movie but, when placed in the similar situation, imitated many of his actions. Indeed, after vanquishing the original owner of the toys, she turned to the experimenter and inquired, "Do you have a sack here?" Thus, the influence of witnessing a successful aggressive model apparently overrides observers' stated opinions about the model's behavior.

Another determining factor in the effectiveness of models is the media through which they are presented. For example, Bandura, Ross, and Ross (1963a) compared the effects of showing the same content in three different forms: as a cartoon, on film, or as a live drama. The subjects who watched either the live performance or the film saw an experimenter beating a Bobo doll with a mallet, hitting it, kicking it, and verbally berating it with statements such as "Hit him down," and "Pow!" The cartoon presentation featured similar actions, but the protagonist was dressed as a black cat and typical cartoon music was included.

After presenting one of these versions, the experimenters frustrated the youngsters by inviting them to play with a collection of highly attractive toys and then informing them that these toys were actually being reserved for other children and that the youngsters, therefore, would have to be content with the toys that were in the next room. These toys included some that the subjects had viewed earlier, such as Bobo dolls and mallets, in addition to various toys that were not well adapted to aggressive play. The results showed that children in all three conditions engaged in more aggressive play than did children in a control group who had not seen any of the presentations. As it turned out, the cartoon and the film appeared to be more effective than the live presentation.

This finding suggests that violence portrayed by the media might be especially influential in promoting aggressive behavior among young children. In fact, a topic of great contemporary interest concerns the effects of media violence on people's social behavior in general and aggressive behavior in particular. We will consider this issue again in a later section. At this point, suffice it to say that experimental studies have clearly shown that experimental subjects (especially children) will imitate *some* actions that may be considered moderately ag-

DISPOSITIONS AND SITUATIONS

WHO WATCHES MEDIA VIOLENCE?

Watching violence on the media can induce aggressive behavior. But is the opposite also true? Do aggressive people choose to watch violence on the media? If so, people may get caught in a vicious circle: viewing violence can produce aggressive feelings and behavior, which can make people choose to watch more violence, which can create more aggressive feelings and behavior, which can make people choose more violence, and so on.

Is there any evidence for this possible chain of effects? Correlational studies suggest there may be some truth to these links. In a study at the University of Illinois, the more aggressive male subjects became, the more they enjoyed a violent program (Diener and DeFour, 1978); in Madison, Wisconsin, attendance at a violent movie increased markedly after a brutal local murder (Boyanowsky, Newtson, and Walster, 1974); and residents of high-crime areas of Toronto, Canada, watched more violent programs than residents of low-crime areas (Doob and Macdonald, 1979). But because these studies are correlational, they do not clearly establish cause and effect. We are still left with our original question: Do aggressive people prefer violence on the media?

One study speaks clearly to this question. Allan Fenigstein (1979) conducted a study in which he manipulated a person's level of aggressiveness and then noted how it influenced that person's choice of watching violent or neutral films. To carry out this study, Fenigstein asked male and female undergraduates at the University of Virginia to make up fantasy stories that included each of twenty-four words in a list supplied by the experimenter. For half of the subjects, the list contained ten words with aggressive connotations (for example, "hurt," "insult," "knife," "anger"). The other half of the subjects were given ten matching nonaggressive words (for example, "help," "praise," "pen," "joy"). The remaining fourteen words were the same for both groups. A later questionnaire confirmed that students who used the aggressive words did in fact rate their own stories as significantly more aggressive than those students who used the nonaggressive words.

After the students had made up their stories, they were then given a chance to select several one- or two-minute film clips to watch out of a total pool of twenty-six films. Each film had previously been rated for its aggressiveness content and was described to the students with a brief phrase, such as "rioting at a rock concert," "a downhill ski run," "a fist fight," or "a student taking a test."

Fenigstein found that men preferred more aggressive films than women. More important, the amount of aggression in subjects' fantasy stories had no effect on the films chosen by women but increased the amount of violence in films chosen by men.

Next, Fenigstein wondered whether aggressive *behavior* would also affect men's film choices in the same way that aggressive fantasies did. He also sought to test the combined effects of aggressive fantasies and aggressive behavior on choice of violent films. To answer these questions Fenigstein asked undergraduate men to make up the same type of fantasy stories as before. But this time, half of the subjects were also led to aggress against another individual. This was achieved by asking the subjects to deliver

gressive against *some* targets (the evidence that children will attack live targets physically in the laboratory is somewhat tenuous) under special, laboratory conditions and after the subjects have been frustrated by the experimenters in a manner described above.

REWARD AND PUNISHMENT

The previous section was concerned, among other things, with the effects of *vicarious* rewards and punishments—that is, with how people are affected by witnessing the consequences

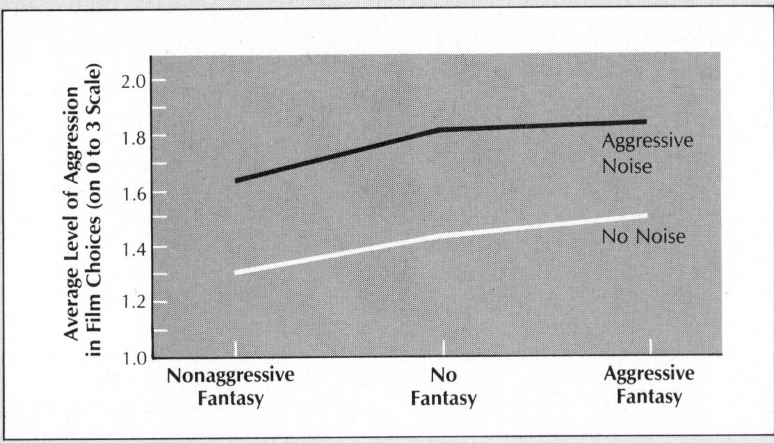

(From Fenigstein, 1979)

loud bursts of static noise to another student wearing headphones. The noises ranged over ten levels from very low and soft to very loud and painful, and were supposedly a means of evaluating the other person's creativity on a task. However, the subjects were restricted from using the noise levels on the low end of the range. Thus, subjects in this group were forced to be moderately aggressive in their behavior toward another person. The other half of the subjects administered no noise but simply pressed buttons that lighted up the numbers 1 through 10 in front of the other person. Thus subjects in this group were nonaggressive. All subjects were then given the same opportunity to choose films as before.

As shown in the graph above, the men who made up aggressive fantasies chose more violent films than the men with nonaggressive fantasies. But the men who engaged in aggressive behavior chose films that were even more violent than those who did not engage in aggressive behavior.

The implications of this research are clear. Men overall choose more violent programs than women. But aggressive fantasies and aggressive behavior lead to still more violent film choices. Thus we can infer that men who dispositionally have violent imagery or who dispositionally behave aggressively are most likely to select violent programming. Furthermore, we know from previous research that viewing violence can increase aggressive imagery and behavior, as explained in the accompanying sections of the text. Apparently, then, there is a high possibility of a vicious circle in which dispositions and situational factors interact and aggravate each other. And while it is hard to say exactly which comes first—aggressive behavior or media violence—Fenigstein's research suggests a definite reciprocal relationship between the two.

of others' behavior rather than directly experiencing the rewards and punishments themselves. In contrast, in this section we will focus mainly on *direct* rewards and punishments, those administered to the "doers" themselves.

Given the effectiveness of reward and, to some extent, of punishment in determining various types of behavior, it is not surprising that these factors influence aggression as well. Gerald Patterson, Richard Littman, and William Bricker (1967) have studied the effects of rewards and punishments on the *development* of

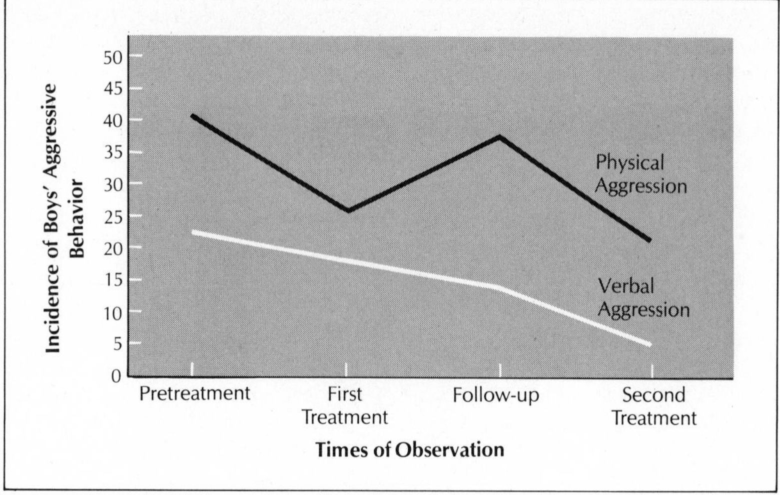

FIGURE 8.1 When teachers ignored aggression and rewarded cooperation and other desirable behaviors, physical and verbal aggression among nursery-school boys decreased substantially. (Adapted from Brown and Elliott, 1965.)

aggressive behavior in a natural environment. They entered a nursery school and observed sixty class meetings, each lasting two and one-half hours. In the course of their observations, they witnessed 2,583 aggressive incidents among the children and in each case recorded the aggressor, the victim, the form of the aggressive act (whether hitting, verbal insult, or some other form), and its consequence. They had hypothesized that when a child is praised for his or her aggression or wins his or her objective, the next act of aggression he or she undertakes will tend to be against the same victim and will tend to assume the same form. On the other hand, if the aggressive act is met either by counteraggression or by the victim regaining a toy or territory, the child's next aggressive act will either be directed at a different victim, will assume a different form, or both. These two predictions were both confirmed. Furthermore, children who were passive when they entered the nursery school learned that counteraggression usually met with success. They therefore became increasingly ready to resort to action when aggressed against. Patterson and his associates concluded that children learn to be aggressive and to respond forcefully when attacked because in doing so they are rewarded directly or indirectly by adults and peers.

These findings raise an interesting question: can classroom aggression in young children be reversed by changing reinforcement contingencies? In a naturalistic study, Paul Brown and Rogers Elliott (1965) observed the aggressive patterns of twenty-seven male nursery-school children for one week and then requested that the teachers not attend to any but the most severe aggressive actions. (It was intended that the teachers' nonattention would, in the terminology of learning theorists, extinguish the bad behavior.) In addition, Brown and Elliott asked the teachers to reward cooperative and other desirable behaviors. Within fourteen days, both verbal and physical aggression decreased substantially. Several weeks later, the experimenters returned and found that the incidence of physical aggression had returned to its former level, although verbal aggression had continued to decline. Brown and Elliott again recommended nonattention to fights and other disruptions. As indicated in Figure 8.1, this second round of efforts to extinguish aggressive behavior produced even greater reductions in both forms of aggressive behavior than before. This study carries special promise because, following the extinction periods, two of the most violent boys in the class "became friendly and cooperative to a degree not previously thought possible."

Reinforcement of aggression is seldom accomplished through a conscious effort on the part of parents, teachers, and other socializing agents, but it nevertheless occurs. Attention per se is a rewarding experience, and human beings of all ages go out of their way to obtain it. But if attention is not usually given to children unless they are acting out some form of aggression, it is likely that they will learn to rely on aggressive acts to gain attention. Brown and Elliott's observations provide dramatic evidence that aggression can be deconditioned by ignoring aggressive behavior.

The effects of punishment are far more complicated than those of reward. Whereas some authorities—parents, educators, political and religious leaders, and so on—have claimed that only the threat of punishment deters many individuals from acting aggressively (Walters and Llewellyn-Thomas, 1963), others have contended that punishment only temporarily suppresses aggression and that as soon as the threat becomes less imminent, the suppressed behavior will recur (Estes, 1944).

In some situations, punishment can eliminate aggressive responses, although the effects may depend on the regularity with which it is applied. For example, Jan Deur and Ross Parke (1970) observed first-, second-, and third-grade children playing a game that involved putting on boxing gloves and hitting a toy clown in the stomach. Deur and Parke reinforced some children by giving them a marble after half of their punches and punished them by sounding a loud buzzer after the other half of their punches. The researchers also informed the children that marbles meant that they were playing the game well and that buzzes meant that they were playing poorly. After two minutes of this inconsistent feedback, half of the children received neither rewards nor punishments (extinction) and the remainder were punished by the buzzer for all subsequent punches. Punishment worked more quickly than extinction did in persuading the children to stop playing the game.

There was another important finding, however. Youngsters who had received the combination of 50 percent reward and 50 percent punishment on their first several trials were far more resistant to the schedules of both continuous extinction and continuous punishment than were children who had been treated more consistently. Thus, it would appear that it was the inconsistent practice of both rewarding and punishing aggression that produced behavior resistant to extinction and minimally affected by punishment. This finding suggests a distressing analogy. In most families and schools, children who aggress sometimes are rewarded (for example, they succeed in taking the toy away from their playmate or they are told that they are brave for winning fights) and at other times punished (for example, they are called bullies, or their playmate successfully defends his or her possession). If Deur and Parke's findings are generally applicable, inconsistencies of this nature may lead to considerable resistance to later punishment, possibly resulting in incorrigibility.

Clearly, then, both in the laboratory and in naturalistic settings, the consequences of aggression substantially influence both its frequency and the form it takes. Reward is an effective shaper of aggressive acts, and systematic extinction in combination with rewards for desirable (nonaggressive) behavior appears to be particularly effective in controlling excessive aggression, at least among children. Punishment, on the other hand, also has some suppressive influence on aggression. However, a problem that often accompanies the use of punishment should not be overlooked: punishment often provides compelling examples of the very behavior that it is employed to eliminate. Many punishing acts, such as yelling or spanking, require the punisher to behave aggressively himself or herself and thus, in a sense, provide effective models of aggressive behavior.

INTERPERSONAL DETERMINANTS AND CONSEQUENCES OF AGGRESSION

Much human aggression occurs in face-to-face situations, often between people who know each other well, such as family members or coworkers. Unlike the more institutionalized forms of aggression—such as that which occurs in a war—interpersonal aggression is more influenced by the exact nature of the instigation, by subtle situational influences, and by the emotional states experienced by the participants in the aggressive exchange. In this section, we will examine some social, cognitive, and emotional determinants, as well as behavioral and other consequences, of interpersonal aggressive behavior.

VERBAL ATTACK, PHYSIOLOGICAL AROUSAL, AND ANGER

Social aversive events (that is, aversive events caused by other people) can have a profound effect on a person exposed to them, especially if he or she perceives others' action as being arbitrary or capricious and performed with the clear intent of producing physical, economic, or psychological harm (Cohen, 1955; Pastore, 1952). Examples of such social aversive events are being verbally or physically attacked or being threatened by such attacks; being slighted or humiliated; losing income or property due to others' actions; being obstructed by other people in the gratification of basic needs or in the achievement of important goals; observing that any of the above has occurred to others with whom one has an emotional bond; and so on (Konečni, 1979). Both everyday experience and the scientific literature indicate that many of these social events are powerful and frequent causes of interpersonal aggression. This is perhaps best documented in the case of people's exposure to what may be considered the prototypic social aversive events—namely, humiliating or slighting remarks and insults (Buss, 1961, 1966).

Verbal attack is a common form of interpersonal aggression. *(© Leonard Freed / Magnum)*

Like other powerful stimuli, insults produce a large number of changes in a person exposed to them. One of these is a dramatic increase in the level of *physiological arousal*, a term that for our present purposes can be taken to include hormonal changes (especially in the level of epinephrine and norepinephrine), changes in the cardiovascular system (increases in blood pressure, heart rate, etc.), and a host of other changes ranging from rate of respiration to pupil diameter, posture, and level of muscular activity (Ax, 1953; Kahn, 1966). These physiological fluctuations are usually considered to be a part of the "fight/flight" reaction by which people and other organisms prepare themselves for high-level activity often involved in aggression and escape. The elevation of arousal is likely to persist for the duration of the insults or other noxious stimulation. Once the insults have ceased and their source has been removed from the vicinity of the target of the insults, the target person's arousal gradually subsides toward the base line, providing that additional aversive events do not occur. It is uneconomical and maladaptive for an organism to maintain arousal at an excessively high level for long periods of time after the noxious stimulation has ceased and there is no further need for energizing aggressive or escape behaviors.

In addition to causing physiological fluctuations, insults also activate a variety of cognitive processes in the person exposed to them. For example, an insulted person must evaluate the situation, making sure that a meaning has been interpreted correctly or that a particular remark was not made jokingly. The person must also

FOCUS ON APPLICATIONS

RAGE AND AGGRESSION: THE MIAMI RIOTS

For two nights in May 1980 the city of Miami, Florida, became a war zone. Black citizens took to the streets in a riot that left blocks of burning buildings, millions of dollars in property damage, and six people dead. One white body was mutilated as cars repeatedly ran it over, and a boy had his tongue cut out.

What factors led to these riots? Many of the causes parallel exactly the "social aversive events" described in the accompanying section.

First, the precipitating event involved perceived "attack and threat of attack." An all-white jury acquitted four Miami police officers in the alleged beating death of a black insurance salesman. This event occurred against a historical background of poor community relations between police and blacks. Benjamin Hooks, the executive director of the NAACP, said: "It's hard to describe the feelings of rage you have when men and women in uniform, who are agents of the state, beat or kill someone and you follow due process of law and the Constitution and they're let go."

Later, when police tried to disperse the crowd at a rally, one black man yelled, "Hell, no, we ain't going nowhere. What are you going to do, shoot us too?"

A second important factor involved "losing income or property due to others' actions." As thousands of refugees streamed into Florida from Castro's Cuba, local and national authorities gave them a warm welcome. Special processing centers were set up, food stamps were distributed, and aid was provided for resettlement and employment. At the same time black refugees from Haiti were given a much cooler reception. Furthermore, the presence of the Cubans threatened black jobs. Blacks resented both the Cuban refugees and their special treatment. As one black man said at a rally, "We blacks, who have fought for this country, still have to beg for food stamps, while Cubans get them with no trouble."

Thirdly, there was a pervasive sense among Miami blacks that they were "being obstructed by other people in the gratification of basic needs." Unemployment, which was at 9 percent nationally in the spring of 1980, was 28 percent among Miami blacks and over 50 percent among black young people. Housing was in short supply, and Miami city officials conceded that, despite the influx of Cuban refugees over the past fifteen years, "not one new unit of government housing had been built." The local rental vacancy rate was less than 1 percent. But black leaders warn that Miami is not unique. As Benjamin Hooks said, "The ingredients for racial disturbances are everywhere in every big city in this country. That's where the unemployment is greatest. That's where the misery is greatest. All it takes is a spark to set it off."

In Miami that spark amounted to the acquittal of four police officers.

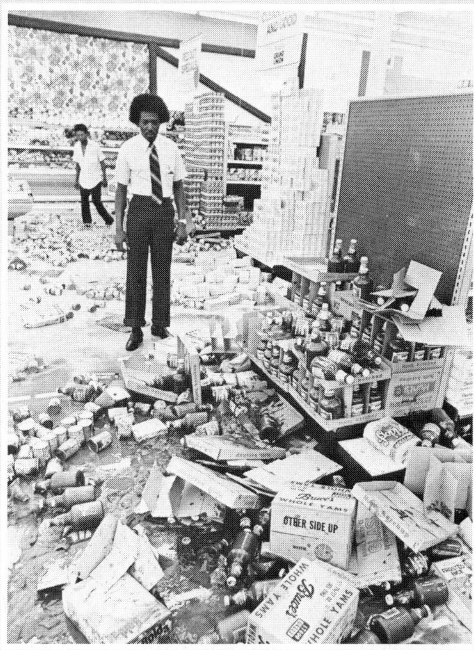

A supermarket manager surveys the aftermath of a night of looting during the Miami riots in May 1980. *(Tom Salyer / UPI)*

monitor internal bodily processes, noting such sensations as blood "surging into one's head" and the heart pounding very fast. And external sources of information must be monitored as well such as the posture and actions of one's opponent. According to some researchers (Konečni, 1976–1977; Schachter, 1964; Zillmann, 1971), these various cognitive processes—monitoring and interpreting information from both external and internal sources and integrating various cues—play a major part in how a person comes to decide that he or she is experiencing a particular emotion, such as anger, fear, or even love (see Chapter 7).

As explained in Chapter 6, an emotional state is a joint product of physiological changes and cognitive processes—an idea elaborated by Schachter and his colleagues (Schachter, 1964; Schachter and Singer, 1962; Schachter and Wheeler, 1962). More specifically, while an increase in the level of physiological arousal is necessary for a pronounced emotional state to occur, such an increase is not sufficient. The labeling of anger, or that of any other pronounced emotion, is arrived at by considering *both* fluctuations in physiological arousal *and* the details of the stimulus situation that produced them.

There are several important implications of such a view of emotion. First, the above position suggests that a person may be highly aroused (for example, by jogging for an hour) without experiencing any emotional state in particular. Second, a given state of high physiological arousal may result in any number of different emotional states, depending on the precise conditions which generated the arousal and on the particular interpretation of these conditions. For example, a person may be highly aroused by someone else's remarks, but would label this arousal state very differently depending on whether the person considers the remarks to be insulting or uttered in jest (the emotional labels of anger and mirth, respectively, would presumably be adopted). Third, once an emotional label (such as anger) has been arrived at, the higher the arousal level, the more intense the emotional state in question. Finally, a person who is not aroused but merely has negative attitudes or thoughts about another person, would not, by definition, be considered as experiencing an emotional state.

These considerations are very important, because many researchers have suggested that anger, rather than merely an increase in the level of physiological arousal, on the one hand, or simply hostile thoughts and attitudes about another person, on the other, is the principal precursor of interpersonal aggression, especially physical aggression (Doob and Wood, 1972; Donnerstein and Wilson, 1976, Konečni, 1975a; Rule, Ferguson, and Nesdale, 1978; Zillmann, Katcher, and Milavsky, 1972).

A recent experiment by Vladimir Konečni (1975b) examined the role of mere arousal versus the emotional experience of anger as determinants of aggression. In the first part of the experiment, some subjects were insulted by an "experimental confederate," whereas others were treated neutrally. In the insult condition, a subject worked on a difficult task in the same room as the confederate. The latter pretended to finish the task quickly and then proceeded to insult the subject by making disparaging comments about the subject's ability, intelligence, and personal characteristics. In contrast, in the control condition, the confederate behaved in a neutral manner. In the next part of the experiment, the subject had to decide on each of fifty trials whether or not to administer an "electric shock" to the confederate in the context of an ambiguous task. While deciding whether or not to punish the confederate, the subject heard, on each trial, a tone sequence that was presented at a comfortable listening level in the control group, but at an aversively loud level in the experimental group. The tones were administered to subjects on each trial irrespective of whether or not they shocked the confederate. Prior work had shown that both of these manipulations—that is, insults and loud noise—independently raise the level of physiological arousal. However, only insults could be expected to result in the cognitive label of anger, since it was made clear to subjects that the noise was not in any way caused by the confederate's behavior, and was instead a "part of the experiment."

The main experimental hypotheses were strongly supported by the results presented in Figure 8.2. Whereas the loudness of the noise

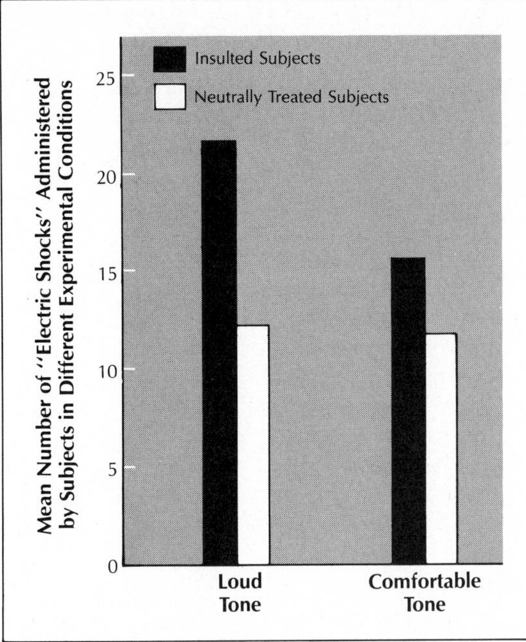

FIGURE 8.2 Noise, insults, and aggression under experimental conditions. Loud noise had no significant effect on subjects who had not been insulted by the confederate. In the case of insulted subjects, however, aggression was far greater among those who were exposed to the loud tone than among those who were exposed to a comfortable noise level. (Adapted from Konečni, 1975b.)

had no differential effects on the number of shocks given by subjects who had not been insulted by the confederate, the insulted subjects who were exposed to loud tones were far more aggressive than subjects exposed to tones presented at a comfortable listening level. In other words, the physiological arousal by itself, when not accompanied by the cognitive label of anger, did not increase the level of aggression. However, exposing the insulted objects (who were both aroused *and* angry) to loud noise further increased their already high level of aggression, presumably because of the added physiological arousal due to the noise. These results were successfully replicated by Edward Donnerstein and David Wilson (1976). Moreover, Dolf Zillmann and his colleagues (1972) similarly found that subjects aroused by the strenuous physical activity of riding an exercise bike delivered more intense shocks to an abusive confederate than nonaroused subjects did.

In summary, verbal insults seem to be a particularly potent cause of interpersonal aggression. These stimuli not only raise the level of physiological arousal, but also lead to the label of anger, unlike many other manipulations that merely increase arousal level. Anger by itself seems to be a powerful determinant of aggressive behavior; and its impact can be further increased by exposing the angry person to additional sources of arousing stimulation, even though such stimulation by itself may not be directly related to either anger or aggression. Thus, interpersonal aggressive behavior depends to a large extent on a complex interplay of social, cognitive, physiological, and emotional factors.

CONSEQUENCES OF DIRECT AND "SUBLIMATED" AGGRESSION FOR FURTHER AGGRESSION

Several modern theories of aggression share a degree of kinship with the Aristotelian concept of catharsis. Although their theoretical positions differed in many details—as we discussed earlier—the psychoanalysts, some ethologists, and even the frustration-aggression theorists all espoused some version of the "catharsis" hypothesis. Many of these theorists assumed that observation of aggressive activity—both by people who are angered and by those who are not—may reduce the level of the observers' subsequent aggressive behavior. In addition, at least some of these theorists also thought that other forms of indirect or sublimated aggressive activity, such as having aggressive fantasies or attacking inanimate targets (for example, cutting off dolls' heads or throwing darts at pictures of human faces) would also increase the level of subsequent aggression.

Many experimental studies have been conducted to test these ideas, in part because of their considerable practical implications. For instance, several types of clinical therapies for maladjusted children rest on the assumption that aggressive play with dolls or other objects should decrease both immediate expressions of aggression as well as long-term "deep-seated" hostility. Also, many educators, politicians, and other public figures, not to mention average parents, believe that "letting off steam" has beneficial consequences, including a reduced level of aggression.

Unfortunately, these expectations have not been borne out by experimental results. On the contrary, experimental studies have been almost unanimous in their findings that both indirect and sublimated forms of aggression, whether performed by angry or nonangry people, if anything, *increase* the level of subsequent direct and indirect aggression rather than "drain off" hostility and reduce aggression.

For example, the studies by Albert Bandura that we mentioned earlier showed that children who watched models beat up dolls were *more likely* to aggress against these dolls at a later time than children who had not observed aggressive models. In a large number of investigations, Leonard Berkowitz and Russell Geen (Berkowitz, 1965; Berkowitz and Geen, 1966; Geen and Berkowitz, 1966) found that when angry people viewed violent films, they were subsequently *more* aggressive toward people who had angered them than were others who did not view violent films. Moreover, the effects of violent films on angered people were further increased when a character in the film was similar in some way to the confederate who had initially made the subject angry. For example, in some of the studies, the confederate had the same first name—Kirk—as the actor involved in the prize fight in the film (Kirk Douglas).

Other studies showed that even films with erotic content (such as sexual foreplay) served to increase the amount of viewers' subsequent aggression (for example, Zillman, 1971). These findings cast doubt on some contentions derived from psychoanalytic theory to the effect that erotic activity may have aggression-decreas-

The brutal "kung fu" films, starring Bruce Lee, enjoyed wide popularity in the mid-1970s. Research shows that such films do not have a cathartic effect. Rather, they may *increase* the possibility of aggressive behavior. *(The Museum of Modern Art / Film Stills Archive)*

ing "cathartic" values because of the aggressive aspects of eroticism.

Still other studies tested the psychoanalytic notion that strenuous physical activity, contact sports, or aggression against inanimate targets should reduce the amount of subsequent aggression (Hornberger, 1959; Husman, 1955; Johnson and Hutton, 1955; Kenny, 1953; Mallick and McCandless, 1966). Although many of these studies leave much to be desired in the way of tight methodology, the sheer frequency of their findings that such activities *increase* rather than decrease aggression tends to raise our confidence in their findings.

The results of studies examining indirect *verbal* aggression lead to similar conclusions. In a study of M. Kahn's (1966), subjects in one condition were insulted by the experimenter in the first part of the study and then either had an opportunity to retaliate verbally by criticizing this person's behavior to another experimenter or did not have such an opportunity. It was found that the opportunity to aggress verbally against the rude experimenter made subjects' subsequent ratings of this person even *less* favorable than the ratings of those subjects who had no opportunity to vent verbal aggression. Similarly, in a field study conducted by Ebbe Ebbesen, Birt Duncan, and Vladimir Konečni (1975), people who were laid off their jobs in an aerospace company (and thus were assumed to be angry) were given an opportunity to aggress verbally against the company or their immediate supervisor. Others being laid off were assigned to a control group that discussed neutral topics. A different group of people who were leaving their jobs for other reasons (and thus were assumed not to be angry) were also given the opportunity to verbally attack the company or not. Afterward, all subjects filled out aggression questionnaires concerning the company and their supervisors. The results indicated that when angered subjects were given an opportunity to express verbal aggression, their subsequent verbal aggression *increased,* but only when aggression was directed against the same target on both occasions. Thus, these two studies showed that indirect verbal aggression increases subsequent verbal aggression, but only when the subjects are angry and under conditions when the same person or entity is attacked twice in succession.

In summary, contrary to the predictions of catharsis theorists, an overwhelming amount of evidence suggests that various sublimated or indirect forms of aggression do *not* decrease the amount of subsequent aggression; instead, under many circumstances, a greater amount of aggressive behavior is a more likely consequence. There is, however, one set of conditions under which aggression expressed by angered people does lead to a decrease in the amount of subsequent aggression: if an angry person is given an opportunity to *physically aggress against the individual who caused the anger* and subsequently has another opportunity to aggress physically against this same individual, the angry person will be less aggressive in the second instance. This situation has been intensively studied by Anthony Doob, Vladimir Konečni, and their colleagues.

In an experiment by Doob and Wood (1972), subjects were first either insulted by a confederate or treated neutrally, and were then given an opportunity to "hurt" the confederate repeatedly by administering "electric shocks" to this person. Subjects in another condition did not have the opportunity to "shock" the confederate and merely waited alone in a room during this period. In the final part of the experiment, all subjects were asked to judge the "creativity" of the confederate's responses to certain stimulus words by administering electric shocks for "noncreative" responses. The results presented in Figure 8.3 clearly show that for angered subjects only, a prior opportunity to physically punish the insulting confederate reduced the amount of subsequent physical aggression against this person. Similar results were obtained in a number of other responses (Konečni and Doob, 1972; Konečni and Ebbesen, 1976).

The question that remains is why should an angry person be less aggressive in a second assault upon an attacker than in the first? In their research Doob, Konečni, and their colleagues ruled out the possible explanations that their angry subjects felt they had already retaliated sufficiently, or that they felt guilty about the first assault, or that they were distracted from

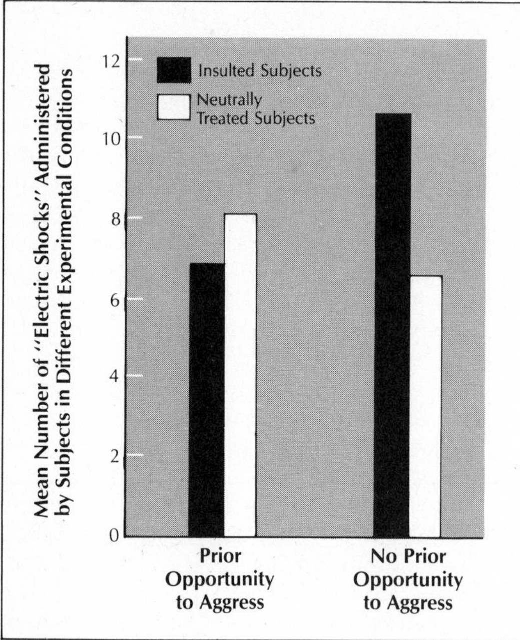

FIGURE 8.3 If an angry person has an opportunity to aggress physically against the individual who caused the anger, the angry person will be less aggressive in a second encounter. (Adapted from Doob and Wood, 1972.)

their anger by intervening activity (see Konečni, 1975a). What, then, accounts for the effect?

The answer to this question may lie in the reduced level of physiological arousal an angry person feels after aggressing toward an insulting individual. In a study by Hokanson and Shetler (1961), insulted and neutrally treated subjects subsequently had an opportunity either to aggress against an insulting confederate or not. These people's systolic blood pressure was measured at various points in the experiment. It was found that the blood pressure of subjects who had an opportunity to aggress against the confederate decreased almost to the level of the neutrally treated subjects, whereas the blood pressure of the insulted subjects who had no opportunity to aggress remained high.

This finding was subsequently investigated in many experiments. Although the results are not unanimous, the most frequent finding seems to be that aggressive actions against an insulting individual tend to decrease the level of the angered subjects' cardiac arousal. As Konečni and Doob (1980) have pointed out, aggressive behavior not only affects the target of aggression—by inflicting injury—but may also affect the aggressor as well—by decreasing the level of physiological arousal. Such a decrease may be due to the fact that physical aggression is often successful in terminating the aversive social stimulation that produced the arousal in the first place. Once such aversive stimulation (for example, obnoxious or threatening people) has been removed, there is no reason for the person to maintain arousal at a high level. Over time, there may be repeated instances of pairing of aggressive activity with a decrease in the aggressor's arousal level. Therefore, subjects may well arrive at the laboratory with a learning history in which aggressive actions performed in anger have become associated with arousal reduction.

The Hokanson-Shetler finding helps explain the results obtained by Doob, Konečni, and their colleagues by virtue of the previously discussed connection between physiological arousal and emotional labeling. Because the degree of an emotional state is presumably influenced both by the level of physiological arousal and by the cognitive labeling processes, we can expect that insulted people who had a prior opportunity to express aggression enter the final stage of this experiment not only less aroused (as in the Hokanson-Shetler study), but also *less angry*, because there is less physiological justification for the emotion of anger. Given that the degree of anger is such a powerful predictor of interpersonal aggression, it is perhaps not surprising that people who are less aroused and less angry would be less aggressive than those insulted subjects who had no prior opportunity for aggression and whose levels of both arousal and anger were, therefore, presumably higher.

Thus, whereas most indirect and sublimated forms of aggressive behavior seem to increase the amount of subsequent aggression, direct physical aggression by angered people seems to have the opposite effect. These results appear to support the contention of another Greek philosopher. In *The Republic* Plato asserts, "If one man is angry with another, he can take it out on him on the spot, and will be less likely to pursue the quarrel further." However, Plato notwithstanding, this finding does not offer much to rejoice about in terms of practical applications aimed at reducing interpersonal aggression.

The first problem lies in the fact that one would hardly want to use aggression to reduce subsequent aggression. Second, if aggressive responses, as we have hypothesized above, are indeed more effective than nonaggressive responses in removing threats and terminating aversive social stimulation, as well as in decreasing the level of physiological arousal labeled as anger, it follows that the effectiveness of such aggression would *increase the probability that aggression would occur in future cases when anger is again present.* Direct experimental support for this suggestion has indeed been obtained in recent research (Konečni, 1976–1977, 1979). Thus, in the long run aggression may breed aggression despite—or perhaps because of—its capacity for reducing arousal and anger in the short run, as demonstrated by the findings of Hokanson and Shetler, on the one hand, and Doob and Konečni, on the other.

Incidentally, with regard to the accuracy of his opinions about human aggressive behavior, Plato bested Aristotle in yet another way. Unlike Aristotle, Plato felt that dramatic performances should be banned because they provided inducements for aggressive actions on the part of the presumably peaceful citizens. Plato thus anticipated the results obtained by Bandura, Berkowitz, and others that we discussed earlier.

INSTITUTIONAL AGGRESSION

This chapter has concentrated so far on the aggressive behavior of individuals who have been insulted or attacked on a one-to-one basis. Yet personalized aggression is hardly the only type of violence existing in our society. Many agressive acts are committed by people who are merely "doing their jobs" or who find themselves in violent situations because of their jobs and then become angered and commit aggressive acts.

PASSING ON THE MISERY

Bruno Bettelheim noted in 1943 that more acts of violence have been committed in the name of obedience than ever have been motivated by rebellion. The Nazi concentration camps, the central metaphor for evil in the twentieth century, provide especially compelling evidence for Bettelheim's contention. In addition to frequent beatings, stabbings, shootings, and genocide in the gas ovens, the prisoners endured daily hardships, including inadequate food, minimal clothing, and exposure to heat, rain, and freezing temperatures seventeen hours per day, seven days per week. Bettelheim was imprisoned in two of the most notorious camps for several years. As a means of "maintaining his sanity" he interviewed prisoners about their reactions to life in the camps (Bettelheim, 1943). He describes his fellow prisoners as a mixed group, including Jews, political opponents of the Nazis, Jehovah's Witnesses, homosexuals, and others whom the regime wanted either to intimidate or destroy.

There were great variations in individual reactions to their plight, but Bettelheim observed that a relatively small group of prisoners—members of the middle class who had not been involved in political activity—were particularly vulnerable to the physical and verbal torments:

> They found themselves utterly unable to comprehend what had happened to them. . . . They had no consistent philosophy which would protect their integrity as human beings, which would give them the force to make a stand against the Nazis. They had obeyed the law handed down by the ruling classes, without ever questioning its wisdom. And now this law, or at least the law-enforcing agencies, turned against them, who always had been its staunchest supporters. . . . They could not question the wisdom of law and of the police, so they accepted the behavior of the Gestapo as just. What was wrong was that *they* were made objects of a persecution which in itself *must* be right, since it was carried out by the authorities. The only way out of this particular dilemma was to be convinced that it must be a "mistake." (Bettelheim, 1943: p. 426)

Of additional interest was the behavior of long-time prisoners—those who had been pris-

The Nazi concentration camps represent one of the most chilling examples of institutional aggression in human history. The prisoners—Jews, homosexuals, political opponents of Hitler's regime, and others who were deemed "undesirable"—were denied adequate food, clothing, and shelter. Millions of them were exterminated. *(Culver Pictures)*

oners in the camps for several years and had, in a certain sense, adjusted to the conditions. Bettelheim noted that it was common for these prisoners to copy the guards' every action: the way they walked, their language, even their abuse of other inmates. One game that the guards played was to beat a group of prisoners and to bet on who could withstand the punishment for the longest time. Some long-time prisoners adopted this same activity as recreation among themselves. Others collected scraps of guards' old uniforms and sewed them onto their own clothing so as to closely resemble their captors, despite the fact that these prisoners often were severely punished by the guards for doing so. At first impression, such behavior seems nothing short of incredible. But in the light of studies like the one conducted by Bandura, Ross, and Ross (1963b), which was described earlier in the chapter, victims' *identification with the aggressor* becomes slightly more believable, although no more easily understandable.

When tried at Nuremberg following World War II, those responsible for the concentration-camp atrocities claimed that they were only obeying orders. Because the tribunal considered this defense to be insufficient justification, it convicted and executed or imprisoned for life many former Nazis. Although in no way implying that punishment is not warranted under such circumstances, a series of experiments by Stanley Milgram has demonstrated that under certain circumstances most individuals will inflict harsh pain on innocent persons in order to follow instructions.

REACTIONS TO AUTHORITY: "JUST DOING MY JOB"

In the guise of a verbal learning experiment, Stanley Milgram (1963) asked his subjects to administer electric shocks to another person. The "learner" was seated in the next room, and whenever the "learner" made an error, the subject, playing the role of "teacher," had to push a lever on the "shock machine." After each error, the "teacher" was also asked to increase the shocks, which were labeled from "mild" to "extreme danger—xxx."

In reality the "learner" was not actually receiving the electric shocks, but was a confederate who activated a tape recorder that played a standardized sequence of screams and pleadings over an intercom. The experiment actually tested how far the "teacher" would go in shocking the "learner" in obedience to the experimenter's orders.

To the surprise and shock of both psychologists and the general public, Milgram found that 65 percent of his subjects obeyed the experimenter's commands to deliver increasingly severe shocks to a man in an adjoining room who they believed was a fellow subject. They did this even though the man pounded on the wall, presumably in pain and begging the subject to stop, and then fell completely silent. No physical efforts were made to prevent subjects from leaving if they got up or refused to push the shock buttons. The experimenter limited his prompting to verbal commands that they continue.

The "learner's" indications of pain were somewhat effective, as nine of the forty participants stopped after hearing the pounding on the wall. But for a large majority of subjects, the experimenter's insistence overcame any misgivings they had about what they were doing. Twenty-six of forty subjects continued until they had pressed the switch that administered the most intense shock.

Although most subjects went all the way, it was clear that they were very uneasy about the situation. Profuse sweating, trembling, groaning, and nervous laughter were common. Many requested permission to stop, and many expressed fear for the "learner's" health. Nevertheless, the authority represented by the experimenter was sufficiently compelling that his demands overcame any inhibitions the subjects had against harming another human being.

A later study revealed some cause for optimism. By providing subjects with social support for disobedience, Stanley Milgram (1965) found that he could dramatically reverse the blind obedience that nearly two-thirds of his subjects had demonstrated when pitted alone against the experimenter. In this study, two confederates shared the teaching task with the subject. When the "learner" first pounded on the wall, one confederate announced that he would not continue further and resisted all of the experimenter's efforts to dissuade him. After the second pounding on the wall, the other teaching confederate followed the lead of the first and sat down on the other side of the room. If the subject was still participating, he assumed the entire teaching task, as he had in the first experiment.

In sharp contrast to the initial findings, only four of forty subjects who witnessed the nonconforming models continued to the end. After the second confederate left, only fifteen subjects continued, and most of them stopped on one of the later trials. Thus, given the misgivings that subjects were almost certainly experiencing, the influence exerted by the two disobedient models liberated subjects from the compulsion they otherwise felt to obey the experimenter's order.

DEINDIVIDUATION: THE FACELESS VILLAIN

The phenomenon of deindividuation, discussed in Chapter 3, is particularly conducive to aggressive behavior. When feelings of anonymity lead to abdication of personality responsibility, there results a weakening of the social and the inner constraints that normally guard against impulsive acts of aggression. Institutional settings that include groups of people with uniformity of roles and clothing often foster such feelings of personal anonymity and lead to spontaneous aggression. One such setting is the prison.

Was the extreme aggression of the New Mexico State Prison riots, described at the beginning of the chapter, caused by an especially vicious collection of prisoners? Or was the aggression due in part to the deindividuation encountered in prisons? To help answer this type of question, Philip Zimbardo, Craig Haney, Curtis Banks, and David Jaffe (1973) set out to see how well-adjusted Americans would respond to one of the most depersonalizing of situations—that in which people are assigned either the role of "prisoner" or the role of "guard." The investigators converted the basement of

SOCIAL PSYCHOLOGY AND THE ARTS

DEINDIVIDUATION AND INSTITUTIONAL AGGRESSION

(Museo del Prado, Madrid)

Paralleling events in revolutionary Europe, painting in the early nineteenth century broke with its classic past and exploded into romanticism and realism. Painters expressed subjective feelings in their art and began to explore human experience as never before. Among the foremost masters of this movement was the Spanish painter Francisco Goya. In *The Third of May, 1808*, shown here, Goya protests the massacre of Spanish townspeople by Napoleon's invading forces. The painting also embodies many of the social-psychological processes that make such institutional aggression possible.

The French soldiers are perfect models of deindividuation in their long uniforms and dark fur helmets, and Goya heightens their deindividuation by hiding their faces from view. Firing as a group out of the darkness of night, and no doubt acting in obedience to orders, they ignore the pleas of their victims. Like subjects in the experiments of Milgram or Zimbardo, these soldiers demonstrate the power and horror of institutional aggression.

the Stanford University psychology building into a mock prison. The prison included three-man cells, with only mattresses, sheets, and pillows; a "yard" for exercise and recreation; and an unlit closet for solitary confinement. From seventy-five male volunteers, they selected the twenty-one who appeared most mature, most stable, and least involved in antisocial behavior and assigned them randomly to be guards or prisoners. To enhance the realism of the situation, they secured the cooperation of the Palo Alto Police Department. Officers drove to the prisoners' homes, charged them with suspicion of armed robbery or burglary, "arrested" them, and delivered them to the station for fingerprinting and preparation of identification files. The prisoners were next taken to the mock prison, where they were stripped, sprayed for lice, and forced to stand naked and alone in the prison yard. They were then issued shapeless smocks to be worn as uniforms, placed in their cells, and ordered to remain silent. After this, the prisoners stayed in their prison twenty-four hours a day. Their schedule included exercise, meals, and free time.

The guards, on the other hand, worked in three eight-hour shifts and went home when not on duty. Physical violence toward prisoners was strictly forbidden. Guards, like prisoners, were dressed impersonally.

During the first five days, four of the ten prisoners had to be released as a result of fits of rage, crying, and acute anxiety. A fifth was released because he developed a rash that covered large portions of his body. Their instructions allowed guards a high degree of latitude in the postures they could assume toward prisoners. In practice, however, the guards' actions ranged from tough-but-fair to excessively cruel. Virtually no friendliness or helpfulness toward the prisoners was observed. The guards stretched the ten-minute line-up periods that had been established for counting prisoners into two-hour interrogation sessions that featured verbal insult and abuse. They did this on their own initiative—no instructions the investigators had given them could have predisposed the guards to this sort of cruelty.

None of the investigators foresaw how easily the subjects would fall into these roles, nor how traumatic and destructive these temporary roles would be. The researchers originally planned an experiment that would last fourteen days, but they called it off after six days in order to prevent what they felt might be permanent psychic damage to their subjects. Whereas during the initial stage of the study both prisoners and guards indicated general unhappiness with the situation, by the sixth day, when the study was terminated, only the prisoners were glad it was over. The guards appeared to have become sufficiently involved in their work that they were reluctant to relinquish their position of power.

Even among individuals selected for their emotional stability and altruistic orientations, then, prison life may elicit considerable aggression. Thus, the brutality rampant in modern prisons may be as much a function of the *situation*—or, more precisely, of prevailing conceptions of the situation even among those who have never set foot in a prison—as it is a function of any predispositions to violence that may characterize those who are imprisoned or those who choose careers as guards.

Riots, lynchings, and other instances of mass violence represent other situations in which individuals are likely to commit aggressive acts that they ordinarily would not engage in. All of these situations can produce a state of deindividuation, and, according to Zimbardo's research (1970), this condition can result in increased and indiscriminate aggression. For example, as discussed in Chapter 3, when college women were deindividuated by wearing hoods and sitting together in a dark room, they delivered longer and less discriminate shocks to another person than did women who wore name tags and sat in a bright room. Similar phenomena can be observed in the real world. For example, during riots in the United States, the stores of both white and black merchants—those who are considered exploiters as well as those who are not—have frequently been destroyed with equal abandon by angry inner-city residents.

AGGRESSION AND PUBLIC POLICY

Both personalized and institutional forms of aggression are so pervasive in daily life that it is not surprising that these aspects of human behavior have attracted the attention not only of researchers but also of the media, the public, and public officials. In this section, we will examine some research findings that are closely related to several forms of aggressive behavior observed in daily life.

As is the case with other branches of psychology and science in general, there is often a two-way street between research findings, on the one hand, and practical applications to problems of daily living, on the other. In some instances, research studies are designed to answer questions, under controlled conditions, that were initially raised by real-life events. For example, for many thousands of years it has been informally observed that the consumption of alcohol and certain other drugs is associated with an increase in aggression. Such informal observations and police statistics eventually inspired contemporary researchers to examine the link between alcohol and aggression in the laboratory. Their goals were to demonstrate the link experimentally, to discover the underlying mechanism responsible for it, and to formulate certain practical recommendations that may help alleviate the problem in the real world.

In other instances, certain questions had been long investigated experimentally in large part because of their theoretical significance, such as principles governing observational learning, or "modeling." As violence became more pervasive in American society, suddenly these studies were seen as providing a great deal of relevant information about an important social problem—namely, the effect of televised violence on interpersonal aggression and criminal behavior.

These and other research findings pertaining to aggression in daily life are discussed in this section. Other chapters in this book also contain information relevant to aggression in daily life (see, for example, Chapter 12 on environmental psychology for information regarding the effects of heat and crowding on aggression, and the implications of this relationship for the "long, hot summer" explanation of riots and other civil disturbances).

TELEVISED VIOLENCE AND AGGRESSION

Principles of learning by imitation have been investigated in psychology for some time. The studies by Bandura and his colleagues, which we discussed earlier, represented pioneering efforts to understand the conditions under which aggressive models will be imitated. The work of Berkowitz, Geen, and their colleagues, on the other hand, represented an attempt to investigate the combined effects of a powerful negative emotional state, such as anger, and the viewing of aggressive content (for example, a film portraying a prize fight) on an entirely different form of aggressive behavior—namely, the administration of "electric shocks" to the experimental confederate. Although these two types of studies are different, they both examined theoretical questions of long standing in psychology, and both were concerned with the effects of viewing aggressive materials on aggressive behavior.

As people became more concerned about the effects of the media in general, and of television in particular, the laboratory studies on the effects of viewing aggressive content suddenly came into the limelight. The findings of these studies were frequently used as evidence that TV portrayals of violence are important causes of aggressive behavior in the general population (see, for example, Comstock, 1975; Liebert, Neale, and Davidson, 1973). As a result, various suggestions were made to restrict TV portrayals of violence (Rothenberg, 1975; Sommers, 1976).

But is the research evidence strong enough and conclusive enough to justify censorship of TV programming or economic pressures against sponsors of programs containing a great deal of violence? Although many social scientists would probably endorse at least some restrictive measures, a recent detailed review of the literature by Kaplan and Singer (1976) casts serious doubts on the justifiability of doing this.

As Kaplan and Singer point out, when the results of research studies are used to formulate large-scale social policy, the question of paramount importance becomes the extent to which the research studies have "external validity"—namely, to what extent their findings can be safely generalized to real-life situations. The generalizability of an experiment is increased, among other things, when the subjects in the experiment, the experimental conditions, the behaviors observed, and the general context are as representative as possible of the real-life populations and contexts about which one wishes to generalize.

Kaplan and Singer argue that psychological laboratories are not representative of the settings and situations in which average Americans view television programs. Furthermore, the violent films used in most experiments and the behaviors that are observed are not generally representative of real-life conditions. Therefore, the research demonstrating that violent films or models can cause an increase in aggressive behavior in the laboratory does not necessarily prove that these materials would have the same effect in the real world. As we pointed out before, aggressive behavior is multiply determined, and the effects of other situational variables may well offset those of aggressive films. Furthermore, even if TV portrayals of violence do cause an increase in aggressive behavior in the real world, the question is whether the contribution of this factor, relative to other causes of aggression in the real world, is a significant one. In other words, the question is not so much whether TV portrayals of violence cause aggressive behavior in the real world, but, rather, what percent of real-world aggression and violence is attributable to television. The issue of the extent of contribution of a particular variable in the determination of a particular behavior is especially important when costly policy changes and administrative restrictions are involved. As it happens, few, if any, laboratory studies—or even groups of laboratory studies—can help answer the question of the percent of the variation in a real-world behavior that is accounted for by a particular real-world factor, such as TV violence.

Apart from these methodological concerns, the review of the evidence provided by Kaplan and Singer offers additional reasons to question the wisdom of programming restrictions on the basis of the current research evidence. With regard to the experiments by Bandura and his colleagues, the studies typically involved very young children and "aggression" against inanimate objects that is closer to "aggressive play" than to more destructive forms of aggression. Moreover, social sanctions against aggression are typically absent in these experiments, even though studies show that children in the real world often watch TV in the presence of adults and that these adults often disapprove of the portrayed aggression. In fact, one study suggested that children who viewed an aggressive model in the presence of an adult who disapproved of the aggression subsequently aggressed less than the controls (Hicks, 1968). Moreover, as Kaplan and Singer point out, findings by Bandura and his colleagues demonstrate that aggressive models who are rewarded for their aggression are imitated far more than those who are punished. To the extent that much television violence incorporates quick punishment of criminal aggressive behavior, one might argue that television programs could in fact help suppress the incidence of criminal behavior, at least when punishment is likely.

In response to these criticisms by Kaplan and Singer, the point is often made that television serves to model or "teach" new and often bizarre forms of aggression that members of the viewing population would otherwise never be exposed to in their daily lives. For example, a San Francisco girl was raped by other girls with a beer bottle soon after a TV movie portrayed a similar incident. Dramatic and convincing as such a case appears with regard to the detrimental role of television violence, it should be kept in mind that the frequency of such bizarre incidents is quite low, and, more importantly, in the absence of a control group, we have no information about whether or not those girls would have committed *some* violent criminal act—perhaps different in form—had they not seen the television program in question.

With regard to the research by Berkowitz, Geen, and their colleagues, in addition to the problems of generalizability already mentioned, an increase in aggressive behavior is observed in their studies only in subjects who had previously been made angry and only when the portrayed violence is somehow justified. These facts alone would seriously limit the range of real-life situations to which the results would be applicable. Moreover, there is additional evidence that the key aspect of the aggressive films used by Berkowitz and Geen is not the films' aggressive content, but their arousingness (Tannenbaum and Zillman, 1977). If so, many other television programs that are arousing, although not at all violent, would have to be banned because they could increase the aggressive behavior of certain people, notably those who had been made angry.

Proponents of restrictions on TV violence often cite a nonlaboratory study by Leonard Eron, Lowell Huesmann, Monroe Lefkowitz, and Leopold Walder (1972). This was a longitudinal study that examined the long-term effects

A great deal of research has focused on the relationship between the viewing of televised aggression by young children and their subsequent aggressive behavior. The evidence remains inconclusive, however, and the percentage of real-life aggressive behavior that is clearly the effect of watching TV violence has yet to be determined. *(© Joel Gordon 1979)*

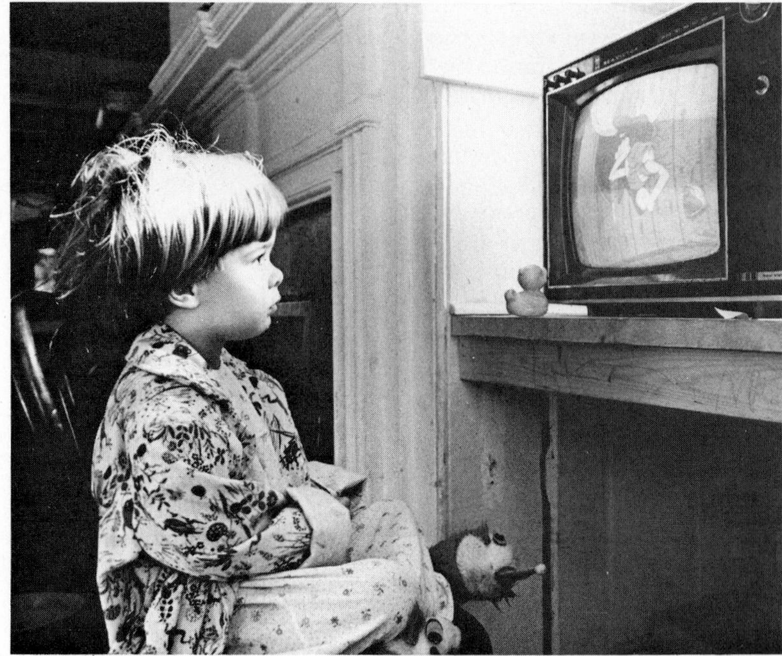

of violent television programs on aggressive behavior. A significant correlation was obtained between the amount of TV violence children watched during the third grade and the amount of aggressive behavior the same people displayed at age nineteen. However, it should be noted that the correlation accounted for, or explained, only 9 percent of the variation in aggressive behavior at age nineteen. Moreover, many different methodological and statistical problems with this study have been noted (Armor, 1976; Kaplan and Singer, 1976; Surgeon General's Committee, 1972).

Thus, for a number of methodological and other reasons, many studies and lines of research that are typically interpreted as providing conclusive evidence that TV violence causes aggression, when taken either individually or jointly, do not prove that aggressive behavior in real life is necessarily augmented by watching TV violence. Furthermore, they do not provide any evidence about the percent of aggressive behavior in real life that can be clearly attributed to the effects of watching TV violence. While there are admittedly very few studies in the literature that suggest that watching violence has "cathartic" value in the Aristotelian sense of decreasing subsequent aggression, Kaplan and Singer, in their review of the literature, did find a large number of studies in which watching aggressive content had *no* effect on the amount of subsequent aggression (that is, neither an increase nor a decrease in aggression was observed). Such studies, perhaps because they are not exciting or do not appear informative, are rarely included in reviews of the literature. In addition, it is often assumed that a study that does not find any effect must have been poorly designed, although that is not necessarily the case. When these studies are considered, the weight of evidence in favor of the view that watching TV violence increases real-life aggression diminishes further.

Consequently, it seems premature to some investigators to recommend restrictions on TV violence on the basis of the research evidence gathered so far. However, the research in this area has drawn attention to the important role that TV programs may play in establishing or maintaining a context of violence in society and has demonstrated that, at least theoretically, TV portrayals of violence can influence aggressive behavior.

PORNOGRAPHY AND AGGRESSION

Paralleling public concern about the effects of televised violence, there has been mounting concern over the possibly detrimental effects of pornography on various aspects of social behavior. As pornographic films, books, and magazines became more easily available and more abundant, this concern culminated in the report of the Presidential Commission on Obscenity and Pornography (1971).

One main goal of the commission was to examine the evidence linking exposure to pornographic materials with aggressive behavior. In particular, the question was whether the easy availability of pornography might increase the frequency of sexual crimes, especially rape and child molestation, both of which often involve extreme aggression. Yet, after examining various types of studies and statistics, the commission's conclusion was that there was little, if any, evidence that exposure to pornographic materials led to aggressive behavior. This position was reflected in other studies as well (Howard, Liptzin, and Reifler, 1973; Mann, Sidmann, and Starr, 1973).

Recently, however, experimental research has investigated in detail the relationship between exposure to erotic materials and aggressive behavior. It now appears that exposure to very weak erotic materials (such as *Playboy* centerfolds) in fact *reduces* aggressive behavior (Baron and Bell, 1973; Frodi, 1977). However, for erotic materials with more impact, it appears that the more explicit and arousing the stimuli are, the more aggression is observed (Donnerstein, Donnerstein, and Evans, 1975; Baron and Bell, 1977), although this relationship is typically obtained only in subjects who have previously been made angry. In contrast, the aggressive behavior of nonangered subjects does not seem to be affected by exposure to erotica at all (Jaffe, Malamuth, Feingold, and Feshbach, 1974; Zillmann, 1971). The reason that pornography can make angry people more aggressive has to do with the phenomenon of emotional labeling we have discussed before: if you are already angry, anything that increases your level of physiological arousal, whether it be loud noise or pornography, will intensify your labeling of anger.

The implications of these results are unclear. Just as aggressive behavior in general is caused and affected by many factors in addition to televised violence, so are sexual crimes multiply determined. Again, we do not know whether the relationship between pornography and aggressive sexual crimes does exist in the real world or what the *size of the contribution* of easily available pornography to the frequency of such crimes is. Moreover, the fact that even in the laboratory exposure to erotic materials increased aggressive behavior only in people who had previously been made angry limits the applicability and relevance of these findings to the real world (although it should be noted that the victims of sexual crimes often resist the initial "friendly overtures" of their assailant, thus producing frustration and anger in the aggressor). Finally, it is important to note that most of these laboratory studies did not systematically examine the aggressive behavior of males toward females, but were generally concerned with same-sex aggression, primarily male-to-male aggression.

A laboratory study by Edward Donnerstein and Gary Barrett (1978) attempted to correct this last problem. The subjects in the experiment were male undergraduates who interacted with either a male or a female confederate. In the first part of the experiment, some subjects were angered by having an essay of theirs evaluated very negatively by the confederate and by receiving an inordinately large number of electric shocks from the confederate as a part of the evaluation. In contrast, other subjects were treated neutrally and were given very few shocks. In the next part of the experiment, subjects either saw a neutral film (a wildlife documentary) or a highly explicit "stag" film depicting various forms of sexual intercourse. In the final part of the experiment, in the course of a pseudo-learning task, all subjects were free to choose, on each of a number of trials, the intensity and duration of electric shocks to be delivered to the confederate (male or female, depending on the experimental condition). The subjects' blood pressure was measured throughout the experiment.

In terms of physiological arousal, the male subjects who had been angered by a female were far more aroused by the erotic film than by the neutral film. In contrast, the erotic film had little physiological effect on the male subjects who had previously been angered by a male. Any number of after-the-fact explanations can be given regarding the failure of the erotic film to arouse these male subjects who had been angered by another male. The important thing is, however, that looking at just the physiological results, we might assume that the angered male subjects could attribute at least a part of their high arousal following the erotic film to the earlier unpleasant encounter with the female. Thus we might expect that these subjects would subsequently be more aggressive toward females than toward males.

The results presented in Table 8.1, however, show that this was not the case. Although erotic films did increase the amount of aggressive behavior in subjects who had been previously angered (part A of Table 8.1), the angered subjects, in fact, aggressed more toward the male than toward the female confederate (part B of Table 8.1), regardless of the type of film they had viewed.

TABLE 8.1 MEAN INTENSITY TIMES DURATION OF ELECTRIC SHOCKS ADMINISTERED BY SUBJECTS IN DIFFERENT EXPERIMENTAL CONDITIONS

PART A

TREATMENT OF SUBJECTS	TYPE OF FILMS	
	EROTIC	NEUTRAL
Insulted Subjects	1.90	1.45
Neutrally Treated Subjects	.93	1.15

PART B

TREATMENT OF SUBJECTS	SEX OF TARGET OF AGGRESSION	
	MALE	FEMALE
Insulted Subjects	1.86	1.55
Neutrally Treated Subjects	.95	1.13

Source: Adapted from E. Donnerstein and G. Barrett, "Effects of Erotic Stimuli on Male Aggression Toward Females," *Journal of Personality and Social Psychology* 36 (1978): 180–188.

The Donnerstein-Barrett experiment is important in that it directly compared males' aggression toward males with males' aggression toward females. Although the results of the study further confirmed the link between exposure to erotic materials and aggression in people who had been previously angered, this link pertains more to aggression toward males than to females. This finding somewhat limits the applicability of the laboratory research with regard to the real-world question of whether exposure to pornography increases sexual crimes, since the overwhelming proportion of such crimes involves male offenders and female targets.

However, it is important to note that in the Donnerstein-Barrett study the experimental situation may have been stacked too heavily against subjects' expressing much aggression toward women, since the pervasive social norms against such aggression may have been salient in a psychology laboratory involving fellow students. In comparison with college students and laboratory aggression, sex offenders in the real world are likely to be far less restrained by such norms. In fact, a study by Edward Donnerstein and John Hallam (1978) found that even college-student subjects aggress a great deal against women when the inhibitions against this type of behavior are weakened by certain experimental procedures.

GUNS AND AGGRESSION

Since the political assassinations of the 1960s, there has been considerable public concern over the distribution, control, and use of firearms in the United States. According to many sources (for example, Newton and Zimring, 1970), about two-thirds of all homicides in this country involve firearms. These facts, along with increasingly vocal public debate about the necessity of strict gun-control legislation, have motivated social psychologists to examine the relationship between aggression and the presence of firearms. This research has been conducted under controlled laboratory conditions, despite the criticisms that laboratory situations are artificial and remote from the conditions under which homicides occur in real life. The assumption behind the research is that experimental studies can help us, at least in a general way, to understand better the conditions under which the presence of firearms may increase the probability and the amount of extreme aggression in criminal behavior.

In a seminal study by Leonard Berkowitz and Anthony LePage (1967), angered and nonangered subjects were given the opportunity to aggress against an experimental confederate in the presence of either a gun that was conspicuously placed in the laboratory or of a neutral object—namely, a badminton racket. It was found that angered subjects gave more "electric shocks" to the confederate when a firearm was in the room than did subjects in the neutral conditions.

This finding, which quickly became known as the "weapons effect," was subsequently investigated in a number of experiments. Ann Frodi (1973) obtained similar results with Swedish students; and other researchers—in a conceptual replication of the Berkowitz-LePage study—obtained the effect using horn honking by automobile drivers as a measure of aggression (Simons, Turner, and Layton, 1974). Some failures to replicate the effect (for example, Buss, Booker, and Buss, 1972) seemed to be due to the use of experimental subjects who were either suspicious of the purpose of the experiment or highly apprehensive about expressing aggression (see Simons and Turner, 1974). Despite some evidence to the contrary (Page and Scheidt, 1971), it appears that when nonapprehensive and nonsuspicious subjects are used, the weapons effect can be generally obtained (Simons and Turner, 1974; Turner and Simons, 1974).

There are several possible theoretical explanations for the occurrence of the weapons effect, one of which again follows from our previous discussion about arousal and emotional labeling. The sight of weapons may have arousing properties, which, however, may have no effect on subjects who are not angry. In the case of angry subjects, however, the additional arousal due to the presence of firearms may further augment the already adopted emotional label of anger and thus lead to an increase in the amount of aggression when compared with the amount of aggression expressed by angry subjects in the presence of a neutral object.

The weapons effect is at least indirectly relevant to the issue of gun control because a very substantial proportion of all homicides is committed not by professional criminals, but by family members, coworkers, and neighbors with a negligible or nonexistent prior criminal record. More importantly, in many of these instances, the homicides are precipitated by powerful emotional states (such as anger or jealousy) or other arousing conditions (such as various drugs). Therefore, if the ownership of firearms were severely restricted, one could expect a drastic decrease in the number of homicides, in part because even if the would-be murderers were to switch to other weapons (such as knives), these would be less efficient or lethal (Diener and Crandall, 1979; Seitz, 1972).

Such questions cannot be investigated in the laboratory. However, social psychologists Edward Diener and Rick Crandall (1979) wanted to find out how closely the suggestive but inconclusive laboratory studies related to real life. In order to investigate further the relationship between guns and aggressive/criminal behavior, they ingeniously took advantage of a comprehensive, large-scale social experiment to combat crime in Jamaica.

To combat rising crime, Jamaica enacted in 1974 some sweeping gun-control laws. These included complete banning of possession of all guns, indefinite sentences (up to life in prison) for crimes involving guns and for gun possession, and a considerable increase in police surveillance in order to discover and confiscate firearms (including curfews and searches without warrants). By examining trends in crime statistics both before and after the new legislation in Jamaica, Diener and Crandall hoped to answer questions concerning the relationship between gun ownership and criminal behavior, and the effects of gun-control legislation on this relationship.

Before examining the results and conclusions of this study, we should remember the differences that exist between Jamaica and the United States and the difficulties in generalizing from one to the other. However, there are also a number of similarities between Jamaica and the United States, and Diener and Crandall articulate them very clearly: "The homicide rates are rather similar; both countries are English speaking, capitalistic and have constitutional governments and an English system of law; both have subcultures of poverty and these subcultures are predominately responsible for violent crime; crime is on the rise in both locations; gun ownership is enormous in both countries; and the majority of crime occurs in the cities in both locales. . . . As always, one must be cautious in generalizing from one geographical area to another, but the U.S. and Jamaica are not as dissimilar as one might imagine based solely on their relative size and wealth" (p. 16).

The study found that in the first year after comprehensive gun-control laws went into effect, homicides decreased by 14 percent and nonfatal shootings decreased by 37 percent. The decrease in the number of homicides involving firearms was in fact far greater, but this decrease was in part offset by an increase in homicides not involving firearms. Prior to this new legislation, 53 percent of all homicides involved firearms; after the law took effect, only 28 percent of all homicides involved firearms.

To the extent that many homicides are crimes of passion involving intense emotions, it is tempting to interpret the above data as supporting the laboratory conclusions regarding the weapons effect. However, additional data obtained by Diener and Crandall cast serious doubts on such an interpretation. In the first place, during the first year after the law was passed, only about 500 guns were removed from circulation, either because they were turned in by the citizens or confiscated by the police. Of the guns that were turned in, many were probably turned in by law-abiding citizens who would not have committed a crime anyway. In other words, since the amount of guns removed from circulation was estimated at less than 1 percent of the total, there was no substantial decrease in the availability of firearms: angry people were probably just as likely to find themselves in the presence of guns after, as before, the law was passed.

The components of antigun legislation that Diener and Crandall credit most with the reduction in crime were fear of long-term imprisonment and increased police surveillance. The fear explanation is supported by the fact that many murderers simply switched from guns to other weapons that did not carry as severe penalties as firearms. Also, there was a sharp drop in all types of crimes immediately after the new legislation first went into effect. The importance of increased police surveillance is underlined by the fact that robbery and rape not involving guns also dropped considerably. Since the law imposed no new penalties for crimes not involving guns, such a drop in nonhomicide crimes can probably be attributed to police surveillance rather than fear.

The investigation by Diener and Crandall is a fine example of research motivated both by a concern over a real-world social problem as well as the suggestive, but inconclusive, laboratory results on the weapons effect. The study's implications are both practical (in terms of the usefulness of gun-control legislation) and theoretically important in that new variables such as fear and surveillance may now be investigated in the laboratory in order to shed light on the weapons effect.

ALCOHOL AND AGGRESSION

Both psychological theory and research and folk wisdom suggest that alcohol consumption releases inhibitions and thus makes more likely various forms of behavior that are ordinarily kept in check, notably impulsive acts of aggression (Cameron, 1963; Jones, Schainberg, and Byer, 1973; Medina, 1970; Tucker, 1970).

Criminal statistics tend to support this point of view. For example, one study examined the records of almost 1,000 persons arrested for committing a violent crime and found that more than 70 percent were under the influence of alcohol at the time the crime was committed (Shupe, 1954), and almost two-thirds had alcohol concentrations over .1 percent. Another study investigated the relation between alcohol and homicides in hundreds of cases over a five-year period and found that alcohol was a possible factor contributing to the crime in more than 60 percent of the cases (Wolfgang and Strohm, 1956).

Popular culture frequently portrays a relationship between alcohol consumption and impulsive acts of aggression; the barroom brawl is a recurrent example in Westerns. Research by social psychologists has confirmed this correlation. *(Culver Pictures)*

Although these statistics are suggestive, they are correlational and inconclusive. A causal link between alcohol consumption and aggression cannot be inferred on the basis of these findings. For example, regular or excessive alcohol consumption may be frequent in certain subcultures, certain personality types, or people with certain life styles, any of which characteristics could be the actual cause of the high frequency of criminal behavior, making the correlation between alcohol intake and violent criminal behavior spurious.

For these reasons, several social psycholgists have undertaken to study experimentally in the laboratory the relationship between alcohol intake and aggressive behavior. In a study by Richard Shuntich and Stuart Taylor (1972), male college students were assigned to one of three experimental conditions: alcohol, placebo, or control. Subjects in the alcohol group consumed .9 milliliter of 100-proof bourbon per kilogram of body weight. Subjects in the placebo group drank a mixture of ginger ale and a sugar solution. In order to conceal from the placebo subjects the nature of the experimental condition to which they had been assigned, some bourbon was spilled on a cloth coaster at the base of the glass. After consuming the liquid, subjects in both the alcohol and placebo conditions waited awhile for the second part of the experiment to begin; the same was true for subjects in another control condition who did not consume any liquids.

In the second part of the experiment, all subjects participated in a pseudo-reaction-time task in which they supposedly competed against an opponent. Over a number of trials, the subject and the (fictitious) opponent each decided on the intensity of electric shock that they wanted their opponent to receive if he lost the trial by having a slower reaction time. The entire procedure was rigged in such a way that subjects won 50 percent of the trials, and the shock settings chosen by the fictitious opponent increased over trials. The main measure of aggression was the average intensity of shock settings chosen by the subject for his opponent over all the trials.

The results of the experiment were clear. The subjects who drank the alcohol set significantly higher shock intensities than either of the other two groups, which did not differ from each other. Also it is important to note that the difference in aggressive behavior across the three conditions was determined by the difference in the *actual* amount of alcohol consumed, rather than the subjects' *expectations* about how much alcohol they had consumed. Both the subjects who drank alcohol and the subjects who drank the placebo were asked after drinking the liquid how much alcohol they thought they had consumed. The subjects who drank alcohol believed that they had consumed significantly more alcohol than did the subjects who drank the placebo, but the latter nevertheless believed that they had consumed approximately 4 ounces of alcohol! Despite this expectation, the placebo group did not differ from the control group in the amount of aggressive behavior subjects subsequently expressed.

Evidence for the causal relationship between alcohol intake and aggressive behavior was subsequently obtained in a number of additional studies. For example, Stuart Taylor and Charles Gammon (1975) found that a high dose of both vodka and bourbon increased the amount of aggression in comparison to a no-alcohol control group, but that a low dose of alcohol in fact decreased aggression in comparison to the control group. Taylor and Gammon thus suggested a curvilinear relationship between aggressive behavior and the quantity of alcohol ingested. A small dose of alcohol was assumed to produce a feeling of tranquility that was incompatible with aggressive responses, whereas a large dose produced excitation that was compatible with aggression.

Another finding of the Taylor-Gammon study was that subjects who had drunk vodka were more aggressive than those who had drunk bourbon, although equally high doses of both types of drinks were consumed. Apparently, because of chemical differences between the two drinks, vodka leads to a faster rate of absorption of alcohol into the bloodstream than does bourbon. Thus, although the two alcoholic beverages used in the test were both 100 proof (50 percent ethyl alcohol), subjects who drank vodka may have had a higher level of alcohol in the blood during the competitive task than those who drank bourbon.

In a later study, Taylor and his colleagues (Taylor, Vardaris, Rawtich, Gammon, Cranston, and Lubetkin, 1976) compared the effects on aggressive behavior of alcohol versus marijuana. As shown in Table 8.2, while a high dose of alcohol resulted in more aggressive behavior than a low dose—thus replicating previous experiments—a high dose of marijuana made people less aggressive than a low dose. Moreover, both doses of marijuana led to significantly less aggression than the high dose of alcohol. Since the high dose of marijuana (.3 milligram of delta-9-tetrahydrocannabinol) was in the range that is known to produce a reliable marijuana "high," the aggression-arousing effects of each drug are interesting in light of the legality of the two substances.

TABLE 8.2 MEAN ELECTRIC-SHOCK SETTINGS CHOSEN BY SUBJECTS IN DIFFERENT EXPERIMENTAL CONDITIONS*

	DOSAGE	
SUBSTANCE CONSUMED	LOW	HIGH
Alcohol	2.1	5.4
Marijuana (THC)	3.1	1.9

*No-treatment control: 4.0.

Source: Adapted from S. P. Taylor, R. M. Vardaris, A. B. Rawtich, C. B. Gammon, J. W. Cranston, and A. I. Lubetkin, "The Effects of Alcohol and Delta-9-Tetrahydrocannabinol on Human Physical Aggression," *Aggressive Behavior* 2 (1976): 153–161.

Despite some isolated evidence to the contrary (for example, Lang, Goeckner, Adesso, and Marlatt, 1975), the causal effect of alcohol consumption on aggressive behavior seems to be relatively well established. Moreover, the effect does not seem to be due to the possibility that high-dose subjects were so intoxicated by the alcohol that they chose shock settings in a haphazard manner (which could have inflated the average setting for this condition). Various additional results collected by Taylor and his colleagues indicate that subjects who drank a large amount of alcohol were not significantly more variable in their shock-setting behavior than were subjects who drank a small amount of alcohol. Perhaps the most likely explanation of the alcohol effect is that a high dose of alcohol impairs judgment and disinhibits aggressive modes of behavior that are ordinarily held in check.

Here, then, we have an example of a phenomenon about which folk wisdom, correlational evidence from police statistics, and experimental laboratory evidence all basically agree.

SUMMARY

Aggression is defined as any real or planned act of physical or verbal abuse that one human directs at another. Whether or not a behavior will be labeled aggressive depends on the culture in which it occurs; thus, the labeling of aggression is both a social and a cultural process.

Almost every instance of aggressive behavior is multiply determined, involving social, biological, situational, cultural, and learning-related factors. Perhaps for this reason, the various "grand" theories of aggressive behavior—psychoanalytic, ethological, and frustration-aggression—have not been successful in explaining research findings and are not as popular as they used to be. Contemporary research has led social psychologists to compartmentalize the field of aggression and to develop small-scale theoretical models that more successfully account for specific sets of findings.

Aggression does not differ from other behaviors in that many of its aspects are learned. Under certain circumstances, experimental subjects, especially young children, will imitate aggressive behavior displayed by adults toward inanimate targets. Subjects who see models rewarded for violent actions are more likely to imitate the models than are those who see the models punished. Also, like other behaviors, aggression is in part governed by its consequences in terms of reward and punishment. For example, if a child's aggression is rewarded in some way, aggression is likely to increase; if it is ignored, however, aggressive behavior is likely to become less frequent. Punishment mixed with reward makes aggressive behavior difficult to extinguish.

One of the most important instigators of interpersonal aggression is a verbal attack consisting of insulting remarks. This prototypic social aversive event raises the level of physiological arousal in the person who is the target of the insult and is likely to result in the emotion of anger. Anger, like other emotions, depends on both physiological fluctuations and various cognitive processes. These processes include the monitoring and interpretation of information obtained from both external and internal sources and the integration of various cues. Research has shown that anger, rather than merely the level of physiological arousal, is an important determinant of interpersonal aggression.

Contradictory to the predictions of catharsis theories, various forms of sublimated aggression, including viewing violent attacks against inanimate targets, aggressive sport, and so on, are likely to increase rather than decrease aggressive behavior. Only under specific circumstances—when angry people are given the opportunity to physically aggress against the person who had made them angry—does the expression of aggression tend to reduce the amount of immediate subsequent aggression toward the same person. Apparently, this effect may occur when aggression serves to terminate a noxious threat, thereby reducing the level of physiological arousal and the accompanying emotion of anger. However, precisely because such aggression may be effective in removing a threat, it would seem that aggression would breed more aggression in the long run.

In terms of institutional aggression, orders by authority figures to do violence are often able to overcome an individual's inhibitions against violence, especially if this authority confronts a lone individual. Personal anonymity and diffused responsibility further encourage aggression in an institutional context.

Although much of the research on aggressive behavior can contribute to our understanding of aggression in daily life, generalizations must be made with a great deal of caution, especially when large-scale public-policy changes are in question. The evidence is inconclusive whether TV violence or exposure to pornography have a major, important effect on aggressive and criminal behavior in the real world. Alcohol seems to increase aggression, but its effect, too, is modified by other factors. Finally, research indicates that gun-control legislation may reduce the number of violent crimes, but the effect appears to be due mainly to a fear of punishment rather than to a decrease in availability of firearms.

CHAPTER NINE

ALTRUISM

THE CURRENT SIGNIFICANCE OF ALTRUISM

THEORIES OF ALTRUISM
- Normative Influences
- Sociobiology
- Empathic Concern
- Equity

CHARACTERISTICS OF THE INDIVIDUAL
- Personality Factors and Altruism
- Transitory Psychological States

INFLUENCE OF THE SURROUNDING SITUATION
- Influence of Others
- Long-Term Effects of Models
- Effects of Others on Bystander Intervention in Emergencies
- Effects of the Environment
- The Recipient: The Face of the Fortunate

THE EFFECTS OF ALTRUISM
- The Changer and the Changed
- Reciprocity: Balancing the Seesaw
- When Reciprocity Fails
- The Repercussions of Failing to Help
- Receiving Help: When Is Aid Appreciated?

THE SALVATION ARMY
Sharing is Caring

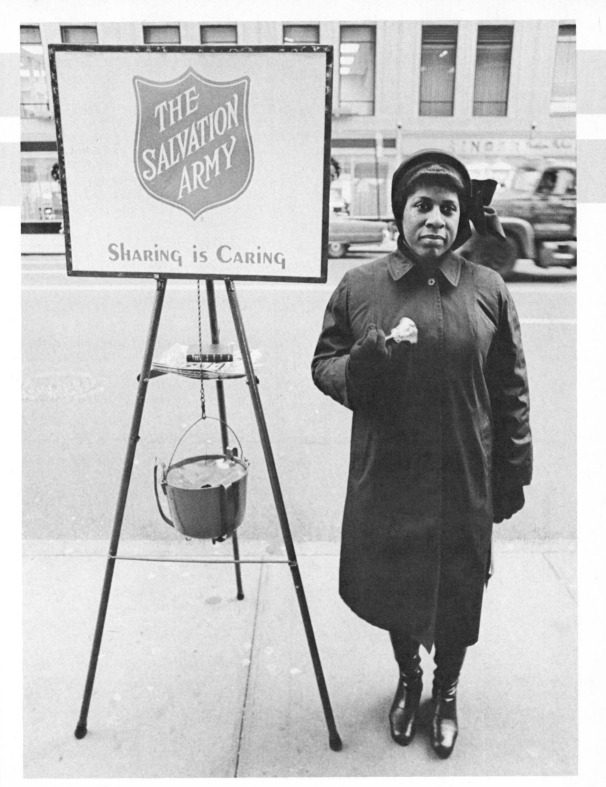

Late one afternoon in the spring of 1979, a man named Ray McKenzie was riding a Chicago Transit Authority train a couple of miles north of the Loop. His car was two-thirds full. Because he was late for an appointment, McKenzie kept glancing at his expensive watch. Another passenger—a burly, heavy-set man—also looked at McKenzie's watch. The man came up and stood over McKenzie, growling something like, "I want your watch." When McKenzie refused, the man went for the watch and started slugging his victim.

McKenzie tried to block his assailant's punches, but he was cornered and could not stand up. McKenzie yelled for help repeatedly, but the other passengers looked away, as if they wanted to avoid what was happening. The mugger kept slugging McKenzie, who finally gave in. The man took the watch off McKenzie's wrist, backed away slowly, and jumped off the train at the next stop.

McKenzie, bruised and incredulous, stood up and confronted the other passengers. "Hey, why didn't anybody help me?" he asked. They all ignored him. When he got off the train, a girl who had witnessed the crime said that she had heard him, but she didn't know what she could do. She said she told the man next to her that someone was being beaten up, but he just stared out the window.*

This incident is not unique; people frequently have the opportunity to help a fellow human being in need or distress. Sometimes people intervene. Often they don't.

In a now-famous incident, Kitty Genovese was stabbed to death in Queens, New York, while thirty-eight of her neighbors looked on from the windows of her apartment house. Although the assailant made three separate attacks and took half an hour to murder her, no one came to her assistance or even called the police. Yet in another case, when a young woman was stabbed by her estranged husband at an urban university, a fellow student rushed to her aid and struck the attacker with a chair. Other students threw books at the assailant. The man was disarmed, and the woman recovered from her injuries.

In Los Angeles a woman was abducted and raped. She managed to escape from the car of her attacker and ran nude along a busy freeway, calling for help and trying to flag down cars. No one stopped, and the rapist eventually recaptured her and dragged her back into his car. Yet in Austin, Texas, when a sniper in the tower of the University of Texas gunned down students on the campus, several people risked their lives to drag the wounded to safety.

Why is it that human beings vary so much in their response to crises that endanger others? It is easy to answer that "some people" care about their fellow beings and "other people" do not. Undoubtedly, most people would be tempted to feel that they are among the "some" but that they know lots of the "others." Yet, when this question is considered closely, the answer becomes increasingly complex. What would *you* do if confronted with one of the above situations, in which danger threatens and you must decide in a split second whether to act or not?

Most of us have experienced situations in which we have not acted when we felt that we should. Many feelings can prevent people from acting on their judgments of what they "ought" to do—feelings such as uncertainty that they are competent to help, fear of making a spectacle of themselves, depression, and inertia. Interviews with witnesses to tragedies such as the Kitty Genovese slaying do not reveal these people as callous misanthropes. Rather, these bystanders are everyday citizens who for various reasons construe the situation as one not requiring *their* action. If one is to understand, then, what inspires and what blocks helping, it is important to suspend for the moment the desire for simplistic some-people-do-and-others-don't interpretations of altruistic acts and to examine instead the various factors that influence a given person to help or not to help in a particular situation.

In this chapter we will discuss a broad category of diverse behaviors that have been

*This incident was reported by Mike Royko in the *Chicago Sun-Times*, June 26, 1979, p. 2.

lumped together by social psychologists under the term *prosocial behavior*, commonly known as *altruism*. Prosocial behavior is simply behavior that shows concern and caring for one's fellow human beings. We shall examine personal characteristics of individuals who are most likely to help their fellow beings as well as aspects of situations that encourage or inhibit prosocial action regardless of an individual's personal characteristics.

The domain of prosocial behavior is broader than the crisis reactions described at the start of the chapter. Acts that may be considered prosocial include a wide range of behavior—from saving a person who is drowning to helping someone carry his or her packages, from donating a kidney to donating a penny, from the heroic to the merely thoughtful. The common denominator of these acts is their apparent selflessness, the voluntary doing of "good" for another person where the motivation does not appear to be self gain.

Dennis Krebs (1970) has identified three aspects by which conventional wisdom defines prosocial acts: a prosocial act is performed voluntarily by an actor; the actor intends for the act to benefit another person or group of persons; and the act is performed as an end in itself and not as a means to fulfilling an ulterior personal motive of the actor. Obviously, this way of describing prosocial behavior highlights people's *motivations* for performing acts of helping. In fact, Irving Staub (1978b) distinguishes between prosocial and altruistic behavior on the basis of a person's motivation. He says, "Prosocial behavior refers to behavior benefitting others. A prosocial act may be judged altruistic if it appears to have been intended to benefit others than to gain either material or social rewards" (p. 10). Staub goes on to say that, doubtlessly, there may be internal rewards associated with the performance of prosocial acts, such as a sense of self-satisfaction or virtuousness. While we can never fully know the motives of another person's behavior, we will focus in this chapter on behaviors that are done with the apparent intent of benefiting another more than oneself; we will regard the terms altruism and prosocial behavior as synonymous.

THE CURRENT SIGNIFICANCE OF ALTRUISM

Altruism is interesting to social psychologists as a social problem as well as a scientific puzzle. The complexity of our mass technological society makes us increasingly vulnerable and dependent on each other. At the same time, because of depersonalization and increased mobility, we may no longer rely on traditional sources of aid such as family and long-term friends. We are struck by examples such as the transit robbery and the Genovese slaying, where people apparently like us in most ways failed to intervene to help another individual. Thus, we seek reassurance that, in fact, we can expect help and concern from those around us. We want to understand when people will act with compassion toward others and when they will not.

Prosocial behavior is also interesting from the perspective of psychological theory. Most psychological theories have tended to conceptualize human behavior as egoistic—emphasizing the self-interested and reinforcing aspects of human functioning. Prosocial behavior is unusual because of its seeming independence from the usual notions of reinforcement. How is effort and sacrifice for another reinforcing in the traditional sense? Furthermore, many psychologists are seeking to understand behavior that is governed by volition and self-regulation rather than by the controlling influence of the surrounding environment (Mahoney, 1974; Kimble and Perlmuter, 1970).

So, both for social and scientific reasons, psychologists have become interested in prosocial behavior. We shall first examine theoretical explanations for prosocial behavior and then turn to research about specific processes.

THEORIES OF ALTRUISM

Because interest in prosocial behavior is fairly recent, there has not been a great deal of theorizing about the causes of this somewhat paradoxical form of behavior. As we mentioned,

Mother Teresa, who won the 1979 Nobel Peace Prize, has dedicated her life to helping the homeless men, women, and children of Calcutta, India. Although altruism such as hers is widely admired and advocated, we do not realistically expect others to follow her example. *(J. P. Laffont / Sygma)*

most psychological theories have emphasized human beings as being primarily self-interested. Thus, the question that theories of altruism must address is: How do we account for self-sacrifice?

NORMATIVE INFLUENCES

People have espoused ideals of selflessness and concern for others for thousands of years, and altruism is one of the most universally accepted ethics. Almost every culture embraces a norm that concern for others is good and that selfishness is bad. A norm is a standard of action that specifies what behavior is expected, or "normal," and what behavior is abnormal. The unwritten rule in most societies is that when the cost is not very great and another person is in need, one should do all that one can to aid that person. Some societies have even legislated the conditions under which one member must come to the aid of another or suffer punishment. The universality of some type of norm of social responsibility indicates that this standard has functional value and that it operates to facilitate social life.

So one way of "explaining" altruism is to say that the behavior is normative and that there are social rewards for behaving in accord with the norms and sanctions for violating the norm. These sanctions may range from mild disapproval to incarceration or even more severe forms of censure, depending on the threat to the established social order posed by the offenses. For example, when the shah of Iran was overthrown, the new Muslim leaders made it a crime for banks to charge interest on loans, since the Muslim religion forbids usury.

If it is truly normative in Western culture to show concern for others and to help others whenever possible, it is relatively easy to understand the horror people express when they read of failures to aid others who are in danger. But if helpfulness is a norm, why, then, are people surprised and approving when others *do* act altruistically? If "norm" defines expected behavior—"normal" behavior—then one might expect the system of rewards by which Western society encourages adherence to a prosocial norm, such as medals for lifesavers or newspaper articles about people who run into burning buildings to save parakeets. But why do we feel mild surprise at seeing someone stop on the freeway to help a stranded motorist fix a flat tire?

Allan Teger (1970) has suggested that the norm of helping, although frequently endorsed verbally, is actually an *ideal* norm—neither a true expectation of behavior nor even a very morally compelling force. As an ideal norm, the prosocial ethic is an expression of the fact that people value socially responsible behavior.

Adherence to social norms may not seem to be a sufficient explanation of prosocial behavior. However, Schwartz (1977) has identified certain conditions that determine whether or not an individual is sensitive to internalized norms or feelings of moral obligation. Later, in the section on situational influences, we will examine some of those conditions that influence how obligated we might feel to a person in need.

SOCIOBIOLOGY

Recently there has been a great deal of interest in the possibility that altruism might be a trait that has evolutionary survival value (Campbell, 1975; Wilson, 1978). This interest is partly due to the universality of norms regarding helping and partly due to ethologists' observations that "altruistic behavior" is not unique to humans but can be found in many species of animals. The basic contention is that we may be biologically predisposed to respond with aid to the suffering of others (Barash, 1977).

The idea that we have a biological predisposition to help others is a fascinating one and has generated a great deal of debate between psychologists and sociobiologists. The intricacies of these debates are beyond our scope here, but we will highlight the salient issues. Sociobiologists such as Wilson (1975, 1978) have argued that genes responsible for self-sacrificial behavior might be selected for over generations because in the long run self-sacrifice increases the probability that the species will survive.

Wilson and ethologists such as Konrad Lorenz and Nicholas Tinbergen have drawn heavily on observations of animals in reaching conclusions about human prosocial behavior. For example, many kinds of birds give a warning cry when a predator is sighted. The cry seems to serve the good of the species, since it alerts others to the presence of danger. However, it may work to the detriment of the individual who gives the warning by attracting the attention of the predator. Why do animals, who do not have religious or ethical systems encouraging altruism, engage in such self-sacrifice for the good of another?

A child is saved from drowning by a St. Bernard, a breed of dog long celebrated for its good deeds. Sociobiologists have pointed to such phenomena to advance their claim that altruism has evolutionary survival value. *(Culver Pictures)*

This issue raises an interesting dilemma for evolutionary theory. If altruism is selected for, what is the mechanism of selection? For if the bird who gives the warning is increasing its chance of being killed, then the altruistic gene will be lost; thus it appears that the less altruistic birds who do not self-sacrifice would eventually be left.

Several mechanisms have been proposed by which self-sacrificial behavior might have been selected for. Wilson (1978) argues that *kinship selection* might account for the evolution of altruism. If an individual organism's self-sacrificial behavior benefits a relative, then altruistic genes will be selected for because the relative (who shares some of the genes with the altruist) will probably survive. This seems to be a plausible possibility because much of the self-sacrificial behavior we see in humans and other species is directed toward kin; for example, a mother bird feigns injury to lead a predator away from the nest of her young.

A variation of this view has been proposed by Trivers (1971). He argues that the behavior with the most survival value is not altruism but *reciprocal altruism*. What has actually evolved, Trivers suggests, is a tendency to exchange benefits by prosocial acts. According to Trivers (1971, 1974), it is not only possible that reciprocal altruism is selected for, but it is also possible that the tendency to *enforce* altruism and moral behaviors in others is selected for. This idea is appealing because it suggests that the costs of being altruistic are offset by the subsequent benefits that an individual would receive from prosocial behavior of other members of the group.

Arguing against biological evolution of altruism is Donald Campbell. In his presidential address to the American Psychological Association, Campbell (1975) contends that the extreme examples of altruism found among human beings could not have been biologically selected for because the altruists would eventually sacrifice themselves while the selfish would benefit and reproduce. Campbell concedes that certain primitive forms of prosocial behavior probably did evolve biologically, such as care for the young. However, biological evolution cannot easily account for the complex forms of prosocial action found among humans. To understand behaviors such as donating kidneys or running into a burning building to save a child, Campbell says that we must look at *social evolution*. He says that for the culture to function optimally, norms have developed to promote prosocial concern. These norms evolved in order to balance genetically based selfishness. The optimal balance seems to be a compromise between the greatest good for a particular person and the greatest good for the social group as a whole.

Psychologists and biologists disagree about a possible genetic basis for altruism. There is general consensus, however, that to understand such behavior in humans we must look to specific personality differences and situational factors that affect prosocial behavior.

EMPATHIC CONCERN

A very different explanation of altruism is that it is unpleasant to watch another organism suffer. When we come to the aid of others, we are actually seeking to alleviate the unpleasant feelings that their distress arouses in us. Piliavin, Piliavin, and Rodin (1975) have developed a theory to explain when people will intervene in an emergency, but their point can probably be applied to prosocial behavior in general. They believe that the observation of an emergency is physiologically arousing in an unpleasant way and that the individual will seek some means to reduce this aroused state. So, in their analysis, "altruism" is not that at all; rather it is the attempt of an organism to reduce unpleasant arousal in itself that motivates the helping. The specific response chosen is whatever behavior will most rapidly and most completely reduce the arousal but at the same time maximize the rewards and minimize the costs. The balance of costs is complex. The costs for acting might be danger, loss of time, involvement with an unpleasant situation, expending effort, or acting inappropriately. The rewards might be social approval, increased self-esteem, or relieving a negative mood. In addition, there may be certain costs of not helping, such as self-blame or criticism from others. Piliavin, Piliavin, and Rodin believe we weigh all these factors in a complex calculus before deciding to help someone in need.

In a somewhat similar explanation of altruism, Dennis Krebs (1975) also asserts that we feel physiological arousal when we witness the suffering of another. However, Krebs thinks the arousal results from *empathy*, or the ability to sense another's experience. He argues that altruism is mediated by empathy and that empathy is in turn mediated by similarity. People are likely to feel empathy toward someone they perceive as similar to themselves, and altruism is often the result of this empathy. Krebs argues that the "altruist" obtains vicarious pleasure from giving something of value to a person with whom he or she empathizes. Although it appears that the "altruist" is giving something of value and receiving nothing in return, Krebs believes that the "altruist" actually receives vicarious pleasure in return. In Krebs's words: "it is possible for people to behave altruistically without violating the principle of hedonism." Consistent with this explanation, Krebs has found that people respond physiologically when someone like themselves is being shocked; the greater the similarity, the greater the arousal and also the greater the subsequent altruism to the victim. Thus, both the Krebs and the Piliavin, Piliavin, and Rodin positions interpret prosocial behavior as essentially motivated by self-interest, even though, at least for Krebs, there is also empathy for the other.

Other authors such as Batson, Cole, Jasnoski, and Hanson (1978) agree that empathy mediates helping, but they argue that the helper may feel genuine concern for the person being helped. They say that "we should not too quickly assume that people are always motivated to help others out of an egoistic desire to reduce their own distress. Empathic emotion may produce an altruistic desire to have the distress of others reduced."

EQUITY

A final explanation of altruism is offered by Elaine and William Walster and Ellen Berscheid (1978). In their book *Equity: Theory and Research* (also discussed in Chapters 7 and 10), these authors emphasize that our societal structure is based on a system of social exchange. From this perspective, we behave altruistically partly because we strive for equity or balance in our relationships with others. If we help others, then we can expect them to return the favor when we are in need, and vice versa. In support of this view is the surprisingly large number of people who send substantial sums of money to the federal government or to charities because they were helped at some point in their past and they want to "help someone else in turn." According to this formulation, then, altruism results from having been treated altruistically or from an expectation that our own altruism will be reciprocated by another.

While each of these explanations helps us understand some aspects of human beings' caring and concern for each other, no one of them is a general theory of altruism. That may be because we are still gathering information from research, and a sufficient theory of altruism has just not emerged yet; or it may be that the sorts of behavior included under the label "altruism" are so diverse that no single explanation will be sufficient to explain them. Any general theory of altruism will have to address both the universality of prosocial acts—which suggests biological or social evolution—and the specificity of prosocial behavior—which suggests individual differences in such things as empathic concern as well as situational influences on helping. Some of the research we examine in the rest of the chapter relates to the theoretical mechanisms we have discussed. Much of it is general in nature and is not related to any specific theoretical position.

Now we turn from general theories about prosocial behavior to experimental research aimed at identifying factors that affect prosocial behavior. This review of research can be divided into three general sections. First we will examine *characteristics of the individual* who engages in prosocial action. In this section we will look at attempts to define personality factors associated with prosocial concern. Can we identify people who are altruistic "by nature"? We will also examine the effects on altruism of momentary moods or temporary states of the individual.

The second general section examines *situa-*

FOCUS ON APPLICATIONS

ALTRUISM IN REAL LIFE

The incidents below were all recently reported in the *Los Angeles Times.* Each incident describes a different form of altruism, and each can be traced to a different theory of altruism.

For example, the Road Ranger seems to be motivated by *normative influences.* About his highway helpfulness, he says, "I wonder what Clayton Moore [the actor who played the original Lone Ranger] would think of this. I revere him so much. He was a model of self-control and helping his fellow man."

On the other hand, the women who assaulted the purse snatcher may have been motivated by *empathic concern.* They had just met with the police to plan a rally protesting street violence against women. They no doubt felt solidarity with each other and with women in general. As one of them said, their counterattack on the purse snatcher "was an example of what the rally is going to be all about—an example of women refusing to view themselves as passive victims."

Finally, the man who tried to settle up for a unpaid bill forty-six years later seems to have been motivated by a sense of *equity.* He had benefited from an unpaid-for purchase of gasoline during the Depression of the 1930s and he wanted to settle the balance, with anonymous thanks.

These examples demonstrate that there can be very different motivations for altruism. As the accompanying section makes clear, no single theory or explanation will be sufficient to account for them all.

The Road Ranger and Vigilante. *(L.A. Times Photo)*

I

SCOTTS VALLEY—Dressed in a gray polyester jump suit, black boots, beaver-skin Stetson and wide black leather belt with chrome studs and a silver buckle enscribed "The Road Ranger," the man climbed behind the wheel of his trusty truck named Vigilante.

Just as this modern knight of the road pulled onto busy California 17 in search of truth, justice, adventure and fame, a California Highway Patrol car passed by, pushing a disabled auto from the traffic lanes to the shoulder of the mountain road.

"To the rescue" the Road Ranger shouted with a flourish, flooring Vigilante's throttle and roaring to the spot where the CHP officer had left the disabled auto.

The Road Ranger pulled ahead of the stranded motorist and fairly leaped to the rescue. But a quick check under the hood revealed the engine had succumbed to lack of oil. There was nothing the Road Ranger could do but offer the driver a lift into town, eight miles away.

Rene Dorantes of San Jose declined the offer, but he did take a business card from the mechanical marvel. And as the Road Ranger walked back to his pickup, Dorantes turned to an observer and exclaimed, "He's terrific. Who is that man?"

The man is Allen Norman Little, a former infantry sergeant in Vietnam who is trying to bring to life the ideals of his hero, actor Clayton Moore's Lone Ranger.

"I wonder what Clayton Moore would think of this," Little mused as he cruised the winding road that connects coastal Santa Cruz with metropolitan San Jose in his daily search for stranded motorists.

"I revere him so much," Little said of his idol. "He was a model of self-control and helping his fellow man. I have to accept filthy money for what I do but, then, the Lone Ranger was a fantasy and I'm real."

Little puts in eight or more hours each day looking for stranded travelers and helping as many as two dozen a day with such simple remedies as driving a screw into a tire puncture to keep the car rolling into town or wrapping aluminum foil around a fuel line so the gasoline won't boil and cause a vapor lock.

"What I'd like is to be a legend in my own time," Little explained. And with that he put his foot to the gas pedal and was off again on his quest.

II

HOLLYWOOD—No purse snatcher ever made a worse choice of victims—they were exactly the wrong women at exactly the wrong time and in exactly the wrong mood.

As a result, he did not get away with snatching the purse. What's more, he wound up being administered a severe purse-pummelling, then was chased five blocks by his would-be victims, and, finally, arrested and taken to jail.

The women were Sue Embrey, president of the Los Angeles City Commission on the status of Women; Vickie Smith, acting director of the agency; Annette Louise Lopez, secretary of the same group; and Noreen Hill-Duffy, a planner for the upcoming Women Take Back the Night Rally.

It happened Thursday night.

As Smith recounted it later, she and her three feminist colleagues had been to a city Police Commission meeting at which they had won approval of the Women Take Back the Night Rally, a march through Hollywood on April 19.

The march, as irony would have it, is to protest violence on the streets—specifically, violence against women, including purse snatchings.

Smith said they were so happy that the march had been OKd that they went to a Little Tokyo restaurant for a celebration dinner.

They were leaving the 2nd Street restaurant a little after 7 P.M. when, before they could get to their car, the unfortunate purse snatcher made his move.

"He lunged at Annette and grabbed her purse," Smith said. "And she just held on. He threw her up against the car but she just held on."

And then all hell broke loose.

"I jumped on his back and started hitting him with my purse," Smith said. "Noreen started hitting him with *her* purse and fist and Sue Embrey grabbed a stick from the car and started beating him with it."

Smith said the purse snatcher seemed absolutely boggled by the indignity of all this.

"I can't remember his exact words," she said, "but it was something like, 'I can't believe it! What are you doing!' "

It was about then that the would-be purse snatcher pulled a knife.

"I swung my purse at his head," Smith said, "and then we all backed away from him and started screaming for help."

The suspect gave up the purse and decided on a strategic withdrawal, moving off at a semi-trot.

However, he didn't figure on the determination of the feminist four. While Embrey tailed him in her car, Lopez and Hill-Duffy followed the suspect on foot, and Smith called police.

Five blocks away, two Los Angeles Police Department patrol cars—one of them carrying Smith—closed in on the suspect and arrested a man later identified as 25-year-old Leonard Jordan. He was booked on suspicion of robbery.

"It was," Smith said, "an example of what the rally is going to be all about—an example of women refusing to view themselves as passive victims."

The suspect's reaction was not recorded.

III

SANTA ANA—Somewhere among the 20,000 inhabitants of the Missouri boot-heel town of Poplar Bluff, there is at least one very honest old soul.

How else can one explain the one-page unsigned letter containing $10 that arrived recently in the Orange County recorder's office bearing a Poplar Bluff, Mo., postmark and an April 1 date?

The letter was addressed to the recorder's office at the "Court House Annex"—an extension of the old county courthouse that was vacated by the recorder and his staff nearly 10 years ago.

"In what used to be Santa Ana Gardens, at corner of Edinger and Sullivan St., was a filling station owned by a Mr. Forbes—I think," the handwritten letter read.

"Anyway I or we left there owing $1.50 for gas which was forgotten. I do not know how to settle this unless someone there will look up records and forward half of $10 enclosed to heirs and keep the other half for yourself.

"Thanks."

There was no signature, but there was a postscript.

"PS," the letter closed, "this was in 1934."

Source: David Johnston, "It's Road Ranger—the Fastest Wrench in West," *Los Angeles Times*, May 16, 1980, Section A, p. 3; Jerry Belcher, "Victims Turn Purse Snatching into Rout," *Los Angeles Times*, April 12, 1980, Part 2, p.1; Doris A. Bryon, "46 Years Later, Oldster Tries to Pay $1.50 Bill," *Los Angeles Times*, April 22, 1980, Part 2, p. 1.

tional variables as determiners of altruistic intervention. Here, the focus will be on factors that seem to have general effects on prosocial behavior in most people.

The third section focuses on the *consequences* of having acted or failed to act altruistically on the victim as well as the potential benefactor. The question posed here is how we respond to having helped someone and how we respond to being helped. We also look at the other side. What happens when we have an opportunity to help and fail to do so?

In reading these subsequent sections, try to keep in mind the theories we have briefly described and see how helpful they are in explaining the diverse sorts of prosocial behaviors that have been investigated experimentally. Also think about situations you encounter in your everyday life and see if the experiments help you to understand better how you and those around you respond to opportunities to help.

CHARACTERISTICS OF THE INDIVIDUAL

PERSONALITY FACTORS AND ALTRUISM

As we mentioned at the beginning of the chapter, our intuitive feeling is that people differ widely in their concern for others and their tendencies to act unselfishly toward others. Literature abounds with examples of the noble and generous who live lives of self-sacrifice for the betterment of others.

Psychologists have shared the assumption that some people are more helpful than others, and these scientists have sought to identify personality characteristics that account for these differences. Although there may be a number of different personality factors that lead to prosocial action, people who somehow have altruistic personalities should show this inclination in a number of different types of situations.

In this section we will examine whether specific personality factors seem to be associated with prosocial concern. We will also ask whether people in fact show generality in their prosocial behavior across different types of situations. For example, is a person who donates blood also more likely to stop and aid someone with a flat tire?

Most of the initial attempts to relate personality differences to helping behavior were unsuccessful (for example, Schwartz and Clausen, 1970), but recent studies have revealed that it is possible to identify personality variables associated with helpfulness. In one such effort Satow (1975) hypothesized that people who were strongly motivated to gain the approval of others would be more likely to engage in helping behavior than those low in need for social approval, and that this tendency would be greatest when others witnessed the helping. As expected, female subjects who scored high on the Crowne-Marlowe Need-for-Approval Scale donated more of their $1.50 research earnings to the university research fund than subjects who scored low on the approval scale, but only when the high-need subjects thought their donation was being observed by the experimenter behind a one-way mirror.

Another personality dimension that relates to prosocial behavior has been referred to as a "belief in a just world" (Lerner, Miller, and Holmes, 1975). According to this theory, people want to believe that the world is just and that people get what they deserve. In order to maintain this belief while we encounter the abundant evidence of innocent victims being mugged, natural disasters devastating the homes of the helpless, and the just suffering while the unjust escape punishment, we must selectively attend only to certain aspects of our environment and adjust our perceptions so that they accord with our view that the world is fair and just. For example, on seeing a person victimized for apparently no reason, we may seek out reasons why that individual actually deserved his or her fate.

Dale Miller (1977) conducted an experiment examining the relationship between altruism and an individual's motivation to believe in a just world or, as he called it, "justice motivation." Miller found that subjects who were high in justice motivation were generous when a victim's plight was seen as an isolated example. However, when the victim was described as a member of a whole group of similar unfortunates, those with a high justice motivation tended to be unwilling to volunteer to help. According to Miller, when people with a high belief in a just world have a prosocial response available that will help restore that belief, they are motivated to behave altruistically. However, when confronted with a victim who is only one of many, then those with a high belief in a just world will avoid the situation in order not to contradict their beliefs, since nothing they can do will alleviate the suffering.

These two studies represent attempts to relate specific personality dimensions to specific opportunities to behave prosocially. However, if personality characteristics are potent determiners of prosocial behavior, then we should expect some cross-situational generality of such behaviors. Psychologists Kenneth and Mary Gergen and Kenneth Meter (1972) studied the relationship between personality and helping behavior across situations. College students who were enrolled in a personality course took ten different personality tests, including tests of self-esteem, dominance, affiliation, and self-consistency. A few days later, the professor handed out a mimeographed sheet from the Psychology Department indicating that voluntary help was much needed for five different types of tasks. These activities involved counseling troubled students at a local high school, helping to collate and assemble the class's test data, and assisting other professors in carrying out some research. In actuality, the investigators had made up the notice for volunteer aid and had purposely varied the helping activities so that they could learn whether or not a person who volunteered to help with one of these tasks would also volunteer to help with the others.

Correlations were computed among each of the ten traits and each of the five prosocial behaviors, with the male and female groups separated in order to help develop an accurate set of statistics. In all, more than one-fourth of the 100 correlations were significant beyond chance, 13 for males and 16 for females. Interestingly, however, only 5 of the correlations between personality traits and helpfulness that were found for male subjects were also found in the female group. This finding indicates that if there are people who habitually do good, their personal qualities are different depending on whether they are male or female.

The researchers were especially interested in the relationship between nurturance and altruism. The nurturant person is defined as giving warmth, service, acceptance, and as being helpful. The researchers did find that male and female college students who scored high on nurturance were likely to volunteer to counsel troubled high-school students of the same sex. However, nurturance did not correlate with any other form of helping, though this may be because the only option to help other people by interpersonal means in this experiment was the counseling task.

The data also show that for both sexes, high sensation-seeking scores correlate with offering to assist in research on unusual states of consciousness. Certainly, this type of helping would be gratifying to a sensation seeker.

The results of this study by Gergen, Gergen, and Meter indicate that some types of people are likely to be helpful in some situations while other types will emerge as the "good guys" in other situations. *When* people help depends heavily on how the situation happens to interact with their personal dispositions at the time.

An experiment by Staub (1974) has also addressed the complex question of whether we can predict a person's tendency to behave prosocially from knowing his or her personality. Staub's study is important because it is one of the few that attempt to access individuals' prosocial orientation and relate it to specific prosocial behaviors. Male undergraduate subjects took several personality tests chosen to measure their concern about the welfare of others, their feeling of responsibility for others' welfare, and their belief in moral and prosocial values. Later, while working on a task, these subjects heard sounds of distress coming from an adjoining room. The sounds were made by a male confederate and were supposed to indicate that the victim had severe stomach cramps. The subjects had several opportunities to help the so-called victim: the subject was given 135 seconds to enter the adjoining room and see about the confederate; if the subject did not act within this time, the confederate then entered the subject's room and asked to lie down on a sofa; after a

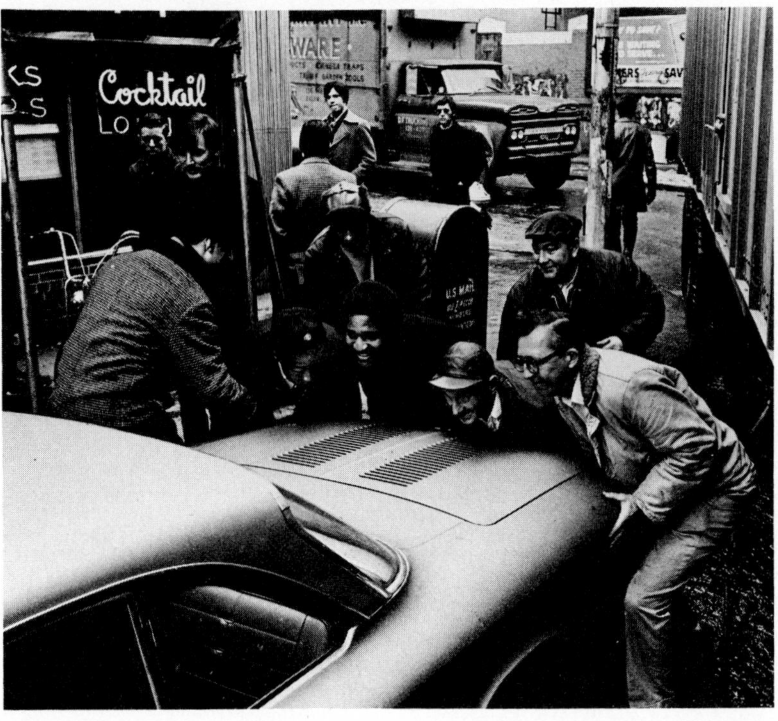

Research indicates that an "altruistic personality" is too simple an explanation of prosocial behavior. It is more probable that altruism in a specific instance results from an interaction of dispositional and situational factors at that time. *(© Jim Freeman)*

few minutes the confederate offered to go to another room where he wouldn't bother the subject; finally, the confederate asked the subject for a favor, either to call the confederate's roommate or to get a prescription filled for the confederate.

The general findings of this study support both the idea that personality is related to prosocial behavior and that personality factors alone are insufficient to predict whether a person will behave prosocially across all situations. For example, subjects with a high prosocial orientation were likely to intervene during the first 135 seconds to help the confederate. They also showed a high tendency to perform each of the other helping acts allowed for in this experiment. However, Staub also emphasized the importance of looking at how personality variables interact with aspects of the situation. In a follow-up report Staub (1979a) says: "Our findings clearly show that a general personality characteristic which I referred to as prosocial orientation . . . tends to lead people to behave prosocially. It is also true that this personality orientation tended to exert influence jointly with other characteristics of the person or with characteristics of the situation."

These results of Staub's study are consistent with current movements in personality (Endler and Magnusson, 1978) that emphasize the interaction of characteristics of the person with characteristics of the situation. That is, we might expect certain personality types to respond to certain situations with prosocial concern while other types would be more prosocial in different circumstances. So it is probably too simple to expect there to be an "altruistic personality"; instead we should try to discover what types of people are likely to behave prosocially in which contexts.

Another way of thinking about individual determinants of prosocial action is in terms of transitory states of the person rather than stable personality characteristics. We will examine several of these transitory states in the following section.

TRANSITORY PSYCHOLOGICAL STATES

Transitory states such as guilt, happiness, or failure can each affect a person's responsiveness to others. These states sometimes result from the individual's own thoughts or actions; at other times, the actions of others produce them.

All of us have experienced the exhilaration that accompanies the successful completion of a difficult task. When success comes our way, we feel that the world, for once, is indeed just and can do us no wrong. This state of mind can produce intense feelings of good will toward our fellow human beings. Do these benevolent feelings affect subsequent behavior, or are they simply a private reaction to past accomplishments? When we perceive ourselves as generous, are we inclined to be kinder toward others, or are we merely deluding ourselves? These questions have provided the focus for a rapidly growing body of psychological research.

SUCCESS AND FAILURE: BOUQUETS AND BRICKBATS Isen's (1970) work is illustrative of research into the comparative effects of success and failure. She asked teachers and college students to take a battery of perceptual and motor tests, randomly telling some subjects that they had done extremely well and others that they had done poorly. Still other subjects received no feedback on their performance or did not perform the tasks at all.

Isen found that subjects who thought they had been successful on the tasks subsequently donated more generously to a school fund *and* more frequently volunteered assistance to a person struggling with an armload of books than did subjects who believed they had failed or who had received no feedback. However, subjects who received negative evaluations were not significantly less helpful than subjects who received no feedback at all. Neither group showed a special interest in being generous.

This study indicates that the experience of success does indeed increase altruistic behavior toward others. However, success produces a complicated mix of reactions in most people. Increased generosity in Isen's experiment may have derived from several sources, including a positive feeling that can accompany success, which Isen referred to as the "warm glow of success," a feeling of competence that can follow success, an enhanced expectation that success will lead to more rewards in the future, or from a combination of these factors (Kazdin and Bryan, 1971; Midlarsky and Midlarsky, 1972).

MOOD STATE In order to control for the alternative explanations mentioned above, Alice Isen and her colleague Paul Levin (1972) set out to see if they could induce a positive mood in subjects by some means other than the complex experience of success. They decided that a small unexpected gift might have the same effect. One experimenter approached students in a library and gave them each a cookie. In a seemingly unrelated encounter, the second experimenter subsequently asked the students who had received cookies, as well as some who had not, if they would help her out by being in her experiment. As it turned out, there were more volunteers among the students who had received cookies than among those who had not.

These findings seem to establish that a positive mood leads to increased helpfulness. It could still be argued, however, that the researchers had merely uncovered an instance of modeled altruism—that is, the students' generosity had not resulted from positive mood at all but merely from observing an altruistic model. So Isen and Levin eliminated any possibility of modeling in a second study. This time, they arranged for some people to find a dime in a telephone booth. The recipients would be made happy by their unexpected profits, the experimenters reasoned, but would not have been exposed to an altruistic model, because nobody *gave* them the dime. More people who found dimes did indeed subsequently help the experimenter pick up spilled papers than did people who had not found dimes.

You may feel at this point that the effects of giving someone a cookie or leaving a dime to be found in a phone booth are not matters of great import. Most psychologists would agree that knowledge of the effects of cookie giving per se is not particularly interesting. What is significant is the fact that these simple manipulations distinguish between two important psychological processes—reaction to success and reaction to positive feelings. The Isen and Levin study has established that people are more altruistic during a positive than a negative mood state, whether the mood is aroused by successful performance on an examination, by a pleasant interaction with another person, or simply by finding an unexpected small reward.

Although the conclusion is warranted that positive moods increase altruism, there are still other questions to explore about the effects of mood on altruism. For one thing, not all positive mood states arise from such gratuitous windfalls as finding a dime in a telephone booth or receiving a cookie from a stranger. Some positive mood states are cognitively mediated, such as the memory of a week when everything seemed to go right, the recollection of a particularly happy time during one's past, or quiet meditation while walking through the woods. Second, the possible effects of *negative* moods on altruistic behavior have not yet been discussed. It has been shown that failure in the laboratory has typically not rendered subjects any more or less altruistic than control groups, although this effect may be due to other components of the failure experience that cancel out the effect of melancholy.

Bert Moore, Bill Underwood, and David Rosenhan (1973) have investigated cognitive components of mood states as well as the effects of bad moods. These investigators asked some children to recall events from their lives that had made them particularly happy. Other children were asked to recount events that had made them particularly sad. Each child was then asked to think briefly about one of the experiences and about how it had made him or her feel. Children in the control groups either waited quietly or were asked to do an innocuous counting task. The results of this study are summarized in Figure 9.1. As the experimenters had expected, children who had remembered happy events were subsequently more generous in sharing their money with other children than were subjects who had had neutral experiences. Moreover, children who had thought about sad events gave significantly less of their money than did those in control groups. Moore, Underwood, and Rosenhan interpreted these results as indicating that positive mood leads to increased responsiveness to others while negative affect promotes a turning inward and a conserving of resources.

Cialdini and his associates (1973, 1976) have challenged these results for negative affect. Because prosocial action is valued by society, we are able to feel good about ourselves when we help others. Thus, one would expect that people in a negative mood should be more helpful to others than people in a neutral mood, since the negative people should want to improve their mood by doing something as socially desirable and reinforcing as altruism. Why, then, did the subjects tested by Moore and his colleagues (1973) behave less altruistically when they were in a negative mood? Cialdini and Kenrick (1976) contend that these findings may be specific to children. Perhaps children would not have fully internalized the norms regarding al-

FIGURE 9.1 Moore, Underwood, and Rosenhan (1973) investigated the influences of mood on altruistic behavior. They found that children who reminisced about happy events were most likely to share their money and those who recalled sad events were least likely to do so.

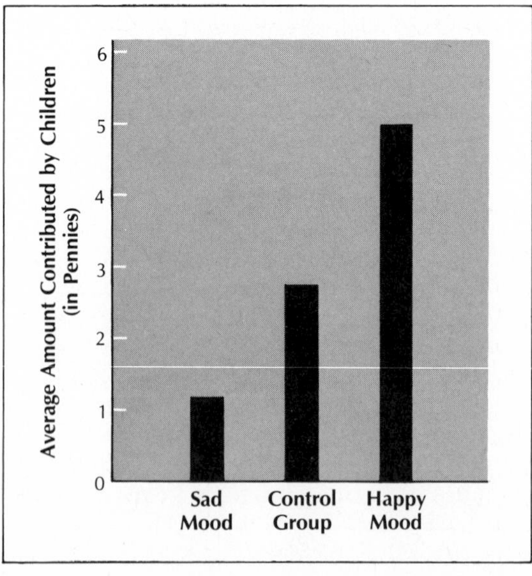

truism, so that engaging in such behavior might not serve to terminate the negative affect.

To test their explanation, Cialdini and Kenrick replicated the procedures used by Moore and his colleagues but with children at three different age levels in order to see if negative affect had different consequences for altruistic behavior at different ages. They found that young children tended to donate little money after reminiscing about sad experiences; however, by the time students are in the tenth and twelfth grades, negative affect leads to increased rates of donation as compared to neutral controls. The authors interpret these results as supporting their ideas regarding the acquired reinforcing value of prosocial action.

However, two studies using adult subjects (Underwood, Bevenson, Berenson *et al.*, 1977; McMillan, Sanders, and Solomon, 1977) point out the need for further clarification of this issue. Underwood *et al.*, using movies prerated for affective content, and McMillan *et al.*, using negative personality feedback, found low donations and helping respectively under conditions of negative affect. So while the general results are fairly consistent regarding the facilitative effects of positive moods on prosocial behavior, the role of negative affect is more complex and appears to involve counteracting tendencies.

This confusion may be partially reconciled in recent work that shows that negative mood can result in increased helping when the costs of helping are low and the potential benefits are high (Weyant, 1978; Kenrick, Bauman, and Cialdini, 1979). This suggests that when we are sad or depressed, helping someone else may be *one* way to terminate those negative feelings. However, it also suggests that we must not perceive the costs of helping as too great and that we expect to derive some benefits in terms of recognition and feeling good about ourselves.

GUILT AND SYMPATHY Another transitory psychological state with implications for altruism is guilt. A widely espoused norm of our society is that one should help people whom one has injured. But beyond restitution to the injured party, does guilt produce a generalized impulse to be helpful that extends to others? Perhaps when we have injured someone, a generalized urge to be helpful serves as a form of compensation, so that we can still see ourselves as the good people we wish to be. Furthermore, can a generalized tendency toward helpfulness result simply from witnessing someone being wronged—whether or not the observer is the wrongdoer? Is there some sense of fair play, some desire to ensure justice, that quite apart from any feelings of personal responsibility promotes increased helpfulness?

In order to answer these questions Edna Rawlings (1970) set up an experiment in which student subjects observed a coworker receiving shocks. Some students thought they were responsible for the coworker's suffering (guilt condition), while others merely watched (observer condition). The coworkers of control subjects did not receive shocks. When the students were later given an opportunity to help out a third person who was not in the original experiment, both the guilty students and the observers were more helpful than were control subjects, but guilty and observing subjects did not significantly differ in their willingness to help. This finding would seem to indicate that guilt-produced altruism does generalize to persons other than those wronged and, furthermore, that altruism may be prompted merely by witnessing an injury for which the observer is not responsible.

Restitution Rawlings demonstrated that guilt can promote charitability toward persons other than those the guilty party has injured. But what about restitution—reparation by the guilty to the injured party? Early research had suggested that guilty persons who were responsible for an accident were no more likely to help out the injured than nonguilty persons, though they were likely to help someone *other* than the injured party (Freedman, Wallington, and Bless, 1967). However, if those responsible for the accident did not have to meet their victims face to face, then the guilty were more likely than the nonguilty to help the victim (Freedman, Wallington, and Bless, 1967).

Apparently, the effects of guilt in promoting altruism can be negated by the distress of having to confront one's victim. However, if injury itself occurs in a face-to-face encounter (Ko-

SOCIAL PSYCHOLOGY AND THE ARTS

GUILT AND ALTRUISM

One of the world's greatest novelists is the nineteenth-century Russian writer Fyodor Dostoyevsky. In *The Brothers Karamazov*, his last and perhaps most respected work, Dostoyevsky uses one of his characters to portray the making of a saint and to demonstrate the power of selfless love. In the passage below, Father Zossima recounts how he came to resign his prestigious commission as an officer in the czar's army and to take up the life of a wandering monk. The transformation occurred the night before a duel, to which the jealous young officer challenged a respected landowner, who has married a woman the officer finds attractive. In selfish conceit and fury that the beautiful woman has not saved herself for him alone, the young officer intends to kill her husband.

> It was the end of June, and our meeting was to take place at seven o'clock the next day on the outskirts of the town—and then something happened that in truth was the turning point of my life. In the evening, returning home in a savage and brutal humor, I flew into a rage with my orderly and gave him two blows in the face with all my might, so that it was covered with blood. He had not long been in my service and I had struck him before, but never with such ferocious cruelty. And, believe me, though it's forty years ago, I recall it now with shame and pain. I went to bed and slept for about three hours; when I waked up the day was breaking. I got up—I did not want to sleep any more—I went to the window—opened it, it looked out upon the garden. I saw the sun rising. It was warm and beautiful, the birds were singing.
>
> What's the meaning of it, I wondered. I feel in my heart as it were something vile and shameful. Is it because I am going to shed blood? No, it's not that. Can it be that I am afraid of death, afraid of being killed? No, that's not it, that's not it at all. . . . And all at once I knew what it was: it was because I had beaten my orderly the evening before! It all rose before my mind, as it were repeated over again; he stood before me and I was beating him straight on the face and he was holding his arms stiffly down, his head erect, his eyes fixed upon me as though on parade. He staggered at every blow and did not even dare to raise his hands to protect himself. That is what a man has been brought to, and that was a man beating a fellow creature! What a crime! It was as though a sharp dagger had pierced me. I stood as in a trance, while the sun was shining, the leaves were rejoicing and the birds were trilling the praise of God. . . . I hid my face in my hands, fell on my bed and broke into a storm of tears. And then I remembered my brother Markel and what he said on his deathbed to his servants: "My dear ones, why do you wait on me, why do you love me? Am I worth your waiting on me?"
>
> "Yes, am I worth it?" flashed through my mind. After all what am I worth, that another man, a fellow creature, made in the likeness and image of God, should serve me? For the first time in my life this question forced itself upon me. My brother had said: ". . . in truth we are each responsible to all for all, it's only that men don't know this. If they knew it, the world would be a paradise at once."

Several social-psychological variables are involved in the above passage. The Christian norm of selfless love is expressed by the officer's brother Markel, who also serves as an important social model. However, the officer's conversion is directly precipitated by his intense guilt over beating his servant and by his empathic concern with the servant's suffering. Indeed, the officer's pain is so intense that it disrupts his sleep, and he feels as though he had been pierced by a sharp dagger. In an effort to reduce his own suffering, the officer dashes back to his servant's quarters and begs forgiveness. In the morning, he refuses to fire a shot in the duel. He then resigns his military commission and devotes the rest of his life to serving others.

Source: Fyodor Dostoyevsky, *The Brothers Karamazov* (New York: Signet, 1957; originally published, 1881): 273.

nečni, 1972), then the guilty are more helpful than nonguilty observers, toward both the injured party (specific guilt, resulting in restitution) or a different person (generalized guilt). Furthermore, when people witness a misfortune caused by someone who does not stop to help, or even to apologize, then the witnesses are more likely to volunteer help to the victim than are the guilty parties themselves (Konečni, 1972). This finding indicates that perceiving an injustice produces an even stronger incentive to be altruistic than does guilt.

The preceding research supports both guilt and sympathy explanations of altruism. But perhaps what we are calling guilt or sympathy is really just a negative mood that can be escaped by performing a helpful act but that also can be reduced by other means as well. For example, in one study, when subjects who had inflicted or witnessed harm received an unexpected monetary reward, they were *less* likely to help than subjects who received no unexpected rewards and were left in the negative moods (Cialdini, Darby, and Vincent, 1973). This points out that "altruistic" behavior may sometimes be motivated by a desire to terminate the negative affect associated with guilt; if alternative ways of terminating the state arise, prosocial action is not likely. One interesting demonstration of this phenomenon showed that male subjects who were entering a church for confession were more likely to donate to a charity than subjects who were leaving confession (Harris, Benson, and Hall, 1975).

Thus, it appears that harm-doing, whether committed or simply witnessed by the actor, can increase prosocial action. Rawlings established that the desire to be helpful increases after seeing an injustice; Konečni added the knowledge that helpfulness increases still fur-

The United States has traditionally offered refuge to victims of persecution and oppression in other parts of the world. However, when South Vietnamese refugees fled the communist takeover in 1975, restitution—in this case, compensation for losses and hardships caused in part by the American military involvement in Vietnam—was an additional factor in the decision to welcome them. *(Tony Korody / Sygma)*

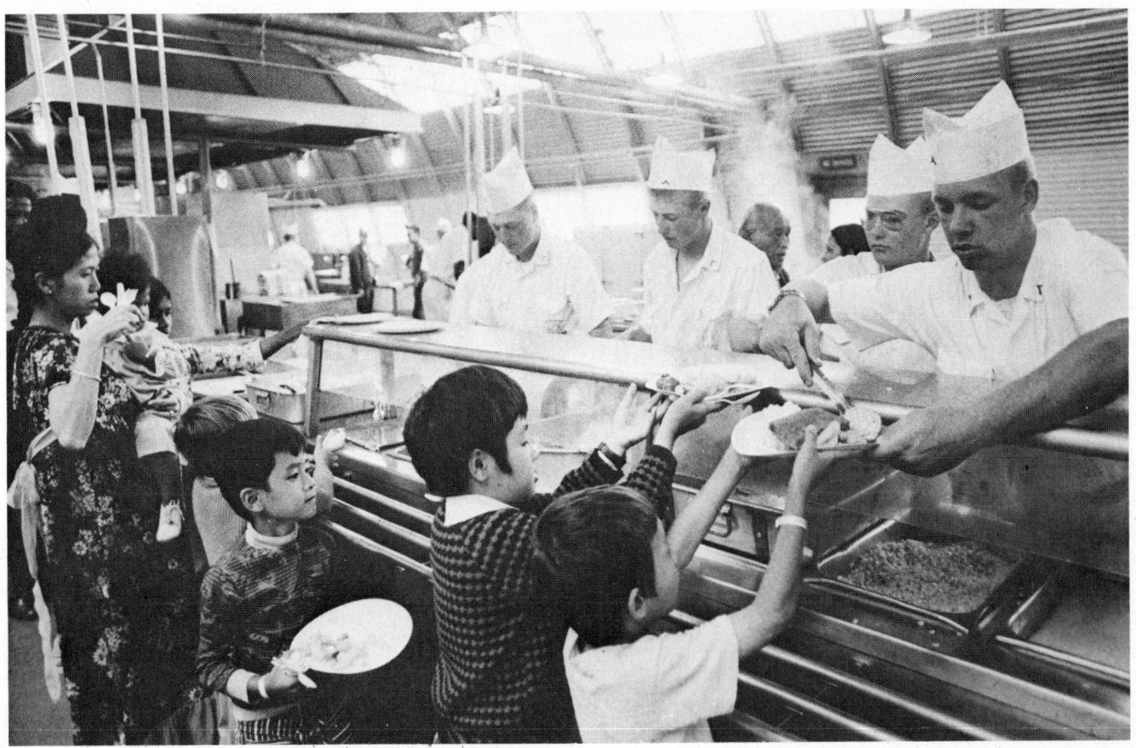

ther if the potential benefactor did not himself or herself injure the victim. But later research showed that other events, such as confession or receiving an unexpected reward, can reduce the extent of prosocial behavior.

Guilt or Image Repair? The effects of guilt and sympathy on altruism seem to have been elaborated satisfactorily by the line of research just described. But one nagging question remains: Are the effects of guilt on altruism really attributable to an internalized feeling of guilt, or are they merely the results of having been *observed* transgressing? In other words, is helpfulness caused merely by a desire to repair one's flagging image in the eyes of others, or is it due to genuine feelings of guilt? The image-repair explanation seems unfounded when Ruth Fisher's (1971) report is considered: unwitnessed transgression motivates donations to charity that are every bit as generous as those prompted by witnessed transgression. It seems safe to conclude, therefore, that the effects of transgression on altruism are at least partly caused by feelings of guilt and not necessarily by a quest for image repair. This final observation serves to solidify our previous conclusions about the effects of guilt and sympathy on altruism.

We have now examined how characteristics of the individual—both personality factors and affective states—may influence prosocial behavior. We have also seen that we often need to know the particular context in which an act occurs to know how the individual will respond. Therefore, we now turn to an examination of how the surrounding situation influences altruism. As you read about the various situational determinants of prosocial behavior, keep in mind that these situational factors generally interact with characteristics of the individuals involved.

INFLUENCE OF THE SURROUNDING SITUATION

In this section we will examine how the surrounding situation influences prosocial behavior. The surrounding situation can consist of a large number of different kinds of factors: the presence or absence of others, the nature of others present, a big city or small town, a relaxed environment or a stressful one, the nature of the recipient of aid. All of these have been found to affect the way in which we respond to others. One of the most important factors in the surrounding situation is other people. So first we will examine some ways that those around us may influence our tendency to behave prosocially.

INFLUENCE OF OTHERS

Perhaps the simplest way that others affect us is through modeling—how watching another perform prosocial acts affects our own tendency to do so. Our discussion will focus first on the relative effects of what models say versus what they do. Then we will examine how the presence of others influences a bystander to intervene in an emergency. Finally, we will consider how altruism is affected by the personal characteristics of the potential recipient.

DOING UNTO OTHERS AS OTHERS DO One of the central themes of this book is that people are affected by the presence of others, and altruism is no exception. By observing others' altruism, we are reminded of what we "ought" to do when someone is in need; we can learn new patterns of behavior in situations we have never confronted before; or we can become aware of the possible consequences of helping.

Several studies have demonstrated the potent effect that observing prosocial behavior may have on eliciting prosocial behavior. Bryan and Test (1967) found that simply watching someone change a flat tire or donate to the Salvation Army makes one likely to do the same. Similar effects have been found for such diverse behaviors as aiding in a search (Ross, 1970), volunteering to be in an experiment (Rosenbaum and Blake, 1955), or donating to a charity (Rushton, 1975). The evidence from both naturalistic and laboratory settings seems to establish that an altruistic act by one person can substantially increase the chances of altruistic acts by others.

However, the effects of models are not always so straightforward. For example, Macaulay (1970) studied the effects of generous and stingy models in a Christmas-time field experiment. Upon approaching a street-corner Santa Claus ringing a bell for needy children, a female model either contributed some money along with some kind words about giving or rudely refused to donate and rushed on. Donations from real passers-by were noted immediately after the model had acted charitably or uncharitably and also in control periods. As expected, donations increased when a model had donated money; but, surprisingly, the model who refused to donate also led to increased donations as compared to the control periods, although not to the extent of the generous model. Macaulay suggests that this "Scrooge" figure may have had a "boomerang effect," reminding others of what was actually an appropriate response. Another possible explanation may be the just-world hypothesis, already discussed, which suggests that we will act to restore a belief that the world operates in a just and humane fashion.

Although we learn important information from models about what behaviors are appropriate, it is also clear that we don't always model the behaviors that we see around us. Research summarized in the next section explores factors that affect our tendency to emulate prosocial action.

Model-Observer Similarity The effect of a model depends on who the model is as well as on what the model does. This point was demonstrated in an interesting field experiment by Hornstein, Fisch, and Holmes (1968). These researchers carefully "lost" several open envelopes on the sidewalks of Manhattan. From each envelope protruded a man's wallet containing money. Also, in each envelope was a brief note from someone who apparently had previously found the wallet and was returning it to its owner. In other words, the finder of the envelope was led to believe that the wallet had been lost once before, but that the writer of the note had lost it again before he or she was able to return it. The writer of the note thus constituted a model.

Hornstein and his colleagues reasoned that a model who seemed dissimilar from the observer would not have as strong an effect on the observer as would a model who was similar (see Table 9.1). In order to vary the similarity between observer and model, they created the impression that the model was from a different cultural background. One set of notes accompanying the wallet was composed in broken English and explained that the writer was a visitor to the United States. Another set of notes, on the other hand, was composed in normal English prose. For example, one of the normal notes stated, "I found your wallet which I am returning. Everything is here just as I found it." The contrasting note from the culturally dissimilar model said, "I am visit your country finding your ways not familiar and strange. But I find your wallet which I here return. Everything is here just as I find it." The notes also mentioned the pleasure of being able to help someone in need (positive condition) or were neutral, as in the examples above.

The experimenters stationed observers where the observers could see when an enveloped was picked up and record the characteris-

TABLE 9.1 RETURNS OF WALLETS

CONDITION	TOTAL RETURNS	TOTAL NOT RETURNED*
Similar model		
Neutral note	**12**	**8**
Positive (courteous) note	**14**	**6**
Negative (complaining) note	**2**	**18**
Dissimilar model		
Neutral note	**4**	**11**
Positive (courteous) note	**5**	**10**
Negative (complaining) note	**6**	**9**

***Includes *no return* and *returned but not intact*.**

***Source:* Adapted from H. Hornstein, E. Fisch, and M. Holmes, "Influence of a Model's Feeling About His Behavior and His Relevance as a Comparison Other on Observers' Helping Behavior," *Journal of Personality and Social Psychology* 10 (1968): 225.**

tics of the person who retrieved it, such as sex and estimated age. Altruism was measured by the number of wallets that people returned intact with the money.

The results showed that almost two-thirds of the finders returned the wallet when the model was similar to them, but more than half failed to do so when the model was dissimilar, as shown in Table 9.1. However, if the similar model complained of the inconvenience (the negative condition in Table 9.1), the enhanced altruism was eliminated—unlike the effects of the positive and neutral notes.

Factors other than similarity also influence whether a modeled behavior will be performed or not. The nurturance of a model as well as the power or prestige of a model are potent determinants of the model's effectiveness (Rushton, 1976). Parents, respected others, people in positions of power, warm, effective people are all likely to attract our attention and perhaps lead us to model their behaviors. But what happens when a model's verbal admonitions are discrepant with the model's actual behavior? We will look at this question in the next section.

Do as I Say but Not as I Do A problem confronted by parents the world over is to get their children to do as they say. While most of us verbalize lofty values of concern, fairness, and altruism, our behavior may be less than noble. And parents often find that children are quick to pick up on discrepancies between verbal admonitions and actual behavior. Most studies of modeling have used behavioral models of one sort or another. Some researchers (for example, Harris, 1968; Rosenbaum and Blake, 1955) have utilized verbal cues as well, but only a few attempts have been made to compare the relative effectiveness of behavioral and verbal models.

In one such study, Joan Grusec and Sandra Skubiski (1970) exposed elementary-school children either to a *behavioral model*—who donated to charity half of his or her winnings from a game—or to a *verbal model*—who did not play the game but strongly endorsed the idea that winnings should be shared equally with charity. No model was witnessed by a control group. The results indicated that behavioral modeling elicited larger donations from the children than did verbal exhortations. In fact, only under fairly specific circumstances was verbal modeling more effective than no model at all—only when the potential donor was female *and* the model had previously established a warm, nurturant relationship with the subject.

What do these results suggest to parents, who from time immemorial have urged their children to do as they are told and not as they see others do? The parents of daughters may be able to rely somewhat on verbal modeling, if Grusec and Skubiski's findings are any indication. But must the parents of sons expect verbal appeals to have little effect on altruistic behavior? The answer is complicated. James Bryan and Nancy Walbek (1970) found that verbal exhortations can have an effect on observers, regardless of their sex, but only on their *verbal* behavior. Their child subjects observed films of a model who either donated winnings to charity or refused to donate and who simultaneously made statements that were approving, disapproving, or neutral about sharing. The subsequent behavior of these children showed that their tendency to share was affected by the model's behavior but not by the model's words. However, when each child was asked to tape-record a statement telling the next child what to do, the child's statement typically reflected the influence of the original model's words. The children advocated more sharing when the model had either approved or disapproved of sharing than when the model had made neutral statements. It is as if *any* statement about sharing—greedy or generous—calls forth the norm of altruism. Thus, the children's statements were virtually unrelated to what they had seen and done themselves, but were related only to what they had heard. Apparently, behavioral modeling influences an observer's behavior, whereas verbal modeling influences his or her verbalizations.

These results do contain a message for parents: if parents only want their children to *say* that people should help others, it is probably sufficient that the parents just tell the children so; but if parents want their children to help others, the parents must act altruistically themselves rather than simply talk about it. To their surprise, Bryan and Walbek found that modeling of hypocrisy—that is refusing to share while verbally approving sharing—works in very much the same way as does the modeling of other behaviors: the modeled behavior produces more of the same, regardless of what children hear.

LONG-TERM EFFECTS OF MODELS

The research thus far has focused on short-term effect of models. What evidence exists that witnessing prosocial action has any long-term consequences for people's behavior? This question has great societal importance, for if the effects of models are only momentary, then we must turn to other means for increasing prosocial concerns.

In one study of the delayed effects of models, children who observed a model share resources were more generous immediately afterward as well as after an eight-week interval than children who did not see this, even when the experimental context was varied and different measures of altruism were used (Rushton, 1975). Other research has investigated the effects of socialization and child-rearing practices on altruism. For example, Hoffman (1975a) asked fifth graders to nominate three same-sexed classmates who were most likely to "care about how other kids feel and try not to hurt their feelings" and "to stick up for some kid that the other kids are making fun of or calling names." At the same time, their parents were asked to rank eighteen values in order of importance in their own value systems. These included values like "showing consideration of others' feelings," "putting work before play," "going out of one's way to help other people." Presumably, parents who placed high values on altruism will provide good models of caring, helping, and consideration.

Hoffman found that the fathers of the most helpful and considerate boys and the mothers of the girls with these same characteristics ranked altruism high in their own hierarchy of values. Apparently, the degree of altruism shown by the parent of the same sex has the most impact on the child's propensity to perform altruistic acts. This is undoubtedly related to the fact that, at this age, children are likely to identify most strongly with the parent of their own sex and, consequently, to incorporate and imitate that parent's behavior, attitudes, and motives.

Along the same lines Yarrow, Scott, and Waxler (1973) have tried to duplicate aspects of the family setting in the laboratory in order to see what variables affect the internalization of altruistic behavior. Two groups of preschool children spent extensive amounts of time over a two-week period with a caretaker who was nurturant and responsive with one group but with the other was somewhat cold and aloof. Then each child participated in two modeling sessions, separated by two days, in which she or he worked individually with the caretaker. The caretaker modeled sympathy, comfort, and help in distress situations that took place in either a diorama—a miniature playhouse with toy people and animals—or were realistically staged with another adult who appeared to bang her head against a table while getting some supplies. Two days after the last training session, the altruistic responses of the children were tested with a new series of pictures and dioramas and two behavioral incidents. Then, two weeks later, there was an additional session to evaluate the durability and generalization of the effects of training. In this session, the children were taken individually to a neighboring house to visit a mother and her baby, and, while there, they could help the mother by picking up a basket of spools or buttons that had spilled or by retrieving toys the baby had dropped out of her crib.

The two types of modeling had vastly different effects. If children had only seen symbolic altruism (the dioramas), they did not necessarily behave altruistically in real-life situations. However, those who had seen both forms of altruism modeled, symbolic and real, were likely to perform actual deeds of altruism. This effect was enhanced if the model had been warm and nurturant. In the follow-up test two weeks after the training, those who had been exposed to extended modeling by the nurturant caretaker were more likely to express sympathy and to help the mother or baby in the home setting than children in any other group.

As these results make clear, both the characteristics of the model (nurturance) as well as how consistent the model is in terms of verbal statements and behavior are important influences on children's prosocial behavior. This finding is borne out by an interesting real-world study of civil-rights workers.

David Rosenhan (1970) studied the background of college students who had given enormously of their time and resources in the civil-rights movement of the late 1950s. When Rosenhan interviewed the students' parents, he could distinguish easily between the most active volunteers and those civil-rights workers who had given but minimal amounts of time. Those who had given most generously had parents who were themselves socially concerned, while those who gave less were brought up by parents who seemed less than fully committed to prosocial action. So models convey a great deal of information to observers about what is appropriate and desirable in a particular situation, and observers are quick to spot inconsistencies. However, it is not always others' actions that influence us. Sometimes it is the mere presence of others that affects our prosocial behavior, as we will see in the next section.

EFFECTS OF OTHERS ON BYSTANDER INTERVENTION IN EMERGENCIES

From the Biblical story of the Good Samaritan to the Kitty Genovese slaying mentioned at the beginning of this chapter, one form of altruism is particularly significant to us as members of the human community: the willingness, in emergencies, of people to break out of their role as bystander and to come to another's assistance. Precipitated by such incidents as the urban violence and subway crimes described earlier, a series of studies have been conducted in search of the conditions that determine when people will respond to one another's distress. This research on *bystander intervention* has grown out of the extensive efforts of two social psychologists, John Darley and Bibb Latané.

Darley and Latané (1968) were particularly struck by the failure of witnesses to the Genovese murder to help the victim in any way. Here was a situation in which thirty-eight people witnessed the slaying of a woman, and no one acted to save her. Although each of us might like to imagine that we would spring instantly into action and, heedless of danger, run to the aid of the victim, the fact that no one confronted Kitty Genovese's murderer will probably not come as a surprise. Even the most idealized notion of helping does not require the chance bystander to face a knife-wielding killer. But what is surprising and seems so incomprehensible is the failure of the bystanders to do anything at all during the thirty-minute assault. No one organized the neighbors to go out and help; the police were not summoned; no one even called an ambulance or checked the victim after the assailant left.

Darley and Latané were impressed by the witnesses' apparent lack of social responsibility. They were also struck by the weak explanations for the bystanders' inaction offered by the newspapers. The effects of living in a megalopolis, increased alienation, apathy, and other assorted theories seemed incomplete explanations of why people fail to intervene to help others; these same factors fail to account for any number of prosocial acts that *are* performed by city dwellers. Darley and Latané discounted these general cultural factors and looked instead to those situational factors that are specific to emergencies.

Because most emergencies are, at least initially, ambiguous events from an observer's point of view, *the definition of the situation* as one requiring action—by anyone—is the first step in the intervention process. If the situation is not defined as an emergency, then obviously no action is required and the decision-making process stops. Because the situation is ambiguous, and because one risks making a fool of oneself by acting inappropriately, the presence of other people who do not appear alarmed will tend to produce a social definition of the situation as one not requiring any action.

Even if the observer defines the situation as an emergency, another decision must be made about the appropriate course of action. People are generally cautious about taking responsibilities; they fear getting blamed if anything goes wrong. The presence of more than one bystander causes the perceived responsibility to be diffused among the observers. As a result, each bystander feels *less personally responsible* for

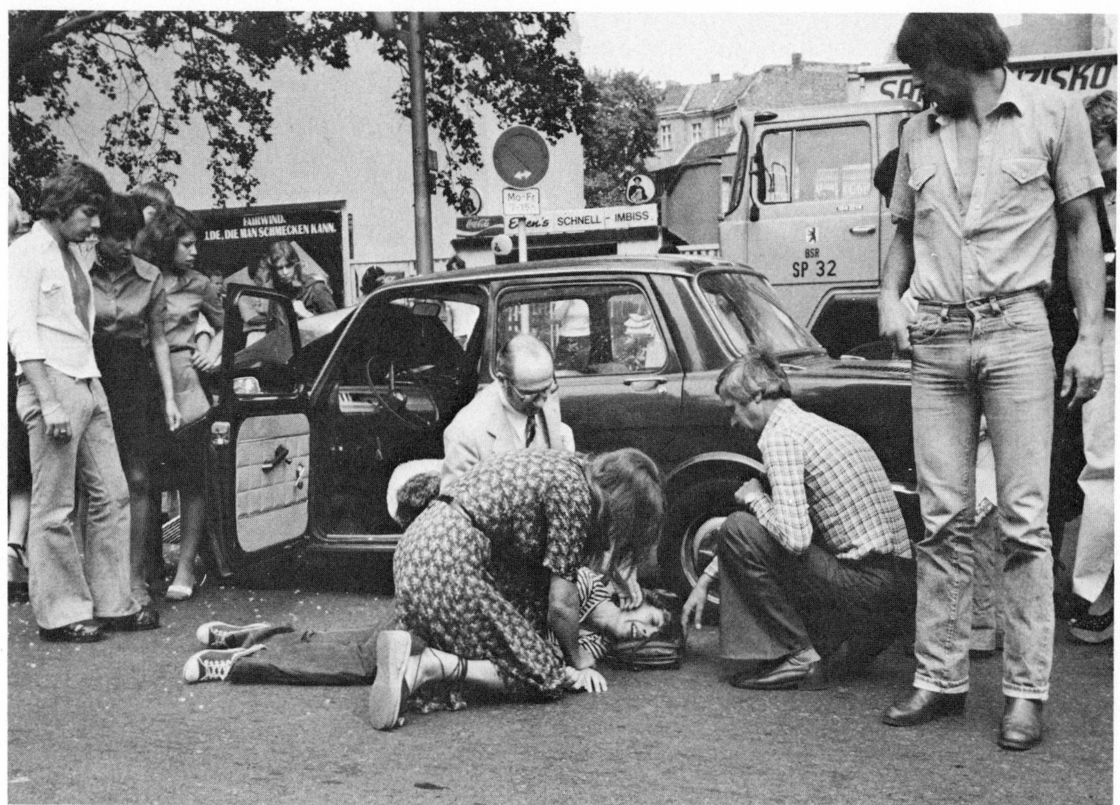

When a number of bystanders witness an accident, each one tends to assess the responses of the others before he or she considers intervention. *(© Bernard Pierre Wolff 1976 / Photo Researchers, Inc.)*

the situation than if he or she were alone. Because the thirty-eight witnesses to the Genovese slaying were in separate apartments, relatively certain that their neighbors were aware of what was happening, each could rationalize that the situation did not directly require his or her personal action.

To test these two ideas regarding the effects of others on bystander intervention, Darley and Latané performed several experiments in which they confronted subjects with simulated emergencies.

DEFINING THE SITUATION In one of their studies, Latané and Rodin (1969) summoned their subjects ostensibly to participate in a market research study. While the subjects thought they were waiting for the experiment to begin, they heard what sounded like someone falling and being injured in the adjoining room. All the while, however, the experimenters were watching to see if responses to this possible emergency differed according to whether the subject was waiting alone, with a friend, or with a passive stranger who was actually a confederate of the experimenters.

From the standpoint of all subjects, the situation was ambiguous; it was not clear to them exactly what had happened. Because of the uncertainty of the situation, the experimenters predicted that whenever another person was present, a desire for *social comparison* would prompt a subject to use the other's reactions to interpret the ambiguous cues. The experimenters reasoned that people do not wish to commit themselves until they are reasonably sure that a particular course of action is appropriate. When alone, each person has only himself or herself to rely on to define a situation. The presence of others adds complexity to the definition process, and when the others are not responding with alarm, the individual may assume that no emergency exists. Furthermore, Latané and Rodin suspected that people in emergency situations tend to keep their responses at a minimum until a consensus is reached about the seriousness of the situation. They expected that strangers would hesitate longer before helping a third person than would friends, because the risk of appearing foolish would seem greater among strangers than friends.

The results confirmed Latané and Rodin's expectations. Subjects in the company of a passive, unconcerned stranger were substantially less helpful than were subjects who waited with a friend. The most helpful of all were those subjects who waited alone.

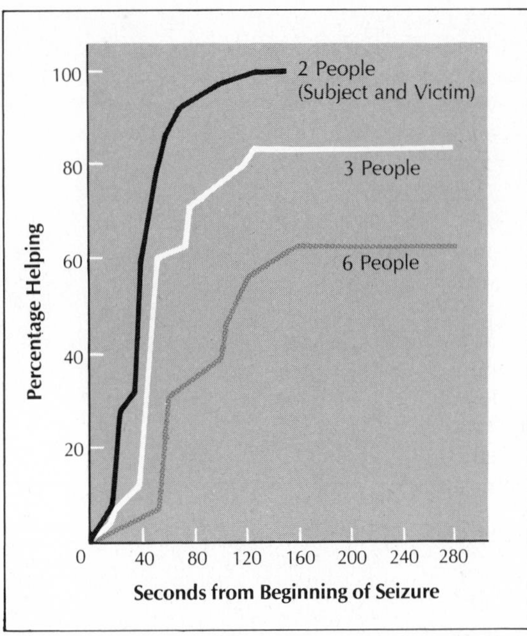

FIGURE 9.2 Darley and Latané (1968) found that the number of bystanders affects diffusion of responsibility. Via an intercom, subjects heard a simulation of a student having a seizure. People tended to act most often and most quickly when they thought they were the sole source of help. The greater the number of witnesses they believed to be hearing the seizure, the less likely they were to assume responsibility.

DIFFUSION OF RESPONSIBILITY A different experiment conducted by Darley and Latané in 1968 involved subjects who thought they were participating in a discussion group. This study varied the number of others who were supposedly present in the discussion. To better understand the effects of an experience like this, consider it from the viewpoint of a subject arriving for the experiment.

When you arrive, the experimenter directs you to a booth. You sit alone but are able to communicate via an intercom with other participants in the group. The experimenter tells you how many other participants are in the group. As the discussion gets under way, the other participants describe, via the intercom, their reactions to college and to city life. Suddenly, one of the other students, who has already mentioned that he had been anxious and upset during his first few months at college and that he is subject to seizures, begins to stutter, and his breathing becomes labored. He complains that he is "having a bit of trouble." His speech becomes increasingly incoherent, he says he needs help, and then there is silence. The experiment requires you to stay in your booth, and you cannot talk to anyone because the intercom opens only into the victim's booth. You have no idea where the experimenter went. Chances are, you have never before confronted a situation such as this. What would you do?

If you react as did most of Darley and Latané's subjects, the fewer the participants you believe are listening to the commotion over the intercom, the more likely you will be to act, and to act quickly. Hence, you will respond most rapidly when you believe yourself to be the sole witness to trouble. Figure 9.2 shows the response patterns of Darley and Latané's subjects.

The results of these two experiments are consistent with the two related hypotheses offered by Darley and Latané to explain why the presence of others inhibits bystander intervention. In the first place, passivity in others generates a tendency to define ambiguous situations as nonemergencies. Second, even when there is no opportunity for communication among bystanders (as in the second experiment), there is a tendency for the presence of others to diffuse responsibility for taking action.

The inhibiting effect of others can be seen not only in emergencies but in almost any situation where the appropriateness of intervention is unclear and responsibility is diffused. For example, Darley (1970) investigated the likelihood of reporting a crime in a drive-in market. Male undergraduates, either alone or with another "witness" (actually an experimental confederate), witnessed the theft of a case of beer. Even after the thief had left and the clerk returned to the room, the subjects who had been the sole witnesses to the theft were more likely to report the crime than if someone else were present.

Other studies have supported the diffusion-of-responsibility hypothesis but have also suggested certain limiting conditions. For example, both Korte (1971) and Bickman (1971) have shown that no diffusion of responsibility occurs when other bystanders are somehow unable to come to the aid of the victim. When subjects knew that the only other person who could assist in an emergency was either in another building (Bickman's study) or strapped down (Korte's study), they responded as quickly as if they were alone. This evidence suggests that the decision to intervene involves assessing not only the *number* of other people present but also their potential as interveners.

CLARIFYING THE SITUATION As Darley and Latané try to point out, when people fail to help another in need, it may not be caused by lack of concern but rather by a number of processes that serve to inhibit individual action. Clark and Word (1972, 1974) varied the ambiguity of the emergency situation and obtained encouraging results. In their study an emergency occurred while a subject was alone, with one other person, or with four other people. A workman carrying a ladder and a Venetian blind walked through the subject's room to the next room; shortly afterward there was the sound of the Venetian blind and the ladder falling. In the ambiguous condition the workman said nothing; in the unambiguous condition he cried out that he was hurt. When there was no cry from the next room, the usual bystander effect was obtained, with subjects who were alone being more likely to help than subjects who were with one other person or with four other people. However, when there was a cry for help and the ambiguity was low, subjects went to the aid of the victim *every time*, despite the number of bystanders.

In still other studies increased rates of intervention are *also* found if subjects are committed ahead of time to be responsible for someone's welfare. For example, if subjects were asked to watch someone's possessions while the owner went on an errand, the subjects pursued and even apprehended the "thief" despite the presence of others (Moriarty, 1975; Shaffer, Rozell, and Hendrich, 1975). In yet another version of Darley and Latané's "phantom discussion group" procedure, when the subjects believed that one member of the group was medically competent to deal with the accomplice's apparent seizure, the least intervention was volunteered. Thus, it seems that the likelihood of intervention is affected not only by the number of other bystanders present but also by their relative responsibility and capacity to be of assistance.

COSTS OF HELPING The decision whether or not to intervene in an emergency is more complex still when personal risk, rather than just embarrassment, is involved.

To determine the effects of personal risk on bystander intervention, Harvey Allen (1972) conducted an experiment on a subway train. One confederate sat next to a subject and gave false information to another confederate who had asked directions. The measure of intervention was how often subjects corrected the misdirections. Before the confederates exchanged the misdirections, however, the experimenters varied the demeanor of the information giver by having him behave in either a sarcastic, a physically threatening, or a neutral manner when yet another confederate tripped over his feet. Therefore, before having an opportunity to intervene, subjects had a chance to form some

DISPOSITIONS AND SITUATIONS

"FROM JERUSALEM TO JERICHO"

A few years ago John Darley and C. Daniel Batson (1973) became interested in the question of what types of people are most helpful to others and under what types of circumstances. In their own words, "for inspiration, we turned to the Bible, to what is perhaps the classical helping story in the Judeo-Christian tradition, the parable of the Good Samaritan."

> "And who is my neighbor?" Jesus replied, "A man was going down from Jerusalem to Jericho, and he fell among robbers, who stripped him and beat him, and departed, leaving him half dead. Now by chance a priest was going down the road; and when he saw him he passed by on the other side. So likewise a Levite, when he came to the place and saw him, passed by on the other side. But a Samaritan, as he journeyed, came to where he was; and when he saw him, he had compassion, and went to him and bound his wounds, pouring on oil and wine; then he set him on his own beast and brought him to an inn, and took care of him. And the next day he took out two denarii and gave them to the innkeeper, saying, 'Take care of him; and whatever more you spend, I will repay you when I come back.' Which of these three, do you think, proved neighbor to him who fell among the robbers?" He said, "The one who showed mercy on him." And Jesus said to him, "Go and do likewise." (Luke 10:29–37 RSV)

What sort of people were the priest, the Levite, and the Samaritan? Darley and Batson suggest that the priest and Levite were prominent religious functionaries, likely to be hurrying about on "church business." Their religiosity was apparently motivated by a concern about how they appeared to others. In contrast, the Samaritan was a religious outcast, less likely to have important business or responsibilities. His religiosity was probably motivated by an inner concern about ethical values.

The parable suggested several hypotheses to Darley and Batson: first, helpfulness may depend on the nature of a person's religiosity; second, helpfulness may depend on whether a person is thinking about ethical values versus business affairs; and third, helpfulness may simply depend on how hurried a person is at the time of an emergency.

Each of these hypotheses was tested in a field experiment. The researchers went to Princeton Theological Seminary, where they first tested sixty-seven seminary students regarding the nature of their religiosity. Later, each student was asked to return for further information. At this point the researchers manipulated two situational variables and set up a fake emergency. In order to lead some students to think about ethical values and others to think about business concerns, each half of the sample was given a different task. One group was asked to record a short talk about careers for seminary students. The other group was asked to read the Bible passages about the Good Samaritan and to record a short talk about this parable. Next, the researchers manipulated how much of a hurry the students were in to record their talks. All subjects were told that the recordings would be made in another building. One-third was told that they were late and should hurry over ("high hurry" condition); one-third was told that an assistant was ready to make the recording and they should go right over ("intermediate hurry" condition); and one-third was told that the assistant wouldn't be ready for a few minutes, but

opinion about the potential risks of antagonizing the information giver. Allen found that when the information giver appeared physically threatening, subjects intervened the least; they were more willing to intervene when the confederate had been merely sarcastic, and they were most helpful when he had made a neutral response. Most interestingly, these effects persisted even after the information giver left the subway. Apparently, once bystanders assess a they might as well head on over ("low hurry" condition).

As each seminary student walked through an alley to get to the other building, he encountered an emergency much like the Biblical parable. Slumped in a doorway, head down, eyes closed, not moving, was a young man. As the subject passed by, the slumped figure coughed twice. If the subject offered help, the victim replied groggily, "Oh, thank you. (Cough) . . . No, it's all right. (Pause) . . . I've got this respiratory condition. (Cough) . . . The doctor's given me these pills to take and I just took one . . . If I just sit and rest for a few minutes I'll be OK. . . . Thanks very much though. (Smiles weakly)" The victim, who was blind to the subject's condition, rated each passing subject on the amount of help offered, using a scale that ranged from 0 (no help) to 5 (refusing to leave the victim).

How helpful were these seminary students? And what factors best predicted their helpfulness? Was it their religiosity? Their concern about ethical versus business affairs? Or how hurried they were? As can be seen in the graph below, only the latter variable—how hurried the subject was—significantly influenced the amount of helping offered. The more hurried these seminary students were, the less likely they were to stop and help the slumped victim—even if they were hurrying to tape a speech about the Good Samaritan. While there was some tendency for students who were going to make the Good Samaritan speech to be more helpful than students who were going to make the career speech, this tendency was not statistically significant. Finally, the nature of a person's religiosity had no relationship to whether or not help was offered. But among those who did stop and help, the more orthodox the student's religious views, the more likely he was to refuse to leave the victim alone, despite the victim's assurances that help was not needed.

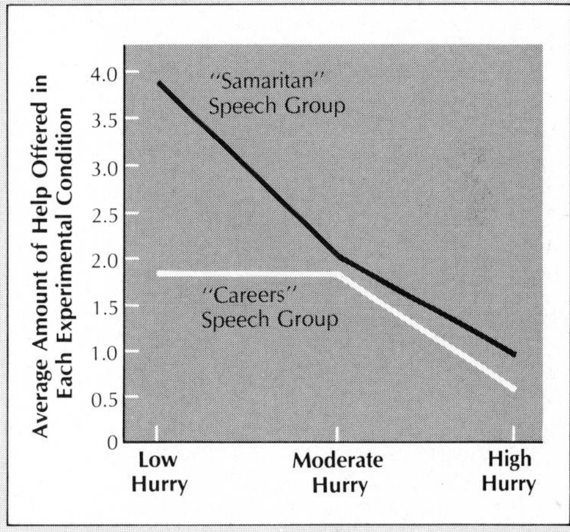

What conclusions can we draw from this research? Helpfulness seems to depend on how much time one has—whether it's convenient to stop and offer help. But once the decision is made to help, then the kind of help offered may reflect one's inner convictions. Ironically, perhaps the Biblical parable makes this same point. The Good Samaritan may have been an unimportant man—someone with time on his hands and no schedule to meet—someone who could afford to stop and help another, on the road "from Jerusalem to Jericho."

situation and decide what to do, they don't change their mind, even after the threat is removed. This apparent intransigence may result from the bystanders' desire to avoid appearing inconsistent—to themselves as well as to others.

We talked about theories of altruism earlier in the chapter and mentioned a model proposed by Piliavin, Piliavin, and Rodin (1975), which argues that the perceived *costs* of intervening are important determinants of an indi-

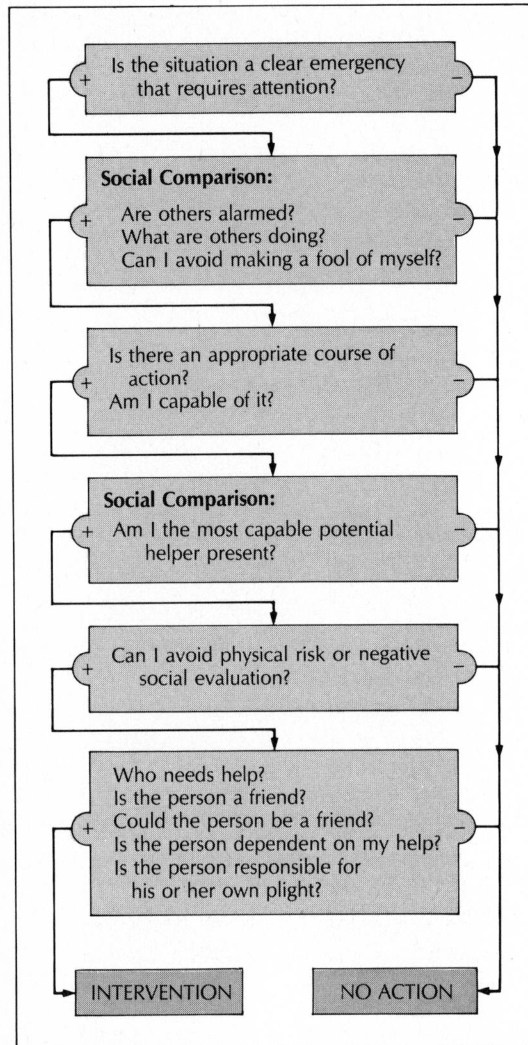

FIGURE 9.3 Whether a bystander will intervene in an emergency is dependent upon many factors, as shown here in schematic form. A negative answer to *any* of these questions will probably lead to nonintervention. However, a positive answer to one question will lead the bystander to the next question, and his or her intervention is likely only if *all* answers are "yes."

vidual's tendency to help. In general as the costs of helping go up, direct intervention becomes less likely. These costs are of two types. The first type is the cost of intervention to the *bystander*. If the attacker of Kitty Genovese is truly a vicious person, then attempting to help could result in a direct physical cost to the bystander (that is, the bystander could be stabbed). If the information giver in the Allen study is really combative, then it is prudent to avoid the situation.

The second type of cost is the cost to the *victim* if the bystander fails to help. How much trouble is the victim in? How much potential benefit can the bystander provide? A person attacked by a mob of people may be in genuine jeopardy, but little extra cost may be involved if the bystander fails to intervene directly, since the bystander may not be able to accomplish very much. Piliavin, Piliavin, and Rodin expect direct intervention to occur when the bystander does not accrue high costs for trying to help and the victim will suffer great harm if the bystander fails to act. When the cost to the bystander is high, then the bystander is motivated to reduce arousal by choosing an alternative method to deal with the situation. The most common alternative may be a redefinition of the situation such that it is viewed as a nonemergency or as a situation that does not call for a response by the bystander. The latter redefinition is akin to Darley and Latané's concept of diffusion of responsibility. If the situation can be responded to by people other than a particular bystander, then that bystander is especially likely to diffuse responsibility when the costs of intervention are high.

Defining a situation and deciding whether to intervene are complicated by both real and imagined consequences of taking the action. In addition to fear for personal safety, people often fear negative evaluation from others. Consider, for example, the agonies of indecision expressed by one of Charles Korte's student subjects when he was confronted with the sounds of an asthmatic attack apparently coming from another participant over the intercom (Korte, 1971: p. 153):

> I am wondering if this is a put-on job and I am the only subject. Is this part of the experiment, not seeming to breathe? I'll bet it is. If not, the other two can take care of him. Am I willing to risk someone's life just to prove I'm right? I guess so—no legal obligation, of course. Should I just feel stupid or guilty the rest of my life?

The particular circumstances faced by this person were engendered by an experimental situation, but it is easy to imagine the same sort of process taking place under normal circumstances. In fact, Staub (1970) found that the older a child gets, the more reluctant he or she is to intervene in an ambiguous situation for fear of doing something inappropriate. It seems that human beings are taught early in life that losing face is one of the worst things that can happen. When asked why they failed to intervene during various emergencies, witnesses said they were afraid they had misconstrued the situation, were afraid they would somehow make things worse if they intervened, or hoped that someone better equipped to deal with the situation would come along.

We have discussed several situational factors that help determine whether or not people will attempt to help their fellow human beings: the social definition of emergencies, diffusion of responsibility, and fear of consequences. An additional factor is the effects of living in a complex urban environment, as discussed in the next section.

EFFECTS OF THE ENVIRONMENT

It is the subjective impression of many city dwellers and social commentators that urban people are less sensitive to the suffering of others than their rural counterparts. Darley (1970) places much of the blame on the daily confrontations urbanites—and particularly the urban poor— face with unresponsive bureaucracies, inadequate public facilities, and uncaring public officials. He feels that constant exposure to these frustrating encounters produces in the individual a pervasive feeling of helplessness in controlling what will happen to oneself or others. When presented with a helping situation, a person with this *low-control-of-effects syndrome* will tend to feel that anything he or she does will be of no avail and, furthermore, may actually have detrimental consequences.

Several studies have in fact revealed that urban dwellers seem less responsive to the needs of others than rural dwellers. For example, rural residents have offered more assistance than their urban counterparts when confronted with a "wrong number" telephone request for help (McKenna, 1976; Korte and Kerr, 1973) and have also been more likely to mail apparently "lost" postcards found on the street and to return overpayments of change to store clerks (Korte and Kerr, 1973). Other research has found that noise (Sherrod and Downs, 1974; Mathews and Canon, 1977), crowding (Bickman, 1971; Cohen and Spacapan, 1978), and environmental overload all tend to make people unresponsive to the needs of others. Exactly how the urban environment may exert these effects on altruism is a complicated question that will be discussed in Chapter 12. Suffice it to say at this point that complex, overloading, and restricting environments often reduce the level of altruism in people. Urban environments, then, may be a pervasive background situational influence on helping behavior.

A final situational influence on helping that we will examine is the identity of the person who needs help. We have discussed how models and bystanders can affect our prosocial behavior. Now we investigate factors about the victims that mediate our helping.

THE RECIPIENT: THE FACE OF THE FORTUNATE

Whether circumstances encourage or discourage prosocial concern depends in part on who the person in need is. Most people do not feel equal concern toward everyone; friends and family usually receive preferred treatment over strangers or brief acquaintances, especially when cost or risk to the benefactor is involved. Close personal ties are not, however, the only assets of potential recipients that make us willing to help them, as we will see in this section.

Friendship, almost by definition, refers to a relationship in which the participants can expect to render and receive aid when it is needed. Because this altruistic element in friendship seems so obvious, researchers have not devoted much experimental attention to altruistic patterns among friends. The evidence that does exist, however, is not unequivocal. One study (Sawyer, 1966) found as expected that close friends felt the most altruistic concern for each other and that antagonists felt the least, but a study with child subjects found no preference for friends over strangers when distributing rewards (Floyd, 1964). When questioned, the children said their generosity toward strangers was intended to win new friends, while their relative stinginess to friends was often a retribution for past selfishness from friends. Perhaps many of us may be concerned about appearances with strangers and thus more superficially considerate around those we do not know well, while we may tend to take our friends for granted when bestowing small favors. But when large sacrifices are demanded, it is for our friends that most of us are willing to commit ourselves in a real way.

As noted in Chapter 7, similarity is an important component of friendship, and similarity is equally important in altruism. For example, several studies have found that people are more willing to help members of their own race than members of a different race (Benson, Karabenick, and Lerner, 1976; Gaertner, 1975).

A subtle dimension of similarity was explored by Harvey Hornstein and his colleagues (1971, 1977). They attempted to create a perception of altruism by using the "lost letter" technique (Hornstein, Mason, Sole, and Heilman, 1971). In a predominantly Jewish neighborhood, unsealed stamped letters containing a questionnaire with either pro-Israeli or pro-Arab responses were dropped on the street. Hornstein predicted more helping toward the similar letter writer than the dissimilar one, but, surprisingly, there were no differences in the rates of pro-Israeli and pro-Arab letters that were mailed in. In a later study, temptation was varied by including either a nonnegotiable money order or cash along with the similar or dissimilar attitude questionnaire. Given the temptation of enclosed cash, the rate of helping was then much greater for the similar other than for the dissimilar other (Hornstein, Holloway, and Sole, 1977).

Another characteristic of the recipient that may elicit altruism is *dependence*. Leonard Berkowitz and his colleagues set up a laboratory situation in which "supervisors'" rewards were highly dependent on their "workers'" productivity (Berkowitz and Connor, 1966; Berkowitz and Daniels, 1963). As expected, productivity increased concurrently with the level of the supervisor's dependence on the workers, even when the individual workers thought that the supervisor would not know how much each had produced, a factor that discounted fear of negative evaluation as a motive. Elizabeth Midlarsky (1968) also found that experimental subjects volunteered more help to a partner with broken eyeglasses than to a less dependent recipient, even when the act of helping resulted in electric shocks for the helpers themselves. Similarly, former clients of a vocational rehabilitation center were likely to volunteer assistance to new clients when the new clients' need was made to appear great (Cowan and Inskeep, 1978).

Despite these studies that suggest that help increases with the needy person's dependency, it is important to realize that other social-psychological processes may sometimes counter the effects of dependency. For instance, the donor may feel restricted freedom of action if the dependency is made too strong, and this may produce a boomerang effect—a decrease in helpfulness rather than an increase (Brehm, 1966). This may in part account for a recent finding (Fink, Rey, Johnson, Spenner, Morton, and Flores, 1975) that blood donors were more responsive to appeals emphasizing equity—such as the ability to withdraw blood from the blood bank later on if they themselves needed it—than the dependency of people in need of blood. The effect was most pronounced for males, where 91 percent donated in the equity condition while only 33 percent did so in the dependency condition, versus 82 percent and 75 percent for females respectively.

Research by Schopler (1967) also found decreased helping under conditions of high dependency. An interesting feature of these studies, though, is that they involved situations in which any one of several people could have helped the person in need; therefore, subjects could have rationalized that someone else would help. As the research on diffusion of responsibility makes clear, because someone is in dire need does not guarantee that others will come to his or her aid. Dependence may evoke altruism only when the potential benefactors feel that attention is focused on them.

One factor that seems to mediate the effects of dependence is the perceived origin of that dependence. At one extreme, when people appear to have gotten themselves into a jam or seem to have "made their own bed," the obligation to help is not compelling. For example, when male college students were given an opportunity to help a peer at cost to themselves in a money-earning situation, they were likely to help when they perceived the other person as having been made dependent by the experimenter rather than by his own decisions (Schopler and Matthews, 1965).

In addition to actual dependence, our perceptions of other people's moods—how emotionally needy they are—also affect our tendency to help. Enzle and Harvey (1979) investigated whether people are more likely to help a person who seems sad than someone in the same situation who does not seem sad. They found that female subjects tend to offer more help than males to others who are portrayed as being depressed, but only when the subjects felt that there was some likelihood of alleviating the person's sadness. When the others were portrayed as having been depressed for a long time, sadness did not lead to increased helping. So sadness may evoke helping only when we have hopes of doing something to change that need that produced the sadness.

The number of the victims as well as the nature of the victims can also affect helping. Remember that when the number of *witnesses* is increased, intervention in emergencies is reduced. Wegner and Schaefer (1978) hypothesized that increasing the number of victims might have the opposite effect because it would increase the salience of norms regarding an obligation to help. They were able to demonstrate both effects. In a work situation where some subjects worked at a disadvantage and thus were unlikely to receive a reward, there was a replication of the bystander effect—increased numbers of potential helpers led to reduced helping; but there was also a "concentration of responsibility" effect in which increased numbers of victims led to increased helping overall.

We have seen how a number of situational variables may operate to increase or decrease helping. Presumably, these situational factors combine in complex ways with each other as well as with those characteristics of individuals discussed earlier in the chapter. Thus, the ability to predict specific levels of altruism is always difficult.

Now we turn to a different problem: the effects of helping or not helping. What are the psychological consequences of having intervened to aid another person, and what are the consequences of failing to intervene?

THE EFFECTS OF ALTRUISM

As we have seen, people's helpfulness is affected by numerous circumstances. Often social-psychological analyses stop at this point with statements that certain conditions lead to certain behaviors. However, altruism is such an important topic for all of us that the consequences of our decisions whether or not to help another individual should be clearly understood. These effects have a bearing both on the ways in which we will behave and on those who benefit or suffer as a result of our decisions.

As shown in the following sections, one prosocial act tends to lead to others, but failing to help can create feelings about the victim or the situation that make subsequent helping unlikely. Also, people who receive help are sometimes less than completely grateful for their benefactors' efforts.

THE CHANGER AND THE CHANGED

One of the consequences of behaving prosocially is that we usually feel good about ourselves. As Cialdini and Kenrick (1976) have argued, the desire to feel good may be one of the reasons we engage in altruism. Indeed, one study found that a person's mood improves after helping someone else (Harris, 1977). Another study found that children reward themselves more generously after helping a normal child than a deaf child (Masters and Pisarowicz, 1975), perhaps because they feel that more is "owed" the disabled child than the normal child and thus the helping is less deserving of reward.

A more explicit question is: How do we perceive ourselves after helping someone else?

Dionne Warwick says: "Get your blood into circulation."

Call Red Cross now for a blood donor appointment.

Ad Council A Public Service of This Newspaper & The Advertising Council

An act of altruism, such as giving blood, not only benefits the recipient, but it also boosts the morale of the donor. *(Courtesy, Ad Council)*

What factors allow us to attribute altruism to ourselves when we have performed a helping act, and how do these attributions affect our future behavior? The general issue of attribution is discussed more fully in Chapter 6, but several studies have examined the relationship between helpfulness and self-attributions. In one study Paulhus, Shaffer, and Downing (1977) gave information to half of a group of blood donors stressing the self-sacrifice of donating one's blood. The other half received information emphasizing the personal benefits of the donation (for example, the donor's potential use of the blood bank's blood). Presumably, these different types of information might lead to different attributions in the subjects' own eyes about why they had chosen to donate blood. When the donors were later questioned about how likely they were to give blood in the future, more of those who had read the altruistic literature said they were likely to give blood in the future than those who read about the personal benefits. This was particularly true for first-time donors, who were probably less certain of the attributions to make for their own unfamiliar behaviors.

Batson, Cole, and Jasnoski (1978) found a similar effect. Subjects who were given a very small reward prior to helping someone else subsequently rated themselves as less altruistic than subjects who had received no reward for helping or who received the reward only after having helped. As both of these studies suggest, when people receive rewards or expect personal gain for helping, they are not likely to attribute altruism to themselves and, as Paulhus and his colleagues found, they are not likely to be altruistic in the future.

Once we come to see ourselves as people who help, we may then be likely to help out even more in the future. Freedman and Fraser (1966) demonstrated this effect by first going door to door and asking people to perform a relatively small favor—signing a petition to save the redwoods. Later, different experimenters approached these same people again and requested a much larger favor—allowing a large "Drive Safely" sign to be installed in their front yards. People who granted the initial small favor were more likely to perform the large favor than those who had never been asked to help in the first place. Freedman and Fraser called this the "foot in the door" technique for soliciting help.

RECIPROCITY: BALANCING THE SEESAW

As we mentioned in the theoretical section earlier in the chapter, one of the strongest norms about altruism is the norm compelling the recipient of help to return the favor if the occasion should arise. Indeed, Alvin Gouldner suggested in 1960 that this norm is a universal component of moral codes and that reciprocity is a force that contributes to the maintenance of a stable social structure. A survey of attitudes about social obligations (Muir and Weinstein, 1962) found that people did indeed subscribe to a norm of reciprocity, which they applied both to themselves and to others. Gouldner, however, was careful to distinguish between a *verbal* norm of reciprocity, which the survey seems to have demonstrated, and *behavioral* reciprocity. The norms people preach are sometimes only weakly related to the norms they practice.

Does the norm of reciprocity guide people's behavior as well as their verbalizations? As mentioned earlier, Berscheid and Walster (1978) have written extensively about factors affecting reciprocity of prosocial acts. That reciprocity occurs has been demonstrated frequently. Typical of these studies, for example, is the finding that children were likely to share crayons with another child if that child had previously shared candy with them (Staub and Sherk, 1970).

But what are some of the variables that affect reciprocated altruism? For example, is a large favor more likely than a small favor to stimulate help in return? Wilke and Lanzetta (1970) found evidence that a direct process of exchange may govern reciprocity of altruism: the more help that one of their subjects offered another, the more help the second subject was likely to reciprocate with when the original benefactor was in need.

However, the results of a study by Dean Pruitt (1968) indicate that the exchange may be influenced more by the relative size of the sacrifice than by the objective amount of material assistance. In an experimental game involving money sharing shown in Figure 9.4, a player who gave his or her partner a large percentage of a small sum (80 percent of $1) tended to receive more money from the partner in the next round than those who gave a small percentage of a larger sum (20 percent of $4), even though the actual sums of money yielded by the two percentages were identical. Even more striking was the discovery that people who gave a fixed percentage (20 percent) of their money tended to receive more money in return when they had started with only a small sum of money ($1) to share than if they had started with a larger sum ($4), even though the amount of money shared was actually less for the person with the smaller sum. In other words, the level of reciprocity is determined by the degree of sacrifice rather than by the absolute value of the original gift.

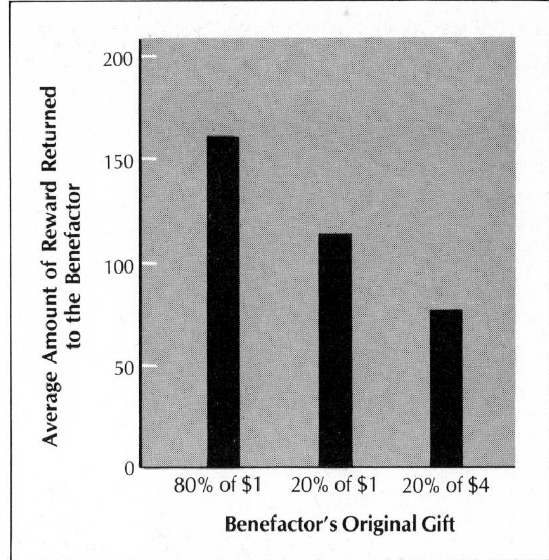

FIGURE 9.4 According to Pruitt (1968), the actual size of a gift has less effect upon a beneficiary's reciprocated generosity than does the size of the sacrifice it involves. Benefactors who gave 80 percent of $1 were likely to receive much greater rewards from beneficiaries than were those who gave 20 percent of $4—even though both amounts are the same. The beneficiaries also seemed to feel that 20 percent of $1 was a larger sacrifice than 20 percent of $4, even though it represents a smaller sum.

WHEN RECIPROCITY FAILS

It is not always the case, however, that receiving a favor increases a person's generosity. For example, if a favor does not appear to have been performed voluntarily, it does not lead to reciprocity (Goranson and Berkowitz, 1966). And a favor can actually decrease reciprocity toward the benefactor if the beneficiary receives that favor in an inappropriate situation, as Schopler and Thompson (1968) found when they offered subjects flowers under awkward circumstances. Furthermore, if help is received inadvertently, it is less likely to be reciprocated than if it is received intentionally (Greenberg and Frisch, 1972).

Even if an individual's motive for helping is not suspect, we may react negatively to help or a gift that seems to limit our freedom. Brehm and Cole (1966) found that when an unsolicited favor appeared to require a response from the recipient, people volunteered less help to the favor doer than did unobligated subjects. Thus an important determinant of our tendency to reciprocate is our perception of the motives of the actor.

THE REPERCUSSIONS OF FAILING TO HELP

We are frequently less helpful than we might be to others. For example, a staggering proportion of the residents in any institution for the aged, the crippled, or the mentally disturbed never receive a single visitor, even though relatives and friends often live nearby. And this plight of having our needs ignored is not limited to persons who are confined in institutions; indeed, it may afflict all of us in our time of need.

As became clear in the discussion of dependence, the fact that someone is in need does not guaranteee that people will rush to his or her assistance; in fact, a needy person may elicit the opposite reaction if the need is too intense or too frequent. Reminders of moral obligations may only make matters worse. As we have seen, if the cost is too great, if the potential benefactor is too depressed, or if there does not appear to be any way of rendering effective assistance, the potential benefactor may resent feeling obligated to help.

One way to cope with negative feelings toward the needy is to avoid thinking about their needs. The decision not to deal with the suffering of others may not be intentional; it probably is not the case, for example, that people say to themselves, "I've got to think of a way to quit feeling bad whenever I see a blind person." Nevertheless, people do use various means, conscious or unconscious, of avoiding their own unpleasant feelings regarding suffering. The solution often chosen by friends and relatives of inmates in various institutions involves simple avoidance of the victim; the relatives of a rest-home patient may find life too busy for visits or may come to believe that their relative "doesn't recognize us anyway" or that "it just upsets him or her." Similarly, most Americans, as soon as they are able, structure their lives so that they do not often confront the abject poor, the infirm, or the oppressed. Perhaps we all avoid confronting the reminders of injustice and of others' needs for assistance in order to preserve sanity in a world that is full of injustice and need.

In addition to physical avoidance of suffering, there is a cognitive process by which people sometimes justify their failures to alleviate suffering by justifying the suffering itself. Melvin Lerner's (1977) "just-world hypothesis" suggests that when a person sees others in need and yet fails to offer help, that observer will be motivated to perceive the victims as "bad" or as in some way deserving of their fate, thus rationalizing his or her passivity toward them. The obverse would also be expected: victims have gained esteem in the benefactor's eyes after he or she has helped them.

Evidence to support Lerner's theory is suggestive rather than direct, but what data exist support the theory. Several experiments have found that subjects who caused pain and difficulty for others (Bramel, 1969; Berscheid and Walster, 1978) or who benefit from others' pain (Lerner and Simmons, 1966) tend to see their victims as deserving of suffering. Lerner (1970: p. 227) explains these reactions as follows:

> When the person becomes aware of a victim who is clearly innocent of any act which might have brought about the suffering, he is confronted with a conflict. He can decide he lives in a cruel, unjust

> world where innocent people can suffer or that the only people who suffer in this world are those who deserve such a fate.

Through this response to misfortune, human beings are able to simplify their world. They need not agonize over the undeserved sufferings of those they like; the people who suffer simply become the people they do not like.

Paradoxically, derogation of victims can be both a *result* of refusing to help someone and also a *cause* of future failures to help. Once we derogate victims, because we have not helped them, we are then even less likely to help them in the future, because we do not like them.

If people come to dislike those they fail to aid, what evidence is there that they like those they do aid? Lerner and Simmons (1966) gave some subjects an opportunity to alleviate the suffering they were observing in an experiment by switching the victim's learning assignment from a punishment procedure to a reward procedure. When subjects were able to alleviate the victim's suffering, they rated her more positively. Mills and Egger (1972) also report that people who alleviated others' miseries were more positively disposed toward them than were subjects who could only watch helplessly.

RECEIVING HELP: WHEN IS AID APPRECIATED?

Most of us expect some sort of gratitude from the recipients of our help and kindness. Yet help does not always elicit gratitude. The amputee selling pencils on the street may feel little love for the people dropping dimes in his or her can. And the people of developing nations, wary of the strings attached to aid, seem remarkably restrained in their expressions of gratitude for wheat shipments, dams, and generators. In field interviews with fifty officials from over a dozen nations receiving foreign aid, Gergen and Gergen (1971) discovered widespread animosity from aid recipients toward their benefactors—even when the benefactors were attempting to use the aid to build bridges of good will.

Berscheid and Walster (1978) point out several reasons why receiving aid may yield hostility rather than appreciation. At least some of the time the altruistic relationship is inequitable, since the recipient is benefiting without being able to return the favor. This may create an unwanted feeling of obligation and a humiliating sense of dependence. Remember Brehm and Cole's finding, mentioned earlier, that beneficiaries of help rated their benefactors as less attractive when a favor had reduced their freedom of action. Also recall Pruitt's finding that the size of a gift is less important than the beneficiaries' appraisal of the size of the sacrifice the gift represents. Similarly, Fisher and Nadler (1976) recently found that recipients of aid feel better about themselves when the aid is costly to the donor. Apparently, if the donor has to sacrifice, then recipients can feel important, but a low-cost effort feels demeaning.

These studies help to explain why aid is often unappreciated, whether the beneficiary is a beggar, a Third World country, or a welfare recipient. Most forms of charity simply do not represent much of a sacrifice. A well-dressed passer-by, the United States government, and most other sources of charity give so small a proportion of their goods that the donor's existence is not substantially altered. Moreover, the beneficiary may perceive that the benefactor's motives may not be benign (Tesser, Gatewood, and Driver, 1968).

When is aid most appreciated? When there is an opportunity to reciprocate the favor, beneficiaries feel most attracted to a donor (Castro, 1975; Gross and Latané, 1974). Furthermore, if aid is unexpected, it is more appreciated (Morse, Gergen, Peele, and Van Ryneveld, 1977), and helpers who spontaneously volunteer help are more liked than those who must be asked for assistance (Broll, Gross, and Piliavin, 1974).

We have seen that conformity to a norm of helpfulness is dependent on the social settings in which people find themselves. These factors affect not only people's behavior but also the ways in which they feel about and perceive one another. Bear in mind, however, that the experimental evidence accumulated so far is but a starting point in understanding the full range of human prosocial concern. Prosocial behavior covers a wide range of activities that may be affected by many different factors. Therefore, generalizations must be made carefully. For ex-

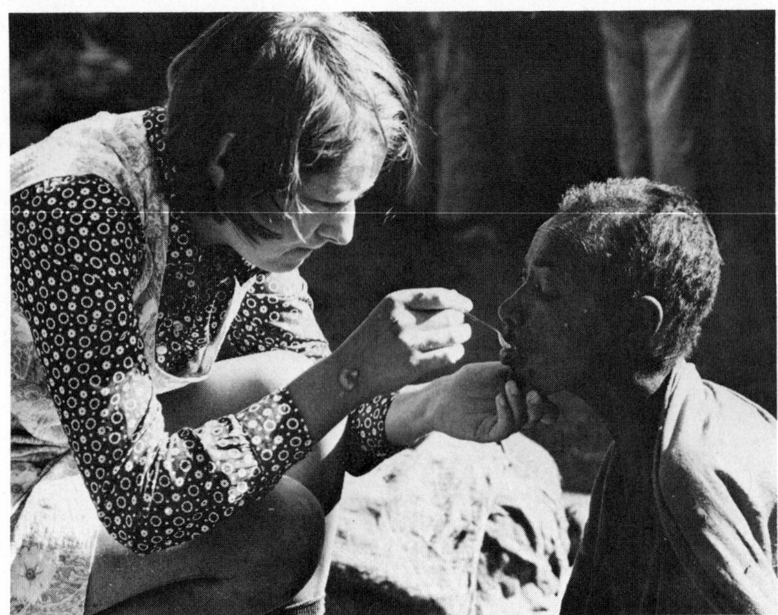

A Peace Corps worker feeds a victim of drought and famine in Ethiopia. Some developing countries do not appreciate assistance from the United States and other wealthy nations; one reason, research suggests, may be that the aid represents only a very small sacrifice to the donor. *(Thomas Höpker/Woodfin Camp & Assoc.)*

ample, whereas mood may increase or decrease a person's tendency to be charitable to others, it may have no bearing on how he or she would respond in an emergency. Or while the presence of others may reduce an individual's tendency to intervene in an emergency, it may increase the probability that he or she will comply with a request.

There are countless examples of great and small sacrifices that people make for one another, and most of us express prosocial concern in some form. It is up to each of us to adapt the insights provided in this chapter to our own circumstances. Each prosocial action that a person undertakes is likely to generate still other prosocial acts—by the original benefactor, by the beneficiaries, and by uninvolved observers as well. To some extent, then, each of us is able to decide what sort of human community we will live in.

SUMMARY

This chapter has focused on a wide variety of behaviors that might be characterized as prosocial. Prosocial behavior is behavior that is done for the apparent purpose of helping others. Whether a prosocial act is considered altruistic depends on our assessment of the actor's motives and the actor's expectation of personal gain. Current interest in explaining altruism derives from both social concerns and reasons specific to psychological theories.

Theories of altruism emphasize cultural norms, possible biological factors, emotional responses to the suffering of others, and expectations of social exchange and equity. However, there are no general theories of altruism, and each of the theories discussed applies to certain domains of prosocial behavior but not to others.

We then turned to three general sections of research into prosocial behavior: characteristics of the individual, the influence of the surrounding situation, and the effects of altruism.

The first section on characteristics of the individual focused on personality factors associated with altruism and psychological states associated with altruism. Such factors as need for approval and belief in a just world may lead people to behave prosocially. However, these personality factors also interact with specific aspects of the situation. The search for a "general altruist" has yielded mixed results, with the general conclusion being that a concern for others' welfare probably does increase prosocial action but that other aspects of the individual's personality as well as situational factors probably mediate that tendency.

Transitory states of the individual may also affect altruism. One such state is produced by prior success in a seemingly unrelated task, which may create a feeling of competence or general good will. The good feeling produced by success appears to increase altruism, as does a positive mood in general. The effect of negative mood on altruism is complex, with different effects being found at various ages and in different situations.

Altruism often arises from guilt or sympathy and a desire to compensate the injured for their pain. However, guilt can generalize from those a person has wronged to other victims he or she has not injured and from a personal act of wrongdoing to an act for which the observer is not responsible.

The surrounding situation was seen to be an important determiner of prosocial behavior. Altruistic behavior is affected by other people, especially models. An important factor in the influence of a model is his or her similarity to us; the similar model is more likely than the dissimilar one to influence our own responses to a person in need of help. However, behavioral modeling and verbal modeling are distinctly different in effect. For instance, a hypocritical model who talks about altruism but does not actually help is likely to evoke that same inconsistent response in an observer.

Research on bystander intervention focuses on conditions that determine when one person will aid another in an emergency. Whether a situation is defined as an emergency and how many other people are present to diffuse responsibility influence an individual's decision to intervene. Other factors that influence bystander intervention include the perceived potential of other bystanders to help; ambiguity of the situation; the physical threat to the bystander; the fear of losing face by acting inappropriately; and the low-control-of-effects syndrome, which produces a cynical view of individual effectiveness against the general dehumanization of mass society.

Specific aspects of the physical environment may also be important determiners of prosocial action. Differences have been found between urban and rural residents in their responsiveness to others. It also has been shown that stressful environments may reduce our helpfulness.

People who need help are not all equally successful in eliciting a particular individual's help. When the need is great, we are more likely to assist our close friends than we are to assist total strangers. In addition, a person's dependence on someone's help can elicit altruism, although if the person seems responsible for his or her own plight, the benefactor may be unlikely to help.

The effects of altruism are varied. We saw how the norm of reciprocity encourages us to return favors. But reciprocity may be blocked if the favor seems to be a very small sacrifice, to be involuntary, to be inappropriate, or to be restrictive of our freedom.

If we perform one prosocial act, we are likely to do others to maintain our altruistic image; but if we fail to help once, we are likely to fail again. We may fail to help if the need is too intense or too frequent, because reminders of suffering are unpleasant. We may either avoid these reminders or come to believe that those who suffer deserve their fate. If we are forced to confront the victims of injustice, we may develop a dislike for those victims. But if we are able to help, the dislike often disappears.

In the same way that the sight of suffering makes us uncomfortable, the needy may be uncomfortable with their dependence on the help of others, perhaps resenting it. Research indicates a variety of factors that can cause recipients of help to react negatively to their benefactors.

Prosocial action can take many forms and can spring from a variety of motivations. But, because one prosocial action often leads to another, we can all facilitate the spread of altruistic behavior.

CHAPTER TEN

SOCIAL INTERDEPENDENCE

In July 1979, the pirate whaling ship *Sierra* dropped anchor outside the harbor of Oporto, Portugal, waiting to unload its cargo of whale products. Defying all international whaling agreements, the *Sierra* made its kills with old-fashioned barbed metal harpoons. These harpoons do little damage to the whale meat, but they prolong a whale's death; as a result, other whales who try to comfort their kin are themselves harpooned as well. Outside the harbor, the hunter suddenly became the prey.

The *Sea Shepherd*, a converted fishing trawler owned by the U.S. conservation group Fund for Animals, had stalked the pirate ship for 180 miles. Its bow packed with 100 tons of cement, the 789-ton *Shepherd* bore down on the lighter *Sierra* at a speed of twelve knots and punched a six-foot gash in its hull. Taking on water, the *Sierra* limped into port for long-term repairs; the conservationists' ship suffered only a battered bow.

At a London meeting in 1979 the International Whaling Commission voted overwhelmingly to prohibit all hunting of whales by factory ships on the high seas. While the ban was expected to spare at least 6,000 sperm whales during its first year, it makes the high seas even more attractive to outlaw whalers who refuse to cooperate with the international community.

Whales are just one example of a scarce resource that can only be preserved through human cooperation. Other examples range from energy supplies to wilderness lands, clean air and oceans, and perhaps human life itself. The basic issues involve cooperation and conflict over things of value and the bargaining processes that lead to cooperation or invite conflict.

Negotiation and bargaining go on daily in our own lives. Between teacher and student, roommates, friends, and lovers there is bargaining. Though the conflicts and consequences may not be as dramatic as in the example above, we are almost always seeking to obtain, preserve, or exchange things of value. Either implicitly or explicitly we are bargaining over what we will give to another in exchange for what they will give to us. Some of these exchanges are brief—a meeting with a professor or a date—while others may last years or even a lifetime—a career or marriage. In all of these cases we experience outcomes or "payoffs" directly or indirectly—good, bad, or indifferent—that depend on the behavior of others. In social-psychological terms, these are situations of *social interdependence.*

This chapter will acquaint you with a general theoretical and experimental approach to social interdependence known as exchange theory. This approach differs from other psychological specialties in terms of its explicit emphasis on "the structure of interdependence." The chapter will focus on this notion of structure. In addition, we will examine the experimental procedures and findings of this research area. We will see what variables are related to behavior in these research settings, and we will examine a recently developed theoretical explanation for these findings.

Finally, we will be concerned with the so-called "ecological validity" of the results provided by exchange-theory research. Specifically, we will ask if the human behavior seen in the exchange theorist's laboratory version of social interdependence is an accurate picture of what goes on in the real world. As you will see, the answer is a careful, and complicated, yes.

SOME BASIC IDEAS OF EXCHANGE THEORY

In 1959, John Thibaut and Harold Kelley published *The Social Psychology of Groups.* Of the several books on exchange theory published around this time, Thibaut and Kelley's had the greatest impact on social psychology. In order to understand the behavior of two or more interdependent persons, they argued, we must understand the "structure" of their relationship. In other words, we must know how specific outcomes or "payoffs" are associated with specific combinations of behaviors.

The notion of structure is valuable because it gives us a way of thinking about any situation of social interdependence, regardless of its specific features. It allows us to see, for example,

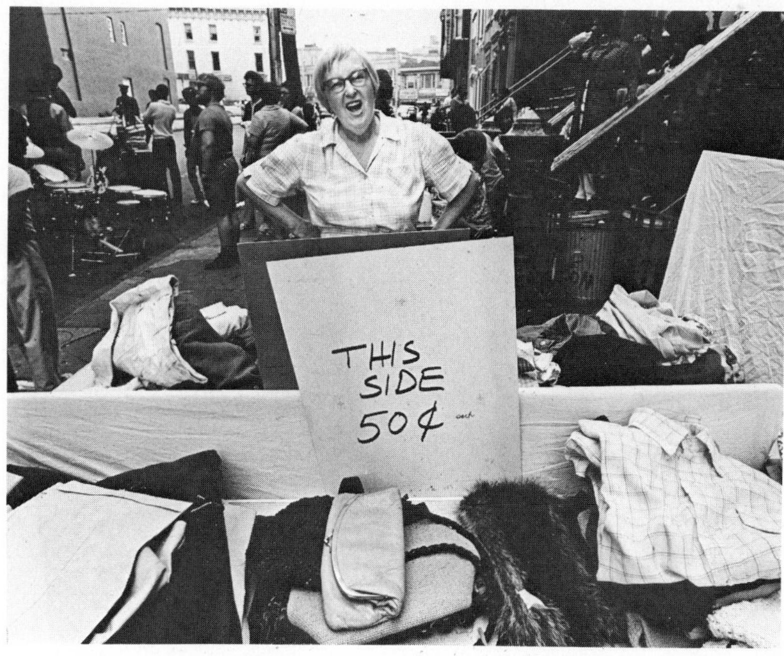

Bargaining and exchange are daily occurrences in our lives. At a flea market, for example, we may feel that an item is being sold at a fair price, or we may haggle with the vendor until we reach a mutually satisfactory agreement. *(© Shalmon Bernstein / Magnum)*

that many interdependent relationships that might appear different on the surface are really similar psychologically. To develop this notion of structure further, let's consider an imaginary interdependent relationship between two bank robbers.

"FLOYD AND BESSIE MAKE A DECISION"

Imagine that Floyd and Bessie robbed a bank last week. After some detective work, Lieutenant Garibaldi tracks them down to their hideout, a room in the Sunrise Motel. But instead of finding the bank's money, which he needs for a conviction, the detective finds only that each suspect possesses an illegal handgun. Floyd and Bessie are arrested for suspicion of robbery. At the station house, Lieutenant Garibaldi sends each one to separate interrogation rooms for questioning.

Each suspect hears the following offer: "Look Bessie (Floyd), I know you two held up the bank. But I need a confession to prove it in court. I think I can make it worth your while to confess. Here's the deal. If you *don't* confess and your partner does, then you're in trouble. We'll send you up for the maximum sentence and let your partner off free for helping us. Of course, if you confess and your partner stonewalls it, then you get off free and your partner gets the maximum sentence."

Bessie (Floyd) shifts in her (his) chair and asks the lieutenant: "What happens if we both confess? What happens if we both stonewall it?"

Garibaldi puffs on his cigar and responds: "If you both confess, I'll get each of you a reduced sentence for bank robbery. You'd each do the same time. But if you both stonewall it, I can't make the robbery charge stick but I can have you both sent up for illegal possession of handguns. You'll do the full time for that violation. So think it over Bessie (Floyd)."

Now let's conceptualize Floyd and Bessie's problem from the point of view of its structure.

THE OUTCOME MATRIX

Recall that in situations of social interdependence, the specific outcome received by each party depends on the actions of that party *and* the actions of the other parties. Bessie cannot avoid a maximum sentence through her own action; neither can Floyd. It's what they do *together* that counts. Thus, actions of all parties become very important.

In a given interdependent relationship each party has a set of potential actions from which he/she chooses. In the present example, each party's action repertory consists of *confessing* or *stonewalling*. The interdependent relationship can be described in terms of the association between each party's outcomes on the one hand and their joint actions on the other. In the present relationship we have several possibilities: (1) if Bessie confesses and Floyd stonewalls, Floyd gets the maximum sentence and Bessie goes free; (2) if Bessie stonewalls and . . . You can work the rest out for yourself until all possible choice combinations and associated outcomes have been listed. Such a list would show you exactly how each party's outcomes depend on joint action. There is, however, a much more efficient and organized method for getting this important information across. It's called the "outcome matrix," and an example is given in Figure 10.1.

The rows of the matrix represent Bessie's available actions; the columns represent Floyd's available actions. The cells of the matrix are divided by diagonal lines, and (by conventional agreement among workers in this area) the lower half of each cell shows the "row chooser's" (Bessie's) outcomes and the upper half shows the "column chooser's" (Floyd's) outcomes. The outcome matrix is valuable primarily because of its ability to clearly represent complicated interdependence structures. It also is a useful device for laboratory research, as we will discuss later.

VALUES

We have just seen that a given interdependent relationship can be conveniently represented by an outcome matrix. Another relationship, be-

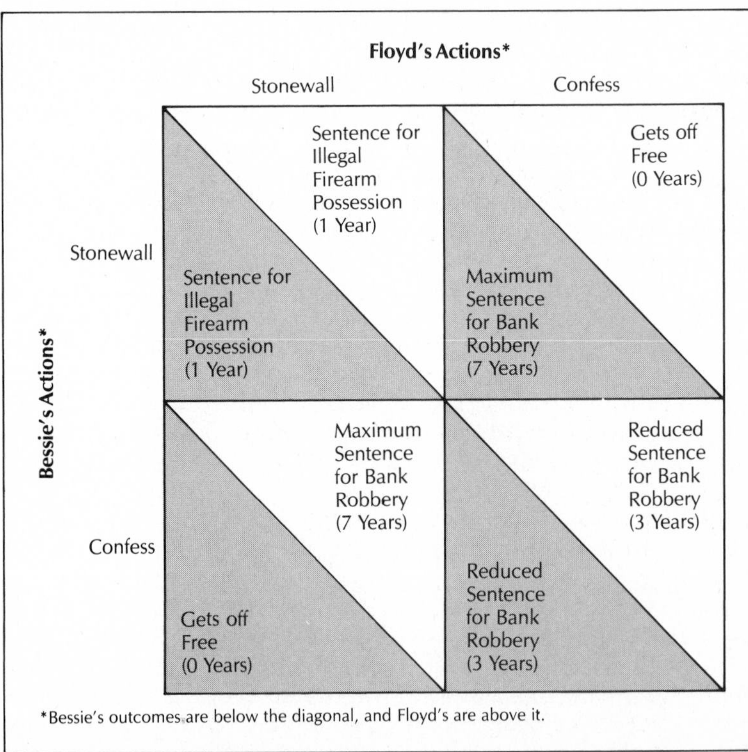

FIGURE 10.1 The possible outcomes associated with Floyd and Bessie's interdependent relationship.

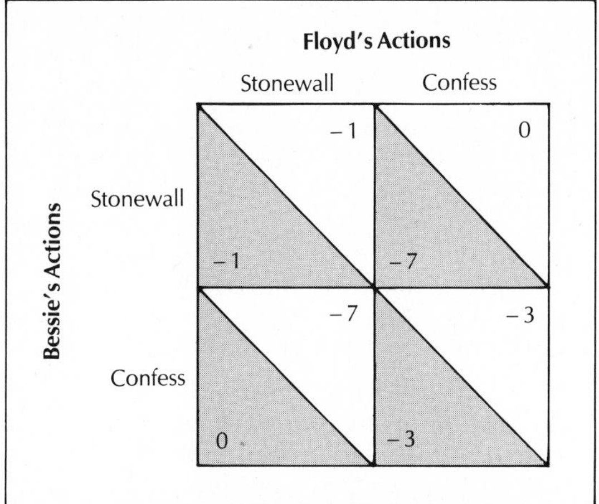

FIGURE 10.2 The values of the outcomes and the respective jail terms associated with Floyd and Bessie's interdependent relationship are inversely proportional.

tween different parties, with different behavioral repertories, and with different outcomes, could also be represented this way. An important question that arises from considering two or more outcome matrices is: Do they have any important features in common? If so, then we might feel safe in assuming that knowledge we gain about behavior in one situation tells us something about behavior in another, and vice versa. We would feel that we were learning not only about Floyd and Bessie's interaction, but about a general class of interdependent relationships, of which our present example is but one specific instance.

You may find it difficult to see how two or more specific outcome matrices could be compared. The physical outcomes themselves—for example, the solution of Floyd and Bessie's dilemma as opposed to the survival of the world's whales—can be so different from one setting to the next that comparison seems absurd. However, our ability to compare interdependence patterns results from a reasonable pair of assumptions made by exchange theorists about human beings. They are (1) each party to the interaction can locate all of his or her outcomes on a single dimension of value; and (2) each party to the interaction prefers outcomes of high value to those of low value.

These assumptions enable us to solve our comparison problem. First, assumption 1 means we can take the available set of outcomes and represent each numerically. This single numerical scale shows us the value attached to each available outcome. The higher the value, the larger the number.

For our present example we'll imagine that the value of each outcome is inversely proportional to the number of years in jail it involves. This would lead to (a) value of maximum robbery sentence = −7; (b) reduced robbery sentence = −3; (c) firearms sentence = −1; and (d) going free = 0. With these values we could reconstruct the outcome matrix as shown in Figure 10.2. This representation of the interdependent relationship allows us to focus on the values of the outcomes rather than on the outcomes themselves.

THE STRUCTURE OF INTERDEPENDENCE

Assumption 2, above, states that we want to obtain outcomes of high value and avoid those of low value. Coupled with this assumption, the present form of the outcome matrix gives us an immediate feel for where Floyd and Bessie want to be in the matrix and where they don't want to be. Also, since their location in a particular cell depends on their specific actions, the present matrix suggests how each person might be likely to respond to particular anticipated actions of the other. For example, if Bessie expects Floyd to confess, we would expect her to confess also.

You can also see from this matrix how likely it is for the two parties to reach a mutually satisfying outcome. For example, since the matrix contains a cell in which both parties receive an outcome that is not too terrible (−1, −1), this outcome should be a likely compromise.

For the time being we'll leave Floyd and Bessie. They have helped us realize that an interdependent relationship has a great deal to do with its *structure*. We have seen that the structure of interdependence is not determined just by the available outcomes themselves; it is defined as a pattern of values that expresses possible outcomes resulting from joint actions.

In order to understand more about the no-

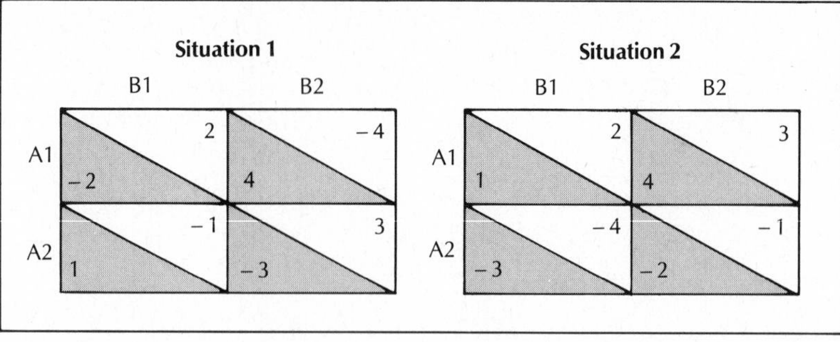

FIGURE 10.3 Two different situations involving the same values. Situation 1 is one of conflict, while situation 2 could easily lead to compromise and allow each person to receive the best possible outcome.

tion of structure, consider the two interdependent relationships shown in Figure 10.3. Person A has the same set of available outcome values (+1, −2, −3, −4) in both cases; so does person B (3, 2, −1, −4). However, the two situations are very different. Situation 1 is one of conflict. In each cell, if one person wins, the other loses. Situation 2, however, is not one of conflict. Each party's best outcome is in the same cell. There is no problem; A will do A1, B will do B2, and they will be fine. In situation 1, however, we would expect these *same two people* to have a difficult time with one another.

Structure is important psychologically because it defines the specific problem the parties have to deal with—namely, obtaining a mutually satisfactory outcome. If two different relationships—such as two kindergarten classmates and a pair of tennis professionals—possess similar structures, they are more psychologically similar than if they possess different structures. Situations with the same structure present their participants with the same problem to solve.

In order to study the structure of interdependence in the laboratory, the researcher begins with some real-world problem and then tries to specify its abstract structure. Based on the researcher's own intelligence, creativity, and intuition, this structure incorporates specific response alternatives and the likely values obtained by each party as the result of different combinations of actions.

Once the researcher is satisfied that the abstract structure adequately represents a real-world problem, the next step is to create that structure in the laboratory. The structure is usually created in the form of an experimental game with different possible outcomes. The outcomes of each player are shown in a matrix. The matrix makes it clear what each player can win or lose as the result of each player's choice. The goal for each player is to maximize outcomes. By observing the strategies that people employ to deal with specific structures, the researcher can learn how people in the real world might respond to a similar problem with the same structure, such as a wage dispute between municipal employees and city government or a conflict between two independent nations over control of nuclear weapons.

This strategy, if it works (and we will argue later that it can), allows us to make controlled observations of important human behavior. We can investigate people's ability to reach mutually satisfying outcomes under the influence of different variables—such as the sex of the interacting parties, the presence or absence of communication channels, the "toughness" or "accommodativeness" of the parties' actions, and so forth. We can understand the circumstances under which a particular interdependent structure will be handled well and when it will not.

The most common form of this research is known as "experimental gaming" (Pruitt and Kimmel, 1977; Rubin and Brown, 1975). In this approach, each subject is shown the entire outcome matrix; each subject also knows that every other subject is aware of the outcome matrix. Such studies show us how people respond to a particular structure *when everyone involved knows what the structure is*. This type of research is discussed in the section below.

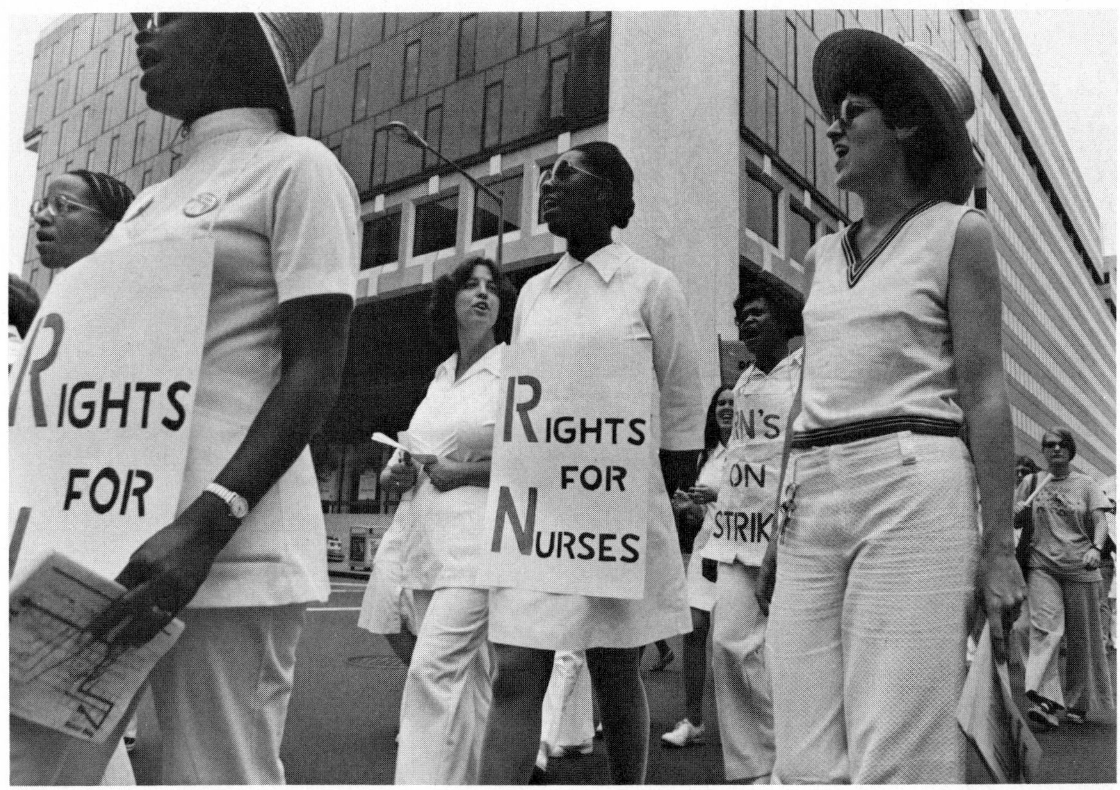

The structure of interdependence in a given situation—say, a strike and its possible outcomes for both workers and employers—may be represented symbolically by a matrix like the ones shown in Figure 10.3. *(Martha Tabor / Working Images)*

EXPERIMENTAL GAMING RESEARCH

If you were to participate in a typical experimental gaming study, you and another student—in most gaming studies, there would be only two of you—would arrive at the laboratory at approximately the same time. In the majority of these studies, you would be unacquainted with one another. After greeting you and the other, the experimenter would escort you to the research area, where you would each be seated. You would not be able to see the other, and he or she would not be able to see you. In addition, you would be requested by the experimenter to avoid speaking with the other for the rest of the experimental session. Let's imagine you are designated as "student 1."

You are now given instructions: you discover that the study will consist of a number of trials, and on each trial you and the other student will have to make a decision about what to do. Most often, each student is given only two alternatives to choose from, and they are described in abstract terms such as "alternative X and alternative Y."

You will all have to make your decision in ignorance of what the other is doing, and you will silently communicate your choices to the experimenter. Most often this is done by providing the students with a set of silent electrical switches that control signal lights on the experimenter's panel.

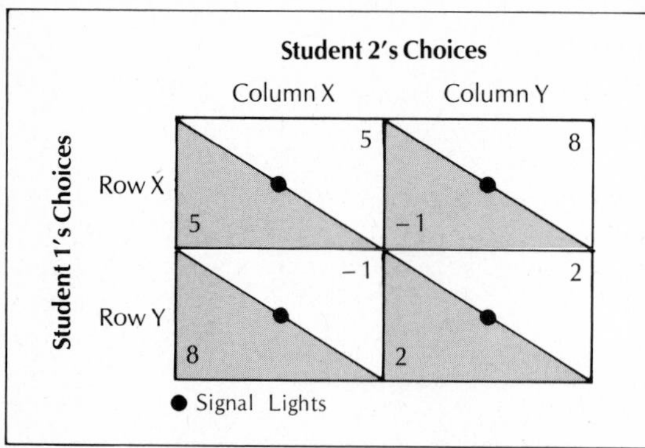

FIGURE 10.4 A payoff matrix as it is presented to students in a gaming experiment.

The instructions continue, stating that once you have all made your choices in a particular trial, you will each receive an outcome; also, the specific outcome you receive depends on what the two of you do together. At this point you are shown exactly how your outcomes depend on your combined choices. Almost invariably for two-person groups, the experimenter makes this point with an outcome matrix. An example is given in Figure 10.4. The matrix often has two rows and columns. As we saw before, each cell of the matrix is divided by a diagonal, and numbers appear in each cell above and below this line. Your outcomes, those of student 1, are below the diagonal, and student 2's are above it.

In addition, the matrix contains a small light bulb in the center of each cell. These are used to signal you and the other student as to the outcomes on each trial. The experimental game is abstract, but it has all the defining properties of social interdependence we mentioned at the beginning of this chapter—negotiation, exchange, and outcomes that depend on the behavior of others. The game matrix also makes a direct and explicit statement about the *structure* of the interdependent situation. This seems desirable given that structure is of such theoretical importance.

Now, let's focus on the outcomes. They are described as "points" or "units." For example, the instructions might be "If you choose row X, and student 2 chooses column Y, the light in the upper-right-hand corner would come on, indicating that you would lose one point, and student 2 would gain eight points." Are the points worth anything? It depends on the particular study. In some, you are told that the points are worth real money; the more points you earn, the more money you will take home with you. In other experiments, though, the experimenter will ask you to attempt to make as many points as possible, but you will not be paid for them.

Why are the outcomes presented in this numerical way? Why not make them more "realistic"? After all, in the real world we don't go around getting "points" from our interdependent relationships. The laboratory outcomes are numerical for a good reason.

Remember that the purpose of experimental gaming research is to study human behavior in an interdependent relationship possessing some particular *structure*. Remember, also, that the structure of a relationship is defined in terms of the association of the *values* of the outcomes rather than the specific outcomes themselves. The gaming researcher wants to present all of his or her dyads with the same interdependence structure. Therefore, the experimenter tries to choose outcomes so that most students will value them in much the same way.

Numbers are things we have been taught to order and compare in the same way. Eight points is larger than five points, which is larger than two points, which is larger than minus one point. By telling the student that points are valuable (either by paying students for points earned or by simply saying "try to get as many as you can"), we come as close as we know how to producing a similar interdependence structure for all dyads.

PRISONER'S DILEMMA

In the last twenty years or so, hundreds of experimental gaming studies have been conducted. Most of these have focused on a single structure called "prisoner's dilemma" (Pruitt and Kimmel, 1977). The term *prisoner's dilemma* derives from the fact that the first story used to describe this structure was the bank-robber problem we presented earlier.

Figures 10.2 and 10.4 are examples of a prisoner's-dilemma structure. Notice in Figure 10.4 that row X (column X) is the choice that can produce a mutual and moderately valued outcome for each of you (five points apiece). Also, if you choose X, you are showing a certain amount of trust in your partner; if your partner were to choose Y, you would lose a point and your partner would win eight. A row X choice, then, seems to represent a desire for both parties to do well and a trust in the other person at the same time. For these reasons, it is appropriate to label row X (and column X) as the "cooperative" choice. In Figure 10.2, the "cooperative" choice is stonewalling, for this is the choice that shows most trust in one's partner. On the other hand, the Y choice in Figure 10.4 and the "confess" choice in Figure 10.2 can be labeled as "noncooperative." Here, one player wins at the expense of the other. You might choose such a strategy for a number of reasons: (1) to beat the other person; (2) to get the most for yourself; or (3) to keep the other from beating you.

Thus, the prisoner's dilemma offers its participants a choice between cooperating and not cooperating. Many important real-world problems are similar to the prisoner's-dilemma structure. In the next section we will examine one of these real-world problems that has been conceptualized in light of prisoner's-dilemma research—the so-called "commons dilemma" (Dawes, 1975).

THE COMMONS DILEMMA

In 1968, the human ecologist Garret Hardin wrote an article entitled "The Tragedy of the Commons," in which he stressed that uncontrolled population growth and free access to natural resources would inevitably destroy the earth's resources. To support his argument, Hardin drew on the work of a nineteenth-century British mathematician, W. F. Lloyd. Lloyd had illustrated a point about the labor force by referring to the example of the commons, which were public pastures in English villages where all citizens could freely graze their livestock. Just as commons pastures often became muddy, barren fields from overuse by too many animals, so the value of labor was reduced when too many people entered the labor market. Commons, whether they are grazing pastures, labor markets, whale populations, or the earth's resources, can only support a certain level of demand. When this demand is exceeded, the commons itself suffers, as well as the people who derive value from the commons. Lloyd and others have argued that the nature of a commons is such as to assure that sooner or later this demand will be exceeded.

To use terms introduced in this chapter, we would say that the interdependence structure of the commons situation encourages each party to be noncooperative. In commons settings, noncooperation (adding livestock to the commons in the above example) makes good sense to each party for the reason that it is profitable. By placing more sheep, pigs, or cattle on the commons, you obtain an increase in the amount of meat the commons supports for you. Those are your animals; that excess meat is yours. So, the rewards of noncooperation come directly to you. Of course, noncooperation has a cost. For each animal added, the amount of available food decreases. But, you share the costs of noncooperation with every other party to the commons. In the short run, then, you receive a reward that goes to you alone, and you share only a small fraction of the cost. Overall, you come out ahead of what you would have had if you had cooperated. The problem is, what's true for you is equally true for everyone else. It is profitable, each person realizes, to be noncooperative.

However, while you realize that noncooperation is profitable, you also realize that if everyone acts in this "reasonable" way, you are all in trouble. And since you can hardly expect your fellow commons participants to be cooperative while you engage in profitable noncooperation, it begins to seem "reasonable" to think about cooperating yourself. But you do not stay convinced of the wisdom of this for very long. Perhaps you think that others, too, have begun to realize the dangers of noncooperation, and so they, too, are going to cooperate. With everyone else cooperating then, you are tempted to be noncooperative. Your single act will not hurt the commons very much, and it will yield you a nice profit.

Or, on the other hand, perhaps you want to

a

(a) Sheep graze on a commons, or public pasture, in medieval England. As villages grew and more and more people used the commons, these lands often became muddy and barren. (b) This situation frequently occurs on a global scale today. Many natural resources—petroleum, for example—have become scarcer due to increased demand over the years. The result is a commons dilemma: noncooperation is the most profitable short-term strategy, but it leads to faster depletion of the resource. *(New York Public Library Picture Collection; J. Giannini / Sygma)*

b

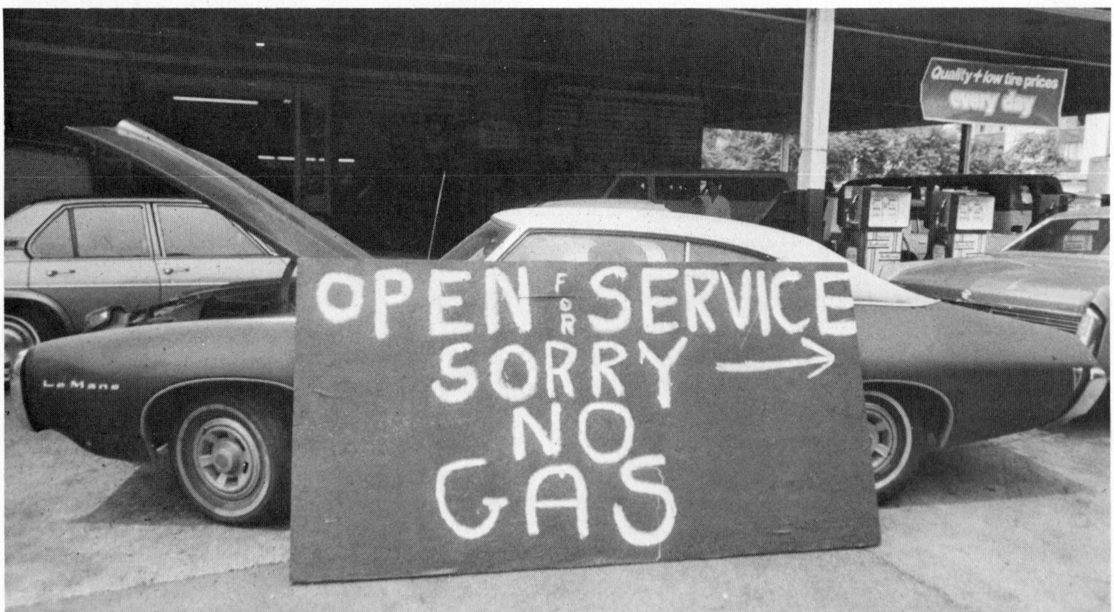

SOCIAL PSYCHOLOGY AND THE ARTS

"NO MAN IS AN ISLAND"

One of the most profound commentaries on social interdependence in the English language comes from the seventeenth-century English poet John Donne. In the last part of the year 1623 Donne fell ill with a fever and for six weeks lay near death. As he daily heard the bells toll out, announcing the deaths of others, the poet wrote down musings on his own sickness and on the meaning of life and death. Donne later published these writings as "Meditations." One of these works, Meditation XVII, dwells on the oneness of humankind in words that hold special relevance for modern-day commons dilemmas.

> **No man is an island entire of itself; every man is a piece of the continent, a part of the main. If a clod be washed away by the sea, Europe is the less, as well as if a promontory were, as well as if a manor of thy friend's or of thine own were. Any man's death diminishes me, because I am involved in mankind, and therefore never send to know for whom the bell tolls; it tolls for thee.**

***Source*: John Donne, "Meditation XVII," *Devotions Upon Emergent Occasions*, in R. P. T. Coffin and A. M. Witherspoon (eds.), *Seventeenth-Century Prose and Poetry* (New York: Harcourt, Brace, 1957): 58–59.**

cooperate, but you believe that your fellow commons members will be seduced by the rewards of noncooperation. But since noncooperation is costly and these costs are shared by every member of the commons, why should you cooperate and pay a part of everyone else's costs when no one is paying anything for you? It isn't fair. So you think about being noncooperative. But then you realize that if everyone is noncooperative, you're all in trouble—and you're right back where you were two paragraphs ago.

By now you should have an intuitive feel for the decision problem created by the commons-dilemma structure. In recent years, social psychologists and other social scientists have suggested contemporary versions of this interdependence structure. Kelley and Grezlak (1972) have suggested that deciding whether or not to turn up your air conditioner in a brown-out has commons-dilemma features. Wilson (1977) has presented persuasive data indicating that uncontrolled lobster fisheries in New England create a commons structure that adversely affects the quality of the yearly catch. Other examples range from the whale-hunting incident described at the beginning of this chapter to everyday decisions, such as whether or not you should leave money for your coffee at the coffee pool at work. Indeed, there are many important real-world settings with such a structure. They may be found in earthshaking contexts that affect our planet and our species as well as in our daily lives.

What do human beings do when they encounter such structures? What factors make people more or less cooperative in a commons dilemma? One way to answer such questions is to create the commons structure in a gaming laboratory and to study how humans respond to it.

To do so, we need to move from our current intuitive understanding of the commons dilemma to a more formal level. Specifically, we will list the properties needed by an interdependence structure in order to consider it a commons dilemma. These properties were developed by Robyn Dawes (1975) in an article on the formal properties of social dilemmas. In light of these properties, we will see that the prisoner's dilemma can really be viewed as an instance of a two-person commons dilemma.

FORMAL PROPERTIES OF THE COMMONS DILEMMA Before reviewing the literature, we will show you a laboratory version of a commons dilemma involving ten people. Figure 10.5 shows the payoff table that *each* person in this experiment would receive. Everyone sees

FIGURE 10.5 This table shows the payoffs each individual would receive in a laboratory version of a commons dilemma. The payoffs for cooperation (X) and noncooperation (Y) are a function of the level of noncooperation in the group.

Action	Number of People in the Group Who Choose Y										
	0	1	2	3	4	5	6	7	8	9	10
X (Cooperation)	10	8	6	4	2	0	−2	−4	−6	−8	*
Y (Noncooperation)	†	18	16	14	12	10	8	6	4	2	0

*It is impossible for you to cooperate if everyone in your group (including you) is noncooperative.

†It is impossible for you to be noncooperative if everyone in your group (including you) cooperates.

the same table. Now try to imagine how you would respond if you were in this experiment.

The rows of the table show the actions available to you and to each of the other players. Row X is the "cooperative" choice (as will be explained shortly) and row Y is the "noncooperative" choice. The numbers in the cells of the table show your final outcome for choosing X (cooperating) or Y (noncooperating) when there is a given number of noncooperators (Y choosers) in your group. For example, if you choose X and only two people in your group choose Y, then you would receive six "points." Figure 10.5 is important because it allows us to see all the structural features of the commons dilemma, each of which is described below.

Noncooperation Dominates Cooperation First, Figure 10.5 shows that for you, the choice of noncooperation "dominates" cooperation. The notion of "dominance" is simple. Consider an example involving a choice between two gambles. If you choose gamble 1, I'll flip a coin. If heads comes up, you win a dollar; if tails, you lose a dollar. But if you choose gamble 2, you win 50 cents for heads and lose $2 for tails. The only reasonable choice is gamble 1. Whatever happens, you do better with gamble 1 than with gamble 2. In other words, we say that gamble 1 *dominates* gamble 2.

Now, you can only guess how many of your fellow game partners are going to choose Y. Imagine that none of them is. What is your best choice? If you cooperate, then there are zero noncooperators in your group and your outcome is 10. If you are noncooperative, then there is one noncooperator in your group (you) and your outcome is 18. Therefore, *if* none of your fellows is noncooperative, your best choice is Y. This is always true, *regardless* of how many of your fellows are noncooperative. If, for example, four others are noncooperative, you obtain two units for X, but you would obtain 10 for Y. Therefore, you realize that no matter how the others behave, you come out ahead by being noncooperative.

For you, then, Y dominates X, just as gamble 1 dominates gamble 2. And this is true for every party in the situation. Therefore, as Dawes says, a commons dilemma presents each party with a dominating strategy. Dominating strategies are compelling; each individual is strongly pushed toward noncooperation.

Mutual Noncooperation Produces a Deficient Equilibrium What happens when all the individuals choose their dominated strategy? Figure 10.5 shows that each person receives an outcome of 0. Now, imagine that you find yourself in this position; you and everyone else are receiving 0. Do you think about cooperating? It is foolish (in one sense) for you to do so. If you switch from Y to X in this situation, your outcome falls from 0 to −8. This consideration applies to every other person in your situation. That is, there are pressures operating to keep each party in the system from changing. Such a state of affairs is called an "equilibrium," and we have as our second feature of the commons that *unanimous choice of the dominated strategy produces an equilibrium*. Also, notice that the equilibrium is not very satisfying. It is not the best state of affairs the group could be in. If everyone cooperated, each individual's outcome would be 10. The equilibrium is thus said to be deficient.

Cooperative Behavior Makes Things Better for Others and for the Group The final two features of the dilemma are concerned with the value of individual and group outcomes as a function of the level of noncooperation. First, as Figure 10.5 shows, *each individual's outcomes increase as cooperation increases.* This is true whether the individual chooses X or Y. Second, *the total group outcome increases with increasing cooperation.* If everyone cooperates, the total outcome is 100; unanimous noncooperation produces a total outcome of 0. Taking an intermediate situation, seven noncooperators and three cooperators produce a total outcome of 36. So, both individual and group welfare increase with increasing cooperation.

That, then, is our formal description of the commons dilemma and its payoff structure. The last thing to do in this section is to show that the two-person prisoner's-dilemma game is a commons dilemma. Let's go back to Floyd and Bessie's problem. For each prisoner (1) confession dominates stonewalling; (2) if both prisoners confess, this produces a deficient equilibrium; and (3) Bessie's (Floyd's) outcomes improve when Floyd (Bessie) switches from confession to stonewalling. Also, collective punishment is minimal when everyone stonewalls (cooperates) and maximum when everyone is noncooperative (confesses).

In light of the above discussion, you can see that prisoner's-dilemma payoff matrices are actually a special (two-person) case of the commons dilemma. In the following sections we will examine research of this gaming structure and consider a recent theory that attempts to explain the results. Finally, we will consider the validity of gaming research as a source of information about the real world.

RESULTS OF STUDIES ON THE TWO-PERSON COMMONS DILEMMA

One of the earliest and most systematic investigations of behavior in the two-person commons was conducted by Anatol Rapoport and Albert M. Chammah (1965b). They studied the responses of many pairs of college students over a large number of trials; each pair played the game 300 times. Such an experiment gives us a good picture of how behavior in the commons dilemma changes (if at all) with experience. Do subjects "learn" to cooperate? Do they become increasingly noncooperative with time? Does experience matter at all? Remember: We are dealing with a dilemma here, so that both courses of action available to each person make sense. This makes it very hard to be sure that our guess about what might happen is accurate.

Figure 10.6 displays the average level of cooperation (across seventy pairs of students) over the 300 trials of the game. Initially, cooperation was less than 50 percent, and it decreased steadily until around trial 30. At this point, it began to increase and continued to do so for the remainder of the session. We could say that experience tends to have a facilitating effect on cooperation. However, Rapoport and Chammah discovered that different students varied in their level of cooperation. Some were very cooperative, some very noncooperative, and as a group they averaged out to the values given in Figure 10.6. Thus, it is not true that experience necessarily leads to cooperation for all persons.

Toward the end of the 300 trials, Rapoport and Chammah also found a strong similarity of choice behavior within each pair of students. That is, if student 1 was highly cooperative, you could be sure student 2 was also. If student 2 was highly noncooperative, so was student 1. Rapoport and Chammah discovered that as trials elapsed, a point would be reached where each student was either cooperating or competing on each trial, and the dyad would "lock in" on a mutually cooperative or mutually competitive result for the remainder of the session. These authors report that by the last 25 trials of the experiment, the majority of their groups had locked in. Of this group 76 percent had become completely cooperative and 24 percent had locked in on competition.

Over time, then, most students developed a cooperative solution to this version of the commons dilemma. Would it be correct to suggest that experience with the game per se is sufficient to produce high levels of mutual cooperation? Although Rapoport and Chammah's work

FIGURE 10.6 The average level of cooperation across seventy pairs of cooperative and noncooperative students over 300 trials of the game. (From Rapoport and Chammah, 1965b.)

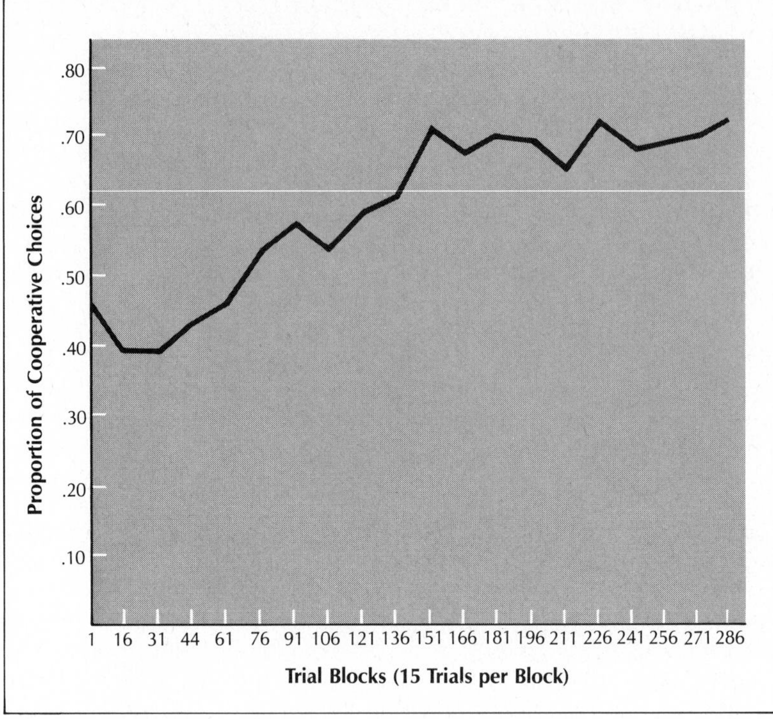

does not allow for an unambiguous answer to this question, a considerable amount of research done by others in this area does. The answer is no.

Shure and Meeker (1968) conducted a study in which half of the participants played prisoner's dilemma in standard fashion over a series of trials. The other half of the participants played with a new and different partner on each trial. Shure and Meeker found that students who kept the same partner were more cooperative than students who switched partners on each trial. Mere experience with the game appears insufficient to produce cooperative responding. It seems that one must perceive some continuity of relationship with one's "partner" for cooperation to have a chance to develop.

At this point it would be reasonable to wonder why this should be so. For the time being, however, we will postpone such speculation until we accomplish two goals: (1) the presentation of more experimental results and (2) the development of a theory of cooperation in prisoner's dilemma put forth by Pruitt and Kimmel (1977). At that time, you will appreciate the role of theory as a conceptual framework that allows us to make sense of a wide collection of experimental facts, including the one provided by Shure and Meeker's study.

THE EFFECTS OF STRATEGY

We have seen that experience with a permanent partner appears sufficient to produce cooperative behavior in most students. Does it matter what the partner does, or is it sufficient just to be paired with one person for a series of trials? No doubt everyone suspects that the answer to this question is "It depends on what the partner does," and everyone is right. But now let's ask the same question more specifically: If you were going to be someone's partner in a prisoner's-dilemma experiment, what should you do to maximize the chance that he or she will play cooperatively? To use a term that appears frequently in this area, we could ask: What *strategy* should you adopt to produce a good chance of cooperation in your partner?

Many experiments have been conducted to determine the effectiveness (measured in level of cooperation) of various strategies in prisoner's dilemma. The experiments all follow basically the same procedure. A student plays some number of trials of the game with a "partner." Although the student believes the "partner" is like himself or herself, in fact the "partner" is an accomplice of the experimenter's. The "partner's" responses in the game are determined by a set of rules generated by the experimenter. This set of rules is called the "partner's" strategy.

Experimenters have studied two general types of strategy, contingent and noncontingent. In noncontingent strategies, the "partner" chooses the "cooperative" row (or column) with some constant probability on each trial. This probability does not change during the course of the game. For example, a "partner" following a 50-percent noncontingent strategy could generate his or her choices by flipping a fair coin before each trial, cooperating if heads comes up and not cooperating if tails comes up. A "partner" following an 83-percent noncontingent strategy could generate his or her choices by rolling a fair die and cooperating if any number other than 6 came up. Perhaps now you see why such strategies are labeled noncontingent. The behavior of the "partner" is completely independent of the behavior of the student.

As you might expect, research (Rapoport, 1973) has shown that a noncontingent strategy of 100-percent cooperation produces more cooperative responses from a real subject (about 50 percent) than a noncontingent strategy of 0-percent cooperation (around 20 percent). Total nondiscriminating cooperation (compared to total noncooperation) thus appears to have some impact on others. But at the same time it does not keep others from taking advantage of you; they still exploit you on about half the trials. Moreover, total noncooperation predictably produces almost total noncooperation from others; after all, why should others put up with being exploited by you?

In addition to noncontingent strategies, psychologists have investigated the effects of contingent strategies on cooperation level. In a contingent strategy the behavior of the "partner" depends in one way or another upon the behavior of the student. The "partner" is responsive to the student.

One contingent strategy that has received much research attention is called "tit for tat." A tit-for-tat "partner" behaves according to the following set of rules: (1) if the student cooperated on the last trial, then the "partner" cooperates on the present trial; (2) if the real student did not cooperate on the last trial, then the "partner" chooses noncooperatively on the present trial. Now imagine how such a "partner" would respond to you if you were highly cooperative: the "partner" would be highly cooperative as well and would not exploit you. On the other hand, if you were highly noncooperative, your "partner" would also be highly noncooperative and would stay this way until you switched over to cooperation. Such a "partner" is more than ready to establish mutual cooperation, but will not tolerate being exploited.

Is such a strategy effective? A study by Chammah (1969) strongly suggests that it is. Playing with a tit-for-tat "partner," students showed an average cooperation level of 70 percent. Against 100-percent and 0-percent noncontingent "partners," however, Chammah's students showed only around 40-percent and 10-percent cooperation levels, respectively. After reviewing several other studies employing a tit-for-tat "partner," Rapoport (1973) concludes that of the strategies studied, tit for tat is most effective in producing high levels of cooperation.

It would appear, then, that unconditional cooperation is a less effective means of inducing others to cooperate than is a strategy that mixes readiness to cooperate with readiness to retaliate. We said in our earlier discussion of the Shure and Meeker study that one needs to feel he or she is interacting with the "partner" on some sort of long-term basis. Now it seems that the "partner" needs to impress the student with the facts that he or she is (1) trustworthy and (2) intolerant of exploitation. Interestingly, national leaders strive to convince potentially hostile nations of just such facts. Both the United States and the Soviet Union, for example, assure each other that they will not be the first to

Unconditional cooperation seems to be a less effective means of persuading others to cooperate than is a strategy that combines willingness to cooperate with willingness to retaliate. The international arms race illustrates this principle: As this cartoon shows, the United States and the Soviet Union talk about peace and cooperation, but each continues to build its missile arsenal to defend itself against possible attack by the other. *(© Eugene Mihaesco 1979 / The New York Times)*

launch missiles toward the other, but if attacked they will not fail to retaliate.

Notice that a subtle shift has just occurred in our discussion. Up to this point, we have been dealing with issues at the purely objective, behavioral level—how choice behavior changes over time, how one strategy influences choice behavior, and so forth. Then we made the reasonable point that a student's view of what his or her partner is like on the "inside" is very important. It is also likely that such internal states are important determinants of the person's actual choices in the dilemma.

THE EFFECTS OF INTERNAL DISPOSITIONS ON BEHAVIOR IN THE COMMONS

THE IMPORTANCE OF MOTIVATIONAL ORIENTATION

One set of internal characteristics that relates to behavior in the commons setting is called *motivational orientation* (MO). The first researcher to study the effects of MO on behavior in the commons was Morton Deutsch, who reported his findings in an influential book, published in 1973, called *The Resolution of Conflict*. Deutsch studied three types of basic MOs, which he defined as follows:

— *Cooperation*: Players have a positive interest in their own welfare and in the welfare of others. In Deutsch's research, cooperative dyads are instructed, "Help yourself and help the other person. Also, be assured that the other person is going to help you."
— *Individualism*: Players have a positive interest in their own welfare but have no interest in the welfare of others. Individualistic dyads are told to do well for themselves but to be indifferent to the other.
— *Competition*: Players have a positive interest in their own welfare and also try to beat the others. Competitive dyads are instructed, "Do better than the other person and also be assured that the other person is trying to do better than you."

The students in Deutsch's study played a prisoner's-dilemma game for ten trials. On the first trial the cooperative choice was made by 78 percent of the cooperative MO students, 40 percent of individualistic students, and 23 percent of the competitive MO students.

Over all ten trials cooperative MO dyads showed no change in cooperation level. Individualistic MO dyads, however, became increasingly competitive, so that by trial 10, they were no different from the dyads with a competitive MO (both showed around 12-percent cooperation on trial 10). In these early stages of interaction individualistic MO dyads are unlikely to be cooperative, even though it is in their best interest to be so. Remember, such dyads are supposed to do well for themselves and not worry about beating the other person.

There is an important point here. Although competitive and individualistic MO dyads were doing the same thing (being noncooperative), this was "reasonable" for the competitive group, but not for the individualistic one. Competitively motivated dyads were avoiding being "beaten," which was the best they could do under the circumstances. Individualistic dyads, however, were not doing as well as they could under their circumstances. Why, according to Deutsch, were the individualistic students so unsuccessful at obtaining their goals in these early trials? Deutsch's answer involves one of the most important processes in situations of interdependence: trust.

THE IMPORTANCE OF TRUST AND COMMUNICATION

We will define *trust* as a belief that your partner(s) will cooperate with you in the commons. As we saw earlier, unless a decision maker expects cooperation from his or her partner, it is foolish to do anything other than be noncooperative. How, then, can dyads develop trust? Deutsch believes that members of a dyad can communicate a willingness to cooperate with their partner. If one's partner perceives one's communication accurately and believes it, then trust is possible. But the development of trust in such a dyad depends on communication itself.

In a third part of his experiment, Deutsch made it possible for the students to communicate with one another; specifically, each student was allowed to write a note to his partner stating anything he felt to be necessary or desirable. If Deutsch's analysis was correct, such a manipulation should have had a large effect on the cooperation of individualistic MO dyads and a much smaller effect on cooperative or competitive ones. The reasons for such predictions are (1) for cooperative dyads, trust already existed between the students; (2) for competitive dyads, there was no basis for the development of trust; (3) for individualistic dyads, however, an open communication channel allowed for the sending of explicit messages that could clearly signal that cooperative behavior was called for.

Deutsch found that the communication channel had just these effects on the three types of dyad. The level of cooperation shown by competitive and cooperative MO dyads did not change significantly from that shown by them in the no-communication condition. For individualistic dyads, however, there was a significant increase in the level of cooperation—71 percent of the students in this condition chose the cooperative alternative. This is almost twice the amount of cooperation shown by individualistic dyads who could not communicate. Furthermore, when Deutsch looked at the kinds of messages the individualistic students were sending, he found that 60 percent of the messages were communications of cooperation.

Deutsch's findings have implications for relations between nations, especially regarding arms control. So long as nations follow a competitive strategy, each seeking to outdo the other in arms production, no country will gain as much as it could under a cooperative strategy. In other words, each nation is forced to commit more and more of its resources to arms production. Yet when nations are interested primarily in their own welfare, following a strategy of individualism in Deutsch's terms, open communication can dramatically increase cooperation and mutual gain, with fewer resources committed to beating the opponent. Thus direct communication channels such as the "hotline" between the United States and the Soviet Union or indirect channels such as orbiting reconnaissance satellites—which monitor a nation's military preparedness—can assure each nation that the other is seeking to cooperate in arms control.

In general, we have seen three things to be true of motivational orientation in the commons. First, MO is importantly related to choice behavior. Second, what seems to be highly important to the development of cooperation is mutual trust. Third, trust can come about as a direct result of MO, or it may depend on some feature of the environment, such as communication channels.

Before we imagine that Deutsch's results shed any light on the findings of studies like Rapoport and Chammah's, let's consider an important point: Deutsch expressly told his students what MO they should have; it was clear to them how they were supposed to approach the game. In the typical commons study, however, the experimenter is much less explicit in giving the students a particular MO. Also, in Deutsch's work, each student in the dyad knew what the MO of his partner was. Such information is typically not provided students in commons experiments.

Therefore, it seems appropriate to ask three questions about students in the typical experimental gaming study. First, what MO (if any) do the students adopt if their experimenter does not explicitly tell them how to be ori-

DISPOSITIONS AND SITUATIONS

CHILDREN, CULTURE, AND COMPETITION

Try to remember what it was like to be a seven year old. You're playing with a friend and you're given a choice: you can have two toys while your friend gets one, or you can have three toys while your friend gets four. Which do you choose? If you are like most seven year olds, you would opt for relative gain rather than absolute gain; in other words, you would rather have more than your friend, even if it leaves you with fewer toys overall. Thus, competition has become an "autonomous motive"—not a strategy to maximize your own gains, but a goal in itself.

How does such a competitive motivation develop? How does it change with the years? How important is culture in establishing such a motive? And how can this motive be modified by situational factors? These are the questions addressed by an international team of social psychologists—Masanao Toda and Hiromi Shinotsuka from Japan and Charles McClintock and Frank Stech from America (1978).

Previous research (McClintock and Moskowitz, 1976; McClintock, Moskowitz, and McClintock, 1977) had shown that very young children—three and a half to four and a half years old—are mainly "egoistic"; that is, they always prefer to maximize their own short-term gain rather than long-term gain or mutual gain with another child. But beginning about age seven, many children start to develop autonomous motives, those motives that serve as ends in themselves rather than as strategies for long-term gain.

To understand how these motives develop with age across different cultures, the researchers studied three groups of children—second-, fourth-, and sixth-grade boys—in five different cultures—Anglo-American, Japanese, Belgian, Greek, and Mexican-American. Pairs of children played a specially adapted laboratory game with the goal of winning points. As shown in the matrix below, there were four options in the game: the children could choose a strategy in which both players won 6 points; a strategy in which one player earned 5 points and the other 0 (and vice versa); or a strategy in which neither player gained a point. The researchers made sure that each child understood all the outcomes, both for themselves and for their partners, and that the points were merely "points," with no economic or ented? Second, is a student's "self-imposed" MO related to his or her choice behavior in the commons? Third, is there a relationship between a student's "self-imposed" MO and his or her views regarding the MO of the "partner"?

DETERMINATION OF SELF-IMPOSED MOTIVATIONAL ORIENTATION

The psychologists most responsible for answering the first question, above, are D. M. Messick and C. G. McClintock. In 1968, they published a paper that presented a technique for determining the MO of a student who had been given no explicit motivational instructions. In the Messick-McClintock procedure the experimental game itself is presented in a new format, called the "decomposed game." In a decomposed game the amount of points received by each player is shown for each choice. For example, if you choose A in game 1 of Figure 10.7, you would receive 6 points and your partner would receive 3. Different combinations of points would be chosen by players with different MOs. Suppose a student with a cooperative MO chose the column in which the sum of points to self and the other person is the largest (column B in the first game and column A in the second). A student with an individualistic MO would choose the column that maximizes

material incentives attached. Finally, to study the influence of situational factors, the researchers varied whether each child knew only his own score or his partner's score as well. The researchers believed that when social comparison was possible, competition would be higher.

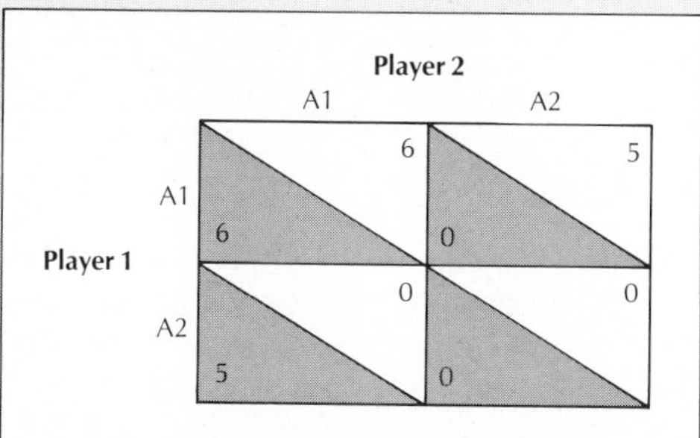

How did the children respond? For each of the cultures, the numbers of competitive choices (5 points for self, 0 for partner) increased steadily with age. The children also became more competitive when they could see their partner's score as well as their own. Although children in all five cultures were about equally competitive by the sixth grade, there were some striking cultural differences at the second-grade level. Here, the Belgian boys were the least competitive and the Japanese boys were the most competitive. The authors interpreted this finding to suggest that Belgian boys become more competitive with schooling, while Japanese boys are made competitive by their culture, even before they start school. Also, as in other gaming research, the children's strategies were influenced by the children's experience together, with some pairs "locking in" on competition and other pairs "locking in" on cooperation. In general, one partner's strategy was reciprocated by the other.

The researchers concluded that in all of these Western-influenced cultures, competition as an autonomous motive increased with age. In addition, competition could be heightened by displaying both children's scores side by side, creating the opportunity for social comparison. Overall, competitive behavior is complexly determined by dispositional factors, situational factors, and cultural factors.

FIGURE 10.7 Examples of two decomposed games. In game 1, cooperation leads to column B, individualism to column A, and competition to column C. In game 2, all three MOs lead to the same choice—column A.

Game 1

	Column A	Column B	Column C
Self	6	5	4
Other	3	5	0

Game 2

	Column A	Column B	Column C
Self	9	5	4
Other	1	3	0

his or her own welfare with no concern for the gains or losses of the other (column A in the first game and column A in the second as well). Finally, a student with a competitive MO would choose the column that would lead to the greatest gains over his or her partner (column C in the first game and column A in the second).

If Deutsch is correct and the three MOs represent the MOs that most people are likely to adopt, which strategy would people actually choose in a decomposed game when no MO had been dictated by the experimenter? In Figure 10.7, game 2, most people should choose column A, since that choice maximizes all three motives. And a recent study (Kuhlman and Marshello, 1975a) found that students did just that, choosing column A 84 percent of the time.

Do students differ as to which of the three MOs they adopt? Yes. In the study by Kuhlman and Marshello (1975a), the researchers found that approximately one-third of their students chose A in game 1 (individualism), one-third chose B (cooperation), and one-third C (competition). Interestingly, males and females did not differ in terms of the MO they adopted.

RELATION OF SELF-IMPOSED MO TO CHOICE IN THE COMMONS

We saw fron Deutsch's work that MO (when it is established by instructions from the experimenter) is significantly related to choice behavior in the commons. Does the MO of a student as determined by the decomposed-game procedure have any relationship to that student's behavior in the commons?

Kuhlman and Marshello (1975b) conducted a study in which each student's MO was assessed via decomposed games. Then the student was placed into a standard two-person commons-dilemma setting. During the actual play of the commons game each student was paired with one of three "partners." In fact, the "partner" was an experimentally controlled stooge following one of three strategies: 100-percent cooperation, 0-percent cooperation, or tit for tat.

As can be seen in Figure 10.8, there was a strong relationship between the student's MO

FIGURE 10.8 Percentage of cooperative choices made by cooperative, individualistic, and competitive students to three preprogrammed strategies. (From Kuhlman and Marshello, 1975b.)

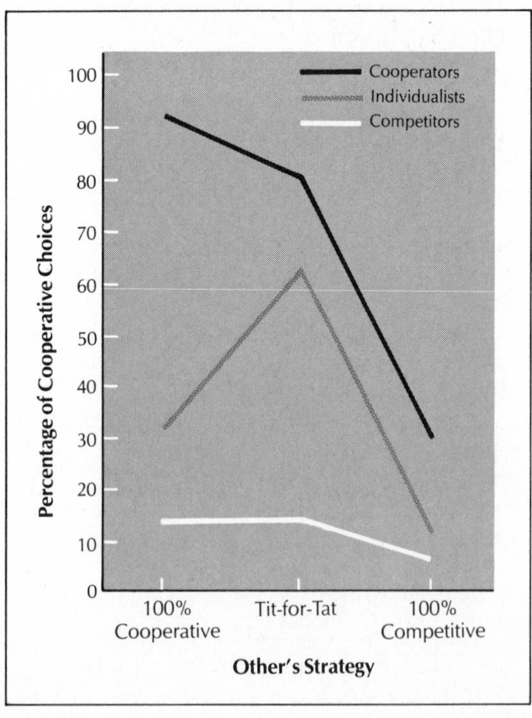

and his or her response to the three preprogrammed strategies. A "partner" who was totally cooperative was exploited by students with a competitive and/or an individualistic MO. A cooperative MO, however, produced very high levels of cooperation with such a "partner."

These data demonstrate the importance of "internal" motivational states to behavior in the commons dilemma. However, features of the setting are important as well. For example, we have just seen that a student with a cooperative MO will only cooperate under certain circumstances. This is another demonstration of the point that we have argued throughout this book—that behavior is a function of persons *and* situations.

With this notion in mind, let us turn to a consideration of how situational factors combine with dispositional factors to determine the likelihood of cooperation in the commons. We will use the work of Dean Pruitt and Melvin Kimmel (1977) to guide us.

HOW EXTERNAL FACTORS INTERACT WITH INTERNAL DISPOSITIONS IN THE COMMONS

PRUITT AND KIMMEL'S GOAL/EXPECTATION THEORY OF COOPERATION IN PRISONER'S DILEMMA

Pruitt and Kimmel argue that in order for cooperation to develop in a dyad, each member must possess four specific cognitions. These include three "insights" and an "expectation." The three insights cause each person to adopt mutual cooperation as the *goal* for the relationship. However, such a goal does not guarantee cooperative behavior. Before the person will cooperate, he or she needs to possess a fourth cognition, which is a particular expectation regarding the characteristics of the partner.

THE INSIGHTS The three insights are as follows:

1. *You must realize that you depend on the behavior of other people for your own best outcomes.* Specifically, you must see that your own outcomes get better and better as your partner becomes more and more cooperative. Once a person acquires this first insight, he/she becomes concerned with the behavior of his/her partner; specifically, the concern is that the partner choose cooperatively.

The next insight is necessary (but not sufficient by itself) to get the person to act in such a way that the chance of cooperation from the partner is not zero.

2. *You must realize that others will not tolerate being exploited.* We have seen that no one (including cooperators) will allow himself or herself to be taken advantage of in this situation. If you are interacting in the commons with an old friend or with a stranger, the most realistic view you can have of him/her is "This person will not let me rip him/her off. If I act noncooperatively with him/her, the response I am going to get back is noncooperation."

When a person comes into possession of this second insight, he/she realizes that noncooperation on his/her part will result in mutual noncooperation in the dyad. Both participants to the interaction will wind up in the undesirable deficient-equilibrium state.

The third insight implies that the other kind of behavior possible in this situation (cooperation) will *also* be mutual, if it is going to occur at all.

3. *The only way you can expect the other to cooperate is if you cooperate yourself.* If we examine the responses of individualistic and cooperative students to the 100-percent cooperative partner, it seems that the two MO groups may differ on this insight. Individualists seem ready to believe that there are others who will cooperate even in the face of unrelenting exploitation. The behavior of the cooperative group in no way suggests such a notion.

To this point, then, we have listed the insights necessary for a goal of mutual cooperation. While it seems reasonable to assume that students with cooperative MOs start out with more of these insights than students with individualistic MOs, we cannot assume that individualists never come into possession of these insights. In fact, individualists can become cooperative in the commons. Therefore, individualists must acquire the insights they lack as interaction proceeds; that is, individualists depend on experience in the game to pick up these insights.

THE EXPECTATION Imagine a student who possesses all three of the insights. Can we be sure he or she will choose cooperatively? No. It is also necessary for our student to have a specific view of the partner with whom he/she is paired. This is the "expectation" component of the theory: *The person must believe that his or her own cooperation will be reciprocated by the other.* That is, you need to trust the other. Even if you realize the wisdom of mutual cooperation and the tragedy of noncooperation in the commons (which happens when you hold the first three insights) you should not cooperate with the other unless you think that (sooner or later) the other will cooperate with you. To be the sole cooperator sticks you with the "sucker's payoff"; you can do better than that by being noncooperative.

Trust in one's partner reappears as a very important determinant of your choice behavior. Do students of differing MOs enter interaction with different levels of trust? Fortunately, we do not need to speculate here. Research provides us with a direct answer.

TRUST AND MOTIVATIONAL ORIENTATION

Harold Kelley and Anthony Stahelski (1970) conducted a series of prisoner's-dilemma studies in which they first determined a student's MO. Then, in several of their studies, they would ask each student to guess what the MO of his or her partner was. Since the partner was a person unknown to the student, and since the game had not yet begun, the student's guess about his or her partner tells us something about the student's trust at the outset of interaction.

These researchers dealt with only two motivational categories: cooperative and competitive. Their cooperative motive is virtually identical to the notion we have been calling "cooperation" so far in the chapter. For competition, however, there was no distinction made between what we have been calling "individualism" and "competition." We cannot be sure how Kelley and Stahelski's competitive group would compare to separate groups of students with individualistic and competitive MOs.

Kelley and Stahelski found that there was a low level of trust in the competitive group. That is, almost all students in this category guessed that their partner was competitive, as they defined the term. In the cooperative group, however, almost half of the students guessed that their partner was also a cooperator.

Since the study of Kelley and Stahelski, another experiment was conducted in which students of all three MO types were asked to guess what "most other people are like in the population at large" (Kuhlman and Wimberley, 1976). The results were clear and consistent with the findings of Kelley and Stahelski. Specifically, both individualists and competitors guessed that almost all people would choose noncooperatively in the commons. Cooperators, however, guessed that around half the population would be cooperative in this game.

These findings relate to goal/expectation theory in a straightforward way. Originally, we speculated only that cooperators were likely to possess some or all of the first three insights. Now, in light of the above research, we can argue that cooperators also possess more trust than individualists at the outset of the interaction. Thus, we are now ready to answer our question concerning the circumstances under which a cooperative MO student will choose cooperatively in the commons: cooperative MO students will behave cooperatively in the commons unless their trust is violated.

How about individualists? We have seen that individualists enter the interaction with the belief that their partner is not worthy of trust (as the Kelley-Stahelski research implies). Yet since individualists do in fact cooperate (as with a tit-for-tat "partner"), they must be "changing their minds" during the interaction. Thus, we can assert that individualistic students will cooperate under two conditions: (1) when they have had sufficient experience in the task to acquire the first three insights; and (2) when they have had sufficient experience with their "partner" to develop a sense of trust.

When students have not had sufficient experience with their "partner," it is difficult to develop trust. For example, in the Shure and

Trust and cooperation generally decrease as group size increases. However, this tendency can be offset in large groups that permit communication among members. *(© Christina Thomson 1980 / Woodfin Camp & Assoc.)*

Meeker study discussed above, students who changed partners on every trial showed much less cooperation than students who kept the same partners. Similarly, if students have simply observed their partner behave cooperatively in a previous game with someone else, they show more cooperation toward the partner than if the partner was observed to behave competitively in a previous game (Braver and Barnett, 1976).

Another factor that affects trust and cooperation in the commons dilemmas is group size. In one study (Bonacich, Shure, Kahan, and Meeker, 1976), as group size increased from three to six to nine, the level of cooperation in the group decreased. However, this tendency can be offset. For example, if each member of the group stands to gain more by cooperating as the group increases in size, then large groups can be more cooperative than small groups. The tendency toward less cooperation in large groups can also be reduced by communication within the group, as we might have expected from Deutsch's early work on trust and communication in two-person games. In a recent experiment, Dawes, McTavish, and Shaklee (1977) had groups of eight strangers play the commons-dilemma game. The groups were allowed to engage in "relevant communication" about the group problem, "irrelevant communication," or "no communication." The researchers found that those groups that engaged in relevant communication showed much higher levels of cooperation (72 percent) than the other two groups (30 percent and 32 percent, respectively). The fact that discussion per se did not reduce conflict supports the emphasis on trust in both Deutsch's and Pruitt and Kimmel's theories. Although it seems likely that the MO of students might moderate these effects of group size, research of this type has yet to be done.

These findings have implications for many of the real-world commons dilemmas discussed earlier. For example, when the number of users in a commons increases to include the population of a large area, such as all the fishers who use a certain bay, or an even larger segment of the world's population, such as citizens of industrialized countries who consume most of the world's oil, then special efforts must be made to create mutual trust. Indeed, why should citizens in one country conserve energy unless they believe that citizens in other nations are conserving energy as well? Otherwise the energy pool is being exhausted and the conserving nations are not benefiting. Thus clear communication becomes imperative in order to build mutual trust.

EFFECTS OF THREAT AND POWER IN TWO-PERSON GAMES

While most interdependence research has followed the matrix-game paradigm we just dealt with, there have been exceptions. These exceptions have produced results that are important to any general theory of social interdependence. In the following paragraphs, we will focus on what might be called the area's second most popular research paradigm—the "trucking game," developed by Morton Deutsch and Robert Krauss (1960). This, in turn, will lead to a consideration of the influence of social power on conflict resolution.

THE EFFECTS OF THREAT Numerous limitations have plagued bargaining researchers. Not the least of these is that the participants are offered very few behavioral alternatives—typically the choice is between pressing a red or a black button. An additional alternative of great interest to psychologists is the use of threat. When a person can threaten another with punishment for behavior the person wants to discourage, what is the effect on their relationship? Can the two of them hope to work together for mutual gain, or does the availability of threat undermine their relationship? Parents often find threats useful in shaping their children: "If you don't stop this instant, you'll be spanked." And diplomats say: "If you help our enemies, you will be destroyed."

Although threats occasionally secure the desired results for the moment, there is reason to believe that at least under some conditions the long-term effect of threats may be less pleasing. For example, Deutsch and Krauss (1960) engaged pairs of subjects in a game in which each player was in charge of a fictitious trucking company—Acme or Bolt. The subjects' chief aim was to carry goods to a destination. For each trip completed, the subjects received sixty cents minus operating expenses at the rate of a penny per second. The object was for subjects to reach their destinations as rapidly as possible.

Each subject received a road map (the basis of Figure 10.9) indicating that each player had two alternate routes, one short and one long. The short route consisted of a one-lane segment to be shared by both players. If both players attempted to cross this segment at the same time, they would meet head-on, be unable to advance, and lose money as the seconds ticked away. To proceed, it would be necessary for one or the other to back down and let the rival pass first. Thus, cooperation was necessary for mutual benefit. The players could also take the longer routes and be assured of reaching their destinations; however, they would sacrifice valuable operating expenses by doing so.

Subjects played the trucking game under various conditions of threat. In the bilateral-threat condition, both Acme and Bolt controlled gates (as indicated in Figure 10.9) that either could use to prevent the other from passing through the one-lane segment. In the unilateral-threat condition, only Acme controlled a gate, thereby gaining an obvious advantage. If both Acme and Bolt reached the lane at the same time and Bolt refused to back down, then Acme could prevent Bolt from ever using the single lane. In the no-threat condition, neither player had a gate. The experimenters did not allow communication between players.

The major experimental question was whether the availability of threat would increase or decrease the players' winnings. And, if

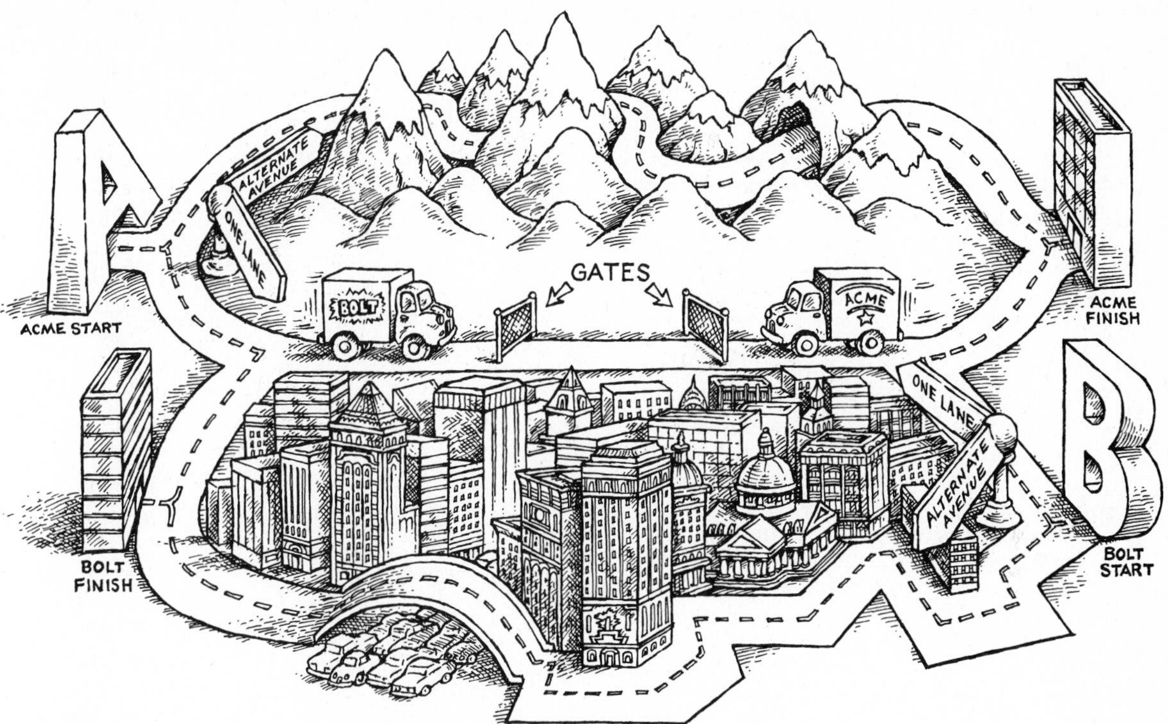

FIGURE 10.9 An elaboration of the road map used in Deutsch and Krauss's (1960) trucking game. In the bilateral-threat condition, shown here, both Acme and Bolt controlled gates on the one-lane road. Because subjects lost one cent for every second it took them to reach their destinations, a cooperative strategy—alternating the use of the road—was mutually beneficial. When both players used their power to close the gates, losses were heavy on both sides. When only one trucking company had the power of threat, it also lost, and the results were even more disastrous for the powerless player.

only one party had threat capability (as is almost always the case in parent-child relations, in international relations between rich and poor nations, and in dictatorships), did only the threatener benefit, or did the threatener tend to share the benefits with the other party?

Table 10.1 indicates the average monetary payoffs won by subjects under all three conditions. Interestingly, only when neither player had a threat option did either player profit from the game. The combined winnings for both players when neither was in a position to threaten the other averaged more than two dollars. When both parties had the power of threat, however, both players lost heavily. And when threat was available only to Acme, Bolt suffered considerably, losing an average of almost three dollars. However, although Acme

TABLE 10.1 AVERAGE WINNINGS AND LOSSES UNDER VARIOUS THREAT CONDITIONS

PAYOFFS	NO THREAT	ACME THREAT ONLY	BILATERAL THREAT
Acme's	$1.22	−$1.19	−$4.07
Bolt's	0.81	− 2.87	− 4.69
Total	2.03	− 4.06	− 8.76

Source: M. Deutsch and R. Krauss, "The Effect of Threat Upon Interpersonal Bargaining," *Journal of Abnormal and Social Psychology* 61 (1960): 181–189

FOCUS ON APPLICATIONS

THREATS

In an interdependent social system, the behavior of one person or group can affect the outcomes of numerous others. One example of such a behavior is threats. Threats can be used either defensively or offensively, as explained in the accompanying section.

In the first example below, a threat is employed defensively for political ends. The federal government had declared the Love Canal neighborhood of Niagara Falls, New York, uninhabitable because a chemical company had dumped toxic wastes on the land years ago. Angered that the government had not followed through on its promised financial assistance for relocation, local homeowners took matters into their own hands and seized representatives of the Environmental Protection Agency as hostages. In the second example below, a terrorist criminal demonstrates just how fragile the social fabric of our lives is. A jar of pickles is poisoned in a San Diego grocery store, and not until the store pays off with loose diamonds will the criminal reveal what other items may have been poisoned as well.

The point is, we are all capable of and vulnerable to threats. Whenever a single individual or a small group decides not to cooperate, they can effectively "negotiate" with threats. Counterthreats can reduce the likelihood of such a threat, but, as the gaming research makes clear, mutual threats can lead to a mutual standoff where no one gains. Threats will no doubt always remain an option, though, so long as participants in the social system do not share mutual trust. As one Love Canal homeowner said of the hostage action, "Why wait? We've paid enough."

I

NIAGARA FALLS, N.Y. (UPI)—Residents of the chemically contaminated Love Canal area held two federal officials "hostage" for several hours Monday night, demanding White House authorization of funds to relocate more than 700 families.

The officials, James Lucas and Frank Napal of the Environmental Protection Agency, were released unharmed, an FBI spokesman said.

Association president Lois Gibbs said no weapons were used in taking the men prisoner, and a telephone line was kept open to receive any response from federal officials to the homeowners' demands.

In Washington, deputy EPA administrator Barbara Blum said the agency spoke to both men by phone while they still were being held and did not feel they were in "any imminent danger at this time." She said the EPA alerted the U.S. attorney's office and the FBI.

suffered less when it controlled the means of threat, it ended up losing money. Acme would have been better off had it not been able to threaten its rival.

These results are frequently taken to mean that bilateral-threat capability will almost invariably make conflicts more difficult to resolve. Recent research, however, shows us that things are not that simple. Consider the nature of the threats used by Deutsch and Krauss. The threats could be either offensive or defensive.

That is, a person could lower his/her gate in order to make one of (at least) two different statements: (1) "If you don't let me go through first, I'm going to hold you up for a long time" or (2) "If you don't stop being so aggressive, I'm going to keep you from getting to your destination." As I've described them, one form of threat (defensive) seems more legitimate or fair than the other (offensive) form.

It could certainly have happened in the Deutsch and Krauss study that when one student lowered the gate thinking of her act as defensive and legitimate, the other student did not see it this way. The threats in this study, then, were imprecise and capable of being misinterpreted.

In a recent study, Pruitt and Gleason (1978)

She denied that the White House had rejected proposals for temporary relocation of Love Canal residents. "These reports are absolutely false," she said.

Niagara Falls police were at the scene but said they were denied access to the office by groups of homeowners blocking the two entrances to the house.

The residents were demanding immediate relocation because of an EPA study released Saturday showing chromosome damage in 11 of 36 Love Canal residents, an abnormally high level. The chromosome aberrations can be an early warning of future health problems such as cancer and birth defects.

Federal officials said they wanted to further verify the results of the study before deciding whether to order relocations. They said there would be no decision before Wednesday.

"Why Wednesday? Why not today?" Gibbs complained. "Why wait? We've paid enough."

II

SAN DIEGO—Deadly concentrations of cyanide have been found in a food product at a second Safeway supermarket here, authorities revealed Monday as they awaited further word from an extortionist who was demanding 50 diamonds before he would identify other food items he has assertedly poisoned.

On Saturday, according to officers, a poisoned 46-ounce jar of Vlasic pickles was found at a Safeway store in La Jolla. It contained 1,400 milligrams of cyanide, said Dr. Georgia Reaser of the San Diego County Health Department. She noted that 250 milligrams is considered a lethal dose.

The extortionist telephoned the La Jolla store Saturday night and told an assistant manager that a jar of poisoned pickles could be found in a cooler.

The employees found the jar, which bore a note reading: "Safeway Stores Inc., Manager. Warning. Warning! This jar of pickles is loaded with deadly cyanide poison.

"Also there are five other food items loaded with cyanide that are now on the shelves of this store. If you comply with our demands, we will give you a list and the exact locations of these food items. Otherwise, we will poison the food in every Safeway store in the area.

"It is up to you what happens next. You have until 6 p.m. today to obtain fifty (50) loose diamonds (one) carat or larger of good quality . . . you will be contacted."

The note was signed, "The Poison Gang."

Deputy Coroner Jay Johnson said there was enough cyanide in the jar of pickles "to kill a family."

Source: "Love Canal Group Releases 'Hostages,' " *Los Angeles Times*, May 20, 1980, p. 20; Ted Vollmer, "Food at 2nd Market Found Poisoned in Extortion Plot," *Los Angeles Times*, April 1, 1980, Part 1, p. 1.

had students play the trucking game under conditions of no verbal communication. One-third of the dyads had gates, one-third had no gates, and a final third had "gates plus threats." In this latter group, each student had a gate, and also possessed a clear, unambiguous defensive threat. Specifically, if one student lowered his or her gate, the other could respond by placing a token on the playing surface. Unless the gate lowerer removed the gate, he or she would be heavily fined on the next move.

Pruitt and Gleason found (as had Deutsch and Krauss) that winnings were much higher in the no-gates group than in the gates group. However, students with the additional and more precise threat option did quite well. There was no significant difference between their winnings and those in the no-gates group.

It would appear, then, that the communication of an unambiguously defensive threat can reduce rather than exacerbate conflict. Before giving in to the temptation to view this result (or any other result you've seen) as a truth that doesn't need qualification, force yourself to examine the experiment for features that might limit the effects we observed.

For one thing, in this study, as in most gaming studies, each student possessed the same

Research has confirmed the popular belief that power corrupts. A notorious case in point is Bokassa I, who seized control of the Central African Republic in 1966 and proclaimed himself Emperor in 1977. He squandered the country's resources for his own glorification and tortured and abused his subjects. He was overthrown in 1979. *(Richard Melloul / Sygma)*

amount of power. Would these results repeat themselves in a dyad in which only one student had the legitimate counterthreat? How about if both students possessed counterthreat, but one could impose heavier penalties than the other? We could only answer these specific questions by conducting specific experiments. Although such studies have not yet been done, there has been research on human behavior in situations of unequal power.

DOES POWER CORRUPT? The threats and punishments to which people resort in a competitive situation are influenced by the magnitude of power that they can wield, according to findings reported by William Smith and Walter Leginski (1970). These investigators had male college students play a bargaining game in which the goal was to agree with an opponent to adopt one of several possible contracts. The participants could resort to bids, threats, and fines in their bargaining. The two bargainers in each pair stood to gain from different contracts. There was actually only one real subject in each pair. The programmed opponent delivered a predetermined sequence of demands, threats, and punishments. The power of the artificial opponent was in all cases less than that of the subjects.

Smith and Leginski found that the greater the individuals' magnitudes of power, the greater are their expectations for the success of their outcomes, as judged by their resistance to compromise. High-power subjects expected the opponent to yield to their demands without having to resort to threat. At first they were reluctant to use their power. But after it became apparent that the opponent would not yield, they increased the frequency and intensity of their threats and punishments. It appears, then, that the greater the power individuals have at their disposal, the more likely it is that they will resist compromise and resort to threats and punishments.

Further indications that power can corrupt have been reported by David Kipnis (1972). He found that power corrupts a powerful person's view of the less powerful and demeans the less powerful in the process. For example, subjects who had more power than others stepped up efforts to influence the less powerful. They also regarded the less powerful as being at the mercy of others. They wanted to minimize their contacts with the less powerful subjects. And they also devalued what less powerful persons did, although this devaluation of others did not seem to boost the self-esteem of the powerful.

THE EFFECTS OF NORMS IN INTERDEPENDENT SITUATIONS

We have dealt with concepts that are fairly specific to the exchange-theory approach to social interdependence: game structure, dominating strategy, motivational orientation, bilateral threat, and so on. In this section we will continue to deal with social interdependence, but we will focus on an idea that is less specific to the exchange-theory approach than the above concepts are. We will examine the concept of social norms and consider the relevance of norms of justice or fairness to behavior in the commons.

NORMS OF DISTRIBUTIVE JUSTICE

Much of the research on rules of distributive justice has been done by Gerald Leventhal (1976). Leventhal argues that we hold several fairness norms, which he calls "justice rules," and that each is based on a different way of determining what a person deserves. Two of these rules are particularly relevant to our discussion here.

The first is the *contributions rule,* which states that a person's outcomes should be directly proportional to his or her contributions (or "inputs") to the social system. For example, if party X has contributed 20 units of value, and party Y only 5 units of value, then by this rule, it would be "unfair" for Y to receive greater outcomes than X.

The most detailed statement of this rule in social psychology is called equity theory (Walster, Walster, and Berscheid, 1978, discussed in Chapters 7 and 9), and a large amount of research on distributive justice has dealt with this single rule. Equity theory says outcomes have been distributed fairly when the ratio of outcomes to inputs for one person is equal to the ratio of outcomes to inputs for the others. In the above example, things would be fair by the equity rule if party X's outcomes were four times greater than party Y's.

Although the contributions rule (or equity theory) applies to a large number of social interactions, Leventhal takes pains to point out that it is not the *only* fairness norm people use. A second rule of distributive justice is the *equality rule,* which states that each person should receive an equal part of the total reward regardless of the individual inputs.

Research by Samuel Komorita and Jerome Chertkoff (1973) demonstrates that both of these rules exist in interdependent situations. In their research on *coalition formation,* three or more students are provided with differing numbers of points, which constitute their "inputs" in the experiment. These points are like the number of votes that a delegate brings with him or her to a nominating convention.

For example, student A might receive 40 points, student B 20 points, and student C 10 points. The experiment offers a prize (let's imagine that it equals 100 points), which no single student can win alone. The students are told something like: "To win the prize, your team needs 45 or more points." The students must decide which team or "coalition" will be formed to win the prize.

The students must also agree how to divide the prize among themselves. It is at this stage that Komorita and Chertkoff's research is most relevant to our current point regarding equity and equality norms. Let's imagine that persons A (40 points) and C (10 points) form a coalition. They now must agree on who gets what.

If you were student A, which of the two justice rules would you use for your "opening" demand? By the equality rule, you would receive one half the prize, or 50 points. By the equity rule, however, you would receive 80 points, because you brought 40 of your team's 50 winning points to the coalition (4/5 of 100 is 80). Invoking the norm of equity, student A can make an initial and legitimate demand for 80 points.

How about student C? Equality provides 50 points. Equity for this person, however, only provides 20 since he/she only brought 10 of the 50 winning points to the coalition. The equality norm, then, allows student C to make an opening and legitimate demand of 50 points. The problem is, of course, that there are only 100 points to be divided.

What do two bargainers do in such a situation? As pointed out by Komorita and Chertkoff, the bargainers probably "split the difference." In this particular situation the difference would be split as follows: student A's best possible legitimate outcome is 80 (by equity); the worst possible legitimate outcome is 50 (equality). Student A would take an outcome halfway between these two extremes, which would be 65. For student C, the two legitimate extremes are 50 (equality) and 20 (equity). By taking the outcome halfway between these two points—a share of 35—student A and student C's bargain is sealed.

If both of these justice norms are salient to each of the bargainers in this situation, we can make quantitative (and nonobvious) predictions about how the bargainers will divide up the prize. In fact, using these two norms, Komorita and Chertkoff were able to predict accurately how the students in their research would actually divide up their points.

As an interesting example of these two norms, consider the United Nations' voting process. In the Security Council, the permanent member nations, which provide most of the financial support for the organization, can veto any measure they disapprove—a privilege that incorporates the contributions, or equity, norm. Yet in the General Assembly, each nation, large or small, has only one vote—a situation based on the equality norm.

Thus, there appears to be good evidence for the idea that both of these distributive justice norms are part of our notions of fairness in interdependent situations. In the preceding analysis of the coalition bargaining process, there was also a hint of when a person might choose one justice rule over another. Specifically, we suggested that each bargainer's opening demand would be based on that fairness norm which was to his/her greatest advantage. In part, then, considerations of self-interest may influence which rules of fairness we subscribe to.

ARE WE FAIR BECAUSE OF OUR BELIEFS OR TO MAKE A GOOD IMPRESSION?

The above research demonstrates that people's sense of fairness is influenced by their self-interest. A more extreme form of self-interest is the possibility that our adherence to norms of fairness in the first place is simply an attempt to make a good impression on others by appearing just. To test this possibility, Rivera and Tedeschi (1976) had female college students work on individual tasks. Each student thought she was part of a pair, working on the same task with another woman who was in the next room. When the experiment was over, the woman was told that she and her partner had each done equally well, and the experimenter would divide a dollar between them. In the equity condition, the student was paid 50 cents and was told that the other person received 50 cents also. In the "overpayment" condition, the student received 75 or 90 cents and was told the other person was being given 25 cents or 10 cents, respectively. The student was then asked to describe her feelings in one of two ways: on either a standard paper-and-pencil measure that would be seen by the experimenter, or through a special technique where she thought her responses would remain anonymous. On the paper-and-pencil measure, the overpaid students reported more distress than students who had been equitably paid. However, when students thought their responses would remain anonymous, there were no differences between the two payment groups in their level of distress.

In light of these studies, our ability to predict an individual's adherence to norms of justice seems to depend on our ability to analyze the impact of each norm on that individual's well-being. These studies also suggest that there will not be a necessary consensus among these members as what is fair and what isn't.

Up to this point we have seen (1) why the experimental gaming researcher uses a particular strategy; (2) examples of the empirical findings produced by this research paradigm; (3) how a theory has been constructed to "rationalize" this set of findings under a small set of basic ideas; and (4) how cooperation in the commons is influenced by threats, power, and norms of justice. At the outset of the chapter, we attempted to show why the questions the gaming researcher asks are important. In the next section we will consider whether this research strategy is helpful in answering these important questions.

CAN WE RELATE BEHAVIOR IN THE GAMING LABORATORY TO THE REAL WORLD?

There is an understandable "unease" that many people experience when hearing about the game paradigm. The situation is so abstract and contrived that it is hard to imagine that what students do in the gaming laboratory tells us anything at all about what they do in interdependent situations in the real world—that is, whether their laboratory behavior has "ecological validity."

But two experiments with different procedures have pointed to such a link between the gaming laboratory and the real world. Although the two studies make their points in different ways, they are both based on one of the reliable game findings we have discussed.

We have seen that different students adopt different strategies in the game lab, some being cooperative, some individualistic, and others competitive. Were these students telling us something about themselves—the way they would react in the real world—or were they simply adopting an arbitrary approach to the game on the spur of the moment? The answer to this question has much to do with the ecological validity of gaming research.

In the first study that helps answer this question, Daryl Bem and Charles Lord (1979) evaluated the ecological validity of gaming research by means of what Bem calls a "template matching technique." With this technique, the experimenter first describes what is meant by a cooperator to an audience of judges (the judges were graduate students in psychology). The cooperator is described only in laboratory-operational terms: for example, the judges are shown a decomposed gaming task, how it works, and then how a cooperator would choose in this task. In the same way, the judges are also shown how an individualist and a competitor would choose.

The judges are then asked to examine a 100-item list of personality statements (Block, 1961) and to decide for each statement whether it is characteristic, uncharacteristic, or unrelated to each of the three types of laboratory orientations (cooperator, individualist, competitor). This process produces three profiles or "templates"—one for each MO type—across the 100 items on the list. The following are some examples of the items describing each of the three types: cooperator "appears straightforward, forthright, candid in dealing with others" and "behaves in a giving way to others"; individualist "has high aspiration level for self" and "is concerned with own body and the adequacy of its physiological functioning"; competitor "behaves in an assertive fashion" and "compares self to others, is alert to real or fancied differences between self and others."

The next step in Bem and Lord's procedure is to observe students' strategies in the laboratory on the decomposed gaming task. Each student is categorized as a cooperator, individualist, or competitor according to the strategy he or she employs. Then the students are asked to get one of their friends from the outside world to describe them, using the 100 personality items described above. The friends are instructed to select statements that describe how the student typically behaves—what he or she "is like as a person." The students' gaming strategy and the friends' descriptions are then compared.

Imagine a student who adopts a cooperative MO in the laboratory. If this behavior is related to the student's actions in the real world, then we should obtain the following result: when we compare the friend's description of the student with the three different MO templates, the best match should occur (in this case) with the cooperative template; if the student showed a competitive MO, the best match should be with the competitive template; and so on.

Bem and Lord's results show just the sort of fit between the friend's descriptions and templates described above. For 70 percent of the students (ten of each MO type), the match indicated that these gaming strategies had ecological validity. In other words, a person who acts cooperatively in the gaming laboratory is likely to behave similarly in the real world and differently than does a person who adopts a different MO in the lab.

The second study on the ecological validity of gaming research dealt with the relationship between an individual's characteristic nonverbal behavior and the game strategy selected by that individual. Previous research (Gottheil, Thornton, and Exline, 1976) had determined that people seem to possess a characteristic nonverbal affective style that is evident regardless of whatever the person might be saying or doing. For example, some people were found to give "background" cues suggesting sadness, some happiness, and others anger, regardless of whether they were telling a sad story, a happy story, or an angry story.

In light of this research Peter Carnevale (1977) conducted a study to determine if an individual's nonverbal affective style was related to his or her gaming strategy. First, he measured students' MOs in a standard laboratory game. Then, four weeks later each student reported for a second study conducted by a different experimenter in a different setting with apparently no connection to the original experiment. Students were asked to tell three stories from their own lives: one happy, one sad, and one angry. The experimenter was not aware of the student's MO (cooperative, individualistic, or competitive) as the stories were being told. The stories were videotaped and then shown without sound to a group of undergraduate judges, whose task was to decide if the story was a happy, sad, or angry one. These judges had no idea that the storytellers had previously been in a gaming study.

The results were surprising and unexpected. Cooperative MO storytellers were judged to be happy much more often than the other two types of MO, regardless of the type of story that was being told. Competitive MO students, on the other hand, gave off less positive nonverbal cues and were more likely to be seen as angry than the other MO groups.

In order to test the reliability of this effect, a second study (Kuhlman, Carnevale, and Mills, 1979) was run much like the first. Students were selected on the basis of cooperative, individualistic, or competitive MOs. Then two months later, a different experimenter contacted them to participate in another study in a completely different building and setting. The second experimenter was "blind" to the MO of the subjects. The students came to the lab, told their stories to a "blind" interviewer, and were videotaped. A group of undergraduates then viewed the tapes without sound and indicated how much anger, happiness, or sadness they detected in the silent segments.

The results of the experiment are shown in Figure 10.10. As the figure shows, the different MO groups have different background affective styles. Cooperators peak on happiness, while competitors show the opposite behavior, producing peaks on anger and sadness. The individualistic group appears somewhere between these two extremes.

Given our assurance that this result is reliable, let's consider why it is also reasonable. First, we will assume that the results from the gaming laboratory have some ecological validity (which these last two studies seem to indicate). We know from our laboratory research that cooperators are more successful at resolving conflicts (that is, experiencing mutually cooperative interactions) than competitors.

FIGURE 10.10 Levels of angry, happy, and sad background affect seen in the stories of cooperative, individualistic, and competitive students. (From Kuhlman, Carnevale, and Mills, 1979.)

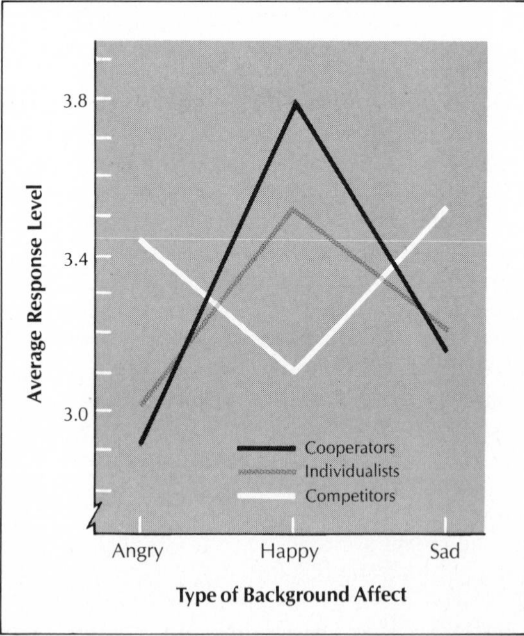

People may act competitively because they either want to win or are afraid of defeat. Research suggests that the latter variety—aversive competition—is the more powerful motivation and may contribute to unhappiness. *(Terry W. Bisbee)*

To the extent that these findings are reflected in the real world, then, cooperators as a group would have had a larger number of "nonconflicted" relationships in the past than competitors, whose relationships would seem to have a good chance of being conflicted, competitive ones. Now, to the degree that such conflicted relationships are negative experiences for the person involved, we might expect those persons to behave differently than a group whose members have had fewer such "bad" times.

What accounts for this effect? Why should cooperators have different nonverbal affective styles than competitors? We know from our laboratory research that cooperators are more successful at resolving conflicts than competitors (that is, cooperators experience more mutually cooperative interactions). To the extent that these findings are representative of the real world, operators as a group would have had a larger number of "nonconflicted" relationships in the past than competitors, whose relationships were more likely to have been conflicted and competitive. Now, if such conflicted relationships may be considered negative experiences, then competitors would be exposed to more negative experiences, and their nonverbal behavior might differ accordingly from someone who has had fewer such "bad" times.

How reasonable is it to view competitive interactions as a negative experience? Couldn't it be argued that competition involves pursuit of goals, defeat of an opponent, and thrill of victory? Perhaps, but gaming researchers Messick and Thornegate (1967) have argued that people can act competitively for two different reasons: (1) the desire to win, or (2) out of fear of being beaten. These researchers call the first instances "positive competition" and the second "aversive competition." In a study measuring the strength of these two types of competition, Messick and Thornegate discovered that aversive competition was more potent.

Other researchers (Steigleder, Weiss, Cramer, and Feinberg, 1978) also suggest that competitive interactions are more negative than positive in tone. These researchers reasoned that if competition produces an aversive internal state, then students should be willing to learn a response that would remove them from competition (that is, they should show "escape" learning). This is just what happened. In five different experiments, when students had to play a maze game in such a way that their performance could be compared with another person, the majority learned the "escape" response.

These results, in combination with those of Messick and Thornegate, suggest that competition is not necessarily a positive experience. Thus it becomes more understandable why competitors may have a nonverbal style that is less happy than cooperators. The reliable nonverbal differences described above help convince us even more that a person's behavior in the gaming laboratory tells us something both real and important about him or her as a person.

CONCLUSION: EVEN WITH ECOLOGICAL VALIDITY WE MUST BE CAREFUL

We have just seen that gaming research can have ecological validity. But we must still be cautious in drawing connections between the real world and laboratory findings. This necessity does not result from the fact that laboratory findings are "untrue." The "truth" of such findings has been the point of the last several paragraphs.

Rather we must be cautious because there may be differences between the laboratory and the real world that make them not entirely comparable. There may even be differences between two similar situations in the real world or between two laboratory settings. In other words, when two settings have important characteristics that are not identical, we should not expect findings from one setting necessarily to generalize to the other.

Let's recall Deutsch's study on MO and choice behavior, and assume the following characteristics: (1) there are two individualists, (2) playing the prisoner's-dilemma structure, (3) who are aware of each other's motives, (4) who cannot communicate, and (5) who are strangers. In this situation we saw a low level of cooperative behavior. However, if the two individualists are given a communication channel, the situation changes drastically even though everything else remains constant. With communication, we observed a high level of cooperation.

We would have been wrong to "generalize" from the first situation to the second in Deutsch's experiment. The two situations had different features. Neither situation was false; each was simply showing us a different truth. As a matter of fact, there are probably many more real-world settings that do not correspond to Deutsch's experiment than settings that do. We learn about a very small and special set of interdependent situations in the real world when we study a single interdependent setting in the laboratory. In order to learn more about the real world in general, we must study many more interdependent situations in the laboratory. The optimal research strategy, then, is one in which the experimenter manipulates different kinds of independent variables so that he or she may learn about behavior in different situations.

Also, it is necessary for social-interdependence researchers to develop a theory that explains all of the research findings with as small a set of notions as possible. Consider what happens when such a research strategy is followed. The theory that is developed to account for the "multisituational" findings becomes very general. It addresses a wide set of socially interdependent relationships in the real world. In both scientific and practical terms, it becomes more useful.

SUMMARY

Exchange theory deals with the mutual outcomes or "payoffs" in situations of social interdependence. According to Thibaut and Kelley, to understand the behavior of two or more interdependent persons, we must understand the structure of their relationship. Structure is the association between specific outcomes and specific behaviors of the interdependent persons. Exchange theorists typically describe a relationship's structure by means of an "outcome matrix," which depicts all possible combinations of outcomes in terms of numerical values.

The structure of interdependence is studied in the laboratory through experimental games. The most common experimental game focuses on a single structure called prisoner's dilemma, which offers its participants a choice between cooperating and noncooperating. A real-world problem that involves the prisoner's-dilemma structure is the commons dilemma. In the commons dilemma everyone can choose to cooperate and win less or not cooperate and win more—at least until the commons is depleted. The dilemma is that it is "reasonable" to be noncooperative, for if no one else is cooperating, then why should you; on the other hand, if everyone else *is* cooperating, then how can it hurt if you act noncooperatively and increase your own gain? Thus in the short run one always maximizes gains and minimizes losses through noncooperation; or, in other words, "noncooperation dominates cooperation."

Research on two-person commons dilemmas finds that over time about three-fourths of the players become cooperative, realizing that cooperation increases gain in the long run. In general, the amount of experience with a partner tends to encourage cooperation. Strategy also influences cooperation, with a tit-for-tat strategy inducing more cooperation from a partner than a strategy of unconditional cooperation.

Individuals' internal characteristics also affect behavior in the commons. One type of individual characteristic—motivational orientation (MO)—was described by Deutsch, who defined three types of MOs: cooperators, individualists, and competitors. By manipulating MO Deutsch determined that MO influenced choice behavior in experimental games, that trust is important for cooperation, and that trust may be fostered by communication. Other research showed that people can be dispositionally categorized according to MO and that each type of MO leads to different strategies.

A number of external situational characteristics have also been found to affect behavior on laboratory games. Pruitt and Kimmel argue that cooperation depends on an individual adopting the goal of cooperation and having the expectation that his or her partner will also adopt this goal and have the same expectation. Such a goal and expectation derive from experience with a partner and are influenced by group size. Also when each player can threaten other players with punishment, cooperation declines, unless the other players possess a defensive counterthreat.

Norms of distributive justice also influence behavior in interdependent situations. Whether players adhere to the equity rule (a share in joint outcomes proportional to individual inputs) or the equality rule (an equal share for all), depends on which rule is more beneficial to each player personally.

The ecological validity of gaming research has been established. For example, Bem and Lord found that an individual's gaming behavior substantially "overlaps" with that individual's behavior in the real world, as perceived by a best friend. Other research determined that people's behavior in a laboratory game reflects their characteristic nonverbal affective style. However, one should be cautious about generalizations from the laboratory to the real world, because the situations may not always be identical.

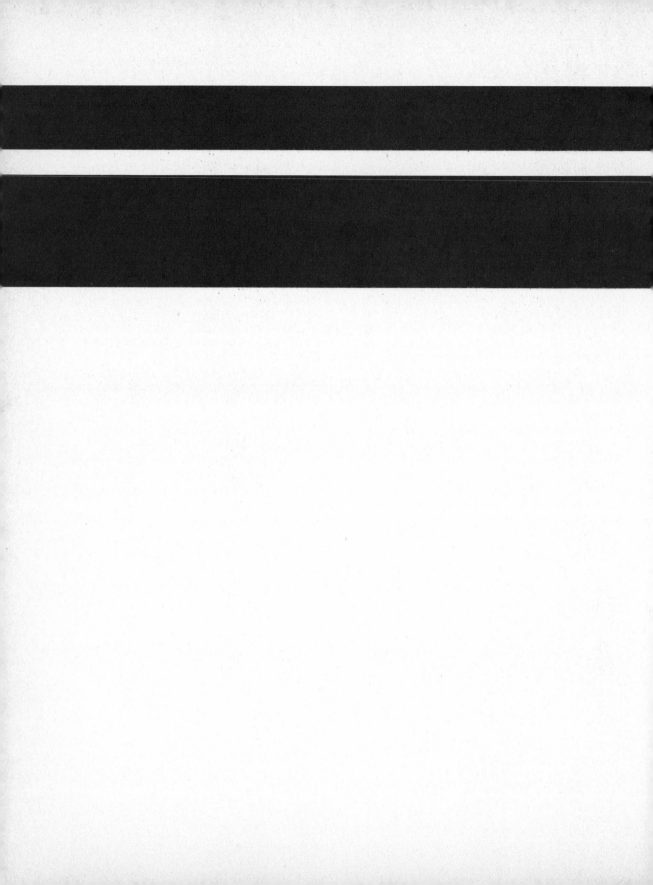

PART FOUR

THE INDIVIDUAL AND SOCIAL ECOLOGY

CHAPTER ELEVEN

GROUPS

Shortly after Thanksgiving 1978, one of the most seemingly incomprehensible human tragedies of modern times occurred in the jungles of Guyana. Here, in a remote religious settlement called Jonestown, more than 900 Americans followed their leader, the Reverend Jim Jones, as he summoned them together over the loudspeaker. "If you love me as much as I love you, we must all die," he told them. Most of his followers willingly filed by the vats of punch and poison set up under the town pavilion. The adults drank cups of fruit-flavored cyanide while the infants had "the potion" sprayed down their throats with hypodermics. A few resisters were marched at gunpoint. Then they were all led away to lie face down in rows. Within minutes they succumbed in violent, choking spasms as Jones's voice intoned over the PA system, "It is time to die with dignity."

What kind of force could lead these individuals from their everyday lives in San Francisco to mass suicide in Guyana? What kind of leader could summon a group of over 900 people to willingly lie down and die? It is tempting, and perhaps comforting, to explain the Jonestown tragedy as the result of an insane leader who twisted the minds of his obedient followers. But as we have argued repeatedly in this book, it is too simplistic to "explain" incomprehensible behavior as caused by "insane" and "twisted" individuals. To understand a tragedy as extreme as Jonestown we must look to the forces inherent in groups. While the theories and research discussed in this chapter generally pertain to small groups of laboratory subjects observed under controlled conditions, they point the way to understanding the powerful forces unleashed in a group of more than 900 people in an isolated jungle with a charismatic leader.

We can begin our exploration of group phenomena with the question: Why do people seek out groups in the first place? It is widely believed—though not proved—that humans have an instinctive tendency to organize themselves into groups, especially nuclear families, kinship groups, cooperative work groups, and organizations (Wilson, 1975). However, the instinctual basis of groups is difficult to establish, both empirically and conceptually. We have no way of verifying either the biological functions groups may have served far back in time or the cause of gregariousness in human beings. But we need not concern ourselves with the role of groups in human evolution in order to understand the nature and power of groups and their effects on individuals.

Groups are pervasive in our society. We can see this pervasiveness from two perspectives: how every individual is a member of many different groups and how much groups dominate the major activities in our society.

Each of us belongs to many groups. We are all identified as members of a gender, a race, a class, an occupation, a family, a neighborhood. And almost all of us belong to many more specific groups, such as garden clubs, fraternities or sororities, a sports team, a dance class. Few people—perhaps only hermits or hobos—can be truly said to live outside groups. And in the case of hobos, it is likely that they, too, form a group that exhibits many of the characteristics of other groups. Hence, to study groups and group behavior is in part to learn about how all of us function in society.

From the other perspective, almost all government, business, and social activity is carried out by groups. From the U.S. Senate—whose innate characteristic is well understood by those who call it "the world's most powerful club"—to local neighborhood planning councils, government is dominated by committees, commissions, and panels. Outside government, there are labor unions, chambers of commerce, and professional societies, and almost all of them have smaller, specialized committees, work groups, and task forces to carry out particular activities.

The specific functions of groups differ widely. Some groups serve very specialized or one-time functions, such as a community-wide committee formed to stop an unwanted freeway or to build a new playground. Other groups have general functions, sometimes serving primarily to provide emotional support. Men who have had heart attacks or women who have had mastectomies sometimes form groups to counsel others in similar situations. In part they may serve as a source of medical information, but in

Commuters cross the Brooklyn Bridge into Manhattan during a strike by New York City's transit workers in April 1980. A group such as a labor union is usually more capable of producing results of this magnitude than is an individual. *(Michelle Bogre / Sygma)*

part they provide support and serve as examples (Schachter, 1959).

All groups are important either because they affect us as individuals or because they affect each other and society. Some groups are important to their members but not to outsiders, like many friendship groups. Other groups have significant effects on nonmembers: for example, the "in group" in a company that informally decides policy, including who gets promoted. Still other groups are significant to virtually everyone, such as a president's "brain trust" that decides national policy.

Groups vary in their degree of effectiveness, too. From one point of view, all groups are powerful relative to the individual. Groups usually have greater ability to influence their environment or to command resources than any individual. One person complaining to a restaurant owner that the air conditioning is too cold will have less impact than twenty persons making the same complaint. There is a force in numbers, but a pooled complaint would probably be even more effective. At a broader level, we have all been affected by the actions of striking workers, such as firefighters or bus drivers, and by the pricing policies of the Organization of Petroleum Exporting Countries (OPEC).

In general, groups are effective when they have a synergistic effect—when the whole is more than the sum of its parts. Brainstorming sessions are an example of one kind of group interaction, in which individuals may correct and amplify each other's ideas and then jointly develop a better plan than the plan of any individual. However, groups sometimes operate in the opposite way, to constrain individual achievements or creativity—so that the whole is less than the sum of its parts. It is also possible for a group to be ineffective because it is too large. The entire student body at a large university, for example, may be too large a group for effective communication and organization of efforts to affect school policies, such as preventing a tuition increase. In fact, in large organizations, members may actually compete with each other for limited resources and for attention from group leaders.

In spite of all these differences among groups and the ways in which groups operate, all groups have some characteristics and processes in common. While not forgetting the wide diversity among groups, we will concentrate in this chapter on what research has revealed about the commonalities among groups. We will describe kinds of groups and their characteristics. We will then look briefly at how groups are formed. Next, we will consider individual roles within a group, the nature of leaders and different styles of leadership, and the effect of different communication patterns in a group. Then, we will examine group dynamics—that is, how groups function and change—and the effects of groups on individuals. Finally, we will apply what is known about group dynamics to the topic of working in groups.

KINDS OF GROUPS

One major set of theories about groups uses the concept of *mere collections.* This approach is exemplified by the restaurant case, above, in which the number of complaints about air conditioning brought about a response from the management. This theoretical approach explains group behavior as simply the logical effect of numbers (Von Neumann and Morgenstern, 1944). It contrasts with theories of synergistic effects, as described in the brainstorming case, above. However, viewing groups as mere collections will take us only so far. While several people working on a problem might each contribute new ideas or correct each other's errors, they still must coordinate their behavior, formulate cooperative goals, and share information (Kelley and Thibaut, 1969). In other words, to be truly effective mere collections must engage in some type of social interaction. Nevertheless, we can begin our analysis of groups from the perspective of mere collections. By describing the limitations of mere collections, we demonstrate what makes groups unique.

NOMINAL GROUPS

Social psychologists use the term *nominal groups* to describe mere collections of individuals. In contrast, the term *psychological groups* applies to groups of people who think, feel, and act together and who care about each other. It is this feeling of being a part of a group that distinguishes true or psychological groups from nominal groups. A nominal group is a group only in the statistical sense, such as all the people who happen to be in a particular supermarket during a survey or all the people who happen to take the same bus to work one morning or all the students who have an eight o'clock class on Monday mornings. In a nominal group people have something in common but it is of no psychological or social significance. We can consider how nominal groups behave, however, as a basis for comparing how psychological groups behave (see, for example, Kelley and Stahelski, 1970; Dawes, McTavish, and Shaklee, 1977).

In a nominal group each person is out for herself or himself: no one feels any responsibility toward the others in the group unless it pays off personally. Imagine, for example, a group of people milling around the opening of a new store. We can think of these shoppers as a nominal group since they share a common interest in the goods for sale, particularly the opening special, a wool sweater for five dollars. Each person wants to buy a sweater, but the manager has stocked only enough to whet the collective appetite. Since each shopper is in competition with every other shopper, the crowd moves toward the sweater display. Will we soon see a mob pushing and shoving? Or will the shoppers stand quietly in line, each hoping that there will be enough? In theory the outcome is a paradox: it is to each shopper's advantage to push others out of the way so as to be first; but if each shopper does that, the result will be a destructive mob.

For another example, consider a new wilderness area in a national park. At first, since the area is difficult to get to and not well known, only a few people go there. They have a wonderful time and the word spreads and more and more people go. The result? An overcrowded "wilderness" area that no one can enjoy as it was planned. This example is not theoretical. At Yosemite National Park, automobile traffic has recently been banned in some places, and limits have been set on the total number of people allowed into the park at any one time.

As detailed in Chapter 10, researchers call these situations the "tragedy of the commons" (Hardin, 1968). In such situations, it is to each person's apparent advantage to get there first and to be selfish; but if everyone always acted that way, our social structure would collapse and each person would lose more than was gained. The other side of this coin, just as tragic, is the situation in which each person in the nominal group could do something that would be beneficial to all, but no one acts. This phenomenon has been called a "social fence" (Platt, 1973). An infamous example of this was the Kitty Genovese case, discussed in Chapter 9, in which a group of onlookers failed to report a stabbing. Each of these examples shows how members of nominal groups can work against their own self-interest by ignoring the interests of one another.

PSYCHOLOGICAL GROUPS

Groups to which people belong are unlike mere nominal groups because their members are connected psychologically and socially. Kurt Lewin (1948: p. 134), one of the founders of modern social psychology, taught:

> Similarity between persons merely permits their classification, their subsumption under the same abstract concept, whereas belonging to the same social group means concrete, dynamic interrelations among persons. A husband, a wife, and a baby are less similar to each other, in spite of their being a strong natural group, than the baby is to other babies.

While all of us belong to many groups, some of them are far more significant to us than others; we identify with some groups, but not others. We can roughly divide psychological groups into two categories: membership groups and reference groups.

A *membership group* is any group to which a person is perceived to belong, including groups based on religion, gender, family, or nationality. In such groups, we share membership with an entire social class or a nation or a neighborhood, though we may not necessarily feel much attachment to the other members. In contrast, a *reference group* is any group whose members are people who matter to us. We compare ourselves to them, and their opinions are important to us. Sometimes a person may not actually be a member of the reference group (as when someone aspires to belong to a certain social set or profession but hasn't made it yet), but still accepts the group's standards and goals. A reference group is one for which a person feels strong involvement. To make the distinction more vivid than it really is, we could say that a membership group is one to which a person is socially connected and a reference group is one to which a person is psychologically connected.

Obviously, many groups to which people belong are both membership groups and reference groups. The family, for example, is a special kind of group and for most people serves as both a membership group and a reference group. You are perceived by others to be a member of your family, and you care what your family thinks of you. The same is true for almost all social groups that people join. You are identified by others as a Chi Omega or a member of the Theater Club; you also accept the group's standards and goals, and you care what the other members think of you.

On the other hand, there are many examples of membership groups that are not reference groups and vice versa. You may be a member of the swimming team, for example, but perhaps you do not care what they think of you or join their weekly beer parties. Conversely, you may try to dress and behave like the campus athletes and hope they think well of you even though you are not a member of a team.

SOCIAL PSYCHOLOGY AND THE ARTS

LONGING FOR A GROUP: AN EXAMPLE FROM FICTION

In her novel *The Member of the Wedding,* Carson McCullers tells the story of Frankie, a twelve-year-old girl growing up in rural Alabama in the 1940s. With her tomboy ways, Frankie is left out of the other girls' parties and clubhouse, and she has no one to play with. When her older brother marries and moves away, Frankie feels completely alone, until she suddenly realizes that her brother and his new wife are now her "group."

> The darkening town was very quiet. For a long time now her brother and the bride had been at Winter Hill. They had left the town a hundred miles behind them, and now were in a city far away. They were them and in Winter Hill, together, while she was her and in the same old town all by herself. The long hundred miles did not make her sadder and make her feel more far away than the knowing that they were them and both together and she was only her and parted from them, by herself. And as she sickened with this feeling a thought and explanation suddenly came to her, so that she knew and almost said aloud: *They are the we of me.* Yesterday, and all the twelve years of her life, she had only been Frankie. She was an *I* person who had to walk around and do things by herself. All other people had a *we* to claim, all other except her. When Berenice said *we,* she meant Honey and Big Mama, her lodge, or her church. The *we* of her father was the store. All members of clubs have a *we* to belong to and talk about. The soldiers in the army can say *we,* and even the criminals on chain-gangs. But the old Frankie had had no *we* to claim, unless it would be the terrible summer *we* of her and John Henry and Berenice—and that was the last *we* in the world she wanted. Now all this was suddenly over with and changed. There was her brother and the bride, and it was as though when first she saw them something she had known inside of her: *They are the we of me.* And that was why it made her feel so queer, for them to be away in Winter Hill while she was left all by herself; the hull of the old Frankie left there in the town alone.

Source: Carson McCullers, *The Member of the Wedding* (New York: Bantam, 1966; originally published, 1946): 39–40.

MEMBERSHIP GROUPS Any membership group to which you belong is important even if it is not consciously a reference group. Sociologists and political scientists have discovered that your social class, for example, predicts in large part such outcomes as the goods and services you will buy, the number of children you will have, your votes in political contests, and your sexual behavior (see, for example, Kohn, 1977). These correlations exist because your social class exerts a wide influence on your behavior, from the type of people you grew up with and who your friends are to where you went to school and what opportunities you have for employment.

Since everyone belongs to many membership groups, the combination of groups is also important. Multiple group memberships may produce conflict. Middle-class blacks, for example, may experience pressure to identify both with poor blacks and with middle-class whites. Such cross pressures can be very strong. In their classic study of school superintendents, Gross, Mason, and McEachern (1958) discovered that as members of both the school board and of the faculty, superintendents were caught in conflicting roles. They escaped the resulting pressures by adhering to the attitudes and standards of a third group, the professional association of superintendents.

A person may also avoid conflict between overlapping membership groups with competing interests by identifying with a larger and more inclusive membership group. For example, a person may be both a worker who seeks higher wages and a consumer who seeks lower prices. To resolve this type of conflict, the individual may be urged by politicians to see him-

a

Three types of groups. (a) A nominal group—such as these travelers—is merely a collection of people who happen to be in a certain place at a certain time. (b) A membership group—based on ethnic background or religious affiliation, for example—is a group to which we perceive a person to belong. (c) A reference group—such as a person's family—is one whose members are important to him or her. Membership groups and reference groups are both psychological groups, and in many cases they are synonymous. *(a—Richard Frieman/Photo Researchers, Inc.; b—© Jill Hartley 1980/Photo Researchers, Inc.; c—© Sylvia Johnson 1980/Woodfin Camp & Assoc.)*

b

c

self or herself as a member in yet a larger group—the nation—and to be mindful of "the national interest." Thus, appealing to the broadest possible membership group can be an effective way to avoid conflict between smaller, competing membership groups.

REFERENCE GROUPS Reference groups are significant because they directly affect values, attitudes, and goals. A person's attitudes and behaviors are heavily influenced by the attitudes and behaviors of those in a reference group, the people he or she looks up to.

Reference groups also help people to think meaningfully. Leon Festinger (1954) wrote that groups construct a view of the world, a social reality that its members use to validate their beliefs and to organize their perceptions and actions. This social reality is especially important when an independent check on physical reality is not possible. Few ideas about life can be measured in the way we measure a hem with a ruler, so we need other people—people who are similar to us—to help us construct a reasonable view of the world, or a set of schemata, to explain our behavior and feelings (Webster and Sobieszek, 1974; Suls and Miller, 1977). Reference groups provide us with these similar people, who serve as an anchor for our feelings and thoughts.

Families are a special kind of reference group. Harold Kelley and John Thibaut (1978) describe their essence as both "close" and "personal." Families, including the husband-wife dyad and larger networks of kin, are close because they are highly interdependent for obtaining material outcomes. The specific behaviors enacted by each person in a family have direct and concrete consequences for the other family members. The relationships in families are also personal in that the attitudes, feelings, and behaviors that are expressed have highly important symbolic consequences for other family members. Of course, there can also be differences within families that are nearly as great as those within any other group. In some families there is a great deal of cooperation, and the interests of each person are felt to be closely tied to the interests of others. In other families, however, the members perceive conflicts of interest, so that interdependence is competitive (when one person wins, another loses).

CHARACTERISTICS OF GROUPS

NORMS

Norms are shared expectations or beliefs about how people in a group (and sometimes others) should act and think. For example, when an entire dormitory corridor takes study breaks at the same time every evening, that is a norm. When the softball team expects public respect shown toward the coach but razzing in private, that is a norm. Or, when scientists on a government advisory committee speak with a frequency that roughly matches their age and number of publications, that, too, is a norm. They are all shared expectations that more or less govern aspects of group life. In almost every realm of our lives we act within (or against) norms constructed and maintained by the groups to which we belong.

Groups have norms of self-presentation, such as how much their members smile and how close they stand to each other; they have norms for dress, for instance, a tailored "preppie" look versus blue jeans and T shirts; and they have norms for addressing people of different status—"sir," "madam," "hey, you." Norms in groups are like the skeleton of the human body: they provide structure and rigidity to keep the organism together and upright, but they also enable plenty of movement and flexibility.

Nominal groups do not have norms. In fact, the absence of norms is one of the things that distinguishes nominal from true, psychological groups. Membership groups have norms, but a member may not care about them. For example, a neighborhood group of senior citizens may spend their time in bridge and lawn bowling, but one lively seventy-year-old may ignore the group and enroll in dancing lessons.

In the case of reference groups, however, norms are extremely important, and violating them is an act of defiance. Usually, we care about the people in our reference groups. Conforming to norms shows respect for others and for their beliefs. Also, it implies continued allegiance to the group. Hence ignoring even a "minor" norm such as using the wrong fork at a fancy dinner may be considered by the group as a sign that the person doesn't really belong to the group or doesn't care about it. Sometimes a reference group is very severe on a person who violates a norm. An example is the infamous practice of "silence" at military academies or totally isolating deviant peers from social contact with any other student.

On the other hand, reference groups may excuse norm breaking by group leaders. According to one theory (Hollander, 1958), the idiosyncracies of a leader are especially pardonable because the group is indebted to them for the leader's past conformity to group norms. Or leaders may be perceived as establishing new norms. Of course, what the group allows to pass as an idiosyncracy or a novelty in a leader might be considered a serious breach of group standards when done by other members of the group.

One of the most important norms in all groups is the norm of reciprocity (Gouldner, 1960), a shared expectation that people will give as they receive—that is, for any benefit that people in a group receive, they incur a debt or obligation to return a comparable benefit. As discussed in Chapter 9, several important theories in social psychology have been developed to explain how the norm of reciprocity affects behavior, such as Lerner's theory of distributive justice (Lerner, Miller, and Holmes, 1976) and the equity theory of Walster, Walster, and Berscheid (1978). Equity theory in particular explains how groups develop specific norms governing social exchange so that self-interest is held in check by regulating trade-offs. In informal groups, such as juvenile gangs, equity may be maintained by direct physical interventions—for example, by "punching out" another person. In formal organizations, people often can restore equity only psychologically—for example, by changing their opinion of a job's value to the group.

A different type of group norm has been labeled by Pruitt (1972) "the norm of mutual responsiveness." This norm pertains to groups where there is a personal level to the relationship, that is, where each person cares about the welfare of the other. In such "communal" relationships (Clark and Mills, 1979), the members of the group assume that each member should strive to benefit every other member. While the norm in this type of group may appear to an observer to be reciprocity, it is not: the benefits given and received are not part of an equal exchange, and the receiver of a benefit does not create a specific debt or obligation to return a comparable benefit. Instead, the aim is simply to satisfy others' needs.

The research of Margaret Clark and Judson Mills (1979) demonstrates an example of this type of norm. In their study unmarried male college students worked on a vocabulary task in conjunction with an attractive woman, who was either married (and therefore unavailable for a "communal" relationship) or unmarried. During the experiment, the woman received help from the subject. In response, she either thanked him for it or gave him one of her "task points" as well as a verbal thank you. Reciprocating help with a task point had a different effect on the male subjects, depending on whether the woman was married or not. When the woman was married, they liked her better when she gave them a point and a "thank you." When the woman was unmarried, they liked her better when she just thanked them. The experimenters concluded that the male subjects may have hoped for a future "communal" relationship with the unmarried woman. Thus, they liked her better when she accepted their help without reciprocating, thereby allowing a potential communal relationship based on mutual satisfaction rather than reciprocity.

Our discussion in this section makes it clear that groups vary in the extent to which norms control behavior. Moreover, people within groups also vary in the extent to which they accept and follow norms. Usually, in fact, there are one or more minority viewpoints regarding norms in a group. In spite of these minority views, however, the norms that do exist are surprisingly resistant to change. Norms bond the individuals together, and as long as the group itself exists, so do the norms.

GOALS

Goals are both the purpose for a group's existence and a way of explaining a group's behavior and attitudes. Some group goals, such as "undying friendship," emerge because they promote group stability; other group goals arise out of negotiation over specific individual or coalition objectives; still other goals amount to reconstructions of actions the group has already taken so as to give the group a good accounting of itself. Sometimes the goal of a group is obvious and not a source of friction. In other groups there is conflict over goals, or the apparent goal is not the real goal of most group members: for example, a country club whose apparent goal is recreation, may have a real goal of providing opportunities for members to discuss business matters in private.

In studies of explicit goals, Alvin Zander (1968) has found that groups often raise their objectives after success rather than lower them after failure. For example, a study (Zander and Newcomb, 1967) of United Fund campaigns in 149 cities over four years found that cities that met their goal one year almost always raised their goal the following year, but cities that did not meet their goal one year rarely lowered their goal the following year. Perhaps it is more satisfying to raise objectives than to admit that objectives should be lowered; alternatively, groups may find it easier to believe that they have succeeded than that they have failed (Zander, 1968).

One of the most interesting aspects of group goals is the "hidden agenda," a term now familiar in the popular vocabulary (Bennis and Shepard, 1965). The hidden agenda is really a goal of a group member or a subset of group members that is not recognized as a group goal, but is nevertheless guiding the group's behavior. For example, members of a high-level government committee may use the group to assert the power of their own position rather than as a means of addressing the particular issues on the committee's public agenda. Sometimes such hidden agendas can develop into group goals; that is, the goals of individuals in the group for using the group become implicit group goals. Meanwhile, the explicit group goal may be some purpose that is far more acceptable publicly.

It is, therefore, somewhat misleading to speak of group goals as though they were all the same. Instead, we would be more accurate to speak of an array of goals for a group, especially superordinate goals and specific objectives about which the group members negotiate; goals of individuals within the groups, including those that provoke hidden agendas; and group rationales, or reasons for the group's existence or behavior—which may or may not be related to the goals for the group. In all groups there are pressures to develop or to protect the whole array of goals.

EGOCENTRISM One way that groups promote their own goals is through *egocentrism*, or a positive view of a group's own members and purposes. Egocentrism seems to be pervasive in groups, even in groups that attempt to be deliberately open and free-thinking. Because egocentric biases of groups are the fundamental origin of such phenomena as prejudice and discrimination as well as championship teamwork, a number of theories have been developed to try to understand the origin of egocentricity and its influence on group behavior.

One explanation has to do with the way people process, remember, and recall information. Groups—like individuals—tend to perceive events in light of their expectations. For example, in the same way that individuals tend to attribute failure to situational factors and to credit themselves for successes (see Chapter 6), so do groups (Schlenker and Miller, 1977). According to Miller and Ross (1975), the reason for such self-serving biases may be that groups tend to recall what they expected to happen better than what actually happened. When expectations are positive but subsequent reality is a mixture of positive and negative events, there is often a distortion of reality in the group's favor.

Another explanation for egocentrism is that group members tend to perceive their own group's responsibility for events as more significant than do outsiders. For example, Ross and Sicoly (1979) conducted five experiments dealing with how a group explains its own achievements. They involved naturally occurring discussion groups, married couples, basketball teams, and groups assembled in the laboratory. In these studies, group members attributed more responsibility for a group's achievements to the group itself than did people outside of the group. Furthermore, group members recalled the group's behavior better than outsiders did. Since group members' biased recall for group behaviors occurred even when the group was unsuccessful, the results suggest that part of the "egocentrism" of groups may simply be an effect of memory processes: you remember better what you do than what others do.

One of the experiments by Ross and Sicoly illustrates how groups account for events involving more than one group—events such as competition, conflict, cooperative work, and the like. The investigators asked players on twelve intercollegiate basketball teams to recall "an important turning point in their last game and to assess why their team had won or lost." More than 80 percent of the players thought their own team had initiated the turning point of the game (significantly higher than a chance expectation of 50 percent). The players remembered that their team was responsible for such events as a strong defense during the last two minutes of the game, defensive steals, and shifts in offensive strategies, each of which was considered the determining condition of the win or loss. Similarly egocentric explanations are seen in many other group situations. Ross and Sicoly cite Dan Rather (Rather and Heskowitz, 1977: p. 307), for example: "CBS [news] became a solid Number One after the Apollo moonshot in 1968. If you are a CBS person, you tend to say our coverage of the lunar landing tipped us over. If you are an NBC person, you tend to cite the breakup of the Huntley-Brinkley team as the key factor."

Other biases in thinking contribute further to group egocentrism. One is the tendency to categorize, stereotype, and label problems according to a group's own frames of reference, or cognitive schemata, and to fit the group's past experience and values into those schemata. What the group does and what happens to the group will be remembered in terms of existing frames of reference (Bruner, 1969). For example, students working on a class project together remember all the time they put into getting organized and carrying out the project. Their frame of reference is likely to emphasize who contributed most in the group and what they did. In contrast, their professors will recall the project in light of how much time was spent in reading and correcting the student papers.

Memory and perceptual processes cannot account for all the egocentrism of groups, however. Part of the tendency comes from a group's motivation to protect itself, especially its goals and its image to outsiders. For example, when two groups are involved in the same event, group A will remember the things about the event that support its behavior. If the event is a conflict situation, the self-interested view of each group would tend to polarize the two groups (Lord, Ross, and Lepper, 1979). Thus, egocentrism in behalf of the group goals can be explained both by memory biases and by a motivation to protect and promote the group's goals.

GROUP FORMATION

How do groups get started? Groups that exist to accomplish specific tasks or purposes are often formed deliberately; groups with an emotional basis usually arise spontaneously. The first kind of group—one deliberately organized for a specific purpose—is usually set up to improve or benefit individuals. These include groups oriented around specific problems, such as alcoholism, drug addiction, or obesity, groups preparing for a special event such as natural childbirth or retirement, or groups organized around a common interest, such as human sensitivity, race relations, drama, or foreign affairs. The second kind of group—one which arises spontaneously—is usually an outgrowth of mutual attraction. Although tasks may be involved in these groups, the tasks are neither as important nor as clear as in deliberate groups. However, the influence of these groups is usually more intense and more broadly felt than in deliberate groups. Spontaneous groups include friendship cliques, informal social groups within a formal organization, social clubs, and even marriages. Sometimes seemingly spontaneous groups arise because people who share something in common—such as race, sex, ethnic origin, or sexual preference—have been treated in a simi-

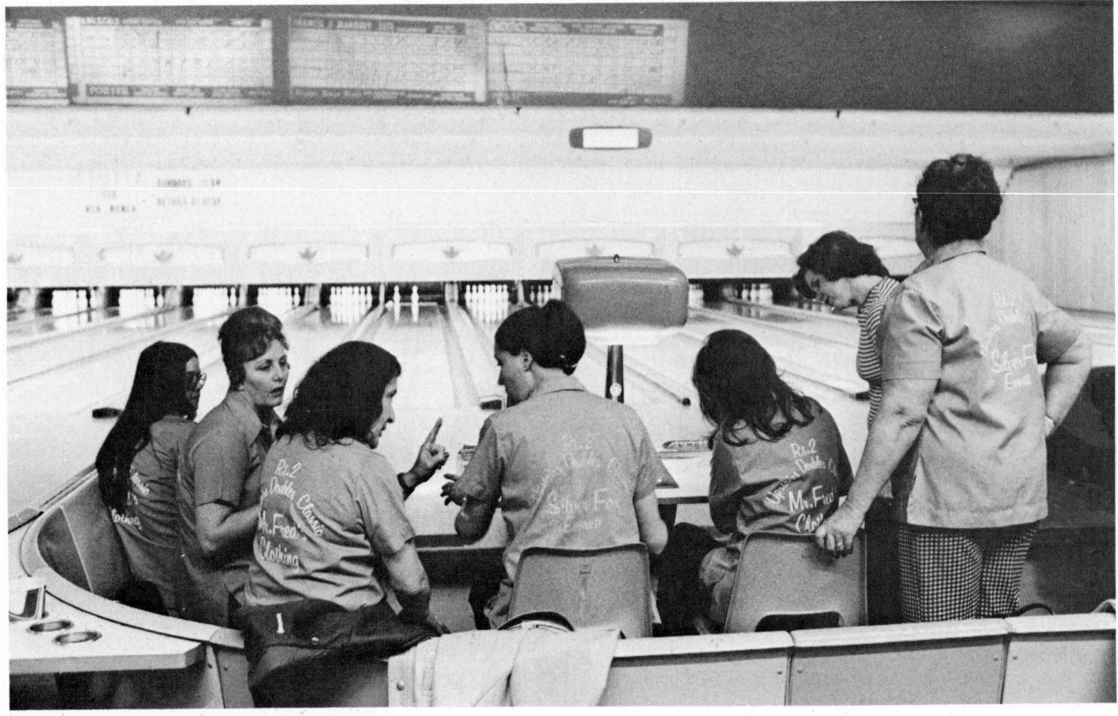

Groups can grow out of a common interest or mutual attraction. Both factors may have contributed to the formation of this bowling team. *(© Elizabeth Hamlin 1976 / Stock, Boston)*

lar manner or categorized in a certain way as people sharing the same fate.

Research shows that it doesn't take much to get a group started. Some of the earliest research in social psychology demonstrates that a group may be formed merely by labeling people as a group, setting them to work on a common task, or informing them that they have an audience in common (Heider, 1958). A critical ingredient seems to be a sense of shared fate, or "outcome," as some theorists call it. The more that people share the consequences of their beliefs and actions—especially dangerous consequences—the more likely it is that they and others will define them as a group.

In the first experimental field studies on this subject, Muzaver Sherif and his colleagues (Sherif, Harvey, White, Hood, and Sherif, 1961) studied the development and resolution of conflict in boys' summer camps. In one study, the investigations deliberately tried to create two groups. They gave distinctive labels to each group, the Rattlers and the Eagles; they isolated each group from the other; and they involved each group in group play. To forge internal solidarity, they chose the strategy of generals and presidents. They promoted conflict between the groups. This was a simple matter of arranging competitive games, such as baseball and tug of war, and emphasizing winning rather than participation for the fun of it. Each group resented losing to the other and became aggressive about winning. Once when the Rattlers had won a game, the Eagles retaliated by burning the Rattlers' flag. Each group stereotyped the other group negatively and began calling the others nasty names. This study showed that the effects of competition could tie a set of individual campers into rival—sometimes violent—gangs.

A second factor that may have contributed to group solidarity in the boys'-camp experiment was the stress of near warfare between the rival factions. A recent study by Dovidio and Morris (1975) demonstrated how stress can increase the consequences of shared fate. In this experiment, pairs of subjects were placed in one of four different situations. In one, there was both high stress and common fate: the subject and another person (a confederate) waited together to participate in an experiment (common fate) involving electric shock (high stress). In a second situation, both the subject and a confederate waited for the same experiment, but it was an innocuous one involving word association. There were also two dissimilar-fate situations in which the subject waited for the shock experiment with a confederate who was waiting for the word association study or vice versa. In order to study coöperation in these four situations, the researchers observed the proportion of subjects in each experimental condition who helped the confederate pick up 100 pencils that he had "accidentally" knocked on the floor. When the subject and confederate shared a common fate—especially when the common fate was the high-stress shock experiment—more than 50 percent of the subjects helped the confederate pick up the pencils. The least altruism occurred when the subjects faced the shock experiment—high stress—but did not share that fate with the confederate. This experiment showed that stress can increase the solidifying effect of shared fate, but by itself may be divisive.

Where stress comes from is important. While stress that arises within the group itself will reduce the group's cohesiveness, external sources of threat or reward can promote feelings of togetherness. When people are exposed to external danger, they are likely to show a remarkable increase in group solidarity. Irving Janis (1963) studied American soldiers during the last months of World War II. Time and again he encountered instances when soldiers failed to act in accordance with their own self-interest in order to ward off separation or guilt about "letting the other guys down." Soldiers who had performed well in combat sometimes refused to accept a promotion if it entailed being shifted to another group. Men who were physically ill or suffering from acute anxiety symptoms avoided going on sick call and struggled against being withdrawn from combat because they didn't want to be separated from their unit. This solidarity also has its less attractive aspects. After World War II, some combat units who were stationed in Germany badly mistreated German civilians. Some of these American soldiers looted private homes, forced old people to give up jewelry in order to receive military food supplies, and pressured young women to submit sexually. Thus, the forces that create particularly strong groups are not necessarily good for other groups, nor do they necessarily lead to outcomes that benefit individual group members.

INDIVIDUALS IN GROUPS: ROLES

Recently, a group of social scientists visited China and asked a Chinese social scientist why so much effort, money, and research were devoted to agriculture and so little to education. After puzzling a bit the scientist answered: "Well, plants are different. We believe that all children are supposed to be the same."

In contrast to this perspective, Western societies generally recognize that each member of a group is an individual who has unique needs and expectations. We rarely expect absolute uniformity, except in combat groups or extremist cults. In friendship groups, work groups, and organizations, we recognize that needs may differ, opinions and goals may differ, and perspectives will differ.

In order to deal with those individual differences, groups assign roles. Roles are also ways for groups to distribute tasks in order to fulfill the various functions of a group. In other words, the role an individual plays within a group is determined partly by dispositional factors—individual differences in members' personalities—and partly by situational factors—the specific tasks that the group faces. In the sections below, we consider how individual differences and group tasks influence the roles people play in groups.

INFLUENCES ON INDIVIDUAL ROLES

We are all familiar with particular social and emotional roles in families. For example, there are some family members who hug and kiss often and others who are uncomfortable with overt expressions of affection. One way that families cope with individual differences in social and emotional behavior is to create different roles for different members of the family. There might be one role for some family member to be overtly emotional; another may require special nurturance; a third might be reserved and cautious. Each of these roles is a set of expectations for an individual—a way for groups to permit, but also to have some control over, individual differences.

People may vary in how well they fulfill the roles expected of them in groups. For example, people who are high self-monitors—those attuned to their own behavior and its social appropriateness (as discussed in Chapter 3)—are likely to be more attentive to a group's expectations and to the behavior of other people in the group than those who are low self-monitors. One study (Eliott, 1979) found that high self-monitors will go to some trouble to obtain useful information about another person whom they wish to impress. Perhaps such high self-monitors could better fill the administrative role in a conflict-prone group than people who are less able to monitor their own behavior and react to the needs of others.

Some roles that individuals are expected to play in groups are dictated by our political and cultural history. For example, the jobs of president or housewife have a large set of expectations attached about how the job should be performed and who should do it. Family roles are similarly influenced by expectations that often vary across different subcultures. The Jewish mother, Irish father, and suburban Wasp parent are stereotypes, but they reflect the powerful effects of ethnic differences in roles (see, for example, Strodtbeck, 1951; Haley, 1967; Straus, 1968).

Other roles evolve in order to help groups deal with crises or to solve problems they have not encountered before. Yet, sometimes these roles themselves create problems. For example, when a group is under stress, such as a family with financial or health problems, it may create a scapegoat role. One group member is viewed as the "dummy" or the "nag" or the "invalid." The person in the scapegoat role is subjected to group social pressures in the form of punishing attitudes and nasty expectations. That person then tends to act out the expected dumb, nagging, or invalid behavior. A typical example of a scapegoat role in families is the "problem child." The problem child takes the blame for the group's problems and is the recipient of all the group's anger and conflict. The rest of the family suffers, too, but often cannot break out of the pattern.

It is unclear who starts such maladaptive roles in a group. A child with particular needs or problems, for example, may be the cause of abnormal parenting, but the abnormal parenting reinforces the child's problem. Roles are a group phenomenon, and they persist because they allow the group to survive as a group. Even individuals who are unhappy in their roles may resist giving them up because the role has protected them in the group. In fact, the entire group may have adapted to this maladaptive role.

When a group member does relinquish a certain role, the group may respond by shifting that role to someone else in the group. For example, in families of schizophrenics, therapists have noticed that the improvement of the "sick person" sometimes results in another family member becoming ill, apparently because the family needs someone in the role of sick person. An analogous situation in "normal" families is the dependency role, whereby there is always someone in the family who has had a bad day and needs special attention. This role may be filled by different family members, depending on circumstances each has encountered.

Roles, then, are not always good. Some roles permit members of a group to go on behaving as they are without facing their own responsibilities for the problems of the group. They allow powerful individuals to collect inequitable rewards from others without challenge, or they allow submissive individuals to absorb special sympathy or help without carrying out equal responsibilities.

LEADERSHIP

Probably the two roles we most closely associate with power in groups are the roles of leader and follower. According to current theories (Hollander, 1978), leadership and followership are a two-way process of mutual social influence. The leader's influence depends more on persuasion and initiation of activity than on coercion, and it involves the cooperative efforts and needs of the followers.

The leader and follower roles do not fall into sharp categories. All leaders at some time and to some degree are also followers, and followers sometimes attain the status of leader. There are also different leadership roles in most groups, particularly large groups: executive, problem solver, arbitrator, advocate, emotional supporter, defender of the group's prestige, and cheerleader. Consequently, sometimes there may be more than one leader role, and each role may be delegated to a different person. There may be a ceremonial leader and a different administrative leader, such as the queen and prime minister in England. Or two leaders may perform different functions, as do the chairman of the board and the president of a corporation.

POWER Power can be defined as social influence. French and Raven (1959) identified five kinds of power, and a leader's influence may rest on any one or on several of these. The five bases of power apply not only to leaders in groups, but also to any situation in which one individual has influence or power over another. According to French and Raven, the five kinds of power are

1. *Referent power*—others like, respect, or identify with the person, who is in turn likely to influence them.
2. *Reward power*—people perceive the individual as having the ability to give others rewards, such as favors, approval, or increased status.
3. *Coercive power*—people perceive the person as having the ability to administer or mediate punishments, such as reprimands, threats, and reduction of privileges or status.
4. *Expert power*—the person has special resources of knowledge or skill that others need.
5. *Legitimate power*—others believe that the person has the right to influence their behavior.

Legitimate, or formally authorized, power is not likely to be a factor in informal groups, but it is important in many formal groups in which one person is officially designated as the leader or boss. Similarly, coercive power is not likely to be a factor in many social and friendship groups. In families, however, both legitimate and coercive power may be factors.

Legitimate power—an influence over the lives of others with their consent—is exercised by many political leaders, such as President Anwar el-Sadat of Egypt. *(Jacques Pavlovsky / Sygma)*

"GOOD" LEADERS Research on leadership reflects both dispositional and situational approaches to the question of what makes someone a good leader. Early studies of leadership emphasized the kinds of personality traits, such as courage and wisdom, that were thought to be associated with a leader. There were many attempts to identify the kinds of people who were effective leaders in organizations. After hundreds of studies, it was discovered that no single quality or set of qualities was associated consistently with effective leadership. Although leaders of work groups and organizations tend to be intelligent, well adjusted, extroverted, and somewhat domineering (Mann, 1959), such personality traits are important only in relation to the particular group and circumstances. A work group that has to produce a product will have a different kind of leader than a discussion group.

These early studies of leadership traits were followed during the 1950s by studies of situations in which certain leadership styles were more appropriate than others. The theory behind these studies was that different situations required different kinds of leaders. One influential example of this kind of research was done by Fred Fiedler (1971), who identified two types of leaders: those who are *task oriented* and those who are *relationship oriented.* Relationship-oriented leaders are permissive, considerate, and sensitive to others. In a number of studies, Fiedler found that this type of leader is most appropriate for situations in which people's feelings are important, particularly if the members' feelings about each other are relatively uncertain and the task is unstructured. In contrast, the task-oriented leader, who is more directive and demanding, performs better when members' relations are good and the task is structured. Because Fiedler's approach relies both on the attributes of a person and on the situation, it is called a *contingency theory of leadership.*

Related to the contingency theory of leadership is a research tradition that was pioneered by Robert Bales and his colleagues. Bales (1970) developed a way of systematically observing group behavior through a technique known as *interaction process analysis.* Bales's system rests primarily on a distinction between two types of behavior: *task-oriented behavior* and *social-emotional behavior.* Task-oriented behavior consists of anything a person says or does that is directed toward accomplishing the group's task, such as "I have an idea; let's put these boxes together this way," or "Let's go to a movie," or "Say, how do you think we should do this?" or "Bill, what do you think the group should do this weekend?" The behavior is directed toward the group's activities, which may be either social or work oriented.

Social-emotional behavior is directed toward the other members of the group. It expresses feelings toward them and may be positive or negative, such as "Say, you really look great," or "What's the matter? You're in a terrible mood!" or, when everyone in a group is dejected, someone lightens the atmosphere by telling a joke. Such behavior is not directed toward the task but toward feelings of the group.

Like Fiedler's model, Bales's interaction process analysis implies that groups have at least two leadership roles that need to be fulfilled: one to lead the group in completing its tasks; the other to maintain social relationships within the group, building its morale and holding people together. These two types of roles may be difficult to carry out by the same person. Getting a task done sometimes involves being harsh or strict with people who are making mistakes or who are not working hard or who need to be discouraged from taking up the group's time. Then, if feelings are hurt, a social-emotional specialist may have to assuage bad feelings, increase enjoyment of the group, and hold the group together.

Another contingency theory of leadership, by Vroom and Yetton (1973), asserts that the effectiveness of a leader depends on how much participation the leader permits on the part of subordinates as compared with how much participation is good for the task. For example, if the members of a work group have much of the information that the leader needs to complete a task, then the leader will achieve more by allowing a great deal of participation by members in decisions. In constrast, if the leader has all the information available, there is less need for the other members to participate in sharing information and opinions.

Although these theories are an advance over

previous, narrowly focused theories, they are still limited because they do not account for change in leaders and leadership roles and in situations. If we consider that groups change over time and across situations, we see that roles in the group also change. They are much less fixed than we often think, even though sometimes the names remain the same. Being a parent of a teenager is certainly not the same role as being a parent of a baby or of an adult.

Much of the research on leadership roles has been conducted on small groups in the laboratory or on small work groups. Thus, the roles that we know most about are the roles that emerge in these kinds of groups. Also, much of the research involves group members who are relatively young and well educated—college students. Therefore, the needs and interests they bring to the group are likely to be different than if we were to study, say, members of a building's cleaning squad. Probably the general principles are the same, but the particular qualities expected in the roles are different.

COMMUNICATION PATTERNS

The role of leader and all other roles in a group are shaped by the structure of the group and how information is exchanged. In a corporation like General Motors, certain kinds of information must be carried up the organizational ladder in order for important decisions to be made. In contrast, the members of a basketball team have to share approximately the same information in order to achieve their goals of scoring and preventing their opponents from scoring.

Early studies on group communication were done in the 1940s and 1950s. Basically, experimenters created groups in which they restricted communication to certain patterns. The most commonly studied patterns were chains, hierarchies, stars, and all-channel networks, as shown in Figure 11.1. Chains (in which person A communicates with person B, who communicates with C, who communicates with D) are typical in governmental organizations, particularly the military. Hierarchies often occur in

FIGURE 11.1 Four patterns of communication in groups: (a) the chain; (b) the star; (c) the hierarchy; (d) the all-channel network. The pattern that a group uses affects its problem-solving efficiency as well as its members' role definitions and satisfaction.

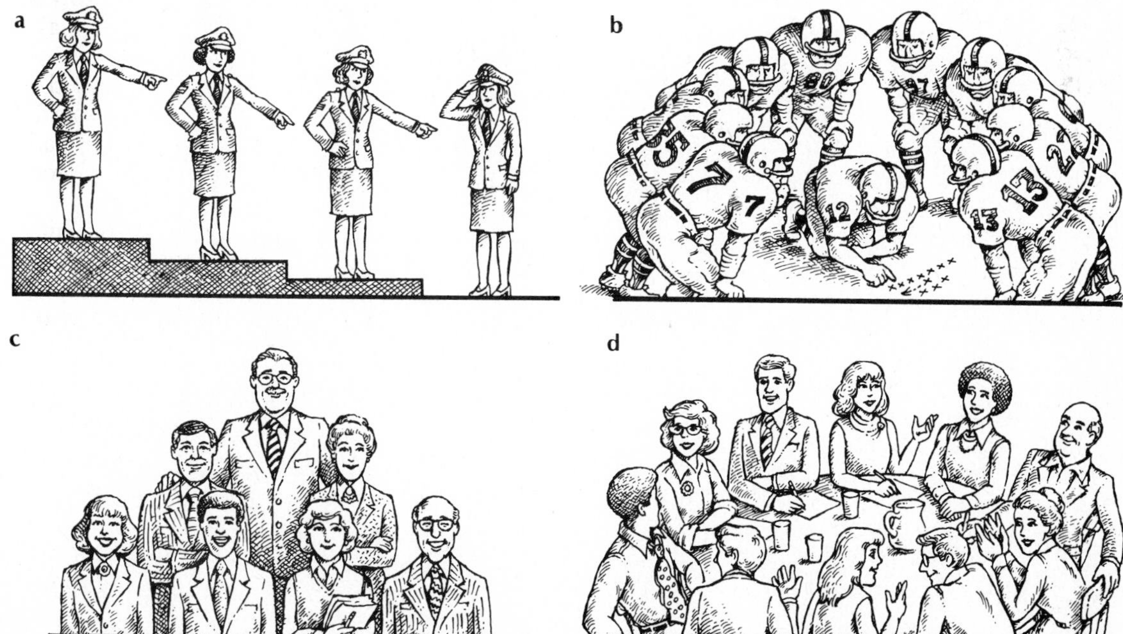

business organizations. Star patterns, in which everyone reports to one central person, often an authoritarian leader, occur in small, task-oriented groups. All-channel patterns are often found in friendship groups. Communication channels are greatly affected by a group's organization. Harold Leavitt (1951) found that a group's organizational structure not only affected who emerged as a leader, but also the satisfaction of the group's members and the group's efficiency in solving problems. For example, if the group is organized around a central person, as in the star pattern, then that person usually becomes the leader rather quickly, probably because this individual has greater access to information than do the others and is in a position to coordinate the activities of the group. However, some of the advantages of centralized groups, such as speed and control, are obtained at the cost of morale and minority influence (Davis, 1973).

GROUP DYNAMICS

Group dynamics refer to groups in action: completing tasks, working out conflicts, helping people, influencing other people and groups, and making decisions.

The study of group dynamics can be traced to two events, one scientific and one historical (Allport, 1968). One of the great theoretical advances of social psychology occurred in the 1940s, when Kurt Lewin developed a theory of group dynamics. Although there had been many scientific studies of groups before Lewin's, these were really studies of "social influence," or the effects of other people on an individual's behavior or attitudes. Lewin expanded the problem to study actual forces within the context of groups. It was he who introduced concepts such as cohesiveness, group decision, styles of leadership, and group attitude change.

The scientific advance grew out of the urgent social problems of the 1930s—the decade of the Great Depression, the rise of Hitler, the influx of German refugees, and the approach of World War II. These events raised grave questions about society in general and about groups in particular. The Society for the Psychological Study of Social Issues was formed in 1936. By the 1940s, books and papers were appearing on such subjects as the authoritarian personality and how groups could function better in a democracy (Adorno, Frenkel-Brunswik, Levinson, and Sanford, 1950; Stouffer, Suchman, DeVinney, Star, and Williams, 1949; Leighton, 1945; Lewin, 1948).

At the same time as these theoretical and historical events turned the focus of social psychology to group processes, improvements in research methodology permitted the study of change in groups. By the 1950s, such phenomena as norms, roles, and communication patterns were being studied as they changed in order to learn more about group dynamics.

COHESIVENESS AND COMMITMENT

One question is inevitably raised in the study of group dynamics: Why do people act so differently in groups? The basic source of the difference is cohesiveness and commitment, phenomena that forge collections of people into a group and lead them to think of the group as a separate entity.

Traditionally, *cohesiveness* has been defined as the sum of *all* of the forces that hold people together as members of a group (Cartwright and Zander, 1968). Two general categories of conditions create cohesiveness: these are factors external to the group and factors internal to the group. The first category includes all of the external conditions that keep a person in a group. For example, people in a prison camp, soldiers in a combat unit, and children in a family are members of highly cohesive groups, even though their membership is caused by external involuntary factors. The second category includes a person's feelings toward the group. This internal factor is known as *commitment*. Charles Kiesler (1971) has defined commitment as the degree to which a person is psychologically bound to a behavior. In a group, commitment can be defined as a person's being psychologically bound to group membership. In most groups we feel some sense of voluntary membership. For example, even in families in which people are beaten or treated cruelly, members typically feel committed to the group and would not leave if given complete freedom.

The degree of commitment in a group affects the maintenance of relationships among group members. When there is little commitment, people react to conflict by attacking other members or leaving the group. When commitment is high, people attempt to negotiate, compromise, and accommodate other group members.

One of the most interesting aspects of voluntary commitment to a group is that it seems to grow in reverse proportion to external pressures. Experiments show that the more money people are paid to be members of groups, the less psychologically committed to it they tend to be. Moreover, the more costly or effortful is membership in a group, the more important the group becomes (Aronson and Mills, 1959; Staw, 1974). In general, as the discussion of cognitive dissonance in Chapter 5 made clear, the harder people work for a group and the more they sacrifice, the higher is their commitment to the group.

CONFORMITY

Perhaps the most important result of cohesiveness is *conformity*—the change in an individual's behavior or attitude that occurs in groups (Kiesler and Kiesler, 1969). Conformity is not a simple process through which all group members become carbon copies of one another. Instead, the degree of conformity in a group depends on a variety of factors, which affect some members more than others. There are two important kinds of conformity. The first is *compliance*, or the change of overt behavior that occurs as a result of group pressure. The second is *private acceptance* of group attitudes. Compliance need not be accompanied by private attitude change. In fact, when group cohesiveness is mainly caused by external forces, compliance is likely to be unaccompanied by private attitude change. Still, it is surprising the extent to which people comply in nonvoluntary groups or in groups to which they feel little commitment.

COMPLIANCE Compliance is not a phenomenon unique to groups. It occurs in almost all social situations, but it tends to be stronger in groups.

Suppose you are asked to participate in a group that is working on a perceptual task requiring a group judgment. With everyone else, you examine a picture in which there are three parallel lines of different lengths—A, B, and C—alongside a comparison line. If you are asked which of the three lines most closely matches the comparison line, you would correctly answer B. But how would you respond if the other members of a group had already answered C? What if you were certain they were wrong? However inaccurate the group's judgment, most of us would feel some pressure to comply with the group. We don't expect people to be wrong about the obvious, and when they are, we face an ambiguous social situation. Perhaps they had some other reason for answering as they did. In an ambiguous situation like this, it is easier to comply with the group—to go along with its judgment—than to face the uncertainty of going our own way.

The situation we have just described was the subject of a classic social-psychological experiment conducted by Solomon Asch (1956). Asch discovered that about one-third of the time an individual in a group will answer the same way a unanimous group of confederates answered even though the confederates' judgment was clearly wrong. Since the subjects in these studies knew very well which lines were correct matches and which were not, the subjects were only complying publicly.

Why did one-third of the people comply with an obvious error? The answer has to do with individuals' perceptions of the group in that particular situation. For example, under conditions when some of the confederates disagreed with each other and there was a minority opinion that supported the subjects' correct opinion, compliance was drastically reduced. But when the subjects had no other support, compliance was highest. Thus, conditions that decrease a person's certainty and confidence in a judgment situation also increase that person's tendency to comply with a group (see Allen, 1975; Allen and Levine, 1975).

Uncertainty and compliance are also related to how much opposition there is in a group. In one version of the Asch experiment, a person whose judgment was challenged by three subgroups of two members each complied much more than a person who was challenged by one subgroup of six people (Wilder, 1977). With three disagreeing groups it probably seems as though one faces more total opposition than with one disagreeing group, and uncertainty would be higher. (Interestingly, this principle is sometimes applied in real-life groups by demagogues, who scatter supporters through the crowd to yell encouragement.)

Other versions of the Asch paradigm have shown that ambiguity increases compliance. For example, in the line-judging study, if the lines are more nearly equal in length, a much larger number of subjects will comply with the group and misjudge the line as equal. Other types of ambiguous tasks, such as evaluating attitude statements, also increase the degree of conformity. The overall finding is that task ambiguity increases uncertainty and thereby results in more compliance.

Another major reason for compliance in groups is the search for social support. People who need emotional support or who fear social isolation are more likely to comply than people who are secure in their acceptance by others. People who want approval from their friends or the other members of their group will often comply with behavior they would not engage in on their own. But what type of group member is most likely to comply out of a need for support and approval? Research has revealed a paradoxical finding: sometimes it is the marginal members of a group who often conform the most closely to group norms; yet in other groups the highest compliance with group norms is seen in group leaders and other central members. There are logical reasons why both phenomena occur. People who are marginal may comply a great deal because they are trying to fit in, to be accepted.

In contrast, group leaders and central members often comply with group norms in order to maintain power and respect and to control the development of group norms. Although leaders have the freedom to deviate from norms because they have power, they are expected to lead the group in achieving its goals. Thus, there is implicit pressure on leaders to adhere to group norms even to a greater extent than is expected of the average group member. Curiously, then, the two types of people who must conform most closely to group norms are the leaders, who are highly accepted by the group, and the marginal members, who are not well accepted in the group but would like to be.

A classic experimental study of compliance and its relevance to group goals was conducted by Stanley Schachter (1951). Schachter induced college students to volunteer for discussion clubs, ostensibly involving various current topics, such as movies, human relations, and so forth. At their first meeting, members in all of the clubs read a report about "Johnny Rocco," a juvenile delinquent. The report was a biography which ended as Johnny was awaiting sentence for a minor crime. The club was asked to discuss and answer the question: What should be done with this person?

Because the report sympathetically portrayed Johnny's case and because the club members were about his age, they usually favored leniency. But the experimenter had placed three confederates in the group, whose behavior prevented immediate consensus. The first confederate was a "deviate" who always took a position favoring extreme discipline for Johnny; the second confederate was a "modal" person who aways chose the majority position, which recommended greater leniency; and the third confederate was a "slider"—someone who first argued for extreme discipline, but then allowed himself to be gradually influenced so that by the end of the discussion he agreed with the majority. Schachter found that club members vehemently tried to persuade the deviate and the slider, addressing more remarks to them than to anyone else. When the slider began to agree with the group, the group members turned to the deviate. But the deviate did not change his position and continued to advocate discipline for Johnny. As a result, he was eventually ignored in all the groups. This public isolation was echoed in private. When members were asked to name one person to exclude from the group should the size become too unwieldy for discussion, they overwhelmingly named the deviate.

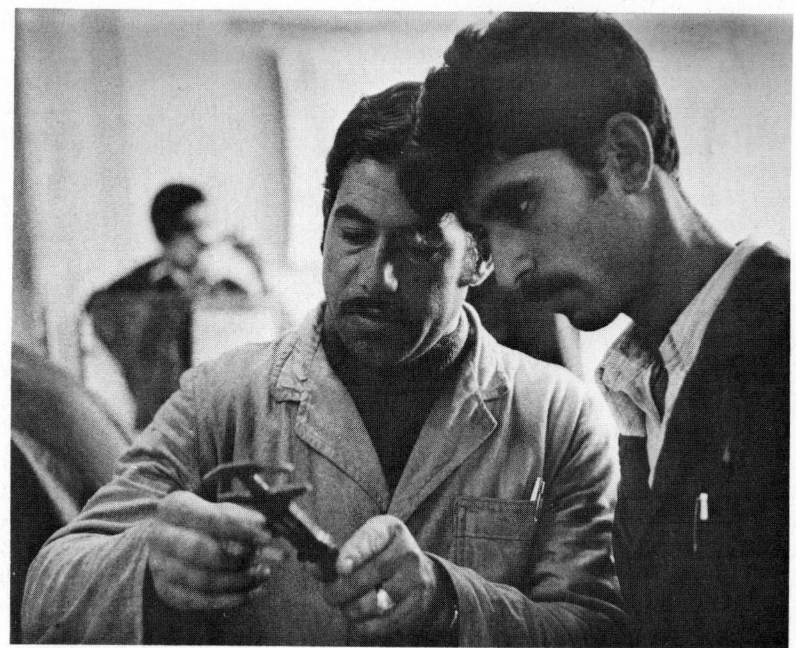

Research shows that on-the-job assistance from a co-worker can affect a person's self-esteem. *(© Marc Riboud / Magnum)*

The amount of conformity pressures in Schachter's study depended on whether agreement about Johnny Rocco was related to the group's goals. When the club was a human-relations club, the members tried harder to reach consensus and ostracized the deviant more severely. When the club was a movie club or a radio club, they seemed to care less about agreement on the issue.

Schachter's study also showed that voluntary commitment to the group's goals is important. When group members had chosen each other instead of just being assigned to the club, they tried harder to reach consensus and were more likely to reject the deviant.

PRIVATE ACCEPTANCE OF GROUP ATTITUDES Because groups have a strong impact on their members' beliefs and values, attitude change in groups can be more extreme than attitude change outside groups. One reason people can experience greater attitude change in groups is because the groups to which they belong are their source of information, emotional support, and self-identification. Studies of feedback in groups (see, for example, Cooper and Duncan, 1971) show that even in laboratory settings people's self-esteem is strongly affected by the evaluations of other group members, particularly others who are high in status or competence. And in real-life settings such as office or factory groups, receiving help from a coworker can similarly affect self-esteem (Fischer and Nadler, 1974, 1976).

Part of the influence groups exert over members' self-esteem is probably due to the social-influence process called "the self-fulfilling prophecy." In other words, people tend to act in ways that confirm other people's attitudes and behavior. For example, if a person on a baseball team is expected to be the poorest hitter, he or she may act hesitantly when approaching the plate, which may give the pitcher enough confidence to get a strike-out. Or if a teacher believes a student is not very smart, the teacher will be unlikely to call on the student for answers to difficult problems or to challenge the student, which may in turn cause the student to define his or her skills as limited (see, for example, Word, Zanna, and Cooper, 1974).

Another way that groups can intensify attitude change is through their control over group members' behavior. Groups usually demand some overt signs of membership, such as special hand clasps, dress, speech, gestures, or an endorsement of people or objects valued by the group, such as political candidates, musical preferences, or dance styles. Such behavior is considered important as a sign of loyalty or of acceptance of a group's norms and goals. As group members express these signs of commitment to the group, the process of self-justification and dissonance reduction affects their private attitudes toward the group. Group goals become individual objectives, and group norms become individual beliefs.

The process of deindividuation further increases a group's influence over individual attitudes. As discussed in Chapter 3 and Chapter 8, deindividuation is a perception of oneself as an anonymous part of a group rather than as a distinct individual. Deindividuation causes individuals to feel emotionally close to the group as a whole and distant from people outside the group (see, for example, Emswiller, Deaux, and Willits, 1971). Deindividuation also tends to diminish an individual's sense of personal identity and responsibility to inner beliefs and values. People who are deindividuated are more than usually susceptible to influence from authoritarian leaders and unreasonable group pressures that they would ordinarily resist. An extreme case of deindividuation can be seen in the opening example of this chapter, the mass suicides in Guyana in 1978, in which individuals gave up their final sense of identity—their lives—for the group.

However, groups are not all-powerful in their control over individual behavior. Under certain circumstances a group's influence may wane. For example, a group may try so hard to control the behavior of individual members that the group's efforts backfire. Teresa Amabile (1979) found that when individuals expect a group to evaluate and explicitly reward "creativity," individuals may be less creative than when the group ignores creativity. At the other extreme, when an individual's attitudes and behavior are completely irrelevant to a group's goals, the group may again lose its influence over individual behavior. For example, if a group's goals are unrelated to attitudes toward minorities, a prejudiced group member will probably feel little pressure to change his or her attitudes (see Brockner and Holton, 1968). In contrast, if prejudice runs counter to the group's goals and the group is highly committed to its goals (as in a civil rights organization), the individual will experience great pressure to change. Hence, private attitude change in groups is often an either/or situation, depending on the importance of the attitude to a group's goals.

WORKING IN GROUPS

All groups have work to do. The work may involve making decisions, solving specific problems, or providing emotional support. For some groups the work is obvious, such as that of the Nuclear Regulatory Commission to formulate policies and guidelines for building nuclear power plants. Such tasks require a group to work together on a continuing basis, combining the knowledge, values, and wisdom of individual members. Other groups are established in order to make a one-time decision, such as a group of officers to plan an advertising strategy, a club subcommittee to plan a dance, or an informal group of friends getting together to attend a concert. In all of these cases the work of the group includes making decisions. Other groups mainly work to solve problems that have correct solutions that must be found. Problem-solving groups may range from groups of students working on algebra problems to engineers planning a bridge. Finally, most groups must also work on social problems and social tasks, such as resolving conflict and maintaining group relations. Those social tasks are the major work of emotional-support groups such as families and friendship groups.

GROUP PERFORMANCE

There is a good deal of research concerning how groups do their work. This research shows that there are at least three categories of factors that affect group performance. The first of these concerns the *characteristics of the task itself* (see Hackman and Morris, 1975). For example, if the task is to find the one correct solution to a problem, the group works differently than if the task is to suggest several alternative solutions that are efficient and practical.

The second major category of factors that affect group performance has to do with the *cohesiveness, commitment,* and *conformity* in the group. In cohesive groups, where there are strong pressures for uniformity, varied viewpoints may not be heard, even when there is diversity of opinion.

Finally, group performance is also affected by the *individual characteristics* of group members. For example, a group made up of heterogeneous and highly tolerant individuals will be more likely to consider a variety of ideas than a group made up of individuals who are very similar to each other and also intolerant of new ideas.

One technique for increasing group members' tolerance for each other's ideas was the brainstorming technique suggested by Osborn in 1957. Originally formulated as a means of boosting creativity in advertising teams, the brainstorming technique includes a free period during which group members explore even the most harebrained suggestions without criticism or evaluation. At first the technique seemed to be an ideal way to consider all suggestions without discarding any of them, but brainstorming turned out not to be a panacea. Studies of brainstorming (Taylor, Berry, and Block, 1958; Bouchard, 1969) suggested that brainstorming groups still follow particular lines of thought and fail to use all members' ideas. One study found that while brainstorming groups produced many more ideas than other groups did, the extra ideas they generated tended to be poor and unimaginative (Weisskopf-Joelson and Eliseo, 1961).

When a problem has only one correct solution, the more tolerant members are of each other's ideas, the more likely they are to find the correct solution. An example is the classic missionary/cannibal problem.

> Three missionaries and three cannibals are on one side of the river. The problem is to get them to the other side by means of a boat that holds only two. All the missionaries and one cannibal can row. Never under any circumstances or at any time may the missionaries be outnumbered by the cannibals.

A task like this is relatively simple for a group because it only requires that the group members recognize the correct solution. The solutions to such problems usually reflect the ability of the group's most competent member. In one study demonstrating the effect, researchers (Blake, Shepard, and Mouton, 1964) had subjects watch part of *Twelve Angry Men,* a film about a murder trial and the suspenseful deliberations of a jury trying to reach a verdict. Each person in the group tried to predict individually what would happen in the rest of the film. Later the subjects as a group were asked to discuss the film and make a collective prediction about what would happen. Some of the individual predictions were accurate, and some were inaccurate. The group prediction usually followed the most accurate individual predictions.

The problems of real-life groups are often more complicated than finding the correct solution to a simple problem. For example, a group may have to decide between two different policies when each one pertains to several different goals (Braybrook and Lindblom, 1970).

Or the problem may be a multiple-stage task, requiring a series of steps to reach a solution, with each step depending on a previous step (see Kelley and Thibaut, 1969). Because a consistent strategy is needed to solve the problem, group members may interfere with, rather than complement, one another's efforts. An example of such a problem was reported by James Davis and Frank Restle (1963), who found that groups working through long problems requiring sequential solutions had difficulty in identifying their best members. All of the members tended to make comments, whether or not the comments were worthwhile. As a result, discovery of correct solutions depended on factors other than competence, such as feelings about who should contribute to the group and who shouldn't, the authority and status of those making suggestions, the legality of procedures for deciding, and the incentives for not paying attention to the correct answers.

Much of the research on group problem

solving has emphasized two processes that affect group performance. One is the "weighting process" by which various solutions are selected and rejected in real groups. The other is the "decision rules" by which the group decides its strategy and how these rules affect minority opinions (Davis, 1973).

An example of research on the weighting process is that of Hoffman (1978), who proposed that potential solutions to group tasks gain or lose support in proportion to the number of positive versus negative comments made about them in the group discussion. Hoffman and his colleagues have discovered that once proposed solutions have received a greater number of favorable than critical comments, these solutions tend to be adopted forthwith and group members then spend little energy searching for better solutions. One reason for this phenomenon is that the norms of work groups usually are to praise popular ideas.

In a recent review of work groups, J. Richard Hackman and Charles Morris (1975) suggested that problem-solving groups are usually guided by conservative norms: for example, members should avoid personal references and anxiety-arousing behavior; they should not take interpersonal risks; and they should save face when their ideas are rejected. These norms protect the group against conflict and uncertainty and help "close ranks" around popular ideas.

However, there are also costs of such conservative norms. For example, people tend to avoid disagreement with a prestigious group member, to go along with the wishes of high-status members, to copy other groups and old decisions, and to avoid thinking about issues or decisions when previous decisions or procedures can be used instead. As a result, groups often fail to pursue the most "rational" methods of discovering solutions.

In summary, researchers have discovered important aspects of group tasks or goals that affect a group's ultimate performance. In real-life groups, however, these "task variables" combine with individual variables—such as skill, talent, and attitudes—and with group variables—such as norms and roles. Therefore, the total mix of all these variables must be considered in order to understand how groups work.

An interesting example of this total mix of task variables, individual variables, and group variables is a study by Jones (1974), dealing with the performance of professional athletic teams. As would be expected, he found a high relationship between individual team members' skills and the performance of the team; that is, teams with good athletes did well. However, the relationship was much higher in some sports than in others. In baseball a team's effectiveness was nearly 90-percent predictable by measuring team members' skills, but in basketball only about 35 percent of the team's effectiveness was predictable from the skill of individuals. Jones noted that success in basketball is especially dependent on personal relationships and teamwork. If these conditions are not favorable, then basketball team effectiveness is impaired, even if individuals are highly skilled. Thus, in order to improve group performance, one would have to train people to improve not only their individual skills but also their coordination of these skills with the demands of the task and the goals of the group. In other words, groups should develop effective strategies and plans for carrying out goals.

STRATEGIES AND PLANNING Any group, explicitly or implicitly, elects different strategies for doing its work. For example, in one group the members might decide to free-associate in order to get ideas; another group might discuss specific agendas and alternative sequences of events; still another group might call on each person in turn.

Research shows that the performance of groups is markedly affected by the strategies they use. An example of this is seen in a study by Richard Hackman and his colleagues (Hackman, Brousseau, and Weiss, 1976). They set up an experiment to test whether groups with specific strategies about group discussions were more productive than groups without such strategies. Groups composed of four persons each were assigned to three different conditions: a "strategy" condition, an "antistrategy" condition, and a control condition. In the strategy condition, group members were asked to spend the first five minutes of a thirty-five-minute period discussing their goals and how they might best work together. As a guide to this discussion, the members were given suggestions about how they might choose a performance strategy. In the antistrategy condition, group members were asked explicitly not to waste time discussing strategies, but to move immediately into their work. In the control-group conditions, group members were given no special instructions other than to try to maximize performance.

The experimental task required group members to assemble various kinds of electrical components described on lists given to each group member. In order to test the effects of strategies on different types of groups, members' task information was varied. In half of the groups each member had all the necessary information to perform the task. In the other half, each member's list was different, and members presumably had to share information and coordinate their work. It was hypothesized that planning and strategy would be much more beneficial in the unequal information condition.

As shown in Figure 11.2, when group members had unequal information, those groups who planned a strategy were the most productive. (They decided to share their information.) However, when all members had equal information, the groups who were told to proceed with no strategy at all were most productive. When all members of a group have all the information needed, planning can be detrimental to the group's work. Figure 11.2 also reveals an interesting paradox: both the "strategy" and the "antistrategy" instructions had some beneficial effects on performance as compared with leaving the groups alone. This indicates that part of the effect of any intervention may be the so-called placebo effect of intervening; in other words, just appearing to "treat" a group in some way may positively affect its performance. This phenomenon is also known as the "Hawthorne effect," after studies carried out in the 1930s in the Hawthorne factory, in which it was discovered that any attention given to work groups at all—whether conditions were improved, for example, by brightening illumination or worsened by dimming illumination—resulted in increased performance. Apparently, any intervention affects workers' sense of their own importance and results in improved performance.

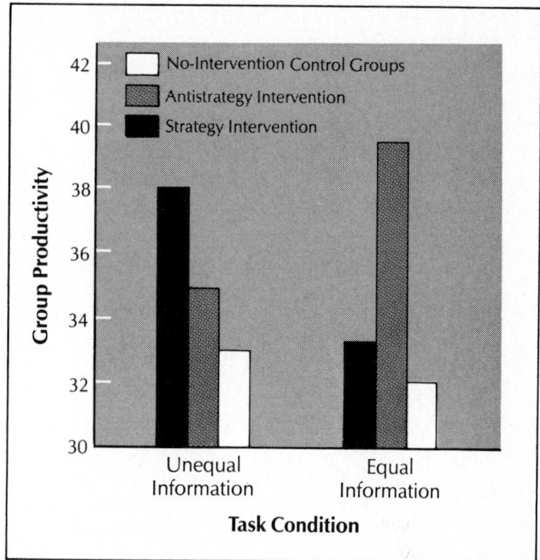

FIGURE 11.2 Productivity of groups in a strategy study. When each member was given different information, the "strategy" groups—those that were told to map out a plan before beginning—were most productive. When group members all had the same information, the "antistrategy" groups—those that were told to proceed without planning—worked best. In both cases, the strategy and antistrategy groups were more productive than the control group, which received no special instructions. (Adapted from Hackman, Brousseau, and Weiss, 1976.)

SOCIAL FACILITATION

Some of the earliest research in social psychology deals with the effects of groups on individual performance. As discussed in Chapter 1, in 1897 a teacher named Triplett had his students wind fishing reels either alone or in the presence of other students. He discovered that the students who worked in the presence of others wound their fishing reels more quickly than those who worked alone (Triplett, 1897). This was one of the first experimental studies demonstrating that the presence of other people may enhance the performance of individuals.

DISPOSITIONS AND SITUATIONS

COMPETITIVE PEOPLE IN GROUPS

How competitive are you? Are you a high-pressure achiever who pushes herself or himself to near capacity to achieve her or his goals, and do you get frustrated and angry when something interferes with your progress? Or are you a relaxed, easygoing individual who takes things as they come? Researchers have labeled the former, competitive personality as "Type A" and the latter, easygoing personality as "Type B."

Type A and Type B people react to stress differently. In one study students walked a motorized treadmill at a sharper and sharper angle until they finally gave up. Physiological monitoring showed that Type A students reached 91.4 percent of their aerobic capacity while Type B's reached only 82.8 percent. However, A's admitted to less fatigue than B's, suggesting that A's ignore or deny their body's tiredness (Glass, 1979). Not surprisingly, Type A's also show a high risk of heart disease. In fact, Type A behavior is also referred to as the "coronary-prone behavior pattern" (Friedman and Rosenman, 1974).

How do Type A's behave in groups? As explained in the accompanying section, one effect of groups on individuals is social facilitation. The presence of other people is arousing and facilitates performance on simple tasks but hinders performance on complex tasks. If Type A's are competitive and hard-driven, then we might assume that they would become more aroused and competitive in groups and thus more subject to social facilitation. This was the hypothesis tested by John Gastorf, Jerry Suls, and Glenn Sanders (1980).

At the State University of New York at Albany, 240 undergraduate students—120 males and 120 females—were classified as Type A or Type B, based on their answers to an activity survey adapted for college students (for example, "Has some friend ever told you that you eat too fast?" "How would your closest friend rate you—hard-driving and competitive or relaxed and easygoing?"). Each student was then asked to work either on a simple task (recopying a digit printed in a box) or a complex task (reading a digit, consulting a code, copying a second digit based on the code, and periodically switching to a new code). The students were told that the task was an important measure of concept formation and their performance would be evaluated. In addition, the students worked either alone or with another person under conditions that made it easy to compare progress on the tasks.

How did these students perform? As shown in the graph below, only Type A's were significantly affected by the presence of another person. For these hard-driven, competitive people the presence of someone else facilitated their performance on the simple task and caused them to copy many more digits, but hindered their performance on the complex task and caused them to copy significantly fewer digits. There were no significant differences between males and females.

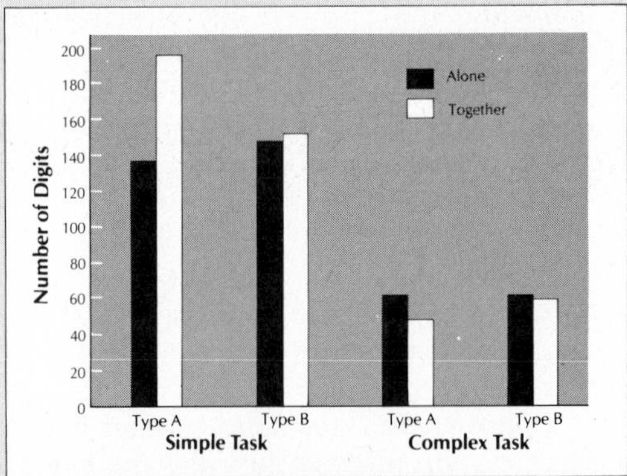

This experiment involved groups of only two people. However, it demonstrated that Type A's will behave differently than B's in the presence of others. A group's effect on an individual, then, partly depends on the nature of the individual. If you are a Type A, you are likely to become aroused, competitive, and concerned about your performance when you're in a group. If you are a Type B, you will probably be much less affected by the group.

The phenomenon has come to be called "social facilitation" even though the presence of others may sometimes detract from individual performance as well as facilitate it.

For many years, psychologists have wondered about the conditions under which the presence of others enhances or impairs individual performance. The question can be conceptualized in two different ways, depending on whether the presence of others involves "audience effects" or "coaction effects." *Audience effects* are those that influence an individual's performance when he or she is working alone on a task but knows that other people are watching. Audience effects are most obvious in performances of a speaker, a dancer, or a pole-vaulter, but they also operate in groups and in all social situations. *Coaction effects* are those that influence an individual's performance when the others who are present are also working on the same task, either individually or collectively.

Research on coaction and audience effects has produced conflicting findings. Sometimes individuals do better alone; sometimes they work best in groups. In an influential article published in *Science* in 1965, Robert Zajonc theorized that the presence of others usually serves to increase arousal and motivation. Anyone who has taken a timed test while being watched has probably felt this arousal. This results in a faster speed of performance and greater reliance on habitual, well-learned responses. An increase in work speed and reliance on habitual responses, however, does not necessarily improve performance on tasks. Errors and distraction may also increase. Therefore, performance may be improved only when the task is simple to perform or is well learned. In contrast, when the task requires finely tuned skills and concentration or learning new material, Zajonc proposed that the arousal produced by the presence of others would have a negative effect on performance.

The presence of others tends to increase arousal and motivation and may improve performance on a task such as an exam. *(© Arthur Grace / Stock, Boston)*

The effect of arousal on performance was demonstrated in a study by Zajonc and Nieuwenhuyse (1964). Subjects had to learn nonsense words that the experimenter claimed were Turkish. Those words were presented in a tachistoscope for brief periods of time, but some of the words were presented so often that subjects could remember them easily. Then, in the test phase of the study, the words were shown for such a brief period of time that none of the words could actually be seen. The researchers predicted that on these "blank" trials the subjects would "see" some of the well-learned words, and indeed they did, especially when the subjects were highly aroused. A second and follow-up study by Zajonc and Sales (1966) demonstrated that the effect of arousal could be duplicated by merely having another person watch the subject, thus suggesting that the presence of others is arousing and that arousal increases the rate of well-learned or simple responses. Further research showed that even cockroaches ran faster in the presence of other cockroaches (Zajonc, Heingarther, and Herman, 1969). In humans, however, other investigators (Cottrell, 1968, for example) have found that the social-facilitation effect can be nullified if the observing audience is blindfolded. In these conditions subjects' performance on well-learned tasks and their speed of behavior did not differ from their performance alone. Hence, it seems that the presence of others is not automatically arousing, but that it has something to do with being watched, evaluated, or distracted by others.

Although we now know *how* audiences and coworkers affect individual performance, research has not yet answered the basic question of *why* a person's reactions speed up on well-learned behavior in the presence of others. Zajonc's explanation is that the arousal caused by the presence of others is not learned, but is innate to several animal species. Other researchers (Cottrell, 1968) suggest that the presence of others arouses a person's apprehension about being evaluated and, therefore, leads people to try harder to succeed. Still a third explanation is that the presence of others is distracting, an effect that reduces performance on complex tasks but enhances performance on simple tasks. All of these theories are competing explanations for why people in the presence of others act more quickly and with greater reliance on habit than when they are alone.

CHOICE SHIFTS

Another way that groups affect individual performance is the so-called "risky-shift phenomenon." Typically, when a person makes a decision as a member of a group, it is generally a less cautious, more "risky" decision than that same individual would make alone. Whether the decision involves an individual buying a house, a company introducing a new product, or a government invading a foreign country, individuals will shift from a less extreme to a more "risky" decision after participating in group discussion. This "risky" shift is an intriguing idea with many practical applications. But why does it happen?

An idea popular in social science in the nineteenth century was that groups think, feel, and behave differently than the individuals who make up the group. Phrases such as the "collective mind" or the "group mind" implied that the whole is more than the sum of its parts. For example, a group may engage in a lynching although its individual members never would (LeBon, 1896). Floyd Allport (1924), one of the early social psychologists, disagreed. He suggested that the antisocial behaviors performed by groups are actually present in each individual member's repertoire, but that these behaviors are not expressed unless the group sanctions them. If the group's action implies that a certain behavior is acceptable, then this activity becomes acceptable to individuals (even if society does not condone it). The responsibility for a lynching is defused among group members so that no individual can view himself or herself as fully responsible for the action.

The risky-shift phenomenon, which parallels this early theoretical development in social psychology, was first studied by James Stoner in 1961. Stoner presented his subjects with a set of decision problems called the "choice dilemmas questionnaire" (CDQ). For example, the subjects are told that Mr. A is an electrical engineer who graduated from college five years ago, is married, has one child, and has been working for a large electronics firm. The company pays him a modest but adequate salary, which will probably not increase much over time. Mr. A is offered a job with a new, small company, which would pay more and would give him a chance for part ownership. However, it is not certain that the new company will survive. Subjects are then asked to advise Mr. A whether or not he should take the job with the new company, given a specified set of probabilities (odds) that the new company will survive: 1 in 10, 3 in 10, 5 in 10, 7 in 10, or 9 in 10.They are asked to pick the lowest acceptable probability that would make it reasonable for Mr. A to take the job, if they think he should take the job at all.

Typically, the experimenters have first asked their subjects to respond individually to a series of items of this kind. Then the subjects are brought together in groups and asked to discuss each of the items. After the discussion, the group makes a joint decision. On most items of the CDQ, groups usually make riskier decisions than the average of the decisions made by the individuals composing the group.

In subsequent work, Michael Wallach, Nathan Kogan, and Daryl Bem (1962, 1964) attributed the risky shift to diffusion of responsibility. They suggested that groups can afford to take greater risks than individuals because none of the members would be fully responsible should things go wrong. However, problems with this explanation of the risky shift became apparent rather quickly. For instance, the risky shift does not occur for all kinds of decisions, nor even on two of the original CDQ items, one of which typically yields a conservative shift. In this item (number 12 on the CDQ) the group members are told that Mr. M is considering marriage to Miss T, whom he has known for more than a year. Recently Mr. M and Miss T, who view a number of things quite differently, have repeatedly argued; they seek the advice of a marriage counselor and are told that a happy marriage is possible but not certain. On this item, subjects acting as individuals are more likely to recommend a risky marriage for Mr. M than when they are acting as a group.

Because group discussions can sometimes result in such conservative shifts as the example above, the term "choice shift" has been proposed as a more accurate label for the phenomenon. Recent research has suggested two major processes whereby group decisions can lead to choice shifts in either a more risky or more conservative direction. The first process emphasizes the influence of norms already present in the group; the second process emphasizes the influence of information and persuasion.

The roots of the first explanation lie in Festinger's social-comparison theory (1954). In order to evaluate the appropriateness or "correctness" of our behavior and attitudes, we often compare ourselves with others. When we enter into group discussions we find that some people have positions that are more extreme than our own toward some desirable goal. Because cultural norms generally favor risk taking—in whatever direction is consistent with one's goal—we realize that our own more moderate positions fall short of group norms, as represented by the more extreme group members. In order to bring our own attitudes and behavior into alignment with the norms made salient by group discussion, we shift our own position to become more extreme. Thus, according to Roger Brown (1965), choice shifts are explained by cultural values that are highlighted by group discussion.

The second explanation concerns the effects of information and persuasion. According to this view, the mere knowledge of others' positions per se is not a sufficient ingredient for choice shifts. Instead, information that is exchanged during the course of discussion plays a critical role. Group discussion often produces a number of arguments in favor of extreme positions, so individual group members become aware of additional reasons for either risk taking or conservatism and therefore shift their positions in a more extreme direction (Vinokur, 1971; Burnstein and Vinokur, 1973).

Although we still do not know exactly why choice shifts occur, it is important to have learned that this group process does occur. The fact that a group's opinions become more uniform as its members interact, combined with the movement of groups toward extreme judgments or decisions, has important implications for how groups work.

GROUPTHINK Several other factors also contribute to groups making extreme, one-sided decisions that are often "wrong" in light of all the evidence. Irving Janis (1972) has coined the term *groupthink* to describe these factors, and he has analyzed several foreign-policy actions of the United States government in order to understand how groupthink works. For example, not long after his inauguration, President John F. Kennedy accepted his advisors' recommendation for an invasion of Cuba—an invasion that turned out to be a dismal failure and a major embarrassment for Kennedy. As shown in the accompanying box, Kennedy's advisors failed to consider many factors that made the invasion unlikely to succeed. In Janis's view, the president's advisors were victims of groupthink.

What are the symptoms of groupthink? Janis has identified several. One is an *illusion of invulnerability*, which often results from high morale and optimism. Although this illusion is

FOCUS ON APPLICATIONS

CUBA 1961/IRAN 1980: THE PROBLEM OF GROUPTHINK

In the spring of 1961 some of the most respected statesmen in American history formed a group that unanimously made one of the worst foreign-policy decisions in recent times. The group was the inner circle of advisors to incoming President John F. Kennedy. The decision was to carry out plans for an invasion of Cuba, staged by Cuban exiles trained by the CIA. The invasion took place at the Bay of Pigs, and despite assistance by the U.S. Navy, Air Force, and the CIA, within three days 1,200 of the 1,400 exiles had been captured and their supply ships had been sunk by Castro's air force.

What accounts for this failure of judgment? According to Irving Janis (1972), Kennedy's advisors committed several of the errors of groupthink. Specifically, they failed to consider available information about the size and strength of Castro's forces, about the deteriorating morale of the exile invaders, and about the likelihood that the invasion would touch off uprisings behind the lines in the Cuban underground. In some cases, the advisors even neglected to *seek* relevant information. They also engaged in stereotyping, leading them to underestimate the military strength and morale of the Cuban people.

Although Kennedy's advisors seemed to reach the Bay of Pigs decision unanimously, it has since been revealed that there were "silent dissenters"—people who had private doubts about the invasion but had failed to mention them. As Arthur Schlesinger, Jr., described the meetings in his book *A Thousand Days* (1965): "Our meetings were taking place in a curious atmosphere of assumed consensus. Had one senior adviser opposed the adventure, I believe that Kennedy would have canceled it. Not one spoke against it."

Almost twenty years later, some of the same problems may have beset President Carter's advisors when they decided to try to rescue the American hostages held in the U.S. embassy in Iran. The mission failed in a fiery explosion in the Iranian desert early one morning when one of the rescue helicopters crashed into the support plane. Eight men were killed, the Iranians hardened their demands, and America suffered a major loss of international prestige.

The newspaper article below suggests that the rescue mission was more risky than the advisors may have acknowledged. Perhaps groupthink combined with the risky-shift phenomenon to quiet doubts that would have blocked the mission. Even after the failure, the Joint Chiefs of Staff still be-

generally characteristic of highly cohesive groups, it has also been shown to occur even in groups that are not cohesive. A second symptom has to do with *shared stereotypes*, which leads a group to act unwisely with regard to the objects of its stereotyping. Another symptom is rationalization—the tendency of a group to pool the resources of its individual members in inventing justifications for whatever action it decides on. A related symptom is an *illusion of morality*—the tendency to assume that the group's actions are morally justified. Another symptom is *self-censorship*—members of the group partly censor their own views, which results in an illusion of unanimity.

Some of these symptoms have been demonstrated in recent laboratory research conducted by Matie Flowers (1977). She discovered that a closed-leadership style—a leader who encourages unanimity at all costs and focuses discussion only on his or her preferred solutions—can lead to or intensify groupthink. In this study, forty experimental teams (each consisting of three people and a leader) "role-played" school administrators faced with serious redistricting and personnel problems. Half of the teams were

lieved the plan was workable; the chief of naval operations said, "We would do it again."

WASHINGTON—In all the second-guessing about the Iran raid, a recurring question has been how the Joint Chiefs of Staff decided that the mission would have "a very good chance of success," as their chairman, Gen. David C. Jones, later said.

President Carter invited similar questions when he said there had been a "general consensus" that each of the three phases of the mission would have a different chance of success: "most difficult," to put the U.S. rescue team into Iran undetected; "easiest," to actually rescue the hostages, and "second most difficult," to get the rescuers and hostages out of Iran.

Analysts dubious about such broad and subjective assessments ask, "Where are the calculations in that calculated risk?" More kindly put, the question is, "What is the basis of those risk assessments?"

No answers are yet available and there have been no assurances that a professional examination was conducted to assess the chances of success for each stage of the operation.

Defense Secretary Harold Brown said that to preserve secrecy, knowledge of the overall operation was confined to a "very, very small group of people—only those who had an absolutely essential part in the preparations." Whether any specialists in war games were among those who participated is not known.

Such experts normally conduct the so-called "scenario analysis" of each phase, then multiply each probability to arrive at the odds of success for the overall mission.

Thus, if the chances were 90% for success in the easiest phase, 70% for the hardest and 80% for the other one, the product of these probabilities—$0.9 \times 0.7 \times 0.8$—would be the predicted odds for the full mission. In this hypothetical example, it comes out to be 50%, or one chance in two. . . .

The failure rate for helicopter components is better known than the likelihood of a fierce sandstorm or the chance passage of a busload of Iranians. Yet the risk that could be most precisely predicted for the Iran raid turned out to be radically wrong, because three out of eight helicopters failed and the mission was called off. . . .

When the risks of such mechanical failures are combined with subjective estimates on the performance of men—such as how hard the Iranian terrorists might resist the rescuers—the overall assessment of a mission's chances is extremely difficult to make.

Asked how quantitative and qualitative estimates can be combined, one authority answered, "By praying a lot." . . .

Source: Robert C. Toth and Norman Kempster, "Iran Rescue Mission: How Were Risks Assessed?" *Los Angeles Times*, May 3, 1980, part I, p. 6.

made up of acquaintances and half of strangers. One-half of these groups had a leader who adopted the closed style. The other half of the groups had an "open" leader who encouraged wide discussion and a "wise" decision. The experimenters measured the quantity and quality of solutions offered, the number of facts considered, and members' own perceptions. As shown in Table 11.1, they found that groups with "closed" leaders discussed fewer alternatives and considered fewer facts in reaching a decision than groups with "open" leaders. It made no difference whether the groups were composed of strangers or acquaintances. Surprisingly, however, all groups rated the quality of their decisions about equally, despite an open- or closed-leadership style. Perhaps this suggests that all groups are interested in "closing ranks" after a decision is made and in promoting the value of their decisions, regardless of the process leading to the decision or the facts supporting the decision.

When groupthink phenomena are combined with factors leading to choice shifts as well as the conformity pressures discussed earlier, it is easy to understand the extreme actions

TABLE 11.1 SOLUTIONS PROPOSED AND FACTS THAT EMERGED DURING GROUP DISCUSSION IN FLOWERS'S STUDY OF GROUPTHINK

EXPERIMENTAL CONDITION	AVERAGE NUMBER OF SOLUTIONS PROPOSED	AVERAGE NUMBER OF "FACTS" DISCUSSED	
		BEFORE DECISION	AFTER DECISION
"Open" Leader			
Strangers	6.20	15.10	.80
Acquaintances	6.70	15.90	.90
"Closed" Leader			
Strangers	5.35	7.10	4.60
Acquaintances	4.94	7.30	2.50

Source: M. L. Flowers, "A Laboratory Test of Some Implications of Janis's Groupthink Hypothesis," *Journal of Personality and Social Psychology* 35 (1977): 888–896.

taken by groups. Even "the best and the brightest"—as David Halberstam labeled the White House advisors who initiated the Vietnam War—can make terrible mistakes. When the picture is clouded still further by deindividuation, social isolation, and the demands of an autocratic leader, even such extreme behavior as the mass suicide in Guyana seems possible.

SUMMARY

Each of us belongs to many groups—groups that affect us individually and those that affect society as a whole. Nominal groups are mere collections of individuals, while psychological groups are made up of people who are connected socially and psychologically. Psychological groups are designated as either membership groups—any group to which a person belongs—or reference groups—a group with which a person identifies and that influences values and attitudes. Psychological groups are characterized by norms such as reciprocity or mutual responsiveness that govern members' behavior. Such groups are also characterized by goals that justify the group's existence and explain members' values and attitudes. One way that groups promote these goals is through egocentrism, or a positive view of the group's own members and purposes. Egocentrism occurs partly because of perceptual and memory processes that focus a group's attention on its own behavior and partly because of a group's motivation to protect itself.

Groups are formed either deliberately for a specific purpose, such as alcoholism or weight watching, or spontaneously out of mutual attraction. Groups are strengthened when members must perform a common task, face a common adversary, or cope with a stressful situation.

Individuals in groups enact various roles. Roles are determined by both dispositional factors—such as individual members' needs and personalities—and situational factors—such as political or social expectations, or a problem or crisis to solve. Two of the best-known roles in groups are those of follower and leader. Much research on leadership has determined that different types of leaders emerge in different kinds of situations: social-emotional leaders attend to members' feelings and are most effective when tasks are unstructured; task-oriented leaders are more directive and demanding and are most effective when tasks are clearly structured. Roles in groups are partly influenced by communication patterns within groups.

Group dynamics is the term used to refer to groups in action. A common question in group dynamics research is, why do people behave so differently in groups? One factor has to do with the degree of cohesiveness and commitment within a group. When cohesiveness is high there is greater conformity. One type of conformity is compliance—a change of behavior that occurs as a result of group pressure. Compliance is highest when group members appear to be unanimous in their decisions and when information is ambiguous, as demonstrated in Asch's classic research paradigm. Deviants who resist the decision of a group's majority are subject to intense pressures to conform. Another type of conformity is private acceptance of a group's attitude. Because of the power of groups over an individual, attitude change is often more intense in a group context.

How people perform in a group is determined by several factors having to do with the nature of the task, the group, and the individual members, as well as the problem-solving strategies adopted by the group. Behavior in groups is also affected by social facilitation—the tendency for the presence of other people to increase arousal, which facilitates performance of a simple, well-learned behavior but hinders performance of a novel, not-well-learned behavior. Groups also lead people to make more extreme decisions than they might make by themselves, a tendency that is further enhanced by the phenomenon of groupthink. When these factors are combined, the extreme behavior often observed in groups becomes more comprehensible.

CHAPTER TWELVE

THE PHYSICAL ENVIRONMENT AND SOCIAL BEHAVIOR

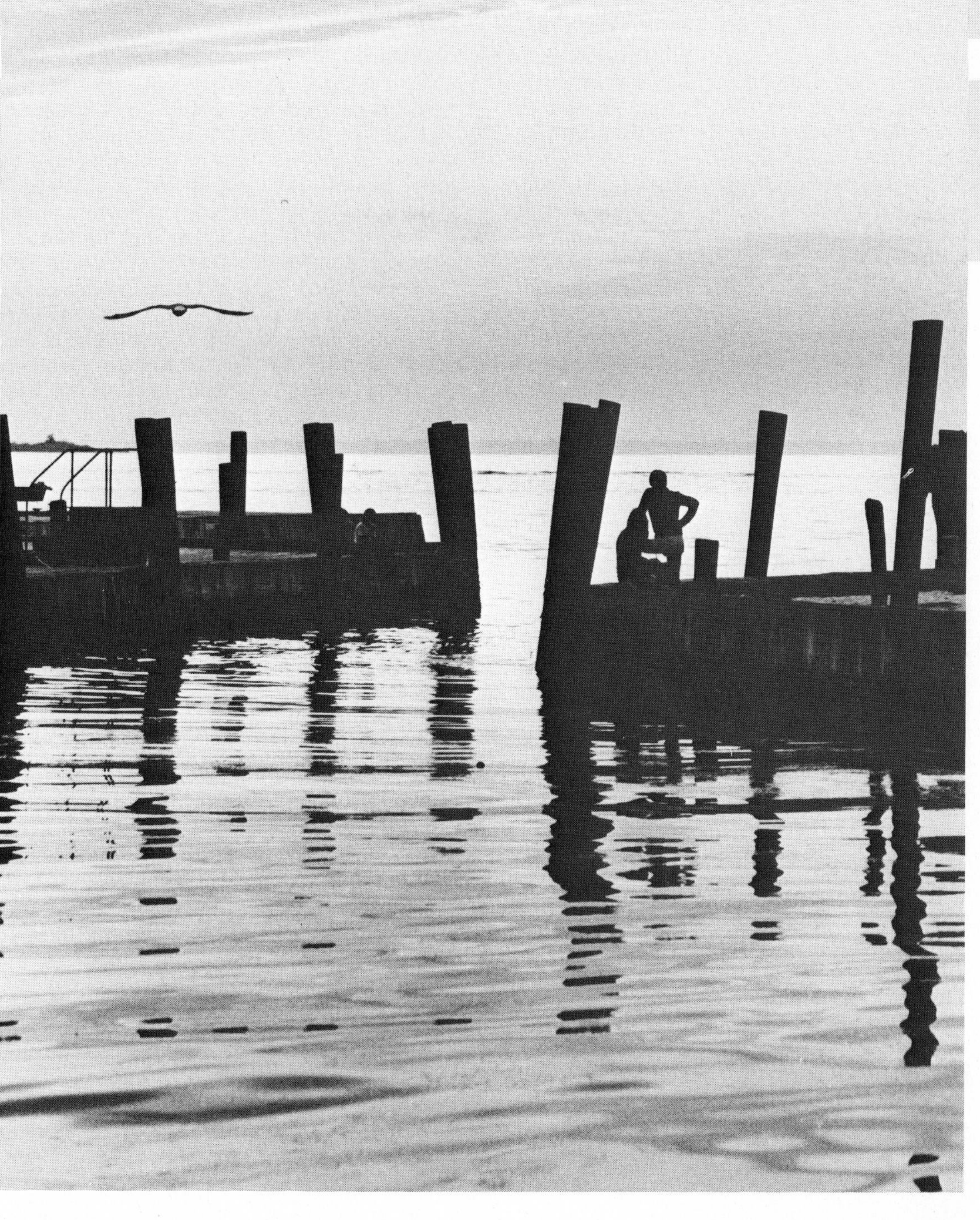

Imagine yourself living in each of the following environments. The first is a crowded college dormitory. Your room is cramped. Most of the furniture is bolted down or built permanently in place. You share your few square feet with another person who was assigned to you by some bureaucratic office. Outside your door is a long hallway with forty other doors leading to forty other rooms just like yours. Outside your window is a parking lot, and across the parking lot is another dormitory. Beyond your door, the hallway is almost always noisy with the comings and goings of the seventy-nine other people who share your floor. There are five other floors above you and two below you, and the lobby and lounges are usually littered. The campus is a clutter of nondescript institutional buildings, and the grounds are largely asphalt. The surrounding neighborhood is a declining section of a large city. Beyond the blocks of crowded college shops are freeways, small businesses, and cheap apartment houses. The general feeling of the whole place is crowding, noise, unpleasantness, and a sense of unmanageable confusion.

Now compare this with a second environment. You've been loaned a friend's mountain cabin for the summer. The cabin backs up to an aspen forest and overlooks a meadow dotted with wildflowers. Off to the right you hear the rush of a mountain stream. Across the valley the glow of the sun on the rocky peaks contrasts with the unbelievably blue sky. The air smells of fir and pine, and a nearby trail leads you through these woods to high lakes and snowy peaks. The cabin where you're staying is large, with a private loft for yourself and plenty of space in the other rooms for the close friends you've invited to join you. If you want to seek out more people or other diversions, there's an interesting resort community a few miles away. You can get there easily on a road that winds among the trees and then cuts across a broad valley with distinctive mountain peaks all around. In the town you can find sports, music, entertainment, and people from around the country. When you're tired, it's an easy trip back to your cabin. The general feeling in this environment is one of privacy, natural beauty, freedom of choice, and release from regimentation.

Consider how you might feel about yourself, your work, and your social relationships if you lived in each of these two environments. In the first environment—the crowded, overloaded, and unpleasant dormitory—chances are you would feel frustrated, unable to concentrate, unwilling to offer much help if a friend asked, and generally like a "pawn," moved around by forces beyond your control. But in the second environment—the mountain cabin surrounded by natural beauty and space with friends and pleasures nearby—chances are you could feel capable, focused, open to others, and generally in control of yourself and your world. How does the physical environment exert such an effect on the way people feel and behave toward themselves and others? And how can we alter the environments we inhabit as well as our responses to those environments in order to gain more control over ourselves? These are the kind of questions that concern psychologists interested in the effects of the physical environment on social behavior.

PERSONAL SPACE

One way to begin to understand how physical environments affect human social behavior is to phrase the question in the broadest terms and ask: How much space does the average person need to feel comfortable? Of course, a question that general is unanswerable, but it is possible to describe conditions under which people need more or less space around their bodies, what kinds of others people will allow to encroach on their space, and how people respond to unwanted intruders. These questions relate to a phenomenon called *personal space*—that is, *an amount of space with an invisible boundary surrounding a person's body into which intruders may not come.*

In 1959, Edward T. Hall was able to say: "Personal space is like sex. It's always there but no one ever talks about it." Today, like sex, personal space is the subject of much discussion and investigation, yet it is still not entirely understood.

Personal space varies from culture to culture. In the Middle East, for example, people prefer a very limited personal space. In the United States, we tend to favor a greater personal space. *(© Esaias Baite/VIVA 1980/Woodfin Camp & Assoc.; Michael Weisbrot & Family)*

Hall set the stage for research into the personal-space phenomenon with his insightful descriptions of the way people use space in different cultures. In his book *The Hidden Dimension* (1966), Hall noted, for example, that Americans and Arabs have very different personal-space needs when engaged in public conversation. An American diplomat speaking to an Arab government official might prefer a conversational distance of 4 to 7 feet. In contrast, the Arab would prefer a much closer distance, close enough, in fact, to smell the body and breath of the person being spoken to and to actually feel the other's body heat.

In Western cultures, social interaction is regulated by standardized zones of personal space, and much is communicated by the distances people adopt when they're speaking to each other. Hall has identified four different distances that Americans employ, depending on what they wish to communicate.

1. Intimate Distance
   a. Close phase: bodily contact; the distance of love-making and wrestling, comforting and protecting.
   b. Far phase: 6 to 18 inches; the distance of whispering and intimate conversation.
2. Personal Distance
   a. Close phase: 1½ to 2½ feet; conversational distance between close friends—or the distance of crowded parties.
   b. Far phase: 2½ to 4 feet; conversations between acquaintances, literally keeping someone "at arm's length."
3. Social Distance
   a. Close phase: 4 to 7 feet; the distance of impersonal business.
   b. Far phase: 7 to 12 feet; the distance of formal business and social discourse.
4. Public Distance
   a. Close phase: 12 to 25 feet; the distance of formal public speaking, allowing only one-way communication.
   b. Far phase: 25 feet or more; the very formal public-speaking distance of extremely important persons, such as the president of the United States.

MEASUREMENT OF PERSONAL SPACE

One of the first attempts to measure the personal-space needs of different individuals was conducted by a group of psychiatrists who were interested in what they called the "body buffer zone" of schizophrenics versus normal persons (Horowitz, Duff, and Stratton, 1964). These researchers asked people to walk over to one of three different objects: a hatrack, a man, or a woman. Then they measured the distance from the object at which people stopped. Normal persons approached the human beings closer than did the schizophrenics, and all persons walked closer to the hatrack than to the humans. In addition normal persons approached the female closer than the male.

A number of subsequent studies have adopted this *experimental approach* to measuring people's personal-space needs. In the typical experiment, one person is asked to walk across a room toward someone else or to enter a room and sit down beside someone else. Often the floor may be marked into small squares so that distances can be easily measured. Sometimes videotapes are made of the interaction, and the distance is subsequently measured by counting the floor squares on the videotape.

A second popular measurement technique involves a *simulation*. In this approach, a particular type of interaction is described—for example, a "getting-acquainted conversation"—and people are then asked to position cutout silhouettes on a felt board at a comfortable distance for conducting that type of interaction. The distance between the silhouettes is then measured in terms of centimeters. A variant of this technique asks people to trace around cardboard silhouettes on a piece of paper at a distance that seems most comfortable to them.

A third technique involves *observing* people in the real world as they go about their normal interactions. For example, observers may watch or photograph people sitting in airports, students studying at library tables, or friends talking in a park. Relative distances can be gauged in terms of the number of chairs that separate people or the number of floor tiles or cracks in the sidewalk between them.

One problem in personal-space research has been that the three measurement techniques described above—experimental manipulation, simulation, and field observation—do not always intercorrelate highly. For example, one study (Dosey and Meisels, 1969), which explored the effects of stress on personal space, employed each type of measure as subjects were asked to (1) approach a stranger, (2) position cardboard silhouettes on a felt board, and (3)sit down at a table with a stranger. There was no significant correlation among any of these measures. This suggests that research findings on personal space may be highly specific to the particular measures employed. While this may create a problem in interpreting research based on only a single measure, most of the findings described below have been replicated over several experiments, often involving different types of measures.

RESULTS OF PERSONAL-SPACE RESEARCH

Researchers have explored a variety of factors influencing people's personal-space needs. As summarized by Gary Evans and Roger Howard (1973) and by Leslie Hayduk (1978), these factors include the following:

— *Age*: Children do not seem to have a well-developed personal-space zone like adults, although they usually develop this zone by about the age of twelve.
— *Personality disorders*: People with personality disorders, such as adult schizophrenics or teenagers with behavior problems, generally maintain larger personal space zones than normal persons, though they may sometimes invade others' personal space too closely. At the very least, people with personality disorders seem to have more variable personal space needs than "normal" persons.
— *Anxiety*: When people feel anxious—for example, if college students expect to be judged on their "sex appeal" or to face an unpleasant encounter—they tend to maintain larger personal space zones.
— *Social stigma*: When people have some sort of stigma or abnormality, such as a physical handicap or epilepsy, others keep a larger distance from them than from people who appear normal.
— *Sex*: In general, two males will keep a larger distance between themselves than will two females, while an acquainted male and female pair will keep the smallest personal space.
— *Friendliness*: In general, people who are friends or who wish to communicate friendliness will stand closer than people who are not friends.

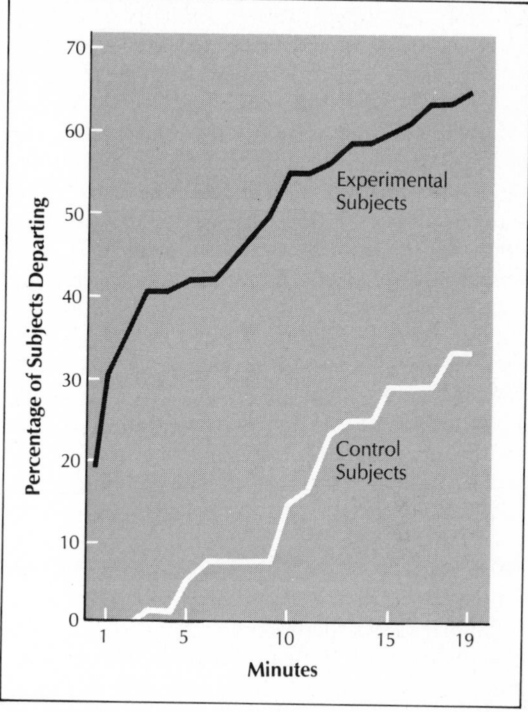

FIGURE 12.1 Robert Sommer (1969) sat down next to subjects on a bench and kept a six-inch distance from them when they edged away. These subjects were more likely to get up and leave after a short time than were the control subjects, whose personal space was not invaded.

PERSONAL SPACE AND SPATIAL INVASION

Another way to investigate people's spatial needs is to physically invade their personal space and see how they react. One of the first investigators to use this technique was Robert Sommer, a pioneer in personal-space research (Sommer, 1959, 1969). Sommer began his studies with patients in a mental hospital. While strolling in the hospital's garden, Sommer would approach a patient sitting alone on a bench and proceed to sit down on the same bench just six inches away, occasionally jangling his key ring to assert his authority. If the patient moved farther away, Sommer moved too, so as to maintain the six-inch distance. After two minutes of this invasion, Sommer found that a third of the patients had fled, and by nine minutes half of the victims had been driven away, as shown in Figure 12.1. Those who did not move reacted to the invasion by facing away from Sommer, fidgeting, or trying to erect a barrier by putting their hands against their chin or face. Even the most extremely withdrawn patients, who generally made no social responses, were affected by the invasion. In contrast, a group of control subjects who were not invaded but who were observed for comparison purposes maintained their seat for a much longer period of time. Sommer's students obtained similar results when they invaded the personal space of normal college students studying at library tables. Other researchers have found that people in shopping centers will flee more quickly from a male invader than from a female invader, while female shoppers who are invaded flee more quickly than male shoppers (Bleda and Bleda, 1976)

When people cannot escape a personal-space invasion by a stranger, they often become anxious and physiologically aroused. Arousal can be measured in terms of galvanic skin response (GSR), a measure of skin conductance based on the fact that when people are anxious, their palms sweat and thus conduct more electric current. In one study, for example, people who were invaded at distances of 1 and 3 feet had higher GSRs than people who were invaded at a distance of 9 feet (McBride, King, and James, 1965). Another study found that GSRs increased as the space between oneself and an invader decreased (Evans and Howard, 1972).

One of the most unusual measures of physiological arousal and personal-space invasion was conducted in men's restrooms by Dennis Middlemist, Eric Knowles, and Charles Matter (1976). These researchers knew that one effect of physiological arousal in males is pressure in the bladder and in the sphincter muscles in the urethra. This pressure acts to delay the onset and persistence of urination. Since personal-space invasion produces arousal, these researchers reasoned that close spatial invasions in the lavatory could delay urination. To conduct their experiment, the researchers stationed an observer in a toilet stall and provided him with a stopwatch and a periscope to monitor the three urinals nearby. Whenever someone came in to use the urinal, another confederate of the experimenter would also enter the restroom and step up to the adjacent urinal or to one two spaces away. In a control condition, restroom users' personal space was not invaded (except, of course, for the concealed observer with the periscope and the stopwatch). The results suggested that the closer a man's personal space is invaded, the greater is his delay of urination and the shorter is his persistence of urination. Not surprisingly, the ethics of this study created a lively controversy. One critic (Koocher, 1977) branded the research an intrusion on human dignity, since subjects were not informed in advance that they would be observed. The researchers (Middlemist, Knowles, and Matter, 1977) countered that men who were invaded in an early pilot study were interviewed afterwards, and none were bothered to have been observed; and in any case, the identity of the subjects in the final study remained anonymous, since the periscope was not aimed at subjects' faces.

THEORETICAL EXPLANATIONS OF PERSONAL SPACE

Why have humans developed personal-space needs, and what purpose does it serve in our social behavior? Why, indeed, would each of us, especially if we are males, be likely to stand farther away from another human being when we are feeling stressed, unstable, unfriendly, or uncertain about how to respond to a peculiar person or situation? As commonplace as the phenomenon is, like many other social behaviors, it is not clear why we do it. Several tentative theories have been advanced, and these are summarized in recent reviews (compare Altman, 1975; Evans and Eichelman, 1976; Hayduk, 1978). Drawing on these summaries, we can identify three possible explanations for a human being's need for personal space: (1) as a protection against stress; (2) as a way to reduce stimulation overload; and (3) as a means of regulating privacy and intimacy. Each of these approaches is discussed below.

STRESS/PROTECTION MODEL If people maintain large personal-space zones when they are feeling stressed, then perhaps personal space literally serves as a protective "buffer zone" around one's body. Some research, in which anxious or angry people maintain large personal space (see, for example, Dosey and Meisels, 1969; Meisels and Dosey, 1971), suggests this may be the case. The theory also helps explain why males typically have larger and less permeable personal-space zones than females, if one assumes that males are generally socialized to be the aggressors and defenders.

As plausible as this explanation sounds, there are a number of complexities in the theory, and all the evidence is not in yet. For instance, do people have different reactions to threats of a physical attack than to emotional threats that have no spatial implications? Do people's personal-space needs adapt over time in stressful situations, gradually decreasing as the stressor becomes familiar? And how are spatial needs affected by different types of common stressors, such as noise or sleep deprivation? While the stress/protection approach is a possible explanation for personal space, the specific connections between stress and personal space are unclear and the extent of the effects are unknown.

STIMULATION-OVERLOAD THEORY One consequence of standing close to another person is that we may receive more sensory stimulation than we wish. This is particularly true if the situation is beyond our control, as on a crowded elevator or in the subway. We see a myriad of tiny details on our invaders, from blood vessels in their eyes to pores in their skin. We smell their bodies, their perfume or their shaving lotion, and maybe their lunch. We feel the heat of their bodies, their breath on our skin, and possibly their spittle if they speak to us. In other words, we are forced to process more information than we normally do. This can "overload" our information-processing system and cause confusion and stress.

Edward Hall seems to lean toward this explanation when he suggests that people from a "far" personal-space culture like the British feel overwhelmed by sensory inputs when they are "invaded" by individuals from a "close" personal-space culture like the Arabs. Other theorists have suggested that the close proximity of people in a crowd produces a state of attentional overload that uses up too much of our attentional capacity. As a result, spatially invaded persons perform less well on tasks requiring strict attention to detail than persons who are not spatially invaded (see Cohen, 1978; Saegert, 1973).

One interesting prediction of the stimulation-overload approach to personal space was tested by Nesbit and Steven (1974). They reasoned that if spatial invasion produces sensory overload, then people who are already overloaded with sensory inputs should stand farther apart than persons who are not overloaded. As predicted, they found that people who were experiencing intense levels of stimulation in an amusement park spaced themselves farther apart than people who were not in an overstimulating environment, though other factors may account for this result.

Despite the evidence in favor of the stimulation-overload view, several questions can be raised. Evans and Eichelman (1976) have pointed out that human beings respond more to the meaning of sensory stimulation than to the quantity of stimulation. Furthermore, we can easily tune out irrelevant stimulation when we wish, like the faces in a crowd. Also, other types of intense stimulation, such as highly complex visual patterns presented at close range, have been shown to have no effect on people's task performance, whereas personal-space invasion has produced a strong negative effect (Evans and Eichelman, 1974). Therefore, personal-space invasion seems to involve more than a simple overload of sensory stimulation.

INTIMACY/PRIVACY REGULATION A third explanation of personal space emphasizes interpersonal distance as a means of regulating desired levels of intimacy and privacy. In one version of this approach, Michael Argyle and Janet Dean (1965) argue that in any social interaction, individuals desire a certain level of intimacy. Intimacy is determined by several factors, including eye contact, the topic of discussion, smiling, and physical proximity. Argyle and Dean suggest that when one of these factors deviates from the desired level of intimacy, individuals compensate by changing one of the other factors. An example that is well supported by research is that when physical closeness exceeds a desired level, people compensate by reducing eye contact or turning slightly away so as not to face the other directly (see Patterson,

Mullins, and Romano, 1971; Patterson, 1973). Thus, in Argyle and Dean's view personal space is one behavior among several that helps to maintain a desirable level of intimacy.

In a related approach Irwin Altman (1975) has described personal space as a privacy regulation mechanism. People increase the distance between themselves and another person when they are concerned about maintaining the boundary between self and nonself.

Finally, Evans and Eichelman have reminded us that in any social situation, people hold certain expectations about their encounters with others. These expectations depend on the specific environment as well as the individual. For example, Daniel Stokols (1976) has suggested that spatial invasions are more disruptive when they occur in *primary* environments—those in which we live and work and over which we expect to have control—than when they occur in *secondary* environments—those public spaces that we inhabit only briefly and seldom expect to control. Consequently, we are less concerned about personal-space violations at a crowded soccer match than in our private rooms.

Expectations also vary across different individuals. According to Marshal Duke and Stephen Nowicki (1972), individuals who feel generally in control of their environments are able to maintain less personal space between themselves and others because they are less threatened by others. In contrast, individuals who generally expect to be unable to control their environments maintain greater space between self and others because they feel more vulnerable to others, especially strangers.

This explanation of personal space as a means of regulating intimacy and privacy appears most adequate given all the evidence. As we have argued elsewhere in this book, human behavior is almost always a complex response to individual expectations and situational requirements. Personal space is no exception. While it would be tempting to conclude that personal space is a protective response to stress or a direct reaction to stimulation overload, the available evidence does not support such neat conclusions. Personal space is one technique among many that helps people achieve control over their environments. The answer to the question of how much space people need is: it depends. It depends on where one is, how much control one expects to have, and what other forms of control are available.

TERRITORIALITY

Do humans express their need for personal space by staking out and defending physical territories? If you're like most people, you probably do, and your territorial behavior extends throughout the day. When you get up in the morning, chances are you rise from your familiar side of the bed, no matter who is sleeping across the mattress. If you shower at a group facility—in a dormitory, for example—you probably have your preferred shower head or shower stall. At the dining table or cafeteria, you probably take your regular seat or usual table. If you drive to work or school and find another car in "your" parking space, you may feel slightly annoyed. When you go to class, you probably sit in the same section of the room or even the same exact row and seat. At the library you no doubt have your own favorite study table or special carrel. In the gym locker room, even when the lockers are unassigned, you probably think of a certain locker as yours. Around the places you inhabit most—your work space, office, room, or apartment—you're likely to have numerous indicators that this space is yours. Photographs, posters, and plants announce that this territory belongs to you, and signs may even make the message clearer as well as warn off intruders. When your territory is disrupted by your moving out or another person moving in, you're likely to feel considerable strain until your own space is reestablished.

Why do we do this? Why do we identify, mark off, and sometimes defend territories that are ours? What are the implications of this territorial behavior for our lives as social beings? Can we ever successfully adapt to sharing our territories as required by dense urban living? These are the questions that social-environmental psychologists have only begun to explore.

HUMAN AND ANIMAL TERRITORIALITY

Robert Sommer was one of the first psychologists to study human territoriality. In his early work (1959), Sommer noted several distinctions between personal space and territoriality: (1) personal space is carried around while territory is relatively stationary; (2) territorial boundaries are usually visible to others while personal-space boundaries are invisible; (3) personal space has the body as its center while territory does not; (4) animals, and sometimes humans, will fight to maintain dominion over their territory, but will generally withdraw if others intrude into their personal space.

Fierce territorial behavior is easily observed in animals. Even the usually docile family dog becomes a growling beast when another animal approaches its territories. Territorial markings are clearly established when the animal leaves its scent around the perimeter of its territory by depositing urine and feces, a warning to other animals not to enter. And in one anecdote, even a woodsman in the wilds kept the timber wolves at some distance from his tent by urinating on all the trees surrounding his campsight.

Human territoriality is often traced back to animal territorial behavior. As discussed in Chapter 8, some theorists such as Robert Ardrey (1966) and Konrad Lorenz (1969) see human territoriality as instinctual remnants of our animal roots. In their view, these remnants may doom us as a species, confronted as we are with ever-increasing numbers and ever-diminishing space over which to exercise our instinctual territorial claims. The inevitable aggression, coupled with our technological expertise and destructive capacity, could release territorial conflicts of cataclysmic proportions.

Despite the provocative parallels between animals and humans in their territorial behavior, Eric Sundstrom and Irwin Altman (1974) have pointed out serious flaws in the view that human territoriality is an instinctive, animallike response. For animals, territoriality serves specific biological needs. Animals must control a certain territory in order to protect their food sources, their shelter, and, depending on the species, their mating and nesting grounds. Animals generally use one territory at a time for a continuous period of time, while humans utilize a number of territories, from home to office to beach, for example. Humans will release their temporary spaces to others when they are through with them, whereas animals seldom release their spaces. Humans generally do not fight to defend their day-to-day territories, whereas animals generally do. Most important, human use of space varies widely, depending on individual learning and cultural norms, whereas animals relate to space in a stereotypic, genetically determined way.

HUMAN TERRITORIALITY DEFINED

Human territoriality has been defined in a variety of ways (compare Edney, 1974; Altman, 1975), and all the definitions have certain features in common. Sommer (1969) defined territoriality as "geographical areas that are personalized or marked in some way and that are defended from encroachment." Other theorists disagree on whether the territories must be actively defended. In many of the examples that opened this section—for instance, seeking one's usual parking spot or place at the table—territorial defense is not a necessary component. Thus, other theorists avoid the concept of defense, preferring instead to associate territoriality with control of space. For example, Harold Proshansky, William Ittelson, and Leanne Rivlin (1970) see territoriality as "achieving and exerting control over a particular segment of space." Perceived control over space is probably the most important function of territoriality, and in order to maintain their perception of control, humans sometimes defend their space, though not always. Irwin Altman (1975) has provided a useful definition of territoriality that combines the idea of control over spatial boundaries with the possibility of territorial defense: "Territorial behavior is a self/other boundary-regulation mechanism that involves personalization of or marking of a place or object and communication that it is 'owned' by a person or group. Personalization and ownership are designed to regulate social interaction and to help satisfy various social and physical motives. Defense responses may sometimes occur when territorial boundaries are violated."

Territoriality also provides another type of perceived control over space. Several theorists have suggested that territoriality allows for organization and predictability in our daily lives (Edney, 1974; Evans and Eichelman, 1976). As a result, our attention is freed to focus on other matters, and our behavior can be more efficient and more rewarding than if we had to monitor an unfamiliar environment constantly. Overall, then, when we determine the boundaries around ourselves, we control who has access to our persons. And when we are familiar with the surrounding space, we can predict and thus be better prepared to control what takes place there.

RESEARCH ON HUMAN TERRITORIALITY

What does the research reveal? First we should note that special problems constrain researchers

SOCIAL PSYCHOLOGY AND THE ARTS

TERRITORIALITY IN NEW ENGLAND

Robert Frost's classic poem "Mending Wall" uses a ritual of New England farm life to ask a basic question about human territoriality. To Frost, mending walls is "just another kind of outdoor game"; but to his flinty companion, " 'Good fences make good neighbors.' " " 'Why do they make good neighbors?' " asks the poet. But the neighbor does not answer. Instead, he carries stones "like an old-stone savage armed" and "moves in darkness." In a less poetic way, social psychologists search for answers to Frost's question and seek to remove some of the darkness from the issue of human territoriality.

Something there is that doesn't love a wall,
That sends the frozen-ground-swell under it,
And spills the upper boulders in the sun;
And makes gaps even two can pass abreast.
The work of hunters is another thing:
I have come after them and made repair
Where they have left not one stone on a stone,
But they would have the rabbit out of hiding,
To please the yelping dogs. The gaps I mean,
No one has seen them made or heard them made,
But at spring mending-time we find them there.
I let my neighbor know beyond the hill;
And on a day we meet to walk the line
And set the wall between us once again.
We keep the wall between us as we go.
To each the boulders that have fallen to each.
And some are loaves and some so nearly balls
We have to use a spell to make them balance:
'Stay where you are until our backs are turned!'
We wear our fingers rough with handling them.
Oh, just another kind of out-door game,
One on a side. It comes to little more:
There where it is we do not need the wall:
He is all pine and I am apple orchard.
My apple trees will never get across
And eat the cones under his pines, I tell him.
He only says, 'Good fences make good neighbors.'
Spring is the mischief in me, and I wonder
If I could put a notion in his head:
'Why do they make good neighbors? Isn't it
Where there are cows? But here there are no cows.
Before I built a wall I'd ask to know
What I was walling in or walling out,
And to whom I was like to give offense.
Something there is that doesn't love a wall,
That wants it down.' I could say 'Elves' to him,
But it's not elves exactly, and I'd rather
He said it for himself. I see him there
Bringing a stone grasped firmly by the top
In each hand, like an old-stone savage armed.
He moves in darkness as it seems to me,
Not of woods only and the shade of trees.
He will not go behind his father's saying,
And he likes having thought of it so well
He says again, 'Good fences make good neighbors.'

Source: Robert Frost, "Mending Wall," *Complete Works of Robert Frost* (New York: Holt, Rinehart and Winston, 1947): 940–941.

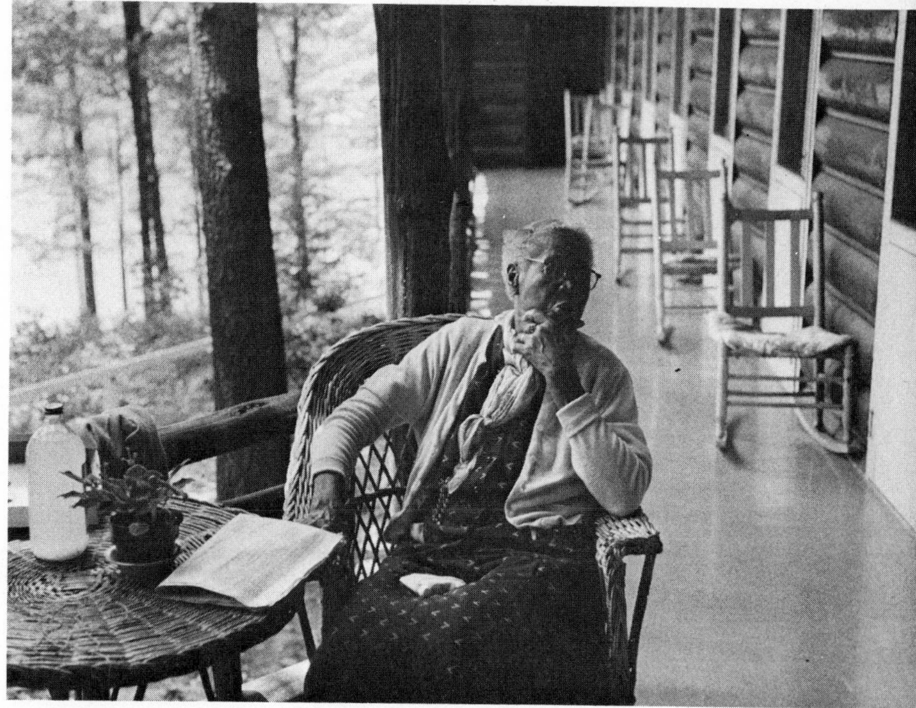

Secondary territories—for example, this porch—are semipublic spaces where we can converse with neighbors and acquaintances. *(© Bruce Davidson / Magnum)*

interested in human territoriality. Unlike personal space, which can be studied fairly easily in the lab or field using approach and invasion techniques, convincing feelings of territoriality are difficult to establish and observe under laboratory conditions. Because territoriality typically involves a long period of association between person and place, researchers have usually investigated real-world phenomena or sometimes employed simulation techniques.

Irwin Altman has distinguished three types of territories over which people exert control, and his distinctions help organize the research.

Primary territories are spaces like homes, apartments, or bedrooms, owned or used exclusively by an individual or group on a relatively permanent basis, clearly marked as theirs, and central to the day-to-day functioning of the occupants.

Secondary territories are semipublic spaces like your porch or yard, the hallway in front of your door, or the lounge on your dorm floor—spaces that are used for interaction with neighbors and acquaintances on a fairly regular basis.

Public territories are places like beaches, parks, or shopping malls, where everyone has free access and property rights.

A recent study supported Altman's distinctions by presenting people with descriptions of places that fell in each of these three types of territories (Taylor and Stough, 1978). Subjects were asked to rate how much time they would spend and how much control they would feel in each of the places. People indicated that they would spend most time and feel most control in primary spaces, less in secondary, and least in public spaces. Thus, territoriality is associated with how much control people feel over the spaces they inhabit. The research reported below explores how people behave in these three types of territories.

RESEARCH IN PRIMARY TERRITORIES Several field studies have established that people do in fact feel in control when they are on their own, clearly marked primary territories. Julian Edney (1972) rang doorbells of houses that were either clearly marked with territorial signs such as "No

Trespassing" or similar homes that had no markers. Compared to residents of unmarked homes, residents of marked homes answered their doorbells much more quickly, apparently asserting more control. Similarly, Arthur Patterson (1978) found that elderly homeowners who displayed territorial markers—such as signs, personalized doormats, or initials—expressed less fear of crime than residents of unmarked homes, again suggesting a connection between territoriality and control. When the focus switches from homeowners to college students, Edney (1975) found that dormitory residents felt they were more able to resist another person's control in their own dormitory rooms than similar students who were merely visitors in the same room.

When people must share primary territories, the arrangement is often more successful if each individual can personally control some portion of the territory. Anyone who has lived with another person in a confined space for a period of time knows that conflicts inevitably arise. However, Altman and his colleagues found that when pairs of male U.S. Navy volunteers were confined together for eight to ten days, the most compatible pairs were those whose members initially established clear territorial control over individual beds, chairs, and other parts of the room (Altman and Haythorn, 1967; Altman, Taylor, and Wheeler, 1971). Furthermore, the pairs that were territorial were also successful in performing various tasks, resisting stress, and organizing their daily activities.

Because these studies do not involve manipulation of variables, they do not establish that territoriality *causes* people to feel in control, not to fear crime, to interact compatibly with others, or to perform tasks successfully. Nevertheless these studies do establish that territoriality and feelings of control are connected.

RESEARCH IN SECONDARY TERRITORIES The only research on territoriality in secondary spaces is a simulation study by Ralph Taylor and Roger Stough (1978). As described above, this study compared people's responses to descriptions of various places, representing primary, secondary, and public spaces. While all of the subjects felt less control in the secondary than in the primary territories, an interesting difference emerged between urban and suburban dwellers. Suburban dwellers felt more control over secondary territories such as their porch, stoop, or sidewalk in front of their residence than did urban dwellers. Taylor and Stough hypothesized that suburban residents felt more control over their secondary territories because of the greater homogeneity of the suburbs. Thus, they were less likely to encounter strangers or unpredictable others in their secondary territories than were urban dwellers.

RESEARCH IN PUBLIC TERRITORIES Some of the early research on territoriality explored how people use, mark, and defend public territories. Robert Sommer and Frank Becker (1969) wondered how college students expressed their territoriality when they wanted to study undisturbed in the college library. In a simulation study, a number of students were shown the diagram below, representing library tables and chairs. "Where would you sit," students were asked, "if you wanted to discourage anyone else from using the table?" As shown in Figure 12.2, students who wanted to defend their table from encroachment chose the middle chairs. If students were then told that the table was situated in a large study room, those preferring isolation chose to sit near the end of the room, near a wall, facing away from the room's entrance; those intending to defend their territories chose to sit facing the entrance near an aisle.

Sommer and Becker then began to wonder how students used markers to delineate "their" territories at snack bars or library tables. In a field experiment the researchers left various types of personal possessions in front of an unoccupied chair at a university snack bar when the room was either crowded or fairly empty. Possessions ranged from personal items like jackets or sweaters to less personal items such as books and newspapers. The researchers found that under low density, all items prevented others from occupying the chair, while only the most personal items defended the chair under high density. Then, finally, Becker and Clara Mayo (1971) extended this work further in an attempt to see how people actually responded when their territorial markers were ignored and

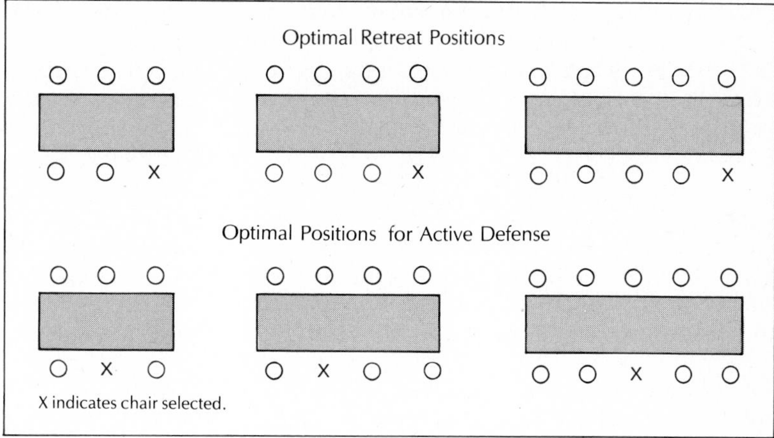

FIGURE 12.2 In their research in public territories, Sommer and Becker (1969) found that students who wanted to isolate themselves in the college library chose end chairs. Those who wanted to keep their table to themselves chose middle chairs.

their spaces were invaded. The researchers went to a university cafeteria and looked for tables where people had left their clothes or books to hold a seat. A confederate invaded these spaces by sitting (1) in the exact marked seat, (2) adjacent to the marked seat, or (3) across from the marked seat. The researchers found that almost all of the people who were invaded either directly or in the adjacent seat moved away, while almost all of those invaded across the table remained and ignored the invader. These results show that people do not "defend"—in the true sense—their public territories even when these territories are marked. If equivalent territories are available, they simply move away. Perhaps markers in public territories are utilized more to maintain personal space than to stake out territories, at least when occupancy is intended to be only short-term.

Another study of public territories dealt with how groups on the beach perceive and mark their group spaces. Edney and Jordon-Edney (1974) measured the radii of territories claimed by groups of beach users. They found that groups perceived a large surrounding circular space as "their" territory, that male groups claimed larger territories than female groups, and that the longer people were on the beach, the larger the territory became for same-sex groups and the more markers were deployed by mixed-sex groups. While these findings are complex, they demonstrate that even in public territories, the longer people occupy a space, the more control they assert by increasing the size of their territories or the number of markers.

A second tradition of research on public territories is concerned not with free public space like libraries, cafeterias, and beaches, but with the limited public space available to residents of institutions such as psychiatric hospitals or juvenile homes. When space is limited, people cannot shift their territories in response to invasion, but must rely on more active forms of defense. In this situation, *dominance hierarchies* frequently emerge as a means of regulating occupancy of "public" places.

One of the first researchers to notice this phenomenon was Aristide Esser. Esser and his colleagues observed inmates' use of space in a mental ward and concluded surprisingly that the *least* dominant patients exhibited the most territorial behavior—for example, by claiming certain chairs or corners as their own. In contrast, the most dominant patients moved so freely through the ward that they defended no particular space as their own (Esser, Chamberlain, Chapple, and Kline, 1965; Esser, 1968). However, the relationship between dominance and territoriality is complex and variable. Other studies of people in institutional settings have found that dominant people are more territorial than nondominant people (Esser, 1973; Sundstrom and Altman, 1974; DeLong, 1973). Perhaps the relationship between dominance and territoriality depends on the desirability of the setting: when certain territories are more desirable than others, dominant persons may be expected to stake them out for their own personal use; but when no territory is more desirable than any other, perhaps dominant persons roam freely throughout the entire space.

TERRITORIALITY AND ARCHITECTURAL DESIGN

How can research on territoriality contribute to architectural design? Consider the example of the Pruitt-Igoe housing project. Built in St. Louis in the early 1950s, Pruitt-Igoe consisted of forty-three eleven-story buildings situated in a common territory and separated by open courtyards. Each building included wide hallways that the architects envisaged as public "galleries," spaces where children could play and residents could congregate while using the laundry rooms. But, instead of the pleasant community life that planners anticipated in the outdoor courtyards and inner galleries, these areas became a wasteland. The public spaces were littered with broken glass and smeared with graffiti. Hallways, stairways, and elevators reeked of urine and garbage. The wide galleries and open courtyards became the province of gangs and criminals. Almost all of the public facilities were vandalized or broken and left in disrepair. Residents lived in fear. Occupancy rates dropped, leaving many apartments vacant, boarded up, and inviting further abuse. The project was eventually abandoned by the city, and the buildings were dynamited. The lesson of Pruitt-Igoe remains as one of the most conspicuous failures in the history of public housing.

Why did Pruitt-Igoe fail? One answer has been suggested by Oscar Newman in his book, *Defensible Space* (1973). As an architect and urban planner, Newman was interested in the connection between architecture and behavior. To explain what happened at Pruitt-Igoe, he took a clue from one of the forty-three buildings that curiously escaped the deterioration of the others. While new play equipment and

A building in the Pruitt-Igoe project, one of the worst failures in the history of public housing. Due to litter, crime, and vandalism, the vacancy rate reached 70 percent, and the complex was eventually demolished. *(© George W. Gardner)*

seats were being installed in the adjacent courtyard, this particular building was fenced off from the others to prevent pilferage of construction materials. The only break in the fence was a gate opposite the main entrance to the building. During the six-month construction period, crime and vandalism in this building decreased significantly, and the residents asked that the fence be left in place when the construction was completed. Two years later, the fence was still there and, according to Newman, the crime and vandalism rate in this building was 80 percent below the Pruitt-Igoe norm. Furthermore, residents of this building were the only ones who began to show some concern about the maintenance of the interior, picking up litter, sweeping the corridors, and replacing light bulbs. The vacancy rate in this building varied from 2 to 5 percent, in contrast to the overall vacancy rate for Pruitt-Igoe of 70 percent.

Why was this building so unlike the others? Newman draws on the concept of territoriality for an explanation. Residents of the fenced-off building, he suggests, identified the space as "theirs," probably because they felt more control over their territory. The fence with a single gate served both as a territorial marker and as a means of defending the public space around the building. Residents may have then felt safe enough to venture outside and utilize the courtyard and galleries. When the residents became more visible and people got to know each other, the building's public territory probably came to function more like a secondary or semipublic territory. Individual residents could extend their lives beyond their apartments and into the galleries as the architects intended. With an increasing number of people identifying with and using the semipublic spaces, these people took an interest in maintaining these spaces, and the public surveillance helped decrease crime.Thus, Oscar Newman's technique for crime control in public housing involves applying the principles of territoriality through urban design. When housing projects and apartment blocks are built on a human scale, encouraging familiarity among the residents and use of the public territories, then residents' sense of territoriality and control should increase and crime should decrease.

CROWDING

We have seen that people employ personal space and territoriality to control the environment that surrounds their body, and we have learned that personal space and territoriality can affect social behavior in a variety of ways. With this background, we will now consider the effects of crowding on human behavior. Initially, it might seem that crowding should have uniformly negative effects on human beings. After all, crowding causes other people to intrude into our personal space—for example, on tightly packed elevators, on buses or subways, in classrooms or cafeterias. Crowding also threatens our needs for territoriality—for instance, in inner-city ghettos, in people-packed campgrounds and beaches, in overly dense apartment houses and dormitories, or in any space where others come too close. We can each supply our own examples of the frustrations and tensions that appear to be caused by crowding. Almost daily we read that crowding is blamed for a wide variety of social evils. Steven Zlutnick and Irwin Altman (1972) conducted a ten-year review of the *Reader's Guide to Periodical Literature* and found popular articles attributing at least seventeen dire social problems to the effects of overcrowding. These problems ranged from mass starvation, pollution, and disease through riots, crime, and war to mental illness, drug addiction, and the breakdown of the family.

The only problem with the proposition that crowding is the cause of so many human ills is that there is very little research that *directly* supports this conclusion. Unquestionably, crowding has negative effects on *some* people *some* of the time, especially when people are helpless and unable to escape crowding. Yet crowding itself is not necessarily bad and may often be a positive experience for people. Consider the fact that parties are more enjoyable, sports events more exciting, and comedies funnier when there are many people present than when there are few people present.

To understand when and how crowding affects human beings involves following a trail of research with several surprising findings and some interesting controversies. The trail begins in the 1960s, when the only research on crowding dealt with animals, mainly rats. By the early 1970s overpopulation and urban dilemmas had become serious enough threats that field and lab researchers began studying the effects of crowding on human behavior. Currently, the trail has led to investigations of the many factors that help people cope with crowding when they are subjected to high-density conditions. These studies are often conducted in shopping centers, department stores, dormitories, or housing complexes as well as in the laboratory. In ten years, human crowding has become a prominent concern of many social psychologists.

EFFECTS OF CROWDING ON ANIMALS

The best-known study of crowding in animals was conducted by John B. Calhoun in 1962. Although this study deals with rats, Calhoun's findings are relevant because they strongly influenced later research on humans. In his Rockville, Maryland, barn, Calhoun divided a ten-by-fourteen-foot room into four pens, each furnished with enough nesting places and nesting materials to comfortably satisfy about twelve wild rats. A colony of wild rats was introduced into the room and allowed to breed until its population size reached eighty, or about twice the number of animals that could be comfortably accommodated in the pens. Adequate food and water were supplied for all the animals.

As the population increased, two pens were staked out and defended by dominant males for their harems of eight to ten females, while the rest of the sixty-odd rats were forced to congregate in the two remaining pens. Calhoun labeled these pens "behavioral sinks" because their crowded conditions produced an astonishing array of antisocial behaviors. Some male rats in the "sinks" became hyperaggressive sex offenders, attempting to mount everything from nesting females to adolescent males. Other male rats became socially withdrawn and passive, while female rats became delinquent mothers, ignoring their young and the care of their nests. Thus, merely by crowding rats together in pens, it appeared that Calhoun had dramatically produced many of the same conditions that characterize urban slums. And other researchers obtained similar results (Marsden, 1972).

Why should crowding affect animals so adversely? One explanation has been adapted by John Christian (see Christian, 1950; Christian, Flyger, and Davis, 1960) from Hans Selye's theory of stress (1956). According to this view, the stress of crowding sets off an automatic physiological process in the organism's body. When an invader crowds one's space, the stress sets off a biochemical *alarm* that results in a discharge of adrenaline, a faster heartbeat, and a generally aroused state. This condition energizes the organism to respond to the stressor. If the stress continues, a second automatic *resistance* process comes into play, as the body tries to repair any damages by diverting certain hormones to produce antibodies and releasing other chemicals from the liver to help resist the stressor. It is in this second stage that hormones normally regulating sexual and maternal instincts are diverted to resist the stressor, thus disrupting sexual and maternal instincts. Finally, if these two processes of alarm and resistance continue unsuccessfully, the organism enters a state of *exhaustion* during which most of the body's functions slow down or stop altogether.

It is the third stage of exhaustion that Christian believed was responsible for a mass die-off of deer on a small island near the coast of Maryland in Chesapeake Bay. Over a period of years the deer population increased until the small island was densely packed with the animals. But suddenly, in one season, half their number strangely died, despite an adequate food supply and no natural predators. Christian performed autopsies on several of the dead deer and found enlarged adrenal glands, indicative of the automatic biochemical processes of alarm and resistance. Christian suggested that the continual stress of crowding allowed no relaxation of these processes until exhaustion finally led to death for many of the weaker animals.

SOCIOLOGICAL RESEARCH ON HUMAN CROWDING

Does crowding lead to the same behavioral and physiological effects in humans as it does in animals? One group of investigators tried to answer this question by looking for human parallels to Calhoun's rat experiments. Instead of crowding people into pens, Omer Galle, Walter Gove, and J. Miller McPherson (1972) selected an area of Chicago that was very densely populated. Then they gathered data paralleling the kinds of observations that Calhoun made on his rats. For instance, they collected information on community death rates, fertility rates (the number of births in the community per 1,000 women ages fifteen to forty-four), the effectiveness of parental care of young (the number of recipients of public assistance under eighteen years of age), the incidence of aggressive behavior (the number of juvenile males brought before Family Court per 1,000 males in the population), and the incidence of social withdrawal and other psychotic behavior (rates of admissions to mental hospitals). When they statistically controlled for ethnic background and social class—factors frequently associated with high-density slum living—they found no relationship between community density per se and social problems. Only when the researchers changed their focus from general community density to the number of persons per room were they able to find a small relationship between density and social problems. However, even this relationship has been criticized because of the complex statistical techniques involved. When Jonathan Freedman, Stanley Heshka, and Allan Levy (1975) performed a similar study in New York City but used more rigorous statistical procedures, they found no significant relationship at all between any measure of crowding and any type of social pathology.

In general, sociological studies of human crowding in the real world have found little or no negative effects when other confounding factors are controlled for. Only on very specific subgroups within the general population, such as the elderly or children, has crowding produced any undesirable consequences. Yet, as discussed in Chapter 13, these effects seem to be caused not by crowding itself, but by the lack of control that these relatively powerless groups exercise over their crowding.

LABORATORY RESEARCH ON HUMAN CROWDING

Many researchers were surprised that the effects of crowding on humans were so insignificant in comparison with the effects of crowding on animals. Of course, animals respond to the environment largely through instinctive biological programming, while human behavior is filtered through culture and custom. Nevertheless, there was still a widespread feeling that crowding *should* have negative effects on humans. Many investigators turned their attention to the laboratory, where they could create intense short-term crowding, hold other factors constant, and observe the results, uncontaminated by real-world problems such as income, ethnic background, social class, or education. In the laboratory, it was hoped, the true effects of crowding might emerge.

Another surprise awaited researchers. In the first important laboratory study of human crowding, Jonathan Freedman, Simon Klevansky, and Paul Ehrlich (1971) asked California high-school students to sit for three hours in a group of nine people in a room about the size of a large closet—30 square feet. For three days in a row the participants sat in these crowded conditions working on a variety of tasks, ranging from simple performance measures, such as crossing out sevens on a page of random numbers, to measures of creativity, such as thinking up as many uses as they could for common objects like a brick. Hundreds of subjects were run, some in the tiny room and others in large rooms. After months of experimenting, the researchers found that room size made no difference on any of their task measures. Doubting their findings, they replicated the study with middle-aged women hired through a temporary employment service. But they again obtained the same results. The researchers finally concluded that crowding was apparently not a stressful phenomenon for humans, since it produced no negative effects that the researchers could measure.

A major controversy ensued. Many researchers felt that Freedman and his colleagues had stated their conclusions too soon and that they had overlooked other negative effects of crowding that didn't happen to show up on the measures Freedman and associates used in their study. In fact, in the years after Freedman published his findings, a number of researchers have conducted experiments revealing a wide variety of crowding effects on human behavior. The most important of these are summarized below.

COMPLEX-TASK PERFORMANCE How well people perform on complex, demanding tasks is a good measure of how much stress they feel, since it is well established that stress disrupts complex-task performance. If crowding is stressful for people, then it should interfere with their performance on difficult, demanding tasks. This is exactly what several researchers found when they asked crowded people to work on difficult tasks. For example, Gary Evans (1979) crowded groups of ten people in a small room so that they had about 3 square feet per person. He then asked them to listen to random numbers announced every second and to classify each number as odd or even and high or low (above 32 or under 32). Subjects also had to categorize complex shapes on several dimensions while listening to a story on which they would later be quizzed. Evans found that crowded people performed more poorly on these tasks than people who were in larger less crowded rooms. Similar findings were also obtained by Paul Paulus and his colleagues when they asked subjects to learn a complicated electronic maze in either crowded or noncrowded conditions (Paulus, Annis, Seta, Schkade, and Matthews, 1976).

DELAYED EFFECTS ON TASK PERFORMANCE Another way to measure the effects of a stressor such as crowding is to look for delayed consequences. It may be that people can learn to adapt and perform their jobs well under stress, but that the cost of adapting will show up on subsequent performance. From this perspective, we might expect crowded people to perform all right while they are crowded but to do less well after they have left the crowded situation. Again, this is exactly what several researchers found. Drury Sherrod (1974) asked groups of eight students to sit in a little room so cramped that their shoulders and knees were touching and to work on tasks similar to Freedman's for two hours. Then the students were taken to a much larger room and given a frustration tolerance test. The people from the crowded room became frustrated much more quickly than students who had worked initially in a large uncrowded room. Similar results were obtained by Evans (1979), using exactly the same measure, and by Dooley (1978), using a different manipulation and measure.

PHYSIOLOGICAL EFFECTS OF CROWDING Perhaps the most important indicator of stress is whether or not people become physiologically aroused when they are exposed to the stressor. At least two studies have shown that crowding can produce an increase in physiological arousal. John Aiello, Yakov Epstein, and Robert Karlin (1975) found that crowded people experience greater skin conductance (a measure of arousal) than people in a noncrowded situation. Similarly, Evans (1979) found that crowded people experience higher blood pressure and increased heart rate when compared to noncrowded people.

ANXIETY, DISCOMFORT, AND SOCIAL BEHAVIOR If crowding is stressful and unpleasant, we should expect crowded people to complain about their situation and to be less sociable than uncrowded people to others who are present. Several experiments have found these kinds of results. For example, crowded laboratory subjects, as opposed to uncrowded laboratory subjects, have rated the other people in their group as less attractive (Griffitt and Veitch, 1971) and more hostile (Evans, 1979), have had a harder time remembering the names of group members, and have thought the experiment lasted longer (Worchel and Teddlie, 1976). Also, members of crowded groups have been found to engage in more nervous laughter (Stokols, Rall, Pinner, and Schopler, 1973) and fidgeting (Evans, 1979) than members of noncrowded groups.

CROWDING AND AGGRESSION Crowding has also produced some curious and inconsistent effects on aggression. Jonathan Freedman and his colleagues have found that when men are crowded, they become more aggressive than uncrowded men, while crowded women become less aggressive than uncrowded women (Freedman, Levy, Buchanan, and Price, 1972). Crowded males also behave more competitively than uncrowded males, while crowded females become less competitive than uncrowded females (Epstein and Karlin, 1975). And men have displayed more hostility in crowded rooms than in uncrowded rooms whereas women have been more hostile in uncrowded rooms than in crowded rooms (Stokols, Rall, Pinner, and Schopler, 1973). However, this general effect of crowding on men and women appears not to take place in mixed-sex groups (Freedman, Levy, Buchanan, and Price, 1972).

The explanation of these sex-linked effects of crowding on aggression probably has to do with the different personal-space needs that men and women learn in our culture. Thus, males, who expect greater personal space when dealing with another male, feel stressed by close spatial invasions and respond aggressively. In contrast, women, who expect less personal space when dealing with another female, may feel stressed by the inappropriately large distances in noncrowded rooms and express their stress through greater aggression.

ESCAPE AND WITHDRAWAL One final indicator of the stressfulness of a phenomenon is whether people try to escape or withdraw when they are exposed to the stressful event. There is evidence that people prefer to avoid crowding if possible. And when crowding can't be avoided, people often withdraw into themselves in order to escape psychologically. Such coping mechanisms may come into play when people merely anticipate crowding, even before they actually experience it. In one study, Andy Baum and Carl Greenberg (1975) asked students participating in a crowding experiment to wait in a room until the rest of the participants arrived. When subjects expected ten people to be involved, the first arrivee sat closer to the corner of the room and avoided looking at the second arrivee more than when subjects expected only four people to be coming. Other studies have found that psychiatric patients (Ittelson, Proshansky, and Rivlin, 1970), children in a playground (Loo, 1973), and college-dormitory residents (Baum and Valins, 1977) also tend to withdraw and engage in little social interaction when they are crowded.

Anthropologists Ruth and Lee Munroe (1972) have discovered that withdrawal mechanisms are even expressed as cultural norms in certain high-density societies in East Africa. For example, the Logali, who live in an average density of 1,400 people per square mile, have strict norms prohibiting hand holding with friends, have difficulty recalling words relating to interpersonal affiliation, and tend to describe family members in negative terms, when compared to the Kipsigis and the Gusii, who live in much lower-density conditions.

THEORETICAL EXPLANATIONS OF CROWDING

Much research can be cited to demonstrate that crowding can produce negative effects on a wide range of human behaviors. Why, then, have so few effects been found for naturally occurring crowding in cities, and why have other laboratory studies suggested that crowding has no harmful effects on people? What accounts for these inconsistencies?

Part of the problem lies in the way one defines *crowding.* While one perspective views crowding as simple density—the number of square feet per person (see Freedman, 1975)—the majority of social psychologists see crowding as a *subjective* experience that can be distinguished from *objective* measures of simple density. In an influential statement, Daniel Stokols (1972) has defined the experience of crowding as a "motivational state directed toward the alleviation of perceived restriction and infringement" caused by spatial limitations. Part of the inconsistency in the research literature is due to confusing *crowding* with *density.* As Stokols asserts, people in high density may not necessarily *feel* crowded. It depends on the circumstances. According to this view, it is not density that is stressful to people, but only the subjective perception of crowding. Consequently, some situations that are characterized by very high levels of density might not actually feel "crowded." Such situations might include heavily attended football games or concerts, parties with many guests, or a number of good friends talking in a very small room.

What factors help determine this subjective perception of crowding? Different theorists emphasize different circumstances (compare Altman, 1975; Stokols, 1976), but the following factors are important.

Crowding is a subjective perception, and it is not always unpleasant. In fact, there are several high-density situations that we are likely to enjoy. *(© David Hurn / Magnum)*

BEHAVIORAL CONSTRAINTS Many writers have emphasized the behavioral constraints imposed by high-density conditions. For example, people in dense cities, homes, and streets may be unable to get what they want when they want it because so many others are in the way. In the words of Harold Proshansky, William Ittleson, and Leanne Rivlin (1970), density "restricts one's freedom of choice," and the resulting frustration and helplessness are stressful. Thus, many of the negative consequences of high density should only appear when people feel restricted due to the close presence of others. When density is not restrictive, people are not likely to feel crowded.

STIMULATION OVERLOAD Other theorists have been concerned with the stimulation overload that may be caused by high density. In this view, somewhat like the overload explanation of personal-space invasions, density presents too many inputs for people to process efficiently. So much stimulation from so many people overloads our mental capacity. Consequently, the individual suffers fatigue or a temporary depletion of attentional capacity that disrupts task performance and social behavior. Both Sheldon Cohen (1978) and Susan Saegert (1973) have argued that high density affects information processing in this way, and Cohen has pointed out that we may feel especially overloaded when we are surrounded by strangers. Because friends and relatives are generally predictable, we can afford to relax in their presence, even under high-density conditions. However, the unpredictability of strangers requires us to be alert and vigilant in their presence, prepared for a possible response. All this vigilance and alertness around strangers requires extra attentional capacity, and when high density increases our vulnerability, we must be extra vigilant still. The consequences of this extra alertness are increased stress and fatigue and an increased sense of crowding.

SITUATIONAL REQUIREMENTS Still other theorists emphasize functional requirements of the situation that influence whether people feel crowded. Ecological psychologists argue that most situations or physical settings contain an inherent "program" regarding what activities are suitable and how many people are required to carry them out. Thus, when the number of people present in a setting exceeds the number required for a particular job or the number appropriate for that setting, people feel crowded. For example, Allan Wicker and Sandy Kirmeyer (1977) have found that people are dissatisfied when there are more persons than there are jobs to be performed in a crowded work-type setting.

Daniel Stokols (1976) has also shown how the implicit program of a setting contributes to an individual's sense of crowding. As we mentioned before, Stokols distinguishes between primary and secondary environments: primary environments are those settings in which we live, work, and engage in personally important activities; secondary environments are places where our encounters with others are relatively transitory, anonymous, and inconsequential. Accordingly, the presence of too many others may affect us more strongly and make us feel more crowded in primary environments than in secondary environments.

"DENSITY/INTENSITY THEORY" One final view departs radically from the above three perspectives on density as restraining, overloading, and dysfunctional. Jonathan Freedman (1975) has suggested that high density produces no negative consequences itself but merely serves to intensify whatever effects are already present in a situation. Calling this view the "density/intensity theory," Freedman and his colleagues have shown, for example, that if people are led to feel elated or depressed, high density can intensify both of these mood states. Freedman fails to distinguish the subjective perception of crowding from the objective circumstances of density. For these researchers high density, or crowding, is not good or bad; it merely intensifies a person's typical responses to a situation.

It is likely that crowding is a complex phenomenon with all of the above effects. Therefore, it is probably most accurate to see these four theories of crowding as complementary rather than contradictory. The research evidence is certainly broad enough to justify each of these theoretical positions.

CROWDING AND CONTROL

Much of the confusion in crowding research and theory can be clarified by the concept of "control." Recall our previous conclusions that personal space and territoriality were techniques by which individuals exercised some control over the surrounding environment. A perception of control appears to be one of the most important human needs in regard to the surrounding physical environment, and certain crowded situations can threaten our perceptions of control. For example, when crowding restricts our freedom of choice, then crowding threatens our control of resources in the surrounding environment. Furthermore, when we are crowded with strangers, then the surrounding environment is not only restrictive, but also unpredictable and therefore even less controllable and more stressful.

Sheldon Cohen and Drury Sherrod (1978; see also Sherrod and Cohen, 1978) have argued that high density is a stressful experience only when it threatens our control of the environment. Rubin Baron and Judy Rodin (1978) also maintain that uncontrollable crowding is stressful, while controllable crowding may produce little or no negative effects on human behavior. One implication of this perspective is that when people perceive some control over their crowded conditions, they should be more resistant to the potential stress of crowding than when they perceive no control of their conditions. It is important to note here that people only need to *perceive* some measure of control over crowding; they do not actually have to exercise this control.

One experiment demonstrates this point clearly. Drury Sherrod (1974) asked groups of eight students to sit in a crowded room for two hours while they worked on various tasks. Some of these students were told that they could leave the room whenever they chose, although the experimenter would prefer that they didn't do so. The decision was entirely up to them. No one actually left the crowded room, although the students with a choice had "perceived control" over their crowding. On a subsequent measure of frustration tolerance, the ones who felt free to leave were much more resistant to frus-

FOCUS ON APPLICATIONS

PERCEIVED CONTROL IN McDONALDLAND

A few years ago the McDonald's Corporation moved into a brand new futuristic national headquarters building in Oak Brook, Illinois. Dubbed "Hamburger Central," the building was a "total concept environment." Rather than traditional hallways and offices with walls and doors, McDonald's headquarters featured an open-plan "landscape" style of architecture in which floor-to-ceiling walls were replaced by shoulder-height partitions, and offices became "task response modules." The place was beautiful, the employee turnover rate declined, and people started dressing more colorfully. However, everything did not work out as the planners intended.

According to the book *Big Mac: An Unauthorized Story of McDonald's* (Boaz and Chain, 1975), the open-plan office at first backfired. Kibitzers leaned over each other's task response modules, workers trespassed on the undefined space of others, people bumped into each other and wandered aimlessly, and rudeness became a problem. In terms of environmental psychology, people lacked a perception of control over their territories.

But then it became clear to the people at Hamburger Central that the total concept environment needed to be balanced by a "counterenvironment." McDonald's president, Ray Kroc, conferred with his architect and concluded that "there are times when people really need to get away from it all." The solution the two came up with was as futuristic as the building itself. On the seventh floor they built a strange conical-shaped structure with a hermetically sealed door, like the hatch of a spacecraft. A panel on the door housed three signal lights: green—PROCEED; yellow—BUZZ; red—STAY OUT. Inside, a soundless winding corridor led to an egg-shaped enclosure lined with beige suede. This was the workroom, equipped with a thick carpet of the same beige color, a beanbag chair and hassock, an adjustable desk, and a machine for monitoring brain waves—a device to help the user find "an ideal creative state of mind." Beyond the workroom was the think tank proper—a womblike room with soft pink fleshy walls and a floor made up entirely of a nine-foot diameter waterbed. The think tank is available to both male and female employees but, according to McDonald's rules, never at the same time. McDonald's executives regularly use the tank for brainstorming sessions, and a few departments even hold meetings there.

The greatest benefit of the tank, however, has been on general office morale. Kibitzing and quarreling declined after the tank was built, and people seemed to be in a pleasant frame of mind. According to the tank's designer, "Before, corporations were on a health-club kick, trying to keep their employees fit. Now corporations live in an age of individuals, and they realize the mind must be healthy, too."

It is not hard to relate McDonald's morale problem and its solution to the research discussed in the accompanying section. The open-plan office threatened employees' sense of perceived control over the environment; the think tank offered an escape. Interestingly, it was not even necessary that people actually use the tank, only that they perceive it as available should they need it. In other words, the employees' sense of psychological satisfaction was determined not by the actual physical environment that immediately surrounded them, but by the environment as they perceived it, one that was escapable and thus potentially controllable.

tration than the ones who had no choice. In other words, when people perceived some measure of control over their crowding, they were less affected by it.

Why should perceived control exert such a positive effect on people's responses to crowding? One theory, proposed by Martin Seligman (1975), asserts that when people have no sense of control over their environment, they feel "helpless" when confronted with environmental stress. Thus, they give up easily when confronted with frustration. In contrast, when people feel some sense of control over their environment, they expect to be effective in dealing with the environment, and when confronted with frustration, they don't give up quickly.

Another experiment demonstrates how residential crowding can produce what Seligman describes as "learned helplessness." As discussed in Chapter 1, Judith Rodin (1976) brought children from a high-density housing project into the laboratory at Yale University. These children had backgrounds that were similar in all important ways, and they lived in apartments that were identical, except that some were more crowded than others. Rodin found that the more crowded the children's home, the more errors the children made on a laboratory puzzle-solving task and the less independence they exercised when given a chance to choose free prizes. In other words, the more crowded the children, the more helpless they became.

In a related study, Rodin and her colleagues found that people on densely packed elevators felt less crowded and perceived the elevator as larger when they were standing in front of the control panel than when they were crowded to the other side (Rodin, Soloman, and Metcalf, 1978). In the same study, people also felt less crowded when they were put in charge of a group's interactions, even though they were exposed to the same crowding as the rest of the group.

Perceived control not only allows crowded people to feel less restricted, but it also reduces the effects of stimulation overload that is associated with crowding. Sheldon Cohen (1978) argues that perceived control allows people to relax their attention in crowded situations, since people don't have to be so alert to potential threats if the crowding is escapable or predictable. The resulting conservation of attentional capacity allows individuals to direct more of their energy into task performance rather than constant monitoring of the environment.

An experiment that relates to Cohen's point was conducted by Ellen Langer and Susan Saegert (1977). These investigators found that shoppers in a crowded grocery store performed better on a realistic shopping task if they were told in advance what to expect from the crowding, in essence making the crowding more predictable. (See also Chapter 13 for a discussion of how perceived control or lack of control affects people's reactions in real-world crowded settings, such as dormitories, prisons, and residential neighborhoods.)

To sum up, crowding is a complex phenomenon influenced by one's expectations and degree of control in high-density environments. The feeling of crowding frequently results in stress and related consequences at the physiological, psychological, and behavioral levels. To the extent that people feel some measure of control over their crowded conditions, the sense of crowding and its consequences may be alleviated.

NOISE AND URBAN STRESS

Excessive noise is becoming a dominant characteristic of urban life. From all sides city dwellers are bombarded with sound: jackhammers, honking cars, machinery, freeway traffic, business, the din of life. In this jangling crush, people must live, work, and relate to each other. What are the costs and consequences?

NOISE AND TASK PERFORMANCE

One of the most influential research programs in environmental psychology has been a series of experiments conducted by David Glass and Jerome E. Singer on noise and social stressors (1972). In their research Glass and Singer sought to simulate an urbanlike din in the laboratory by tape recording a mixture of sounds composed of (1) two people speaking Spanish,

(2) one person speaking Armenian, (3) a mimeograph machine, (4) a desk calculator, and (5) a typewriter. These superimposed sounds were played to human laboratory subjects in random bursts at extremely high volume (110 decibels—about the sound of a jet on the runway) or soft volume (56 decibels—about the sound of ambient background noise in the average room). While listening to this noise, the subjects performed a series of relatively simple tasks, such as crossing out the letter *a* in a page of words or performing math problems. The researchers found that people could adapt fairly well to even the loudest noise, so that they seldom made mistakes on these simple tasks. In fact, not until the tasks became extremely complex did the noise have any adverse effect on subjects' performance (Finkelman and Glass, 1970). However, when the noise stopped, subjects had to perform two additional tasks: a proofreading test and a puzzle-solving measure of frustration tolerance. These tests showed that despite subjects' ability to adapt to the loud noise and perform the prior simple tasks without impairment, the subjects still had problems with these later tests, even though the noise was turned off. In other words, mere exposure to the stressful noise seemed to exact some cost or leave some residue that interfered with subsequent performance.

But the most interesting findings in Glass and Singer's research had to do with subjects' perception of control over the environment. If people believed that they could turn the noise off—even though none of them actually did so—they were much less affected by the stressful sound than if they did not feel in control of the environment. Thus, as we mentioned before in our discussion of crowding, it is not so much the stress of crowding or noise itself that is harmful to human functioning, but the perceived uncontrollability of the stress that is harmful. In fact, subsequent researchers demonstrated that not only does perceived control alleviate the effects of noise, but the more control that people think they have, the better they will do on postnoise tasks, even though the control is never exercised (Sherrod, Hage, Halpern, and Moore, 1977).

Glass and Singer's findings on the effects of laboratory noise have been replicated in interesting ways in real-world environments. Sheldon Cohen collaborated with Glass and Singer to investigate the effects of traffic noise on children who lived in an apartment house built by the New York State Housing Authority in the air space directly over a major Manhattan freeway (Cohen, Glass, and Singer, 1973). They found that children on the lower floors of the apartment house were unable to discriminate subtly different sounds, apparently because they had learned to "tune out" background noise. The children's difficulties with auditory discrimination interfered with their learning to read and caused them to have lower school reading scores than similar children who lived on the upper floors of the same apartment house. Similarly, low reading scores have also been found for children in a New York school located only 220 feet from an elevated train track. On the noisy side of the building, where classes are disrupted every four and one-half minutes by a train registering 89 decibels of noise, the children had reading scores three to four months behind those whose classrooms were on the quiet side of the building (Bronzaft and McCarthy, 1975). More recently, Cohen and his colleagues have studied children whose schools are located directly under the landing path adjacent to the Los Angeles International Airport (see Chapter 2). Not surprisingly, these children have higher blood pressure, perform more poorly, give up sooner on frustrating puzzles, and feel more bothered by noise than children whose schools are not in the flight pattern of the airport (Cohen, Evans, Krantz, and Stokols, 1980). It is interesting to note that airport noise affects children's test performance in much the same way as does the residential crowding, reported in Rodin's study: both stressors made the children more helpless on laboratory tests than children not subjected to these stressors.

Since environmental noise can have such a negative effect on human task performance, we can speculate what the consequences of persistent failure might be on self-esteem and mood and how such failures may help maintain low education, income, and employment opportunities. While specific data are not available, we can imagine that each of these consequences will take its toll on social behavior and interpersonal relations.

NOISE AND SOCIAL BEHAVIOR

AGGRESSION Urban dwellers often become irritated by noises they can't control. A stereo in the next apartment, a barking dog down the block, or construction across the street all help make the city a sometimes annoying and frustrating place to live. But can noise make people more aggressive?

Two experiments have explored this question. Edward Donnerstein and David Wilson (1976) played random bursts of white noise in laboratory subjects' ears at either a very high volume or a soft volume. The experimenters also previously angered some of the subjects by giving these subjects several electric shocks, supposedly as a judgment of the low quality of an essay the subjects had written. Then the subjects were given a chance to shock another person. It turned out that loud noise caused angry subjects to deliver more shocks than soft noise, although it had no effect on nonangry subjects. However, if angry subjects thought they could control the noise, the loud noise no longer served to intensify their subsequent aggression. An experiment conducted by Russell Geen (1978) used a similar approach and found that perceived control of loud noise had the same effect of minimizing aggression occurring *during* noise exposure that it did on postnoise aggression, as in the experiment above. Thus, noise makes angry people more aggressive, but perceived control minimizes this effect, even if control is unexercised.

ALTRUISM If uncontrollable noise makes angry people more aggressive, does it also have a similar effect on the opposite end of the spectrum by making people less altruistic? Numerous investigators have explored this question, spurred partly by the frequently reported incidents in which urban dwellers refuse to aid one another in times of need. While a number of factors influence helping behavior, as discussed in Chapter 9, noise and the general overload of urban life seem to exert a high toll on interpersonal helpfulness. How noise produces this effect and whether or not city dwellers are less helpful to each other than are rural dwellers have been the key research questions in this area.

City dwellers frequently encounter noises that they cannot control. Research has shown that such noise pollution can, in certain circumstances, increase aggression and decrease altruism. *(© Joel Gordon 1978)*

The first and most influential investigation of altruistic behavior in cities was reported by Stanley Milgram. In his paper "The Experience of Living in Cities" (1970), Milgram proposed that cities provide too great an overload of stimulation for city dwellers to respond fully to any one input or to any stranger's need of help. Milgram suggested that urban residents learn to adapt to a life of constant overload by developing certain social norms regarding helping.

These norms include (1) allotting less time to any one input—for instance, offering only minimal assistance if necessary; (2) disregarding low-priority inputs—for example, passing by the figure slumped in the doorway; (3) filtering out highly demanding inputs—for instance, allowing only superficial forms of interaction with others; (4) blocking access to oneself—for example, through unlisted phone numbers; and (5) shifting the burden of helping onto special service institutions like public charities. Although Milgram and his colleagues reported findings suggesting that urban residents were less likely than rural dwellers to admit strangers to their homes and to speak with strangers on the phone, such noninvolvement with others may not necessarily reflect the effects of urban overload. Perhaps the city dwellers were merely afraid of crime or crank calls when they offered little help.

Other researchers undertook to demonstrate more clearly that stimulus overload can diminish helpfulness. In one study, Drury Sherrod and Robin Downs (1974) showed that laboratory subjects who had worked on tasks while overloaded with loud noise were less helpful to a fellow student's request for assistance at the conclusion of the experiment than were subjects who had heard soft noise. In addition, subjects who thought they could control the loud noise were more helpful than people who had no control over the noise. In a related study, Ferne Weiner (1976) found that people who are overloaded with simultaneous auditory and visual tasks were less responsive to a staged accident victim than were less overloaded people who were not working on the two tasks simultaneously. Similarly, Richard Page (1977) discovered that pedestrians on the streets of Dayton, Ohio, were less likely to help a passerby pick up dropped packages or to provide change for the telephone if these incidents took place immediately adjacent to a jackhammer rather than in a quieter part of the street.

Do these effects of noise on helpfulness reflect the learned norms by which urban dwellers adapt to stimulus overload, as proposed by Milgram? Probably not, since they occur among college students in noisy laboratories and on different blocks of the same city streets—places in which one would not expect norms to differ widely. A different explanation for the effects of noise overload on helpfulness is needed.

Recall the explanation of stimulus overload that we introduced elsewhere in the chapter: excessive stimulation demands extra attentional capacity; as a result of this extra effort our attentional capacity is temporarily depleted, so that we may not be responsive to inputs encountered just after exposure to stress. Another consequence of excessive stimulation is that we tend to narrow our attentional focus, zeroing in on only the most important details and ignoring the background noise. For example, we may all have had the experience of driving effortlessly along the freeway with the radio or stereo blaring, yet when our exit comes up and we pull off into heavy street traffic, we invariably turn the radio down. The reason may be that we need more attentional capacity than before to handle the additional inputs and decisions required by stop-and-go street traffic. If we could not turn the radio down, we would have to narrow our focus of attention, ignoring the inputs that were not directly relevant to our ongoing behavior. This same process explains why people may not be responsive to others' needs when they are overloaded with loud noise and other urban stressors. Because of the overload and the consequent narrowing of attentional focus, people may simply be unaware of the social cues that signal help is needed.

Two experiments demonstrate this point especially well. Sheldon Cohen, a major proponent of overload theory, and his colleague Anne Lezak (1977) demonstrated that laboratory subjects were less likely to notice emergency cues presented on photographic slides when they were listening to loud noise than soft noise. For instance, if the slide depicted a service-station robbery, subjects listening to loud noise were less likely to realize what was happening on the slide than subjects listening to soft noise.

Kenneth Mathews and Lance Canon (1975) demonstrated the same point by simulating an emergency situation on a city street. They reasoned that if noise leads to a narrowing of attention, then subjects exposed to loud noise should ignore an emergency cue while subjects exposed to soft noise should be able to attend and respond to the cue. In their study, the emergency cue consisted of a man wearing a full wrist-to-shoulder arm cast and dropping a box loaded with books. This incident occurred immediately adjacent to a power mower that was either turned off or running full blast without a muffler. As shown in Figure 12.3, the results revealed that when the mower was off, people were much more helpful to the man with the cast than to a similar book-dropper without a cast who could help himself. However, when the mower was loudly running, the passersby failed to discriminate between the man with the cast and the man without a cast. In other words, noise led to a narrowing of attention, which prevented people from realizing the nature of the emergency.

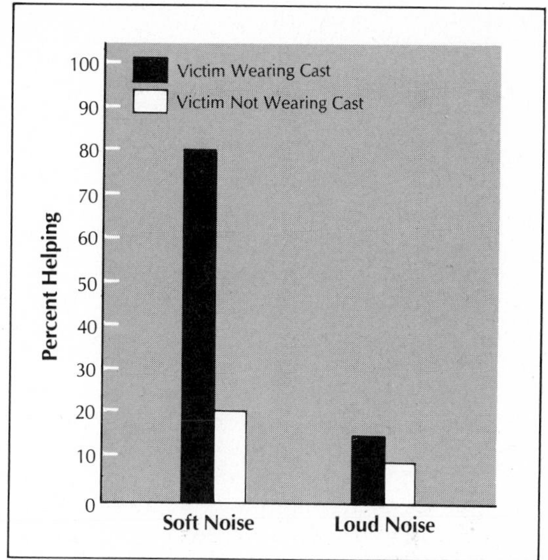

FIGURE 12.3 Amount of helping as a function of noise level and whether victim was wearing a cast. When the power mower was off ("Soft Noise"), people were more helpful to the victim wearing a cast than to the victim not wearing a cast. When the mower was running without a muffler ("Loud Noise"), people tended to be equally unhelpful to both victims. The results suggest that near loud noise, people narrow their focus of attention and fail to discern cues to help. (Adapted from Mathews and Canon, 1975.)

RURAL-URBAN DIFFERENCES IN HELPING

The preceding studies have established that noise and overload can prevent people from helping others. But these studies leave open the question of whether urban overload causes city dwellers to be generally less responsive to others than rural dwellers, as Milgram proposes.

This question was the focus of a study of helping in cities and small towns in Holland. The study is important because it allows a direct comparison of the attentional-overload explanation versus Milgram's view that learned norms reduce helpfulness in cities. Charles Korte, Ido Ypma, and Anneka Toppen (1975) identified "high-input" areas and "low-input" areas adjacent to each other in the same neighborhoods in both cities and towns. In this way, they could control for neighborhood differences and compare urban dwellers in both high- and low-input areas versus rural dwellers in high- and low-input areas. Input level was determined by a count of pedestrian traffic, automobile traffic, the number of buildings, and the level of noise in a particular neighborhood. Helping was measured in terms of citizens' willingness to submit to an interview and to assist a stranger with a map. The results revealed no overall differences in helping between cities and towns. However, people in high-input areas were less likely to offer help than people in low-input areas, regardless of whether they lived in cities or towns. Because there were no overall rural/urban differences, the results do not support Milgram's view that city people learn to be less helpful than rural people in order to insulate themselves against the demands of strangers. Instead the results suggest that both rural and urban dwellers are equally affected by stimulus overload, and it is this attentional overload that affects their helping rather than learned norms.

A second study, conducted in Hawaii, further supports our contention that helpfulness in cities is more influenced by attentional factors than by learned norms. Ferne Weiner (1976) compared the helpfulness of students who had been reared in small towns versus those who had been reared in large cities by exposing them to a simulated accident while they were working in either high- or low-overload conditions. If learned norms are the principal determinant of helpfulness, then one would expect rural or urban backgrounds to be more important than overload conditions in determining helpfulness.

SOCIAL PSYCHOLOGY AND THE ARTS

URBAN STRESS

(Whitney Museum of American Art, N.Y. Juliana Force Purchase Award)

In "The Subway," the twentieth-century American painter George Tooker portrays the urban scene as an alien, sinister place—almost a prison for its helpless, wary residents. The people are isolated and withdrawn, afraid even to make eye contact with one another. Their behavior is similar to the adaptive mechanisms suggested by Milgram as a means of coping with urban overload: disregarding others, blocking access to oneself, and allowing only superficial forms of social interaction. The faces above may also be interpreted as reflecting "attentional overload." The woman in the foreground is anxiously scanning the environment for unpredictable inputs, while the men behind her stare blankly ahead, as if dulled by years of sensory bombardment. As demonstrated in laboratory research, people deal with excessive stimulation by narrowing their attentional focus, effectively "tuning out" the background noise of urban stress. Such overload has been blamed for impairing the quality of social behavior in cities and making people less aware of and less sensitive to the needs of others.

However, Weiner found that regardless of urban or rural background, all students were less helpful in the high- than in the low-overload conditions. Most surprisingly, though, the rural students were less helpful overall than the urban students. Weiner interprets this difference as a possible reflection of the greater cognitive complexity of people with urban backgrounds than people with rural backgrounds; as a result of growing up in a complicated and demanding environment, urban students may have learned to discriminate among more stimuli and respond more effectively to situations than students from less demanding rural environments.

URBAN OVERLOAD: BOON OR BANE?

We have seen that noise and overload may cause people to perform poorly on a variety of tasks, to be aggressive when angry, and to be unresponsive to the needs of others. If cities are truly characterized by noise and stimulus overload, the outlook is not very bright for the quality of social life in cities. Yet we have also seen that cities themselves are not necessarily responsible for such antisocial behavior, only the overload that frequently occurs in cities. At the same time we have learned that perceived control of noise reduces its negative effects and that urban residents who inhabit low-input areas are just as helpful as their small-town counterparts. The implications of this section, then, are not that cities are bad for people, only that overload is bad. In fact, cities offer a variety of options and stimulations that greatly expand one's freedom of choice and enrich one's experience. The goal should not be the abandonment of cities, but the design of cities so as to enhance people's perceptions of control and predictability. Theoretically, controllable cities would allow people to tolerate high levels of intense stimulation while maintaining social responsiveness.

ENVIRONMENTAL QUALITY, HUMAN EMOTIONS, AND SOCIAL BEHAVIOR

In the previous sections we have seen how the *quantity* of stimulation in the surrounding environment can influence human behavior. While most of the research in social/environmental psychology has dealt with excessive stimulation in the form of crowds, noise, and urban overload, a few researchers have been concerned with the effects of environmental *quality* on human behavior. In the current section, we will see how people have been affected by temperature, air pollution, darkness, and the general attractiveness of the natural and built environment.

TEMPERATURE

In the late 1960s and early 1970s, social unrest in the United States led to a number of riots in major cities around the country. Because many of the riots occurred during the summer months, urban leaders and social scientists routinely assumed that heat intensified the social unrest. Popular articles referred to the "long, hot summer" as a major catalyst of social strife. At the time, there was little research on the relationship between heat and human behavior. The few social-psychological studies to have examined this problem seemed to confirm "common sense" in concluding that people become irritable and negative in their reactions to others when they are uncomfortably hot (Griffitt, 1970; Griffitt and Veitch, 1971).

In light of the urban riots and limited research, it seemed reasonable to assume that heat not only makes people irritable, but also aggressive. Yet when Robert Baron and his colleagues began to study this problem in their laboratory, they turned up findings that surprisingly contradicted these common assumptions (see Baron, 1979; Baron and Ransberger, 1978).

When people were given an opportunity to shock another person in either a cool room (low seventies) or a hot room (mid-nineties), it turned out that heat reduced, rather than intensified, the subjects' aggression. Taking a cue from subjects in the hot room, who said that all they wanted to do was to get out of the uncomfortable experiment, Baron and his colleagues modified their hypothesis: perhaps heat intensifies aggression up to a certain point, but after that point people are more concerned about escaping the heat than in expressing their aggression. Indeed, further lab research as well as analysis of local temperature records for the days surrounding the urban riots during 1967 to 1971 revealed a *curvilinear relationship* between heat and aggression. As shown in Figure 12.4, aggression increases with heat up to a temperature in the mid-eighties, but then begins to decrease, apparently as people become more concerned about seeking relief from heat than in venting their anger (Baron and Ransberger, 1978). Consequently, Baron and his colleagues suggest that collective violence is more likely to occur under moderate rather than extreme heat conditions and frequently after a period of gradually rising temperatures.

Other researchers (Carlsmith and Anderson, 1979) have challenged Baron's conclusions about the urban riots of the late 1960s. These

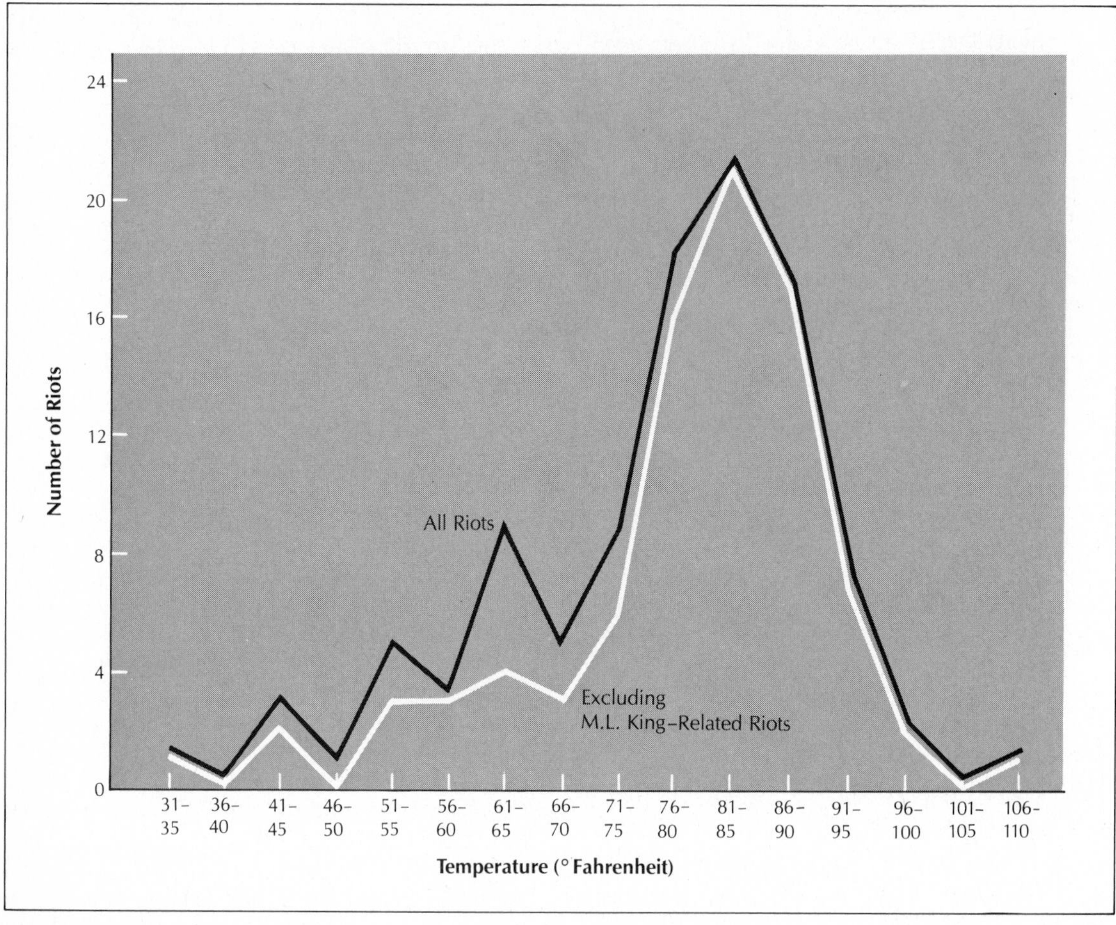

FIGURE 12.4 Baron and Ransberger (1978) studied the relationship between temperature and collective aggression (urban riots). They found that rioting increased with heat until temperatures reached the mid-eighties. When temperature rose beyond that point, aggression decreased sharply; desire to escape the heat probably became more important than anger.

researchers argue that the reason there seemed to be fewer riots on very hot days is simply because there are fewer very hot days than temperate days in the year, and thus fewer opportunities for riots to occur. Accounting for the fewer number of very hot days, these researchers assert that the likelihood of a riot actually increases as temperature increases. Nevertheless, Baron's *laboratory research* is clear: aggression peaks at moderate, not extremely hot, temperatures. The contradiction in the real-world versus laboratory data suggests that other factors associated with heat may have contributed to the urban riots, perhaps factors such as anger, frustration, or a greater number of people outdoors.

AIR POLLUTION

Despite the prevalence of air pollution in almost every major city in America, very little systematic research has been conducted on the effects of polluted air on human social behavior. While pollution has been found to impair health (see Lave and Seskin, 1970) and possibly to influence psychiatric disorders (see Randolph, 1970), only three studies to date have investigated the effects of polluted air on human social relations. One study (Razran, 1940) discovered that putrid odors lower people's evaluations of sociopolitical slogans. In light of this finding and the fact that foul odor constitutes the public's largest complaint about polluted air, James Rotton and his colleagues in Dayton, Ohio, set out to investigate the effects of chemical pollutants on interpersonal attraction (Rotton, Barry, Frey, and Soler, 1978). They asked college students to rate one another in a room that was either odor-free or filled with the odor of ammonium sulfide emanating from the trash in a nearby wastebasket. Foul odor not only caused the students to be unattracted to another person, regardless of whether the other was similar or dissimilar to themselves, it also caused them to feel anxious, aggressive, tired, and sad—as revealed by self-ratings—and to judge the odor-filled room as less pleasant, less comfortable, and less cheerful than the normal room. Later research determined that foul odors even increased the level of interpersonal aggression (Rotten, Frey, Barry, Milligan, and Fitzpatrick, 1979). These findings suggest that pollution in real-world environments may strongly affect human social relations. The findings clearly call for additional research.

DARKNESS

The most intense social behaviors are often those that occur in the dark. People avoid dark streets for fear of crime, but seek out darkened bars or parties for the social license darkness

Preliminary research suggests that air pollution can impair human social relations. *(© Burk Uzzle / Magnum)*

provides. Because darkness cloaks identity, it tends to release the inhibitions that normally restrain a variety of extreme interpersonal behaviors.

In our discussions of deindividuation (see Chapters 3 and 8), we mentioned that people are more aggressive in dark rooms than in light rooms (Zimbardo, 1970). Richard Page and Martin Moss (1976) found that dim lighting also intensifies aggression toward another person, especially when the recipient of the aggression is sitting in the same room. Apparently, darkness not only serves to release the inhibitions that otherwise control aggressive acts, it also tends to isolate aggressors from their victims, making the victims less visible than normal and preventing the attacker from seeing the victim's suffering.

Not all of the effects of darkness are antisocial in character. In another intriguing study of darkness as a disinhibitor, Kenneth and Mary Gergen and William Barton (1973) asked college students to sit for one hour with eight other persons, four male and four female, in a ten-by-twelve-foot chamber that was either totally dark or brightly lighted. Subjects were told that there were no ground rules as to what they should do together. Covert surveillance, assisted by infrared photography in the dark room, revealed that people in the dark were much quieter than people in the light, but at the same time spent much more time moving about and touching each other. Subjects also reported that they felt more sexually aroused in the dark room than in the light room.

The implications of these studies are straightforward. Darkness releases inhibitions for good or ill. To decrease crime, we should brighten the streets; to increase passion, we should dim the lights.

ENVIRONMENTAL ATTRACTIVENESS AND HUMAN BEHAVIOR

Perhaps we have all felt the invigoration of starting the day on a crisp, sunny morning, the refreshment of pausing near a bubbling fountain in a cobbled courtyard, or the satisfaction of being surrounded by a beautiful room or garden. Attractive physical environments can exert a powerful influence on human moods and behavior that researchers are only beginning to explore.

Albert Mehrabian and James Russell (1974) have done extensive work on human emotional responses to the physical environment. Prior research had determined that people respond to any emotionally arousing event mainly in terms of three dimensions: pleasure, arousal, and dominance or controllability. Mehrabian and Russell reasoned that these same three dimensions should also be important determinants of people's responses to the physical environment. To explore this possibility, the researchers selected sixty photographic slides of urban, suburban, and wilderness settings on three continents. The scenes were chosen to represent all possible combinations of the pleasure, arousal, and dominance dimensions. Subjects were asked to view the slides and to imagine how they would feel after spending a couple of hours in each setting. Subjects then rated their desire to affiliate with others in terms of their desire to be friendly with, to talk to, and to explore the environment with another person. Mehrabian and Russell found that people had a greater desire to affiliate with someone else when they were watching the most pleasurable than the least pleasurable slides and that this desire for affiliation increased as the slides also increased from low to moderately arousing. Although such "imaginary" responses do not necessarily relate to actual behaviors, the researchers theorized that the positive emotions stimulated by the environment generalized to other people associated with the environment. If such strong emotions could be generated by merely viewing slides—or by reading written descriptions, as in other research by Mehrabian and Russell (1975)—consider what profound effects may be produced by actual environments with their much greater capacity for pleasure and arousal.

Herbert Leff and his colleagues (Leff, Gordon, and Ferguson, 1974; Leff, 1978) have demonstrated that physical environments not only influence people's experience, but also that people may alter their environmental experiences by changing the way they perceive the environment. Leff and his colleagues showed subjects photographic slides and asked them to imagine

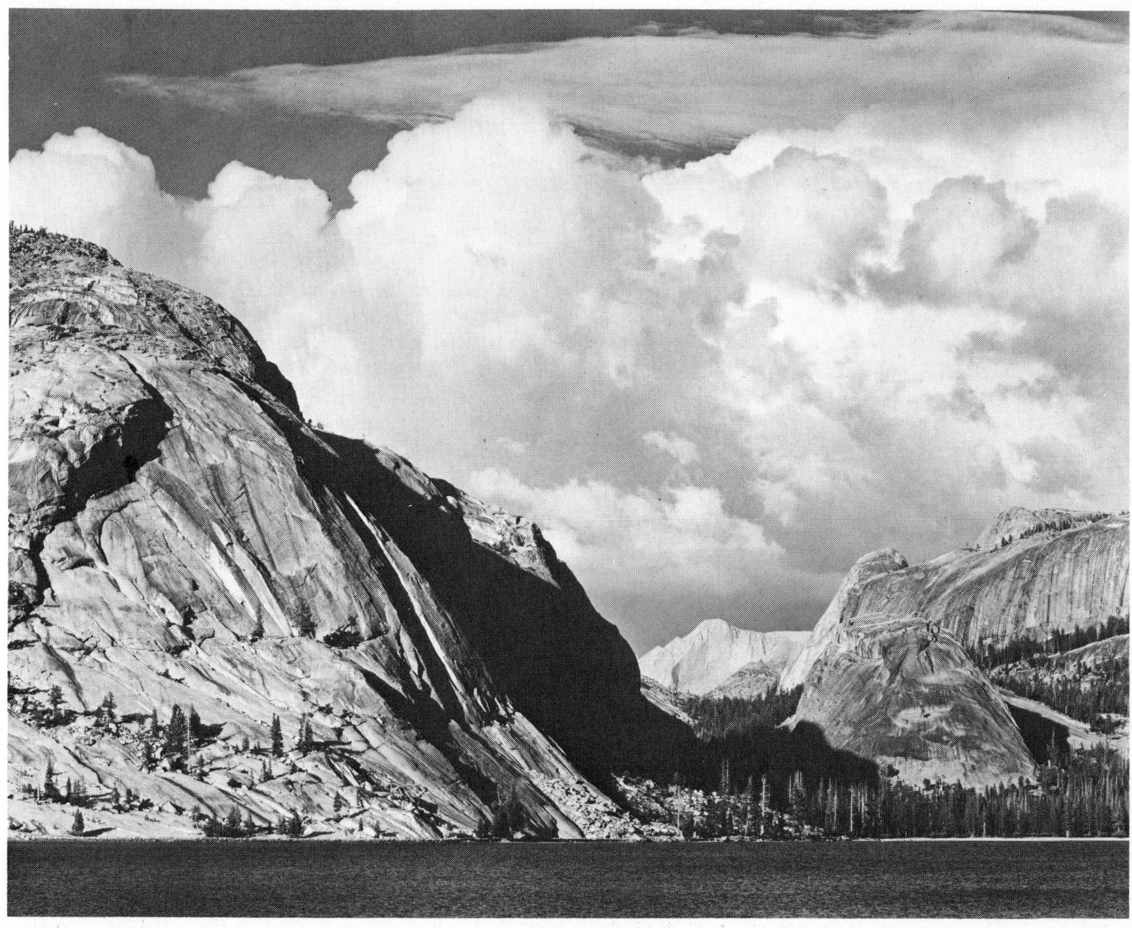

An attractive physical environment—such as Yosemite National Park—may have a positive and powerful impact on our mood and behavior. *(© Ansel Adams / Magnum)*

the slides in different ways—for example, how human construction might alter the natural environments or how the environments would appear if they were seen as abstract lines, shapes, textures, and colors. When people adopted a perceptual set emphasizing human changes in the environment, they saw the slides as less pleasant, while abstract focusing increased the perceived complexity and interestingness of the slides.

The above research has shown that environmental slides can affect people's ratings of their emotions and that individuals can alter their emotional responses by the way they perceive the environments to which they are exposed. In a related research program, Drury Sherrod and his coresearchers (Sherrod, Armstrong, Hewitt, Madonia, and Speno, 1977) found that images of attractive environments can influence people's behavior, and that to some extent people can alter the behavioral impact of positive or negative environments by the way they perceive the environments. College students were asked to reflect for ten minutes on the most or least attractive aspects of their campus environments or to view slides that depicted sunny, beautiful environments versus gray, ugly environments. Afterward, the subjects were given an opportu-

DISPOSITIONS AND SITUATIONS

SUNSHINE, MOOD, AND HELPING

When someone is optimistic, friendly, and helpful, it is often said that the person has a "sunny disposition." The phrase suggests that sunshine is somehow associated with pleasantness, brightness, and an openness to others. If people who behave in this way can be characterized as "sunny," does it also follow that sunshine can influence such behaviors? In other words, do people's dispositions change on sunny days?

Despite anecdotal reports and personal experience regarding the effects of sunshine on mood and behavior, there is little published research on this issue and there are many confounding factors to cloud the results. For example, sunshine is usually associated with temperature changes and with daily and seasonal cycles of behavior, and different types and numbers of people are likely to be out on sunny days than cloudy days. Nevertheless, the research discussed in the accompanying section suggests that environmental factors can have a direct impact on mood and behavior.

Michael Cunningham (1979) conducted a study at the University of Minnesota that sheds some light on the relationship between sunshine, mood, and helping. Cunningham and his colleagues approached 540 individuals on the streets of Minneapolis over thirty-six randomly selected days during the spring, summer, and winter seasons. Each person was presented with an eighty-question survey and was asked how many of the questions he or she would be willing to answer. The reseachers were careful to exclude factors other than sunshine and weather—such as age, sex, or location—that could bias subjects' responses. The investigators found that, independent of temperature, people were more helpful and were willing to answer more of the questions on sunny days than on nonsunny days.

Next, in order to exclude any other comfort factors that might be related to sunshine, the experimenters replicated the study indoors. This time the measure of helping was the size of waitresses' tips on sunny and cloudy days. The study was conducted at a moderately expensive restaurant in a Chicago suburb, where 130 parties of diners were observed over thirteen days in April, May, and June. Here, again, sunshine affected behavior, as tips increased on sunny days. Although the waitresses' moods also improved with sunshine, the researchers determined that neither this factor nor others such as the amount of liquor consumed or the size of the group were significantly related to the amount of the tip.

While this research was basically a correlational study and cannot establish a causal relationship between sunshine and helpfulness, when these findings are combined with the related research on environmentally induced moods and helping, there is a clear possibility that sunshine may produce "sunny dispositions."

How such dispositional changes are wrought by sunshine is not clear. Perhaps sunshine affects mood by stimulating thoughts of pleasant experiences or by making the physical environment more aesthetically pleasing. It is also conceivable that sunshine might affect mood by altering the level of negative ions in the atmosphere or the amount of ultraviolet rays reaching the surface of the earth.

nity to do a favor for another person. The results showed that those who thought about desirable aspects of their campuses or who viewed slides of attractive places were significantly more altruistic than students who were exposed to the unattractive environments. More interestingly, students' altruism decreased if they looked at the beautiful slides but focused only on the unattractive aspects of these scenes, for example, focusing on the intrusion of civilization into an otherwise pristine wilderness. This research implies that physical environments can produce emotional states that mediate social behavior such as altruism. Consequently, other things being equal, beautiful environments should help shape "beautiful" people.

An application of this principle was recently reported by the Soviet news agency, Tass. Workers at a furniture factory in Lithuania can relax during their breaks by watching brief films shown in "rooms of good cheer." Each worker is allowed to select scenes, according to his or her own taste, to view on small individual screens. According to Tass, viewing a picturesque scene of the Baltic coast or the Lithuanian lakes affects workers' moods and motivates them to produce more furniture.

ARCHITECTURE AND SOCIAL BEHAVIOR

Architects frequently cite a statement made by Winston Churchill upon the reopening of the House of Commons after its destruction in World War II: "We shape our buildings, and afterwards our buildings shape us" (Michelson, 1970). While Churchill's quote is undoubtedly true, only a few research studies clearly demonstrate the influence of architecture on behavior. Part of the problem lies in the scale and complexity of such research. Investigations must necessarily be conducted in field settings, where subjects are exposed to two different types of buildings while all other variables are held constant. The behaviors of interest are often subtle and difficult to measure in the field. Nevertheless, the implications of existing research are promising.

We have already mentioned several studies that relate to architecture and behavior. For example, in Chapter 7 we saw that proximity influences liking; the chances of friendship were four times greater between next-door neighbors than between neighbors four doors away (Festinger, Schachter, and Back, 1950). This suggests that apartment houses could be designed with adjacent doors opening onto common courtyards and hallways in order to encourage neighborliness. Indeed, in one study of friendship formation, Lucille Nahemow and Powell Lawton (1975) found that architectural design could even overcome age barriers. In a mixed-age, mixed-race apartment complex, old and young people became friends only when their doorways opened onto common spaces; otherwise, friendships were age-segregated. Thus, one way to prevent the isolation of elderly people in "gray ghettos" is to use architecture to encourage intergenerational friendships.

We also mentioned Oscar Newman's (1973) provocative suggestion that architectural design might reduce crime by fostering territoriality. For example, alcoves surrounding a doorway could create a secondary territory that acts as a buffer between private apartments and public hallways. People might decorate such spaces or personalize them with plants and doormats, thus extending their sense of control into the public territories. Similarly, low-rise buildings and shorter corridors can increase residents' sense of control and predictability in public spaces and thus increase residents' usage and surveillance of these territories, thereby cutting down on crime. Some of the most impressive research on the influence of architecture on social behavior has been conducted in college dormitories, as discussed in the next section.

DORMITORY DESIGN AND RESIDENT SATISFACTION

Although environmental design can bring people together, as in the above examples, it can also lead to too many people being thrown together too often. Andy Baum and Stuart Valins (1977) investigated the effects of architectural design on crowding in college dormitories. On a series of measures, they compared residents of a dormitory made up of small suites versus residents in a conventional long-corridor style of dorm. Working mainly at the State University of New York at Stonybrook, Baum and Valins selected one dormitory in which students lived in six-person suites, sharing three double bedrooms, a lounge, and a bathroom. This group was compared with students in a second dormitory, housing thirty-four people per floor in seventeen double bedrooms along a single long corridor with a common bathroom and lounge. The situation provided an ideal field experiment since all students were initially strangers from similar backgrounds who were randomly assigned by the housing office and enjoyed equivalent amounts of square feet per person, regardless of dormitory style. Nevertheless, after six months of living in the dorms, differences emerged between the two populations.

Corridor residents felt more crowded than suite residents. Corridor residents also felt they had less control over the public space outside their doors, and they had fewer friends and disliked more people on their floor than the suite residents. The two groups also differed in their performance in a number of experiments set up by Baum and Valins. For example, corridor residents placed fewer stick-pin figures in a simulated model room than did suite residents. When corridor residents reported for an experiment in the psychology lab, they sat farther away from other people, spent less time looking at the other people, and felt more uncomfortable with the other people than suite residents who reported for the experiment. Baum and Valins interpret these reactions as evidence of social overload experienced in the corridor dorms, leading to a generalized desire to withdraw from interaction with others. Furthermore, the corridor residents felt less social "cohesiveness" on their dorm floors than suite residents, and in a group problem-solving experiment they performed worse than suite residents in a task requiring cooperation but did better than suite residents on a competitive task. Similar results were obtained when the authors compared long-corridor dorms versus short-corridor dorms at Trinity University in Connecticut. Baum and Valins's work is discussed further in Chapter 13 as an example of how architecture fosters perceptions of control in crowded environments.

SUMMARY

People are influenced by the environments they inhabit in numerous ways. The research in this chapter has shown that individuals react at the physiological, emotional, and behavioral levels when their personal space is invaded or when they feel crowded. In order to prevent such reactions, people seek to control the environments surrounding them by guarding their personal space against threats, by marking their territories, and sometimes by defending their territories. When crowding is stressful, people's task performance and social behavior are less negatively affected if they perceive some measure of control over the crowding than if they have no control over the crowding.

Exposure to noise also disrupts people's performance on complex and frustrating tasks and tends to make people unaltruistic and aggressive, though again, perceived control can reduce these effects.

Humans are also affected by the quality of the environments they inhabit, and they appear to be socially responsive when in pleasant environments. Air pollution, heat, darkness, and environmental attractiveness have all been found to affect behaviors as important as aggression and altruism.

The research suggests that we can intervene at several levels to alter the way we are affected by their surrounding environments. In particular, we can design the physical environments we inhabit so as to maximize actual and perceived control. For example, housing projects may reduce crime by providing defensible spaces, friendships can be fostered through door placement, and dormitories can be built around suites instead of long corridors. In addition, we can change the way we perceive the environments around us—for example, by focusing on the attractive or controllable aspects of the environment instead of on the unattractive or uncontrollable aspects.

Human-environment interaction is a two-way street. We are shaped by the environments we inhabit, but we can also choose what environments we expose ourselves to, how we design them, and how we perceive them.

CHAPTER THIRTEEN

APPLYING SOCIAL PSYCHOLOGY

THE NATURE OF APPLIED RESEARCH

LOSS OF CONTROL IN THE INSTITUTIONALIZED AGED
- Control and Old-Age Homes
- The Intervention
- Pre- and Postintervention Interviews
- A Milder Intervention
- After the Researcher Leaves: The Follow-Up
- Following Up the Milder Intervention

RESIDENTIAL DENSITY, HUMAN BEHAVIOR, AND HEALTH
- Studies of Human Population Density
- The Canadian Urban Crowding Project
- Density in Institutions

RACIAL PREJUDICE AND THE CONTACT HYPOTHESIS
- Early Research: The Housing Studies
- A Laboratory Study of Contact under "Optimal" Conditions

SOCIAL PSYCHOLOGY AND THE LEGAL PROCESS
- Jury Selection
- Extralegal Characteristics
- Methodological Issues

SEXISM AND JOB DISCRIMINATION
- Stereotypes of Males and Females in Our Society
- Effects of Stereotypic Beliefs on Perceptions of Women's Work
- Sexism and Employment
- The Future

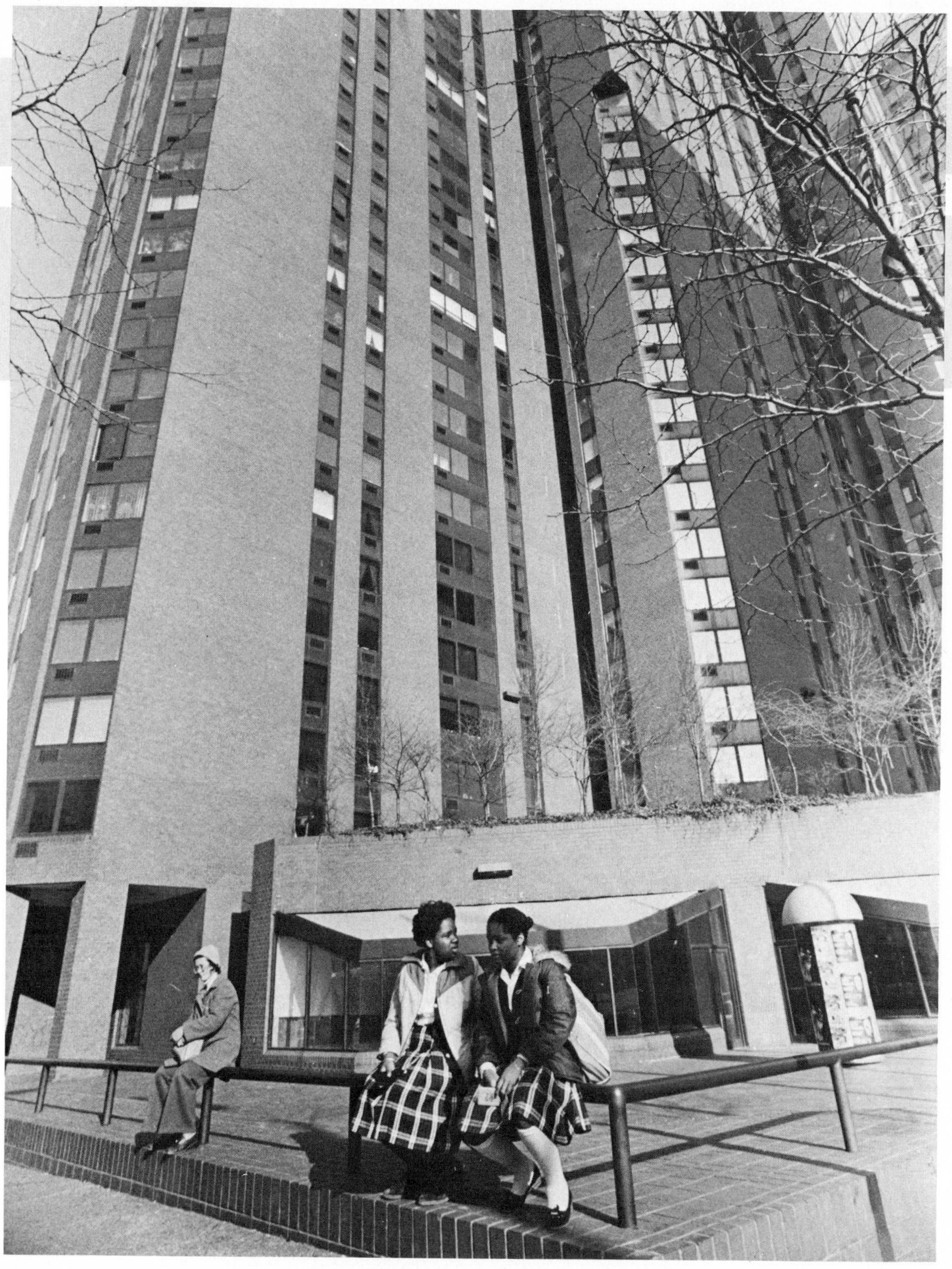

Paulette Barnes is a black woman who was hired in 1973 as an administrative assistant at the Environmental Protection Agency in Washington, D.C. The man who hired her to assist him is also black. At the time, he was the director of the agency's equal employment opportunity division, whose job was to combat discriminatory employment within the agency.

Shortly after she started her new job, Ms. Barnes claimed that the director began to ask her for sexual favors. He repeatedly invited her to join him after work, despite her refusals to do so; he frequently made sexual remarks to her; finally he told her that her employment status would improve if she would have an affair with him and that "many executives have affairs with their personnel." When Ms. Barnes continued to spurn the director's advances, he began, she said, a campaign to belittle her, to harass her, and to strip her of her job duties. Eventually her job was eliminated entirely, and she was fired. After seeking an informal resolution of the matter, Ms. Barnes filed a formal complaint, followed by a suit with the United States District Court.

Was Ms. Barnes the victim of discrimination, as she charged? Both she and her director were black, so race was not the issue. But had she lost her job because of her sex? The Civil Rights Act of 1964 and the Equal Employment Opportunity Act of 1972 prohibit discrimination based on sex. However, the District Court ruled that Ms. Barnes "was discriminated against, not because she was a woman, but because she refused to engage in a sexual affair with her superior," and thus she was not protected by federal law. Ms. Barnes appealed the decision, arguing that were it not for her womanhood, she would never have been solicited for a sexual affair in the first place. Furthermore, she charged that she was solicited only because she was a woman who was subordinate to the man who demanded the affair. The United States Court of Appeals ruled in her favor, finding the employer guilty of sex discrimination and ordering that Ms. Barnes be reinstated with the Environmental Protection Agency.

In its decision, the court referred to numerous studies showing that women, solely because of their sex, are often placed in less challenging, less responsible, and lower-paid jobs than are men. Moreover, the court noted that sex discrimination and racial discrimination possess many of the same characteristics.* Documenting the nature of such discrimination and exploring means of overcoming prejudice and discrimination are among the types of issues to which social psychology has been usefully applied. Such issues—and how social psychology may be used to illuminate or influence them—are the topic of this chapter.

THE NATURE OF APPLIED RESEARCH

Why should this book contain a chapter on applied social psychology? Isn't all social psychology applied? Hasn't everything you have read up to this point dealt with real problems? Topics such as aggression, group conflict, love, and environmental stress are all relevant to important social issues. However, the distinction between applied research and basic research is *not* solely based on the "topic" of study.

What is meant by the basic-applied distinction? The distinction is based on the *immediate* implications of the research. Applied research results in information that is *directly* relevant to assessing and possibly solving a real-life problem. Basic research may or may not provide such information.

The purpose of basic research is *understanding*. Basic research in social psychology is work that provides information that contributes to the development of *general principles* of social behavior. It is research that helps us to understand why and when people behave in a particular manner. This goal is often (but not always) best served by isolating individual variables in laboratory environments.

*"Barnes vs. Costle," *Federal Reporter*, 2nd ed., 56 (1977): 983–1011.

Applied research has a different orientation. Its purpose is to shed light on real-life problems rather than to provide understanding of a general psychological process. This is accomplished by (1) conducting studies to assess whether a problem exists—for example, investigating the impact of residential crowding on social behavior; (2) experimentally comparing the effectiveness of various solutions (what we call interventions) in real-life settings—for example, comparing the effectiveness of two kinds of interracial contact in alleviating prejudice; and (3) testing (actually pretesting) interventions in simulated settings—for example, comparing in a laboratory setting how different instructions a judge gives a jury can affect verdicts.

Many studies are both basic and applied. They teach us some general principle about social behavior and also shed light on a real-life problem. Thus, there is often *no clear dividing line* between applied and basic research. As a result, studies cited in this chapter as solutions to social problems are often informative in a basic way as well. On the other hand, other applied research is so specific in nature that it may successfully deal with a particular problem, but may not provide us with any further understanding as to why or under what conditions such a solution will be effective.

In order to provide an idea of how social-psychological principles can help solve a wide range of social problems, this chapter will consist of five major sections. Each section describes research on a different social problem:

1. What happens when elderly people in nursing homes lose personal control over their daily lives?
2. How do crowded living conditions affect human health and behavior?
3. Under what conditions will interracial contact help reduce prejudice?
4. How do psychological factors influence juries' decisions in court trials?
5. What social processes encourage sexism, and how does this affect women's employment opportunities?

These sections do not encompass all or even a majority of areas in which social psychology is being applied. They do, however, provide a sample of some of the interesting possibilities.

LOSS OF CONTROL IN THE INSTITUTIONALIZED AGED

In the last few years, psychologists have become increasingly interested in the aging process. Several investigators have argued that the aging experience leads to a loss of control over many aspects of everyday life. For example, at sixty-five or seventy, many people are forced out of their jobs. Retirement often means a loss of income, and as a consequence it severely limits an older person's mobility and choice of activities. Retirement also means giving up work roles, which may be a central component of an individual's identity and a means of gaining status and respect among peers. Illness and the physical consequences of aging further deprive both wealthy and poor alike of control even over their own bodies.

Do the senior citizens in our culture feel a loss of control over their lives? If so, does this loss affect their desire to live, their enthusiasm for life, and, most importantly, their ability to survive?

CONTROL AND OLD-AGE HOMES

We have suggested that old age and retirement frequently cause people to feel they have lost control over their own lives. On top of this loss, about 10 percent of the elderly persons in our society are further deprived of everyday choices as a result of living in institutions such as nursing homes or old-age homes. These homes are often designed so that the institutional staff takes over many responsibilities that once were performed by the elderly people themselves—for example, shopping and preparing food, caring for belongings, and making decisions about what to do and when to do it. Because institutionalized elderly persons are a clear example of people who have lost control over a wide range of events in their lives, they have been the subject of several fascinating studies on the importance of personal control for health and well-being. Each of these studies examines whether the decline in health, alertness, and activity often found in the institutionalized aged could be slowed or reversed by providing these people with *increased control* over some aspect of their daily lives.

The first of these studies involved a group of women and men ranging from sixty-seven to ninety-six years old who lived in a retirement home in North Carolina. Drawing from the results of numerous laboratory studies, Richard Schulz (1976) sought to determine whether the psychological and physical health of these people would improve if they could predict or control the regular occurrence of some positive event in their life. The event was a visit from an undergraduate college student. While this intervention may seem unimportant, try for a moment to put yourself in the place of an elderly person living in such a home. Many of these people seldom have any visitors at all and have almost no contact with young people. The importance of the visits for the residents is clearly documented by their responses to a questionnaire administered at the end of the study. Ratings of student visits were comparable to ratings of the residents' favorite activities.

THE INTERVENTION

Each student visited one nursing-home resident at a time. At the first visit the student introduced himself or herself as a member of a class on aging who was interested in having some firsthand interaction experience with the elderly. After a few other opening comments, the visitors allowed the subjects to control the content of the conversations.

Each visitor was randomly assigned a set of three residents. According to plan, the visitors established a different visiting schedule with each of the three residents in their assigned set, and these schedules constituted the three experimental groups: the "controllable visitor" group, the "predictable visitor" group, and the "random visitor" group.

"CONTROLLABLE VISITOR" GROUP Nursing-home residents assigned to this group were allowed to control both the *duration* and the *frequency* of visits they received. After about forty-five minutes of the initial meeting, visitors informed each resident that they didn't want to take any more time than the resident could spare and would be glad to leave whenever the resident wished. At the beginning of each subsequent visit visitors reminded the resident not "to let me stay any longer than you want me to." Visitors then told the resident that they had a lot of free time now and would be glad to leave whenever the resident wished. Moreover, visitors gave the resident their telephone number and added, "If you ever just feel like talking, give me a call and I'll come right over." These arrangements, which allowed home residents to control both the frequency and durations of visits, were maintained throughout the entire experiment.

"PREDICTABLE VISITOR" GROUP Residents assigned to this group were informed when to expect a visitor, but were not given the opportunity to control when a visitor came or how long he or she stayed. Visitors would arrange each visit by telling the resident when they would be in the home and exactly when they would stop by and visit. To make the duration of the visit as predictable as possible, residents were informed at the beginning of each meeting approximately how long the visit would last.

For purposes of the experiment, the "predictable visitor" group was "yoked" to the "controllable visitor" group. This means that each member of the "predictable visitor" group received the same number of visits with the same duration as a matched or "yoked" member of the "controllable visitor" group. This yoking procedure assured that the groups differed only in their level of control over the visits and not in the frequency or duration of the visits.

"RANDOM VISITOR" GROUP Residents in this group were also yoked to the "controllable visitor" group so that they received the same number of visits with the same duration as their matched members in the "controllable visitor" group. The "random visitor" group, however, was not given the opportunity to control either when a visitor came or how long he or she stayed. Nor were members of this group able to predict when a visitor was coming. The visitor would just drop in at various times and then

Research shows that some degree of responsibility for and control over their own lives can enhance the health and well-being of the institutionalized aged. *(© Christina Thomson 1980 / Woodfin Camp & Assoc.)*

leave when the time for the visit had elapsed.

Visitors tried to behave as similarly as possible with all residents regardless of the experimental condition. In all cases visitors were fairly passive, allowing the residents to talk about whatever the residents wished. Ratings of the visits by both the visitors and the residents indicated that visits were enjoyed equally in all three experimental groups.

"NO VISITOR" GROUP A group of residents who did not receive any visits was used as a comparison group. This group was unaware that other members of the home were being visited.

PRE- AND POSTINTERVENTION INTERVIEWS

Before the experimental interventions were begun, each home resident who agreed to participate in the study of aging was interviewed and filled out several questionnaires regarding his or her health, activity level, hopefulness, and so forth. Then, after about two months of the visits described above, the residents were interviewed again. This time they were asked the same questions as before, along with questions about their background, the visits by the undergraduates, their health status, their sense of "usefulness," their happiness, and so forth. Two additional scales evaluating each subject's health status and zest for life were filled out by the activities director of the home. The director did not know anything about the nature of the study or the experimental condition to which each resident had been assigned.

By comparing information collected in the initial interview to that collected after two months of visits, Schulz was able to determine the impact of the various types of visits on the residents of the home. The results were clear and striking. In the case of health status, indicators such as drug intake and number of trips to the infirmary showed an increase over the two months for all four groups. However, this increase was *smaller* for those receiving controllable and predictable visits than it was for those receiving either random visits or no visits at all. Thus, the ability to control or predict a positive event served to inhibit a progressive decline in physical health. But changes in the patients' own ratings of their psychological status and activity level are even more striking, suggesting that the ability to control and predict visits actually *reversed* the pattern of progressive decline. Residents who could control and predict visitors' schedules reported more time spent in active pursuits such as recreation, visiting friends, and attending lectures, more time devoted to planning for the future, and a greater level of general activity than their random-visit and no-visit counterparts. Moreover, while both the no-visit and random-visit groups showed a decline in level of hope over the course of the study, the predict-and-control groups showed an increase in hope.

Schulz's intervention was powerfully successful, and it demonstrates the wide-ranging consequences of increased control over one small life event for the health and well-being of the institutionalized elderly. Schulz's intervention would be difficult to implement on a regular, long-term basis, however. That is, while most homes for the elderly would welcome regular visits to their residents by young people, it would be difficult to find students with the time and dedication necessary to continue regular predictable or controllable visits.

A MILDER INTERVENTION

What about less drastic techniques? Can interventions providing control over mundane life events have similar effects? A more easily implemented and seemingly less powerful intervention than the above was employed by Ellen Langer and Judy Rodin (1976) in a study of the aged residents of a Connecticut nursing home. In this study residents from two different floors of the home were called to a meeting in their respective floor lounges. In both meetings the nursing-home administrator delivered a short speech. However, his prepared speeches differed slightly. In one case, his speech emphasized the *residents' own responsibility* for themselves (responsibility-induced group). For example, they were told that they were responsible for caring for themselves and their rooms. In addition, each member of this group was allowed to choose a small green plant as a present from the home to water and care for. This group was also given a choice over which of two movies they would like to see every Thursday night.

In his speech to the second group, the administrator emphasized the *staff's responsibility* for them (comparison group). For example, the members of this group were told that the nursing-home staff was responsible for caring for the group and the group's rooms. Each member of this group was handed a plant, about which he or she had no choice, as a present from the home and was told that the nurses would water and care for the plant. The group members were also shown a movie every Thursday night, but they had no say in its selection. It is important to point out that although the administrator's speeches to the two groups differed in the degree of personal control and responsibility offered to the residents, each group was promised an equal amount of concern and attention on the part of the home's staff.

Langer and Rodin used two types of questionnaires to assess the effect of their intervention on the home residents. Each questionnaire was administered twice—both one week prior to and three weeks after the home administrator's speech. One of the questionnaires was administered directly to the residents and dealt with how much control they felt over general events in their lives and how happy and active they felt. The second questionnaire was filled out by the nurses who staffed the experimental and comparison floors. The questions included ratings of happiness, alertness, dependence, sociability, and activity of each of the residents.

Residents receiving the responsibility-induction treatment reported feeling happier after the experimental treatment than did the comparison group. They also rated themselves as more active and alert than was indicated by the comparison group's self-ratings. Nurses' judgments indicated that 93 percent of the responsibility-induced group had shown improvement since the experimental intervention, compared to 21 percent of the comparison group. The nurses' ratings also indicated that the responsibility-induced group was generally more active and spent more time with others than the comparison group.

In total, 71 percent of the comparison group was rated as having become increasingly *debilitated* over the three-week period between testing periods. In contrast, 93 percent of the people who were encouraged to make decisions for themselves, given decisions to make, and given responsibility for something outside of themselves showed *overall improvement*.

AFTER THE RESEARCHER LEAVES: THE FOLLOW-UP

While the positive effects of these control-related interventions are impressive and provoking, one wonders if they have any lasting effects on these people. What happens when the researcher leaves and the study ends? Do those subjects who were given increased control over aspects of their lives continue to do relatively well in comparison to those not given control? Both Schulz (1977) and Rodin and Langer (1977) returned after several months to assess the long-term effects of their interventions. The results of these follow-up studies are as powerful as anything ever reported in the literature and perhaps as disturbing in their ethical implications.

Schulz (1977) collected additional data at twenty-four, thirty, and forty-two months after the experiment was terminated. While he was not allowed to interview subjects, the activities director of the home agreed to provide ratings of each of the patients. Ratings were made on scales measuring health status, "zest for life," activity level, sociability, awareness, and pleasantness. The activities director had worked in the home for eleven years, and as a result was personally acquainted with all the participants of the study. While she was aware that a number of residents had participated in the project, she was unaware of any of the details of the study.

RATINGS OF RESIDENTS The results of the follow-up revealed that the home residents who had received predictable and controllable visits, and had originally responded positively to these treatments, surprisingly showed substantial *decline* in their zest for life and health status over time. On the other hand, persons in the random and no-treatment groups exhibited a slight *increase* on these measures over the forty-two-month period. In other words, the groups that originally gained the most as a result of the interventions (predict and control) declined substantially after the intervention was terminated. In contrast, the two groups that originally showed no gains as a result of the experiment (random and no treatment) also showed no losses after the study was terminated. Moreover, at each of the three follow-up periods, ratings of the "predictable visitor" and "controllable visitor" subjects actually *fell below* the "random visitor" and "no visitor" groups.

MORTALITY A total of four of the participants died over the forty-two-month period; two persons in the "predictable visitor" group and one person in the "controllable visitor" group died before the twenty-four-month follow-up; the fourth person, also in the "controllable visitor" group, died between the thirty- and forty-two-month follow-up. Thus all four who died were members of the groups that had shown initial gains. This result, as well as the declines in ratings of health and zest for life mentioned above, suggests that those residents who were given increased control over their lives but were later *deprived of that control* (student visits were terminated for all study participants) were worse off than those who never experienced increased control. While the death rates are not conclusive, they suggest the potentially ominous effects of first giving and then taking away control over important life events.

FOLLOWING UP THE MILDER INTERVENTION

Rodin and Langer (1977) collected their follow-up data eighteen months after the original intervention. A doctor on the nursing-home staff evaluated the medical records of each subject and assigned the subject an overall health score. The records were evaluated for two periods—the six months prior to the intervention and the six months that immediately preceded the final follow-up. The data indicated that those who were given increased control over their lives (the responsibility-induced group) showed an improvement in their overall health, which was greater than the improvement in the comparison group. Again, however, the most striking differences were in the death rates of the two groups. The average death rate in the home for an eighteen-month period was 25 percent of the entire home. Yet, in the eighteen-month period following the intervention, only 15 percent of the responsibility-induced group died (seven of forty-seven), while 30 percent of the comparison group died (thirteen of forty-four). It is important to note that those who died did not differ reliably in the length of time they had been institutionalized or in their overall health status when the study began.

Why did a control intervention have long-term positive effects in the follow-up by Langer and Rodin but negative effects in the follow-up of the Schulz study? One possible explanation lies in an important difference between the two interventions. As pointed out earlier, in the Schulz study, residents were able to control visits for the duration of the study, but when the study was completed, the intervention was terminated. Students no longer visited the residents. In the case of the Langer and Rodin study, however, the intervention was a permanent one. The residents were able to keep and care for their plant, plan their schedules, and care for their rooms indefinitely. Their control was never taken away. Thus, it appears that interventions that increase control over life events of institutionalized elderly persons can have a dramatic positive impact on their health and well-being. However, it is essential that these interventions be *permanent*—in other words, they must provide increased control for the duration of the residents' confinement in the institution (and possibly for the duration of their lives)—or the losses may be equally dramatic.

RESIDENTIAL DENSITY, HUMAN BEHAVIOR, AND HEALTH

During the last ten years, there have been over one hundred studies of the effects of crowding on human behavior. As described in Chapter 12, most of these studies focus on short-term crowding: during laboratory experiments, rides in an elevator, or while shopping at the supermarket or shopping center. While this research indicates that short-term exposures to high-density settings sometimes cause changes in behavior and feelings of stress, it would be a big leap of faith to suggest that this evidence is directly relevant to crowding in residential settings. After all, prolonged exposure to high density might have a more severe effect on people than short exposure. On the other hand, a long exposure may allow people to adapt—to adjust to high density—and thus may have less of an impact than a short exposure. Moreover, most residential crowding involves sharing tight spaces with family and friends while short-term crowding situations are often (especially in laboratory settings) experienced with strangers. These factors suggest that in order to assess whether residential crowding is an important social problem, we should focus on the impact of density in real-life residential settings.

STUDIES OF HUMAN POPULATION DENSITY

For obvious reasons, humans cannot be randomly assigned to high- or low-density environments and confined for months and years while scientists observe their behavior. Therefore, for the most part, studies of residential crowding in human populations are limited to statistical comparisons of people living in real-life environments that are similar except for levels of density. These studies are correlational, not experimental. We cannot make inferences concerning cause and effect. For example, if we find that there are more crimes committed in high- than in low-density neighborhoods, there are a number of alternative conclusions. First, density may be acting as a causal agent. That is, high levels of density may be directly responsible for increases in crime. Second, people who commit crimes may be drawn to high-density neighborhoods. This might be because such areas would provide more people to victimize and there would be fewer police per person than in low-density neighborhoods. Third, a separate factor such as income or education that is correlated with both density and crime might be responsible for the density-crime relationship. For example, high-density neighborhoods are often populated by people with relatively low incomes. If their incomes were substantial, these people might choose to live in low-density neighborhoods. Many types of crime are more likely to be committed by the poor than by the middle or upper class. Thus, the third factor, a lack of income, might cause people both to live under high levels of density and to commit crimes. It follows that results of such studies must be interpreted with caution.

While occasional studies report that high levels of household density are related to various social, mental, and physical disorders, recent critical reviews of the population-density research conclude that there is no convincing evidence that human population density causes pathology, mental disorder, or social disorganization (Fischer, Baldassare, and Ofshe, 1975; Freedman, 1975; Lawrence, 1974). Others (Cohen, Glass, and Phillips, 1979; Cohen and Sherrod, 1978), however, argue that while household density is not a major pathological agent for the *general population*, high levels of density can affect certain *susceptible population groups*. These groups include the very young, the poor, the uneducated, and those living in institutions. Before discussing why these particular groups are affected by density, let us examine one of the studies in this area.

High household density does not seem to lead to physical, mental, or social disorders among the general population, but it may affect certain susceptible groups, such as the very young and the poor. *(© Roland L. Freeman 1973 / Magnum)*

THE CANADIAN URBAN CROWDING PROJECT

The Urban Affairs Ministry of Canada sponsored a study by sociologist Alan Booth (Booth, 1975; Booth and Edwards, 1976; Booth and Johnson, 1975) on the effects of crowding on the health and social behavior of Canadian families. The data were collected from 560 households within the greater metropolitan area of Toronto. All families were white, of European or North American descent, had one or more children, and had resided in their place of residence for at least three months. The sample was selected so that the number of families residing in dwellings that had one or more persons per room was nearly equal to the number in dwellings that had fewer people than rooms. By using a sample of households that were relatively homogeneous in race, ethnic background, and family size, the investigators hoped to compare families that were similar in these respects and differed only in terms of how crowded their living conditions were.

CROWDING MEASURES The investigators employed four separate crowding measures: (1) objective household; (2) objective neighborhood; (3) subjective household; and (4) subjective neighborhood.

Objective household crowding was defined as the number of people per room in a dwelling. People per room has been used in a number of studies and is computed by dividing the number of people by the number of rooms (excluding bathrooms and uninhabited rooms such as closets) in their household. The assumption behind this measure is that fewer rooms result in increased contact among household members.

Objective neighborhood crowding was defined as the number of households per block. Households per block provides a rough representation of the number of people with whom one might have contact in the immediate neighborhood area. Measures of neighborhood crowding in previous studies have included number of persons per acre or per mile and number of residential buildings per acre or per mile. However, the results of these past investigations have been inconsistent. This inconsistency may be partly due to the insensitivity of past measures of neighborhood crowding. For example, the number of persons or buildings per acre do not necessarily reflect potential sources of congestion such as automobile traffic or shared yards and play areas.

Subjective household crowding was assessed through interviews with the residents. People were asked questions such as:

> Are you troubled by the lack of room or space inside the house here? Sometimes people don't invite their friends and relatives into their home as often as they would like because they feel they don't have enough space to entertain them. Do you ever feel that way?

Subjective neighborhood crowding was also assessed through interview questions, such as:

> Are the neighborhood stores in which you shop too crowded? What about the places in the neighborhood where your children play, are they too crowded?

HEALTH MEASURES Husbands, wives, and all children living in the household were asked to undergo a physical exam at a nearby community health center. Health measures included physiological measures of stress (for example, blood pressure and urinary catecholamines), incidence of stress-related diseases (for example, hypertension, ulcers, and asthma), infectious and communicable disease, psychiatric impairments, and estimates of how often people stayed in bed because they were not feeling well and how often they consulted a physician.

FAMILY RELATIONS A number of measures of family relations were employed, including a scale that indicated whether the families' love and affection had dwindled, whether arguments had increased, and whether the parents' sexual activities had been altered. Other measures included the length of time parents spent playing with their children and the number of times parents felt it necessary to discipline their children.

AGGRESSION Measures of aggression were based on interview questions concerning arguments and fights inside and outside the house. Information was collected on the number of households involved in each argument and whether or not hitting and pushing were part of the conflict.

SOCIAL RELATIONS OUTSIDE THE FAMILY Measures of social activity included questions about how often members of the family visited friends, neighbors, relatives; joined voluntary associations; attended religious services; switched jobs; and participated in escapist activities such as excessive sleeping, watching TV, and going on drinking sprees.

POLITICAL ACTIVITY During their interview, respondents were asked about their participation in a wide range of political activities. Measures included whether the subject approved or participated in aggressive political acts such as disobedience and demonstrations and in traditional political activities such as voting, letter writing, petitioning, election campaign work, and so on.

REPRODUCTION From medical histories of the female participants in the study, the investigators collected data on contraceptive use, sexual behavior, family-planning decisions, and number of pregnancies and history of pregnancies, including infant survival during the first year.

CHILD HEALTH AND DEVELOPMENT Three measures were used to assess each child's health and physical development. These included presence of disease as determined by examination by a nurse and physician, the child's body weight, and the child's height.

RESULTS Contrary to the expectations of the investigators, *crowded conditions seldom had any consequences at all,* and even when they did, they were small. Where crowding was correlated with adverse effects, it was generally *household* crowding and not neighborhood crowding. Objective household crowding had a small adverse effect on *child* health and physical and intellectual development. Occasionally, household crowding also affected adults, but only when people were already under stress due to *low income* or other problems.

This work is representative of research on single-family households in high-density residential settings. As mentioned earlier, studies of objective household crowding indicate that high density in these settings does not affect the general population, but does seem to affect certain susceptible population groups such as children or the poor.

Why should residential crowding affect certain subgroups but not the population in general? One explanation has to do with the ability of various subgroups to *control their level of social interaction* in high-density settings (Cohen and Sherrod, 1978; Cohen, Glass, and Phillips, 1979). This argument holds that high levels of density often force people into constant contact with one another. This forced interaction makes it difficult to regulate the quality, the number, and the duration of one's social contacts (Altman, 1975). One means of gaining some control over one's level of social interaction in these situations is temporary escape. Many populations who live under high levels of residential density have the ability to periodically escape. For example, they spend a good part of their day at work and occasionally take vacations, days in the country, and so forth. Populations with a general lack of environmen-

Temporary escape—a day at the beach, for example—can help to offset the effects of forced interactions in a high-density environment. *(© Joel Gordon 1979)*

tal control often lack such opportunities. Due to insufficient income and/or mobility, these people are unable to escape from their high-density environments. This is true of the populations affected by household crowding in the Booth (1976) study: the very young and the poor. This inability to "escape" at will can cause both an increase in feelings of *helplessness* as well as an increase in the overall *duration of high-density exposure.* As a consequence, these groups are more likely to show signs of distress than are groups with more control over their environments.

DENSITY IN INSTITUTIONS

Household density may not be a major contributor to ill health in the general population, but several recent studies suggest that crowding can affect institutionalized populations, such as people in prisons, naval ships, and college dormitories. For example, D'Atri (1975) reports that prisoners housed in dormitories have higher blood pressure than those housed in single-occupancy cells. Similarly, Aiello, Epstein, and Karlin (1975) find that when three females live in college dormitory rooms designed for two, they report more health problems than do females living with only one roommate. These researchers found that "tripling" had no effect on the health of male students. And a similar study (Baron, Mandel, Adams, and Griffen, 1976) also reported no increase in the number of visits to the health center for males tripled in double rooms. Increased visits to the dispensary are, however, reported for males crowded aboard naval ships (Dean, Pugh, and Gunderson, 1975).

Other dormitory research indicates that density can result in interpersonal problems—for example, a desire to withdraw and avoid others (Baum and Valins, 1977) and a dissatisfaction with roommates (Aiello, Epstein, and Karlin, 1975; Baron, Mandel, Adams, and Griffen, 1976). These studies of institutionalized populations suggest that residential crowding with *strangers* may be experienced differently than crowding within a family household. The explanation may be that the nature of social relationships is different between strangers versus family members. Since family members' behaviors are more predictable than the behaviors of strangers, one has more *control over the quality of one's own interactions,* and this may be important in determining the impact of household density. Moreover, many institutionalized populations are not only exposed to the unpredictable behavior of strangers, they are also unable to regain control by escaping from their high-density environment.

Direct evidence that people crowded in institutional, nonfamily settings feel decreased control over their interactions and their lives is provided in Andrew Baum and Stuart Valins's (1977) work on crowding in college dormitories, discussed in Chapter 12. It is important to note that this work did not actually compare students under high or low density. Rather it compared dormitory residents who, because of dormitory design, were exposed to prolonged and repeated personal encounters with large numbers of other residents versus those whose forced encounters included a comparatively small number of others. For example, residents of long-corridor dormitories in which residents shared a hallway, bathroom, and lounge area with thirty-three others were compared with residents of suite-style dormitories in which these facilities were shared by groups of six.

Baum and Valins report a number of behavioral and self-report measures, suggesting that students reacted to the high level of social encounters with strangers by adopting an interpersonal style of "passive surrender" or "learned helplessness." For example, crowded residents used a withdrawal strategy more often in a competitive game and were less likely to assert themselves by asking questions in an ambiguous situation than uncrowded residents. Crowded residents also reported feeling helpless and feeling that their attempts to change things and make them better were, relative to their less-crowded counterparts, worthless. The Baum and Valins data, however, do not indicate a total lack of coping by crowded residents. As cited earlier, crowded residents actively attempted to avoid contact with others. The researchers conclude that crowded residents display helpless-

FOCUS ON APPLICATIONS

THE PRICE OF PRISON CROWDING

Inmates in the Dallas County Jail are confined to their cells twenty-four hours a day. The cells range from individual units with about 65 square feet per person to seventy-bunk dormitories with about ten square feet per person. To put these figures in perspective, you should realize that about 350 square feet of living space per person is considered desirable in American homes. In order for a rather small 1,000-square-foot house or apartment to be as crowded as the Dallas County Jail, it would have to house about fifty residents. To put it mildly, the Dallas County jail qualifies as a high-density environment where people have no control over their crowding. As described in the accompanying section, this is exactly the type of population where the effects of residential density should be most pronounced.

How do prisoners react to these conditions? Psychologist Paul Paulus and his colleagues at the University of Texas at Arlington (Cox, Paulus, McCain, and Schkade, 1979) investigated prisoners' psychological stress as a function of social density (that is, the number of individuals per housing unit). Their research was conducted at the Dallas County Jail as well as at a federal prison in Texarkana, Texas. Previous research had shown that among college students as well as naval personnel there is an increase in the number of complaints about illness as social density increases, even when the illnesses are not the product of increased contagion. Similar results were found for the Texas prisoners. In both Dallas and Texarkana the prisoners who lived in the most crowded conditions complained of twice as many illnesses as prisoners in the same institutions who lived under less crowded conditions.

Other measures also support the apparent connection between crowding and psychological stress in prisons. For example, palmar sweat (sweaty palms) is a standard psychological measure of arousal. In the Texarkana prison, the researchers found palmar sweating to correlate significantly with social density. Since it was also the case that the newest arrivals were housed under the most dense conditions, the researchers considered whether arousal might actually be related to how long an individual had been imprisoned. However, there was no significant relationship between length of stay in prison and arousal, suggesting that the increase in palmar sweating was in fact a reaction to crowding.

The Dallas County Jail and the Texarkana prison are not alone in their overcrowded conditions. The Los Angeles County Central Jail, one of the nation's largest prisons, has recently been sued by its inmates because of overcrowding. It is so crowded that some of the inmates sleep in bunks set up in walkways and dayrooms. When space gets particularly tight, some are even housed in the showers. And so many prisoners must be served at the mess hall that prisoners complain they are sometimes given only five minutes to eat their meals. Although prison officials are doing what they can to relieve the problem, according to the county sheriff's office, there is no money to build more jail space.

ness in situations when interaction with another person is not likely, but that they actively avoid contact when interaction is expected.

In sum, it is clear that *household* density is not a major pathological agent for the general population. But it does seem to affect certain susceptible population groups—in particular, those groups who are crowded with strangers and/or lack the ability to temporarily escape their crowded environments. Evidence on the effects of *neighborhood* density on health and behavior is inconsistent and uninterpretable at this time.

RACIAL PREJUDICE AND THE CONTACT HYPOTHESIS

In its simplest form, the *contact hypothesis* suggests that when members of antagonistic groups meet and interact with one another, the unfavorable attitudes the groups have about one another will lessen, and new, more favorable attitudes will develop. Contact as a solution to intergroup conflict and ethnic and racial prejudice has long been part of our folklore. Moreover, modified versions of the hypothesis have over the years received strong support from social psychologists. For example, in his 1946 presidential address to the Society for the Psychological Study of Social Issues, Theodore Newcomb suggested that the most likely way to reduce group hostility would be intergroup contact with outgroup members of equal status (Newcomb, 1947).

The contact hypothesis has also had an impact on governmental policy. For example, for many years the Israeli government's policy for the settlement of immigrants was to establish new settlements that mixed the poor and uneducated immigrants from Asian and African countries with their relatively wealthy and well-educated European and American counterparts. The assumption was that intergroup contact would help smooth intergroup relations and create a unified, homogeneous nation. (The policy was abandoned since it often produced intergroup conflict rather than accord.)

As we hinted above, there is no longer much support for the simplest form of the contact hypothesis. Over the last forty years, numerous studies have concluded that *intergroup contact will improve the relationship between two groups under some situations, but will have no effect or may even intensify negative feelings under other situations.* In this section, we will try to specify those conditions under which contact is most likely to improve the relationship between two groups. After outlining these conditions, we will describe the results of an experiment that tested the effectiveness of intergroup contact in changing the attitudes of prejudiced southern college students.

EARLY RESEARCH: THE HOUSING STUDIES

Early support for the contact hypothesis stemmed from a study, conducted by Morton Deutsch and Mary Collins (1951), of racially integrated housing projects in New York City and Newark, New Jersey. The investigators interviewed white housewives living in two types of housing projects: *area segregated projects* in which black and white families lived in the same project but were assigned to different buildings or to different parts of the project, and *area integrated projects* in which families were assigned to apartments without consideration of race. The investigators felt that white families living together in integrated projects would have increased neighborly and intimate contacts with their black neighbors and that this contact would lead to positive attitudes toward blacks as a group. On the other hand, those living in area integrated projects would have no increased opportunity for interracial contact and thus would not show any shifts in their level of prejudice toward blacks.

Not surprisingly, the results suggested that those whites living in area integrated housing developed more neighborly and intimate *contacts* with blacks than did those whites living in area segregated projects. (It is likely that most residents of the segregated projects had little or no contact at all with blacks.) More important, however, are the reported differences in the interracial *attitudes* of these two groups. White housewives living in integrated housing reported more favorable attitudes toward blacks than those living in segregated housing.

In considering these results, it is important to remember that this is a correlational study and not an experiment. Thus, it is valid to ask: Which came first, the attitude or the interracial contact? That is, did those families living in integrated housing change their attitudes toward blacks because of the interracial contact? Or did they choose to live in an integrated project because they held relatively positive attitudes

Interracial contact is likely to be friendly when it provides equal status to members of both groups, allows one group to disprove stereotypical beliefs that the other may hold, encourages intimate association, and is supported by social norms. *(© Jeff Jacobson / Magnum)*

toward blacks? Likewise, could those living in area segregated housing have chosen that kind of living situation because they were prejudiced? Deutsch and Collins argue that information collected on demographic and psychological characteristics of the residents of the two kinds of projects indicated that the two populations were *comparable*. This evidence led the researchers to speculate that residents of segregated and integrated projects did not differ in their attitudes prior to living in the projects. (The researchers assume that people with similar occupations, incomes, educational backgrounds, and so forth will have similar interracial attitudes.) Thus, the investigators conclude that the positive attitudes on the part of those living in integrated public housing reflected the differences in interracial contact rather than differences in previously held attitudes. Even so, this is correlational data and should be treated as suggestive and not as conclusive evidence for the effect of contact on intergroup attitudes.

While there are a number of housing studies supporting the contact hypothesis (for example, Wilner, Walkey, and Cook, 1955), other interracial housing studies have reported different findings. A study of residential areas in Chicago (Kramer, 1951) found that those whites living close to blacks were most inclined to make spontaneous prejudiced statements. Another Chicago study (Winder, 1952) reported that only middle-income groups that lived close to blacks showed little prejudice. A number of other studies (see Amir, 1969, for a review) have reported similarly inconsistent results.

After examining these apparently conflicting results, Stuart Cook (1969) identified five characteristics of interracial contact that consistently occurred in studies where contact led to friendly social behavior and favorable attitude change.

1. Contact occurred in a setting that provided *equal status* for the participants from the two racial groups. This would be illustrated by equivalent tenant status in an integrated housing project or equivalent job status in a work situation.
2. The contact situation was one in which *cooperation* was called for.
3. The attributes of the minority person with whom the contact occurred *contradicted stereotypical beliefs* about that group.
4. The setting promoted *personal or intimate association*. That is, the contact would reveal enough about the individual participant to encourage seeing that person as an individual rather than only as a member of a particular minority or ethnic group.
5. The contact took place in a situation in

which *social norms favored interracial association.*

A LABORATORY STUDY OF CONTACT UNDER "OPTIMAL" CONDITIONS

Cook's five points provided a good summary of the studies of interracial contact (reviews of the numerous studies in this area can be found in Amir, 1969). Moreover, he laid out the rules for creating the kind of contact situations that would have a *maximum effect* on prejudice. In order to test the effectiveness of this procedure, Cook (1969) put together a laboratory experiment that combined these optimal characteristics required for producing attitude change.

ATTITUDE PRETESTING Women from a number of colleges in a city in the border South were recruited by a newspaper advertisement offering part-time work "taking paper-and-pencil tests of attitudes and abilities for the Educational Testing Institute." On arriving at ETI potential subjects were tested over a ten-day period for a total of twelve hours. Within this test battery were two scales measuring attitudes toward blacks. The subjects were told that ETI was concerned about the test-retest reliability of the battery of scales—whether people would score similarly if they took the test a second time—and thus subjects would have the opportunity some weeks later to work for another twelve hours. This would allow Cook to com-

DISPOSITIONS AND SITUATIONS

PUBLIC-SCHOOL INTEGRATION AND RACIAL ATTITUDES

In 1954 the U.S. Supreme Court ruled that segregated public schools were unconstitutional. Since that time the desegregation of America's schools has been one of this country's most explosive social issues.

The Supreme Court's ruling was based in part on testimony of social psychologists that segregation was detrimental to black children's self-esteem, that it held down black children's achievement, and that it maintained racial prejudice between blacks and whites. Implicit in this testimony was the assumption that desegregation could help reverse all of these problems. Over the years, numerous studies attempting to measure the effects of desegregation have found that the results are marginal at best and that desegregation often had no effect or even opposite effects than were intended (Stephan, 1978). For example, some studies have found that black and white children in newly integrated schools are more prejudiced toward each other than they were before integration (see, for example, Stephan, 1978).

What accounts for these confusing and often disappointing findings after almost three decades of struggle to achieve integrated public schools? The issues are complex and cannot be adequately addressed in this space, but one explanation has to do with the influence of dispositional factors on children's reactions to integration. In other words, different people react in different ways to interracial contact.

What specific factors influence children's reactions to school integration? This was the question explored by Walter Stephan and David Rosenfeld (1978) in a two-year study of school desegregation in Austin, Texas. The school system was 62 percent white, 23 percent Mexican-American, and 15 percent black. In an initial interview in 1972, 230 white fifth graders were contacted while they were attending either segregated or naturally integrated schools. A second interview was conducted two years later when the children were all attending newly integrated junior high schools. Some children were dropped from the sample because their parents failed to fill out additional questionnaires or because these children could not be located two years later. This left a group pare subjects' attitudes during the first testing to their attitudes a number of months later, after some subjects had been exposed to the optimal contact situation.

SUBJECT SELECTION AND TRAINING Only those people showing high antiblack prejudice on the scales in the test battery were chosen to participate in the study. A number of weeks after the testing, each potential subject received a phone call from a faculty member from one of the colleges in town. She was invited to apply for part-time work involving participation on a simulated management task. The job was at a different college from ETI, and the subjects had no reason to think that the part-time work on the management game was in any way related to the test battery. Those who agreed to participate spent a two-day period during which they were interviewed, were tested (presumably for suitability for the job), received some training in the management game, and were signed to a contract to work two hours a day for a month. It is important to note that payment of salary was made dependent upon completion of the full month of work. These terms helped to assure that the participants would not quit their jobs when they found out that they would have a black coworker.

The management task involved three team members. Each member had a specific job (in running an imaginary railroad system), and as a

of 65 seventh grade subjects in the final sample.

Both before and after integration, the students were asked several types of questions: they rated their attitudes toward blacks and Mexican-Americans on a semantic differential scale (for example, "friendly–unfriendly," "trustworthy–untrustworthy," "similar to me–dissimilar to me"); they rated their own level of self-esteem (for example, "I would say that I am happy"; "I wish that I were different from the way I am"); and they rated their actual degree of contact with other ethnic groups ("been to their house to visit"; "have brought them home from school to play"). The second time around, students also rated how punitive their parents are when the students do something their parents disapprove of as well as how their parents react to positive behaviors.

The statistical analysis of this research is complicated, but the results showed that four factors jointly account for white children's positive attitude changes toward blacks and Mexican-Americans following school integration: the greater the amount of interethnic contact, the more favorable the children's attitudes; the more a student's self-esteem increased over the two years, the more favorable were his or her attitudes; and the more punitive and authoritarian a child's parents, the *less* favorable the child's attitudes after integration. In other words, a student's reactions to school integration were determined by the situational factor of interethnic contact as well as the dispositional factor of increases in self-esteem and the developmental factor of parents' child-rearing practices.

In order for public-school integration to result in favorable attitude changes, the researchers suggest that several things are necessary: actual interethnic contact must be fostered in a context that is likely to raise students' self-esteem; and school systems should avoid authoritarian rules and excessive punitiveness that prevent a positive classroom climate. These recommendations are not simple, but they provide hope that under the right circumstances, school integration can help reduce prejudice, as the Supreme Court envisaged.

group the team members were responsible for various management decisions. The task lasted for forty periods. A period covered twenty to thirty minutes, and two such periods, separated by a thirty-minute break, made up an experimental session.

On her third day of work, each subject met for the first time the two other members of her management team—all strangers. One member was white like herself and the other was black. Both new members were introduced as students from a nearby college and acted as if they were new to the situation. In fact, they were both experimental confederates with clearly defined roles.

CREATING OPTIMAL CONTACT Each of the five characteristics of interracial contact favoring friendly social behavior and favorable attitude change was brought into play in the context of the management game. First, the status of the subject and that of the black confederate were equal within the game situation. The team rotated roles so that each member would have equal responsibility, and the black confederate made an equal contribution to the solution of various game problems.

The second requirement was that it be a cooperative situation where blacks and whites worked together for the same goal. The management game required the participants to work together in order to accomplish the various required tasks. They shared failures as well as successes (winning bonus money) for each day of the twenty-day period.

The third requirement was the black confederate's dissimilarity to commonly held stereotypes about blacks in general. The confederate was selected and presented as being personable, competent, ambitious, and self-respecting.

The fourth component was the extent to which the setting promoted personal associations. This was introduced through the conversation of the confederates. During each food break the black participants mentioned things about themselves, their aspirations, their families, and so forth. Sometimes these comments were elicited by planned questions from the white confederate and sometimes they were volunteered.

The final component was that contact should take place in a situation in which social norms favor interracial association. Both the black confederate and the experimenter's assistant, who also was black, were treated no differently than white participants. It was clear from this overall atmosphere that it was appropriate to treat blacks as equals. Moreover, when alone with the subject, the white confederate made a number of planned comments suggesting her disapproval of segregation.

POSTINTERVENTION ATTITUDE MEASUREMENT Between one and three months after the termination of the part-time job, each subject was recontacted by the Educational Testing Institute and asked to come back to retake the test battery. As mentioned earlier, ETI was located in a different college, and the subjects had no reason to think that the test battery was in any way related to their "part-time job," developing the management-training game.

Subjects who participated in the management game and thus experienced interracial contact under what were presumably optimal conditions were compared with a group of similarly prejudiced students who did not participate in the management game. Cook reports that of the twenty-three women who experienced contact, eight (35 percent) showed significantly positive changes in attitude and only one (4 percent) showed a significant shift in the negative direction. Of the twenty-three women with equally antagonistic attitudes who were used as controls, two (8 percent) showed significant shifts in the positive direction and two (8 percent) showed strong negative shifts.

SUCCESS OR FAILURE? After years of research, Cook was able to specify a type of situation that should have had a maximum effect in eliminating prejudice. He was able to choose highly prejudiced individuals and expose them to forty hours of controlled interracial contact. Yet the experience succeeded in changing the attitudes of only about one-third of the participants. Was the intervention a success? Is it the most we can hope for?

First, this procedure was successful in changing the attitudes of a sizable proportion of a college population of highly antiblack, highly anti-integration individuals. These changes might be thought of as having considerable practical meaning. Cook suggests that while there are a number of explanations as to why the intervention was unsuccessful for the majority of subjects, individual differences in personal make-up probably cause some people to be more resistant to attitude-change procedures than others. It is also important to ask what percentage of people we should expect to change their attitudes, even assuming these are optimal conditions. These women lived in a society that advocated discrimination. Moreover, *they were not removed from that environment.* They spent most of each day outside the laboratory in a small southern city where there were constant reminders that prejudice and discrimination were socially approved. Considering these facts, the influence of Cook's procedures on one-third of his subjects seems impressive. Moreover, it suggests that this kind of optimal contact in a community setting, where the community social norms support positive treatment of minority groups, may be highly effective.

SOCIAL PSYCHOLOGY AND THE LEGAL PROCESS

Psychologists are becoming increasingly active in applying psychological techniques and principles to the legal system. The notion that psychology could be fruitfully applied to legal issues was first suggested in the late 1890s by researchers interested in the psychology of testimony and eyewitness reports. In 1908 Hugo Munsterberg, an experimental psychologist from Germany who had come to America to head the Harvard Psychological Laboratory, published a now-classic book entitled *On the Witness Stand.* This collection of essays triumphantly heralded psychology's entrance into the legal system, but met with some resistance from lawyers and jurists who maintained that psychology had little or no place in the courtroom. Nevertheless, collaborations between lawyers and psychologists on legal issues, particularly on the fallibility of eyewitness testimony, began to increase (for example, Hutchins and Slesinger, 1928; Marshall, 1966), and in the past decade the number of psychologists working in the law field has grown rapidly. In this section we will take a brief look at several areas in which psychologists have conducted research on legal questions. Longer reviews of this research area can be found in Sales (1977) and Bermant, Nemeth, and Vidmer (1977).

JURY SELECTION

The jury trial is generally seen as the hallmark of the Anglo-American legal system. A central concern of any trial lawyer is selecting a jury whose members will be as impartial and open-minded as possible in reaching a verdict: "The defendant has the right to have the conscience and mind of the juror tested by a declaration under oath, not simply that he will be governed by the evidence, but by declarations which show that he believes he is in such a state of mind, so free from bias and prejudice, that he can weigh the evidence impartially, uninfluenced by any opinion or impression that he has formed" (*People* v. *Casey*, 96 N.Y. 115, 1884).

In the vast majority of jury trials, lawyers double as "amateur" psychologists in evaluating jurors. An extensive folklore has developed in the legal profession about the factors thought to be important in jury selection (see, for example, Busch, 1959; Adkins, 1969). For example, occupation is often thought to be a key variable. Cabinetmakers and accountants, it has been said, should be avoided because they require everything in the case to fit together perfectly. Salespeople are said to be good for the defense, since they sympathize with the difficulties involved in selling a "bill of goods" to people. Ethnic background has also been suggested as an important factor. Jurors of southern European or of Irish extraction are said to be sympathetic to defendants, while jurors of Scandinavian or German descent are sympathetic to the prosecution.

In recent years, lawyers have had doubts about the effectiveness of these informal generalizations. Plutchik and Schwartz (1965), in one of the first articles to advocate the scientific approach to jury selection, dryly noted that "the suggestion that the Irish are most desirable to the defense leads inevitably to the conclusion that Ireland, where jurors are monotonously

Irish, must be utopian for the practice of criminal law. . . . [However,] an examination of the prisons of the land reveals that, as a general proposition, the cells are occupied."

These doubts have led some lawyers to look to psychologists and sociologists for help in assessing prospective jurors. While social scientists have been actively involved in the jury selection of only about 15 of some 150,000 jury trials in the past ten years, the trend will undoubtedly increase as lawyers become aware of the techniques and as social scientists become qualified to consult with trial attorneys.

One of the first cases in which social scientists were consulted by the defense was the 1972 Harrisburg Seven conspiracy trial (Schulman, Shaver, Colman, Emrick, and Christie, 1973). Among the defendants in the case were several Catholic clergy members, including Father Daniel Berrigan. The charges included conspiracy to raid draft boards and destroy draft records, and conspiring to kidnap then-presidential advisor Henry Kissinger. The Justice Department chose to have the trial held in Harrisburg, Pennsylvania, a relatively conservative city that at that time had three Republicans for every two Democrats, an unusually low proportion of Catholics, several military installations and war-related industries, and an active Ku Klux Klan chapter. The government's choice of Harrisburg as the site of the trial prompted several social scientists, including sociologist Jay Schulman and psychologists Richard Christie and Philip Shaver, to offer their help to the defense, with the goal of selecting a jury that would be less conservative than the prosecution had hoped.

The first step was to conduct a telephone survey of the registered voters in the Harrisburg area, since this was the population from which the jury ultimately would be selected. The team first obtained the demographic characteristics (for example, sex, age, race, education, occupation) of the existing jury panel in order to compare the panel with a random sample of registered voters. If the panel, the group from whom the actual jury would be selected, were representative of the population of registered voters, the two groups should be statistically similar. The team found that members of the random sample of voters were younger on the average than people in the jury panel. Using this evidence, the defense was successful in convincing the judge to rule in favor of their motion to select a new panel before the actual jury was chosen.

In the second stage, in-depth interviews were conducted with a subset of the original group interviewed previously. These in-depth interviews focused on several areas that the social scientists thought would be relevant to a prospective juror's attitudes and impartiality, including degree of contact and familiarity with the media, level of trust in government, organizational memberships, religious attitudes, spare-time activities, and several attitudinal measures related to the trial itself. Interviewees were also asked to rate their feelings about political protest on a scale that ranged from "Accept what the Government is doing and keep quiet about one's feelings" to "Become part of a revolutionary group which attempts to stop the Government from carrying on the war by bombing buildings or kidnapping officials."

Some of the findings were useful to the defense. For example, religion was significantly related to the key attitudes: Catholics, Lutherans, and "no preference" tended to favor the defense point of view, while Episcopalians, Presbyterians, and Methodists did not. Thus, the social scientists recommended that the lawyers ask each prospective juror about religion. In addition, low trust in government was related to liberal attitudes, and so it was also recommended that the lawyers attempt to assess the juror's trust in government during the questioning of the prospective jurors. Furthermore, high levels of education and media contact, two factors usually thought of as linked with liberal attitudes, were in this case associated with conservative attitudes. (This was thought to be due to the liberal—and young—college graduates leaving Harrisburg for more liberal areas of the country, resulting in a college-educated population made up primarily of businessmen.) Finally, sex and political party were not importantly related to attitudes, although women and Democrats were slightly more liberal on several questions than men and Republicans.

From this information, the social scientists constructed a profile of the ideal juror: a female

Democrat with no religious preference who had a white-collar or a skilled blue-collar job. This ideal juror would also sympathize with at least some elements of the defendants' views about the war, would tolerate peaceful protest of government policy, and would show some willingness to presume the defendants innocent until proven guilty. Armed with this information, the defense lawyers began the voir dire, or questioning of the jurors.

After each court session, the defense team (lawyers, defendants, and social scientists) met to discuss and rate each prospective juror on a scale of one (very good) to five (very bad), for the purpose of deciding which jurors to retain and which to oppose. At the completion of the jury selection process, the jury was composed of two "ones," five "twos," and five "threes." The ultimate outcome of the trial was a hung jury, with ten members voting for acquittal and two for conviction. Schulman and his colleagues note that the two votes to convict came from jury members who had been rated as "twos." Nevertheless, the outcome was generally favorable to the defense in that the defendants were not convicted, and the predictions of the social scientists had been relatively accurate.

Similar techniques have been used in other criminal cases with similar success (see Sage, 1973; Buckhout, 1978; Chevigny, 1975; Rokeach and Vidmer, 1973; Zeisel and Diamond, 1976). However, there are still many obstacles that prevent the routine participation of social scientists in jury selection. Some lawyers are resistant to the techniques. Others simply do not receive jury lists far enough in advance of a trial for any analysis to be done. Another problem is the expense involved. June Tapp, a psychologist who participated in the jury selection during the trial of the Wounded Knee defendants, has estimated that the actual costs of the work done in that case, including supplies and computer time, would have been close to $50,000 (Tapp charged no fees). In addition, it is important to remember that while the record of social-science techniques in jury selection is remarkably good, it is difficult to ascertain exactly how important social-science techniques are in determining trial outcomes since we have no information on how many times the defendants would have been acquitted without the use of the techniques. Nevertheless, empirical techniques can refine the intuitive generalizations often used by lawyers in jury selection. (Note, for example, the finding in the Harrisburg trial that education was associated with conservative attitudes rather than liberal attitudes.)

EXTRALEGAL CHARACTERISTICS

Another issue that has received attention from social psychologists interested in law is whether "extralegal" characteristics affect a jury's verdict. Extralegal characteristics may be thought of as attributes of the various participants in a trial—such as a defendant's race, sex, or looks—which, according to the rules of the system, should have no effect on the verdict in the case. One such extralegal characteristic that has been investigated experimentally is attractiveness. Attractiveness has two aspects, both of which have been examined in research studies: *character* attractiveness and *physical* attractiveness. In addition, the attractiveness of both the defendant and the victim may influence the verdict.

VICTIM ATTRACTIVENESS David Landy and Elliot Aronson (1969) suggested that a crime may seem more serious when the victim is perceived as a good person with an attractive character, someone undeserving of such an unfortunate fate. If so, it is possible that people would judge an accused defendant more harshly when the victim has an attractive character than when the victim has an unattractive character, although the law deems attractiveness to be irrelevant. Indeed, criminal defense lawyer Percy Foreman has suggested that the best defense in a murder case is that the deceased deserved to be killed. Foreman recounts a case in which he successfully defended a woman who had confessed to shooting her husband by so effectively denouncing the dead man that he felt that "the jury was ready to dig up the deceased and shoot him all over again" (Smith, 1966).

To test their hypothesis, Landy and Aronson (1969) presented simulated jurors with the details of a case involving a negligent automobile homicide. The details of the accident were identical for all subjects, but half the subjects received a description of a victim with an unattractive character ("a notorious hoodlum and ex-convict who had been convicted of assault and extortion") while the other half were given a description of an attractive victim ("a senior partner of a successful stock brokerage firm and an active member of the community welfare board"). The defendant in the case was described similarly for all subjects. When the victim had an attractive character, subjects sentenced the defendant to 15.77 years in prison, while the alleged assailant of an unattractive victim was given only 12.90 years. Similar findings have been reported in other studies as well (Shaw, 1972; Fulero and De Lara, 1976), though no published study has yet examined the effect on jurors of the *physical* attractiveness of the victim.

DEFENDANT ATTRACTIVENESS In some criminal cases, jurors may not have any information about the crime victim. However, jurors are virtually always given information about the defendant, such as a prior criminal record, and they are often able to see and hear the defendant as well. Does the defendant's character or physical attractiveness affect a jury's verdict?

Landy and Aronson (1969) ran a second study in which the character attractiveness of both the defendant and the victim were manipulated. The experiment used the same basic design as the first experiment, described above. The results replicated the finding that the more attractive the victim, the more severe the punishment for the defendant, although the effect was only marginally significant. In addition, it was found that a defendant with an unattractive character was sentenced more harshly than an attractive defendant or a defendant described in a neutral way (11.75 years versus 8.58 and 8.22 years, respectively). Other researchers have found the same effect (for example, Shaw, 1972; Sigall and Landy, 1972; Nemeth and Sosis, 1973; Gray and Ashmore, 1976). While these studies manipulated a defendant's character attractiveness, Michael Efran (1974) used a modified version of the Landy and Aronson technique to vary physical attractiveness. When a defendant's photograph was attached to the information read by the simulated jurors, the unattractive defendant was judged more severely than the attractive defendant.

Thus, it seems that attractiveness, based on both character and physical appearance, can affect jury verdicts, at least in the mock-jury context. But will the effect hold in all cases? Sigall and Ostrove (1975) reasoned that under most circumstances, physically attractive defendants are viewed by jurors as less likely to commit future offenses and are therefore treated more leniently than an unattractive defendant, who may be thought of as more likely to be a repeat offender. However, when the offense is linked to the attractiveness of the perpetrator, as in a con game or swindle, an attractive defendant may be regarded as more dangerous than an unattractive defendant and the effects of "beauty" may be reversed.

Sigall and Ostrove presented their simulated jurors with one of two case accounts: a swindle in which the female defendant had ingratiated herself to a middle-aged bachelor and induced him to invest $2,200 in cash and merchandise (attractiveness-related), or a burglary in which the female defendant obtained a passkey and entered an apartment, burglarizing it for $2,200 in cash and merchandise (attractiveness-unrelated). In addition, a photograph of the female defendant was attached. This photograph had previously been rated as either attractive or unattractive. As expected, in the burglary—a crime unrelated to the defendant's looks—the unattractive defendant was sentenced to a significantly longer term than the attractive defendant (5.20 and 2.80 years, respectively). However, in the case of the swindle—a crime related to the defendant's looks and charm—the attractive defendant was sentenced to 5.45 years, and the unattractive defendant to 4.35 years. Thus, when the crime is seen as being related to the defendant's attractiveness, the advantage otherwise held by good-looking defendants is lost. The attractive defendant is seen as "taking advantage" of his or her attractiveness and is treated more harshly as a result.

METHODOLOGICAL ISSUES

The studies that we have cited above all involve simulated or "mock" juries. Of course, the optimal technique would be to utilize real cases and

Physical attractiveness can affect the treatment of both victims and defendants in court, as illustrated by this scene from *Madame Q*, an early motion picture. *(Culver Pictures)*

real participants in real courtrooms. This use of real juries was attempted in 1954 by a group of legal researchers and behavioral scientists from the University of Chicago. The researchers, with the permission of the judge but without the knowledge of the jurors, "bugged" a jury room in order to record the jury deliberations for later analysis. Some of the results of this analysis were presented at a judicial conference in Estes Park, Colorado, shortly afterward. The resulting controversy over the legal and ethical issues involved in using real-jury deliberations for research purposes triggered a congressional investigation (see House Committee on Judiciary, 1955). Eventually, a law was passed specifically prohibiting such techniques. The concerns that prompted passage of the law included the legal doctrines of the sanctity of the jury and the inviolability of what goes on behind the locked doors of the jury room, as well as ethical concerns about invasions of the privacy of both the jurors and the defendant. It should be noted, however, that even if use of real juries were possible, the "one shot" nature of a trial would make control of independent variables impossible, leading to data at the correlational level rather than at the cause-and-effect level.

Thus, most of the psychological research done on issues relevant to the legal system are conducted with "mock" or simulated juries. The simulated-jury technique has several problems, including the fact that the "jurors" are aware that their decisions will not have real consequences for the "defendant" whom they are asked to judge. Does this variable really make a difference?

Donald Wilson and Edward Donnerstein

(1977) ran a series of studies to investigate this question. In one study, subjects were told by the experimenter that a fellow college student in another course had kept an exam after taking it and then had distributed it to students who were to take the same exam in a later section of the course. Four of these students admitted receiving the exam and described the student who gave it to them. Their description matched the instructor's description of the student he suspected of not returning the exam. Still, the instructor did not actually catch the student with the exam, and the instructor had only the indirect testimony from the four witnesses to go on. At this point, half of the subjects were told that the instructor thought it would be best if the student's peers judged the student's guilt or innocence, and that the instructor had agreed to accept the decision made by the majority of the students in the class (the subjects). This was the real-consequences condition. The other half of the subjects were told that the theft was only a hypothetical case for the purposes of the experiment and that the experimenters were interested in learning how students in the role of jurors make decisions (the hypothetical-consequences condition).

The second variable manipulated in the study was the character attractiveness of the defendant. Half of the subjects in each of the two consequences conditions were told that the accused student was a very good student who had received several honors, had a grade point average of 3.60 on a four-point scale, and was a very articulate student who had attended class every day. The other half of the subjects were told that the student had a grade point average of 1.60, had been on academic probation for several quarters, did not belong to any campus organizations, and had missed class frequently. At this point, the subjects were asked to make a judgment of guilty or innocent.

The results showed that more guilty verdicts occurred in the real-consequences condition than in the hypothetical-consequences condition (83 percent versus 47 percent). More importantly, within the hypothetical-consequences group, the unattractive offender was found guilty by 59 percent of the subjects, and the attractive offender was found guilty only 33 percent of the time, while in the real-consequences condition, both the attractive and unattractive offenders were found guilty 83 percent of the time. This finding suggests that there may be important differences between experimental studies of simulated juries and the operation of real juries in actual courtroom cases, where the verdicts do have real consequences for the persons involved. Thus, we need to be cautious in extrapolating laboratory findings to the legal system. Nevertheless, the research suggests that justice may not always be as blind as we would hope. In fact a recent review of mock-jury research is entitled "Justice Needs a New Blindfold" (Gerbasi, Zuckerman, and Reis, 1977).

SEXISM AND JOB DISCRIMINATION

Discrimination based on sex is a phenomenon at least as old as discrimination based on race, nationality, and ethnicity. The history of Western civilization is one of subordination of women. In ancient Greece, wives were confined to a small area in the rear of the house. The ancient Jews viewed wives as a form of property, and longer purification rites were required if a mother gave birth to a daughter rather than to a son. Christianity maintained this tradition of subordination by portraying women as being ruled by their husband "even as the church is ruled by Christ" (Watson and Johnson, 1972).

Many social scientists argue that discrimination based on sex is not confined to the history books. The argument that present-day American women are an oppresed group was clearly stated by Swedish sociologist Gunnar Myrdal (1944). Myrdal noted a number of similarities between the situation of blacks in a white-dominated culture and that of women in a male-dominated culture. These similarities included the following: (1) both blacks and women had relatively high social visibility due to physical appearance or dress; (2) both were viewed as forms of property; (3) both were judged inferior in mental ability and at the same time were given only limited educational opportunities;

(4) both were assigned a "place" in the social system and earned approval only if they remembered their "place"; (5) both were kept in their place by similar myths, those of the "contented woman" and "contented black" who did not *want* to have equal rights or opportunities; (6) both groups were allocated certain jobs, usually ones low in salary and prestige.

As our society has grown and changed, there has been increasing resistance to the "traditional" feminine stereotype in our culture, as well as an increasing recognition of ways in which this stereotype has led to adverse treatment of women. These changes have paralleled those that have taken place with regard to blacks in our society. In this section, we will examine the content of the traditional view of women and how this view is transmitted culturally. Finally we will look at how these beliefs lead to job discrimination.

STEREOTYPES OF MALES AND FEMALES IN OUR SOCIETY

In one study, when psychologists asked a group of male and female college students to describe the "typical" characteristics of men and women, the psychologists found considerable agreement between the sexes' descriptions (Rosenkrantz, Vogel, Bee, Broverman, and Broverman, 1968). Men were described by both sexes as being independent, objective, active, competitive, adventurous, self-confident, and ambitious—traits rated by a separate group of male and female students as being positive or socially desirable for people in general. Women, on the other hand, were seen as dependent, subjective, passive, noncompetitive, nonadventurous, and unambitious—traits rated by the separate group of college students as being negative and undesirable.

In 1972 these same researchers asked a group of mental-health professionals—both male and female psychologists, psychiatrists, and social workers—to fill out a questionnaire regarding male and female traits (Broverman, Broverman, Clarkson, Rosenkrantz, and Vogel, 1972). A second group was asked to check only the items that described a "healthy, mature, socially competent female." And a third group was asked to describe a "healthy, mature, socially competent adult person." The results were striking. As in earlier studies of sex-role stereotyping, both male and female subjects showed a high level of agreement about the male and female stereotypes. But while the traits and behaviors judged to be typical of the healthy adult *person* were nearly identical to those describing the healthy adult *male*, the healthy adult woman was described much differently. For example, the healthy man and the healthy adult were described as independent, competent, and objective, while the healthy woman was described in terms of dependency and emotionality.

TRANSMISSION OF STEREOTYPES: PARENTAL SOCIALIZATION We have seen that the culture's stereotypes of men and women are clearly different. How is it that new members of the culture acquire these stereotypes?

It is through the process of *socialization* that people take on the roles, norms, and values appropriate to the culture to which they belong. The most direct form of socialization is interaction with other people, most importantly a child's parents. The differential treatment of male and female infants begins very early. In one study researchers interviewed a group of thirty first-time parents (fifteen had boys and fifteen had girls) within twenty-four hours after the baby's birth (Rubin, Provenzano, and Luria, 1974). Each baby had been given the routine hospital examination for such characteristics as color, muscle tone, and reflex irritability, and no objective differences were found between the male and female infants, even in size. Yet the parents of girls rated their babies as softer, more finely featured, smaller, and less alert than did the parents of boys. This effect was less strong in mothers than in fathers, who described their sons as firmer, better coordinated, stronger, more alert, and hardier. Fathers thought their daughters were less alert, weaker, and more delicate than the mothers did.

It is no wonder that such perceptions are carried over to treatment of male and female infants. From the beginning, parents treat their infants differently according to sex: a father will tend to "roughhouse" with a boy, but to pet and cuddle a girl. Both fathers and mothers tend to discourage dependent behaviors such as clinging in male infants, but to encourage such behavior in female infants (Lewis, 1972). Differential treatment persists throughout childhood as well (Rothbart and Maccoby, 1966). During the preschool years, the child is often supplied with what our culture defines as sex-appropriate toys such as footballs for boys and dolls for females. This practice was dramatically demonstrated by psychologists who observed eleven mothers as they played (individually) with a six-month-old child (Will, Self, and Datan, 1974). Since infants that age are often alike in appearance, the researchers were able to tell six of the mothers that the child was a boy named Adam, and the other five that the child was a girl named Beth. There were three toys in the playroom: a doll, a train, and a fish. The researchers looked at which toys the women would offer the child. Those mothers who thought they were playing with Beth handed "her" the doll more often than those mothers who thought they were playing with Adam. In addition, Adam got the train more often than did Beth. In fact Adam/Beth was male. But more importantly for our purposes, all of the women in the study claimed to believe that males and females are alike at six months of age, and none thought that she would treat her own son differently than her daughter. Moreover, nine of the eleven claimed that they encouraged rough play in their daughters, and ten said that they encouraged their sons to play with dolls.

TRANSMISSION OF STEREOTYPES: THE MEDIA AND LITERATURE Mass communications media (television, newspapers, books, magazines, and so forth) also teach the sex-role stereotypes prevalent in our culture. At the earliest age, children's literature begins to define culturally appropriate sex roles. Key (in Unger and Denmark, 1975) summarized a dozen studies of children's books as follows: "In general, children's books show that boys climb, dig, build, fight, fall down, get dirty, ride bikes, and have many adventures, while girls sit quietly and watch. Boys are taught to express themselves; girls to please." These portrayals continue throughout the school years. One study of high-school history texts found that females were pictured as domestics and caretakers of children, while men were shown as workers of all types. In one history text, 98 percent of the people discussed were males, and female achievement was frequently ignored. For example, Mary Shelley, the author of *Frankenstein*, was described as the poet Shelley's wife (Chafetz, 1974).

Television commercials tend to reinforce sex-role stereotypes. Women, for example, are typically shown as product-oriented homemakers. *(© Ellen Pines Sheffield 1980/Woodfin Camp & Assoc.)*

The same patterns of sex stereotyping are found in studies of children's television programming. In the mid-1970s more than two-thirds of all leading characters on Saturday-morning network TV were male (McArthur and Eisen, 1976b). Furthermore, males were portrayed as more active, more autonomous, and better at solving problems than females. Even the commercials featured four times as many males as females, and the males were likely to appear as expert authorities while females were likely to be shown as dependent product users.

What are the effects of such media stereotypes on children's behavior, and how can changes in these stereotypes lead children to engage in decreased stereotyped behavior? These questions were explored in two studies by Leslie McArthur and Susan Eisen. In the first (McArthur and Eisen, 1976a), male and female preschool children were read one of three different versions of a story. One-third of the children heard a "stereotype" story, which portrayed successful achievement behavior by a male, but not by a female; another third heard a "reversal" story in which the female engaged in the achievement behavior, but not the male; and the rest of the children heard a "control" story, which did not include any achievement behavior. When the children were later given an opportunity to perform a task, boys who heard the "stereotype" story persisted longer at the task than did boys who heard the "reversal" story, while girls who heard the "reversal" story tended to persist longer at the task than did girls who heard the "stereotype" story. Similar findings were obtained in the second study, which employed videotapes rather than written stories (McArthur and Eisen, 1976b). These findings suggest that alterations in the way males and females are portrayed in media for children may have an impact on the future achievement-related behavior of young people.

EFFECTS OF STEREOTYPIC BELIEFS ON PERCEPTIONS OF WOMEN'S WORK

We have seen that there is general agreement on the content of male and female stereotypes in American society, and we have examined how these stereotypes are transmitted to new members of the culture through interaction with parents and others and through the media. A major consequence of such male and female stereotypes is the effect that such beliefs have on the *evaluation of women's performance* in the work context. As a result, women receive lower salaries than their male counterparts and are less likely than men to be considered for jobs and promotions.

One example of sexism in the work world is the perceived status of occupations that are traditionally male or female. John Touhey (1974) examined this issue by giving male and female subjects information about various traditionally male occupations—architecture, law, medicine, science, and college teaching. One group of subjects was told that the percentage of women in these fields was increasing rapidly, so that in just a few years women would constitute a majority of the people working in these areas. The other subjects were told that the percentage of women in these fields was relatively stable and was not expected to increase. All subjects were then asked to rate the prestige of each occupation. Both male and female subjects who expected increasing numbers of women in the field rated all of the occupations lower in prestige than did those who expected the occupation to remain male-dominated.

This bias is not limited to specific occupational groups. Several studies have found that work attributed to women is evaluated less favorably by both males and females than work attributed to men, even when the work is in "female-related" fields such as dietetics or education (see, for example, Goldberg, 1968; Bem and Bem, 1970). However, not all studies have found this discrimination. For example, more recent research has found that male and female high-school students tend to rate male workers higher than female workers in male-dominated fields and female workers higher than male workers in female-dominated fields (Mischel, 1974). But this finding may offer little comfort, since we have already learned that female-dominated fields may be perceived as being less prestigious than male-dominated fields.

Can we expect that perceptions of female workers will change as women enter the labor force in increasing numbers? Perhaps. But, again, the research is not encouraging. A study by Shirley Feldman-Summers and Sara Kiesler (1974) suggests that sexist attitudes can be maintained even in the face of evidence that a woman has in fact succeeded. These researchers gave their subjects sheets of problems that had supposedly been worked on by either a man or a woman. In some cases 90 percent of the problems were answered correctly, and in some cases only 20 percent had been answered correctly. In reality, the sheets had all been filled out by the experimenters. The subjects were then asked to indicate the extent to which they felt that the supposed worker's performance was due to ability, motivation, luck, or the difficulty of the task problems. When the male worker had succeeded (90 percent correct), subjects indicated that it was due to his ability. When the woman succeeded, the subjects explained her success in light of her motivation rather than her ability. Thus, despite equal performance, different reasons were ascribed for the success of each. Successful women were seen as having to be especially motivated to succeed in order to overcome their "lack" of ability. Other researchers have obtained similar results: successful work by males is attributed to ability, while successful work by women is attributed to "luck" by both men and women (Deaux and Emswiller, 1974).

SEXISM AND EMPLOYMENT

Do these views have an effect on women in the work world? The evidence suggests that they do, and that these effects may even have increased. For example, in 1955 women earned about 64 percent as much as men did in the same job; in 1970 they earned only about 58 percent as much; in 1977 the figure was still about 58 percent. This gap even remains when male and female workers are matched for tenure on the job, rated skill, education, and other variables (Suter and Miller, 1973; Levitin, Quinn, and Staines, 1973).

Sex discrimination affects not only women's salary and rank, but basic employment opportunities as well. This type of discrimination was documented in a study of corporate hiring practices by Stephen Cohen and Kerry Bunker (1975). These researchers contacted 150 male job recruiters whose job entailed interviewing students at college placement offices throughout the country. Each researcher was given a packet of information, including a job description and an application form from a job seeker. The job description was either for a traditional male-related job—personnel technician—or for a traditional female-related job—editorial assistant. Identical information was provided for each applicant regarding background, education, college activities, past job experience, career objectives, and references. Even transcripts of an alleged interview were provided. All information was the same except the applicant's sex and first name. Recruiters were asked to indicate whether or not the applicant was acceptable for the job. The results showed that while a majority of the applicants were considered acceptable for each job regardless of sex, the recruiters were much more likely to prefer males to females for the personnel-technician job and females to males for the editorial-assistant job. In another study, male and female college students responded to 256 classified employment advertisements and were met with clear-cut sex discrimination from over one-third of the employers (Levinson, 1975).

Does awareness of such sex-role stereotyping help alleviate the problem of job discrimination against women? If so, one might imagine that psychologists would be immune to sex discrimination. Unfortunately, this does not seem to be the case. In a 1970 study (Fidell, 1970), descriptions of prospective job applicants were sent to the chairpersons of each of the 228 colleges and universities in the United States that offers graduate degrees in psychology. Each description contained ten paragraphs detailing the professional activities of a hypothetical psychologist. The chairperson was asked to judge his or her "current impression about the chances of getting an offer for a full-time position." Each prospective job applicant was described in some of the descriptions as being male and in some of the descriptions as being female. The chairpersons were predominantly male, and the male applicants were consistently favored over the female applicants. While females were most of-

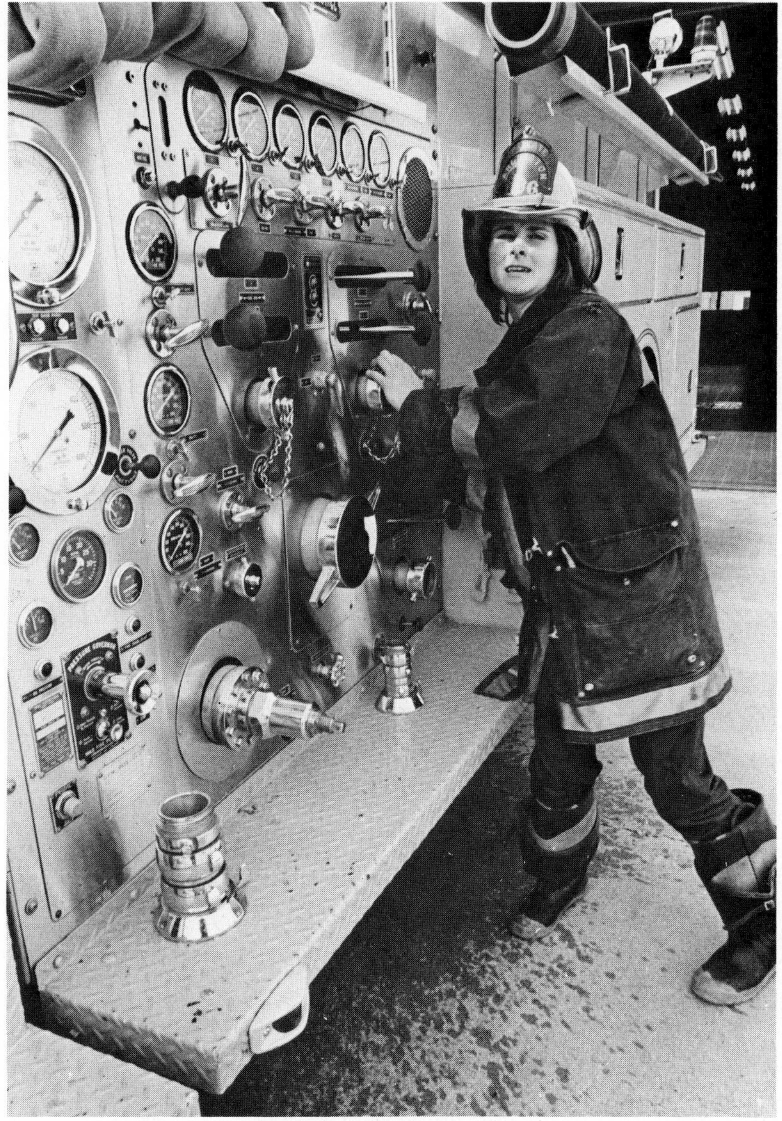

Sex discrimination has restricted women's salary, status, and job opportunities. Recently, however, alternatives to traditional sex roles have become acceptable, and women have begun to enter "male" occupations, such as firefighting. *(© Abigail Heyman / Magnum)*

ten recommended for assistant-professorships (the lowest professorial rank), males were most often recommended for associate-professorships (the middle level). In addition, the men were more often recommended for jobs that would lead to tenure than were the women. Finally, while at least one of the men was recommended for the highest rank of full professor, no woman was.

THE FUTURE

There are some signs that conditions are changing in the direction of freeing women from the rigidity of traditional sex-role expectations (Harrison, 1976). First, as technological development advances, the physical differences that exist between men and women will mean less in terms of job requirements and skills. Second,

FOCUS ON APPLICATIONS

SEX DISCRIMINATION ON THE JOB: THE CASE OF THE WONDER BREAD FIVE

Five middle-aged clerical workers at the Wonder Baking Company in Beverly Hills, California, have learned firsthand about sexism in employment. Although they refer to each other as "girls," they have also been known as "the Wonder Bread Five" since they began a four-year legal battle with one of the world's largest conglomerates, International Telephone and Telegraph, the multinational corporation that bakes Wonder Bread. As one complainant said, "They thought we were a bunch of dippy broads. . . .They thought it would all go away because we would get tired of fighting." But the case has not gone away, and the story of the Wonder Bread Five was recently told in the *Los Angeles Times*, as follows.

The setting is unique: Right in the heart of the Beverly Hills industrial area stands the Wonder Bread bakery, one of more than 60 facilities operated by ITT Continental Baking Co.

The plot is controversial: The Wonder Bread Five filed sex discrimination and harassment charges against their employer, alleging in court and in government agency complaints that they became victimized by a management campaign initiated in 1976 to rid the office of women who either were sexually unattractive to male managers or who did not respond to their sexual advances.

Further, government documents and court records show the women to have alleged that:

—Female office employees received written reprimands for errors and tardiness and were given additional duties, while male employees were not treated in the same manner; at the same time, women were denied equal opportunities for overtime pay.

The Wonder Bread Five. *(L.A. Times Photo)*

—Women were denied promotional opportunities and were not given the chance to be placed in management-training programs or educational assistance-tuition refund programs.

—Sexual remarks and advances were made by the general manager to female employees, who were treated in a demeaning manner when they failed to respond to his remarks and advances.

The federal Equal Employment Opportunity Commission (EEOC) unsuccessfully tried to negotiate an out-of-court settlement based on these charges. Later the charges were dismissed by a federal court judge.

However, a recently released U.S. Department of Labor report substantiates a number of the Wonder Bread Five's allegations based on a three-month investigation of the facility.

The six-page summary report concluded that ITT Continental Baking Co. was in violation of more than 20 provisions of Labor Department regulations.

Specifically, in regard to preferential treat-

the changing patterns of employment in our society suggest that role models for young girls have changed and will continue to do so. Thus, the proportion of married women holding down jobs has increased from 30.5 percent in 1960 to almost 60 percent in 1978. While women accounted for only 4 percent of the students in law school in 1960, they accounted for 19 percent in 1974. In medical school, the comparable figures were 6 percent in 1960 and 18 percent in 1974. If such changes continue, there is room for cautious optimism about the options that will be available to men and women in the years ahead.

ment, the report states: "An analysis of the personnel files for employees working in the Accounting Department revealed that during the period 1970 to 1977, 70 reprimands were given to females and only one to males . . . An analysis of personnel files for all employees working in the Accounting Department revealed many documented errors for females but no documented errors for males."

Besides pointing out that there were 204 male sales representatives and only one woman, the report states that Wonder Bread employed 26 male transport drivers and no females in 1977.

In addition, the investigation report states that the female office supervisor, who managed the office where four of the five women worked, told government investigators that "she was required to take disciplinary action against her employees while this was not required of male supervisors. These actions included issuing reprimands to her female employees for lateness, overstaying on break time and job performance."

(The supervisor, Jean Bacon, quit her job with the company and filed her own sex-discrimination suit against ITT Continental Baking Co., asking for $425,000 compensation after alleging that she was doing the same job as a man but getting less pay and that she was promised educational-training benefits she never received. Her case recently was settled out of court.)

On overtime pay: "A review of the time cards for office employees . . . for October and November, 1977, showed that males worked 49.9 more overtime hours than females."

On promotional opportunities: "A file search revealed that there were 29 promotions at the facility in 1976; only one was a female . . . (In 1978) a file review of employees in the office . . . revealed that there were 11 female promotions. However, they were limited to office and clerical positions and lead clerk in the thrift store."

On management-training opportunities: "Our investigation revealed that no female employee had been given the opportunity to participate in the Office Management Trainee Program even though several females employed by the company possess work experience and qualifications equal to and at times exceeding those of males in managerial jobs . . . A sample analysis was made to determine if managerial employees possess the education requirement delineated in the Office Management Trainee Position Description . . .The sampling revealed that several males did not meet the requirements of the position description."

On educational-assistance opportunities: "Our investigation further revealed that the company provides an Educational Assistance–Tuition Refund Program for all nonbargaining personnel who have been employed on a permanent and full-time basis for six months or more. The program is not available to union employees. This department has concluded that this practice is discriminatory . . ."

On sexual harassment: "An investigation was conducted to substantiate or refute the allegation that female employees were subjected to sexual remarks and advances by the general manager and that their refusal to respond to such remarks and advances resulted in their being treated in a demeaning manner. These allegations were substantiated."

Finally, the Labor Department said, "Our investigation further indicates that the contractor has taken no remedial action to resolve the complainants' allegations other than general affirmative-action commitments."

***Source*: *Los Angeles Times*, June 18, 1980, Part V, p. 1.**

From an applied-psychology point of view, interesting questions remain as to what kinds of intervention techniques would be effective in encouraging these trends. Such programs as Affirmative Action are no doubt partly responsible for the lessening of sexism in employment. According to the technique mentioned repeatedly in this book, "when behaviors change, attitudes will follow." Psychological work in this area has so far been directed toward assessing the problem of sexism, documenting its existence and its development. Future work should focus on appropriate intervention programs and seek to assess the effectiveness of these programs.

SUMMARY

In contrast to basic research, which seeks to understand general principles of social behavior, applied research in social psychology seeks to shed light on real-life problems. Applied research approaches this task in three ways: (1) by assessing the nature of a problem, such as racial or sexual discrimination; (2) by experimentally comparing the effectiveness of various solutions in real-life settings, such as providing increased control over life events to institutionalized elderly persons; and (3) by testing interventions in simulated settings, such as giving different types of information to subjects in mock juries. The five topics discussed in this chapter demonstrate these techniques.

Institutionalized elderly persons have lost a wide range of control over their lives, but research demonstrates that increased control can slow the decline in health, alertness, and activity. When nursing home residents could predict or control visits from college students, the residents were healthier, more active, and more hopeful than similar residents who had no control over visits. Similar results were obtained among residents who could choose plants and weekly movies, when compared to residents who could not. These results suggest that interventions that provide increased control over life events can have dramatic positive benefits for the health and well-being of the institutionalized aged.

Research on household density shows that high density by itself does not negatively affect the health and behavior of the general population. However, population subgroups who lack control over their level of social interaction—for example, children, the elderly, or prisoners—do experience such negative effects of high density as high blood pressure, higher incidences of illness, and social withdrawal.

According to the contact hypothesis, racial prejudice can be reduced by increasing contact between races, and this assumption has guided many government policy decisions. However, research suggests that the effect only occurs under certain circumstances, which include: (1) the participants are of equal status; (2) the participants must cooperate on a task; (3) the attributes of minority participants contradict existing stereotypes; (4) the setting promotes personal or intimate associations; and (5) social norms favor interracial association. In one experiment that met all these conditions, 35 percent of the prejudiced college student subjects changed their attitudes from negative to positive.

Social psychologists are becoming more active in the legal process. Their efforts have helped to identify potential jurists who are likely to favor defense attorneys' arguments in trials such as the Harrisburg Seven conspiracy trial. Researchers have also investigated the importance of the victim's and the defendant's physical attractiveness in the decisions of simulated juries. Although other research cautions against applying laboratory findings to the legal system, simulated jury studies suggest that justice may not be as blind as we would hope.

Sexism is based on widely shared stereotypes about the abilities and characteristics of men and women. Such stereotypes are transmitted through mass media and have been especially prevalent in children's literature and television. A major consequence of such stereotypes is the differential evaluations of men's and women's performance both on laboratory tasks and in the work world. As a result, female job applicants with skills equal to male applicants are frequently limited to "female-type" jobs.

Each of these sections demonstrates how applied social psychology contributes to assessing social problems and testing interventions both in the laboratory and in the real world.

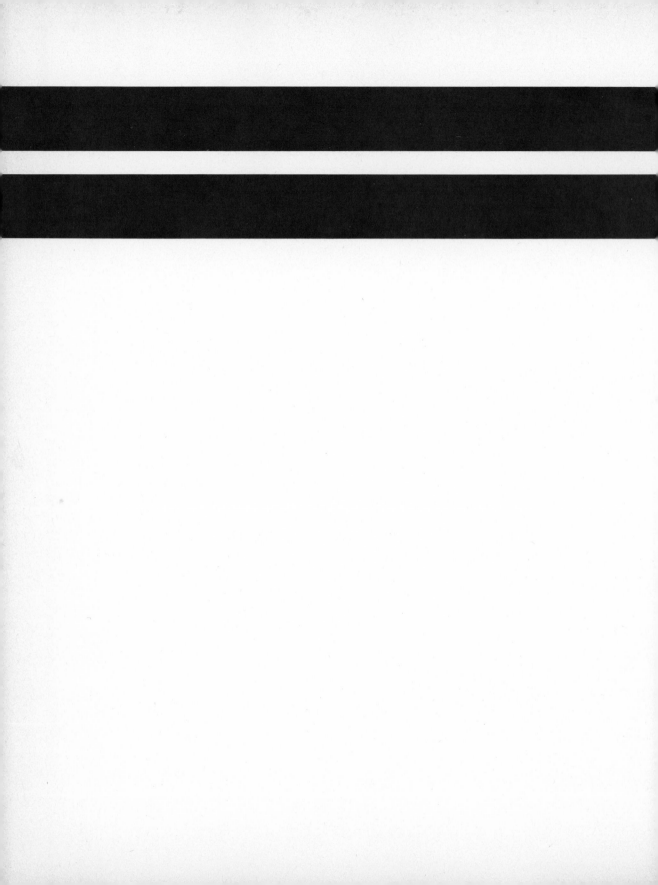

PART FIVE

EPILOGUE

CHAPTER FOURTEEN

SOCIAL PSYCHOLOGY: EXPLORING THE HUMAN CONDITION

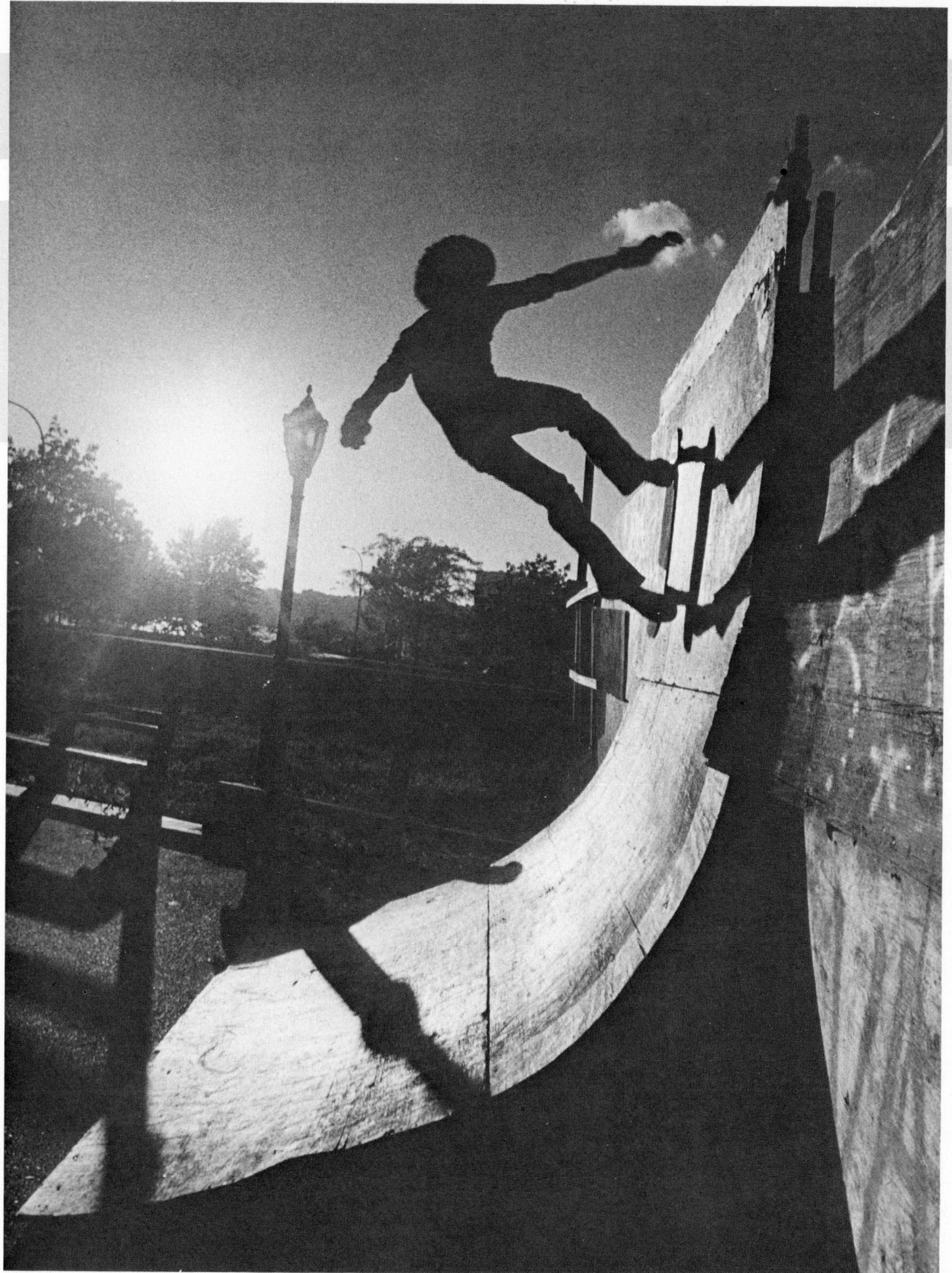

We began this book with a broad definition of social psychology as the empirical study of human social experience—of the people and social situations in our life and how they affect us. We said that historically social psychologists have had two concerns: a desire to understand social processes and a desire to help solve social problems. We endorsed the view of Kurt Lewin that human behavior is influenced by both persons and environments. And we added that the environment not only influences our behavior directly but also indirectly, as it shapes the type of persons we become over time. Therefore, social situations can have an enormous impact on the way we act, think, and feel. However, our own behavior is also affecting the environments that are affecting us. The process, therefore, is reciprocal: we encounter the environment, the environment affects us, and we affect the environment. Social psychology attempts to understand this process and to apply this understanding to social problems.

How successfully is social psychology achieving its goals? Let's consider some examples drawn from the chapters of this book.

INDIVIDUAL PROCESSES

In Chapter 3 we learned that our self-concept is shaped by several types of social forces: by the reactions of others to our behavior, by the ways we compare ourselves with others, and by the way other people influence our behavior. At the same time, we are also observing our own behavior and theorizing about our identities, developing a self-theory. Then, as we develop a sense of our own "self," this self influences our behavior. The self functions as a schema that affects the way we perceive the world and process information. The self also helps regulate our behavior, and, to the extent that we are more or less aware of our self, it exerts more or less control over our behavior. But, once again, the factors that determine our degree of self-awareness are often the social situations that surround us.

The same case can be made for the development and functioning of attitudes, as we saw in Chapter 4. A variety of social forces shape our attitudes: attitudes can be learned through social conditioning; they can be inferred from observing our own behavior; and they can be acquired in order to maintain consistency among our already established attitudes and behaviors. And like our self-concept, attitudes exert more or less influence over our behavior, depending on their strength and salience versus the strength and salience of the surrounding social environment.

Similarly, attitudes can be changed in the same way they are acquired, as explained in Chapter 5, through learning and conditioning, consistency needs, and self-inferences. Understanding how and when attitudes affect behavior as well as how they can be changed is important for solving social problems such as racial prejudice, sexism, conservation of resources, or health practices.

We have seen that social situations influence the development and functioning of "inner states" such as our self-concept, values, and attitudes. We have also seen that social situations render these inner states more or less important in controlling our behavior. For example, when the surrounding situation is fairly neutral—as in a voting booth—our attitudes and values may predict our behavior fairly well; but when the surrounding situation is extreme—as in an uncontrolled mob—our values and attitudes may exert little influence over our behavior, and we may be strongly influenced by the powerful forces around us.

What happens when we turn our attention from these inner states and focus instead on interpersonal behavior? What mixture of internal and external factors accounts for how we perceive others, whom we are attracted to, when and why we are aggressive and altruistic, and how we respond in situations of social interdependence?

INTERPERSONAL PROCESSES

When we turn from individual processes to interpersonal processes, we again find the dispositional/situational distinction useful. When we

A group gathers in a candlelit New York City bar during a blackout. When such crises occur they bring fear and uncertainty, and almost all people become more affiliative than usual. *(© Jim Anderson 1980 / Woodfin Camp & Assoc.)*

focused on person perception and attribution in Chapter 6, the dispositional/situational distinction became an important way to organize and comprehend the behavior of other people. In order to interact with others, we need to be able to understand and predict their behavior. To do this, we need to know whether their behavior reflects stable personal dispositions or temporary situational influences. How we attribute responsibility for behavior affects our responses in most of the social settings of our lives—from understanding the behavior of a lover to stereotyping a whole class of people. And as we learned, our attributions depend in part on the specific social events that happen to attract our attention, whether we play the role of actor or observer, and numerous other factors that influence how we process social information and how we retrieve it from memory.

When we considered affiliation and attraction in Chapter 7, we saw that some people, such as firstborns, have higher affiliative needs than others due to social conditions of their upbringing. But more importantly, we saw that almost all people become increasingly affiliative under certain situational circumstances—for example, when they are afraid or uncertain. Furthermore, our attraction to specific others often hinges on such seemingly innocuous situational factors as proximity and frequency of exposure. Even passionate love—one of the most significant and intense human experiences—is influenced by the situational factors that produce arousal and provide the appropriate labels to explain the arousal.

In Chapters 8 and 9 we learned that some people may be more aggressive or altruistic than others "by nature"—that is, dispositionally. However, we also saw that a major influence on such dispositional tendencies was whether people were exposed to aggressive or altruistic social models while they were growing up. Furthermore, we learned that regardless of dispositions, the majority of people can become increasingly aggressive or altruistic as the result of a variety of situational factors. If we can understand how these factors influence aggression and altruism, then we can begin to apply this knowledge to social problems—for instance, how we can evaluate the controversial effects of television violence on behavior, or how we can encourage people to intervene in emergencies and be responsive to others' needs.

Chapter 10 focused on social interdependence as revealed in gaming research on cooperation and conflict. Even in these laboratory games, cooperation between partners hinged on such situational factors as the amount of communication between partners, the history of interaction between partners, and the resulting level of trust. At the same time, we saw that some people are dispositionally more cooperative or competitive than others, and their responses on experimental games reflect these characteristic tendencies. Yet, understanding what factors lead most people to behave cooperatively, regardless of their dispositional tendencies, can help solve real-world problems of cooperation such as energy usage and conservation.

SOCIAL ECOLOGY AND INDIVIDUAL BEHAVIOR

Human behavior is influenced by social factors not only at the individual and interpersonal level, but also at the level of the surrounding sociophysical environment. In Part IV we examined how people respond in groups, how behavior is shaped by the physical spaces people inhabit, and how knowledge of social psychology can be applied to solving social problems.

Chapter 11 examined how groups work and how they affect individuals. We saw that different people play different roles in a group—for example, social-emotional leaders versus task leaders—and these roles reflect dispositional characteristics. At the same time, we saw that roles shift with the nature and function of the group. Furthermore, the majority of people are affected by group pressures to become more conforming, more extreme in the direction of the group's values, more self-censoring, and sometimes more aroused and activated than usual. Understanding these typical reactions to group pressures can help groups to make good decisions and act with increasing rationality.

Social psychologists have begun to study how the physical environment influences behavior, as discussed in Chapter 12. Here, too, we can find the same dispositional/situational distinction. For example, certain people have larger personal-space needs than others, yet almost all personal-space needs are affected similarly by personal-space invasions or situational stressors. Moreover, while most people can be affected by potential environmental stressors such as crowding or noise, how an individual appraises these environmental events and how much control is felt over the environment can significantly affect reactions to these external forces. Thus, a goal of environmental psychology is not only to understand the effect of surrounding environments on human social behavior, but also how people can be given a sense of personal control over the environment. And these findings have clear implications for environmental design.

In Chapter 13, we focused on five social problems. We made explicit how an understanding of social processes can contribute to solutions and analyses of major social problems. The concern may be with people's inner states—such as attitudes toward minorities or women—or with external environmental conditions—such as residential crowding, homes for the aged, or the social conditions that lead to prejudice. The point is that social problems cannot be understood and changed unless we also understand the social processes that underlie them.

PERSONS, ENVIRONMENTS, AND BEHAVIOR

Is it possible to specify the relative importance of dispositional versus situational factors in this complicated interplay of persons and environments? When researchers have tried to specify the relative importance of "person" factors versus "situation" factors in accounting for social behavior, they find that neither one by itself can account for sizable amounts of variance (Bowers, 1973; Jaccard, 1974; Block, 1977; Mischel, 1977). However, the *interaction* of person factors and situation factors can account

a

b

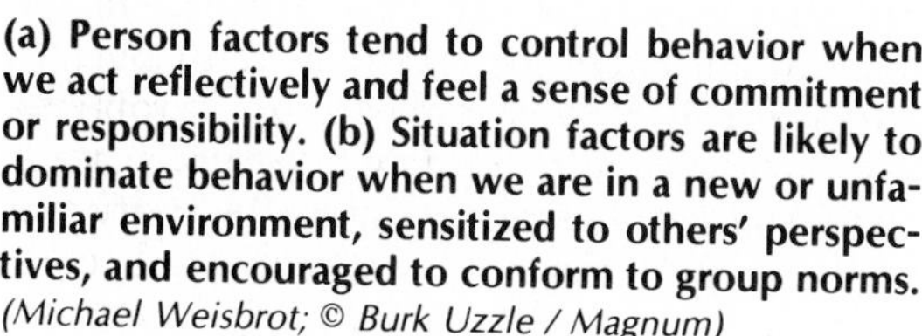

(a) Person factors tend to control behavior when we act reflectively and feel a sense of commitment or responsibility. (b) Situation factors are likely to dominate behavior when we are in a new or unfamiliar environment, sensitized to others' perspectives, and encouraged to conform to group norms. *(Michael Weisbrot; © Burk Uzzle / Magnum)*

for almost twice as much of the variance as either factor by itself. In other words, to understand behavior involves an understanding of how persons and environments interact.

What form does this interaction take? Under what conditions can we expect person factors to be more influential than situation factors on behavior and vice versa? Mark Snyder (1978) has outlined a number of circumstances that render person factors relatively more important than situation factors in controlling behavior. These include environments that

1. encourage a reflective, contemplative approach to action;
2. enhance one's sense of commitment or personal responsibility for one's actions;
3. heighten one's awareness of self as a potential cause of behavior;
4. make it impossible to define one's beliefs and attitudes as irrelevant to one's behavior;
5. provide normative support for congruence between behavior and beliefs.

On the other hand, Snyder has also proposed a number of circumstances that favor situation factors over person factors in controlling behavior. These include environments that

1. are novel, unfamiliar, and contain relevant sources of social comparison;
2. make individuals uncertain of or confused about their inner beliefs;
3. suggest that one's attitudes are socially undesirable;
4. sensitize one to others' perspectives and motivate conformity with group norms;
5. motivate individuals to maximize gains in their self-presentation strategies.

Note, however, that even when person factors are likely to be paramount, it is the external social situation that boosts their importance. Thus, even here it is the interaction of situation and disposition that produces behavior. Social behavior, then, is largely determined by the social situations that surround us, either as they influence our behavior directly or as they have influenced the development of our personal dispositions and thus affect our behavior indirectly.

A CONCLUDING OBSERVATION

We have argued that social psychology is the empirical study of human social experience and that its subject is the human condition. Yet students often resist an empirical view of human experience. "If I become so aware of all the social situational factors that influence my behavior," one might ask, "how can I ever just take life as it comes? What if I become so objective about myself that I no longer feel spontaneous?"

The answer, we believe, is that social psychology does not detract from an individual's capacity for subjective experience; instead, it sharpens the capacity for objective analysis. As a result, the individual should be able to approach life not only subjectively but also objectively, with a scientific understanding of the phenomena that one feels and experiences. To use an analogy, the student and professional in the field are left somewhat like a meteorologist viewing a sunset. The scientist knows that the spectacle is a product of light rays, water droplets, and smog, but, at the same time, he or she can marvel at the view and feel humbled before such a heavenly display; to be able to explain a phenomenon does not diminish one's capacity to experience it.

Let us close by urging you not to lose the "feel" of human experience as you seek to explain it. After all, the data of social psychology are human thoughts, emotions, and actions, and the research ultimately makes sense when it enriches human experience at an immediate, personal level. Our hope is that social psychology will not only help you to understand the data of your own experience, but that it will also enlarge your capacity for experience itself. Like the Zen master who wished his students to learn that true enlightenment is beyond reasoning and understanding, we close with a proverb:

Nothing is left to you at this moment
But to have a good laugh.

GLOSSARY

Affiliation A learned drive to associate with others.

Aggression Intentional and unjsutified verbal or physical abuse.

Alarm The first stage in Hans Selye's theory of stress; it is characterized by a discharge of adrenaline, a faster heartbeat, and a generally aroused state that energizes the organism to respond to the stressor. *See also* Exhaustion; Physiological arousal; Resistance.

Altruism (Prosocial Behavior) Behavior that shows concern and caring for one's fellow human beings and is performed without expectation of personal gain.

Attitude A relatively enduring disposition to evaluate persons, events, or objects in a favorable or unfavorable way.

Attitude Scaling Method Any system by which a researcher measures the strength and direction of a subject's attitudes. *See also* Guttman scale; Likert scale; Semantic differential; Thurstone scale.

Attribution Boomerang Effect According to Michael Storms and Richard Nisbett, a reduction in an individual's anxiety that occurs if he or she can attribute the physiological state to an external source.

Attribution Theory The psychological perspective that is concerned with how individuals explain the causes of behavior in themselves and in others.

Audience Effects Forces that influence an individual's performance of a task when he or she is alone but knows that other people are watching. *See also* Coaction effects.

Balance Theory A cognitive consistency theory that studies the relationships among three elements in a triangle comprised of two perceivers and an attitude object or two attitude objects and a perceiver and that determines which structures are imbalanced and will change to restore balance.

Behaviorism The school of psychology that emphasized events in the environment and the consequences of behavior as the determinants of what people do, think, and feel.

Bystander Intervention An individual's breaking out of his or her role as a bystander and helping another person in an emergency.

Catharsis The release of violent or aggressive emotions, which, according to Freudian theory, allows an organism to return to an equilibrium state.

Causal Schema Stored knowledge that an individual may draw on in lieu of a full-fledged attributional analysis in order to understand and react to social situations quickly.

Central Trait A descriptive adjective that colors a perceiver's impression of an individual because of its high intercorrelation with other adjectives in a list of descriptive trait terms.

Classical Conditioning A procedure in which a conditioned response is established through the association of one stimulus with a second stimulus that is known to elicit an unconditioned response.

Close Relationship According to Harold Kelley, a relationship in which the partners are characterized by three qualities: interdependence—being affected by each other's moods and actions; responsiveness—sensitivity to each other's needs; and understanding each other's enduring dispositions—a desire to know what the other person is "really like."

Coaction Effects Forces that influence an individual's performance of a task when others who are present are working on the same task. *See also* Audience effects.

Coercive Power Social influence acquired through an individual's ability to administer or mediate punishments to group members.

Cognitive Consistency Theory A set of related theories that propose that people seek harmony, balance, or consistency among their attitudes, beliefs and behaviors and that people are motivated to change their attitudes, beliefs, or behaviors in order to reduce the psychological tension caused by inconsistency among these cognitive elements.

Cognitive Dissonance A state of psychological tension, produced by holding two simultaneous and opposing cognitions, that motivates the individual to reduce the tension, often by changing or rejecting one of the cognitions.

Cognitive Psychology The branch of psychology that is concerned with the processing of information and the acquisition of knowledge.

Cohesiveness The sum of all the forces that hold people together as members of a group.

Commitment The degree to which an individual is psychologically bound to a behavior such as group membership.

Commons Dilemma a real-world problem in which the available supply of a resouce is threatened by overuse. In the short term, noncooperation is more profitable among members of a commons, but in the long term, cooperation is more profitable.

Communicator Credibility The degree to which a communicator is perceived as having expertise and trustworthiness.

Companionate Love According to E. Berscheid and E. Walster, the comfortable warmth and caring we feel for those people who have shared experiences with us over time. *See also* Passionate love.

Compliance The change of overt behavior that occurs as a result of group pressure. *See also* Private acceptance.

Conformity The tendency of a group member to change his or her behavior or attitudes in order to correspond with the behavior or attitudes of other group members. *See also* Compliance; Private acceptance.

Consensus According to Harold Kelley, one of three qualities necessary to attribute causal responsibility for behavior. It is the degree to which an individual's responses are similar to those of others in the same situation. *See also* Consistency; Distinctiveness.

Consistency According to Harold Kelley, one of three qualities necessary to attribute causal responsibility for behavior. It is the degree to which an individual responds similarly across time and modalities. *See also* Consensus; Distinctiveness.

Contingency Theory of Leadership The theory that different types of situations require different types of leaders.

Contributions Rule A standard of justice that bases the amount of benefits an individual should receive on his or her contributions to the community. *See also* Equality rule.

Convergent Validation An indication of an experiement's validity that occurs when several different research methods converge on the same findings.

Correlational Research A research method that examines the degree to which two or more variables are related. *See also* Correlation coefficient; Positive correlation; Negative correlation.

Correlation Coefficient A mathematical indication of the extent to which two variables are related. A correlation coefficient can vary from +1.0 (perfect positive correlation) to −1.0 (perfect negative correlation).

Counterarguing A process in which a person who is listening to or reading a persuasive message thinks up arguments that attack the communicator's points.

Counterattitudinal Advocacy Advocating a position opposed to one's initial attitude.

Covariation According to Harold Kelley, the principle by which people observe a behavior under a number of conditions to determine whether the behavior should be attributed to internal or external factors.

Crowding Objectively, defined as density, or the amount of physical space per person in a particular setting; subjectively, defined as a perceived restriction or intrusion that may motivate the individual to escape or seek less crowded conditions.

Danger Control *See* Parallel response model.

Deindivuation A loss of self-awareness and self-regulation due to sensory overload or immersion.

Demand Characteristics Qualities of the experimental laboratory situation that encourage a subject to act or react in ways that he or she would not consider in real life.

Density-Intensity Theory The contention that crowding (objectively defined as high density) will intensify whatever response an individual is having to a situation.

Dependent Variable A variable in an experiment that is affected by (or "depends on") as experimenter's deliberate manipulation of the independent variable. *See also* Independent variable.

Discounting In attribution theory, the rejection of one explanation for behavior in favor of another more plausible explanation.

Dispositionally Controlled Individuals In Snyder's self-monitoring theory, people who are less attuned to the social appropriateness of their behavior than to their internal feelings concerning their behavior. *See also* Situationally controlled individuals.

Dissonance *See* Cognitive dissonance.

Distinctiveness According to Harold Kelley, one of three qualities necessary to determine the cause of a behavior. It is the extent to which a behavior is unique to a specific situation. *See also* Consensus; Consistency.

Divergent Perspectives Hypothesis Edward Jones and Richard Nisbett's contention that actors are likely to attriubte responsibility for a given behavior to situational influences, while observers are likely to attribute responsibility for that behavior to stable dispositions within the actors.

Egocentrism In group dynamics, a positive view held by a group of its own members and purposes.

Emotional Loneliness The lack of a personal, intimate relationship. *See also* Social loneliness.

Emotional Role Playing Acting out a role that has implications for one's own life (such as a smoker role-playing a lung-cancer victim), often resulting in attitude changes.

Empathy The ability to sense another person's experiences.

Empiricism An approach to knowledge that relies on observable facts or experience.

Environmental Force In Heider's version of attribution theory, any circumstance or entity outside of an individual that influences the outcome of his or her actions.

Equality Rule A standard of justice that grants all individuals an equal share in the benefits of a community regardless of their contribution to it. *See also* Contributions rule.

Ethology The study of animal behavior.

Exhaustion The third stage of Hans Selye's theory of stress. It is characterized by a slowing of the body's functions as a result of uusuccessful attempts to cope with a chronic stressor. *See also* Alarm; Resistance.

Expectance-Value Theory A cognitive theory of attitude formation that examines peoples' evaluations of attitude objects in light of their expectations about those attitude objects.

Experimental Approaches Methods of understanding phenomena that rely on the systematic control and observation of relevant variables in order to reveal cause-and-effect relationships among them. *See also* Dependent variable; Independent variable.

Experimenter Effects The unintentional influences that an experimenter's voice, dress, behavior, or other attributes may have on the behavior of his or her subjects.

Expertise In communicator credibility, how well informed and intelligent the audience believes the source to be.

Expert Power Social influence an individual gains when he or she is perceived as having a skill or knowledge needed by other members of a group.

External Attribution Assigning casual responsibility for an individual's behavior to environmental or social circumstances.

Fear-as-a-Drive Model The theory that an individual can be more persuaded by a communication when its reassuring recommendations help relieve the fear produced by a frightening message.

Fear Control *See* Parallel response model.

Field Experiments Experiments that take place in natural settings, in which manipulations of the independent variable and observations of the dependent variables may be naturally occurring phenomena. Cause-and-effect analysis is possible when the subjects have been randomly distributed and all other variables are equal.

Frustration-Aggression Hypothesis A theory that contends that aggressive behavior always presupposes the existence of frustration, and the existence of frustration always leads to some form of aggression.

Gain-Loss Hypothesis The hypothesis that we are more attracted to people who initially dislike us but who warm up later on than to people who like us initially but who then turn cold.

Gestalt Psychology The school of psychology concerned with perceptual processes and the ways in which individuals organize varied stimuli into orderly wholes and patterns.

Group Dynamics A general term for group behavior: completing tasks, resolving conflicts, helping and influencing others, and making decisions.

Groupthink A group decision-making process that results in unrealistic outcomes because of shared illusions of the group's invulnerability, morality, or unanimity.

Guttman Scale An attitude measurement scale that contains either favorable or unfavorable statements arranged hierarchically, so that if a subject agrees with the strongest statement, he or she will agree with the weaker ones as well. Conversely, if a subject disagrees with the weakest statement, he or she will disagree with the stronger ones also.

Hedonic Dissonance The psychological conflict that occurs when an individual willingly engages in behavior he or she considers unpleasant.

Imbalance In Heider's balance theory, the state of psychological tension that arises when an individual holds conflicting attitudes and beliefs and that motivates an individual to change his or her cognitive structure in order to restore balance.

Immunization In attitude change theory, a technique that induces resistance to subsequent persuasion by exposing an individual to weak forms of the persuasive message in order to stimulate the individual's attitudinal defenses. *See also* Refutational defense treatments.

Implicational Molecule According to Robert Abelson, a self-contained set of statements that, taken together, is psychologically consistent.

Implicit Theory of Personality A person's understanding of which traits are usually associated with or implied by other traits. This theory enables an individual to form integrated impressions of another person based on limited information.

Impression Formation The process by which people form their initial impressions about other people, usually based on a few pieces of discrete information.

Impression Management An individual's deliberate alteration of his or her behavior in order to create a desired perception of himself or herself by others.

Independent Variable A variable in an experiment that is manipulated by the experimenter in order to observe its effects on the dependent variable as a means of inferring cause-and-effect relationships. *See also* Dependent variable.

Information Integration Theory Anderson's theory that a person's attitude toward an object can be estimanted by averaging the degree of positive and negative evaluation of that object as expressed by his or her beliefs toward it.

Information Processing Approach to Attitudes According to many social psychologists, a complex cognitive process by which individuals acquire knowledge and form and change attitudes. These researchers emphasize the individual's role as an evaluator of information received from the environment.

Ingratiation Behavior designed to impress people in order to gain personal advantage.

Institutional Aggression Aggressive acts committed by people who are merely "doing their jobs."

Instrumental (Operant) Conditioning A procedure in which an organism's responses, including attitudes, are shaped by their rewarding or punishing consequences.

Interaction Process Analysis Bales's system for the observation of group behavior based on a distinction between two types of behavior within groups: one to direct the group toward the completion of its goals and one to maintain social relationships during the process.

Internal Attribution Assigning causal responsibility for an individual's behavior to dispositional factors within the actor.

Intimacy/Privacy Regulation A theory explaining the need for personal space as a means of controlling the levels of intimacy and privacy we desire with other people.

Latitude of Acceptance A range of statements about an attitude object with which an individual will agree.

Latitude of Rejection A range of statements about an attitude object with which an individual will not agree.

Learned Helplessness The expectancy that an individual's responses have no effects on the environment, which results in a cessation of responding. It has been theorized that learned helplessness may be one result of uncontrollable crowding or noise.

Learning Theory Approach to Attitudes The belief that attitudes are formed and changed through the conditioning of stimulus-response relationships.

Legitimate Power Social influence gained when an individual is perceived as having the right to influence the behavior of others in a group.

Level of Significance The probablility that the findings of an experiment could have occurred by chance. A .05 level of significance means that the findings would have occurred by chance as rarely as 5 times in 100, and thus the findings are probably reliable; a .01 level of significance means that the findings would have occurred by chance as rarely as 1 time in 100, and thus the results are almost certainly reliable.

Likert Scale An attitude measurement scale that evaluates how strongly respondents agree or disagree with favorable and unfavorable statements about an attitude object.

Like Scale A scale constructed by Zick Rubin to measure the extent of a person's liking, respect, and admiration for another person. *See also* Love Scale.

Love Scale A scale constructed by Zick Rubin to measure the extent of a person's love, attachment to, caring for, and intimacy with another person. *See also* Like Scale.

Low-Control-of-Effects Syndrome The tendency to feel powerless against external circumstances and actions.

Matching Hypothesis The hypothesis that people choose dating and marriage partners whom they perceive as being as attractive as themselves.

Membership Group Any group to which a person is perceived to belong.

Modeling In social learning theory, a type of learning in which an individual observes another person's behavior and its consequences and then performs the same behavior later on under appropriate incentive conditions.

Motivational Orientation A term for an individual's characteristic behavior in laboratory games, that refers to an interaction strategy such as cooperation, competition, or individualism.

Multiple-Act Critierion Fishbein and Ajzen's term for a general behavioral index based on an average or combination of several specific behaviors. Attitudes have been found to correlate more highly with a multiple-act criterion than with specific behaviors.

Multiple Selves Kenneth Gergen's view of the self as a flexible process, rather than a single entity, thus allowing for the possibility of several "real" selves in one person.

Mutuality According to G. Levinger and J. D. Snoek, a relationship with another person that involves interpersonal closeness and interdependence. *See also* Surface contact; Unilateral awareness.

Negative Correlation A relationship between two variables in which an increase in one is associated with a decrease in the other. *See also* Positive correlation.

Nominal Group A collection of people who happen to be in a given place at a given time. They act independently and feel no responsibility for the other members of the group.

Norms Shared expectations or beliefs about how people should act and think.

Observational Approaches Methods of studying social behavior that rely on observation rather than manipulation of variables; such an approach does not allow a cause-and-effect analysis.

Operant Conditioning *See* Instrumental conditioning.

Oversufficient Justification Receiving external rewards for engaging in behavior that is already intrinsically motivated; according to self-perception theory, such rewards may undermine the indivudual's internal motivations for the act.

Parallel Response Model The theory that fear-arousing communications produce two parallel and distinct reactions, fear control and danger control, which motivate the individual to reduce fear (an emotional process) and to cope with the danger at hand (a cognitive problem-solving process).

Participant Observation An observational approach to understanding social behavior that relies upon the researcher's direct involvement in the social processes and the group being studied.

Passionate Love According to E. Berscheid and E. Walster, a strong sexual and emotional attraction to another person. *See also* Companionate love.

Personal Force In Heider's version of attribution theory, any quality within an individual, resulting from ability and effort, that influences the outcome of his or her behavior.

Personal Space A space with an invisible boundary around an individual into which intruders may not enter.

Person Perception The act of encountering and forming an impression of another person, either through direct or indirect contact.

Persuasibility Individual differences in reactions to persuasive messages.

Phenomenology The school of psychology that is concerned with an individual's subjective experience and perceptions of the world.

Physiological Psychology The branch of psychology that studies individual behavior at the level of internal physiological systems and processes.

Population In statistical analysis, the total membership of a group, class of objects, or class of events.

Positive Correlation A relationship between two variables in which an increase in one is associated with an increase in the other. *See also* Negative correlation.

Primacy Effect In person perception, the impression of an individual based on initial information received about that individual. *See also* Recency effect.

Primary Environments Those environments in which we live and work and over which we expect to have control.

Primary Territories Spaces used exclusively by an individual or a group on a permanent basis, clearly marked as theirs, and central to the day-to-day functioning of the occupant(s).

Prisoner's Dilemma An experimental gaming structure that offers its participants a choice between cooperation and noncooperation. The strategy chosen affects the outcomes of both players.

Private Acceptance Private change of attitude that may result from group membership. *See also* Compliance.

Prosocial Behavior *See* Altruism.

Psychological Group A collection of people who feel, think, and act together and who care about each other's needs.

Public Territories Spaces where all individuals have free access and property rights.

Recency Effect In person perception, the impression of an individual based on the most recently received information rather than initially received information. *See also* Primacy effect.

Reception In persuasion research, the ability of an individual to understand and evaluate the message being transmitted. *See also* Yielding.

Reciprocity In interpersonal attraction, developing a liking for those people who are attracted to us.

Reference Group Any group whose members matter to a given individual, even if the individual is not a member of that group.

Referent Power Social influence an individual gains when he or she is liked, respected, or identified with by the members of a group.

Refutational Defense Treatments Weak attacks on an individual's beliefs that often motivate the individual to argue against subsequent stronger attacks. *See also* Immunization.

Relationship-Oriented Leaders Leaders who are permissive, considerate, and concerned about the feelings of others.

Resistance The second stage in Hans Selye's theory of stress. It is characterized by the diversion of hormones to produce antibodies in an attempt to enable the organism to resist the stressor. *See also* Alarm; Exhaustion.

Reward Power Social influence gained when other members of a group perceive an individual as having the power to give rewards.

Role The expected behavior attached to a position in a group or social situation.

Sample In statistical analysis, a representative group of the entire population.

Secondary Environments Those public spaces that we inhabit briefly and seldom expect to control.

Secondary Territories Semipublic spaces that are used for social interaction on a fairly regular basis.

Self-Awareness A temporary state in which an individual's attention is focused on his or her own appearance, thoughts, emotions, and inner states, induced by situational circumstances such as mirrors, cameras, or observers.

Self-Concept A person's subjective interpretation of himself or herself.

Self-Consciousness An enduring trait or predisposition to focus attention on oneself.

Self-Disclosure The process of revealing oneself fully to significant others.

Self-Monitoring Mark Snyder's term for an individual's awareness of the social appropriateness of his or her behavior as it appears to others. *See also* Dispositionally controlled individuals; Situationally controlled individuals.

Self-Perception Theory Daryl Bem's view that people observe their own behavior and the situational circumstances in which it occurs in order to infer inner states and assign causal responsibility for the behavior.

Self-System Albert Bandura's belief that the individual has several self-concepts, each pertaining to specific circumstances and behaviors.

Semantic Differential An attitude measurement technique that asks respondents to rate an object on a scale composed of bipolar (opposite) adjectives.

Sentiment Relationship According to Fritz Heider, a relationship between one person and another person or object based on that individual's feelings toward the person or object. *See also* Unit relationship.

Significant Others Individuals—such as parents, teachers, and lovers—whose evaluations of oneself are important and who thus play major roles in shaping one's self-concept.

Simulation An experiment in which the variables are too complex or dangerous to manipulate and observe directly and which are thus presented in a preprogrammed way that is entirely controlled by the experimenter.

Situationally Controlled Individuals People who monitor and alter their behavior according to its social appropriateness. *See also* Dispositionally controlled individuals.

Sleeper Effect In attitude formation, the phenomenon that occurs when messages received from low-credibility sources become more believable over time because of dissociation of source and message.

Social-Comparison Theory Leon Festinger's theory that we evaluate the worth or appropriateness of our own behavior in light of the behaviors of similar others.

Social-Emotional Leaders Group leaders who specialize in making group members feel satisfied within the group by attending to the feelings of one or more group members. *See also* Task-oriented leaders.

Social Evolution An explanation of altruism as the result of prosocial norms that have developed to offset genetically based selfishness.

Social Facilitation A phenonmenon that occurs when an individual's performance is improved by the presence of others. *See also* Audience effects; Coaction effects.

Social Interdependence An exchange of benefits that depends on the behavior of the parties involved.

Social Learning The process of acquiring attitudes or behaviors not only by direct experience, but also by observing the outcomes of others' responses.

Social Loneliness The feeling that one is not socially integrated into the community or is not part of a group that shares common interests. *See also* Emotional loneliness.

Social Psychology The objective, empirical study of human social experience.

Sociobiology A controversial school of thought that contends that many types of social behavior, including altruism, have a genetic, evolutionary basis.

Statistics Mathematical techniques that enable

meaningful inferences to be made from collections of data; also, the numerical date themselves.

Stereotyping Forming oversimplified and biased generalizations about a group of people.

Stimulation Overload a phenomenon that may occur in noisy or high-density environments when a person receives too many inputs to process efficiently.

Surface Contact According to G. Levinger and J. D. Snoek, a relationship with another person that involves minimal closeness and remains fairly restricted. *See also* Mutuality; Unilateral awareness.

Survey Research The use of questionnaire responses to obtain and understand data on a broad range of issues.

Symbolic Interactionism A sociological theory that assumes that individuals imagine how they will appear to others and then shape their behavior accordingly.

Task-Oriented Leaders Group leaders who specialize in moving the group toward achievement of a group goal through behavior that is demanding, directive, and well organized. *See also* Social-emotional leaders.

Territorialty The marking of an area by both animals and humans to indicate control and ownership of it.

Thurstone Scale An attitude measurement scale that contains twenty-five or fewer statements about a given attitude object. Each statement is given a predetermined rating from 1 (very unfavorable) to 11 (very favorable). Subjects are then asked to indicate the statements with which they agree, and each respondent's attitude is the average numerical value of the statements that he or she endorses.

Trustworthiness An aspect of communicator credibility relating to how valid and accurate the audience believes the source's presentation to be.

Type A Personality A person who is hard-driving, competitive, and easily angered or frustrated.

Type B Personality A person who is relaxed and easygoing.

Unilateral Awareness According to G. Levinger and J. D. Snoek, a superficial relationship based on minimal information about the other person. *See also* Mutuality; Surface contact.

Unit Relationship According to Fritz Heider, a relationship that exists when two persons or objects are perceived as belonging together. *See also* Sentiment relationship.

Unobstrusive Measures Observational approaches to understanding social behavior that do not intrude on the social processes being observed and do not cause individuals to behave in an "unnatural" way (as they might if they knew they were being studied).

Validity The extent to which a test measures what it intends to measure.

Yielding In persuasion research, an individual's integration of a message into his or her own belief structure. *See also* Reception.

REFERENCES

Chapter 1 The Nature of Social Psychology

BANDURA, A. 1977. *Social learning theory.* Englewood Cliffs, N.J.: Prentice-Hall.

BREHM, J. 1966. *A theory of psychological reactance.* New York: Academic Press.

COHEN, S. 1978. Environmental load and the allocation of attention. In *Advances in environmental psychology,* eds. A. Baum, J. E. Singer, and S. Valins. vol. 1. Hillsdale, N.J.: Lawrence Erlbaum Associates.

FESTINGER, L. 1957. *A theory of cognitive dissonance.* Stanford: Stanford University Press.

GERGEN, K. J. 1973. Social psychology as history. *Journal of Personality and Social Psychology* 26:309–320.

GILLEY, M. 1975. Don't the girls all get prettier at closing time. In *The best of Mickey Gilley,* vol. 2. Columbia. Written by Baker Knight, Singletree Music Company: BMI.

HEIDER, F. 1958. *The psychology of interpersonal relations.* New York: Wiley.

HENDRICK, C. 1976. Social psychology as history and as traditional science: an appraisal. *Personality and Social Psychology Bulletin* 2:392–403.

MACCOBY, N., and FARQUHAR, J. W. 1975. Communication for health: unselling heart disease. *Journal of Communication* 25:114–126.

PENNEBAKER, J. W., DYER, M. A., CAULKINS, R. S., LITOWITZ, D. L., ACKREMAN, P. L., ANDERSON, D. B., and MCGRAW, K. M. 1979. Don't the girls all get prettier at closing time: a country and western application to psychology. *Personality and Social Psychology Bulletin* 5:122–125.

RODIN, J. 1976. Density, perceived choice, and response to controllable and uncontrollable outcomes. *Journal of Experimental Social Psychology* 12:564–578.

SCHLENKER, B. 1974. Social psychology and science. *Journal of Personality and Social Psychology* 29:1–5.

WEISS, J. M., STONE, E. A., and HARRELL, N. 1970. Coping behavior and brain norepinephrine in rats. *Journal of Comparative and Physiological Psychology* 72:153–160.

WYER, R. S., JR. 1974. *Cognitive organization and change: an information processing approach.* Potomac, Md.: Erlbaum.

Chapter 2 Research Methods in Social Psychology

CAMPBELL, D. T., and FISKE, D. W. 1959. Convergent and discriminant validation by the multitrait-multimethod matrix. *Psychological Bulletin* 56:81–105.

CIALDINI, R. 1977. Littering as a function of extant litter. Unpublished manuscript, Arizona State University.

COHEN, S., EVANS, G. W., KRANTZ, D. S., and STOKOLS, D. 1980. Physiological, motivational, and cognitive effects of aircraft noise on children: moving from the laboratory to the field. *American Psychologist* 35:231–243.

DEUTSCH, M. 1973. *The resolution of conflict.* New Haven: Yale University Press.

DRABECK, T. E., and STEPHENSON, J. S. 1971. When disaster strikes. *Journal of Applied Social Psychology* 1:187–203.

FINNIE, W. C. 1973. Field experiments in litter control. *Environment and Behavior* 5:123–144.

FRANK. J. D. 1944. Experimental studies of personal pressure and resistance: I. Experimental production of resistance. *Journal of General Psychology* 30:23–41.

GOODCHILDS, J. D., JOHNSON, P. B., ZELLMAN, G. L., and GIARRUSSO, R. 1980. *Non-stranger rape: the role of sexual socialization.* Report to National Center for Prevention and Control of Rape.

HUMPHREYS, L. 1971. *Tearoom trade: impersonal sex in public places.* Chicago: Aldine.

KRAUSS, R. M., FREEDMAN, J. L., and WHITCUP, M. 1978. Field and laboratory studies of littering. *Journal of Experimental Social Psychology* 14:109-122.

LIPSEY, M., CORDRAY, D., and BERGER, D. In press. The use of multiple lines of evidence to evaluate a juvenile diversion program. *Evaluation Review.*

MINDICK, B., and OSKAMP, S. 1979. Longitudinal and predictive research: an approach to methodological problems in studying contraception. *Journal of Population* 2:259–276.

ORNE, M. T. 1962. On the social psychology of the psychology experiment: with particular reference to demand characteristics and their implications. *American Psychologist* 17:776–783.

ORNE, M. T., and EVANS, F. J. 1965. Social control in the psychology experiment: antisocial behavior and hypnosis. *Journal of Personality and Social Psychology* 1:189–200.

ROBINSON, S. N. 1976. Littering behavior in public places. *Environment and Behavior* 8:363–384.

ROSENTHAL, R. 1966. *Experimenter effects in behavioral research.* New York: Appleton-Century-Crofts.

SAVINAR, J. 1980. Social psychological factors in the decision to adopt residential solar technology. Unpublished dissertation, Claremont Graduate School.

STREUFERT, S., KLIGER, S. C., CASTORE, C. H., and DRIVER, M. J. 1967. Tactical and negotiations game for analysis of decision integration across decision areas. *Psychological Reports* 20:155–157.

WEBB, E., CAMPBELL, D., SCHWARTZ, R., and SECHREST, C. 1966. *Unobtrusive measures: nonreactive research in the social sciences.* Chicago: Rand McNally.

ZIMBARDO, P., HANEY, C., BANKS, C., and JAFFE, D. 8 April 1973. A Perandellian prison: the mind is a formidable jailer. *New York Times Magazine*, pp. 38–60.

Chapter 3 The Self

ARKIN, R. M., and DUVAL, S. 1975. Focus of attention and causal attributions of actors and observers. *Journal of Experimental Social Psychology* 11:427–438.

ARONSON, E., and CARLSMITH, J. M. 1962. Performance expectancy as a determinant of actual performance. *Journal of Abnormal and Social Psychology* 62:178–182.

BANDURA, A. 1978. The self system in reciprocal determinism. *American Psychologist* 33:344–358.

BEAMAN, A. C., KLENTZ, B., DIENER, E., and SVANUM, S. 1979. Self awareness and transgression in children: two studies. *Journal of Personality and Social Psychology* 37:1835–1846.

BEM, D. J. 1965. An experimental analysis of self persuasion. *Journal of Experimental Social Psychology* 1:199–218.

———. 1972. Self perception theory. In *Advances in experimental social psychology*, vol. 6, ed. L. Berkowitz. New York: Academic Press.

BEM, D. J., and ALLEN, A. 1974. On predicting some of the people some of the time: the search for cross-situational consistencies in behavior. *Psychological Review* 81:506–520.

BERGIN, A. E. 1962. The effect of dissonant persuasive communications upon changes in self referring attitudes. *Journal of Personality* 30:423–438.

BUSS, A. H., and SCHEIER, M. F. 1976. Self consciousness, self awareness, and self attribution. *Journal of Research in Personality* 10:463–468.

CANNAVALE, F. J., SCARR, H. A., and PEPITONE, A. 1970. Deindividuation in the small group: further evidence. *Journal of Personality and Social Psychology* 16:141–147.

CANTOR, N., and MISCHEL, W. 1977. Traits as prototypes: effects on recognition memory. *Journal of Personality and Social Psychology* 35:38–48.

CARVER, C. S. 1975. Physical aggression as a function of objective self-awareness and attitudes toward punishment. *Journal of Experimental Social Psychology* 11:510–519.

———. 1979. A cybernetic model of self-attention processes. *Journal of Personality and Social Psychology* 37:1251–1281.

CARVER, C. S., BLANEY, P. H., and SCHEIER, M. F. 1979. Reassertion and giving up: the interactive role of self-directed attention and outcome expectancy. *Journal of Personality and Social Psychology* 37:1859–1870.

CARVER, C. S., and SCHEIER, M. F. 1978. The self focusing effects of dispositional self consciousness, mirror presence and audience presence. *Journal of Personality and Social Psychology* 36:324–332.

CHAIKIN, A. L., and DERLEGA, V. J. 1974. *Self disclosure.* Morristown, N.J.: General Learning Press.

COOLEY, C. H. 1922. *Human nature and the social order.* New York: Scribner.

COZBY, P. C. 1973. Self disclosure: a literature review. *Psychological Bulletin* 79:73–91.

DERLEGA, V. J., HARRIS, M. S., and CHAIKIN, A.L. 1973. Self disclosure reciprocity, liking and the deviant. *Journal of Experimental Social Psychology* 9:277–284.

DERLEGA, V. J., WILSON, M., and CHAIKIN, A. L. 1976. Friendship and disclosure reciprocity. *Journal of Personality and Social Psychology* 34:578–582.

DIENER, E. 1978. Causal factors in disinhibition by deindividuation. Unpublished manuscript, University of Illinois.

———. 1979a. Deindividuation: the absence of self awareness and self regulation in group members. In *The psychology of group influence*, ed. P. Paulus. Hillsdale, N.J.: Erlbaum.

———. 1979b. Deindividuation, self awareness, and disinhibition. *Journal of Personality and Social Psychology* 37:1160–1171.

DIENER, E., FRASER, S. C., BEAMAN, A. L., and KELEM, R. T. 1976. Effects of deindividuating variables on stealing by Halloween trick-or-treaters. *Journal of Personality and Social Psychology* 33:178–183.

DIPBOYE, R. L. 1977. Alternative approaches to deindividuation. *Psychological Bulletin* 84:1057–1075.

DUVAL, S., and WICKLUND, R. A. 1972. *A theory of objective self awareness.* New York: Academic Press.

———. 1973. Effects of objective self awareness on attribution of causality. *Journal of Experimental Social Psychology* 9:17–31.

EPSTEIN, S. 1973. The self concept revisited: or a theory of a theory. *American Psychologist* 28:404–416.

FENIGSTEIN, A., SCHEIER, M. F., and BUSS, A. H. 1975. Public and private self consciousness: assessment and theory. *Journal of Consulting and Clinical Psychology* 43:522–527.

FESTINGER, L. 1954. A theory of social compression. *Human Relations* 14:48–64.

FESTINGER, L., PEPITONE, A., and NEWCOMB, T. 1952. Some consequences of deindividuation in a group. *Journal of Abnormal and Social Psychology* 47:382–389.

GELLER, V., and SHAVER, P. 1976. Cognitive consequences of self awareness. *Journal of Experimental Social Psychology* 12:99–108.

GERGEN, K. J. 1965. Interaction goals and personalistic feedback as factors affecting the presentation of self. *Journal of Personality and Social Psychology* 1:413–424.

———. 1968. Personal consistency and the presentation of self. In *The self in social interaction*, ed. C. Gordon and K. J. Gergen, pp. 299–308. New York: Wiley.

GERGEN, K. J., and WISHNOV, B. 1965. Others' self evaluations and interaction anticipation in determinants of self presentation. *Journal of Personality and Social Psychology* 2:348–358.

GIBBONS, F. X. 1978. Sexual standards and reactions to pornography: enhancing behavioral consistency through self focused attention. *Journal of Personality and Social Psychology* 36:976–987.

GIBBONS, F. X., and WICKLUND, R. A. 1976. Selective exposure to self. *Journal of Research in Personality* 10:98–106.

GORDON, C. 1968. Self-conceptions: configurations of content. In *The Self in Social Interaction*, ed. C. Gordon and K. J. Gergen. New York: Wiley.

ICKES, W. J., WICKLUND, R. A., and FERRIS, C. B. 1973. Objective self awareness and self esteem. *Journal of Experimental Social Psychology* 9:202–219.

JAMES, W. 1892. *Principles of psychology*. New York: Holt.

JONES, E. E., GERGEN, K. J., and DAVIS, K. E. 1962. Some determinants of reactions to being approved or disapproved as a person. *Psychological Monographs*, Whole No. 521.

JOURARD, S. M. 1971. *The transparent self*. New York: Van Nostrand.

KELLY, G. A. 1955. *The psychology of personal constructs*. New York: Norton.

LEBON, G. 1879. *The crowd: a study of the popular mind*. London: Unwin.

LIEBLING, B. A., SEILER, M., and SHAVER, P. 1974. Self awareness and cigarette smoking behavior. *Journal of Experimental Social Psychology* 10:325–332.

LYNN, S. J. 1977. Three theories of self disclosure exchange. *Journal of Experimental Social Psychology* 14:466–479.

MCGEE, M. G., and SNYDER, M. 1975. Attribution and behavior: two field studies. *Journal of Personality and Social Psychology* 32:185–190.

MARKUS, H. 1977. Self schemata and processing information about the self. *Journal of Personality and Social Psychology* 35:63–78.

MASLACH, C. 1974. Social and personal bases of individuation. *Journal of Personality and Social Psychology* 29:411–425.

MASLOW, A. 1968. *Toward a psychology of being*. New York: Van Nostrand Reinhold.

MEAD, G. H. 1934. *Mind, self and society*. Chicago: University of Chicago Press.

MISCHEL, W. 1968. *Personality and assessment*. New York: Wiley.

———. 1973. Toward a cognitive social learning reconceptualization of personality. *Psychological Review* 80:252–283.

———. 1979. On the interface of cognition and personality: beyond the person-situation debate. *American Psychologist* 34:740–754.

MOORE, B. S., SHERROD, D. R., LIU, T. J., and UNDERWOOD, B. 1979. The dispositional shift in attribution over time. *Journal of Experimental Social Psychology* 15:553–569.

MORSE, S. J., and GERGEN, K. J. 1970. Social comparison, self consistency, and the concept of self. *Journal of Personality and Social Psychology* 16:148–156.

PRYOR, J. B., GIBBONS, F. X., WICKLUND, R. A., FAZIO, R. H., and HOOD, R. 1977. Self focused attention and self report validity. *Journal of Personality* 45:513–527.

ROGERS, C. R. 1959. A theory of therapy personality and interpersonal relationships as developed in the client centered framework. In *Psychology: a study of a science*, vol. 3, ed. S. Koch. New York: McGraw-Hill.

ROGERS, T. B. 1977. Self reference in memory: recognition of personality items. *Journal of Research in Personality* 11:295–305.

ROGERS, T. B., KUIPER, N. A., and KIRKER, W. S. 1977. Self reference and the encoding of personal information. *Journal of Personality and Social Psychology* 35:677–678.

ROGERS, T. B., ROGERS, P. J., and KUIPER, N. A. 1979. Evidence for the self as a cognitive prototype: the 'false alarms effect.' *Personality and Social Psychology Bulletin* 5:53–56.

RUBIN, Z. 1975. Disclosing oneself to a stranger: reciprocity and its limits. *Journal of Experimental and Social Psychology* 11:233–260.

SCHEIER, M. F. 1976. Self awareness, self consciousness, and angry aggression. *Journal of Personality* 44:627–644.

SCHEIER, M. F., BUSS, A. H., and BUSS, D. M. 1978. Self consciousness, self report of aggression. *Journal of Research in Personality* 12:133–140.

SCHEIER, M. F., and CARVER, C. S. 1977. Self focused attention and the experience of emotion: attraction, repulsion, elation, and depression. *Journal of Personality and Social Psychology* 35:625–636.

SCHEIER, M. F., CARVER, C. S., and GIBBONS, F. X. 1979. Self-directed attention, awareness of bodily states, and suggestibility. *Journal of Personality and Social Psychology* 37:1576–1588.

SCHEIER, M. F., CARVER, C. S., SCHULTZ, R., GLASS, D. C., and KATZ, I. 1978. Sympathy, self consciousness and reactions to the stigmatized. *Journal of Applied Social Psychology* 8:270–282.

SCHEIER, M. F., FENIGSTEIN, A., and BUSS, A. H. 1974. Self awareness and physical aggression. *Journal of Experimental Social Psychology* 10:264–273.

SECORD, P. F., and JOURARD, S. M. 1953. The appraisal of body cathexis: body cathexis and the self. *Journal of Consulting Psychology* 17:343–347.

SHERROD, D. R., and GOODMAN, C. L. 1978. Effects of sex-of-observer on female actors' causal attributions for success and failure. *Personality and Social Psychology Bulletin* 4:277–280.

SKINNER, B. F. 1971. *Beyond freedom and dignity*. New York: Knopf.

SNYDER, M. 1974. Self-monitoring of expressive behavior. *Journal of Personality and Social Psychology* 30:526–537.

SNYDER, M., and MONSON, T. C. 1975. Persons, situations, and the control of social behavior. *Journal of Personality and Social Psychology* 32:637–644.

SNYDER, M., and SWANN, W. B., JR. 1976. When actions reflect attitudes: the politics of impression management. *Journal of Personality and Social Psychology* 34:1034–1042.

SNYDER, M., and TANKE, E. D. 1976. Behavior and attitude: some people are more consistent than others. *Journal of Personality* 44:501–517.

STEENBERGER, B. N., and ALDERMAN, D. 1979. Objective self-awareness as a non-aversive state: effect of anticipating discrepancy reduction. *Journal of Personality* 47:330–339.

STORMS, M. D. 1973. Videotape and the attribution process: reversing actors' and observers' points of view. *Journal of Personality and Social Psychology* 27:165–175.

STORMS, M. D., and NISBETT, R. E. 1970. Insomnia and the attribution process. *Journal of Personality and Social Psychology* 16:319–328.

STUART, R. B. 1972. Situational versus self control. In *Advances in behavior therapy: proceedings of the fourth conference of the Association for Advancement of Behavior Therapy*, vol. 3, ed. R. D. Rubins, H. Fensterheim, J. D. Henderson, and L. D. Ullman. New York: Academic Press.

TURNER, R. H. 1968. The self conception in social interaction. In *The self in social interaction*, ed. C. Gordon and K. Gergen, pp. 93–106. New York: Wiley.

VALINS, S. 1966. Cognitive effects of false heart-rate feedback. *Journal of Personality and Social Psychology* 4:400–408.

VIDEBECK, R. 1960. Self conception and the reaction of others. *Sociometry* 23: 351–362.

WATTS, ALAN. 1966. *The book: on the taboo against knowing who you are*. New York: Random House.

WICKLUND, R. A. 1975. Objective self awareness. In *Advances in experimental social psychology*, vol. 8, ed. L. Berkowitz. New York: Academic Press.

WORTHY, M., GARY, A. L., and KAHN, G. M. 1969. Self disclosure as an exchange process. *Journal of Personality and Social Psychology* 13:59–63.

WYLIE, R. C. 1974. *The self concept*, vol. 1. Lincoln: University of Nebraska Press.

ZIMBARDO, P. 1969. The human choice: individuation, reason, and order versus deindividuation, impulse, and chaos. In *Nebraska symposium on motivation*, ed. W. J. Arnold and D. Levine. Lincoln: University of Nebraska Press.

Chapter 4 Attitudes, Beliefs, and Behavior

ABELSON, R. P. 1968. Psychological implication. In *Theories of cognitive consistency: a sourcebook*, ed. R. P. Abelson. Chicago: Rand McNally.

———. 1972. Are attitudes necessary? In *Attitudes, conflict, and social change*, ed. B. T. King. New York: Academic Press.

AJZEN, I., and FISHBEIN, M. 1973. Attitudinal and normative variables as predictors of specific behaviors. *Journal of Personality and Social Psychology* 27:41–57.

ALLPORT, G. W. 1935. Attitudes. In *Handbook of social psychology*, ed. C. Murchison. Worcester, Mass: Clark University Press, 798–844.

ANDERSON, N. H. 1971. Integration theory and attitude change. *Psychological Review* 78:171–206.

ANDERSON, N. H. 1980. Integration theory applied to cognitive responses and attitudes. In *Cognitive responses in persuasion*, ed. R. E. Petty, T. M. Ostrom, and T. C. Brock. New York: Erlbaum.

ARONSON, E., and COPE, V. 1968. My enemy's enemy is my friend. *Journal of Personality and Social Psychology* 8:8–12.

BANDURA, A. 1972. *Social learning theory*. Morristown, N.J.: General Learning Press.

BEAR, G., and HODUN, A. 1975. Implicational principles and the cognition of confirmatory, contradictory, incomplete, and irrelevant information. *Journal of Personality and Social Psychology* 32:594–604.

BEM, D. J. 1965. An experimental analysis of self-persuasion. *Journal of Experimental Social Psychology* 1:199–218.

———. 1970. *Beliefs, attitudes, and human affairs*. Belmont, Calif.: Brooks/Cole.

BEM, D. J., and ALLEN, A. A. 1974. On predicting some of the people some of the time: the search for cross-situational consistencies in behavior. *Psychological Review* 81:506–520.

BERLYNE, D. E. 1960. *Conflict, arousal, and curiosity*. New York: McGraw-Hill.

BIERI, J. 1966. Cognitive complexity and personality development. In *Experience, structure, and adaptability*, ed. O. J. Harvey. New York: Springer.

BOGARDUS, E. S. 1928. *Immigration and race attitudes*. Boston: D. C. Heath.

BOWMAN, C., and FISHBEIN, M. 1978. Understanding public reaction to energy proposals: an application of the Fishbein model. *Journal of Applied Social Psychology* 8:319–340.

CARTWRIGHT, D., and HARARY, F. 1956. Structural balance: a generalization from Heider's theory. *Psychological Review* 63:277–293.

DAVIDSON, A. R., and JACCARD, J. J. 1975. Population psychology: a new look at an old problem. *Journal of Personality and Social Psychology* 31:1073–1082.

ENDLER, N. S., and MAGNUSSON, D. 1976. Toward an interactional psychology of personality. *Psychological Bulletin* 83:956–974.

EPSTEIN, S. 1979. The stability of behavior: I. On predicting most of the people much of the time. *Journal of Personality and Social Psychology* 37:1097–1126.

FAZIO, R. H., and ZANNA, M. P. 1978. Attitudinal qualities relating to the strength of the attitude-behavior relation. *Journal of Experimental Social Psychology* 14:398–408.

FESTINGER, L. 1957. *A theory of cognitive dissonance*. Stanford: Stanford University Press.

FISHBEIN, M., and AJZEN, I. 1975. *Belief, attitude, intention and behavior: an introduction to theory and research*. Reading, Mass.: Addison-Wesley.

FISHBEIN, M., and COOMBS, F. S. 1974. Basis for decision: an attitudinal analysis of voting behavior. *Journal of Applied Social Psychology* 4:95–124.

GALIZIO, M., and HENDRICK, C. 1972. Effect of musical accompaniment on attitude: the guitar as a prop for persuasion. *Journal of Applied Social Psychology* 2:350–359.

GUTTMAN, L. 1944. A basis for scaling quantitative data. *American Sociological Review* 9:139–150.

———. 1950. The third component of scalable attitudes. *International Journal of Opinion and Attitude Research* 4:285–287.

HARVEY, O. J., HUNT, D. E., and SCHRODER, H. M. 1961. *Conceptual systems and personality organization*. New York: Wiley.

HEIDER, F. 1958. *The psychology of interpersonal relations*. New York: Wiley.

HOVLAND, C. I., JANIS, I. L., and KELLEY, H. H. 1953. *Communication and persuasion*. New Haven: Yale University Press.

HUNT, J. M. 1963. Motivation inherent in information processing and action. In *Motivation and social interaction*, ed. O. J. Harvey. New York: Ronald Press.

JANIS, I., KAYE, D. and KIRSCHNER, P. 1965. Facilitating effects of eating-while-reading on responsiveness to persuasive communications. *Journal of Personality and Social Psychology* 1:181–186.

KING, G. W. 1975. An analysis of attitudinal and normative variables as predictors of intentions and behavior. *Speech Monographs* 42:237–244.

LAPIERE, R. T. 1934. Attitudes versus actions. *Social Forces* 13:230–237.

LIKERT, R. 1932. A technique for the measurement of attitudes. *Archives of Psychology* 140:44–53.

MCGUIRE, W. J. 1972. Attitude change: the information-processing paradigm. In *Experimental social psychology*, ed. C. G. McClintock. New York: Holt, Rinehart & Winston.

MISCHEL, W. 1968. *Personality and assessment*. New York: Wiley.

MYSTER, A. M. 1944. Further validation of the Wert-Myster farming attitude scale. *Rural Sociology* 9:226–232.

NORMAN, R. 1975. Affective-cognitive consistency, attitudes, conformity, and behavior. *Journal of Personality and Social Psychology* 32:83–91.

OSGOOD, C. E., SUCI, G. J., and TANNENBAUM, P. H. 1957. *The measurement of meaning*. Urbana: University of Illinois Press.

OSGOOD, C. E., and TANNENBAUM, P. H. 1955. The principle of congruity in the prediction of attitude change. *Psychological Review* 62:42–55.

PAGE, M. M. 1969. Social psychology of a classical conditioning of attitudes experiment. *Journal of Personality and Social Psychology* 11:177–186.

———. 1974. Demand characteristics and the classical conditioning of attitudes experiment. *Journal of Personality and Social Psychology* 30:468–476.

POMAZAL, R. J., and JACCARD, J. J. 1976. An informational approach to altruistic behavior. *Journal of Personality and Social Psychology* 33:317–326.

PRICE, K. O., HARBURG, E., and NEWCOMB, T. M. 1966. Psychological balance in situations of negative interpersonal attitudes. *Journal of Personality and Social Psychology* 3:265–270.

RAZRAN, G. 1961. The observable and inferable conscious in current Soviet psychophysiology: interoceptive conditioning, semantic conditioning, and the orienting reflex. *Psychological Review* 68:81–147.

ROKEACH, M. 1960. *The open and closed mind*. New York: Basic Books.

ROSENBERG, M. J. 1956. Cognitive structure and attitudinal affect. *Journal of Abnormal and Social Psychology* 53:367–372.

ROSENBERG, M. J., and ABELSON, R. P. 1960. An analysis of cognitive balancing. In *Attitude organization and change*, ed. C. I. Hovland and I. L. Janis. New Haven: Yale University Press.

STAATS, A. W., and STAATS, C. K. 1958. Attitudes established by classical conditioning. *Journal of Abnormal and Social Psychology* 57:37–40.

THURSTONE, L. L. 1928. Attitudes can be measured. *American Journal of Sociology* 33:529–554.

———. 1931. *The measurement of social attitudes*. Chicago: University of Chicago Press.

WEIGEL, R. H., and NEWMAN, L. S. 1976. Increasing attitude-behavior correspondence by broadening the scope of the behavioral measure. *Journal of Personality and Social Psychology* 33:793–802.

WEIGEL, R. H., VERNON, D. T. A., and TOGNACCI, L. N. 1974. Specificity of the attitude as a determinant of attitude-behavior congruence. *Journal of Personality and Social Psychology* 30:724–728.

WICKER, A. W. 1969. Attitudes versus actions: the relationship of verbal and overt behavioral responses to attitude objects. *Journal of Social Issues* 25:41–78.

WYER, R. S., JR. 1974. *Cognitive organization and change: an information-processing approach*. Potomac, Md.: Erlbaum.

ZAJONC, R. B. 1968. Cognitive theories in social psychology. In *The handbook of social psychology*, vol. 1, ed. G. Lindzey and E. Aronson. 2d ed. Reading, Mass.: Addison-Wesley.

ZANNA, M. P., and FAZIO. R. H. 1977. Direct experience and attitude-behavior consistency. Paper presented at the annual meeting of the American Psychological Association, San Francisco.

ZANNA, M., KIESLER, C. A., and PILKONIS, P. A. 1970. Positive and negative attitudinal affect established by classical conditioning. *Journal of Personality and Social Psychology* 14:321–328.

Chapter 5 Attitude Change

ANDERSON, N. H. 1980. Integration theory applied to cognitive responses and attitudes. In *Cognitive responses in persuasion*, ed. R. E. Petty, T. M. Ostrom, and T. C. Brock. New York: Erlbaum.

ANDREOLI, V., and WORCHEL, S. Effects of media, communicator, and message position on attitude change. *Public Opinion Quarterly* 42:59–80.

ARONSON, E. 1969. The theory of cognitive dissonance: a current perspective. In *Advances in experimental social psychology*, vol. 4, ed. L. Berkowitz. New York: Academic Press.

ARONSON, E., and CARLSMITH, J. M. 1963. Effect of the severity of threat on the devaluation of forbidden behavior. *Journal of Abnormal and Social Psychology* 66:584–588.

AUSUBEL, N., ED. 1948. Applied psychology. In *A treasury of Jewish folklore*. New York: Crown.

BARTHEL, J. 1976. *A death in Canaan*. New York: Dutton.

BEM, D. 1965. An experimental analysis of self-persuasion. *Journal of Experimental Social Psychology* 1:199–218.

———. 1967. Self-perception: an alternative interpretation of cognitive dissonance phenomena. *Psychological Review* 74:183–200.

BEM, D., and MCCONNELL, H. K. 1970. Testing the self-perception explanation of dissonance phenomena: on the salience of premanipulation attitudes. *Journal of Personality and Social Psychology* 14:23–31.

BIRNBAUM, M. H., WONG, R., and WONG, L. 1976. Combining information from sources that vary in credibility. *Memory & Cognition* 4:330–336.

Bochner, S., and Insko, C. A. 1966. Communicator discrepancy, source credibility, and opinion change. *Journal of Personality and Social Psychology* 4:614–621.

Brehm, J. 1956. Postdecision changes in the desirability of alternatives. *Journal of Abnormal and Social Psychology* 52:348–389.

Cantril, H., and Allport, G. W. 1935. *The psychology of radio.* New York: Harper Brothers.

Chaiken, S., and Eagly, A. H. 1976. Communication modality as a determinant of message persuasiveness and message comprehensibility. *Journal of Personality and Social Psychology* 34:605–614.

Cook, T. D., and Flay, B. R. 1978. The persistence of experimentally induced attitude change: an evaluative review. In *Advances in experimental social psychology*, vol. 11, ed. L. Berkowitz. New York: Academic Press.

Cooper, J., and Worchel, S. 1970. Role of undesired consequences in arousing cognitive dissonance. *Journal of Personality and Social Psychology* 16:199–206.

Cooper, J., Zanna, M. P., and Goethals, G. R. 1974. Mistreatment of an esteemed other as a consequence affecting dissonance reduction. *Journal of Experimental Social Psychology* 10:224–233.

Deaux, K. 1976. *The behavior of women and men.* Monterey, Calif.: Brooks/Cole.

Deci, E. L. 1975. *Intrinsic motivation.* New York: Plenum.

Eagly, A. H. 1978. Sex differences in influenceability. *Psychological Bulletin* 85:86–116.

———. 1980. Recipient characteristics as determinants of responses to persuasion. In *Cognitive responses in persuasion*, ed. R. E. Petty, T. M. Ostrom, and T. C. Brock. New York: Erlbaum.

Eagly, A. H., Wood, W., and Chaiken, S. 1978. Causal inferences about communicators and their effect on opinion change. *Journal of Personality and Social Psychology* 36:424–435.

Elms, A. C., and Janis, I. L. 1965. Counter-norm attitudes induced by consonant versus dissonant conditions of role-playing. *Journal of Experimental Research in Personality* 1:50–60.

Fazio, R. H., Zanna, M. P., and Cooper, J. 1977. Dissonance and self-perception: an integrative view of each theory's proper domain of application. *Journal of Experimental Social Psychology* 13:464–479.

Festinger, L. 1957. *A theory of cognitive dissonance.* Stanford: Stanford University Press.

———. 1964. Behavioral support for opinion change. *Public Opinion Quarterly* 28:404–417.

———. 1964. *Conflict, decision, and dissonance.* Stanford: Stanford University Press.

Festinger, L., and Carlsmith, J. M. 1959. Cognitive consequences of forced compliance. *Journal of Abnormal and Social Psychology* 58:203–210.

Festinger, L., and Maccoby, N. 1964. On resistance to persuasive communications. *Journal of Abnormal and Social Psychology* 68:359–366.

Freedman, J. L. 1965. Long-term behavioral effects of cognitive dissonance. *Journal of Experimental Social Psychology* 1:145–155.

Gillig, P. M., and Greenwald, A. G. 1974. Is it time to lay the sleeper effect to rest? *Journal of Personality and Social Psychology* 29:132–139.

Greenwald, A. G. 1969. The open-mindedness of the counterattitudinal role player. *Journal of Experimental Social Psychology* 5:375–388.

———. 1970. When does role playing produce attitude change? Toward an answer. *Journal of Personality and Social Psychology* 16:214–219.

Gruder, C. L., Cook, T. D., Hennigan, K. M., Flay, B. R., Alessis, C., and Halamaj, J. 1978. Empirical tests of the absolute sleeper effect predicted from the discounting cue hypothesis. *Journal of Personality and Social Psychology* 36:1061–1074.

Haaland, G. A., and Venkatesan, M. 1968. Resistance to persuasive communications: an examination of the distraction hypotheses. *Journal of Personality and Social Psychology* 9:167–170.

Horai, J., Naccari, N., and Fatoullah, E. 1974. The effects of expertise and physical attractiveness upon opinion agreement and liking. *Sociometry* 37:601–606.

Hovland, C. I., Harvey, O. J., and Sherif, M. 1957. Assimilation and contrast effects in reactions to communication and attitude change. *Journal of Abnormal and Social Psychology* 55:244–252.

Hovland, C. I., and Janis, I. L., eds. 1959. *Personality and persuasibility.* New Haven: Yale University Press.

Hovland, C. I., Janis, I. L., and Kelley, H. H. 1953. *Communication and persuasion.* New Haven: Yale University Press.

Hovland, C. I., Lumsdaine, A., and Sheffield, F. 1949. *Experiments on mass communication.* Princeton: Princeton University Press.

Hovland, C. I., and Weiss, W. 1951. The influence of source credibility on communication effectiveness. *Public Opinion Quarterly* 15:635–650.

Janis, I. L., and Feshbach, S. 1953. Effects of fear-arousing communications. *Journal of Abnormal and Social Psychology* 48:78–92.

Janis, I. L., and King, B. T. 1954. The influence of role-playing on opinion change. *Journal of Abnormal and Social Psychology* 49:211–218.

Janis, I. L., and Mann, L. 1965. Effectiveness of emotional role-playing in modifying smoking habits and attitudes. *Journal of Experimental Research in Personality* 1:84–90.

Kelman, H. C. 1961. Processes of opinion change. *Public Opinion Quarterly* 25:57–78.

Kelman, H. C., and Baron, R. M. 1974. Moral and hedonistic dissonance: a functional analysis of the relationship between discrepant action and attitude change. In *Readings in attitude change*, ed. S. Himmelfarb and A. H. Eagly. New York: Wiley.

King, B. T., and Janis, I. L. 1956. Comparison of the effectiveness of improvised versus non-improvised role-playing in producing opinion changes. *Human Relations* 9:177–186.

Lepper, M. R., and Greene, D. 1975. Turning play into work: effects of adult surveillance and extrinsic rewards on children's intrinsic motivation. *Journal of Personality and Social Psychology* 31:479–486.

Lepper, M. R., Greene, D., and Nisbett, R. E. 1973. Undermining children's intrinsic interest with extrinsic rewards: a test of the overjustification hypothesis. *Journal of Personality and Social Psychology* 28:129–137.

Leventhal, H. 1970. Findings and theory in the study of

fear communications. In *Advances in experimental social psychology*, vol. 5, ed. L. Berkowitz. New York: Academic Press.

LEVENTHAL, H., and PERLOE, S. I. 1962. A relationship between self-esteem and persuasibility. *Journal of Abnormal and Social Psychology* 64:385–388.

LINDER, D. E., COOPER, J., and JONES, E. E. 1967. Decision freedom as a determinant of the role of incentive magnitude in attitude change. *Journal of Personality and Social Psychology* 6:245–254.

MCGUIRE, W. J. 1964. Inducing resistance to persuasion: some contemporary approaches. In *Advances in experimental social psychology*, vol. 1, ed. L. Berkowitz. New York: Academic Press.

———. 1968. Personality and susceptibility to social influence. In *Handbook of personality theory and research*, ed. E. F. Borgatta and W. W. Lambert. Chicago: Rand McNally.

———. 1972. Attitude change: the information-processing paradigm. In *Experimental social psychology*, ed. C. G. McClintock. New York: Holt, Rinehart & Winston.

MANN, L., and JANIS, I. L. 1968. A follow-up study on the long-term effects of emotional role-playing. *Journal of Personality and Social Psychology* 8:339–342.

MILLER, N., MARUYAMA, G., BEABER, R. J., and VALONE, K. 1976. Speed of speech and persuasion. *Journal of Personality and Social Psychology* 34:615–624.

NISBETT, R. E., and VALINS, S. 1971. *Perceiving the causes of one's own behavior*. Morristown, N.J.: General Learning Press.

NORMAN, R. 1976. When what is said is important: a comparison of expert and attractive sources. *Journal of Experimental Social Psychology* 12:294–300.

O'LEARY, K. D., and DRABMAN, R. 1971. Token reinforcement programs in the classroom: a review. *Psychological Bulletin* 75:379–398.

OSTERHOUSE, R. A., and BROCK, T. C. 1970. Distraction increases yielding to propaganda by inhibiting counterarguing. *Journal of Personality and Social Psychology* 15:344–358.

PETTY, R. E., WELLS, G. L., and BROCK, T. C. 1976. Distraction can enhance or reduce yielding to propaganda: thought disruption versus effort justification. *Journal of Personality and Social Psychology* 34:874–884.

SHERIF, M., and HOVLAND, C. 1961. *Social judgment*. New Haven: Yale University Press.

SISTRUNK, F., and MCDAVID, J. W. 1971. Sex variable in conformity behavior. *Journal of Personality and Social Psychology* 17:200–207.

TEDESCHI, J. T., SCHLENKER, B. R., and BONOMA, T. V. 1971. Cognitive dissonance: private ratiocination or public spectacle? *American Psychologist* 26:685–695.

WICKLUND, R. A., and BREHM, J. W. 1976. *Perspective on cognitive dissonance*. Hillsdale, N.J.: Erlbaum.

WILHELMY, R. A. 1974. The role of commitment in cognitive reversibility. *Journal of Personality and Social Psychology* 30:695–698.

WILHELMY, R. A., and DUNCAN, B. L. 1974. Cognitive reversibility in dissonance reduction. *Journal of Personality and Social Psychology* 29:806–811.

WYER, R. S., JR. 1974. *Cognitive organization and change: an information-processing approach*. Potomac, Md.: Erlbaum.

WYER, R. S., and GOLDBERG, L. 1970. A probabilistic analysis of the relationships among beliefs and attitudes. *Psychological Review* 77:100–120.

Chapter 6 Attribution and Person Perception

ABELSON, R. P. 1976. A script theory of understanding, attitude, and behavior. In *Cognition and social behavior*, ed. J. S. Carroll and J. W. Payne. Hillsdale, N.J.: Erlbaum.

ALLPORT, G. W. 1954. *The nature of prejudice*. Reading, Mass.: Addison-Wesley.

ANDERSON, N. H. 1965. Adding versus averaging as a stimulus combination rule in impression formation. *Journal of Experimental Psychology* 70:394–400.

———. 1968a. Likableness ratings of 500 personality trait words. *Journal of Personality and Social Psychology* 9:272–279.

———. 1968b. Applications of a linear serial model to a personality-impression task using special presentation. *Journal of Personality and Social Psychology* 10:354–362.

ASCH, S. E. 1946. Forming impressions of personality. *Journal of Abnormal and Social Psychology* 41:258–290.

BEM, D. J. 1967. Self-perception: an alternative interpretation of cognitive dissonance phenomena. *Psychological Review* 74:183–200.

———. 1972. Self-perception theory. In *Advances in experimental social psychology*, vol. 6, ed. L. Berkowitz. New York: Academic Press.

BROVERMAN, I. K., VOGEL, S. R., BROVERMAN, D. M., CLARKSON, F. E., and ROSENKRANTZ, P. S. 1972. Sex-role stereotypes: a current appraisal. *Journal of Social Issues* 28:59–78.

BRUNER, J. S., and TAGIURI, R. 1954. Person perception. In *Handbook of social psychology*, vol. 2, ed. G. Lindzey. Reading, Mass.: Addison-Wesley.

COHEN, A. R. 1961. Cognitive tuning as a factor affecting impression formation. *Journal of Personality* 29:235–245.

CUNNINGHAM, J. D., and KELLEY, H. H. 1975. Causal attributions for interpersonal events of varying magnitudes. *Journal of Personality* 43:74–93.

DEAUX, K. 1976. Sex: a perspective on the attribution process. In *New directions in attribution research*, vol. 1, ed. J. H. Harvey, W. J. Ickes, and R. F. Kidd, pp. 335–352. Hillsdale, N.J.: Erlbaum.

DEAUX, K., and EMSWILLER, T. 1974. Explanations of successful performance on sex-linked tasks: what is skill for the male is luck for the female. *Journal of Personality and Social Psychology* 29:80–85.

EISENGER, R., and MILLS, J. 1968. Perception of the sincerity and competence of a communicator as a function of the extremity of his position. *Journal of Experimental Social Psychology* 4:224–232.

FISCHHOFF, B. 1976. Attribution theory and judgment under uncertainty. In *New directions in attribution research*, vol. 1, ed. J. H. Harvey, W. J. Ickes, and R. F. Kidd, pp. 421–452. Hillsdale, N.J.: Erlbaum.

FISHBEIN, M., and HUNTER, R. 1964. Summation versus balance in attitude organization and change. *Journal of Abnormal and Social Psychology* 54:505–510.

FRIEZE, I., and WEINER, B. 1971. Cue utilization and attributional judgments for success and failure. *Journal of Personality* 39:591–606.

GILBERT, G. M. 1951. Stereotype persistence and change among college students. *Journal of Abnormal and Social Psychology* 46:245–254.

HAMILTON, D. L., and GIFFORD, R. K. 1976. Illusory correlation in interpersonal perception: a cognitive basis of stereotypic judgment. *Journal of Experimental Social Psychology* 12:392–407.

HARVEY, J. H., ARKIN, R. M., GLEASON, J. M., and JOHNSTON, S. 1974. Effect of expected and observed outcome of an action on the differential causal attributions of actor and observer. *Journal of Personality* 42:62–77.

HARVEY, J. H., HARRIS, B., and BARNES, R. D. 1975. Actor-observer differences in the perceptions of responsibility and freedom. *Journal of Personality and Social Psychology* 32:22–28.

HARVEY, J. H., ICKES, W. J., and KIDD, B. F., EDS. 1976–1978. *New directions in attribution research.* 2 vols. Hillsdale, N.J.: Erlbaum.

HARVEY, J. H., WELLS, G. L., and ALVAREZ, M. D. 1978. Attribution in the context of conflict and separation in close relationships. In *New directions in attribution research,* vol. 2, ed. J. H. Harvey, W. J. Ickes, and R. F. Kidd. Hillsdale, N.J.: Erlbaum.

HEIDER, F. 1958. *The psychology of interpersonal relations.* New York: Wiley.

———. 1976. A conversation with Fritz Heider. In *New directions in attribution research,* vol. 1, ed. J. H. Harvey, W. J. Ickes, and R. F. Kidd, pp. 3–18. Hillsdale, N.J.: Erlbaum.

HEIDER, F., and SIMMEL, M. 1944. An experimental study of apparent behavior. *American Journal of Psychology* 57:243–259.

HENDRICK, C., and COSTANTINI, A. F. 1970. Effects of varying trait inconsistency and response requirements on the primacy effect in impression formation. *Journal of Personality and Social Psychology* 15:158–164.

JANOFF-BULMAN, R. 1979. Characterological versus behavioral self-blame: inquiries into depression and rape. *Journal of Personality and Social Psychology* 37:1798–1809.

JANOFF-BULMAN, R., and WORTMAN, C. B. 1977. Attributions of blame and coping in the "real world": severe accident victims react to their lot. *Journal of Personality and Social Psychology* 35:351–363.

JONES, E. E., and DAVIS, K. E. 1965. From acts to dispositions. In *Advances in experimental social psychology,* vol. 2, ed. L. Berkowitz. New York: Academic Press.

JONES, E. E., DAVIS, K. E., and GERGEN, K. J. 1961. Role playing variations and their informational value for person perception. *Journal of Abnormal and Social Psychology* 63:302–310.

JONES, E. E., and KELLEY, H. H. 1978. A conversation with Edward E. Jones and Harold H. Kelley. In *New directions in attribution research,* vol. 2, ed. J. H. Harvey, W. J. Ickes, and R. F. Kidd, pp. 371–388. Hillsdale, N.J.: Erlbaum.

JONES, E. E., and MCGILLIS, D. 1976. Correspondent inferences and the attribution cube: a comparative reappraisal. In *New directions in attribution research,* vol. 1, ed. J. H. Harvey, W. J. Ickes, and R. F. Kidd, pp. 389–420. Hillsdale, N. J.: Erlbaum.

JONES, E. E., and NISBETT, R. E. 1971. *The actor and the observer: divergent perceptions of the causes of behavior.* Morristown, N.J.: General Learning Press.

KAHNEMAN, D., and TVERSKY, A. 1973. On the psychology of prediction. *Psychological Review* 80:237–251.

KARLINS, M. T., COFFMAN, L., and WALTERS, G. 1969. On the fading of social stereotypes: studies in three generations of college students. *Journal of Personality and Social Psychology* 13:1–16.

KATZ, D., and BRALY, K. 1933. Racial stereotypes of one hundred college students. *Journal of Abnormal Psychology* 28:280–290.

KELLEY, H. H. 1950. The warm-cold variable in the first impression of persons. *Journal of Personality* 18:431–439.

———. 1967. Attribution theory in social psychology. In *Nebraska symposium on motivation,* ed. D. Levine. Lincoln: University of Nebraska Press.

———. 1971a. *Causal schemata and the attribution process.* Morristown, N.J.: General Learning Press.

———. 1971b. *Attribution in social interaction.* Morristown, N.J.: General Learning Press.

LANGER, E. J. 1978. Rethinking the role of thought in social interaction. In *New directions in attribution research,* vol. 2, ed. J. H. Harvey, W. J. Ickes, and R. F. Kidd, pp. 35–58. Hillsdale, N.J.: Erlbaum.

LANGER, E. J., BLANK, A., AND CHANOWITZ, B. 1978. The mindlessness of ostensibly thoughtful action: the role of "placebic" information in interpersonal interaction. *Journal of Personality and Social Psychology* 36:635–642.

LIPPMANN, W. 1922. *Public opinion.* New York: Harcourt Brace.

LUCHINS, A. S. 1948. Forming impressions of personality: a critique. *Journal of Abnormal and Social Psychology* 43:318–325.

MCARTHUR, L. A. 1972. The how and what of why: some determinants and consequences of causal attribution. *Journal of Personality and Social Psychology* 22:171–193.

MONSON, T. C., and SNYDER, M. 1977. Actors, observers, and the attribution process: toward a reconceptualization. *Journal of Experimental Social Psychology* 13:89–111.

NATIONAL COMMISSION OF THE CAUSES AND PREVENTION OF VIOLENCE. 1969. *Crimes of violence,* vol. 2. Washington, D.C.: U.S. Government Printing Office.

NISBETT, R. E., BORGIDA, E., CRANDALL, R., and REED, H. 1976. Popular induction: information is not always informative. In *Cognition and social behavior,* ed. J. S. Carroll and J. W. Payne. Hillsdale, N.J.: Erlbaum.

NISBETT, R. E., CAPUTO, C., LEGANT, P., and MARECEK, J. 1973. Behavior as seen by the actor and as seen by the observer. *Journal of Personality and Social Psychology* 27:154–164.

NISBETT, R. E., and VALINS, S. 1971. *Perceiving the causes of one's own behavior.* Morristown, N.J.: General Learning Press.

ORVIS, B. R., KELLEY, H. H., and BUTLER, D. 1976. Attributional conflict in young couples. In *New directions in attribution research,* vol. 1, ed. J. H. Harvey, W. J. Ickes, and R. F. Kidd, pp. 353–386. Hillsdale, N.J.: Erlbaum.

REGAN, D. T., and TOTTEN, J. 1975. Empathy and attribution: turning observers into actors. *Journal of Personality and Social Psychology* 32:850–856.

ROSENHAN, D. L. 1973. On being sane in insane places. *Science* 173:250–258.

ROSS, L. D., RODIN, J., and ZIMBARDO, P. G. 1969. Toward an attribution therapy: the reduction of fear through induced cognitive-emotional mis-attribution. *Journal of Personality and Social Psychology* 12:279–288.

ROTHBART, M., FULERO, S., JENSEN, C., HOWARD, J., and BIRRELL, P. 1978. From individual to group impressions: availability heuristics in stereotype formation. *Journal of Experimental Social Psychology* 14:237–255.

SCHACHTER, S., and SINGER, J. E. 1962. Cognitive, social and physiological determinants of emotional state. *Psychological Review* 69:379–399.

SHAVER, K. G. 1975. *An introduction to attribution process.* Cambridge, Mass.: Winthrop.

SKINNER, B. F. 1957. *Verbal behavior.* New York: Appleton-Century-Crofts.

SLOVIC, P., FISCHHOFF, B., and LICHTENSTEIN, S. 1977. Behavioral decision theory. *Annual Review of Psychology* 28:1–39.

———. 1980. Risky assumptions. *Psychology Today* 14:44–48.

STORMS, M. D. 1973. Videotape and the attribution process: reversing actors' and observers' points of view. *Journal of Personality and Social Psychology* 27:165–175.

STORMS, M. D., and NISBETT, R. E. 1970. Insomnia and the attribution process. *Journal of Personality and Social Psychology* 16:319–328.

TAGIURI, R., and L. PETRULLO, eds. 1958. *Person perception and interpersonal behavior.* Stanford: Stanford University Press.

THIBAUT, J. W., and RIECKEN, H. W. 1955. Some determinants and consequences of the perception of social causality. *Journal of Personality* 24:113–133.

WEINER, B. 1974. *Achievement motivation and attribution theory.* Morristown, N.J.: General Learning Press.

WEINER, B., FRIEZE, I., KUKLA, A., REED, L., REST, S., and ROSENBAUM, R. M. 1971. *Perceiving the causes of success and failure.* Morristown, N.J.: General Learning Press.

WEINER, B., and PETER, N. V. 1973. A cognitive-developmental analysis of achievement and moral judgments. *Developmental Psychology* 9:290–309.

WEISS, R. S. 1975. *Marital separation.* New York: Basic Books.

WELLS, G. L., and HARVEY, J. H. 1977. Do people use consensus information in making causal attributions? *Journal of Personality and Social Psychology* 35:279–293.

WISHNER, J. 1960. Reanalysis of "impressions of personality." *Psychological Review* 67:96–112.

ZAJONC, R. B. 1960. The process of cognitive tuning in communication. *Journal of Abnormal and Social Psychology* 61:159–167.

Chapter 7 Interpersonal Attraction

ARONSON, E. 1970. Who likes whom—and why. *Psychology Today* 74:48–50.

ARONSON, E., and LINDER, D. 1965. Gain and loss of esteem as determinants of interpersonal attractiveness. *Journal of Experimental Social Psychology* 1:156–171.

ARONSON, E., WILLERMAN, B., and FLOYD, J. 1966. The effect of a pratfall on increasing interpersonal attractiveness. *Psychonomic Science* 4:227–228.

BANTA, T. J., and HETHERINGTON, M. 1963. Relations between needs of friends and fiancés. *Journal of Abnormal and Social Psychology* 69:401–404.

BELL, R. R. 1979. *Marriage and family interaction.* 5th ed. Homewood, Ill.: Dorsey Press.

BERSCHEID, E., BROTHEN, T., and GRAZIANO, W. 1976. Gain/loss theory and the "law of infidelity": Mr. Doting vs. the admiring stranger. *Journal of Personality and Social Psychology* 33:709–718.

BERSCHEID, E., DION, K., WALSTER, E., and WALSTER, G. W. 1971. Physical attractiveness and dating choice: a test of the matching hypothesis. *Journal of Experimental Social Psychology* 7:173–189.

BERSCHEID, E., and FEI, J. 1977. Romantic love and sexual jealousy. In *Jealousy*, ed. G. Clanton and L. G. Smith, pp. 101–109. Englewood Cliffs, N.J.: Prentice-Hall.

BERSCHEID, E., and WALSTER, E. 1971. Adrenaline makes the heart grow fonder. *Psychology Today* 5:46–50.

———. 1974a. Physical attractiveness. In *Advances in experimental social psychology*, vol. 7, ed. L. Berkowitz, pp. 158–216. New York: Academic Press.

———. 1974b. A little bit about love. In *Foundations of interpersonal attraction*, ed. T. L. Huston. New York: Academic Press.

———. 1978. *Interpersonal attraction.* 2d. ed. Menlo Park, Calif.: Addison-Wesley.

BOWLBY, J. 1969. *Attachment and loss—Vol.1: attachment.* London: Hogarth.

BROCKNER, J., and SWAP, W. D. 1976. Effects of repeated exposure and attitudinal similarity on self-disclosure and interpersonal attraction. *Journal of Personality and Social Psychology* 33:531–540.

BYRD, R. E. 1938. *Alone.* New York: Putnam.

BYRNE, D. 1971. *The attraction paradigm.* New York: Academic Press.

CARNEGIE, D. 1937. *How to win friends and influence people.* New York: Simon and Schuster.

CARTER, H., and GLICK, P. 1970. *Marriage and divorce: a social and economic study.* Cambridge, Mass.: Harvard University Press.

CIMBALO, R. S., FALING, V., and MOUSAW, P. 1976. The course of love: a cross-sectional design. *Psychological Reports* 38:1292–1294.

CLORE, G. L., and BYRNE, D. 1974. A reinforcement-affect model of attraction. In *Foundations of interpersonal attraction*, ed. T. L. Huston, pp. 143–165. New York: Academic Press.

CLORE, G. L., WIGGINS, N., and ITKIN, S. 1975. Gain and loss in attraction: attributions from nonverbal behavior. *Journal of Personality and Social Psychology* 31:706–712.

CURRAN, J. P., and LIPPOLD, S. 1975. The effects of physical attraction and attitude similarity in dating dyads. *Journal of Personality* 44:528–539.

DARLEY, J. M., and ARONSON, E. 1966. Self evaluation versus direct anxiety reduction as determinants of the fear-affiliation relationship. *Journal of Experimental Social Psychology* 2:66–79.

DARLEY, J. M., and BERSCHEID, E. 1967. Increased liking as a result of the anticipation of personal contact. *Human Relations* 20:29–40.

DICKOFF, H. 1963. Reactions to evaluations by another person as a function of self evaluation and the interaction context. *Dissertation Abstracts* 24:2166.

DION, K. 1972. Physical attractiveness and evaluations of children's transgressions. *Journal of Personality and Social Psychology* 24:207–213.

DION, K., BERSCHEID, E., and WALSTER, E. 1972. What is beautiful is good. *Journal of Personality and Social Psychology* 24:285–290.

DITTES, J. E. 1959. Attractiveness of group as function of self-esteem and acceptance by group. *Journal of Abnormal and Social Psychology* 59:77–82.

DITTES, J. E., and KELLEY, H. H. 1956. Effects of different conditions of acceptance upon conformity to group norms. *Journal of Abnormal and Social Psychology* 53:100–107.

DUTTON, D. G., and ARON, A. P. 1974. Some evidence for heightened sexual attraction under conditions of high anxiety. *Journal of Personality and Social Psychology* 30:510–517.

EBBESON, E., KJOS, G., and KONEČNI, V. 1976. Spatial ecology: its effects on the choice of friends and enemies. *Journal of Experimental Social Psychology* 12:505–518.

EPLEY, S. W. 1975. The presence of others may reduce anxiety—the evidence is not conclusive. *Psychological Bulletin* 82:886–899.

FESTINGER, L. 1954. A theory of social comparison processes. *Human Relations* 7:117–140.

FESTINGER, L., SCHACHTER, S., and BACK, K. 1950. *Social pressures in informal groups: a study of human factors in housing.* New York: Harper.

FROMKIN, H. L. 1972. Feelings of interpersonal undistinctiveness: an unpleasant affective state. *Journal of Experimental Research in Personality* 6:178–185.

GERARD, H. B., and RABBIE, J. M. 1961. Fear and social comparison. *Journal of Abnormal and Social Psychology* 62:586–592.

GOLDMAN, W., and LEWIS, P. 1977. Beautiful is good: evidence that the physically attractive are more socially skillful. *Journal of Experimental Social Psychology* 13:125–130.

GOODE, W. J. 1959. The theoretical importance of love. *American Sociological Review* 24:38–47.

GRUSH, J. E., MCKEOUGH, K. L., and AHLERING, R. F. 1978. Extrapolating laboratory exposure research to actual political elections. *Journal of Personality and Social Psychology* 36:257–270.

HARVEY, O. J. 1962. Personality factors in resolution of conceptual incongruities. *Sociometry* 25:336–352.

HEER, D. 1974. The prevalence of black-white marriage in the United States, 1960 and 1970. *Journal of Marriage and the Family* 36:246–258.

HEIDER, F. 1958. *The psychology of interpersonal relations.* New York: Wiley.

HENLEY, N. M. 1977. *Body politics: power, sex and nonverbal communication.* Englewood Cliffs, N.J.: Prentice-Hall.

HILL, C. T., RUBIN, Z., and PEPLAU, L. A. 1976. Breakups before marriage: the end of 103 affairs. *Journal of Social Issues* 32:147–168.

HINDE, R. A. 1978. Interpersonal relationships—in quest of a science. *Psychological Medicine* 8:373–386.

HOYT, M. F., and RAVEN, B. H. 1973. Birth order and the 1971 Los Angeles earthquake. *Journal of Personality and Social Psychology* 28:126–134.

HUSTON, T. L., and LEVINGER, G. 1978. Interpersonal attraction and relationships. In *Annual review of psychology,* ed. M. R. Rosenzweig and L. W. Porter. Palo Alto, Calif.: Annual Reviews.

JACOBS, L., BERSCHEID, E., and WALSTER, E. 1971. Self esteem and attraction. *Journal of Personality and Social Psychology* 17:84–91.

JONES, E. E. 1964. *Ingratiation.* New York: Appleton-Century-Crofts.

JONES, S. C. 1973. Self and interpersonal evaluations: esteem theories versus consistency theories. *Psychological Bulletin* 79:185–199.

KATZ, A. M., and HILL, R. 1958. Residential propinquity and marital selection: a review of theory, method and fact. *Marriage and Family Living* 20:327–335.

KELLEY, H. H. 1950. The warm-cold variable in first impressions of persons. *Journal of Personality* 18:431–439.

———. 1979. *Personal relationships: their structure and process.* Hillsdale, N.J.: Erlbaum.

KELLEY, H. H., CUNNINGHAM, J. D., and STAMBUL, H. B. 1980. Types of problems and sex differences in young couples' reported conflicts. Unpublished manuscript. University of California at Los Angeles.

KERCKHOFF, A. C., and DAVIS, K. E. 1962. Value consensus and need complementarity in mate selection. *American Sociological Review* 27:295–303.

KIPNIS, D. M. 1957. Interaction between members of bomber crews as a determinant of sociometric choice. *Human Relations* 10:263–270.

KOMAROVSKY, M. 1976. *Dilemmas of masculinity: a study of college youth.* New York: Norton.

KRULEWITZ, J. E., and NASH, J. E. 1980. Effects of sex role attitudes and similarity on men's rejection of male homosexuals. *Journal of Personality and Social Psychology* 38:67–74.

LEVINGER, G. 1964. Note on need complementarity in marriage. *Psychological Bulletin* 61:153–157.

———. 1977. Re-viewing the close relationship. In *Close relationships: perspectives on the meaning of intimacy,* ed. G. Levinger and H. L. Raush, pp. 137–162. Amherst: University of Massachusetts Press.

LEVINGER, G., SENN, D. J., and JORGENSEN, B. W. 1970. Progress toward permanence in courtship: a test of the Kerckhoff-Davis hypothesis. *Sociometry* 33:427–443.

LEVINGER, G., and SNOEK, J. D. 1972. *Attraction in relationships: a new look at interpersonal attraction.* Morristown, N.J.: General Learning Press.

LIPETZ, M. E., COHEN, I. H., DWORIN, J., and ROGERS, L. 1970. Need complementarity, marital stability and marital satisfaction. In *Personality and Social Behavior,* ed. T. L. Huston, pp. 143–165. New York: Academic Press.

LOPATA, H. Z. 1969. Loneliness: forms and components. *Social Problems* 17:248–261.

MARWELL, G., and HAGE, J. 1970. The organization of role relationships: a systematic description. *American Sociological Review* 35:884–900.

METTEE, D. R. 1971. The true discerner as a potent source of positive affect. *Journal of Experimental Social Psychology* 7:292–303.

MILLER, A. G. 1976. Constraint and target effects in the attribution of attitudes. *Journal of Experimental Social Psychology* 12:325–339.

MOLES, O. C., and LEVINGER, G., eds. 1976. Divorce and separation. *Journal of Social Issues* 32: whole issue.

NEWCOMB, T. M. 1956. The prediction of interpersonal attraction. *American Psychologist* 11:575–586.

———. 1961. *The acquaintance process.* New York: Holt, Rinehart & Winston.

NOVAK, D. W., and LERNER, M. J. 1968. Rejection as a consequence of perceived similarity. *Journal of Personality and Social Psychology* 9:147–152.

PEPLAU, L. A. 1976. Impact of fear of success and sex-role attitudes on women's competitive achievement. *Journal of Personality and Social Psychology* 34:561–568.

———. 1979. Power in dating relationships. In *Women: a feminist perspective,* 2d ed., ed. J. Freeman, pp. 106–121. Palo Alto, Calif.: Mayfield.

PEPLAU, L. A., and PERLMAN, D. 1979. Blueprint for a social psychological theory of loneliness. In *Love and attraction,* ed. M. Cook and G. Wilson, pp. 99–108. Oxford: Pergamon.

PERLMAN, D., and OSKAMP, S. 1971. The effects of picture content and exposure frequency on evaluations of Negroes and whites. *Journal of Experimental Social Psychology* 7:280–291.

PERLMAN, D., and PEPLAU, L. A. 1980. Toward a social psychology of loneliness. In *Relationships in disorder,* ed. R. Gilmour and S. Duck. London: Academic Press.

PLECK, J. H. 1976. Male threat from female competence. *Journal of Consulting and Clinical Psychology* 44:608–613.

RUBENSTEIN, C., and SHAVER, P. 1979. Loneliness in two northeastern cities. In *The anatomy of loneliness,* ed. J. Hartog and J. R. Audy. New York: International Universities Press.

RUBENSTEIN, C., SHAVER, P., and PEPLAU, L. A. 1979. Loneliness. *Human Nature* February:58–65.

RUBIN, Z. 1970. Measurement of romantic love. *Journal of Personality and Social Psychology* 16:265–273.

———. 1973. *Liking and loving: an invitation to social psychology.* New York: Holt, Rinehart & Winston.

RUBIN, Z., HILL, C. T., PEPLAU, L. A., and DUNKEL-SCHETTER, C. 1978. Self-disclosure in dating couples: sex roles and the ethic of openness. Unpublished manuscript, Brandeis University.

SAEGERT, S., SWAMP, W., and ZAJONC, R. 1973. Exposure, context and interpersonal attraction. *Journal of Personality and Social Psychology* 25:234–242.

SARNOFF, I., and ZIMBARDO, P. G. 1961. Anxiety, fear and social affiliation. *Journal of Abnormal and Social Psychology* 62:356–363.

SCHACHTER, S. 1959. *The psychology of affiliation.* Stanford: Stanford University Press.

SEGAL, M. W. 1974. Alphabet and attraction: an unobtrusive measure of the effect of propinquity in a field setting. *Journal of Personality and Social Psychology* 30:654–657.

SHEPOSH, J. P., DEMING, M., and YOUNG, L. E. 1977. The radiating effects of status and attractiveness of a male upon evaluation of his female partner. Paper read at the annual meeting of the Western Psychological Association, April 1977, Seattle, Washington.

SIGALL, H., and LANDY, D. 1973. Radiating beauty: the effects of having an attractive partner on person perception. *Journal of Personality and Social Psychology* 28:218–224.

SIGALL, H., and OSTROVE, N. 1975. Beautiful but dangerous: effects of offender attractiveness and the nature of the crime on juridic judgment. *Journal of Personality and Social Psychology* 31:410–414.

STANG, D. J. 1974. Methodological factors in mere exposure research. *Psychological Bulletin* 81:1014–1025.

SULLIVAN, H. S. 1953. *The interpersonal theory of psychiatry.* New York: Norton.

THIBAUT, J. W., and KELLEY, H. H. 1959. *The social psychology of groups.* New York: Wiley.

WALSTER, E., ARONSON, V., ABRAHAMS, D., and ROTTMAN, L. 1966. Importance of physical attractiveness in dating behavior. *Journal of Personality and Social Psychology* 4:508–516.

WALSTER, E., and WALSTER, B. 1963. Effects of expecting to be liked on choice of associates. *Journal of Abnormal and Social Psychology* 67:402–404.

WALSTER, E., and WALSTER, G. W. 1978. *A new look at love.* Reading, Mass.: Addison-Wesley.

WEISS, R. S. 1973. *Loneliness: the experience of emotional and social isolation.* Cambridge, Mass.: The M.I.T. Press.

———. 1974. The provisions of social relationships. In *Doing unto others,* ed. Z. Rubin. Englewood Cliffs, N.J.: Prentice-Hall.

———. 1976. The emotional impact of marital separation. *Journal of Social Issues* 32:135–146.

WHYTE, W. J., JR. 1956. *The organization man.* New York: Simon and Schuster.

WINCH, R. 1958. *Mate selection: a study of complementary needs.* New York: Harper & Row.

WISH, M., DEUTSCH, M., and KAPLAN, S. J. 1976. Perceived dimensions of interpersonal relations. *Journal of Personality and Social Psychology* 33:409–420.

WRIGHTSMAN, L. S. 1960. Effects of waiting with others on changes in level of felt anxiety. *Journal of Abnormal and Social Psychology* 61:216–222.

ZAJONC, R. B. 1968. Attitudinal effects of mere exposure. *Journal of Personality and Social Psychology,* monograph supplement, part 2:1–29.

Chapter 8 Aggression

ARDREY, R. 1966. *The territorial imperative.* New York: Atheneum.

ARMOR, D. J. 1976. *Measuring the effects of television on*

aggressive behavior. Santa Monica: The Rand Corporation.

AX, A. F. 1953. The physiological differentiation between fear and anger in humans. *Psychosomatic Medicine* 15:433–442.

BANDURA, A. 1965. Influence of models' reinforcement contingencies on the acquisition of imitative responses. *Journal of Personality and Social Psychology* 1:589–595.

———. 1973. *Aggression: a social learning analysis*. Englewood Cliffs, N.J.: Prentice-Hall.

BANDURA, A., ROSS, D., and ROSS, S. A. 1963a. Imitation of film-mediated aggressive models. *Journal of Abnormal and Social Psychology* 66:3–11.

———. 1963b. Vicarious reinforcement and imitative learning. *Journal of Abnormal and Social Psychology* 67:601–607.

BARON, R. A., and BELL, P. A. 1973. Effects of heightened sexual arousal on physical aggression. *Proceedings of the 81st Annual Convention of the American Psychological Association* 8:171–172.

———. 1977. Sexual arousal and aggression by males: effects of type of erotic stimuli and prior provocation. *Journal of Personality and Social Psychology* 35:79–87.

BERKOWITZ, L. 1965. The concept of aggressive drive: some additional considerations. In *Advances in experimental social psychology*, vol. 2, ed. L. Berkowitz. New York: Academic Press.

BERKOWITZ, L, and GEEN, R. G. 1966. Film violence and the cue properties of available targets. *Journal of Personality and Social Psychology* 3:525–530.

BERKOWITZ, L., and LEPAGE, A. 1967. Weapons as aggression-eliciting stimuli. *Journal of Personality and Social Psychology* 7:202-207.

BETTELHEIM, B. 1943. Individual and mass behavior in extreme situations. *Journal of Abnormal and Social Psychology* 38:417–452.

BOYANOWSKY, E. O., NEWTSON, D., and WALSTER, E. 1974. Film preferences following a murder. *Communications Research* 1:32–43.

BROWN, P., and ELLIOTT, R. 1965. Control of aggression in a nursery school class. *Journal of Experimental Child Psychology* 2:103–107.

BUSS, A. H. 1961. *The psychology of aggression*. New York: Wiley.

———. 1966. Instrumentality of aggression, feedback, and frustration as determinants of physical aggression. *Journal of Personality and Social Psychology* 3:153–162.

BUSS, A., BOOKER, A., and BUSS, E. 1972. Firing a weapon and aggression. *Journal of Personality and Social Psychology* 22:296–302.

CAMERON, N. 1963. *Personality development and psychopathology: a dynamic approach*. Boston: Houghton Mifflin.

COHEN, A. R. 1955. Social norms, arbitrariness of frustration and status of the agent of frustration-aggression hypothesis. *Journal of Abnormal and Social Psychology* 5:222–226.

COMSTOCK, G. A. 1975. *Effects of television on children: what is the evidence?* Santa Monica: The Rand Corporation.

DEUR, J. D., and PARKE, R. D. 1970. Effects of inconsistent punishment on aggression in children. *Developmental Psychology* 2:403–411.

DIENER, E., and CRANDALL, R. 1979. The effects of the Jamaican anticrime program. *Journal of Applied Social Psychology* 9:135–146.

DIENER, E., and DEFOUR, D. 1978. Does television violence enhance program popularity? *Journal of Personality and Social Psychology* 36:333–341.

DOLLARD, J., DOOB, L. W., MILLER, N. E., MOWRER, O. H., and SEARS, R. R. 1939. *Frustration and aggression*. New Haven: Yale University Press.

DONNERSTEIN, E., and BARRETT, G. 1978. Effects of erotic stimuli on male aggression toward females. *Journal of Personality and Social Psychology* 36:180–188.

DONNERSTEIN, E., DONNERSTEIN, M., and EVANS, R. 1975. Erotic stimuli and aggression: facilitation or inhibition. *Journal of Personality and Social Psychology* 32:237–244.

DONNERSTEIN, E., and HALLAM, J. 1978. Facilitating effects of erotica on aggression against women. *Journal of Personality and Social Psychology* 36:1270–1277.

DONNERSTEIN, E., and WILSON, D. W. 1976. Effects of noise and perceived control on ongoing and subsequent aggressive behavior. *Journal of Personality and Social Psychology* 34:774–781.

DOOB, A.N., and MACDONALD, G. E. 1979. Television viewing and fear of victimization: is the relationship causal? *Journal of Personality and Social Psychology* 37:170–179.

DOOB, A. N., and WOOD, L. 1972. Catharsis and aggression: the effects of annoyance and retaliation on aggressive behavior. *Journal of Personality and Social Psychology* 22:156–162.

EBBESEN, E. B., DUNCAN, B., and KONEČNI, V. J. 1975. Effects of content of verbal aggression on future verbal aggression: a field experiment. *Journal of Experimental Social Psychology* 11:192–204.

ERON, L. D., HUESMANN, L. R., LEFKOWITZ, M. M., and WALDER, L. O. 1972. Does television violence cause aggression? *American Psychologist* 27:253–263.

ESTES, W. K. 1944. An experimental study of punishment. *Psychological Monographs* 57, no. 263.

FENIGSTEIN, A. 1979. Does aggression cause a preference for viewing media violence? *Journal of Personality and Social Psychology* 37:2307–2317.

FESTINGER, L., PEPITONE, A., and NEWCOMB, T. 1952. Some consequences of deindividuation in a group. *Journal of Abnormal and Social Psychology* 47:382–389.

FRODI, A. 1973. The effects of exposure to aggression-eliciting and aggression-inhibiting stimuli, on subsequent aggression. *Goteborg Psychological Reports* 3, no. 8.

———. 1977. Sexual arousal, situational restrictiveness, and aggressive behavior. *Journal of Research in Personality* 11:48–58.

FROST, R. O., and HOLMES, D. S. 1975. Effects of displacing aggression by annoyed and nonannoyed subjects. Paper read at the 83rd Annual Convention of the American Psychological Association, August, Chicago.

GEEN, R. G., and BERKOWITZ, L. 1966. Name-mediated aggressive cue properties. *Journal of Personality* 34:456–465.

HICKS, D. J. 1968. Short- and long-term retention of affectively varied modeled behavior. *Psychonomic Science* 11:369–370.

Hokanson, J. E., and Shetler, S. 1961. The effect of overt aggression on physiological arousal. *Journal of Abnormal and Social Psychology* 63:446–448.

Hornberger, R. H. 1959. The differential reduction of aggressive responses as a function of interpolated activities. *American Psychologist* 14:354.

Hovland, C., and Sears, R. R. 1940. Minor studies in aggression—VI: correlation of lynchings with economic indices. *Journal of Psychology* 9:301–310.

Howard, J. L., Liptzin, M. B., and Reifler, C. B. 1973. Is pornography a problem? *Journal of Social Issues* 29:133–145.

Husman, B. F. 1955. Aggression in boxers and wrestlers as measured by projective techniques. *Research Quarterly of the American Association of Health and Physical Education* 26:421–425.

Jaffe, Y., Malamuth, N., Feingold, F., and Feshbach, S. 1974. Sexual arousal and behavioral aggression. *Journal of Personality and Social Psychology* 30:759–764.

Johnson, W. R., and Hutton, D. C. 1955. Effects of a combative sport upon personality dynamics as measured by a projective test. *Research Quarterly of the American Association of Health and Physical Education* 26:49–53.

Jones, K. L., Schainberg, L. W., and Byer, C. O. 1973. *Drugs and alcohol.* New York: Harper & Row.

Kahn, M. 1966. The physiology of catharsis. *Journal of Personality and Social Psychology* 3:278–286.

Kaplan, R. M., and Singer, R. D. 1976. Television violence and viewer aggression: a reexamination of the evidence. *Journal of Social Issues* 32:35–70.

Kenny, D. T. 1953. *An experimental test of the catharsis theory of aggression.* Ann Arbor: University Microfilms.

Kerner, O., chairman. 1968. *Report of the National Advisory Commission on Civil Disorders*, ed. *New York Times*. New York: Dutton.

Konečni, V. J. 1975a. Annoyance, type, and duration of postannoyance activity, and aggression: the "cathartic effect." *Journal of Experimental Psychology: General* 104:76–102.

———. 1975b. The mediation of aggressive behavior: arousal level vs. anger and cognitive labeling. *Journal of Personality and Social Psychology* 32:706–712.

———. 1976–1977. Quelques déterminants sociaux, émotionnels et cognitifs des préférences esthétiques relatives à des mélodies de complexité variable. *Bulletin de Psychologie* 30:688–715.

———. 1979. The role of aversive events in the development of intergroup conflict. In *The psychology of intergroup relations*, ed. W. G. Austin and S. Worchel. Monterey, Calif.: Brooks/Cole.

Konečni, V. J., and Doob, A. N. 1972. Catharsis through displacement of aggression. *Journal of Personality and Social Psychology* 23:379–387.

———. 1980. A new conceptualization of catharsis of aggression. In *Advances in experimental social psychology*, vol. 13, ed. L. Berkowitz. New York: Academic Press.

Konečni, V. J., and Ebbesen, E. B. 1976. Disinhibition vs. the cathartic effect: artifact and substance. *Journal of Personality and Social Psychology* 34:352–365.

Lang, A. R., Goeckner, D. J., Adesso, V. J., and Marlatt, G. A. 1975. Effects of alcohol on aggression in male social drinkers. *Journal of Abnormal Psychology* 84:508–518.

Liebert, R. M., Neale, J. M., and Davidson, E. S. 1973. *The early window: effects of television on children and youth.* Elmsford, N.Y.: Pergamon Press.

Lorenz, K. 1966. *On aggression.* New York: Harcourt, Brace and World.

Mallick, S. K., and McCandless, B. R. 1966. A study of catharsis of aggression. *Journal of Personality and Social Psychology* 4:591–596.

Mann, J., Sidmann, J., and Starr, S. 1973. Evaluating social consequences of erotic films: an experimental approach. *Journal of Social Issues* 29:113–131.

Medina, E. 1970. The role of alcohol in accidents and violence. In *Alcohol and alcoholism*, ed. R. E. Popham. Toronto: University of Toronto Press.

Milgram, S. 1963. Behavioral study of obedience. *Journal of Abnormal and Social Psychology* 67:371–378.

———. 1965. Liberating effects of group pressure. *Journal of Personality and Social Psychology* 1:127–134.

Miller, N. E. 1941. The frustration-aggression hypothesis. *Psychological Review* 48:337–342.

———. 1951. Comments on theoretical models illustrated by the development of a theory of conflict behavior. *Journal of Personality* 20:82–100.

——— 1959. Liberation of basic S–R concepts: extensions to conflict behavior, motivation, and social learning. In *Psychology: a study of science*, ed. S. Koch. New York: McGraw-Hill.

Montagu, M. F. A. 1968. *Man and aggression.* Fairlawn, N. J.: Oxford University Press.

Newton, G. D., and Zimring, F. E. 1970. *Firearms and violence in American life.* Washington, D.C.: U.S. Government Printing Office.

Page, M. M., and Scheidt, R. J. 1971. The elusive weapons effect: demand awareness, evaluation apprehension, and slightly sophisticated subjects. *Journal of Personality and Social Psychology* 20:304–318.

Pastore, N. 1952. The role of arbitrariness in the frustration-aggression hypothesis. *Journal of Abnormal and Social Psychology* 47:728–731.

Patterson, G. R., Littman, R. A., and Bricker, W. 1967. Assertive behavior in children: a step toward a theory of aggression. *Monographs of the Society for Research in Child Development* 32, no. 5 (serial no. 113).

Report of the Presidential Commission on Obscenity and Pornography. 1971. Washington, D.C.: U.S. Government Printing Office.

Rothenberg, M. B. 1975. Effects of television violence on children and youth. *Journal of the American Medical Association* 234:1043–1046.

Rule, B. G., Ferguson, T. J., and Nesdale, A. R. 1978. Emotional arousal, anger, and aggression: the misattribution issue. In *Perception of emotion in self and others, advances in the study of communication and affect*, vol. 4, ed. P. Pliner, L. Krames, and K. Blankstein. New York: Plenum.

SCHACHTER, S. 1964. The interaction of cognitive and physiological determinants of emotional state. In *Advances in experimental social psychology*, vol. 1, ed. L. Berkowitz. New York: Academic Press.

SCHACHTER, S., and SINGER, J. E. 1962. Cognitive, social, and physiological determinants of emotional state. *Psychological Review* 69:379–399.

SCHACHTER, S., and WHEELER, L. 1962. Epinephrine, chlorpromazine, and amusement. *Journal of Abnormal and Social Psychology* 65:121–128.

SEITZ, S. T. 1972. Firearms, homicides, and gun control effectiveness. *Law and Society Review* 6:595–613.

SHUNTICH, R. F., and TAYLOR, S. P. 1972. The effects of alcohol on human physical aggression. *Journal of Experimental Research in Personality* 6:34–38.

SHUPE, L. M. 1954. Alcohol and crime: a study of the urine alcohol concentration found in 882 persons arrested during or immediately after the commission of a felony. *Journal of Criminal Law, Criminology, and Police Science* 44:661–664.

SIMONS, L. S., and TURNER, C. W. 1974. A further investigation of the weapons effect. In *Proceedings of Division 8 of the American Psychological Association*. New Orleans: APA.

SIMONS, L. S., TURNER, C. W., and LAYTON, J. F. 1974. A naturalistic study of the weapons effect: effect of aggressive stimuli and deindividuation on horn-honking. Paper read at the meeting of the Western Psychological Association, April 1974, San Francisco.

SMITH, D., KING, M., and HOEBEL, B. 1970. Lateral hypothalamic control of killings: evidence for a cholinoceptive mechanism. *Science* 167:900–901.

SOMMERS, A. R. 1976. Violence, television, and the health of American youth. *New England Journal of Medicine* 294:811–817.

STARK, R., and MCEVOY, J. 1970. Middle class violence. *Psychology Today* 4:52–54, 110–112.

SURGEON GENERAL'S SCIENTIFIC ADVISORY COMMITTEE ON TELEVISION AND SOCIAL BEHAVIOR. 1972. *Television and growing up: the impact of televised violence. Report to the Surgeon General, United States Public Health Service.* Washington, D.C.: U. S. Government Printing Office.

TANNENBAUM, P. H., and ZILLMANN, D. 1977. Emotional arousal in the facilitation of aggression through communication. In *Advances in experimental social psychology*, vol. 8, ed. L. Berkowitz. New York: Academic Press.

TAYLOR, S. P., and GAMMON, C. B. 1975. Effects of type and dose of alcohol on human physical aggression. *Journal of Personality and Social Psychology* 32:169–175.

TAYLOR, S. P., VARDARIS, R. M., RAWTICH, A. B., GAMMON, C. B., CRANSTON, J. W., and LUBETKIN, A. I. 1976. The effects of alcohol and delta-9-tetrahydrocannabinol on human physical aggression. *Aggressive Behavior* 2:153–161.

TUCKER, I. F. 1970. *Adjustments, models and mechanisms.* New York: Academic Press.

TURNER, C. W., and SIMONS, L. S. 1974. Effects of subject sophistication and evaluation apprehension on aggressive responses to weapons. *Journal of Personality and Social Psychology* 30:341–348.

WALTERS, R. H., and LLEWELLYN-THOMAS, E. 1963. Enhancement of punitiveness by visual and audiovisual displays. *Canadian Journal of Psychology* 17:244–255.

WOLFGANG, M. E., and STROHM, R. B. 1956. The relationship between alcohol and criminal homicide. *Quarterly Journal of Studies on Alcohol* 17:411–425.

ZILLMANN, D. 1971. Excitation transfer in communication-mediated aggressive behavior. *Journal of Experimental Social Psychology* 7:419–434.

ZILLMANN, D., KATCHER, A. H., and MILAVSKY, B. 1972. Excitation transfer from physical exercise to subsequent aggressive behavior. *Journal of Experimental Social Psychology* 8:247–259.

ZIMBARDO, P. G. 1970. The human choice: individuation, reason and order versus deindividuation, impulse, and chaos. In *Nebraska symposium on motivation, 1969*, ed. W. J. Arnold and D. Levine, pp. 237–307. Lincoln: University of Nebraska Press.

ZIMBARDO, P. G., HANEY, C., BANK, W. C., and JAFFE, D. 8 April 1973. The mind is a formidable jailer: a Pirandellian prison. *The New York Times*, pp. 38–60.

Chapter 9 Altruism

ALLEN, H. 1972. Bystander intervention and helping on the subway. In *Beyond the laboratory: field research in social psychology*, ed. L. Bickman and T. Henchy. New York: McGraw-Hill.

BARASH, D. P. 1977. *Sociobiology of behavior.* New York: Elsevier.

BATSON, C. D., COLE, J. S., JASNOSKI, M. L., and HANSON, M. 1978. Buying kindness: effect of an extrinsic incentive for helping on perceived altruism. *Personality and Social Psychology Bulletin* 4:86–91.

BENSON, P. L., KARABENICK, S. A., and LERNER, R. M. 1976. Pretty pleases: the effects of physical attractiveness, race, and sex on receiving help. *Journal of Experimental Social Psychology* 12:409–415.

BERKOWITZ, L., and CONNOR, W. H. 1966. Success, failure, and social responsibility. *Journal of Personality and Social Psychology* 4:664–669.

BERKOWITZ, L., and DANIELS, L. R. 1963. Responsibility and dependency. *Journal of Abnormal and Social Psychology* 66:429–436.

BERSCHEID, E., and WALSTER, E. 1978. *Interpersonal attraction.* Reading, Mass.: Addison-Wesley.

BICKMAN, L. 1971. The effect of another bystander's ability to help on bystander intervention in an emergency. *Journal of Experimental Social Psychology* 7:367–379.

———. 1972. Environmental attitudes and actions. *Journal of Social Psychology* 87:323–324.

BRAMEL, D. 1969. Interpersonal attraction, hostility, and perception. In *Experimental social psychology*, ed. J. Mills, pp. 1–120. New York: Macmillan.

BREHM, J. 1966. *A theory of psychological reactance.* New York: Academic Press.

BREHM, J., and COLE, A. 1966. Effect of a favor which reduces freedom. *Journal of Personality and Social Psychology* 3:420–426.

BROLL, L., GROSS, A. E., and PILIAVIN, I. M. 1974. Effects of offered and requested help on help seeking and reactions to being helped. *Journal of Applied Social Psychology* 4:244–258.

Bryan, J., and Test, M. 1967. Models and helping: naturalistic studies in aiding behavior. *Journal of Personality and Social Psychology* 6:400-407.

Bryan, J., and Walbek, N. 1970. Preaching and practicing generosity: children's actions and reactions. *Child Development* 41:329–353.

Campbell, D. T. 1975. On the conflicts between biological and social evolution and between psychology and moral tradition. *American Psychologist* 30:1103–1126.

Castro, M. A. 1975. Reactions to receiving aid as a function of cost to donor and opportunity to aid. *Dissertation Abstracts International* 35:3644–3645.

Cialdini, R. B., Darby, B. L., and Vincent, J. E. 1973. Transgression and altruism: a case for hedonism. *Journal of Experimental Social Psychology* 9:502–516.

Cialdini, R. B., and Kenrick, D. T. 1976. Altruism as hedonism: a social development perspective on the relationship of negative mood state and helping. *Journal of Personality and Social Psychology* 34:907–914.

Clark, R. D., and Word, L. E. 1972. Why don't bystanders help? Because of ambiguity? *Journal of Personality and Social Psychology* 24:392–401.

———. 1974. Where is the apathetic bystander? Situational characteristics of the emergency. *Journal of Personality and Social Psychology* 29:279–288.

Cohen, S., and Spacapan, S. 1978. The aftereffects of stress: an attentional interpretation. *Environmental Psychology and Nonverbal Behavior* 3:43–57.

Cole, J. S., Batson, C. D., and McDavis, K. 1978. Empathic mediation of helping: a two-stage model. *Journal of Personality and Social Psychology* 36:752–766.

Cowan, P. A., and Inskeep, R. 1978. Commitments to help among the disabled-disadvantaged. *Personality and Social Psychology Bulletin* 4:92–96.

Darley, J. 1970. Diffusion of responsibility and helping behavior. Paper read at the 78th annual meeting of the American Psychological Association, September 1970.

Darley, J. M., and Batson, C. D. 1973. "From Jerusalem to Jericho": a study of situational and dispositional variables in helping behavior. *Journal of Personality and Social Psychology* 27:100–108.

Darley, J., and Latané, B. 1968. Bystander intervention in emergencies: diffusion of responsibility. *Journal of Personality and Social Psychology* 8:377–383.

Endler, N. S., and Magnusson, D. 1978. But interactionists do believe in people! Response to Krauskopf. *Psychological Bulletin* 35:590–592.

Enzle, M. E., and Harvey, M. D. 1979. Recipient mood states and helping behavior. *Journal of Experimental Social Psychology* 15:170–182.

Feldman, R. E. 1968. Response to compatriot and foreigner who seek assistance. *Journal of Personality and Social Psychology* 10:202–214.

Fink, E. L., Rey, L. D., Johnson, K. W., Spenner, K. I., Morton, D. R., and Flores, E. T. 1975. The effects of family occupational type, sex, and appeal style on helping behavior. *Journal of Experimental Social Psychology* 11:43–52.

Fisher, J. D., and Nadler, A. 1976. Effect of donor resources on recipient self-esteem and self-help. *Journal of Experimental Social Psychology* 12:139–150.

Fisher, R. 1971. The effects of guilt and shame on public and private helping. *Dissertation Abstracts* 31:6897–6898.

Floyd, J. 1964. Effects of amount of reward and friendship status of the other on the frequency of sharing in children. *Dissertation Abstracts* 5396–5397.

Freedman, J., and Fraser, S. 1966. Compliance without pressure: the foot-in-the-door technique. *Journal of Personality and Social Psychology* 4:195–202.

Freedman, J., Wallington, S., and Bless, E. 1967. Compliance without pressure: the effect of guilt. *Journal of Personality and Social Psychology* 7:117–124.

Gaertner, S. L. 1975. The role of racial attitudes in helping behavior. *Journal of Social Psychology* 97:95–101.

Gergen, K. J., and Gergen, M. M. 1971. International assistance from a psychological perspective. In *Yearbook of world affairs*, vol. 25, pp. 87–103. London: Institute of World Affairs.

Gergen, K. J., Gergen, M. M., and Meter, K. 1972. Individual orientations to prosocial behavior. *Journal of Social Issues* 8:105–130.

Goranson, R., and Berkowitz, L. 1966. Reciprocity and responsibility reactions to prior help. *Journal of Personality and Social Psychology* 3:227–232.

Gouldner, A. 1960. The norm of reciprocity. *American Sociological Review* 25:161–178.

Greenberg, M. S., and Frisch, D. M. 1972. Effect of intentionality on willingness to reciprocate a favor. *Journal of Experimental Social Psychology* 8:99–111.

Gross, A. E., and Latané, J. G. 1974. Receiving help, reciprocation, and interpersonal attraction. *Journal of Applied Social Psychology* 4:210–223.

Grusec, J. E., and Skubiski, S. L. 1970. Model nurturance, demand characteristics of the modeling experiment, and altruism. *Journal of Personality and Social Psychology* 14:352–359.

Harris, M. B. 1968. Some determinants of sharing in children. *Dissertation Abstracts* 29:2633.

———. 1977. Effects of altruism on mood. *Journal of Social Psychology* 2:197–208.

Harris, M. B., Benson, S. M., and Hall, C. L. 1975. The effects of confession on altruism. *Journal of Social Psychology* 67:751–756.

Heider, F. 1958. *The psychology of interpersonal relations.* New York: Wiley.

Hoffman, M. L. 1975a. Altruistic behavior and the parent-child relationship. *Journal of Personality and Social Psychology* 31:937–943.

———. 1975b. Developmental synthesis of affect and cognition and its implications for altruistic motivation. *Developmental Personality* 11:607–622.

Hornstein, H. A., Fisch, E., and Holmes, M. 1968. Influence of a model's feeling about his behavior and his relevance as a comparison other on observer's helping behavior. *Journal of Personality and Social Psychology* 10:222–226.

Hornstein, H. A., Holloway, S., and Sole, K. 1977. The effects of temptation and information about a stranger on helping. *Personality and Social Psychology* 3:416–420.

Hornstein, H. A., Mason, H. N., Sole, K., and Heilman,

M. 1971. Effects of sentiment and completion of a helping act on observer helping: a case for socially mediated Zeigarnik effects. *Journal of Personality and Social Psychology* 17:107–112.

House, J. S., and Wolf, S. 1978. Effects of urban residence on interpersonal trust and helping behavior. *Journal of Personality and Social Psychology* 36:1029–1043.

Isen, A. M. 1970. Success, failure, attention, and reaction to others. *Journal of Personality and Social Psychology* 15:294–301.

Isen, A. M., and Levin, P. F. 1972. Effect of feeling good on helping: cookies and kindness. *Journal of Personality and Social Psychology* 21:384–388.

Kazdin, A. E., and Bryan, J. H. 1971. Competence and volunteering. *Journal of Experimental Social Psychology* 7:87–97.

Kenrick, D. T., Bauman, D. J., and Cialdini, R. B. 1979. A step in the socialization of altruism as hedonism: effects of negative mood on children's generosity under public and private conditions. *Journal of Personality and Social Psychology* 37:747–755.

Kimble, G., and Perlmuter, L. C. 1970. The problem of volition. *Psychological Review* 77:361–384.

Konečni, V. J. 1972. Some effects of guilt on compliance: a field replication. *Journal of Personality and Social Psychology* 23:30–32.

Korte, C. 1971. Effects of individual responsibility and group communication on help-giving in an emergency. *Human Relations* 24:149–159.

Korte, C., and Kerr, N. 1973. Response to altruistic opportunities in urban and nonurban settings. *Journal of Social Psychology* 9:556–562.

Krebs, D. L. 1970. Altruism—an examination of the concept and a review of the literature. *Psychological Bulletin* 73:258–302.

———. 1975. Empathy and altruism. *Journal of Personality and Social Psychology* 32:1134–1146.

Latané, B., and Rodin, J. 1969. A lady in distress: inhibiting effects of friends and strangers on bystander intervention. *Journal of Experimental Social Psychology* 5:189–202.

Lerner, M. J. 1970. The desire for justice and reactions to victims. In *Altruism and helping behavior*, ed. J. Macaulay and L. Berkowitz, pp. 205–230. New York: Academic Press.

———. 1977. The justice motive: some hypotheses as to its origins and forms. *Journal of Personality* 45:1–52.

Lerner, M. J., Miller, D. T., and Holmes, D. 1975. Deserving versus justice: a contemporary dilemma. In *Advances in experimental social psychology*, vol. 12, ed. L. Berkowitz and E. Walster. New York: Academic Press.

Lerner, M. J., and Simmons, C. H. 1966. Observer's reactions to the "innocent victim": compassion or rejection? *Journal of Personality and Social Psychology* 4:203–210.

Macaulay, J. 1970. A shill for charity. In *Altruism and helping behavior*, ed. J. Macaulay and L. Berkowitz. New York: Academic Press.

McKenna, R. H. 1976. Good samaritanism in rural and urban settings: a nonreactive comparison of helping behavior of clergy and control subjects. *Representative Research in Social Psychology* 7:58–65.

McMillen, D. S., Sanders, D. Y., and Solomon, G. S. 1977. Self-esteem, attentiveness, and helping behavior. *Personality and Social Psychology Bulletin* 3:257–262.

Mahoney, M. J. 1974. *Cognition and behavior modification*. Cambridge, Mass.: Ballinger.

Masters, J. C., and Pisarowicz, P. A. 1975. Self-reinforcement and generosity following two types of altruistic behavior. *Child Development* 46:313–318.

Mathews, K. E., and Canon, L. K. 1975. Environmental noise level as a determinant of helping behavior. *Journal of Personality and Social Psychology* 32:571–577.

Midlarsky, E. 1968. Some antecedents of aiding under stress. In *Proceedings of the Seventy-sixth Annual Convention of the American Psychological Association*.

Midlarsky, M., and Midlarsky, E. 1972. Additive and interactive status effects on altruistic behavior. *Proceedings of the Eightieth Annual Convention of the American Psychological Association* 7:213–214.

Miller, D. T. 1977. Altruism and threat to a belief in a just world. *Journal of Experimental Social Psychology* 13:113.

Mills, J., and Egger, R. 1972. Effect on derogation of a victim of choosing to reduce his distress. *Journal of Personality and Social Psychology* 23:405–408.

Moore, B. S., Underwood, B., and Rosenhan, D. L. 1973. Affect and self-gratification. *Developmental Psychology* 8:209–214.

Moriarty, T. 1975. Crime, commitment, and the respective bystander: two field experiments. *Journal of Personality and Social Psychology* 31:370–376.

Morse, S. J., Gergen, K. J., Peele, S., and Van Ryneveld, J. 1977. Reactions to receiving expected and unexpected help from a person who violates or does not violate a norm. *Journal of Experimental Social Psychology* 13:397–402.

Muir, D., and Weinstein, E. 1962. The social debt: an investigation of lower-class and middle-class norms of social obligation. *American Sociological Review* 27:532–539.

Paulhus, D. L., Shaffer, D. R., and Downing, L. L. 1977. Effects of making blood donor motives salient upon donor retention. *Personality and Social Psychology Bulletin* 3:99–102.

Piliavin, I. M., Piliavin, J. A., and Rodin, J. 1975. Costs, diffusion and the stigmatized victim. *Journal of Personality and Social Psychology* 32:429–438.

Pruitt, D. G. 1968. Reciprocity and credit building in a laboratory dyad. *Journal of Personality and Social Psychology* 8:143–147.

Rawlings, E. 1970. Reactive guilt and anticipatory guilt in altruistic behavior. In *Altruism and helping behavior*, ed. J. Macaulay and L. Berkowitz, pp. 163–178. New York: Academic Press.

Rosenbaum, M., and Blake, R. 1955. Volunteering as a function of field structure. *Journal of Abnormal and Social Psychology* 50:193–196.

Rosenhan, D. L. 1970. The natural socialization of altruistic autonomy. In *Altruism and helping behavior*, ed. J. Macaulay and L. Berkowitz, pp. 251–268. New York: Academic Press.

Ross, A. S. 1970. The effect of observing a helpful model on helping behavior. *Journal of Social Psychology* 81:131–132.

Rushton, J. P. 1975. Generosity in children: immediate and long-term effects of modeling, preaching, and moral judgment. *Journal of Personality and Social Psychology* 31:459–466.

———. 1976. Socialization and the altruistic behavior of children. *Psychological Bulletin* 83:898–913.

SATOW, K. L. 1975. Social approval and helping. *Journal of Experimental Social Psychology* 11:501–509.

SAWYER, J. 1966. The altruism scale: a measure of co-operative, individualistic, and competitive interpersonal orientation. *American Journal of Sociology* 71:407–416.

SCHOPLER, J. 1967. An investigation of sex differences on the influence of dependence. *Sociometry* 30:50–63.

SCHOPLER, J., and BATESON, N. 1965. The power of dependence. *Journal of Personality and Social Psychology* 2:247–254.

SCHOPLER, J., and MATTHEWS, M. 1965. The influence of the perceived causal locus of partner's dependence on the use of interpersonal power. *Journal of Personality and Social Psychology* 2:609–612.

SCHOPLER, J., and THOMPSON, V. 1968. The role of attribution processes in mediating amount of reciprocity for a favor. *Journal of Personality and Social Psychology* 10:243–250.

SCHWARTZ, S. H. 1977. Normative influences on altruism. In *Advances in experimental social psychology*, vol. 10, ed. L. Berkowitz. New York: Academic Press.

SCHWARTZ, S. H., and CLAUSEN, G. T. 1970. Responsibility, norms, and helping in an emergency. *Journal of Personality and Social Psychology* 16:299–310.

SHAFFER, D. R., ROZELL, M., and HENDRICH, C. 1975. Intervention in the library: the effect of increased responsibility on bystanders' willingness to prevent a theft. *Journal of Applied Social Psychology* 5:303–319.

SHERROD, D. R., and DOWNS, R. 1974. Environmental determinants of altruism: the effects of stimulus overload and perceived control on helping. *Journal of Experimental Social Psychology* 10:468–479.

STAUB, E. 1970. A child in distress: the influence of age and number of witnesses on children's attempts to help. *Journal of Personality and Social Psychology* 14:130–140.

———. 1974. Helping a distressed person: social, personality, and stimulus determinants. In *Advances in experimental social psychology*, vol. 7, ed. L. Berkowitz. New York: Academic Press.

———. 1978a. Predicting prosocial behavior: a model for specifying the nature of personality-situation interaction. In *Internal and external determinants of behavior*, ed. L. Pervin and M. Lewis. New York: Plenum.

———. 1978b. *Positive social behavior and morality, Vol. 1: social and personal influences.* New York: Academic Press.

———. 1979a. Understanding and predicting social behavior with special emphasis on prosocial behavior. In *Personality: basic issues and current research*, ed. E. Staub. Englewood Cliffs, N.J.: Prentice-Hall.

———. 1979b. *Positive social behavior and morality, Vol. 2: socialization and development*. New York: Academic Press.

STAUB, E., and SHERK, L. 1970. Need for approval, children's sharing behavior, and reciprocity in sharing. *Child Development* 41:243–253.

TEGER, A. 1970. Defining the socially responsible response. Paper read at the 78th annual meeting of the American Psychological Association, 1970.

TESSER, A., GATEWOOD, R., and DRIVER, M. 1968. Some determinants of gratitude. *Journal of Personality and Social Psychology* 19:233–236.

TRIVERS, R. L. 1971. The evolution of reciprocal altruism. *Quarterly Review of Biology* 46:35–57.

———. 1974. Parent-offspring conflict. *American Zoologist* 14:249–264.

TUCKER, L., HORNSTEIN, H. A., HOLLOWAY, S., and SOLE, K. 1977. The effects of temptation and information about a stranger on helping. *Personality and Social Psychology Bulletin* 3:416–420.

UNDERWOOD, B., BEVENSON, J. F., BERENSON, R. J., CHENG, K. K., WILSON, D., KULIK, J., MOORE, B. S., and WENZEL, G. 1977. Attention, negative affect, and altruism: an ecological validation. *Personality and Social Psychology Bulletin* 13:541–542.

UNDERWOOD, B., FROMING, W. J., and MOORE, B. S. 1977. Mood, attention, and altruism: a search for mediating variables. *Developmental Psychology* 13:541–542.

WALSTER, E., WALSTER, G. W., and BERSCHEID, E. 1978. *Equity: theory and research.* Boston: Allyn & Bacon.

WEGNER, D. M., and SCHAEFER, D. 1978. The concentration of responsibility: an objective self awareness analysis of group size effects in helping. *Journal of Personality and Social Psychology* 36:147–155.

WEYANT, J. M. 1978. Effects of mood states, costs, and benefits on helping. *Journal of Personality and Social Psychology* 36:1169–1176.

WILKE, H., and LANZETTA, J. T. 1970. The obligation to help: the effects of amount of prior help on subsequent helping behavior. *Journal of Experimental Social Psychology* 6:488–493.

WILSON, E. O. 1975. *Sociobiology: the new synthesis.* Cambridge, Mass.: Belknap Press of Harvard University Press.

———. 1978. *On human nature.* Cambridge, Mass.: Harvard University Press.

YARROW, M. R., SCOTT, P. M., and WAXLER, C. Z. 1973. Learning concern for others. *Developmental Psychology* 8:240–261.

Chapter 10 Social Interdependence

BEM, D. J., and LORD, C. G. 1979. Template matching: a proposal for probing the ecological validity of experimental settings in social psychology. *Journal of Personality and Social Psychology* 37:833–846.

BLOCK, J. 1978. *The Q-sort method in personality assessment and psychological research.* Palo Alto, Calif.: Consulting Psychologists Press. (Originally published, 1961).

BONACICH, P., SHURE, G. H., KAHAN, J. P., and MEEKER, R. J. 1976. *Journal of Conflict Resolution*, 20:678–706.

BRAVER, S. L., and BARNETT, B. 1976. Effects of modeling on cooperation in a prisoner's dilemma game. *Journal of Personality and Social Psychology* 33:161–169.

CARNEVALE, P. 1977. Cooperators, competitors, and individualists encode nonverbal affect. Paper read at the Eastern Psychological Association Convention, 1977, Boston.

CHAMMAH, A. M. 1969. Sex differences, strategy, and communication in mixed motive games. Ph.D. dissertation, University of Michigan.

CONRATH, D. W. 1972. Sex role and cooperation in the

game of chicken. *Journal of Conflict Resolution* 16:433–443.

DAWES, R. 1975. Formal models of dilemmas in social decision making. In *Human judgment and decision processes*, ed. M. F. Kaplan and S. Schwartz. New York: Academic Press.

DAWES, R. M., MCTAVISH, J. and SHAKLEE, H. 1977. Behavior, communication and assumptions about other peoples' behavior in a commons dilemma situation. *Journal of Personality and Social Psychology* 35:1–11.

DEUTSCH, M. 1973. *The resolution of conflict.* New Haven: Yale University Press.

DEUTSCH, M., and KRAUSS, R. M. 1960. The effect of threat upon interpersonal bargaining. *Journal of Abnormal and Social Psychology* 61:181–189.

GOTTHEIL, E., THORNTON, C. C., and EXLINE, R. 1976. Appropriate and background affect in facial displays of emotion. *Archives of General Psychiatry* 33:565–568.

GRANT, M., and SERMAT, V. 1969. Status and sex of other as determinants of behavior, in a mixed motive game. *Journal of Personality and Social Psychology* 12:151–157.

HARDIN, G. 1968. The tragedy of the commons. *Science* 162:1243–1248.

HOMANS, C. G. 1950. *The human group.* New York: Harcourt Brace.

KELLEY, H. H. 1975. An attribution analysis of social interaction. Paper read as the Katz-Newcomb lecture, April 1975, University of Michigan.

KELLEY, H. H., and GREZLAK, J. 1972. Conflict between individuals and common interest in an N person relationship. *Journal of Personality and Social Psychology* 21:190–197.

KELLEY, H. H., and STAHELSKI, A. J. 1970. Social interaction bases for cooperators' and competitors' beliefs about others. *Journal of Personality and Social Psychology* 16:66–91.

KIPNIS, D. 1976. Does power corrupt? *Journal of Personality and Social Psychology* 24:33–41.

KOMORITA, S. S., and CHERTKOFF, J. M. 1973. A bargaining theory of coalition formation. *Psychological Review* 80:149–162.

KUHLMAN, D. M., CARNEVALE, P., and MILLS, J. 1979. Differences in background affect as a function of social motivation. Unpublished manuscript, University of Delaware.

KUHLMAN, D. M., and MARSHELLO, A. 1975a. Individual differences in the game motives of own, relative, and joint gain. *Journal of Research in Personality* 9:240–251.

———. 1975b. Individual differences in game motivation as moderators of preprogrammed strategy effects in prisoner's dilemma. *Journal of Personality and Social Psychology* 32:922–931.

KUHLMAN, D. M., and WIMBERLEY, D. L. 1976. Expectations of choice behavior held by cooperators, competitors, and individualists across four classes of experimental game. *Journal of Personality and Social Psychology* 34:69–81.

LEVENTHAL, G. S. 1976. Fairness in social relationships. In *Contemporary topics in social psychology*, ed. J. W. Thibaut, J. T. Spence, and R. C. Carson. Morristown, N.J.: General Learning Press.

LLOYD, W. F. 1977. On the checks to population. In *Managing the Commons*, ed. G. Hardin and J. Baden. San Francisco: Freeman.

MCCLINTOCK, C. G., and MOSKOWITZ, J. M. 1976. Children's preferences for individualistic, cooperative, and competitive outcomes. *Journal of Personality and Social Psychology* 34:543–555.

MCCLINTOCK, C. G., MOSKOWITZ, J. M., and MCCLINTOCK, E. 1977. Variations in preferences for individualistic, competitive, and cooperative outcomes as a function of age, game class, and task in nursery school children. *Child Development* 48:1080–1085.

MESSICK, D. M., and MCCLINTOCK, C. G. 1968. Motivational bases of choice in experimental games. *Journal of Experimental Social Psychology* 4:1–25.

MESSICK, D. M., and THORNEGATE, W. B. 1967. Relative gain maximization in experimental games. *Journal of Experimental Social Psychology* 3:85–101.

PRUITT, D. G., and GLEASON, J. M. 1978. Threat capacity and the choice between independence. *Personality and Social Psychology Bulletin* 4:252–255.

PRUITT, D. G., and KIMMEL, M. J. 1977. Twenty years of experimental gaming: critique, synthesis, and suggestions for the future. *Annual Review of Psychology* 28:363–392.

RAPOPORT, A. 1973. *Experimental games and their uses in psychology.* Morristown, N.J.: General Learning Press.

RAPOPORT, A., and CHAMMAH, A. M. 1965a. Sex differences in factors contributing to the level of cooperation in the prisoner's dilemma game. *Journal of Personality and Social Psychology* 2:831–838.

———. 1965b. *Prisoner's dilemma: a study in conflict and cooperation.* Ann Arbor: University of Michigan Press.

RIVERA, A.N., and TEDESCHI, J. 1976. Public versus private reaction to positive inequity. *Journal of Personality and Social Psychology* 34:895–900.

RUBIN, J. Z., and BROWN, B. R. 1975. The social psychology of bargaining and negotiation. New York: Academic Press.

SHURE, G., and MEEKER, R. J. 1968. Empirical demonstration of normative behavior in the prisoner's dilemma. In *Proceedings of the Seventy-sixth Annual Convention of the American Psychological Association.* Washington, D.C.: American Psychological Association.

SMITH, W. P., and LEGINSKI, W. A. 1970. Magnitude and precision of punitive power in bargaining strategy. *Journal of Experimental Social Psychology* 6:57–76.

STEIGLEIDER, M. K., WEISS, R. F., CRAMER, R. E., and FEINBERG, R. A. 1978. Motivating and reinforcing functions of competitive behavior. *Journal of Personality and Social Psychology* 36:1291–1301.

THIBAUT, J. W., and KELLEY, H. H. 1959. *The social psychology of groups.* New York: Wiley.

TODA, M., SHINOTSUKA, H., MCCLINTOCK, C. G., and STECH, F. J. 1978. Development of competitive behavior as a function of culture, age, and social comparison. *Journal of Personality and Social Psychology* 36:825–839.

WALSTER, E., WALSTER, G. W., and BERSCHEID, E. 1978. *Equity: theory and research.* Boston: Allyn & Bacon.

WILSON, J. A. 1977. A test of the tragedy of the commons. In *Managing the commons*, ed. G. Hardin and J. Baden. San Francisco: Freeman.

Chapter 11 Groups

Adorno, T. W., Frenkel-Brunswik, E., Levinson, D. J., and Sanford, R. N. 1950. *The authoritarian personality.* New York: Harper.

Allen, V. L. 1975. Social support for nonconformity. In *Advances in experimental social psychology,* vol. 8, ed. L. Berkowitz. New York: Academic Press.

Allen, V. L., and Levine, J. M. 1975. Social support and conformity: the role of independent assessment of reality. *Journal of Experimental Social Psychology* 7:48–58.

Allport, F. H. 1924. *Social psychology.* Boston: Houghton Mifflin.

Allport, G. W. 1968. Six decades of social psychology. In *Higher education in social psychology,* ed. C. C. Lundsted, pp. 9–19. Cleveland: The Press of Case Western Reserve.

Amabile, T. M. 1979. Effects of external evaluation on artistic creativity. *Journal of Personality and Social Psychology* 37, no. 2:221–233.

Aronson, E., and Mills, J. 1959. Effect of severity of initiation on liking for a group. *Journal of Abnormal and Social Psychology* 59:177–181.

Asch, S. E. 1956. Studies of independence and conformity: a minority of one against a unanimous majority. *Psychological Monographs* 70, no.9: whole no. 416.

Bales, R. F. 1970. *Personality and interpersonal behavior.* New York: Holt, Rinehart & Winston.

Bennis, W. G., and Shepard, H. A. 1965. A theory of group development. *Human Relations* 9:415–457.

Blake, R. R., Shepard, H. A., and Mouton, J. S. 1964. *Managing intergroup conflict in industry.* Houston: Gulf.

Bouchard, T. J. 1969. Personality, problem-solving procedure, and performance in small groups. *Journal of Applied Psychology* 53:1–29.

Braybrook, D., and Lindblom, C. E. 1970. *A strategy of decisions: policy evaluation as a social process.* New York: The Free Press.

Brockner, J., and Hulton, B. 1978. An evaluation of self-esteem and impression management theories of anticipatory belief change. *Journal of Experimental Social Psychology* 14, no. 6:564–576.

Brown, R. 1965. *Social psychology.* New York: The Free Press.

Bruner, J. S. 1961. The art of discovery. *Harvard Educational Review* 31:21–32.

Burnstein, E., and Vinokur, A. 1973. Testing two classes of theories about group induced shifts in individual choice. *Journal of Experimental Social Psychology* 9:123–137.

Cartwright, D., and Zander, A., eds. 1968. *Group dynamics: research and theory.* New York: Harper & Row.

Clark, M. S., and Mills, J. 1979. Interpersonal attraction in exchange and communal relationships. *Journal of Personality and Social Psychology* 37:12–24.

Cooper, J., and Duncan, B. L. 1971. Cognitive dissonance as a function of self-esteem and logical inconsistency. *Journal of Personality* 39:289–302.

Cottrell, N. B. 1968. Performance in the presence of other human beings: mere presence, audience and affiliation effects. In *Social facilitation and imitative behavior,* ed. E. C. Simmel, R. A. Hoppe, and G. A. Milton. Boston: Allyn & Bacon.

Davis, J. H. 1973. Group decision and social interaction: a theory of social decision schemes. *Psychological Review* 80:97–125.

Davis, J. H., and Restle, F. 1963. The analysis of problems and predictions of group solving. *Journal of Abnormal and Social Psychology* 66:103–116.

Dawes, R. M., McTavish, J., and Shaklee, H. 1977. Behavior, communication, and assumptions about other people's behavior in a common dilemma situation. *Journal of Personality and Social Psychology* 35, no.1:1–10.

Dovidio, J. F., and Morris, W. N. 1975. Effects of stress and commonality of fate in helping behavior. *Journal of Personality and Social Psychology* 31:145–149.

Elliott, G. C. 1979. Some effects of deception and level of self-monitoring on planning and reacting to a self-presentation. *Journal of Personality and Social Psychology* 37:1282–1292.

Emswiller, R., Deaux, K., and Willits, J. 1971. Similarity, sex and requests for small favors. *Journal of Applied Social Psychology* 284–291.

Festinger, L. 1954. A theory of social comparison processes. *Human Relations* 7:117–140.

Fiedler, F. 1971. Validation and extension of the contingency model of leadership effectiveness: a review of empirical findings. *Psychological Bulletin* 76:128–148.

Fisher, J. D., and Nadler, A. 1974. The effect of similarity between donor and recipient on recipient's reactions to aid. *Journal of Applied Social Psychology* 4:230–243.

———. 1976. Effect of donor resources on recipient self-esteem and self-help. *Journal of Experimental Social Psychology* 12:139–150.

Flowers, M. L. 1977. A laboratory test of some implications of Janis's groupthink hypothesis. *Journal of Personality and Social Psychology* 35:888–896.

French, J. R. P., Jr., and Raven, B. H. 1959. The bases of social power. In *Studies in social power,* ed. D. Cartwright, pp. 118–149. Ann Arbor: University of Michigan Press.

Friedman, M., and Rosenman, R. H. 1974. *Type A behavior and your heart.* New York: Knopf.

Gastorf, J. W., Suls, J., and Sanders, G. S. 1980. Type A coronary-prone behavior pattern and social facilitation. *Journal of Personality and Social Psychology* 38:773–780.

Glass, D. C. 1979. *Stress and coronary prone behavior.* Hillsdale, N.J.: Erlbaum.

Goffman, E. 1966. *Behavior in public places: notes on the organization of gatherings.* New York: The Free Press.

Gouldner, A. W. 1960. The norm of reciprocity: a preliminary statement. *American Sociological Review* 25:161–179.

Gross, N., Mason, W., and McEachern, A. 1958. *Explorations in role analysis.* New York: Wiley.

Hackman, J. R., Brousseau, K. and Weiss, J. A. 1976. The interaction of task design and group performance strategies in determining group effectiveness. *Organizational Behavior and Human Performance* 16:350–365.

Hackman, J. R., and Morris, C. G. 1975. Group tasks, group interaction process, and group performance effectiveness: a review and proposed integration. In *Advances in experimental social psychology*, vol. 8, ed. L. Berkowitz, pp. 45–99. New York: Academic Press.

Hackman, J. R., and Oldham, G. R. 1974. Motivation through the design of work: test of a theory. Tech. Report No. 6. New Haven: Department of Administrative Sciences, Yale University.

Haley, J. 1967. Speech sequences of normal and abnormal families with two children present. *Family Process* 6:81–97.

Hardin, G. 1968. The tragedy of the commons. *Science* 162:1243–1248.

Heider, F. 1958. *The psychology of interpersonal relations.* New York: Wiley.

Hoffman, L. R. 1965. Group problem solving. In *Advances in experimental social psychology*, vol. 2, ed. L. Berkowitz, pp. 99–132. New York: Academic Press.

———. 1978. The group problem-solving process. In *Group processes*, ed. L. Berkowitz. New York: Academic Press.

Hollander, E. P. 1958. Conformity, status, and idiosyncratic credit. *Psychological Review* 65:117–127.

Hollander, E. P. 1978. *Leadership dynamics.* New York: The Free Press.

Hollander, E. P., and Willis, R. H. 1967. Some current issues in the psychology of conformity and nonconformity. *Psychological Bulletin* 68:62–76.

Janis, I. L. 1968. Group identification under conditions of extreme danger. Reprinted in *Group dynamics: research and theory*, ed. D. Cartwright and A. Zander. New York: Harper & Row.

———. 1972. *Victims of groupthink: a psychological study of foreign-policy decisions and fiascos.* Boston: Houghton Mifflin.

Jones, M. B. 1974. Regressing groups on individual effectiveness. *Organizational Behavior and Human Performance* 11:426–451.

Jones, R. A. 1977. *Self-fulfilling prophecies.* Hillsdale, N.J.: Erlbaum.

Kelley, H. H., and Stahelski, A. V. 1970. Social interaction basis of cooperators' and competitors' beliefs about others. *Journal of Personality and Social Psychology* 16:66–91.

Kelley, H. H., and Thibaut, J. W. 1969. Group problem solving. In *The handbook of social psychology*, 2d ed., vol. 4, ed. G. Lindzey and E. Aronsen, Reading, Mass.: Addison-Wesley.

———. 1978. *Interpersonal relations: a theory of interdependence.* New York: Wiley-Interscience.

Kiesler, C. A. 1971. *The psychology of commitment: experiments linking behavior to belief.* New York: Academic Press.

Kiesler, C. A., and Kiesler, S. B. 1969. *Conformity.* Reading, Mass.: Addison-Wesley.

Kohn, M. L. 1977. *Class and conformity: a study in values.* 2d ed. Chicago: University of Chicago Press.

Leavitt, H. J. 1951. Some effects of certain communication patterns on group performance. *Journal of Abnormal and Social Psychology* 46:38–50.

LeBon, G. 1895. *Psychologie des foules.* Paris: F. Oléan.

Leighton, A. H. 1945. *The governing of men.* Princeton: Princeton University Press.

Lerner, M. J., Miller, D. T., and Holmes, J. G. 1976. Deserving versus justice: a contemporary dilemma. In *Advances in experimental social psychology*, vol. 9, ed. L. Berkowitz and E. Walster, pp. 133–162. New York: Academic Press.

Lewin, K. 1948. *Resolving social conflict.* New York: Harper.

Lord, C. G., Ross, L., and Lepper, M. R. 1979. Biased assimilation and attitude polarization: the effects of prior theories on subsequently considered evidence. *Journal of Personality and Social Psychology* 37:2098–2109.

McCullers, C. 1946. *The member of the wedding.* New York: Houghton Mifflin.

Mann, R. D. 1959. A review of the relationships between personality and performance in small groups. *Psychological Bulletin* 56:241–270.

Martin, J. 1979. Miss Manners: rudeness by any name is still impolite. *Washington Post*, April 29, pp. N1, N13.

Miller, D. T., and Ross, M. 1975. Self-serving biases in the attribution of causality: fact or fiction? *Psychological Bulletin* 82:213–225.

Olson, M. 1965. *The logic of collective action: public goods and the theory of groups.* Cambridge, Mass.: Harvard University Press.

Osborn, A. F. 1957. *Applied imagination.* New York: Scribner.

Platt, J. 1973. Social traps. *American Psychologist* 28, no. 3:641–651.

Pruitt, D. G. 1972. Methods for resolving differences of interest: a theoretical analysis. *Journal of Social Issues* 28:133–154.

Rather, D., and Heskowitz, M. 1977. *The camera never blinks.* New York: Ballantine.

Ross, M., and Sicoly, F. 1979. Egocentric biases in availability and attribution. *Journal of Personality and Social Psychology* 37, no. 3:322–326.

Schachter, S. 1951. Deviation, rejection, and communication. *Journal of Abnormal and Social Psychology* 46:190–207.

———. 1959. *The psychology of affiliation.* Stanford: Stanford University Press.

Schlenker, B. R., and Miller, R. S. 1977. Egocentrism in groups: self-serving biases or logical information processing? *Journal of Personality and Social Psychology* 35, no. 10:755–763

Sherif, M., Harvey, O. J., White, B. J., Hood, W.R., and Sherif, C. W. 1961. *Intergroup conflict and cooperation: the robber's cave experiment.* Norman, Okla.: University of Oklahoma Book Exchange.

Staw, B. M. 1974. Attitudinal and behavioral consequences of changing a major organizational reward: a natural field experiment. *Journal of Personality and Social Psychology* 29:742–751.

Stoner, J. A. 1961. A comparison of individual and group decisions including risk. Unpublished masters thesis, School of Industrial Management, Massachusetts Institute of Technology.

Stouffer, S. A., Suchman, E. A., DeVinney, L. C., Star, S. A., and Williams, R. M., Jr. 1949. *The American soldier*, vol. 1. Princeton: Princeton University Press.

Straus, M. A. 1968. Communications, creativity and problem solving ability of middle- and working-class families in three societies. *American Journal of Sociology* 73:417–430.

Strodtbeck, F. L. 1951. Husband-wife interaction over revealed differences. *American Sociological Review* 16:468–473.

Suls, J. M., and Miller, R. L., eds. 1977. *Social comparison processes: theoretical and empirical perspectives.* Washington, D.C.: Halsted-Wiley.

Taylor, D., Berry, P. C., and Block, C. A. 1958. Does group participation when using brainstorming facilitate or inhibit creative thinking? *Administrative Science Quarterly* 3:23–47.

Triplett, N. 1897. The dynamogenic factors in pacemaking and competition. *American Journal of Psychology* 9:507–533.

Vinokur, A. 1971. Review and theoretical analysis of the effects of group processes upon individual and group decisions involving risk. *Psychological Bulletin* 74:231–250.

Von Neumann, J., and Morganstern, O. 1944. *The theory of games and economic behavior.* Princeton: Princeton University Press.

Vroom, V. H., and Yetton, P. W. 1973. *Leadership and decision-making.* Pittsburgh: University of Pittsburgh Press.

Wallach, M. A., Kogan, N., and Bem, D. J. 1962. Group influence on individual risk taking. *Journal of Abnormal and Social Psychology* 65:75–86.

———. 1964. Diffusion of responsibility and level of risk taking in groups. *Journal of Abnormal and Social Psychology* 68:263–274.

Walster, E., Walster, G. W., and Berscheid, E. 1978. *Equity: theory and research.* Boston: Allyn & Bacon.

Waxler, N. E., and Mishler, E. G. 1970. Experimental studies of families. In *Advances in Experimental Social Psychology*, vol. 5, ed. L. Berkowitz, pp. 249–304. New York: Academic Press.

Webster, M., and Sobieszek, B. I. 1974. *Sources of self-evaluation: a formal theory of significant others and social influence.* New York: Wiley.

Weisskopf-Joelson, E., and Eliseo, T. 1961. An experimental study of the effectiveness of brainstorming. *Journal of Applied Psychology* 45:45–49.

Wilder, D. A. 1977. Perception of groups, size of opposition, and social influence. *Journal of Experimental Social Psychology* 13:253–268.

Wilson, E. O. 1975. *Sociobiology: the new synthesis.* Boston: Harvard University Press.

Word, C. O., Zanna, M. P., and Cooper, J. 1974. The nonverbal mediation of self-fulfilling prophecies in interracial interaction. *Journal of Experimental and Social Psychology* 10:109–120.

Zajonc, R. B. 1965. Social facilitation. *Science* 149:269–274.

———. 1968. Attitudinal effects of mere exposure. *Journal of Personality and Social Psychology* 9, no. 2 (Part 2):1–27.

Zajonc, R. B., Heingartner, A., and Herman, E. M. 1969. Social enhancement and impairment of performance in the cockroach. *Journal of Personality and Social Psychology* 13:83–92.

Zajonc, R. B., and Nieuwenhuyse, B. 1964. Relationships between frequency and recognition: perceptual process or response bias. *Journal of Experimental Psychology* 67:276–285.

Zajonc, R. B., and Sales, S. M. 1966. Social facilitation of dominant and subordinate responses. *Journal of Experimental Social Psychology* 2:160–168.

Zander, A. 1968. Group aspirations. In *Group dynamics*, ed. D. Cartwright and A. Zander, pp. 418–429. New York: Harper & Row.

Zander, A., and Newcomb, T. 1967. Group levels of aspiration in United Fund campaign. *Journal of Personality and Social Psychology* 6:157–162.

Chapter 12 The Physical Environment and Social Behavior

Aiello, J. R., Epstein, Y. M., and Karlin, R. A. 1975. Effects of crowding on electrodermal activity. *Sociological Symposium.* 14:43–57.

Altman, I. 1975. *The environment and social behavior* Monterey, Calif.: Brooks/Cole.

Altman I., and Haythorn, W. W. 1967. The ecology of isolated groups. *Behavioral Science* 12:169–182.

Altman, I., Taylor, D. A., and Wheeler, L. 1971. Ecological aspects of group behavior in social isolation. *Journal of Applied Social Psychology* 1:76–100.

American Psychological Association, Committee on Ethical Standards in Psychological Research. 1973. *Ethical principles in the conduct of research with human participants.* Washington, D.C.: Author.

Ardrey, R. 1966. *The territorial imperative.* New York: Atheneum.

Argyle, M., and Dean, J. 1965. Eye contact, distance and affiliation. *Sociometry* 28:289–304.

Baron, R. A. 1979. Aggression and heat: the "long hot summer" revisited. In *Advances in environmental psychology*, ed. A. Baum, J. E. Singer, and S. Valins. Hillsdale, N.J.: Erlbaum.

Baron, R. A., and Ransberger, V. M. 1978. Ambient temperature and the occurrence of collective violence: the "long hot summer" revisited. *Journal of Personality and Social Psychology* 36:351–360.

Baron, R. A., and Rodin, J. 1978. Perceived control and crowding stress. In *Advances in environmental psychology*, vol. 1, ed. A. Baum, J. Singer, and S. Valins. Hillsdale, N.J.: Erlbaum.

Baum, A., and Greenberg, C. I. 1975. Waiting for a crowd: the behavioral and perceptual effects of anticipated crowding. *Journal of Personality and Social Psychology* 32:671–679.

Baum, A., and Valins, S. 1977. *Architecture and social behavior.* New York: Erlbaum.

Becker, F. D., and Mayo, C. 1971. Delineating personal distance and territoriality. *Environment and Behavior* 3:375:381.

Bleda, P. R., and Bleda, S. E. 1976. Effects of sex and smoking on reactions to personal space invasion at a shopping mall. Paper read at meeting of the American Psychological Association, 1976, Washington, D.C.

Boaz, M., and Chain, S. 1975. *Big Mac: an unauthorized story of McDonald's.* New York: Mentor.

BRONZAFT, A. L., and MCCARTHY, D. P. 1975. Effect of elevated train noise on reading ability. *Environment and Behavior* 7:517–527.

CALHOUN, J. B. 1962. Population density and social pathology. *Scientific American* 206:139–146.

CARLSMITH, J. M., and ANDERSON, C. A. 1979. Ambient temperature and the occurrence of collective violence: a new analysis. *Journal of Personality and Social Psychology* 37:337–346.

CHRISTIAN, J. J. 1950. The adreno-pituitary system and population cycles in mammals. *Journal of Mammalogy* 31:247–259.

CHRISTIAN, J. J., FLYGER, V., and DAVIS, D. C. 1960. Factors in the mass mortality of a herd of Siku deer, *Ciruis nippon. Chesapeake Science* 1:79–95.

COHEN, S. 1978. Environmental load and the allocation of attention. In *Advances in environmental psychology*, ed. A. Baum, J. E. Singer, and S. Valins. Hillsdale, N.J.: Erlbaum.

COHEN, S., EVANS, G., KRANTZ, D., and STOKOLS, D. 1980. Physiological, motivational, and cognitive effects of aircraft noise on children: moving from the laboratory to the field. *American Psychologist* 35:231–243.

COHEN, S., GLASS, D. C., and SINGER, J. E. 1973. Apartment noise, auditory discrimination, and reading ability in children. *Journal of Experimental Social Psychology* 9:407–422.

COHEN, S., and LEZAK, A. 1977. Noise and inattentiveness to social cues. *Environment and Behavior* 9:559–572.

COHEN, S., and SHERROD, D. R. 1978. When density matters: environmental control as a determinant of crowding effects in laboratory and residential settings. *Journal of Population: Behavioral, Social, and Environmental Issues* 1:189–202.

CUNNINGHAM, M. R. 1979. Weather, mood, and helping behavior: quasi experiments with the sunshine samaritan. *Journal of Personality and Social Psychology* 37:1947–1958.

DELONG, A. J. 1973. Territorial stability and hierarchical formation. *Small Group Behavior* 4:56–63.

DONNERSTEIN, E., and WILSON, D. W. 1976. The effects of noise and perceived control upon ongoing and subsequent aggressive behavior. *Journal of Personality and Social Psychology* 34:774–781.

DOOLEY, B. B. 1978. Effects of social density on men with close or far personal space. *Journal of Population: Behavioral, Social and Environmental Issues* 1:251–265.

DOSEY, M. A., and MEISELS, M. 1969. Personal space and self-protection. *Journal of Personality and Social Psychology* 11:93–97.

DUKE, M. P., and NOWICKI, S. 1972. A new measure and social learning model for interpersonal distance. *Journal of Experimental Research in Personality* 6:119–132.

EBBESON, E., KJOS, G., and KONEČNI, V. 1976. Spatial ecology: its effects on the choice of friends and enemies. *Journal of Experimental Social Psychology* 12:505–518.

EDNEY, J. J. 1972. Property, possession and permanence: a field study in human territoriality. *Journal of Applied Social Psychology* 3:275–82.

———. 1974. Human territoriality. *Psychological Bulletin* 81:959–975.

———. 1975. Territoriality and control: a field experiment. *Journal of Personality and Social Psychology* 31:1108–1115.

EDNEY, J. J., and JORDAN-EDNEY, N. 1974. Territorial spacing on a beach. *Sociometry* 37:92–104.

EPSTEIN, Y., and KARLIN, R. A. 1975. Effects of acute experimental crowding. *Journal of Applied Social Psychology* 5:34–53.

ESSER, A. H. 1968. Dominance hierarchy and clinical course of psychiatrically hospitalized boys. *Child Development* 39:147–157.

———. 1973. Cottage fourteen: dominance and territoriality in a group of institutionalized boys. *Small Group Behavior* 4:131–146.

ESSER, A. H., CHAMBERLAIN, A. S., CHAPPLE, E. D., and KLINE, N. S. 1965. Territoriality of patients on a research ward. In *Recent advances in biological psychiatry* vol. 7, ed. J. Wortis. New York: Plenum.

EVANS, G. W. 1979. Behavioral and physiological consequences of crowding in humans. *Journal of Applied Social Psychology* 9:27–46.

EVANS, G. W., and EICHELMAN, W. 1974. An examination of the information overload mechanism of personal space. *Man—Environment Systems* 4:61.

———. 1976. Preliminary models of conceptual linkages among proxemic variables. *Environment and Behavior* 8:87–116.

EVANS, G. W., and HOWARD, R. B. 1972. A methodological investigation of personal space. In *Environmental design: research and practice (EDRA 3)*, ed. W. J. Mitchell. Los Angeles: University of California.

———. 1973. Personal space. *Psychological Bulletin* 80:334–344.

FESTINGER, L., SCHACHTER, S., and BACK, K. 1950. *Social pressures in informal groups: a study of human factors in housing*. New York: Harper & Row.

FINKELMAN, J., and GLASS, D. 1970. Reappraisal of the relationship between noise and human task performance by means of a subsidiary task measure. *Journal of Applied Psychology* 54:211-213.

FREEDMAN, J. L. 1975. *Crowding and behavior*. San Francisco: Freeman.

FREEDMAN, J. L., HESHKA, S., and LEVY, A. 1975. Population density and pathology: is there a relationship? *Journal of Experimental Social Psychology* 11:539–552.

FREEDMAN, J. L., KLEVANSKY, S., and EHRLICH, P. 1971. The effect of crowding on human task performance. *Journal of Applied Social Psychology* 1:7–25.

FREEDMAN, J. L., LEVY, A. S., BUCHANAN, R. W., and PRICE, J. 1972. Crowding and human aggressiveness. *Journal of Experimental Social Psychology* 8:528–548.

GALLE, O. R., GOVE, W. R., and MCPHERSON, J. M. 1972. Population density and pathology: what are the relationships for man? *Science* 176:26–30.

GEEN, R. G. 1978. Effects of attack and uncontrollable noise on aggression. *Journal of Research in Personality* 12:15–29.

GERGEN, K., GERGEN, M., and BARTON, W. 1973. Deviance in the dark. *Psychology Today* 7:129–130.

GLASS, D. C., and SINGER, J. E. 1972. *Urban stress*. New York: Academic Press.

GRIFFITT, W. 1970. Environmental effects on interpersonal affective behavior: ambient effective temperature and attraction. *Journal of Personality and Social Psychology* 15:240–244.

GRIFFITT, W., and VEITCH, R. 1971. Hot and crowded: influences of population density and temperature on interpersonal affective behavior. *Journal of Personality and Social Psychology* 17:92–98.

HALL, E. T. 1959. *The silent language.* New York: Doubleday.

———. 1966. *The hidden dimension.* New York: Doubleday.

HAYDUK, L. A. 1978. Personal space: an evaluative and orienting overview. *Psychological Bulletin* 85:117–134.

HOROWITZ, M. J., DUFF, D. F., and STRATTON, L. O. 1964. Body-buffer zone. *Archives of General Psychiatry* 11:651–656.

ITTELSON, W. H., PROSHANSKY, H. M., and RIVLIN, L. G. 1970. A study of bedroom use on two psychiatric wards. *Hospital and Community Psychiatry* 21:177–180.

KOOCHER, G. P. 1977. Bathroom behavior and human dignity. *Journal of Personality and Social Psychology* 35:120–121.

KORTE, C., YPMA, I., and TOPPEN, A. 1975. Helpfulness in Dutch society as a function of urbanization and environmental input level. *Journal of Personality and Social Psychology* 32:996–1003.

LANGER, E. J., and SAEGERT, S. 1977. Crowding and cognitive control. *Journal of Personality and Social Psychology* 35:175–182.

LAVE, L. B., and SESKIN, E. P. 1970. Air pollution and human health. *Science* 160:723–733.

LEFF, H. 1978. *Experience, environment and human potentials.* New York: Oxford University Press.

LEFF, H., GORDON, L., and FERGUSON, J. 1974. Cognitive set and environmental awareness. *Environment and Behavior* 6:395–447.

LOO, C. M. 1973. The effect of spatial density on the social behavior of children. *Journal of Applied Social Psychology* 2:372–381.

LORENZ, K. 1969. *On aggression.* New York: Bantam.

MCBRIDE, G., KING, M. G., and JAMES, J. W. 1965. Social proximity effects on galvanic skin responses in adult humans. *Journal of Psychology* 61:153–157.

MARSDEN, H. M. 1972. Crowding and animal behavior. In *Environment and the social sciences: perspectives and applications,* ed. J. F. Wohlwill and D. H. Carson. Washington, D.C.: American Psychological Association.

MATHEWS, K. E., JR., and CANON, L. K. 1975. Environmental noise level as a determinant of helping behavior. *Journal of Personality and Social Psychology* 32:571–577.

MEHRABIAN, A., and RUSSELL, J. 1974. *An approach to environmental psychology.* Cambridge, Mass.: The M.I.T. Press.

———. 1975. Environmental effects on affiliation among strangers. *Humanitas* 11:219–230.

MEISELS, M., and DOSEY, M. A. 1971. Personal space, anger arousal and psychological defense. *Journal of Personality* 39:333–344.

MICHELSON, W. 1970. *Man and his urban environment.* Reading, Mass.: Addison-Wesley.

MIDDLEMIST, R. D., KNOWLES, E. S., and MATTER, C. F. 1976. Personal space invasions in the lavatory: suggestive evidence for arousal. *Journal of Personality and Social Psychology* 33:541–546.

———. 1977. What to do and what to report: a reply to Koocher. *Journal of Personality and Social Psychology* 35:122–124.

MILGRAM, S. 1970. The experience of living in cities. *Science* 167:1461–1468.

MUNROE, R. L., and MUNROE, R. H. 1972. Population density and effective relationships in three East African societies. *Journal of Social Psychology* 88:15–20.

NAHEMOW, L., and LAWTON, M. P. 1975. Similarity and propinquity in friendship formation. *Journal of Personality and Social Psychology* 32:205–213.

NESBIT, P., and STEVEN, G. 1974. Personal space and stimulus intensity at a southern California amusement park. *Sociometry* 37:105–115.

NEWMAN, J., and MCCAULEY, C. 1977. Eye contact with strangers in city, suburb, and small town. *Environment and Behavior* 9:547–558.

NEWMAN, O. 1973. *Defensible space.* New York: Macmillan.

PAGE, R. 1977. Noise and helping behavior. *Environment and Behavior* 9:311–334.

PAGE, R., and MOSS, M. 1976. Environmental influences on aggression: the effects of darkness and proximity of victim. *Journal of Applied Social Psychology* 6:126–133.

PATTERSON, A. H. 1978. Territorial behavior and fear of crime in the elderly. *Environmental Psychology and Nonverbal Behavior* 2:131-144.

PATTERSON, M. L. 1973. Compensation in nonverbal immediacy behaviors: a review. *Sociometry* 36:237–252.

PATTERSON, M. L., MULLINS, S., and ROMANO, J. 1971. Compensatory reactions to spatial intrusion. *Sociometry* 34:114-121.

PAULUS, P. B., ANNIS, A. B., SETA, J. J., SCHKADE, J. K., and MATTHEWS, R. W. 1976. Density does affect task performance. *Journal of Personality and Social Psychology* 34:248–253.

PROSHANSKY, H. M., ITTELSON, W. H., and RIVLIN, L. G. 1970. Freedom of choice and behavior in a physical setting. In *Environmental psychology,* ed. H. M. Proshansky, W. H. Ittelson, and L. G. Rivlin. New York: Holt, Rinehart & Winston.

RANDOLPH, T. G. 1970. Domicilliary chemical air pollution in the etiology of ecological mental illness. *International Journal of Social Psychology* 16:243–265.

RAZRAN, G. H. S. 1940. Conditioning response changes in rating and appraising socio-political slogans. *Psychological Bulletin* 37:481.

RODIN, J. 1976. Density, perceived choice and response to controllable and uncontrollable outcomes. *Journal of Experimental Social Psychology* 12:564–578.

RODIN, J., SOLOMAN, S., and METCALF, J. 1978. Role of control in mediating perceptions of density. *Journal of Personality and Social Psychology* 36:988–999.

ROTTON, J., BARRY, T., FREY, J., and SOLER, E. 1978. Air pollution and interpersonal attraction. *Journal of Applied Social Psychology* 8:57–71.

ROTTON, J., FREY, J., BARRY, T., MILLIGAN, M., and FITZ-

PATRICK, M. 1979. The air pollution experience and physical aggression. *Journal of Applied Social Psychology* 5:397–412.

SAEGERT, S. 1973. Crowding: cognitive overload and behavioral constraint. In *Environmental design research: Vol. 2, symposia and workshops. Proceedings of the Fourth International Environmental Design Research Association Conference*, ed. W. F. E. Preiser. Stroudsburg, Pa.: Dowden, Hutchinson, & Ross.

SELIGMAN, M. P. 1975. *Helplessness: on depression, development, and death.*. San Francisco: Freeman.

SELYE, H. 1956. *The stress of life.* New York: McGraw-Hill.

SHERROD, D. R. 1974. Crowding, perceived control and behavioral aftereffects. *Journal of Applied Social Psychology* 4:171–186.

SHERROD, D. R., ARMSTRONG, D., HEWITT, J., MADONIA, B., SPENO, S., and TERUYA, D. 1977. Environmental attention, affect and altruism. *Journal of Applied Social Psychology* 7:359–371.

SHERROD, D. R., and COHEN, S. 1978. Density, personal control and design. In *Crowding and design*, ed. J. Aiello and A. Baum. New York: Plenum.

SHERROD, D. R., and DOWNS, R. 1974. Environmental determinants of altruism: the effects of stimulus overload and perceived control on helping. *Journal of Experimental Social Psychology* 10:468–479.

SHERROD, D. R., HAGE, J. N., HALPERN, P. L., and MOORE, B. S. 1977. Effects of personal causation and perceived control on responses to an aversive environment: the more control, the better. *Journal of Experimental Social Psychology* 13:14–27.

SOMMER, R. 1959. Studies in personal space. *Sociometry* 22:247–260.

———. 1969. *Personal space: the behavioral basis for design.* Englewood Cliffs, N.J.: Prentice-Hall.

SOMMER, R., and BECKER, F. D. 1969. Territorial defense and the good neighbor. *Journal of Personality and Social Psychology* 11:85–92.

STOKOLS, D. 1972. On the distinction between density and crowding: some implications for future research. *Psychological Review* 79:275–277.

———. 1976. The experience of crowding in primary and secondary environments. *Environment and Behavior* 8:49–86.

STOKOLS, D., RALL, M., PINNER, B., and SCHOPLER, J. 1973. Physical, social and personal determinants of the perception of crowding. *Environment and Behavior* 5:87–115.

SUNDSTROM, E., and ALTMAN, I. 1974. Field study of dominance and territorial behavior. *Journal of Personality and Social Psychology* 30:115–125.

TAYLOR, R. B., and STOUGH, R. R. 1978. Territorial cognition: assessing Altman's typology. *Journal of Personality and Social Psychology* 36:418–423.

WEINER, F. 1976. Altruism, ambiance, and action: the effects of rural and urban rearing on helping behavior. *Journal of Personality and Social Psychology* 34:112–124.

WICKER, A., and KIRMEYER, S. 1977. From church to laboratory to national park: a program of research on excess and insufficient populations in behavior settings. In *Perspectives on environment and behavior*, ed. D. Stokols. New York: Plenum.

WORCHEL, S., and TEDDLIE, C. 1976. The experience of crowding: a two-factor theory. *Journal of Personality and Social Psychology* 34:30–40.

ZIMBARDO, P. 1969. The human choice: individuation, reason and order vs. deindividuation, impulse, and chaos. *Nebraska Symposium on Motivation* 17:237–307.

ZLUTNICK, S., and ALTMAN, I. 1972. Crowding and human behavior. In *Environment and the social sciences: perspectives and applications*, ed. J. F. Wohlwill and D. H. Carson. Washington, D.C.: American Psychological Association.

Chapter 13 Applying Social Psychology

ADKINS, J. C. 1969. Jury selection: an art? a science? or luck? *Trial* 11:37–39.

AIELLO, J. R., EPSTEIN, Y. M., and KARLIN, R. A. 1975. Field experimental research on human crowding. Paper read at the annual meeting of the Western Psychological Association, 1975, Sacramento, California.

ALTMAN, I. 1975. *The environment and social behavior.* Monterey, Calif.: Brooks/Cole.

AMIR, Y. 1969. Contact hypothesis in ethnic relations. *Psychological Bulletin* 71:319–342.

BARON, R. M., MANDEL, D. R., ADAMS, C. A., and GRIFFEN, L. M. 1976. Effects of social density in university residential environments. *Journal of Personality and Social Psychology* 34:434–446.

BAUM, A., and VALINS, S. 1977. *Architecture and social behavior.* Hillsdale, N.J.: Erlbaum.

BEM, S., and BEM, D. 1970. Case study of a non-conscious ideology: training the woman to know her place. In *Beliefs, attitudes, and human affairs*, ed. D. J. Bem. Monterey, Calif.: Brooks/Cole.

BERMANT, G., NEMETH, C., and VIDMER, N., eds. *Psychology and the law.* Lexington, Mass.: D. C. Heath.

BOOTH, A. 1975. *Final report: urban crowding project.* Ministry of State for Urban Affairs, Government of Canada, August 1975.

BOOTH, A., and EDWARDS, J. N. 1976. Crowding and family relations. *American Sociological Review* 41:308–321.

BOOTH, A., and JOHNSON, D. R. 1975. The effect of crowding on child health and development. *American Behavioral Scientist* 18:736–747.

BROVERMAN, I., BROVERMAN, D., CLARKSON, F., ROSENKRANTZ, P., and VOGEL, S. 1972. Sex role stereotypes and clinical judgments of mental health. *Journal of Consulting Psychology* 34:1–7.

BUCKOUT, R. 1978. *U.S. v. Swinton*: a case history in jury selection. *Social Action and the Law* 4:27–29.

BUSCH, F. X. 1959. *Law and tactics in jury trials.* Indianapolis: Bobbs-Merrill.

CALHOUN, J. B. 1962. Population density and social pathology. *Scientific American* 206:139–146.

CHAFETZ, J. S. 1974. *Masculine/feminine or human? An overview of the sociology of sex roles.* Itasca, Ill.: Peacock.

CHEVIGNY, P. 1975. The Attica cases: a successful challenge in a northern city. *Criminal Law Bulletin* 11:157–172.

COHEN, S., GLASS, D. C., and PHILLIPS, S. 1979. Environmental factors in health. In *Handbook of medical sociol-*

ogy, ed. H. E. Freeman, S. Levine, and L. G. Reeder. Englewood Cliffs, N.J.: Prentice-Hall.

Cohen, S., and Sherrod, D. R. 1978. When density matters: environmental control as a determinant of crowding effects in laboratory and residential settings. *Journal of Population: Behavioral, Social, and Environmental Issues* 1:189–202.

Cohen, S. L., and Bunker, K. 1975. Subtle effects of sex role stereotypes on recruiters' hiring decisions. *Journal of Applied Psychology* 60:566–572.

Cook, S. W. 1969. Motives in a conceptual analysis of attitude-related behavior. In *Nebraska symposium on motivation*, ed. W. J. Arnold and D. Levine. Lincoln: University of Nebraska Press.

Cox, V. C., Paulus, P. B., McCain, G. C., and Schkade, J. K. 1979. Field research on the effects of crowding in prisons and on offshore drilling platforms. In *Residential crowding and design*, ed. J. Aiello and A. Baum. New York: Plenum.

D'Atri, D. A. 1975. Psychophysiological responses to crowding. *Environment and Behavior* 7:237–252.

Dean, L. M., Pugh, W. M., and Gunderson, E. 1975. Spatial and perceptual components of crowding: effects on health and satisfaction. *Environment and Behavior* 7:225–236.

Deaux, K., and Emswiller, T. 1974. Explanations of successful performance on sex-linked tasks: what is skill for the male is luck for the female. *Journal of Personality and Social Psychology* 29:80–85.

Deutsch, M., and Collins, M. E. 1951. *Interracial housing: a psychological evaluation of a social experiment*. Minneapolis: University of Minnesota Press.

Deutsch, M., and Hornstein, H. A. 1975. *Applying social psychology*. Hillsdale N.J.: Erlbaum.

Efran, M. 1974. The effect of physical appearance on the judgment of guilt, interpersonal attraction, and severity of recommended punishment in a simulated jury task. *Journal of Research in Personality* 8:45–54.

Feldman-Summers, S., and Kiesler, S. 1974. Those who are number two try harder: the effect of sex on attributions of causality. *Journal of Personality and Social Psychology* 30:846–855.

Fidell, L. 1970. Empirical verification of sex discrimination in hiring practices in psychology. *American Psychologist* 25:1094–1098.

Fischer, C. S., Baldassare, M., and Ofshe, R. J. 1975. Crowding studies and urban life: a critical review. *American Institute of Planners Journal* 41:406–418.

Freedman, J. 1975. *Crowding and behavior*. San Francisco: Freeman.

Fulero, S., and De Lara, C. 1976. Rape victims and attributed responsibility: a defensive attribution approach. *Victimology* 1:551–563.

Gerbasi, K. C., Zuckerman, M. P., and Reis, H. G. 1977. Justice needs a new blindfold: a review of mock jury research. *Psychological Bulletin* 84:323–325.

Goldberg, P. 1968. Are women prejudiced against women? *Transaction* 5:28–30.

Gray, D., and Ashmore, R. 1976. Biasing influence of defendants' characteristics on simulated sentencing. *Psychological Reports* 38:727–738.

Harrison, A. 1976. *Individuals and groups: understanding social behavior*. Monterey, Calif.: Brooks/Cole.

House Committee on Judiciary. 1955. *Recording of jury deliberations.*

Hutchins, R., and Slesinger, D. 1928. Some observations on the law of evidence-memory. *Harvard Law Review* 41:860–873.

Kramer, B. M. 1951. Residential contact as a determinant of attitudes toward Negroes. Ph. D. dissertation, Harvard University.

Landy, D., and Aronson, E. 1969. The influence of the character of the criminal and his victim on simulated jurors. *Journal of Experiment Social Psychology* 5:141–152.

Langer, E. J., and Rodin, J. 1976. The effects of choice and enhanced personal responsibility for the aged: a field experiment in an institutional setting. *Journal of Personality and Social Psychology* 34:191–198.

Lawrence, J. E. 1974. Science and sentiment: overview of research on crowding and human behavior. *Psychological Bulletin* 81:712–720.

Levinson, R. 1975. Sex discrimination and employment practices: an experiment in unconventional job inquiries. *Social Problems* 22:533–543.

Levitin, T., Quinn, R., and Staines, G. 1973. A woman is 58% of a man. *Psychology Today* 6:89–92.

Lewis, M. 1972. Culture and gender roles: there's no unisex in the nursery. *Psychology Today* 5:54–57.

McArthur, L. Z., and Eisen, S. V. 1976a. Achievements of male and female storybook characters as determinants of achievement behavior by boys and girls. *Journal of Personality and Social Psychology* 33:467–473.

———. 1976b. Television and sex-role stereotyping. *Journal of Applied Social Psychology* 6:329–351.

Marshall, J. 1966. *Law and psychology in conflict*. Indianapolis: Bobbs-Merrill.

Mischel, H. 1974. Sex bias in the evaluation of professional achievements. *Journal of Educational Psychology* 66:157–166.

Myrdal, G. 1944. *An American dilemma: the Negro problem and modern democracy*. New York: Harper.

Nemeth, C., and Sosis, R. 1973. A simulated jury study: characteristics of the defendant and the jurors. *Journal of Social Psychology* 90:221–229.

Newcomb, T. M. 1947. Autistic hostility and social reality. *Human Relations* 1:69–86.

Plutchik, R., and Schwartz, A. 1965. Jury selection: folklore or science? *Criminal Law Bulletin* 1:3–10.

Rodin, J., and Langer, E. J. 1977. Long-term effects of a control-relevant intervention with the institutionalized aged. *Journal of Personality and Social Psychology* 35:897–902.

Rokeach, M., and Vidmer, N. 1973. Testimony concerning possible jury bias in a Black Panther murder trial. *Journal of Applied Social Psychology* 3:19–29.

Rosenkrantz, P., Vogel, S., Bee, H., Broverman, T., and Broverman, D. 1968. Sex-role stereotypes and self-concepts in college students. *Journal of Consulting and Clinical Psychology* 32:287–295.

Rothbart, M. K., and Maccoby, E. 1966. Parents' differential reactions to sons and daughters. *Journal of Personality and Social Psychology* 4:337–343.

RUBIN, J., PROVENZANO, F., and LURIA, Z. 1974. The eye of the beholder: parents' views on sex of newborns. *American Journal of Orthopsychiatry* 44:512–519.

SAGE, W. 1973. Psychology and the Angela Davis jury. *Human Behavior* Jan., 37:56-61.

SALES, B. D. 1977. *Psychology in the legal process.* New York: Halsted.

SCHULMAN, J., SHAVER, P., COLMAN, R., EMRICK, B., and CHRISTIE, R. 1973. Recipe for a jury. *Psychology Today* 6:37–44, 77, 79–84.

SCHULZ, R. 1976. Effects of control and predictability on the physical and psychological well-being of the institutionalized aged. *Journal of Personality and Social Psychology* 33:563–573.

SCHULZ, R. 1977. Long-term effects of control and predictability enhancing interventions: findings and ethical issues. Unpublished manuscript, Carnegie-Mellon University.

SHAW, J. 1972. Reactions to victims and defendants of varying degrees of attractiveness. *Psychonomic Science* 27:329–330.

SIGALL, H., and LANDY, D. 1972. Effects of the defendant's character and suffering on juridic judgment: a replication and clarification. *Journal of Social Psychology* 88:149–150.

SIGALL, H., and OSTROVE, N. 1975. Beautiful but dangerous: effects of offender attractiveness and nature of the crime on juridic judgment. *Journal of Personality and Social Psychology* 31:410–414.

SMITH, M. 1966. Percy Foreman: top trial lawyer. *Life* 60:92–101.

STEPHAN, W. G. 1978. School desegregation: an evaluation of predictions made in *Brown v. Board of Education. Psychological Bulletin* 85:217–238.

STEPHAN, W. G., and ROSENFELD, D. 1978. Effects of desegregation on racial attitudes. *Journal of Personality and Social Psychology* 36:795–804.

SUTER, L., and MILLER, H. 1973. Income differences between men and career women. *American Journal of Sociology* 78:962–974.

TOUHEY, J. 1974. Effects of additional women professionals on ratings of occupational prestige and desirability. *Journal of Personality and Social Psychology* 29:86–89.

UNGER, R., and DENMARK, F. 1975. *Woman: dependent or independent variable?* New York: Psychological Dimensions.

WATSON, G., and JOHNSON, D. 1972. *Social psychology: issues and insights.* Philadelphia: Lippincott.

WILL, J., SELF, P., and DATAN, N. 1974. Maternal behavior and sex and infant. Paper read at the annual American Psychological Association convention, 1974, San Francisco, Calif.

WILNER, D. M., WALKEY, R. P., and COOK, S. W. 1955. *Human relations in interracial housing: a study of the contact hypothesis.* Minneapolis: University of Minnesota Press.

WILSON, D. W., and DONNERSTEIN, E. 1977. Guilty or not guilty: a look at the simulated jury paradigm. *Journal of Applied Social Psychology* 7:175–190.

WINDER, A. E. 1952. White attitudes toward Negro-white interaction in an area of changing racial composition. *American Psychologist* 7:330–331.

ZEISEL, H., and DIAMOND, S. 1976. The jury selection in the Mitchell-Stans conspiracy trial. *American Bar Foundation Research Journal* 1:151–174.

Chapter 14 Social Psychology: Exploring the Human Condition

BLOCK, J. 1977. Recognizing the coherence of personality. In *Personality at the crossroads: current issues in interactional psychology*, ed. D. Magnusson and N. S. Endler. Hillsdale, N.J.: Erlbaum.

BOWERS, K. S. 1973. Situationism in psychology: an analysis and a critique. *Psychological Review* 80:307–336.

JACCARD, J. J. 1974. Predicting social behavior from personality traits. *Journal of Research in Personality* 7:358–367.

MISCHEL, W. 1977. The interaction of person and situation. In *Personality at the crossroads: current issues in interactional psychology*, ed. D. Magnusson and N. S. Endler. Hillsdale, N.J.: Erlbaum.

SNYDER, M. 1978. Self-monitoring processes. In *Advances in experimental social psychology*, vol. 12, ed. L. Berkowitz. New York: Academic Press.

NAME INDEX

SUBJECT INDEX

PERMISSIONS ACKNOWLEDGMENTS

Chapter 1 The Nature of Social Psychology
13—From "Don't the Girls All Get Prettier at Closing Time." © 1975 by Singletree Music. Written by Baker Knight. Used by permission. All rights reserved.

Chapter 2 Research Methods in Social Psychology
24—From Webb-Campbell-Schwartz-Sechrest: *Unobtrusive Measures: Nonreactive Research in the Social Sciences.* Copyright © 1966 Rand McNally College Publishing Co. Reprinted by permission of Houghton Mifflin Company.
29—Box figure. From William C. Finnie, "Field Experiments in Litter Control," *Environment and Behavior* 5 (June 1973): 123–144 by permission of the Publisher, Sage Publications, Inc.
33—Figure 2.1. From S. Cohen, G. W. Evans, D. S. Krantz, and D. Stokols, "Physiological, Motivational, and Cognitive Effects of Aircraft Noise on Children: Moving from the Laboratory to the Field," *American Psychologist* 35 (1980): 231–243. Copyright 1980 by the American Psychological Association. Reprinted by permission.

Chapter 3 The Self
53—From STEPPENWOLF by Herman Hesse. Translated by Basil Creighton. Copyright 1929, © 1957 by Holt, Rinehart and Winston. Reprinted by permission of Holt, Rinehart, and Winston, Publishers.
56—Figure 3.1. Based on data from M. D. Storms, "Videotape and the Attribution Process: Reversing Actors' and Observers' Points of View," *Journal of Personality and Social Psychology* 27 (1973): 165–175. Copyright 1973 by the American Psychological Association. Reprinted by permission.
57—Figure 3.2. Based on data from B. S. Moore, D. R. Sherrod, T. J. Liu, and B. Underwood, "The Dispositional Shift in Attribution over Time," *Journal of Experimental Social Psychology*, 1979. Used by permission.
65—Figure 3.3. From A. Fenigstein, M. F. Scheier, and A. H. Buss, "Public and Private Self-Consciousness: Assessment and Theory," *Journal of Consulting and Clinical Psychology* 43 (1975): 522–527. Copyright 1975 by the American Psychological Association. Reprinted by permission.
66—Box table. From M. F. Scheier, C. S. Carver, and F. X. Gibbons, "Self-Directed Attention, Awareness of Bodily States, and Suggestibility," *Journal of Personality and Social Psychology* 37 (1979): 1576–1588. Copyright 1979 by the American Psychological Association. Reprinted by permission.
73—Figure 3.4. From M. Snyder, "Self-Monitoring of Expressive Behavior," *Journal of Personality and Social Psychology* 30 (1974): 526–537. Copyright 1975 by the American Psychological Association. Reprinted by permission.
75—Figure 3.5. From *The Transparent Self* by Sidney M. Jourard. © 1971 by Litton Educational Publishing, Inc. Reprinted by permission of D. Van Nostrand Co.

Chapter 4 Attitudes, Beliefs, and Behavior
98—Pages 21–23 in BRAVE NEW WORLD by Aldous Huxley. Copyright 1932, 1960 by Aldous Huxley. Reprinted by permission of Harper & Row, Publishers, Inc., Mrs. Laura Huxley, and Chatto & Windus Ltd.
108—Figure 4.3. Reprinted by permission of the publisher, the University of Chicago Press, from *Scales for the Measurement of Social Attitudes,* edited by Louis

Leon Thurstone. Scale 21 by C. K. A. Wang, 1930.
109—Figure 4.4. Copyright © by the Rural Sociological Society.

Chapter 5 Attitude Change

120—Figure 5.2. Reprinted by permission of the publisher from C. I. Hovland and W. Weiss, "The Influence of Source Credibility on Communication Effectiveness," *Public Opinion Quarterly* 15 (1951): 635–650. Copyright 1951 by The Trustees of Columbia University.
123—© 1979 by The New York Times Company. Reprinted by permission.
135—Figure 5.3. From M. Sherif and C. Hovland, *Social Judgement*, Yale University Press, 1961. Reprinted by permission.
136—Figure 5.4. From S. Bochner and C. A. Insko, "Communicator Discrepancy, Source Credibility, and Opinion Change," *Journal of Personality and Social Psychology* 4 (1966): 614–621. Copyright 1966 by the American Psychological Association. Reprinted by permission.
141—Figure 5.5. From L. Mann and I. L. Janis, "A Follow-up Study on the Long-Term Effects of Emotional Role Playing," *Journal of Personality and Social Psychology* 8 (1968): 339–342. Copyright 1968 by the American Psychological Association. Reprinted by permission.
145—Table 5.1. Adapted from J. W. Brehm, "Postdecision Changes in the Desirability of Alternatives," *Journal of Abnormal and Social Psychology* 52 (1956): 348–349.
149—Reprinted from A TREASURY OF JEWISH FOLKLORE by Nathan Ausubel. Copyright 1948, 1976 by Crown Publishers, Inc. Used by permission of Crown Publishers, Inc.

Chapter 6 Attribution and Person Perception

168—Figure 6.2. Adapted by permission from E. E. Jones and K. E. Davis, "From Acts to Dispositions," in *Advances in Experimental Social Psychology*, L. Berkowitz, ed., Vol. II., Academic Press, 1966.
177—Figure 6.4. Adapted from M. D. Storms, "Videotape and the Attribution Process: Reversing Actors' and Observers' Points of View," *Journal of Personality and Social Psychology* 27 (1973): 165–175. Copyright 1973 by the American Psychological Association. Reprinted by permission.
178—Extract from John Barth, *The End of the Road.* Copyright © 1958, 1967 by John Barth. Reprinted by permission of Doubleday & Company, Inc.
179—Table 6.1. From B. Weiner et al., *Perceiving the Causes of Success and Failure.* Reprinted by permission of Silver Burdett Company.
183—Table 6.2. Adapted from S. Schachter and J. E. Singer, "Cognitive, Social, and Physiological Determinants of Emotional State," *Psychological Review* 69 (1962): 379–399. Copyright 1962 by the American Psychological Association. Reprinted by permission.
189—Box table. Reprinted from *Psychology Today Magazine.* Copyright © 1980 Ziff-Davis Publishing Company.

Chapter 7 Interpersonal Attraction

196—Copyright 1975, Los Angeles Times. Reprinted by permission.
199—Table 7.1. Adapted from THE PSYCHOLOGY OF AFFILIATION by Stanley Schachter (Stanford: Stanford University Press, 1959), p. 18, with permission of the publisher.
201—Figure 7.1. Adapted from Leon Festinger, Stanley Schachter, and Kurt Back, *Social Pressures in Informal Groups*, with the permission of the publishers, Stanford University Press. Copyright 1950 by Leon Festinger, Stanley Schachter, and Kurt Back. Copyright renewed 1978.
209—Figure 7.2. Adapted by permission from D. Byrne, *The Attraction Paradigm*, Academic Press, 1971, p. 58.
211—Box figure. From J. E. Krulewitz and J. E. Nash, "Effects of Sex Role Attitudes and Similarity on Man's Rejection of Male Homosexuals," *Journal of Personality and Social Psychology* 38 (1980): 67–74. Copyright 1980 by the American Psychological Association. Reprinted by permission.
215—Figure 7.3. Adapted by permission from E. Aronson and D. Linder, "Gain and Loss of Esteem as Determinants of Interpersonal Attractiveness," *Journal of Experimental Social Psychology* 1 (1965): 156–171.
219—Table 7.2. Adapted from G. Levinger and J. D. Snoek, *Attraction in Relationships: A New Look at Interpersonal Attraction* (General Learning Press, 1972). Copyright by G. Levinger and J. D. Snoek. Reprinted by permission of the authors.
222–223—From Z. Rubin, "Measurement of Romantic Love," *Journal of Personality and Social Psychology* 16 (1970): 265–273. Copyright 1970 by the American Psychological Association. Reprinted by permission.
226—Figure 7.4. From "Loneliness" by Carin Rubenstein, Phillip Shaver, and Letitia Anne Peplau, HUMAN NATURE, February 1979. Copyright © 1978 by Human Nature, Inc. Reprinted by permission of the publisher.
227—Figure 7.5. Adapted from A. Peplau and D. Perlman, "Blueprint for a Social Psychological Theory of Loneliness." In M. Cook and G. Wilson, eds., *Love and Attraction* (Oxford: Pergamon Press, 1979): 99–108. Used by permission of Pergamon Press Ltd.

Chapter 8 Aggression

242—Box figure. From A. Fenigstein, "Does Aggression Cause a Preference for Viewing Media Violence?" *Journal of Personality and Social Psychology* 37 (1979): 2307–2317. Copyright 1979 by the American Psychological Association. Reprinted by permission.
244—Figure 8.1. Adapted by permission from P. Brown and R. Elliot, "Control of Aggression in a Nursery School Class," *Journal of Experimental Social Psychology* 2 (1965): 103–107.
249—Figure 8.2. Adapted from V. J. Konečni, "The Mediation of Aggressive Behavior: Arousal Level vs. Anger and Cognitive Labeling," *Journal of Personality and Social Psychology* 32 (1975): 706–712. Copyright 1975 by the American Psychological Association. Reprinted by permission.
252—Figure 8.3. Adapted from A. N. Doob and L. Wood, "Catharsis and Aggression: The Effects of Annoyance and Retaliation on Aggressive Behavior," *Journal of Personality and Social Psychology* 22 (1972): 156–162. Copyright 1972 by the American Psychological Association. Reprinted by permission.
262—Table 8.1. Adapted from E. Donnerstein and G. Barrett, "Effects of Erotic Stimuli on Male Aggression Toward Females," *Journal of Personality and Social Psychology* 36 (1978): 180–188. Copyright 1978 by the American Psychological Association. Reprinted by permission.
266—Table 8.2. Copyrighted by Alan R. Liss, Inc.

Chapter 9 Altruism

276-277—By David Johnston; Jerry Belcher; and Doris Byron. Copyright, 1980, Los Angeles Times. Reprinted by permission.
282—Figure 9.1. Adapted from B. S. Moore, B. Underwood, and D. L. Rosenhan, "Affect and Self-Gratification," *Developmental Psychology* 8 (1973): 209–214. Copyright 1973 by the American Psychological Association. Reprinted by permission.
287—Table 9.1. Adapted from H. Hornstein, E. Fisch, and M. Holmes, "Influence of a Model's Feeling About His Behavior and His Relevance as a Comparison Other on Observers' Helping Behavior," *Journal of Personality and Social Psychology* 10 (1968): 225. Copyright 1968 by the American Psychological Association. Reprinted by permission.
292—Figure 9.2. Adapted from J. Darley and B. Latané, "Bystander Intervention in Emergencies: Diffusion of Responsibility," *Journal of Personality and Social Psychology* 8 (1968): 377–383. Copyright 1968 by the American Psychological Association. Reprinted by permission.
295—Box figure. From J. M. Darley and C. D. Batson, " 'From Jerusalem to Jericho': A Study of Situational and Dispositional Variables in Helping Behavior," *Journal of Personality and Social Psychology* 27 (1973): 100–108. Copyright 1973 by the American Psychological Association. Reprinted by permission.
301—Figure 9.4. Adapted from G. Pruitt, "Reciprocity and Credit Building in a Laboratory Dyad," *Journal of Personality and Social Psychology* 8 (1968): 143–147. Copyright 1968 by the American Psychological Association. Reprinted by permission.

Chapter 10 Social Interdependence

320—Figure 10.6. Reprinted by permission from A. Rapoport and A. M. Chammah, *Prisoner's Dilemma: A Study in Conflict and Cooperation*, The University of Michigan Press, 1965.
325—Box figure. From M. Toda, H. Shinotsuka, C. G. McClintock, and F. J. Stech, "Development of Competitive Behavior as a Function of Culture, Age, and Social Comparison," *Journal of Personality and Social Psychology* 36 (1978): 825–839. Copyright 1978 by the American Psychological Association. Reprinted by permission.
326—Figure 10.8. From D. M. Kuhlman and A. Marshello, "Individual Differences in Game Motivation as Moderators of Preprogrammed Strategy Effects in Prisoner's Dilemma," *Journal of Personality and Social Psychology* 32 (1975): 922–931. Copyright 1975 by the American Psychological Association. Reprinted by permission.
331—Figure 10.9 and Table 10.1. Adapted from M. Deutsch and R. Krauss, "The Effect of Threat Upon Interpersonal Bargaining," *Journal of Abnormal and Social Psychology* 61 (1960): 181–189. Copyright 1960 by the American Psychological Association. Reprinted by permission.
332-333—"Love Canal Group Releases 'Hostages.' " Reprinted by permission of United Press International.
333—By Ted Vollmer. Copyright, 1980, Los Angeles Times. Reprinted by permission.

Chapter 11 Groups

350—From Carson McCullers, *The Member of the Wedding*, published by Houghton Mifflin Company. Copyright 1946 by Carson McCullers. Copyright © renewed 1974 by Floria V. Lasky. Reprinted by permission.
369—Figure 11.2. Adapted from J. R. Hackman, K. R. Brousseau, and J. A. Weiss, "The Interaction of Task Design and Group Performance Strategies in Determining Group Effectiveness," *Organizational Behavior and*

Human Performance 16 (1976): 350–365. Reprinted by permission.
370—Box figure. From J. W. Gastorf, J. Suls, and G. S. Sanders, "Type A Coronary-Prone Behavior Pattern and Social Facilitation," *Journal of Personality and Social Psychology* 38 (1980): 773–780. Copyright 1980 by the American Psychological Association. Reprinted by permission.
375—By Robert C. Toth and Norman Kempster. Copyright, 1980, Los Angeles Times. Reprinted by permission.
376—Table 11.1. From M. L. Flowers, "A Laboratory Test of Some Implications of Janis's Groupthink Hypothesis," *Journal of Personality and Social Psychology* 35 (1977): 888–896. Copyright 1977 by the American Psychological Association. Reprinted by permission.

Chapter 12 The Physical Environment and Social Behavior

383—Figure 12.1. From Robert Sommer, *Personal Space: The Behavioral Basis of Design*, © 1969, p. 33. Reprinted by permission of Prentice-Hall, Inc., Englewood Cliffs, N. J.
388—From THE POETRY OF ROBERT FROST, edited by Edward Connery Lathem. Copyright 1930, 1939, © 1969 by Holt, Rinehart and Winston. Copyright © 1958 by Robert Frost. Copyright © 1967 by Lesley Frost Ballantine. Reprinted by permission of Holt, Rinehart and Winston, Publishers.
391—Figure 12.2. From R. Sommer and F. D. Becker, "Territorial Defense and the Good Neighbor," *Journal of Personality and Social Psychology* 11 (1969): 85–92. Copyright 1969 by the American Psychological Association. Reprinted by permission.
405—Figure 12.3. Adapted from K. E. Mathews, Jr., and L. K. Canon, "Environmental Noise Level as a Determinant of Helping Behavior," *Journal of Personality and Social Psychology* 32 (1975): 571–577. Copyright 1975 by the American Psychological Association. Reprinted by permission.
408—Figure 12.4. From R. A. Baron and V. M. Ransberger, "Ambient Temperature and the Occurence of Collective Violence: The 'Long Hot Summer' Revisited," *Journal of Personality and Social Psychology* 36 (1978): 351–360. Copyright 1978 by the American Psychological Association. Reprinted by permission.

Chapter 13 Applying Social Psychology

446–447—By Joy Horowitz. Copyright, 1980, Los Angeles Times. Reprinted by permission.

About the Authors

DRURY SHERROD (*Editor; Chapter 1, The Nature of Social Psychology; Chapter 2, Research Methods in Social Psychology; Chapter 3, The Self; Chapter 12, The Physical Environment and Social Behavior; and Chapter 14, Social Psychology: Exploring the Human Condition*) received an M.A. in international relations from Johns Hopkins University and an M.A. and a Ph.D. from Stanford University, where he studied communication research and social psychology. He has held academic appointments on the faculties of Kirkland College, Hamilton College, and the University of Oregon. Currently Dr. Sherrod is Visiting Associate Professor at Pitzer College and the Claremont Graduate School. His publications and research interests deal with environmental stressors such as crowding and noise, and with the cognitive processes that mediate the impace of such stressors on human behavior. He has also published research on attribution and self-perception, and his most recent work examined the effect of time on self-attributions.

SHELDON COHEN (*Chapter 13, Applying Social Psychology*) is an Associate Professor of Psychology at the University of Oregon. He received his Ph.D. in social psychology from New York University in 1973. Dr. Cohen's main research interest is the role of cognitive processes as causes and effects of environmental stress. Dr. Cohen has published a number of reviews of theoretical and empirical research on crowding and noise, and he has proposed an information-processing analysis of the impact of environmental stressors on performance and interpersonal behavior. He has also published both laboratory and field research on the impact of environmental stressors on behavior and health. Most recently, he has become interested in the role of social support in buffering people from the pathological effects of stressors.

ALICE H. EAGLY (*Chapter 4, Attitudes, Beliefs, and Behavior; and Chapter 5, Attitude Change*) began studying social psychology during her undergraduate years at Radcliffe College, where she majored in social relations. At the University of Michigan she obtained an M.A. in psychology and Ph.D. in social psychology, which was jointly sponsored by the departments of Psychology and Sociology. She served on the faculty of Michigan State University for two years and the University of Massachusetts at Amherst for twelve years. During this period she also held visiting faculty appointments at the University of Illinois and Harvard University. In 1980 she moved to Purdue University, where she is Professor of Psychological Sciences. Dr. Eagly has served as Associate Editor of the *Journal of Personality and Social Psychology* and is President of the Society for Personality and Social Psychology. Her research deals with social influence and attitude change. Within these areas, her special interests are the cognitive mediation of attitude change and the effects of gender roles on persuasibility.

Solomon Fulero (*Chapter 13, Applying Social Psychology*) holds a Ph.D. and a law degree from the University of Oregon. He now practices law in Dayton, Ohio, where he also consults with other lawyers about psychological issues such as jury selection and eyewitness testimony.

Eugenia Grohman (*Chapter 11, Groups*) is an editor and technical writer with the National Research Council/National Academy of Sciences in Washington, D.C. She writes frequently on behavioral science and related policy issues.

John H. Harvey (*Chapter 6, Attribution and Person Perception*) received his Ph.D. in social psychology from the University of Missouri at Columbia and held a postdoctoral fellowship at the University of California at Los Angeles. He is an Associate Professor at Vanderbilt University and has been a Visiting Associate Professor at Ohio State University. Currently on leave from Vanderbilt, he is serving at the American Psychological Association as Administrative Officer for Educational Affairs. The recipient of several research grants, Dr. Harvey has authored numerous articles on the attribution of causality, perceived choice, and social perception. He has written a textbook on social psychology and has edited and coauthored several other books, including *New Directions in Attribution Research*, Vols. 1, 2 & 3 as well as *Cognition, Social Behavior, and the Environment* and *The Psychology of Close Relationships.*

Sara B. Kiesler (*Chapter 11, Groups*) obtained her graduate degrees at Stanford University and Ohio State University. She has held academic positions at Yale University, Connecticut College, and the University of Kansas. Her research involved experimental studies of groups until 1975. From 1975 to 1979 she was a study director at the National Research Council/National Academy of Sciences in Washington, D.C., where she worked with groups on national science policies. She is currently Professor of Social Science and Social Psychology at Carnegie-Mellon University. Based on her experience in Washington, her research on groups is now interdisciplinary and policy-oriented. She and her collaborators are studying computer conferences in organizations, national standards-setting committees, and community roles in energy policy.

Vladmir J. Konečni (*Chapter 8, Aggression*) was educated in Great Britain, Yugoslavia, and Canada. He received a Ph.D. in social and experimental psychology from the University of Toronto in 1973. Since then, he has been on the faculty of the University of California at San Diego (La Jolla) where he is presently an Associate Professor. In 1979–1980, he held a John Simon Guggenheim Fellowship and was a Visiting Associate Professor at the University of Sydney, University of Western Australia (Perth), University of Rio de Janeiro, and the London School of Economics. Besides aggressive behavior, his research interests and publications deal with the psychology of law, experimental psycho-aesthetics, and human emotions.

Michael Kuhlman (*Chapter 10, Social Interdependence*) obtained his Ph.D. in experimental social psychology from the University of California at Santa Barbara in 1970. He is an Associate Professor at the University of Delaware. His publications and research deal with decision making and with individual differences in situations of social interdependence. His most recent work examined the ecological validity of laboratory gaming research.

Bert Moore (*Chapter 9, Altruism*) received his M.A. in psychology from the University of

Illinois and his Ph.D. from Stanford University. He has held academic appointments at Wellesley College, and the University of California at Santa Barbara, and he has been a visiting faculty member at Stanford University. Currently Dr. Moore is Associate Professor and Chairman of the Department of Psychology at the University of Texas at Dallas. As the author of numerous articles on personality and social psychology, his research has focused on such topics as altruism, self-control, emotions, and attribution. He is currently investigating cognitive and affective processes that mediate a variety of social behaviors.

LETITIA ANNE PEPLAU *(Chapter 7, Interpersonal Attraction)* received a Ph.D. in social psychology from the interdisciplinary program in social relations at Harvard University in 1973. She is an Associate Professor of Psychology at the University of California at Los Angeles. Her research has focused on close personal relationships among friends and lovers. An interest in how sex roles influence relationships led her to study both heterosexual and homosexual couples. The author of numerous articles on love and attraction, she recently coedited *Loneliness: A Sourcebook of Current Theory, Research and Therapy* (to be published in 1982).